THIRD EDITION

The CONFIDENT STUDENT

Carol C. Kanar
Valencia Community College

Houghton Mifflin Company Boston New York

TO STEVE

Assistant Editor: Melissa Plumb
Project Editor: Gabrielle Stone
Senior Production/Design Coordinator: Jennifer Waddell
Senior Manufacturing Coordinator: Priscilla Bailey

Credits for text begin on page 405.

As part of Houghton Mifflin's ongoing commitment to the environment, this text has been printed on recycled paper.

Library of Congress Catalog Card No.:97-72498

Student Edition ISBN: 0-395-84062-7

Instructor's Edition ISBN: 0-395-84991-8

123456789-WC 01 00 99 98 97

Contents

PART 1 Becoming a Confident Student

PART 2 Studying with Power and Confidence

Preface

The Confident Student, Third Edition is informed by my abiding desire to help students gain confidence in their ability to learn and succeed in college and beyond. Almost thirty years of teaching study skills, reading, and English courses have convinced me that confidence comes from knowledge of oneself as well as through the acquisition of vital skills. Therefore, this book has a dual focus that combines thorough treatment of a wide range of practical, immediately applicable study skills and critical thinking strategies with an equally important emphasis on self-discovery and self-management to help students meet the challenge of college, life, and work.

Because of this combined emphasis, *The Confident Student* is suitable for study skills courses, orientation courses, and student success courses taught either in traditional classroom settings or in labs or learning centers. The book's wide array of special features and lively, open format make it especially attractive to students. Since many students are visual learners, the instructional material includes a wealth of illustrations, photographs, tables, charts, and other visual aids to engage and sustain their interest.

Coverage and Organization

The seventeen chapters of the Third Edition have been reorganized into three parts to flow more naturally from less difficult topics, cognitively, to the more challenging ones. The six chapters of Part 1 address students' affective characteristics. The six chapters of Part 2 address students' academic skills, and the five chapters of Part 3 address critical thinking strategies. While this organization suggests a possible sequence that can be followed, no single order is correct for all classes. Instructors are free to pick and choose chapters from each part based on the mix of affective characteristics, academic skills, and critical thinking strategies that they think their students need. Topics and concepts are carefully cross-referenced throughout the text so that there is no loss in continuity no matter what sequence is observed.

After listening to comments and suggestions from my colleagues who have used the Second Edition and who desired a shorter text, I decided to move Chapter 9, "Developing Your Vocabulary" and Chapter 15, "Using Your Library and Doing Research," out of the Third Edition and into the *Instructor's Resource Manual.* Thus, instructors who still may want to use these chapters are free to make copies of them for their students.

New to the Third Edition is a more pronounced focus in every chapter on workplace know-how: specifically on the foundational skills and workplace competencies identified by SCANS (Secretary's Commission on Achieving Necessary Skills). The Third Edition's inside front cover contains a quick-reference chart that correlates chapter objectives and the keys to success in college to workplace competencies. New material in every chapter of the Third Edition now more visibly helps students make the transition from college to work. As we move into the twenty-first century, not only do we need to help students be successful in college, but we also need to help them prepare for the future.

You will also find that many of the exercises and examples in the Third Edition have been updated not only to make them more current, but to provide a more focused learning experience. For example, icons identify exercises in each chapter that address learning styles and collaborative learning.

Part 1: Becoming a Confident Student invites students to assess their academic strengths and weaknesses and discover and learn how to use their learning styles, develop an internal locus of control, set realistic goals, use a problem-solving procedure, and improve listening, note taking, and oral presentation skills. Also, students enter into a discussion of how they can use their college's resources, not only for academic but also for personal success, and maintain their health and well-being. In addition, Part 1 shows students how to use their time more effectively to accomplish their goals, how to make and follow schedules, and how to avoid procrastination.

Part 2: Studying with Power and Confidence introduces students to a range of study techniques to help them better organize information and make study guides according to their personal learning style preferences. It shows them how to adapt the proven study system, SQ3R, and introduces a new system, PREP, for reading skill-development texts such as those used in math and language courses. This part also focuses on two reading strategies to help students determine what is important in a textbook chapter and how to mark and annotate material. Mapping and outlining strategies for organizing information into study guides are introduced as alternative systems for students to consider. Part 2 addresses concentration, learning, and memory, and explains how students can take control of these processes. Finally, Part 2 explains how to prepare for tests of all kinds, and how to develop a test-taking routine to ensure optimum performance.

Part 3: Learning to Think Critically challenges students to think beyond the surface of the issues and content they will encounter in college. At the same time, students learn how to use critical thinking strategies to help them better process the information they are learning, thus helping them to actually *learn* better. The significant cognitive skills of reading, writing, and researching are explored in the process, building on the perspectives from which *The Confident Student,* Third Edition promotes the concept of active learning. The last two chapters outline special strategies for meeting the challenges of two disciplines that often pose the greatest difficulty for students: math and science. WHISK, a method for solving word problems, is a technique students can apply immediately to their math study.

Special Features

Awareness Checks are brief checklists or assessment questionnaires designed to orient students to a chapter or discussion. Fourteen chapters contain at least one Awareness Check; three chapters contain two or more. These Checks help students become aware of what they already know about a topic and their attitude toward it. Answers and explanations follow each Awareness Check. They could become a focus for class activity followed by discussion, or students can use them to prepare for the next day's assignment. The four Checks in Chapter 1 are especially useful in helping students determine their learning style.

Confidence Builders in every chapter supplement topic discussions by reporting on current research, introducing another method for solving a common study problem, or examining a related topic. The purpose of Confidence Builders is to interest and motivate students to succeed. The Third Edition contains several new Confidence Builders that address job and career skills.

Computer Confidence boxes in Chapters 3, 4, 8, 15, and 16 show students how to use personal computers as a study aid to improve time management, organize notes, draft and revise essays, create glossaries of specialized terms, make study guides, and prepare for math tests. The suggestions are simple and easy to follow so that students who have access to a computer either at home or in a lab can use them right away to enhance their study skills.

The pedagogical foundation is enhanced with *Critical Thinking Application* exercises. Each chapter contains at least one such exercise, designed both to prepare students for the concepts presented in Chapter 13, "Using Critical Thinking Strategies," and then to reinforce these principles, applying them to content throughout the text. Students will learn to integrate critical thinking naturally into their approach to studying and classroom interaction, as they continually are asked to question, more fully process, and consider different viewpoints surrounding the issues and concepts presented. In the Third Edition, the pedagogical foundation is further enhanced with learning objectives that are now more visible. They appear as bulleted lists on the first page of each chapter. The objectives are related to the four keys to success explained in Chapter 1 and to the SCANS skills, making it easy for students to see that what they are learning has applications both in college and beyond.

Instructional Approach and Learning Tools

The *Skill Finder* on pages xix–xxi is an excellent point of entry for this book. It introduces key study skills in checklist form, roughly following the organization of the text. The Skill Finder provides a quick assessment of the student's strengths and weaknesses that is fleshed out by more detailed questions in the Awareness Checks. It also provides an overview of the text and will reassure students that they can find help for any difficulties they may already be experiencing in their course work. The SCANS Quick Reference Chart on the inside front cover provides additional support.

The Confident Student, Third Edition speaks to readers simply and directly in a friendly, non-intimidating tone. Students undoubtedly will find themselves in these pages among the numerous *examples of typical college students* who experience common difficulties and resolve them by trying out the strategies suggested in the text.

Exercises are interspersed with discussions of concepts and strategies throughout each chapter so that students can practice applying new knowledge while it is fresh in their minds. In the Third Edition, many of these exercises have been redesigned to be used as the basis for collaborative work, and they are identified by an icon. Learning Styles exercises, too, are identified by an icon.

The *Instructor's Resource Manual* that accompanies the book is an additional resource for collaborative activities. Candy Ready of Piedmont Technical College has contributed exercises used successfully with her own students, greatly bolstering the emphasis on interactive learning running throughout the text. For the Third Edition, Ready updated these exercises to address workplace skills.

Summaries near the end of every chapter focus attention on essential information and provide either a quick preview or a review of chapter material. Each summary includes a concept map or other graphic aid that overviews the chapter's main points. In the Third Edition, Summaries are interactive. For example, maps and charts are only partially filled in for students to complete.

Your Reflections at the end of each chapter is a new feature. This activity poses several questions for students to think about and respond to in writing. Students are asked to assess their progress and to reflect on what they have learned and how they can apply it.

Ancillaries

The *Instructor's Resource Manual* that accompanies *The Confident Student* contains an answer key for appropriate exercises and chapter-by-chapter suggestions on how to use various elements in the text in a classroom or lab. Also included are sample course syllabi, a brief bibliography, and a set of reproducible masters for overhead transparencies and handouts to supplement information contained in the chapters. Additional collaborative activities are provided in the Third Edition. Candy Ready, Piedmont Technical College, has prepared these exercises in worksheet format, helping ease instructors' use in the classroom. New to the Third Edition are sections on how to integrate SCANS workplace competencies with your course objectives and how to use portfolio assessment for student success. Also new are exercises that can be duplicated and used with Houghton Mifflin's Student Success Roundtable Discussion videotapes.

Acknowledgments

I want to thank everyone who helped me in writing this text: my husband, Stephen P. Kanar, for providing the encouragement and support I needed to complete this book; my family, friends, and colleagues who also encouraged me.

I am grateful to Bill Webber who directed this project and to Gabrielle Stone for her expert editorial help. My special thanks go to Melissa Plumb for her many fine suggestions and for her counsel, encouragement, and guidance through two editions of this book. I am indebted to the entire family of Houghton Mifflin editors and others who contributed to the development, design, and production of *The Confident Student,* Third Edition. Thank you, everyone.

I want to acknowledge the contributions of West Cambridge Associates in formulating the Computer Confidence features and selected exercises, and Dr. Clara Wajngurt of Queensborough Community College for her help and suggestions on math study skills, and D. J. Henry of Daytona Beach Community College for sharing her expertise in portfolio assessment and reflective writing. The following reviewers who read my manuscript and provided me with many excellent suggestions for developing *The Confident Student,* Third Edition into its present form deserve special thanks:

Loretto Allen, State University of New York—Brockport
Virgilia Becker, College of the Redwoods (CA)
Frank Doll, Sinclair Community College (OH)
Laura Ecklin, Napa Valley College (CA)
Margaret Fritz, The University of Toledo Community and Technical College (OH)
Sheryl M. Hartman, Miami-Dade Community College (FL)
D. J. Henry, Daytona Beach Community College (FL)
Laurel Krautwurst, Blue Ridge Community College (NC)
Natalie J. Miller, Joliet Junior College (IL)
Kim Papscun, Arizona State University—West
Candy Ready, Piedmont Technical College (SC)
Susan S. Tully, Aiken Technical College (SC)

Finally, I am deeply grateful to my students, for without them I wouldn't have been inspired to write this book.

CCK

To the Student

A new book, like a new semester or quarter, is a new beginning. On the first day of class, everything seems possible. And if you use this book well, starting right now, *The Confident Student,* Third Edition can help you translate your dreams of success into reality, all the way up through graduation and beyond.

You and *The Confident Student*

This book is designed to help you discover the ways in which you learn most easily and most enjoyably, and to help you define your own goals and preferences as you embark on your college career and look ahead to life and work in the future. It includes thorough discussions, illustrations, and easy-to-understand suggestions on ways to develop all the skills you will need to perform well in your classes and build confidence in your ability to learn.

Some sections contain so many ideas for strengthening a particular skill that you might feel overwhelmed at first. As you read each discussion, keep in mind that you can try out as many or as few ideas as you like to see whether they work for you. You will develop the best ways for *you* to study as you adapt the ideas in this book to suit your own needs and personal learning style.

How to Use This Book

To make the most of this book begin with the Skill Finder on pages xix–xxi. Use it to get an idea of what the book covers, to discover which of your study skills might need improvement, and to note which parts of the book you might find most useful. When you begin your assignments, read each discussion carefully, take all of the Awareness Checks to construct a complete profile of your skills and interests, follow the suggestions in the Confidence Builders and Computer Confidence boxes to expand your learning horizons, and do the chapter exercises to reinforce your grasp of each skill.

Follow your instructor's syllabus and complete the chapters he or she suggests, but don't be afraid to skip around. Turn to the Table of Contents for an overview of the topics this book covers.

The Confident Student, Third Edition is a book you will want to keep on your reference shelf when you've finished the course in which you are using it. You can take advantage of all its tools and special features to refresh your knowledge of important skills as you face new challenges in more advanced courses or even after graduation.

Make It a Better Book

When you've completed your course, I'd really like to know your opinion of *The Confident Student,* Third Edition. Tell me what works and what doesn't work for you; suggest ways that I could make improvements. Write to me at the following address:

Carol C. Kanar
c/o Houghton Mifflin Student Success Programs
215 Park Avenue South
New York, NY 10003

Skill Finder

This questionnaire is designed to give you an overview of *The Confident Student* and an opportunity to determine which skills you need to develop or improve. Read each statement. If the statement applies to you, check YES. If the statement does not apply to you, check NO. See the end of the questionnaire for instructions about how to interpret your results.

Motivating Yourself

YES	NO	
❐	❐	**1.** I know what my basic skill strengths and weaknesses are.
❐	❐	**2.** I know what my learning style is, and how to use it.
❐	❐	**3.** I am able to adapt to others' teaching and learning styles.
❐	❐	**4.** I am able to keep myself motivated.

Setting Goals and Using Resources

YES	NO	
❐	❐	**5.** I usually have a goal I am trying to reach.
❐	❐	**6.** I have no trouble making decisions about which courses I should take.
❐	❐	**7.** I know what courses are required at my college.
❐	❐	**8.** I have a college catalog, and I check it often to keep up with important dates and deadlines.

Listening and Note Taking

YES	NO	
❐	❐	**9.** When I am listening to a lecture, I do not become distracted.
❐	❐	**10.** I know the words to listen for in a lecture that will tell me what is important.
❐	❐	**11.** I usually take notes during class.
❐	❐	**12.** When I take notes, I am able to keep up with the lecturer.

Time Management

YES	NO	
❐	❐	**13.** I know how to manage my time.
❐	❐	**14.** I almost always arrive on time for classes.
❐	❐	**15.** Only sickness or emergency prevents me from coming to class.
❐	❐	**16.** When I have a lot of studying to do, I have no trouble getting started.

Memory and Concentration

YES	NO	
❐	❐	**17.** I can usually remember what I've studied well enough to get good grades on tests.
❐	❐	**18.** I associate new material to be learned with what I already know.

YES	NO	
❒	❒	**19.** I have a certain place where I do most of my studying.
❒	❒	**20.** I am not easily distracted when there is something I need to study.
❒	❒	**21.** I do not hesitate to ask questions in class.

Using Textbooks Effectively

❒	❒	**22.** Before I read a chapter, I look it over briefly to see what it is going to be about.
❒	❒	**23.** I am able to follow the writer's ideas in a textbook chapter.
❒	❒	**24.** I am able to maintain my interest in what I read.
❒	❒	**25.** I read chapter headings and turn them into questions I can answer as I read.
❒	❒	**26.** I always take a few minutes to examine the tables and other visual aids in chapters I read.
❒	❒	**27.** I use mapping techniques to organize information.
❒	❒	**28.** I almost always underline or highlight my textbooks.
❒	❒	**29.** I make notes from my textbooks to help me study.
❒	❒	**30.** I review my notes before and after class.
❒	❒	**31.** I keep a list of special terms and definitions of words I need to learn for my courses.

Preparing for and Taking Tests

❒	❒	**32.** I usually know what to study for tests.
❒	❒	**33.** I am almost always prepared for tests.
❒	❒	**34.** Taking a test does not make me nervous if I am prepared.
❒	❒	**35.** If I don't know the answer to a multiple-choice question, I use guessing strategies.
❒	❒	**36.** I do not usually run out of time when I am taking a test.
❒	❒	**37.** It doesn't bother me if someone finishes a test before I do.

Critical Thinking

❒	❒	**38.** Before I attempt to learn anything new, I examine my assumptions about it.
❒	❒	**39.** When I am listening to a lecture, I can usually predict what the lecturer will say next.
❒	❒	**40.** I am good at interpreting, or making sense of, what I learn.
❒	❒	**41.** I am able to evaluate information for its usefulness.

Reading and Writing

❒	❒	**42.** I know what it means to be an "active" reader.
❒	❒	**43.** I am able to understand and remember most of what I read.
❒	❒	**44.** I know how to plan and write an essay.
❒	❒	**45.** I can usually find and correct my errors.

Studying Math and Science

YES	NO	
❒	❒	**46.** I do all math problems at the ends of chapters whether they are assigned or not.
❒	❒	**47.** In a math course, I usually know why I make the errors I make on tests.
❒	❒	**48.** I believe I am capable of doing well in math.
❒	❒	**49.** I know how to prepare for my science class.
❒	❒	**50.** Remembering information from science textbooks is easy for me.

Count the number of "no" answers for each section. If you have more than one per section, you may want to improve or develop the study skill or skills identified by the section heading. Use the list below to locate the part in *The Confident Student,* Third Edition that covers these skills; see the Table of Contents or Index if you want to locate a specific topic or discussion. Your instructor may ask you to answer these questions again at the end of your course to see what skills you have mastered.

SKILL FINDER	CORRESPONDING PART IN *THE CONFIDENT STUDENT,* 3RD EDITION
Questions 1–16	Part One
Questions 17–37	Part Two
Questions 38–50	Part Three

CHAPTER 1

Motivating Yourself to Learn

You're in college now, and you want to succeed. You may be a recent high school graduate, a returning student, or a military veteran. Perhaps you are a working person who wants to upgrade your job skills, or a homemaker who never had an opportunity to attend college until now.

Whatever your background, you are one of a diverse group of students who represent many cultures, nationalities, and ethnic groups. Like them, you have a unique contribution to make to the learning community of which you are now a part. Like them, you want to get off to a good start.

Begin with these thoughts in mind: Learning is a complicated process. Although some strategies or methods work well for many people, no two people learn exactly the same way. The motivation to learn lies within you—it is your responsibility, not anyone else's. In fact, a personal quality that is extremely valuable to develop, if you do not already possess it, is individual responsibility. This quality is essential not only in college but in the workplace, where you will be challenged with tasks that require you to upgrade your skills.

To help you get motivated and stay motivated, this chapter explains four keys to success in college. They will help you unlock your learning process and free the confident student within you. Moreover, they may open doors for you in the workplace.

- Assess your strengths and weaknesses.
- Discover and use your learning style.
- Develop critical thinking and study skills.
- Adapt to others' styles.

Your academic advisors can help you select courses that take your academic strengths and weaknesses into account and enable you to build new skills.

© Jean Claude Lejeune

ASSESS YOUR STRENGTHS AND WEAKNESSES

One important key to your success in college is a realistic assessment of your strengths and weaknesses in the basic skills of reading, writing, and math. If you do not know what your strengths and weaknesses are in these areas, you may overestimate your skills, believing that if you try hard enough, you can pass a course for which you are unprepared. Or you may underestimate the value of your experiences outside college, which can make up for some skill deficiencies. For example, you may have gained knowledge and abilities from reading, working, traveling, or serving in the military that you can apply to your college courses. Knowing what you can and cannot do, and making decisions based on that knowledge, will help you make the right course selections.

Your self-assessment should take into consideration the advice you have received from helpful people at your college. Your academic advisors and instructors are eager for you to be successful. That is why they have invested so much time in testing you, advising you, and perhaps requiring you to take courses that will help you develop your reading, writing, or math skills.

They also know that employers expect competence in reading, writing, and math, and that a strong foundation in these skills is a career asset.

Self-assessment is a key to success in the workplace as well as in college. When confronted with any new learning situation, ask yourself questions such as "What do I already know about this?" "What skills do I have that I can use?" "What personal qualities apply?" "What knowledge, skills, or qualities do I need that I don't have?" Your answers will provide the self-knowledge you need to make the right choices.

For an informal assessment of your strengths and weaknesses in the basic skills, complete the following Awareness Check.

AWARENESS CHECK #1

What Are Your Strengths/Weaknesses in Basic Skills?

Check *yes* or *no* to the following statements.

Yes	No	
☐	☐	1. I can read college textbooks without difficulty.
☐	☐	2. I know the meanings of most of the words used in my textbooks.
☐	☐	3. I have usually done well in subjects that require a lot of reading.
☐	☐	4. I know how to write an essay.
☐	☐	5. I rarely make grammatical errors.
☐	☐	6. I am a good speller.
☐	☐	7. I consider myself a good writer.
☐	☐	8. I can do basic math, such as addition, subtraction, multiplication, and division, with few or no errors.
☐	☐	9. I passed algebra in high school with a grade of B or A.
☐	☐	10. Math has always been one of my best subjects.
☐	☐	11. According to an assessment test score or an advisor, my reading skills need improvement.
☐	☐	12. According to an assessment test score or an advisor, my writing skills need improvement.
☐	☐	13. According to an assessment test score or an advisor, my math skills need improvement.

If you checked *no* to statements 1–3 and *yes* to statement 11, you may need to improve your reading skills. If you checked *no* to statements 4–7 and *yes* to statement 12, you may need to develop your writing skills. If you checked *no* to statements 8–10 and *yes* to statement 13, you may need to strengthen your math skills. Since strong reading, writing, and math skills are essential to success in college, you will want to build on your strengths and overcome your weaknesses in these three areas. However, academic skills alone are not what make you intelligent. You may be smart in other ways.

CONFIDENCE BUILDER

Your Kind of Intelligence

"Book learning" is only one kind of intelligence. Researchers have found other categories of intelligence that have changed our definition of what it means to be smart.

In *Using Your Head: The Many Ways of Being Smart,* Sara Gilbert explains five ways in which people are intelligent: They may be *book smart, art smart, body smart, people smart,* or *street smart.* According to Gilbert, we all possess some of each kind of intelligence, though we may have more of one kind than another. We can also develop intelligence. For example, book smart people can develop their creativity, which is something that comes naturally to art smart people.

- *Book smart* people do well in school, score high on tests, and are likely to be well organized and logical. They excel in some or all of the academic skills of reading, writing, and math. If you are book smart, you probably learn best by reading.
- *Art smart* people make music, paint pictures, write novels, or have a strong interest in and potential for creative expression. If you are art smart, you may feel you get more out of listening and observing than reading.
- *Body smart* people often have good muscular development and natural coordination. They excel at sports. If you are body smart, you may be able to learn more effectively by combining studying with some physical activity.
- *Street smart* people can turn almost any situation to their advantage and are often good at solving problems. If you are street smart, you probably do best in subjects that you think will help you in your career or chosen field.
- *People smart* individuals are good at empathizing with others and guessing what they may think or are likely to do. If you are people smart, you may have strong analytical skills, and you probably can figure out what your instructors expect.

Do you think you are mostly book smart, art smart, body smart, street smart, or people smart? Do you have characteristics that fit more than one of these categories? The value of recognizing the many ways of being smart is that you learn to appreciate others for the diverse contributions they are able to make. Moreover, you gain confidence in knowing that not only can you do some things well, but you can also develop new skills.

DISCOVER AND USE YOUR LEARNING STYLE

Discovering and using your learning style is another key to success in college. Like everything else about you, your learning style is uniquely your own, different from anyone else's. *Your learning style is your characteristic and preferred way of learning.* Another way to look at learning style is to think of it as the conditions under which you find it easiest and most pleasant to learn and work. For example, suppose you buy a new piece of software. What would be the easiest, quickest, and most pleasant way for you to learn how to use it? Would you read the manual, follow the instructions on a tutorial disk, ask a friend who knows how to use it, or sign up for a course? None of these ways is the *best* way to learn how to use new software, but one of these ways, or a combination of them, may be the best way for *you* to learn.

EXERCISE 1.1

Try this experiment for a vivid example of the way your learning style affects you.

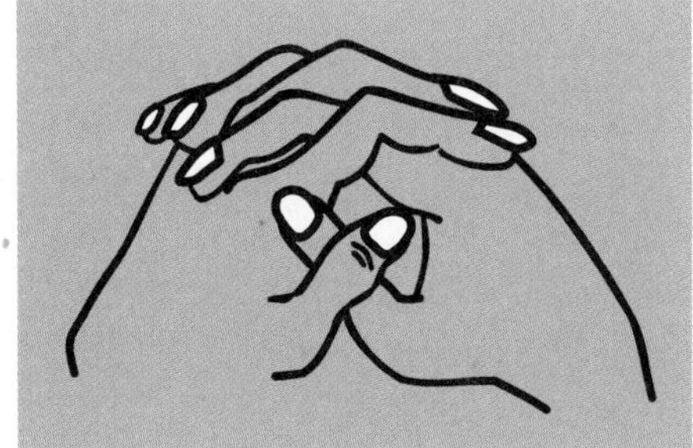

1. Fold your hands.
2. Look at which thumb is on top. Is it your left or right?
3. Now fold your hands again so that the other thumb is on top. Does this position feel uncomfortable to you?
4. Fold your hands your preferred way, and notice the difference in feeling.

Folding your hands is something you do automatically, and because you always do it your preferred way, you feel comfortable. But when you fold your hands differently, you feel uncomfortable because that position is not natural for you. Your learning style is automatic in a similar way. When you are in a classroom environment that matches your learning style, everything feels right. But if the environment does not match your style, you may feel out of place, uncomfortable, unable to do your best. To combat feelings of discomfort in a classroom environment, understand your learning style. Find ways to adapt your style to fit the environment, and you will be successful. Adapting your style is like learning to live with the wrong thumb on top. At first, it may feel a little strange, but with practice the difference will not be as noticeable.

Your learning style has many components. We will discuss four of them:

1. Your five senses
2. Your body's reactions
3. Your preferred learning environment
4. Your level of motivation

Your Five Senses

Is your learning style primarily visual, auditory, or tactile? *Visual learners* prefer to learn by reading or watching. *Auditory learners* like to learn by listening. *Tactile learners* learn by doing, by touching or manipulating objects, or by using their hands. The following chart provides examples of each learning style and shows how learning style preference affects how you go about completing a task such as learning how to use a computer or assembling a child's toy. As you read the chart, remember that it illustrates learning *preferences*: what each type of learner feels most comfortable doing. The most successful learners are those who can adapt to whatever mode of instruction is in use and who use a combination of learning methods.

Though people can learn to adapt to learning styles that are not their preferred ones, most people have difficulty at first when asked to do something that seems unnatural to them. Imagine the frustration of a secretary, an auditory learner, whose boss says, "Now watch how I fix this copy machine, because the next time it breaks down, I'll expect you to fix it"—or the child, a visual learner, whose teacher says, "I am going to explain how to turn on your computer and start the program. Listen to the steps, and do exactly as I say." You may have felt a similar frustration in classrooms when the instructor presented material in a sensory mode other than your preferred one. For example, if you are a student who dislikes lecture courses, loses concentration, or has trouble following ideas, maybe you're not an auditory learner. To be successful in a lecture class, you may need to develop strategies that will help you adapt to auditory modes of instruction. For one thing, you could concentrate on developing good note-taking skills and listening techniques as explained in Chapter 3. To fill in gaps in your notes, compare them with those of someone in the

LEARNING PREFERENCE	EXAMPLE	LEARNING TO USE COMPUTER	ASSEMBLING A CHILD'S TOY
Visual	Prefers visual sense. Must *see* to understand. Learns best by reading and watching.	Looks at diagrams. Reads a manual. Watches someone demonstrate the process.	Tries to duplicate picture on the box. Reads instructions silently while assembling toy.
Auditory	Prefers auditory sense. Must *hear* to understand. Learns best by listening to an explanation.	Attends a class or workshop to hear explanation. Listens to someone read the instructions.	Reads instructions aloud while working. Asks someone to read each step.
Tactile	Prefers tactile sense. Must *touch* or *feel* to understand. Learns best by engaging in hands-on activity.	Uses trial-and-error approach. Attends a hands-on workshop.	May ignore the instructions or resort to them only when trial-and-error method fails.

class who does have a strong auditory preference and who is good at taking notes.

Because instructors may use a variety of techniques, it is important for you to learn to adapt your learning style preference to whatever instructional mode is in use. The following chart illustrates some common instructional modes, the learning style preferences they appeal to, and adaptive strategies for you to try.

TEACHING TECHNIQUES	LEARNING STYLE/ SENSORY PREFERENCE	ADAPTIVE STRATEGIES TO TRY
Lecture/class discussion	Auditory	Take notes. (tactile and visual) Watch for visual cues such as gestures and facial expressions that emphasize important points. (visual) Pay attention to visual aids or information written on chalkboard. (visual)
Videotaped presentations Use of visual aids	Visual	Listen to instructor's explanations or comments and copy them into your notes. (auditory and tactile) Summarize presentation in your notes and read it aloud to review. (auditory)
Hands-on activity	Tactile	Summarize the activity in your notes to read later. (auditory and visual) Listen to any explanation that accompanies the activity. (auditory)

AWARENESS CHECK #2

What Are Your Sensory Preferences?

Put a check beside all the statements that seem true of you. An explanation of your responses follows the Awareness Check.

☐ 1. I learn best by reading on my own.

☐ 2. I get the best results from listening to lectures.

☐ 3. I enjoy courses where there is some physical activity involved.

☐ 4. I can learn how to do something by watching a demonstration of how it's done.

☐ 5. Class discussions are helpful to me.

☐ 6. I like to type and to use computers.

☐ 7. Illustrations, charts, and diagrams improve my understanding.

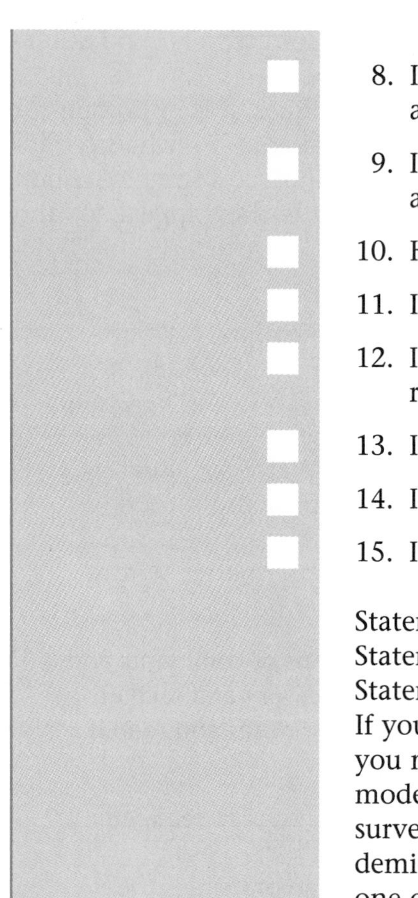

8. I'd rather listen to the instructor's explanation than do the assigned reading.
9. I get more out of labs than lectures because of the hands-on approach.
10. How-to manuals and printed directions are helpful to me.
11. I like to use audiocassette tapes of lessons and exercises.
12. I prefer to work with machines and equipment than listen to or read explanations.
13. I can learn to do something if someone shows me how.
14. I can follow directions best when someone reads them to me.
15. It's not enough to show me; I have to do it myself.

Statements 1, 4, 7, 10, and 13 are characteristic of visual learners. Statements 2, 5, 8, 11, and 14 are characteristic of auditory learners. Statements 3, 6, 9, 12, and 15 are characteristic of tactile learners. If your checks are spread evenly among two or more categories, you may be equally comfortable using one or more of your sensory modes. But remember that this Awareness Check is only an informal survey. For a formal assessment of your learning style, see an academic or career development counselor, who may be able to give you one of several well-known tests.

Your Body's Reactions

When you are in a classroom or study area, lighting, temperature, and the comfort of the furniture may or may not affect your ability to pay attention or to get your work done. If your body does react strongly to these and other influences, such as hunger, tiredness, or mild illness, then you may lose concentration. You should take care of these physiological needs before attempting to do anything that demands your full attention. Determining your physiological preferences and building your schedule accordingly is one way to use your learning style to create the conditions under which you will stay most alert.

Like most people, you probably have a peak time of day when you are most alert and energetic. Throughout the day your concentration, attention, and energy levels fluctuate; in the morning you might be alert and ready for anything, but by afternoon you might feel sapped of energy. If you *are* a morning person, for example, then it would make sense to schedule your classes in the morning if you can. But if you are more alert and can concentrate better in the late afternoon or at night, then schedule as many of your courses as possible in the evening hours. If you anticipate that a certain course will be difficult, make every effort to schedule it at your peak time of day. You should also plan to do as much of your studying as possible at this time of day.

If you learn to accept what you cannot change, then you can adapt to situations that don't meet your preferences, knowing you will have to try harder to pay attention and remain on task. Moreover, although you have limited control over your classroom environment, you can set up your own study environment to reflect all of your important preferences. See Chapter 10 for a detailed discussion and suggestions.

The next Awareness Check will help you understand how your body's reactions might affect your ability to learn.

AWARENESS CHECK #3

How Does Your Body React?

Put a check beside the statements that best describe you.

1. I feel most alert in the morning hours.
2. I don't "come alive" until afternoon or early evening.
3. I am definitely a night person.
4. I concentrate and work best in a brightly lighted room.
5. Bright light distracts me; I prefer natural or non-glare lighting.
6. Overhead lighting is never right; I need an adjustable lamp.
7. The temperature in a classroom does not usually affect my concentration.
8. I can't work or concentrate in a room that is too hot or too cold.
9. I usually get chills next to a fan, air conditioner, or open window.
10. If my chair or desk in class is uncomfortable, I am usually able to ignore it and concentrate.
11. If my chair is not the right height, my back or neck aches.
12. If I feel a little ill or headachy, I can't think about anything else.
13. I can ignore feelings of hunger or tiredness long enough to keep my attention on my work.
14. Mild feelings of illness usually don't distract me from my work.

Your answers to the Awareness Check indicate the following about your body's reactions: The time of day when you are most alert (items 1–3); your lighting preferences (items 4–6); your temperature preferences (items 7–9); your comfort in relation to furnishings in your classroom (items 10–11); the extent to which hunger, tiredness, and illness affect your ability to concentrate in class (items 12–14).

EXERCISE 1.2

Answer the following questions about one of your classes. First determine to what extent your learning is affected by the classroom environment. Then decide what you can do to adapt to the environment.

1. What time does this class meet? Does it meet at the time of day when you feel most alert?______

____

2. Is the temperature in the classroom generally comfortable for you?______

____

3. What type of lighting is available in the classroom, and do you find the lighting acceptable?______

____

4. Are you generally rested or tired when you go to this class?______

____

5. Have you eaten recently before this class, or do you become hungry during class?______

____

6. Would you describe the seating arrangement and the furniture in the classroom as comfortable or uncomfortable?______

____

Your Preferred Learning Environment

A learning environment is much more than the place where your class meets. The way the class is structured is an important part of the learning environment. In what kind of learning environment are you most comfortable? Do you like a traditional classroom, where desks are arranged in rows and the instructor directs activities? Or are you more comfortable in a looser arrangement, where instructor and students sit together in a circle, for example?

Perhaps you are a self-directed student who prefers to work alone in a self-paced class or lab. Or maybe you need a lot of direction and supervision while you learn. You may be a student who learns more from the instructor's lectures and comments than from class discussions. Or you may be a student who doesn't get much out of class unless you have opportunities to work with other students in small groups. The following comments illustrate three learning environment preferences. Can you hear yourself in one of these comments, or do you have yet another preference?

1. **Carol:** The instructors are the ones I've paid my money to listen to; they're the experts. I resent it when a lot of class time is taken up answering questions that are covered in the reading assignments.

The learning environment for your course may affect your feelings about the subject matter as well as your performance.

© Beringer-Dratch/The Image Works

2. **Andy:** I hate this class. All the instructor does is lecture. I learn more in classes where there is a lot of discussion and I can find out what different people think about a topic.

3. **Grant:** I don't like it when I have to adjust my pace to the rest of the class. It seems that the class is always ahead of or behind me. I prefer to work independently in labs where I can progress at my own pace and spend as much time on a topic as I need to.

The first student likes a traditional, teacher-centered classroom. The second student prefers a student-centered environment. The third student, who likes to work alone, prefers individualized instruction.

Most of the time you will have to adapt to whatever learning environment is available. However, understanding your preferences will enable you to select the kind of class in which you are most comfortable, if you have a choice. Counselors and other students are good sources of information about the type of learning environment a specific course or instructor provides.

© Michael Newman/ PhotoEdit

EXERCISE 1.3

Do this exercise by collaborating with a group or partner. Successful group interaction depends on each member's full participation. First, decide who will perform the following roles and duties. In a group, each member should have a role. Partners can share the duties. Next, follow the directions to complete the exercise.

Leader	The leader is responsible for interpreting the exercise directions, keeping the discussion on target, and making sure that everyone participates.
Recorder	The recorder acts as secretary to take notes and summarize the group's findings or record answers after the group achieves consensus (agreement).
Researcher	The researcher consults the textbook, the instructor, or other resources as needed to settle matters of confusion or controversy.
Reciter	The reciter reports back to the class, using the recorder's notes for reference.

Apply what you have learned about the way learning environment affects your classroom performance. Discuss the following questions and record your answers. When you have finished, evaluate your performance.

1. Discuss the similarities and differences in the learning environments of the courses you are taking this term. What conclusions can you draw about the kinds of learning environments available at your college?

2. Discuss your group's learning environment preferences. In what type of learning situation does each group member feel most comfortable, and why?

3. Consider your performance in each of your classes so far. Is there a relationship between learning environment and grades? Explain the relationship.

4. Although you can't change the learning environment, what can you do to adapt to it and improve your performance?

Evaluate your discussion. Did everyone contribute? Did you accomplish your task successfully? What additional questions do you have about learning environment? How will you find answers to your questions?

Your Level of Motivation

Your motivation and your attitude, positive or negative, toward college, work, instructors, and your abilities may depend on your *locus of control.* J. B. Rotter, a psychologist, first explained the concept in 1954 as part of his social learning theory. *Locus* means place. Your locus of control is where you place responsibility for control over your life. Do you believe you are in charge? If so, then you may have an *internal* locus of control. Do you believe others more powerful than you are in control of what happens to you? If so, then you may have an external locus of control.

What does locus of control mean to you as a student, and how can it affect your motivation? To find out, complete the next Awareness Check, and then read the explanation that follows.

AWARENESS CHECK #4
What Is Your Locus of Control?

Yes No

Check *yes* if you agree with a statement; check *no* if you do not agree.

1. If I can do the work, I can get a good grade in any course no matter how good or bad the instructor is.
2. If the teacher isn't a good speaker or doesn't keep me interested, I probably won't do well in the class.
3. I believe that I have the power to control what happens to me.
4. I believe that I have very little control over what happens to me.
5. When I make a mistake, it's usually my fault.
6. When I make a mistake, it's usually because someone didn't make clear to me what I was supposed to do.
7. My grades are the result of how much studying I do.
8. My grades don't seem to be affected by the amount of studying I do.
9. I can adapt easily to a change of plans or events.
10. Adapting to change has always been difficult for me. I like things to be as predictable and orderly as possible.
11. When I fail a test, it's either because I didn't study or I didn't understand the material.
12. When I fail a test, it's either because the test was unfair or the instructor didn't cover the material.
13. I usually don't need anyone to push me or make me study.
14. I can't seem to make myself study.
15. I am a self-motivated person.
16. I need someone to motivate me.

If you checked yes to mostly odd-numbered statements, then you may have an internal locus of control. If you checked yes to mostly even-numbered statements, then you may have an external locus of control. Now read the following descriptions of students who have an internal or external locus of control and decide which most accurately describes you.

The Internal Locus of Control. Students who have an internal locus of control can see a connection between the effort they put forth in a course and the grades they receive. These students tend to be self-motivated, positive thinkers. They believe they can do whatever they set out to accomplish. They are not afraid of change. They welcome challenges. When they make mistakes, they can usually trace the mistake to something they did wrong or something they did not understand. These students don't believe in luck or fate. They are in charge of their lives. When things go wrong, they try to figure out what they can do to put things right again.

The External Locus of Control. Students who have an external locus of control cannot see a connection between the effort they put forth in a course and the grades they receive. They may believe teachers award grades on the basis of personal feelings or that their grades result from good or bad luck. These students tend to be negative thinkers who need someone to motivate them and give them a push to succeed. They believe that many of the things they want in life are out of reach or that other people are holding them back. They may be afraid of change and prefer to follow familiar routines. When they make mistakes, they blame others for being unfair or for not giving them the right information. They believe they have little control over their lives. When something goes wrong, they may feel there is nothing they can do about it.

Research shows that locus of control affects achievement. The more internal your locus of control, the greater your chances for success in college. Thinking positively about yourself and your abilities, accepting responsibility for motivating yourself, and believing that your own best effort will produce results will lead to success in your job or career as well. If you already have an internal locus of control, and many older students do, recognize it for the asset that it is. Use your ability to motivate yourself to stay in control and on track. If your locus of control is external, it is well worth your time to begin developing a more internal one. Here are some ways to do it:

1. **Become a positive thinker.** Earlier in this chapter, you assessed your strengths and weaknesses. Focus on your strengths. Remind yourself of all the things you do well and believe that you will overcome your weaknesses.

2. **Take responsibility for motivating yourself.** Realize that only you can make yourself study. When you study as you should, congratulate yourself and enjoy your good grades. When you don't study, accept the consequences and don't blame others.

3. **Accept the fact that success results from effort.** If you are not getting where you want to go, then apply yourself with more determination. The harder you try and the greater your effort, the more likely you are to get what you want.

4. **Start listening to yourself talk.** Eliminate the nameless "they" from your vocabulary. "*They* made me do it," "*they* keep me from succeeding," if only "*they* had told me" are comments externally motivated students make when things go wrong. Bring the "I" back into your vocabulary and take charge of your life.

In conclusion, the internal and external locus of control represent extremes of behavior. The more internal you are, the more you believe you are in control of your life. The more external you are, the more you believe that someone or something outside yourself is controlling the circumstances that affect your life. In other words, the degree to which you *believe* you can control what happens to you largely determines the amount of control you *actually* have.

EXERCISE 1.4

Discuss the following situations with your group members. Follow the guidelines for group activities on page 12. Determine whether each situation is one you can control, and be able to explain why or why not. Share your answers with the rest of the class.

1. You arrive late to class because:

   Your alarm didn't go off.
   Your ride didn't come.
   You had to work late the night before.
   You had car trouble.

2. Studying is difficult for you because:

   There are too many distractions at home.
   You have a family to take care of.
   The textbooks are difficult or boring.
   You don't know what to study.

3. You never seem to have enough time because:

   People are always interrupting you.
   Your instructors assign too much outside work.
   You have too many things to do.
   You often procrastinate.

4. You are often too hungry to concentrate in class because:

   You usually don't have time for breakfast.
   You can't eat a snack in class to tide you over.
   You have no breaks between classes.
   Class and work make scheduling lunches and snacks difficult.

5. You often leave homework undone because:

   You are too tired to do it.
   You can't seem to turn down your friends' offers to socialize.
   You get stuck or don't understand how to do the assignment.
   You put work or family obligations first.

DEVELOP CRITICAL THINKING AND STUDY SKILLS

Read the following student comments about studying and learning. Do any of them sound like statements you have made? Can you think of another one? Add it to the list in the space provided.

Student A: "My academic skills are OK, but I still don't make the grades I want."

Student B: "I study a lot, but I often study the wrong things."

Student C: "I usually get the point but forget the details."

Student D: "I never seem to have enough time for studying."

Your Comment: ______________________________________

____

____

____

These statements illustrate common problems students encounter as they attend classes and study. You can solve these problems by learning to think critically and study efficiently, though you may have to work hard to overcome your difficulties and may need to devote some time to skill development.

Developing critical thinking and study skills is your third key to success in college. Knowing how to study helps you apply your knowledge and use your skills so that you can be successful in your courses. For example, if you learn how to listen effectively and take good notes, then you will be able to follow lectures and record essential information for study and review. If you learn how to manage your time, then you will be able to keep up with assignments and hand them in on time. If you learn how to prepare for and take tests, then you will be able to make the grades you want.

Learning styles, critical thinking, and study skills overlap. Thinking critically is the means by which you make sense of the world around you. The learning activities that college students must do require critical thinking. For example, you must be able to make decisions, solve problems, reason logically, use your creativity, and know how to learn. Developing critical thinking skills will also make you more employable in the future. Those who can think critically and who know how to gather and use information will get the best jobs and advance more rapidly in their careers than those who don't. Studying is a kind of concentrated thinking that, at its best, involves more than one of your senses. For example, when you read and underline a textbook chapter, you are using your visual and tactile senses. Studying is easier and more efficient when you use what you know about your learning style to create the conditions under which your concentration will be greatest. Figure 1.1 shows how critical thinking and study skills work together to help you complete typical tasks your instructors might ask you to do.

FIGURE 1.1 Using Critical Thinking and Study Skills

CRITICAL THINKING	TASKS TO DO	STUDY SKILLS NEEDED/USED
Making Decisions	Decide when to study.	Set up a schedule.
	Decide what's important.	Read for point, details, key terms.
	Select courses.	Know requirements; use resources.
	Decide what to study.	Review notes, old tests, assignments.
Solving Problems	Solve math problems.	Record problems and solutions on notecards.
	Avoid procrastination.	Make and follow a schedule.
	Reduce test anxiety.	Practice relaxation techniques.
Reasoning	Write a speech.	Make an outline.
	Follow writers' ideas.	Look for patterns of organization.
	Compare theories.	Make a chart or information map.
Knowing how to learn	Learn from reading.	Locate, understand, interpret information.
	Learn from listening.	Use listening and note-taking skills.
Thinking creatively	Compose an original piece of work.	Keep an "idea" journal.
	Develop a project.	Combine ideas in new ways.

ADAPT TO OTHERS' STYLES

Everyone has a learning style. Throughout college you will find yourself in situations where you must acknowledge and accept the different ways that people learn. Being able to adapt to others' styles is the fourth key to your success.

When working collaboratively with a group, or when speaking in front of a class, be aware of others' styles. For example, a person who prefers to work alone may have to be encouraged to participate with the group. Similarly, if you are planning to give an oral presentation, you may need to supplement it with visual aids for the visual learners in the class.

You probably won't find it difficult to adapt to your classmates' styles. Many of them are your friends, and even among those you don't know there is a natural tendency to try to get along since you are going to be working with these people throughout the term. The greatest challenge lies in adapting to your instructors' styles.

Just as you have a learning style, your instructors have teaching styles. An instructor's teaching style determines, to some extent, the instructional methods he or she prefers to use. Although educational researchers define a number of teaching styles, we will consider only two basic types: *independent* and *interactive*. Each of these styles represents an extreme of behavior. Many instructors' styles fall somewhere between the extremes.

The instructor whose style is independent is usually formal and businesslike with students and places more importance on individual effort than group effort. This instructor expects students to assume responsibility for learning, to work independently, and to seek help when they need it. Lecture is the preferred method of this instructor. He or she will often call on students rather than ask for volunteers. Students often feel competitive in this instructor's class. If you feel most comfortable in lecture courses and like working independently, then you may be able to do your best with an instructor whose style is independent.

The instructor whose style is interactive is usually informal with students and places more importance on group effort than individual effort. This instructor would like students to assume responsibility for learning, but doesn't expect it. Instead, he or she will guide students step by step through tasks and anticipate their need for help. Small group activities and large group discussions are this instructor's preferred methods. Rather than call on students, he or she will usually ask for volunteers. Students often feel cooperative in this instructor's class. If you feel most comfortable in classes where students do most of the talking and if you would rather work with others than by yourself, then you may be able to do your best work with an instructor whose style is interactive.

If you do not like or do not get along with one of your instructors, you may be reacting negatively to a teaching style that differs from your learning style. However, don't let personal feelings keep you from being successful in the course. Instead, focus on what *you* can do to meet the instructor's requirements, and make an extra effort to adapt to his or her style. If you make this effort, you may find that your relationship with your instructor improves dramatically.

In an ideal situation, counselors would match students with instructors who have similar styles. Unfortunately, most of the time you may not have a choice of instructors. By learning to adapt to your instructors' styles now, you are preparing for the future. Throughout your career, you will encounter bosses, coworkers, and others whose styles differ from yours.

EXERCISE 1.5 To analyze an instructor's teaching style, complete the checklist that follows. Fill in the name of one of your courses, and then check each phrase that describes your instructor.

Course: ____________________

1. Formal, businesslike attitude ☐
2. Informal, casual attitude ☐
3. Encourages competition among students ☐
4. Encourages cooperation among students ☐
5. Lectures most of the time ☐
6. Holds class discussion most of the time ☐
7. Stresses importance of individual effort ☐
8. Stresses importance of group effort ☐
9. Often uses visual aids ☐
10. Rarely uses visual aids ☐
11. Calls on students ☐
12. Asks for volunteers ☐
13. Expects students to ask for help ☐
14. Guides students step by step ☐
15. Mainly sticks to facts ☐
16. Often shares personal experiences ☐
17. "Tells" what to do, gives directions ☐
18. "Shows" what to do, gives directions ☐

Odd-numbered items describe the independent teaching style. Even-numbered items describe the interactive style. If you checked more even- than odd-numbered items, your instructor's style is probably interactive. If you checked some even- and some odd-numbered items, your instructor's style may be independent and interactive.

CRITICAL THINKING APPLICATION

Based on what you have learned about the four keys to success explained in this chapter, create a profile of yourself as a learner. Write an essay in which you analyze your strengths and weaknesses and make suggestions for self-improvement. Conclude your essay by explaining how what you have learned about yourself will help you now and in the future. Title your essay "My Learning Profile." The following questions will help you think through your essay as you plan what to write. Review sections of the chapter as needed.

1. Of reading, writing, and math, which is your strongest skill? Which skill needs improvement?
2. Describe your type of intelligence based on Gilbert's types as explained on page 4.
3. Is your learning style primarily visual, auditory, or tactile? Explain your answer.
4. At what time of day are you most alert? How do temperature, lighting, hunger, and other physiological preferences affect your learning?
5. What is your preferred learning environment? Do you study best alone or with others?
6. Is your locus of control internal or external? Explain your answer.
7. Review the critical thinking and study skills listed in Figure 1.1 on page 18. Which of these are you good at? Which give you difficulty?
8. Do you prefer the independent or interactive teaching style, and why?
9. What can you do to build on your strengths and overcome your weaknesses?

SUMMARY

The first two paragraphs of the following summary are highlighted to make important points stand out. ***Highlighting*** *is a strategy confident students use to help them follow a writer's ideas, maintain concentration, call attention to important ideas, and remind them of what to review. Using the first two paragraphs as models, highlight the rest of the summary on your own.*

Strategies for becoming a confident, successful student include making use of the four keys to success in college discussed in this chapter.

1. **The first key.** Assess your academic strengths and weaknesses.
2. **The second key.** Discover and use your learning style.
3. **The third key.** Sharpen your thinking and study skills.
4. **The fourth key.** Adapt to others' styles.

Assessing your academic strengths and weaknesses when you enter college is the most important key. Being realistic about what you are able to do will help you select courses in which you can succeed.

Discovering and using your learning style is another important key to your success. Use your five senses to help you take in information accurately and remember what you learn. Let your body's reactions tell you when you are most alert; then try to plan your schedule accordingly. Know which learning environment you prefer, but be willing to adapt to others. Increase your level of motivation by developing an internal locus of control.

A third key to your success in college is your effort to develop critical thinking and study skills. Making decisions, solving problems, using creativity, processing information, and reasoning logically are critical thinking skills involved in studying. All the important study skills you will need to develop or improve—such as how to take notes, listen effectively, read with greater comprehension, and prepare for and take tests—are covered in this book.

The fourth key is your willingness to adapt to your instructors' teaching styles. If you make an honest effort to learn, no matter how an instructor approaches a subject, then you will make efficient use of class time and develop good relations with your instructors.

YOUR REFLECTIONS

Reflect on what you have learned about strategies for learning and how you can best apply that information. Use the following list of questions to stimulate your thinking; then write your reflections. Your response may include answers to one or more of the questions. Incorporate in your writing specific information from this chapter.

- What is your greatest strength as a learner? What weakness do you need to overcome?
- How do you plan to use the four keys to success in college—self-assessment, learning style, critical thinking/study skills, adapting to others' styles?
- What can you do to maintain or develop self-motivation?
- As a result of completing the activities in this chapter, what is the most important thing you have learned about yourself?
- What have you learned from this chapter that will help you in your interactions with others as you pursue your academic career?

Date ______________________________

CHAPTER 2

Setting Goals and Solving Problems

Getting what you want from college, a career, or even a relationship takes planning. You can't just wait for something to happen. You must set a goal, make a plan to achieve it, and follow through. If your plan isn't working, you must be flexible enough to make the changes that will lead to success.

How do you react when your plans don't work or your goals seem out of reach? How do you react to problems? Do you take steps to solve them, or do you figure they'll eventually work out without your help? You probably know some students who can't seem to cope with grades, work, relationships, or finances, while others seem to lead problem-free lives. Is it luck? No, the students who cope have learned problem-solving skills.

Your third key to success in college, critical thinking and study skills, unlocks two more valuable life skills explained in this chapter: *goal setting* and *problem solving.* These skills can help you to plan effectively and to solve the problems that are bound to arise as you continue your education. They will also make your life easier and more productive in the workplace.

This chapter will help you accomplish the following objectives:

- Set goals for success in college.
- Set reachable long-term and short-term goals.
- Use the COPE method to solve problems.

SET GOALS FOR SUCCESS IN COLLEGE

You can be successful if you set goals based on what you want to accomplish. If success in college is your goal, determine what you want out of your education. Do you have a career goal, or are you undecided? What other rewards does a college education offer? Ask yourself "Why am I here?" To help you clarify your reasons for coming to college, complete Awareness Check 5.

AWARENESS CHECK #5
What Are Your Reasons for Attending College?

Put a check beside the reasons for attending college that match your own, or add a different reason in the space provided.

1. I want to earn a degree, but I haven't decided what I want to do.
2. My friends are in college, and they wanted me to be with them.
3. My parents want me to get a college education.
4. I want to prepare myself for a career of some kind.
5. I have an athletic scholarship, veteran's benefits, or other source of funding.
6. I want to make a lot of money.
7. I want to improve my skills so I can get a better job than the one I have now.
8. I want to broaden my knowledge.
9. I wasn't able to go to college when I was younger; now I want that experience.
10. Improving my education will help me advance to a higher-level position at work.
11. I am a non-native speaker of English, and one of my goals is to improve my language skills.
12. Your reason?____

A goal should be something that *you* desire and that *you* will be motivated enough to reach. Your answers to the Awareness Check provide the key for understanding how your reasons for attending college can motivate you to reach your goals. If you checked only item 2 or item 3, for example, then you may have difficulty motivating yourself to do well, because your reasons for attending college are based more on others' expectations than your own. You need to decide what *you* want out of college. If you checked only item 7 or item 10, then you have a more specific goal in mind and are probably already working to accomplish it. You may need to find additional motivation only if you encounter a setback. If you checked only item 1 or item 4, then you have a practical reason for being in college, but you have not chosen a career or major. As soon as you do that, course selection will be easier for you. You will be motivated by a clearer sense of direction. If you checked only item 6, then you may have set an unrealistic goal. A college education, though it prepares you for a career, does not guarantee that you will make lots of money. Motivation is easier to find when your goals are realistic and you believe you can achieve them. If you checked item 11, your college may have a special program for non-native speakers of English. You may have recognized this program's value to your success in college and in the workplace.

Perhaps you checked several items. Checks beside items 7, 8, 9, and 10, for example, could mean that you are an older student who strongly desires a college education that will broaden your understanding and provide access to a better job. If you checked items 1, 4, and 5, then you may be a student who wants a degree and has the funding to get it, but you are still exploring the possibilities of what you might do with your education. A visit to your college's career center might help you decide on a major or set a career goal that will keep you motivated.

There are still other reasons for attending college that you may or may not have considered. In the courses you take, you will be exposed to new ideas, beliefs, and ways of looking at the world. At times you will be excited by what you are learning; at times you will be frustrated by opinions and values that challenge your own. A college education can help you develop a flexible and open mind, sharpen your ability to think, and enrich your life. Best of all, you may discover in yourself talents, skills, and interests that you did not know you possessed.

SET REACHABLE LONG-TERM AND SHORT-TERM GOALS

A *long-term goal* takes a while to accomplish. A *short-term goal* is one of several steps you might take to reach a long-term goal. Suppose one of your long-term goals is to get a degree. Completing a course required to earn that degree would be one of many short-term goals you would accomplish in the process. The following chart contrasts long-term goals with some short-term goals you might set to reach them.

LONG-TERM GOALS	SHORT-TERM GOALS
Complete a course successfully.	Attend regularly. Arrive on time each day. Make a study schedule and follow it. Improve note-taking skills. Earn good grades. Keep up with assignments.
Graduate from college.	Complete required courses. Complete additional courses needed. Meet all degree requirements. Apply for graduation and pay fees.
Get a job in a chosen career field.	Get the degree or obtain the experience necessary to qualify. Prepare a résumé. Apply for the job. Have a successful interview. Repeat steps as needed until you are hired.

As you can see from the chart, *long-term* and *short-term* are relative terms. Though graduation from college may be a long-term goal since it takes several years to reach, it may also be a short-term goal when you view it as a step toward getting your dream job—a goal that may take many more years. Similarly, completing a required course may be a short-term goal needed to reach the longer-term goal of graduation. However, completing that course might also seem to be a long-term goal in comparison to the short-term goals of completing daily assignments or weekly quizzes needed to pass the course. The key to successful goal setting is to know what your long-term goals are and what short-term goals you need to set to reach them.

In general, we can think of goals as personal, academic, career, or work related. The chart on page 28 compares three types of goals.

Most students are in college because they seek the skills and knowledge that will make them employable. Although some enter college with a career in mind, many are undecided. Some students, like Ellen, change their minds. Ellen had always wanted to be a nurse even though she knew very little about what nursing entailed. After completing her required courses, she was accepted into her college's nursing program. Ellen's math and science skills were strong, and she enjoyed taking her anatomy and physiology course, as well as the other courses in her program. But when one of her courses required her to spend time in a local hospital tending to the needs of the sick, she realized immediately that nursing was not what she wanted to do for the rest of her life. She was neither suited to working in a hospital environment nor to the stress that accompanies a career in nursing. At first, Ellen was at a loss. She had invested time and money in a career she no longer wanted. To change her major could add a year or more to her graduation time; nevertheless, that is what she

THREE TYPES OF GOALS

Personal Goals	Losing weight Improving fitness Developing a positive attitude Increasing time spent with family Overcoming a bad habit
Academic Goals	Passing a difficult course Making a grade of A on a test Improving reading comprehension Developing good study skills Graduating from college
Career/Work Related	Getting the job you want Getting a raise or promotion Changing jobs or careers Improving relations with coworkers Upgrading job skills or learning new ones

decided to do. Ellen is now the financial manager of an electronics corporation. She can't imagine having a more rewarding career, and she believes that changing her major from nursing to marketing was the right decision for her.

Ellen's story illustrates how personal, academic, and career goals can overlap. Ellen's career goal was to become a nurse. Her academic goal was to complete her degree in nursing. Ellen had hoped to find satisfaction in her work, so her personal goal was to have a career doing something she liked. At the time she thought she would enjoy being a nurse. As she learned more about her chosen career, however, Ellen's personal goal of job satisfaction was not being met. This led to her decision to change her career goal. She decided that she wanted a management-level position within a large business. As a result, her academic goals changed as well. Her new goals were to change her major to marketing and to complete the courses required for her degree.

What about values and ethics? Did they play a role in Ellen's goal-setting? *Values* are your judgments about what is right and wrong. They are your standards of behavior, and they include such standards as reliability, respect, responsibility, fairness, caring, and citizenship. *Ethics,* on the other hand, are community standards of behavior. Cheating in college is unethical because the college community expects students to earn their grades. Making personal calls at work or taking office supplies to use at home are unethical practices because someone else has to pay for the calls and supplies. Employers expect you not to steal from them. Would it have been ethical for Ellen to pursue a nursing career, feeling as she did? No, because the medical community expects its workers to be dedicated. How dedicated could Ellen be to a job she didn't like? Ellen's values shaped her decision to change majors. She did not want to pursue a career in which she might not be able to live up to her employer's and patients' expectations.

EXERCISE 2.1 Complete the items that follow to make a plan for achieving a long-term goal.

1. What is a long-term goal you want to reach? ______________________________
____

2. What time limit will you set for reaching your goal? ______________________________
____

3. On the lines below, list some short-term goals you will have to accomplish before reaching your long-term goal, and your plan for completing them.

Short-term goals	**Plan**
____________________	____________________
____________________	____________________
____________________	____________________

Which of your values play a role in setting this goal? How? ______________________________
____

Personal values and ethical choices not only are an important part of goal-setting; they also influence every aspect of your life. They make up what is called "character." Character is an asset in college, at work, and in all your relations with others. Figure 2.1 lists values that build character. You can build your character by incorporating these values into your life and by considering them as you set goals.

A goal should be *reachable,* with an outcome you can expect to achieve given your skills, motivation, and values. As Figure 2.2 on page 31 shows, reachable goals have six characteristics.

1. **A reachable goal is realistic;** it is based on your abilities, interests, needs, and desires. For example, in choosing a career goal you should consider your skills and interests. If you dislike math and dread balancing your checkbook every month, then accounting may not be a realistic career goal for you. If you like to write, have always done well in English courses, and enjoy working with others to make reports and presentations, then a career as a technical writer might be a realistic goal for you. Your college may have a career center or provide career counseling that will help you evaluate your interests so that you can consider the jobs, professions, or public services best suited to your abilities and preferences. Career counseling can help you determine your chances for employment in specific fields. You might learn that jobs are scarce in a field you have been considering. Or you might discover a new field of interest that offers many employment opportunities.

FIGURE 2.1 Values That Build Character

Trustworthiness	Be honest and sincere. Don't deceive, mislead, or betray a trust. Stand up for your beliefs. Never ask a friend or colleague to do something that is wrong.
Respect	Be courteous and polite. Accept and appreciate differences. Respect others' rights to make their own decisions. Don't abuse, demean, or take advantage of others.
Responsibility	Be accountable for your actions. Think about the consequences of your behavior before you act. Don't make excuses or take credit for others' work.
Fairness	Treat all people fairly, be open-minded, and listen to opposing points of view. Don't take advantage of others' mistakes.
Caring	Show you care about others through kindness, sharing, compassion, and empathy. Be considerate of others' feelings.
Citizenship	Play by the rules and obey the laws. Respect authority. Stay informed and vote.

Adapted from the Character Counts Coalition's "pillars of character." Appearing in Reece/Brandt, *Effective Human Relations in Organizations,* 6th edition, Houghton Mifflin Company, © 1996, pp.179–180.

2. **A reachable goal is believable and possible;** you must believe that you *can* reach your goal and that it is possible to reach it within a reasonable length of time. Suppose you want to buy a CD player, portable tape player, or tape recorder. After doing some comparison shopping, you find that the price is more than you expected, and you decide to wait. You set a goal to save the money. Knowing how much you need and how much you can afford to set aside each month, you determine that it will take five months to save the money. Each month you deposit the amount you have designated. Your goal is believable because you can afford the extra savings. Your goal is possible because you think five months is a reasonable amount of time. Your long-term goal is to save enough money to make your purchase. Each deposit you make represents the achievement of a short-term goal needed to reach the long-term goal.

3. **A reachable goal is measurable;** establish a time frame and a foreseeable outcome. For example, if your goal is "to make a lot of money," decide how you are going to do it, when you are going to do it, and how much is "a lot." Have a foreseeable outcome at the end of which you can say, "I have reached my goal." If you set a goal to graduate from college four years from now, determine which courses to take and plan your schedule so that you can earn a sufficient number of credits each semester or quarter.

FIGURE 2.2 Six Characteristics of Reachable Goals

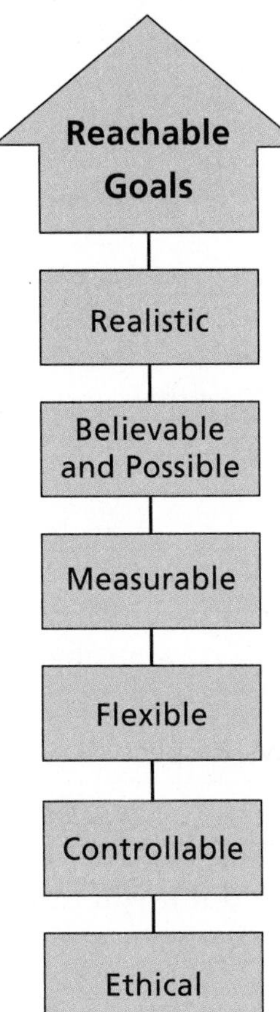

4. **A reachable goal is flexible;** rarely do you set a goal and follow it through to completion without any problems. In working toward your college degree, for example, you may fail or withdraw from one or more courses, or you may change majors and lose credits that have to be made up. These are temporary setbacks that may interrupt your progress but need not keep you from reaching your goal. Reassess your plan for reaching the goal; revise it, or make a new plan. Although it may take you longer to reach your goal, it is time well spent if you are doing what you want to do.

5. **A reachable goal is controllable;** you must be in charge. Set goals *you* can control and determine your own time limit for completing them. No one can, or should, set goals for you. Suppose you need to study for an important exam, and you know from past experience that you need at least three days to prepare yourself. Your study partner says, "We can ace this test with a four-hour study session the night before." That strategy may work for her, but will it work for you? If your goal is to make a good grade, set up your own study schedule and stick to it. You are the best one to determine how much time it will take you to prepare for a test.

6. **A reachable goal is ethical;** it is fair to all concerned. The steps you take to reach your goal should not in any way cause you to violate rules, take advantage of others, or compromise your values. Suppose you are enrolled in a reading class that requires you to spend at least two hours a week in a reading lab practicing the skills you learned in class. The reading class is required as a prerequisite to a composition course that is also required. You have set a short-term goal of completing the course with a grade no lower than B. On your way to lab a friend says, "Let's cut today. We work on our own in there anyway. If we sign in and leave, no one will know." You know this is probably true because the lab is monitored by a technician who sends a copy of the sign-in sheet to the instructor.

   What are the ethics involved in this situation? If you cut the class, you are engaging in unethical conduct for three reasons. First, you are breaking a rule. Second, you are taking advantage of your instructor by signing in and leading him or her to believe that you were there. Third, if honesty is one of your values, then you are compromising it. On the practical side, cutting lab doesn't help you reach your goal. Avoiding practice time prevents your mastery of the skills and may lead to a poor grade. Is it possible to engage in unethical behavior and still reach your goals? In the short term, maybe. But in the long run, unethical conduct catches up with you. Since ethical behavior improves your chances of reaching your goals, it is safe to say that a reachable goal is also an ethical one.

EXERCISE 2.2

Analyze one of your personal, academic, or work-related goals in terms of the six characteristics of reachable goals.

1. State your goal.

____

____

2. Which of your skills and interests make this a **realistic** goal for you?

____

____

3. Explain how your goal is **believable** and **possible.**

____

____

4. Is your goal **measurable?** For example, how long will it take you to reach your goal? When will you know you have achieved it?

____

____

5. Explain how your goal is **flexible,** so that you can continue to progress toward it if you experience a setback.

____

____

6. Is your goal **controllable?** Explain how this is a goal you believe you can reach on your own.

____

____

7. Is your goal **ethical?** Explain how.

____

____

USE THE COPE METHOD TO SOLVE PROBLEMS

As you strive to reach your goals, you will encounter problems. Maintain a positive attitude about your problems by thinking of them as challenges you can meet. To meet a challenge, you need a problem-solving method you can rely on and adapt to any situation.

One Student's Challenge

Kate, a mother of two children, thought the adjustment to college might be easier at a community college than at a university, where most of the students would probably be younger and unmarried. Kate wants a college education and the employment opportunities that will follow. She also wants to complete her education as quickly as she can, so she has enrolled in three morning classes and one night class.

When she first thought about attending college, Kate thought she would have plenty of time to manage the household and do her homework. By the end of the first week, however, Kate realized she would have to do more studying than she had ever done before. By the end of the fifth week she was behind, and her grades were not at all what she had expected. She couldn't find time to do all the reading that was required, so she depended on her notes and what she was getting in class. Unfortunately, most of her instructors' test questions were on material covered in the textbooks. Although Kate understood what she read, she had trouble remembering information and deciding what to study. She could not always tell what was important in a chapter or what was likely to appear on a test. Although Kate was making an A in her algebra class—math had always been her best subject—and a solid C in her English course, she was barely pulling a C in her psychology course, and she was sure she would fail her data processing course.

Kate has always thought of herself as a good student. Now she is beginning to doubt whether she will make it through college. She knows part of the problem is that she has too much to do. She never thought that juggling college and home responsibilities would be so difficult. Although her husband was supportive of Kate in the beginning, he is becoming concerned about the money her education costs and the fact that it interferes with their family life. Kate is always tired, and her study time takes away from her time with him and the children. He feels that if Kate can't be successful, which to him means making an A in every course, she should give it up. What do you think Kate should do? If you were in Kate's place, which of the following options would seem most reasonable?

1. Withdraw from college.
2. Withdraw from the two courses in which she seems most likely to fail.
3. See an academic advisor.
4. Ask her instructors for their advice.
5. Find out what additional help is available and take advantage of it.
6. Find a study partner or join a study group.
7. Take a study skills course.
8. Enlist the help of her husband and children.

Some of these options are better than others. Withdrawing from college would certainly get rid of the problem, but Kate would be wasting the time and money she has already spent, and she would have to make up the credits if she were to continue her education at a later time. Withdrawing from the two courses she is least likely to pass may or may not be a good idea. If there is no possibility that she can pull up her grades, this strategy would leave her more time to devote to the remaining three courses. Since Kate is only five weeks into the term, she may still have time to pull up her grades. Seeing her instructor before making a decision to withdraw would be a better option.

Kate could also see her advisor and explain the problem. The advisor may be able to give her some helpful suggestions for how to manage her time more effectively. Although it would be too late for Kate to sign up for a study skills course, this is an option she should consider for the following term. Kate could also try to identify a person in her class with whom she could study or find a study group to join. Most colleges provide tutorial services at little or no cost for students who are having academic difficulty. Kate could look into the possibility of getting a tutor.

Kate should not let a setback like this in her first term cause her to lose confidence. Adjusting to college is difficult for many students. That Kate is making an A in the algebra course and is passing two other courses demonstrates that she *can* succeed in college. What she needs to do now is find out how to improve her skills in the areas that are giving her difficulty so that she can handle the workload more efficiently. Also, she needs to enlist more support from her family. Her husband needs to realize that success does not mean straight As. Both he and the children should relieve Kate of some of the household chores, and the family should work together to help Kate find the time to study so that she will also have more time for them. Finally, Kate should not set an unrealistic time limit for completing her education. Taking fewer courses a term might be the answer to many of her problems.

As you can see, there is much to consider in trying to solve a problem. Usually there is more than one solution, and each may have advantages and disadvantages. You should always bear in mind that your first solution may not be the best one. Problem solving is a critical thinking skill that can be developed and improved. As you find effective solutions to more and more of your problems, you will gain confidence in your ability to meet difficult challenges.

A problem-solving approach, or method, is a consistent way of thinking through a problem until you find a solution. Some of these approaches are very specific, such as the method you use to conduct an experiment in a biology lab. Other approaches, such as the four-step COPE method discussed in the next section, are more general and can be applied to problems you may have at work, at home, or in your classes.

The COPE Method

COPE stands for *Challenge, Option, Plan, Evaluation.* Figure 2.3 shows the COPE method's four steps.

STEP 1	Clearly identify your **challenge,** *problem,* or its *causes,* and the *result* you want or goal you hope to reach.

This is the most important step. You must be able to identify your problem before you can solve it. Read the following two statements. The first

FIGURE 2.3 **The COPE Method**

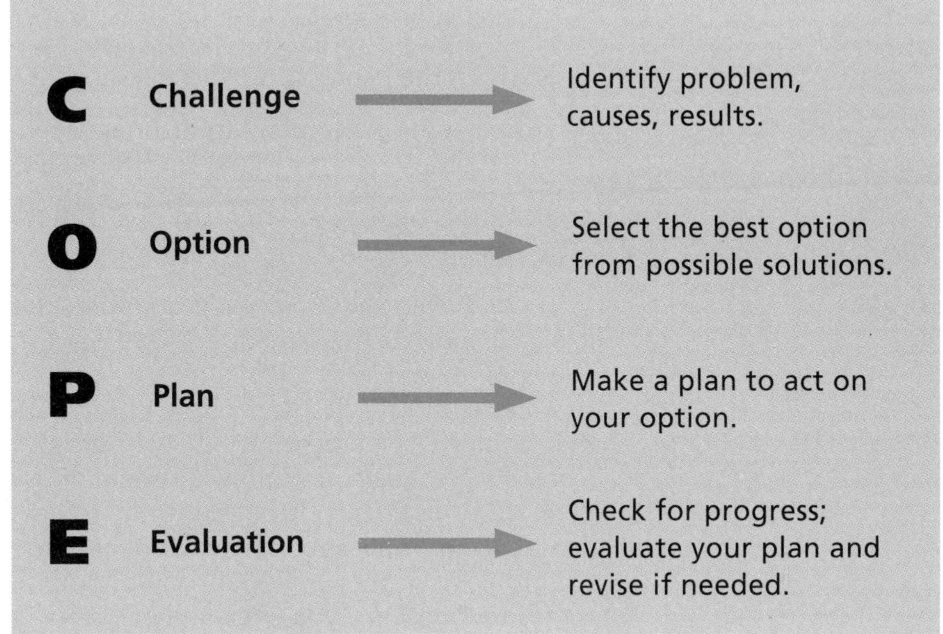

is too general. The second is more specific because it clearly states a problem, its causes, and the desired result.

1. *My problem is that even though I study a lot, I still make poor grades on tests.*
2. *My problem is that even though I study a lot, I still make poor grades on tests because I get very nervous, my mind goes blank, and I can't seem to remember what I have studied until after the test is over. I want to overcome my nervousness so I can take tests calmly and make better grades.*

To meet the challenge, ask yourself three questions. Then answer them. It may help to put your answers in writing.

- What is my problem?
- What causes my problem?
- What result do I want?

STEP 2 Choose the best **option** from the many possible solutions to your problem.

Rosalia says she cannot study at home because it is too noisy. The telephone rings frequently; her husband turns up the TV too loud; her young children make noise playing and fighting with each other. After thinking about her problem and its causes, Rosalia came up with the following list of options.

1. Be assertive with family members about my need for some quiet time for studying. Enlist their cooperation and support so that they feel needed and involved.
2. Study in the bedroom with the door shut.
3. Find a study place away from home such as the library or an empty classroom.
4. Study during the day while my husband is at work and my children are in school.

If you have trouble thinking of options for the solution to your problem, ask yourself this question: *What can I do to eliminate a cause, or the causes, of my problem?*

You might say, "If I knew how to solve my problem, I wouldn't have the problem!" Not necessarily. For example, smoking is a problem for many people. They may know of several options available that might help them quit smoking, yet they continue to have the problem because they do not act on their options. It may be that they don't really want to solve the problem, or they may want to but don't know how to get started. To act on *your* options, you need a plan.

STEP 3 Make a **plan** to solve your problem, within a reasonable length of time, and follow it.

To help you make your plan, ask yourself this question: *What can I do to make my options work?* Then decide how you will act on one of your options. Set a time limit by which you expect to see some progress toward your goal or the elimination of the problem. For example, Rosalia, the student who had trouble studying at home because of the noise, had an algebra test coming up in two weeks. She decided to do all her studying for algebra class in the library for the next two weeks. Her grade on the algebra test would tell her whether studying in a different place had paid off.

Suppose you want to quit smoking and know of several plans available, such as the use of a patch that slowly releases small amounts of nicotine into the bloodstream to stop the craving. Or perhaps a nearby hospital offers a stop-smoking program that uses behavioral modification techniques without the use of drugs. You might want to try one of these methods. If you have tried to stop smoking in the past and failed, evaluate the plan you followed. Why didn't it work? What detracted you from your goal? Make a new plan that allows you to try a different method so that you will be less likely to repeat your past unsuccessful behavior. Then set a reasonable time limit for breaking your habit, and try to stick to your plan.

STEP 4	Give your plan an honest **evaluation** to see what progress you are making.

To help you evaluate your plan, ask yourself these questions:

- Is my plan working?
- Have I given my plan sufficient time to work?
- Do I still have the problem?
- Is the problem situation improving?
- Should I make a new plan?

If you have solved your problem or if the situation is improving, continue what you are doing. If you still have the problem and your situation has not improved, make a new plan.

Until the COPE method becomes second nature for you, try writing out the steps. Writing slows down the thinking process so that you can analyze your problem more carefully. Also remember that when you put your plan into writing, you are making a commitment to yourself. Here is the commitment that Vernon, another student, made:

> *My problem is that I am a procrastinator. One cause of my problem is that I hate to study and will put it off until the last minute. I end up skimming over my notes and not absorbing anything. Another cause is that I'm easily distracted at home. I can think of a million other things to do. Also, I lack self-discipline. I want to overcome my procrastination and give myself plenty of time to study. I know this will make a difference in my grades. My plan is to do most of my homework and studying for tests in the library. I have two hours between classes on Mondays, Wednesdays, and Fridays. Also, I can study at home Tuesday and Thursday mornings when no one is there to distract me. I am going to try to keep weekends free for fun unless I have work that I couldn't get done during the week or a big test on Monday. I'll try this plan for two weeks and see if I'm able to stick to it.*

Notice that Vernon clearly describes his problem, its causes, and the result he wants. He also devises a plan and sets a time limit of two weeks. At the end of two weeks, he can evaluate his plan to see how he is doing. He can then either keep following the plan or revise it if necessary. Vernon's plan is one that can work.

EXERCISE 2.3

Apply what you have learned about problem solving by doing this exercise with group members. Remember to follow the guidelines for group discussion explained in Chapter 1, pages 12–13. Read and discuss the following list of common problem situations. Choose any four of the problems and think of at least two options for solving them. Identify the advantages and disadvantages of each option. After reaching consensus, record your answers on the lines provided. Then evaluate your work.

1. Someone you live with distracts you from studying.
2. You need to lose ten pounds.
3. Your car was damaged in an accident, and it will cost more than the car is worth to fix it.
4. You forgot that you have an important test tomorrow, and you made a date for tonight.
5. A friend of yours wants to drop out of college.
6. Your friend owes you $20.
7. You're taking a required course, and you don't like the teacher.
8. You are not sure whether you will have enough money to pay your tuition next semester or quarter.

1. Problem: ____________________

   Option A: ____________________

   Advantage: ____________________

   Disadvantage: ____________________

   Option B: ____________________

   Advantage: ____________________

   Disadvantage: ____________________

2. Problem: ____________________

   Option A: ____________________

   Advantage: ____________________

   Disadvantage: ____________________

   Option B: ____________________

   Advantage: ____________________

   Disadvantage: ____________________

3. Problem: ____________________

   Option A: ____________________

   Advantage: ____________________

   Disadvantage: ____________________

   Option B: ____________________

   Advantage: ____________________

Disadvantage: __________

4. Problem: __________

Option A: __________

Advantage: __________

Disadvantage: __________

Option B: __________

Advantage: __________

Disadvantage: __________

Evaluate your discussion. Did everyone contribute? Did you accomplish your task successfully? What additional questions do you have about problem solving? How will you find answers to your questions?

____

____

____

EXERCISE 2.4

Marie is a poor problem solver. Read about her problem and think about how she could become a successful problem solver.

I have a big problem this term: my French class. I'm flunking, and I don't know why. I've stopped going to class because it was depressing me to sit there feeling stupid. Now I can forget how much I hate it, and I can sleep late on Friday mornings, too. I'm angry at the college for having so many requirements to fulfill. I'm disgusted at my French instructor, who refuses to speak any English in class. How can I learn if I can't understand what's going on? I passed Spanish in high school, so I know this problem is not mine. It must be their crazy new method of teaching languages. Maybe I should take beginning Spanish again. At least I know I could pass!

1. What is Marie's problem?

____

____

2. Does Marie have an internal or external locus of control? How do you know?

____

____

____

3. What new behaviors could Marie adopt to help her solve her problem?

____

____

____

4. Write a short plan for Marie to follow this week.

____

____

____

CONFIDENCE BUILDER

How to Develop a Positive Attitude

Changing your attitude is the first step toward solving many problems you face in college.

A negative attitude may be a habit you have developed, a characteristic response to problem solving that has prevented you from being successful in the past. As Shakespeare said, "There is nothing good nor bad but thinking makes it so." Choosing to regard your problems as challenges is one way to change your thinking about them. A challenge is like a goal or contest that may be difficult for you to achieve or win. But your chance for success is good if you are motivated and if you do everything in your power to meet the challenge. To develop a more positive attitude, try these four simple proven techniques:

Visualize yourself being successful. Once you have set a goal, picture in your mind what you will have or be able to do once you reach it. Keep that picture in your mind whenever you feel negative, or are concerned about mastering a skill. Some golf instructors advocate using visualization during practice. Golfers picture themselves making a perfect swing, then repeat the process during a game.

Control your inner voice. You talk silently to yourself all the time. If what you say to yourself is mainly negative and derogatory, you are programming yourself for failure. Listen for those times during studying or test taking when you say to yourself, "I can't do this," or "I'm no good at this" and counteract those negative thoughts with positive ones: "I can do this; I just need to practice more" or "I am better at this than I used to be, and I will keep improving."

Reward yourself for doing well. When you know you have done your best or when you have accomplished a short-term goal that will help you reach a long-term goal, treat yourself to a movie, a new paperback novel, or lunch with a good friend. Be sparing with these rewards and save them for when you really deserve them. What you choose as a reward doesn't matter, as long as it acts as a positive reinforcement for good behavior.

Be a positive listener and speaker. If you have trouble screening your own words for negative remarks that you need to change into positive ones, listen carefully to others. When a friend says, "I'm not going to pass algebra," explore this problem with him or her. Ask your friend to think of something he or she might do to bring up his or her grades. Make positive suggestions such as "Why don't you get a tutor to help you with the concepts you don't understand?" Being a positive listener and speaker may help you think more positively about your own challenges as well.

CRITICAL THINKING APPLICATION

A person in each of the following scenarios has a problem and has come up with a solution. Based on your understanding of the COPE method, evaluate their plans. If you decide that one or both of the plans may not work, then suggest alternatives that have a better chance of success.

1. Kevin has been a heavy smoker for ten years. Although he has no physical problems now, his doctor has told him that he should quit smoking to prevent any health problems in the future. Kevin agrees that he ought to quit smoking; after all, his friends who don't smoke are always after him to quit. His family gives him a hard time too. And it is becoming more and more difficult to find places to smoke. Many restaurants and most public businesses are declaring themselves smoke-free. Kevin decides to quit cold turkey. Once he's made a decision, he likes to get on with it.
2. Misako attends a community college. It is now time to register for the next term. She knows that she is scheduled to have surgery shortly after midterm. She figures that she will have to miss two weeks of classes. She knows that many instructors will not permit more than two or three absences, so she decides to register for classes and not mention to her instructors her need to be absent. Instead, she hopes that when the time comes, they will be understanding and let her remain in the class and make up the work.
3. Though Raymond started out making Cs in his composition class, his grades are getting worse, not better. His instructor has said that

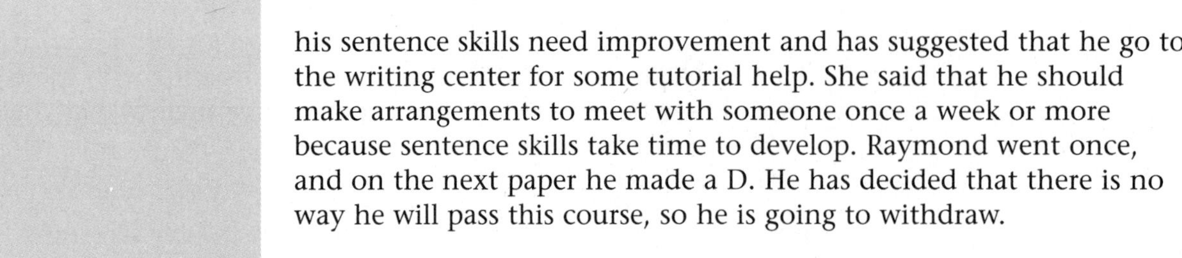

his sentence skills need improvement and has suggested that he go to the writing center for some tutorial help. She said that he should make arrangements to meet with someone once a week or more because sentence skills take time to develop. Raymond went once, and on the next paper he made a D. He has decided that there is no way he will pass this course, so he is going to withdraw.

SUMMARY

The summary is followed by an outline of the chapter. An outline is a helpful way to organize information that you want to remember. The outline is only partially filled in. Based on what is given, and using the summary as a guide, complete the rest of the outline.

Knowing why you are attending college, learning to set goals, and knowing how to solve problems will help you become a more confident student. There are many reasons for attending college. It is important that the reasons you identify be your own and that you use them to motivate yourself.

A *goal* is an outcome, the result of a plan, something you want and are willing to work for. Your goals may be personal, academic, or work related. *Long-term goals* take some time to accomplish and may include such things as graduation from college, a change in career, or planning for a child's college education. *Short-term goals* are intermediate steps between the initiation of a plan and its outcome—the achievement of a long-term goal. For example, when you have successfully completed a course, you have achieved a short-term goal that will help you reach the long-term goal of graduating from college.

Your success will be greatest if your goals are reachable. *Reachable goals* are *realistic, believable,* and *possible.* They are also *measurable, flexible, controllable* and *ethical.* A realistic goal is one you can reasonably expect to achieve given your abilities. A goal is believable and possible if you know what it will take to reach it and where to begin and end. For example, it is possible to complete a bachelor of arts program in four years, perhaps even in three years. But a goal of completing the program in one year would be both unbelievable and impossible. To set measurable goals, give yourself a time limit. Keep your goals flexible and controllable by deciding what you want to do and by being willing to change your plans if necessary. Ethical goals are fair to all concerned.

As you continue your college education, you will encounter some difficulties. You can successfully overcome these problems and meet your goals if you consistently use a problem-solving approach such as the COPE method. COPE is a four-step plan that starts with a *challenge* or problem, its causes, and a result. The second step is to think of *options,* or possible solutions, to your problem. Third, make a *plan* to act on one or more of your options. Finally, make an *evaluation* of your plan after you have given it sufficient time to work. Then revise your plan as needed.

Chapter Outline

I. Setting Goals

A. A goal is a desired outcome, something you want to accomplish.

B. Goals can be personal, ______________, or ______________.

C. Goals are either ______________ or ______________.

1. ______________ goals are intermediate steps taken to reach a long-term goal.

2. Completing a required course is a ______________ goal that leads to the ______________ goal of graduation.

D. You should set goals that you can reasonably expect to achieve.

A ______________ goal has several characteristics.

1. It is ______________.

2. It is ______________ and ______________.

3. It is ______________.

4. It is ______________.

5. It is ______________.

6. It is ______________.

E. ____________________ and ________________ play an important role in goal-setting.

II. Solving Problems

A. You need to know how to solve problems that arise as you work to achieve your goals.

B. Using the ______________ method is one way to solve problems. The four steps of this method are as follows:

1. Identify your ______________, its causes, and the ____________ you want.

2. Think of ______________, or possible solutions.

3. Make a ______________.

4. ______________ and revise it as needed.

YOUR REFLECTIONS

Reflect on what you have learned about strategies for setting goals and solving problems and how you can best apply that information. Use the following list of questions to stimulate your thinking, and then write your reflections. Your response may include answers to one or more of the questions. Incorporate in your writing specific information from this chapter.

- Are you a person who sets goals? Why or why not?
- Describe something difficult you have achieved. How did you achieve it? Was setting goals part of the process?
- Of the goal-setting and problem-solving strategies explained in this chapter, which do you need the most and how will they make a difference in your life?
- Review the values listed in Figure 2.1, page 30. Explain the role that one or more of these values plays in the way you solve problems.
- What have you gained from this chapter that you would recommend to a friend, and why?

Date ______________________________

CHAPTER 3

Sharpening Your Classroom Skills

Do you have difficulty listening to lectures and deciding what is important enough to write in your notes? Do you become distracted and "lose your place" during most lectures? Does your mind wander off to another concern or a pleasant fantasy?

Because most exams and class activities are based on information presented in lectures, your ability to listen and take notes is closely linked to how well you will do in a course. If the lecture method is not your preferred mode of instruction, then you may need to improve or develop listening and note-taking skills that will enable you to gain as much from lectures as you do from other instructional modes.

More and more, learning is becoming a collaborative activity. Sharing your ideas with others builds confidence. Moreover, group work, oral presentations, and class discussion are significant parts of the assessment and learning processes. The give-and-take of these activities helps you build the interpersonal skills needed for effective interaction in class as well as in the workplace.

To sharpen your classroom skills, you must make a commitment to learn, take responsibility for the outcome of every course, and be an active participant in all classroom activities. Your critical thinking and study skills key unlocks five essentials for successful classroom performance.

- Prepare for class.
- Become an active listener.
- Develop a personal note-taking system.
- Learn to make effective oral presentations.
- Participate in class and group activities.

Take the first step toward becoming more actively involved in your own learning process by evaluating your current performance in the classroom: Complete Awareness Check 6.

AWARENESS CHECK #6

How Effective Are Your Classroom Skills?

Check *yes* if the statement applies to you, *no* if the statement does not apply.

Part I: Preparing for Class

Yes	No	
☐	☐	1. I attend class regularly.
☐	☐	2. I usually arrive on time.
☐	☐	3. I use my syllabus, or course outline, to keep up with assignments.
☐	☐	4. I begin studying for tests as soon as they are announced.
☐	☐	5. I always bring my textbook and other necessary materials to class.
☐	☐	6. I do my homework for every class.
☐	☐	7. I usually know what the instructor expects of me.

Part II: Listening to Lectures

Yes	No	
☐	☐	1. I always assume that I can get new information from a lecture.
☐	☐	2. I am able to follow the instructor's ideas.
☐	☐	3. I know what signal words are, and I listen for them.
☐	☐	4. I can ignore most distractions when I am listening to a lecture.
☐	☐	5. I consider students' comments and questions to be part of the lecture, and I listen to them.
☐	☐	6. I keep listening even if I don't agree with the instructor or if I don't understand some part of the lecture.

PREPARE FOR CLASS

Your first essential for classroom success is to prepare effectively for classes. The following tips may seem obvious, but many students do not follow them.

Attend Regularly and Be Punctual. Don't miss classes; when you miss a class, you miss instruction. In any course that teaches a sequence of skills, such as a language or math course, you need to attend regularly because one day's lesson is based on previous lessons. Punctuality and regular attendance are habits valued not only by instructors but by employers as well. If you come to class and arrive on time, then you will know what to expect and you won't miss announcements of upcoming tests or assignments.

Use Your Syllabus. The syllabus helps you keep up with assignments and tests, reminds you of what was covered if you are absent, and summarizes the instructor's requirements. Review it often to keep this information fresh in your mind. Bring it to class every day. Then, if the instructor makes a change or postpones a test, you can note the change directly on the syllabus. Your syllabus is a confidence builder because it gives you a plan to follow.

Bring Textbooks and Other Supplies to Class Every Day. Instructors often call attention to information in the textbook, or they may ask you to do an exercise from the textbook in class. Some instructors lecture on material contained in the book, especially if it's complicated or needs supplementing. If you bring your textbook to class, you will be able to follow along and mark important passages.

Do the Homework. Homework provides the practice you need to acquire new skills. It helps reinforce ideas and concepts discussed in class. Most important, doing the homework provides you with a background of information that will help you make sense of future assignments. Also, you may lose points on tests if you are not able to answer questions that come directly from the homework assignments.

Anticipate the Next Lesson. Try to anticipate what will be covered each day. You can do this by following two simple steps:

1. **Review the previous day's work.** Read your notes from the last class. Review the last chapter you read and the homework assignment, if any. The next class is likely to expand on this information. Reviewing the work from the previous class helps you retain the information and get ready for the next class.
2. **Preview the next day's assignments.** Review your syllabus to determine what will be covered and how it relates to what was covered in the previous class. Formulate some questions in your mind about the topic. Ask yourself, "What do I already know about this?" Previewing helps you relate new information to what you already know, placing it in a meaningful context.

If you attend class regularly, are punctual, use your syllabus, bring your textbook and other supplies to class, do the homework, and anticipate the next lesson, you will always know what to expect from your classes. Also, you will be in the proper frame of mind to listen attentively.

BECOME AN ACTIVE LISTENER

Your second essential for classroom success is active listening. Since lecture–discussion is the preferred style of many college instructors, you probably spend most of your class time listening.

There are two kinds of listeners—those who are passive and those who are active. *Passive listeners* do more hearing than listening. They are aware that the instructor is speaking, but they aren't making sense of what he or she says. Passive listening is characteristic of the external locus of control. Passive listeners may expect instructors to motivate them and to interest them in the topic. *Active listeners* pay attention to what they hear and try to make sense of it. Active listening is characteristic of the internal locus of control. Active listeners tend to be self-motivated, and they expect to find their own reasons for being interested in a lecture topic. Figure 3.1 compares traits of active and passive listeners. Which kind of listener are you?

To get more out of lectures, become an active listener. Follow these six steps:

1. **Decide to listen.** By making this decision, you are strengthening your commitment to learn. Also, by deciding to listen to a lecture, you are taking an *active* role instead of waiting passively to receive information.

2. **Listen with a positive frame of mind.** Expect to find something in the lecture that will interest you. Assume that you will learn something useful, that you will expand your knowledge, and that your understanding of the course will increase.

3. **Focus your attention on the speaker.** If you keep your eyes on the speaker, you should be able to ignore any distractions that are competing for your attention. Keep your mind on the speaker's topic. Do not give in to negative thoughts or feelings about the speaker, the topic, or the speaker's opinions. Your purpose is to learn what the speaker has to say.

FIGURE 3.1 Traits of Passive and Active Listeners

PASSIVE LISTENERS	ACTIVE LISTENERS
Expect a lecture to be dull	Expect to find something in the lecture that interests them
Assume that information in a lecture will not be useful or pertain to their lives	Assume that information in a lecture will be useful—if not now, then later
Look for weaknesses in the speaker's style instead of listening to what the speaker says	May notice weaknesses in the speaker's style but pay attention to what the speaker says
Listen only for major points and ignore details and examples	Listen for major points and the details that support them
Give in to daydreaming and become distracted	Resist daydreaming and ignore distractions
Tune out when they disagree with the speaker	Keep listening even when they disagree with the speaker
Tune out difficult or technical information; do not ask questions	Try to understand difficult or technical information; ask questions as needed
May doze in lectures if tired	Fight to stay awake if tired
Do not take good notes	Take well-organized notes

4. **Encourage the speaker.** Look interested. Sit straight but comfortably, and make eye contact from time to time. Ask questions and make comments when appropriate. Studies of audience behavior indicate that a speaker who is getting positive feedback is encouraged to do an even better job. Your posture and expression can communicate to the speaker that you are trying to follow his or her ideas. Everything you do to encourage the speaker also affects you by making you concentrate on the lecture.

5. **Take notes.** Taking notes helps you concentrate on the lecture. Also, taking notes activates your tactile sense, as explained in Chapter 1, so that you are more likely to retain the information, especially if you review your notes soon after the lecture. Take notes consistently when listening to lectures, and adopt or develop a note-taking system that works for you. (More is said about note taking later in this chapter.)

6. **Decide what is important.** Listen for repeated terms or ideas. Speakers use repetition to emphasize important points. Watch for gestures and facial expressions that may also be used for emphasis. Listen for signal words or phrases. See Figure 3.2 for a list of signal words and phrases and explanations of what they mean.

Listening for signal words helps you listen for ideas. For example, if an English instructor says, "There are seven patterns you can use to organize details in a paragraph," then you should number from one to seven on your paper, skipping lines between, and listen for the seven patterns and the instructor's example of each. If you get to the fifth pattern and realize that you don't have anything written down for the fourth one, then you know you have missed something in the lecture. At this point, you should ask a question.

FIGURE 3.2 Signal Words and Phrases

1. To indicate that another point or example follows:

also	furthermore	another
in addition	moreover	

2. To add emphasis:

most important	above all	of primary concern
remember that	a key idea	most significant
pay attention to	the main point	

3. To indicate that an example follows:

for example	to illustrate	such as
for instance	specifically	

4. To indicate that a conclusion follows:

therefore	in conclusion	finally
consequently	to conclude	so

FIGURE 3.2 Signal Words and Phrases *(continued)*

5. To indicate an exception to a stated fact:

however	although	but
nevertheless	though	except

6. To indicate causes or effects:

because	due to	consequently
since	reason	result
for	cause	effect

7. To indicate that categories or divisions will be named or explained:

types	parts	groups
kinds	characteristics	categories

8. To indicate a sequence:

steps	numbers (1, 2, 3, . . .)
stages	first, second, etc.

9. To indicate that items are being compared:

similar	different	equally
like	in contrast	on the other hand
advantages	disadvantages	contrary to

EXERCISE 3.1

Apply what you have learned about signal words by doing this exercise with group members. Remember to follow the guide lines for group discussion explained in Chapter 1, pages 12–13. Read the following paragraph. Identify as many signal words as you can and discuss their meaning in the sentences in which they appear, using Figure 3.2 as a reference. Then discuss and answer the questions. When you arrive at consensus, record your answers and evaluate your work.

Most of us assume that listening is an innate skill. Aren't most people born with the ability to sleep, breathe, see, and hear? But is hearing the same act as listening? Although most of us can hear perfectly well, we are not all good listeners. What, you might ask, are the characteristics of a good listener? First, a good listener needs a commitment to listening. Second, a good listener focuses attention on what is being said. For example, a good listener is not reading the newspaper or watching television while listening to a friend talk about a problem. Most important, a good listener is genuinely interested in the speaker and in what is being said. In conclusion, listening is not something you should assume you do well. It is a lifelong skill that can be improved with earnest practice and hard work.

1. What signal words indicate that an example is to follow? What example does the writer give?

____

2. Write the signal word that indicates that categories or divisions will be explained.

____

3. Write the signal words that indicate sequence. ______________________

____

4. What does the writer believe is the most important characteristic of a good listener? __________

____

5. What is the writer's concluding idea about listening? ______________________

____

Evaluate your discussion. Did everyone contribute? Did you accomplish your task successfully? What additional questions do you have about signal words? How will you find answers to your questions?

____

____

____

DEVELOP A PERSONAL NOTE-TAKING SYSTEM

The third essential for classroom success is good note taking. There is no one best way to take notes. The suggestions offered in this chapter have worked for many students. Experiment with them, and then adapt them to find the style of note taking that consistently gives you good results. Complete the Awareness Check before you begin reading this section.

AWARENESS CHECK #7

How Effective Are Your Note-Taking Skills?

To see where you need improvement, evaluate your lecture notes from a recent class. Read them over and answer *yes* or *no* to the following questions.

Yes	No	
☐	☐	1. Did you date your notes and number the pages?
☐	☐	2. Did you write the course name or number on your notes?
☐	☐	3. Did you write down the topic of the lecture?
☐	☐	4. Did you use 8 1/2″ by 11″ paper to keep in a looseleaf binder?

Yes	No	
☐	☐	5. Did you take notes with a ball-point pen?
☐	☐	6. Are your notes easy to read?
☐	☐	7. Is this set of notes in the same notebook as all your other notes for this class?
☐	☐	8. Are your notes organized into an informal outline or other logical format?
☐	☐	9. Are you able to distinguish the speaker's main ideas from the examples that explain them?
☐	☐	10. As you read your notes, are you able to reconstruct in your mind what the lecture was about?

If you answered *no* to any of the questions in the Awareness Check—particularly the last two—then your note-taking skills may need improvement. Try the guidelines that follow for improving your note taking.

Guidelines for Note Taking

1. Keep track of your notes by putting a *date* and *heading* on the first page and numbering pages that follow. Be sure to identify the *lecture topic* and the *class* in which the lecture takes place. Later, when you study, you'll be able to match up class notes and textbook notes or assignments on the same topic.

2. Use paper of a standard size, 8 1/2″ by 11″, that will fit into most notebooks or folders. Small sheets of paper won't hold enough and may get lost or out of place.

3. Keep the notes for one class separated from the notes for other classes. Use separate notebooks for each class, or use dividers to set aside different sections in one notebook. Some students like to use spiral notebooks. Others prefer to use a loose-leaf binder so that lecture notes, textbook notes, and the instructor's handouts may be taken out of it and reorganized for study purposes.

4. Use a ball-point pen for taking notes. Ink from felt-tip pens blurs and soaks through the paper, spotting the sheets underneath. Pencil smears and fades over time. Many students prefer to use blue or black ink because other colors, such as red or green, are hard on the eyes.

5. If you know your handwriting is poor, print for clarity. Illegible or decorative handwriting makes notes hard to read.

6. To speed up note-taking, use standard abbreviations, but make up some of your own for words or phrases that you use often. Make a key for your abbreviations so you won't forget what they mean. See Figure 3.3 for a list of some common abbreviations. For even greater speed while taking notes, omit the periods from abbreviations.

FIGURE 3.3 Commonly Used Abbreviations and Symbols

1. equal: =
2. with: w/
3. without: w/o
4. number: #
5. therefore: \
6. and: +
7. and so forth: etc.
8. for example: e.g.
9. against: vs.
10. government: gov't.
11. introduction: intro.
12. information: info.
13. department: dept.
14. advantage: adv.
15. organization: org.
16. maximum: max.
17. individual: ind.
18. compare: cf.
19. association: assoc.
20. politics: pol.

7. Copy into your notes anything that is written on the board or on overhead transparencies. Test questions often come from material that is presented in these ways.
8. Take organized notes. Use a system such as one of those suggested later in this chapter, or devise your own system. Make major points stand out from the examples that support them. Do not write lecturers' words verbatim. Summarize points in your own words so that they will be easier for you to remember.
9. As soon as possible after class, review your notes to fill in gaps while the information is still fresh in your mind. The purpose of taking notes is to help you remember information. If you take notes but don't look at them until you are ready to study for a test, you will have to relearn the information. To retain information in your long-term memory, review it frequently.
10. If you seem to be missing something, compare notes with a classmate or see the instructor.

The Informal Outline/Key Words System

Ideas that are organized into a logical pattern are easier to remember than isolated facts and examples that don't seem to relate to one another. Try this simple, two-step system to improve your note taking.

Draw a line down your paper so that you have a 2 1/2″ column on the right and a 6″ column on the left. Take notes in the 6″ column, using an informal outline. Make major points stand out by indenting and numbering details and examples under them. Skip lines between major points so that you can fill in examples later or add an example if the lecturer returns to a point later on. After the lecture, write key words in the right margin that will help you recall information from your notes.

FIGURE 3.4 The Informal Outline/Key Words System

Study Skills 1620	Sept. 18
Studying on the Right Side of the Brain	
Visual Thinking	
1. Use graphic techniques like diagrams, maps, etc. to organize information into a meaningful pattern.	def.
2. Visual learners need to make verbal information "visual" or they will have a hard time remembering it.	reason for using "visuals"
Fantasy	
1. The ability to create and use mental images is another kind of visual thinking.	def.
2. To understand the stages in an organism's life cycle, imagine you are the organism going through the stages.	ex. of fantasy
Hands-on Experience	
1. Get involved in a direct experience of what you are learning.	def.
2. Do lab experiments, take field trips, role play, look at or touch objects as they are described. Go through the steps of a process.	hands-on activities
Music	
1. Common belief: music distracts while studying.	
2. Music can accelerate learning.	effect of music on learning
3. Studies show retention improved when students read to music.	
4. Instrumentals that match the feeling or mood of the information to be remembered are the best type of music.	

Figure 3.4 shows a student's lecture notes on the topic "Studying on the Right Side of the Brain." The student has used the informal outline/key words system. On the left side of the page, the student has outlined the lecture given in class. Later, on the right side of the page, in the margin, the student has written key words or abbreviations that show at a glance what the lecture covered.

When you use this system, wait to write in the key words until you are reviewing your notes.

The Cornell Method

Developed by Dr. Walter Pauk of Cornell University, the Cornell method is a note-taking system that has worked for many students. One version of this system involves six steps: *recording, questioning, reciting, reflecting, reviewing,* and *recapitulating.*

Begin by dividing an 8 1/2″ by 11″ sheet of notebook paper into three sections, as illustrated in Figure 3.5. Then follow these steps for taking notes from a lecture:

1. **Record** facts and ideas in the wide column. After the lecture, fill in any gaps and neaten up your handwriting, if necessary, so that you will be able to read your notes when you review again.

2. **Question** facts and ideas presented in lectures. Formulate questions about what you don't understand or what you think an instructor might ask on a test. Write your questions in the left margin beside the fact or idea in the wide column. Writing questions helps you strengthen your memory, improve your understanding, and anticipate test questions.

3. **Recite** the facts or ideas aloud from memory and in your own words. If you summarized them in your notes in your own words, then this will be easy to do. If you are an auditory learner, reciting will improve your retention because you will be using listening, your preferred mode. As an awareness check of how much you remember, cover up the wide column of your notes and recite from the key words or questions in the left margin. Recite the key word or question first; then try to recall and recite the whole fact or idea. Check yourself by uncovering the wide column and reading your notes.

4. **Reflect** on what you have learned from the lecture by applying the facts and ideas to real-life situations. Determine why the facts are significant, how you can use them, and how they expand or modify what you already know about the topic.

5. **Review** and recite your notes every day. A good way to begin a study session, especially if you have trouble getting started, is to review your notes. Reviewing reminds you of what you have learned and sets the scene for new information that you will learn in the next assignment.

6. **Recapitulate** by writing a summary of your notes in the space at the bottom of your paper. You can summarize what you have written on each page of notes, or you can summarize the whole lecture at the end of the last page. Doing both a page summary and a whole-lecture summary is even better.

FIGURE 3.5 The Cornell Method: Setting Up the Paper

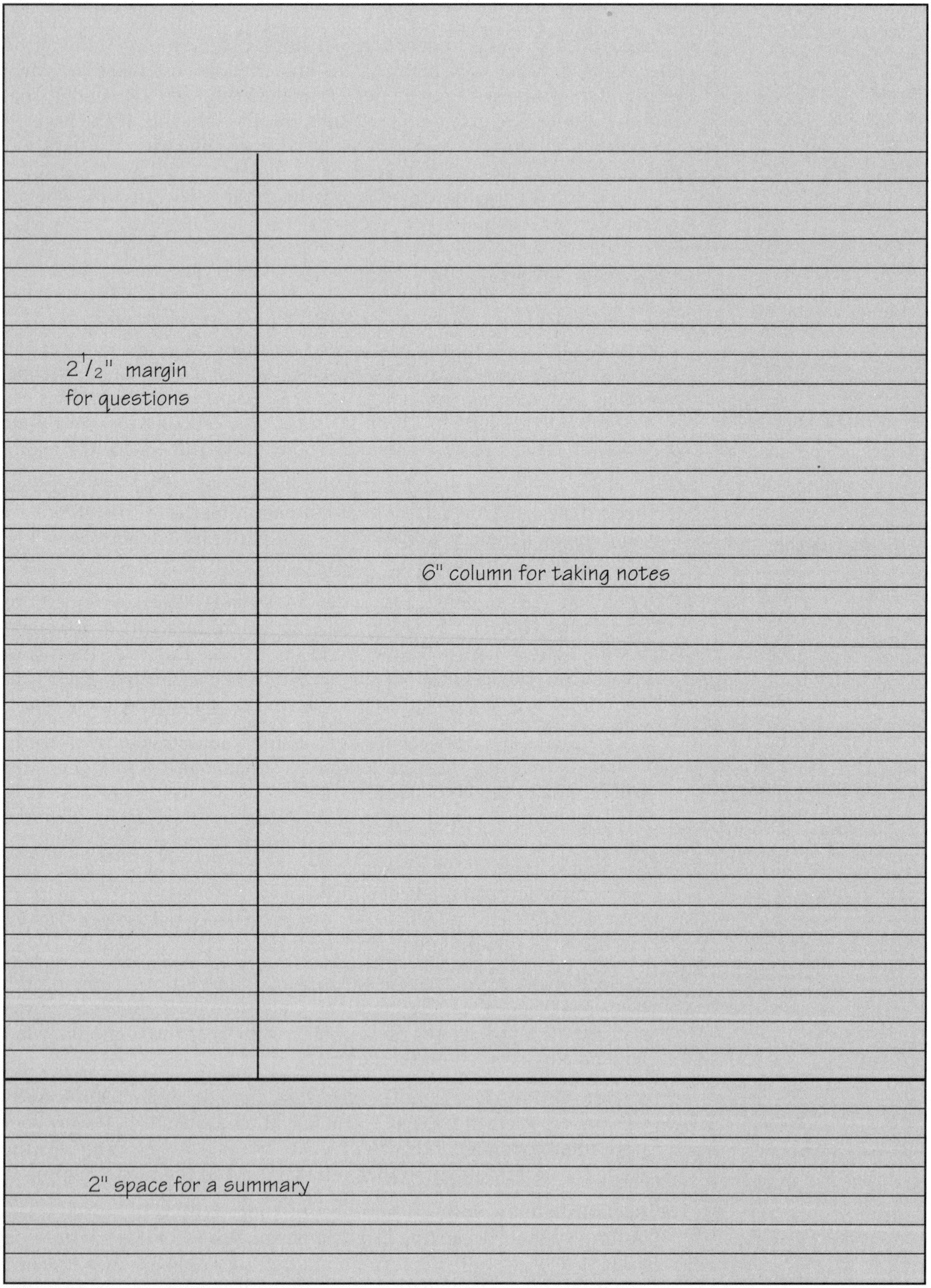

Now, clarify these steps in your mind by examining the student's lecture notes shown in Figure 3.6.

FIGURE 3.6 The Cornell Method: One Student's Notes

Literature 2010 — Sept. 18

Recall column	Notes
	The Five Elements of Fiction
How does the plot of the story develop?	1. Plot a. Events and setting b. Plot development * conflict * complications * climax * resolution
What is the difference between a dynamic and a static character?	2. Character a. Dynamic * well rounded * motives b. Static * flat * stereotype
What are the four points of view?	3. Point of View a. First person b. Omniscient c. Limited omniscient d. Dramatic
How is the theme of the story revealed?	4. Theme a. Meaning or significance b. Revealed through interaction of five elements
What makes one writer's style distinctive?	5. Style / Tone a. Mood or feeling b. Choice of words, use of language

The writer uses five elements of fiction—plot, character, point of view, theme and style/tone—to develop the story. Through the interaction of these elements, the meaning of the story is revealed and the reader can understand its significance.

COMPUTER CONFIDENCE

Use a Computer to Organize Your Notes

Taking notes in class and while you're reading is an important first step toward understanding new material. But the next step is even more important—organizing your notes into a format from which you can study effectively. That's where a computer can make a big difference.

Whichever style you prefer—the informal outline/key words system, the Cornell method, or a system of your own—using the computer to reorganize your notes offers several advantages:

1. **It's easy to move whole blocks of words around to rearrange information in a format that makes sense to you.**
2. **It's easy to add new ideas to your notes as you go along or to combine class and textbook notes to give you the most complete coverage of the information.**
3. **The actual process of putting your notes into the computer will help you remember them because it engages your tactile and visual senses.**

Many word-processing programs offer easy-to-use outlining features. These programs automatically provide an outline format into which you can type your notes. If you like to use outlines but the computer you're using does not have an outlining feature, you can create your own outlines by following these simple steps:

1. **Open a separate file for each of your courses. Create a name for the file.**
2. **Try to get to the computer soon after each class, while the lecture is still fresh in your mind. Put the date and topic of each lecture at the top of a new page.**
3. **Review your class notes. Whatever note-taking system you're using, this is a good time to focus on the main ideas or key questions. Then type your notes into the computer. The computer makes it easy to highlight the main ideas—use the boldface or underlining functions. You can also use the tabs to set special margins for key words or questions.**
4. **At this point, you may wish to add comments or questions, insert notes from your reading, or move sections of your outline around. The computer's "block-and-move" functions make this easy. To create a formal outline, insert Roman numerals and upper-case letters to mark major divisions, and move each line so that it aligns correctly. Then insert Arabic numerals and lower-case letters in front of the details, and align them also.**
5. **Print out the final version. Double-space the printed copy so that you have room to insert additional notes.**

Matching Note-Taking Style and Learning Style

What if you are not a linear thinker? What if a 1, 2, 3 order of information does not appeal to you because you don't think that way and instructors don't always stick to their lecture outline? You may prefer a more visual style of note taking. Try *clustering*. Start a few inches from the top of the page and write the speaker's first major point in a circle near the middle of the page. If the speaker gives an example, draw an arrow to another circle in which you write the example. If the speaker presents a new major point, start a new cluster. Figure 3.7 presents an example of the cluster note-taking technique. This student's notes help her picture in her mind's eye the information she wants to remember.

An advantage of clustering is that if the speaker leaves a point and returns to it later, it is easy to draw another arrow from the circle and add the example. Clustering is a nontraditional note-taking procedure, but if it works for you and if it makes note taking easy and relatively pleasant, then don't hesitate to use it.

FIGURE 3.7 Clustering: A Visual Form of Note Taking

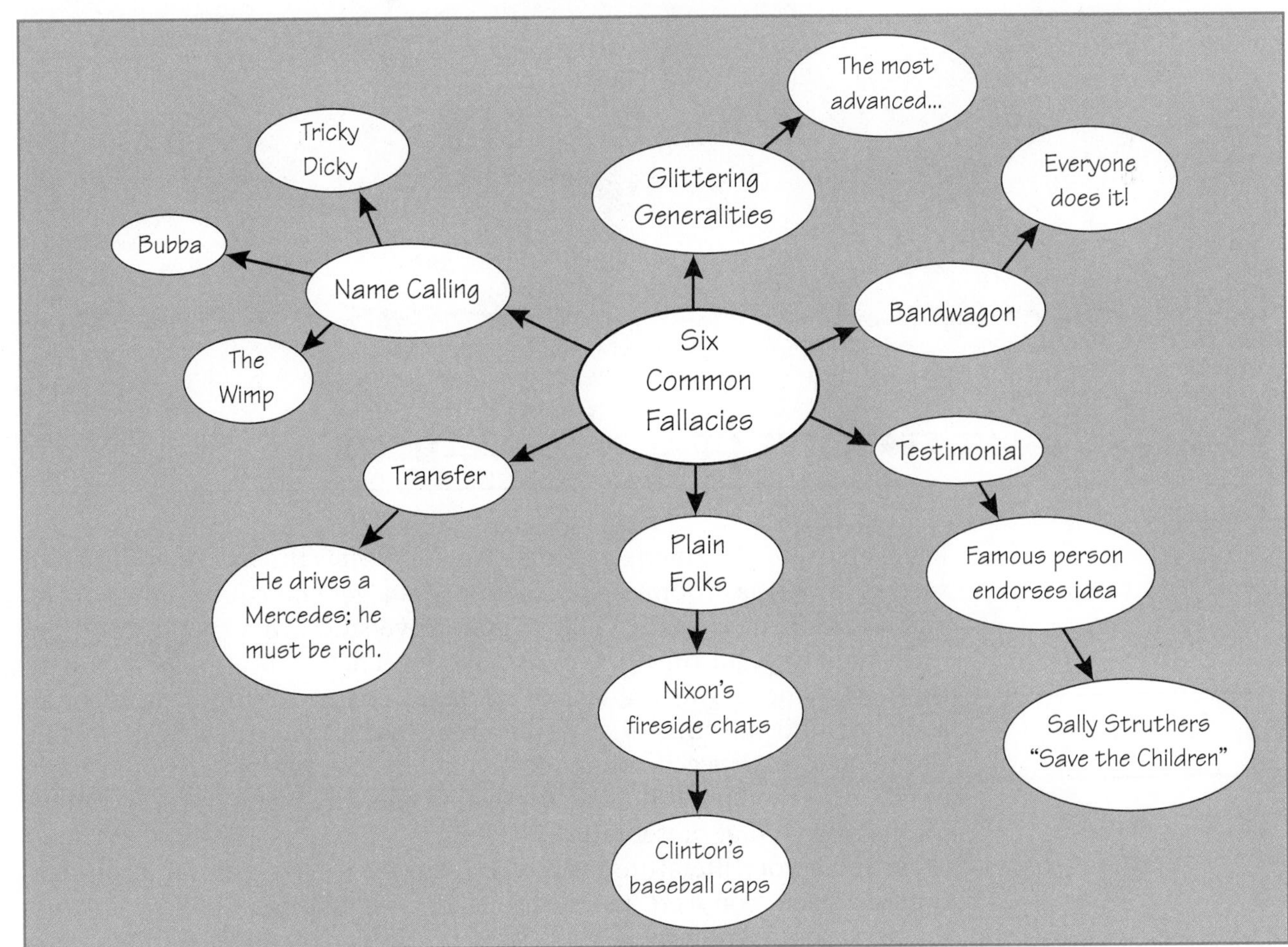

EXERCISE 3.2

In this chapter you have learned about three effective ways to organize your notes: (1) the informal outline/key words system, (2) the Cornell method, and (3) clustering. Reread the sections of this chapter that describe these three techniques, and then use the diagram below to try clustering. Fill in each circle. Then add arrows and circles to the cluster to complete your notes about the three techniques.

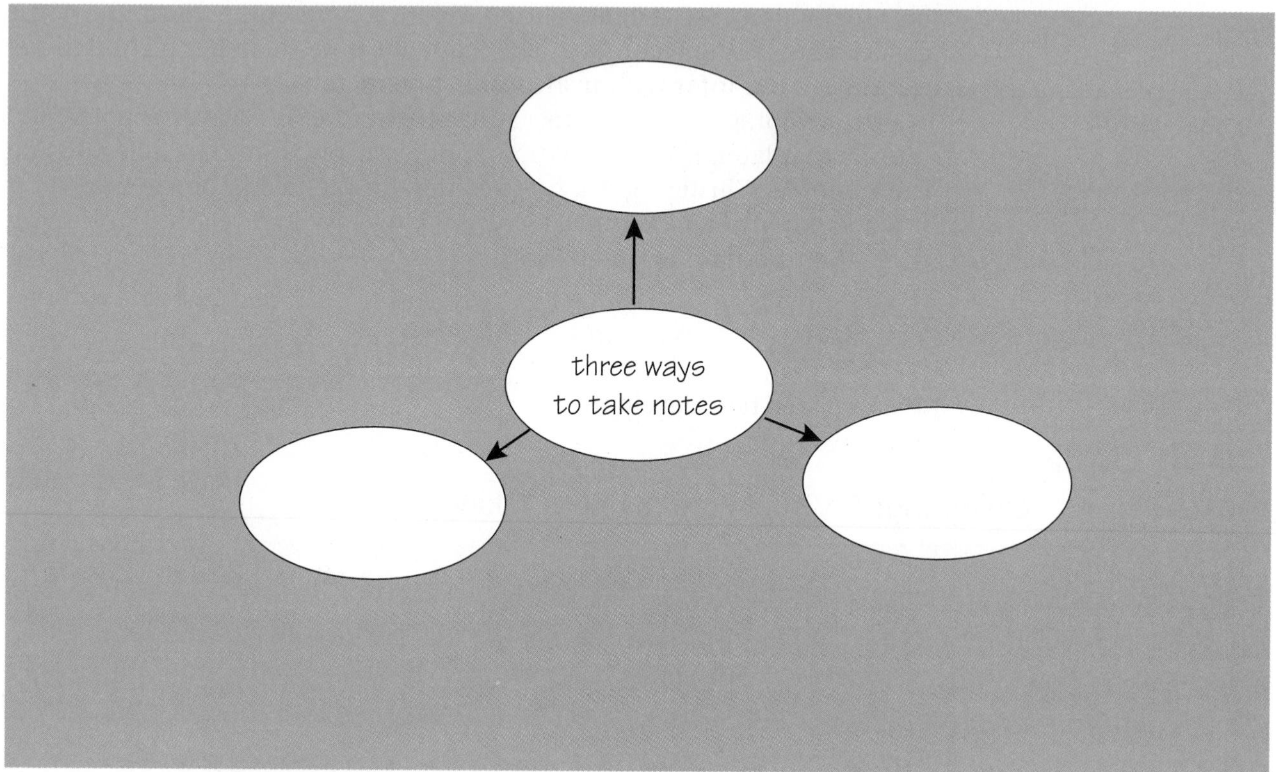

LEARN TO MAKE EFFECTIVE ORAL PRESENTATIONS

Being able to make an effective oral presentation is the fourth essential for success in the classroom. A speech course is a general education or liberal arts requirement at many colleges and universities. In a speech class you learn how to plan, organize, and make speeches. You also learn how to cope with *stage fright,* the fear of speaking or performing in front of an audience, and the stress that results from that fear. If it has been a while since you took a speech course, or if you have not yet had an opportunity to take one, then the following suggestions may help you prepare yourself for making an oral presentation.

Suppose your literature instructor asks you to give an oral interpretation of a poem you were assigned to read. Or maybe your biology instructor asks you to report to the class the results of an experiment you performed in the lab. Perhaps a finance professor asks you to analyze and make an oral report on several properties a company might purchase. You are to explain which purchase would net the company a greater return on its investment. In each case, you would first decide what your *purpose* is. For example, the purpose of your interpretation of a poem might be to explain what you think the writer's theme is. In your report about your lab results, your purpose would be to tell the conclusion you reached as a result of your experiment. In your report to your finance class, your purpose might be to convince them that the purchase of one of the properties is best for the company.

Once your purpose is clear, you can *plan* and *organize* your speech. Make an outline of the points you want to make and the evidence that supports your opinions. Recite from your outline several times until you know what you want to say. Try out your speech on a friend or family member, and ask for suggestions on how to improve your delivery or how to explain your ideas more clearly. If you think you might forget something, summarize your points and evidence on three-by-five cards. The notes will jog your memory, and holding the cards will give you something to do with your hands.

In general, a good plan to follow in preparing an oral presentation is to use a three-part development:

1. **Tell your listeners what you're going to say.** Introduce your topic and make your point.

2. **Say it.** Support your point with evidence in the form of facts, reasons, and examples. Draw a conclusion from the evidence.

3. **Tell them what you have just said.** Briefly summarize your point, evidence, and conclusion.

Don't forget to make eye contact with the audience; speak loudly enough for everyone in the back of the class to hear; speak distinctly and watch your pace. If you go too fast or too slowly, you will interrupt the flow of ideas, and your listeners may have trouble following you.

If you get nervous, try not to focus your attention on your feelings. Thinking about your nervousness will only make it worse, and you may forget what you want to say. Instead, keep your attention focused on the task of making your speech or completing the report. Think about your audience and how they may benefit from the information you are giving them.

Making oral presentations is like any other skill. With practice, you gain confidence. Being able to express yourself clearly in speaking is an asset in any course and in the world of work as well. Look upon oral presentation assignments as opportunities to practice and improve your skill.

EXERCISE 3.3

Imagine that you have been asked to give a three-minute speech on a topic from Chapters 1, 2, or 3 that interests you. Select a topic by looking at the headings in these chapters. Then, using the three-part development plan for oral presentations, plan a speech by answering the questions that follow.

Part 1 Tell your listeners what you're going to say.

1. What is your topic?

____

2. How will you introduce your topic—in other words, how will you interest your listeners?

____

3. What is your point—in other words, why have you chosen the topic?

____

____

Part 2 Say it.

1. What is your evidence? What facts, reasons, or examples support your topic?

____

____

____

2. What is your conclusion—in other words, why is what you've said important or how is it useful?

____

____

Part 3 Tell them what you have just said.

1. What is your summary?

____

____

____

PARTICIPATE IN CLASS AND GROUP ACTIVITIES

The fifth essential for classroom success is to become involved in whatever is happening in class. Contribute to class discussions and ask questions even if you are reluctant to do so. You may find that other students have similar questions or comments but are afraid to speak up. They'll be grateful to you. Speaking out in class will give you confidence. In time, you will become less self-conscious. You will learn to express yourself with clarity and authority, and this skill will serve you well in whatever career you pursue.

When other students do take risks and speak out, give them your full attention. After all, you know how they feel. During a class discussion, maintain eye contact with whoever is speaking, and listen attentively. Students soon overcome their nervousness when they realize that others are interested in what they have to say.

Make your contribution to small group activities. Try to get something accomplished, and follow these rules for polite discourse:

1. **Allow each person equal time to contribute to the discussion.**
2. **Question points of view; do not attack the person asserting the point of view.**
3. **Volunteer to do your part of the work.**
4. **If you are a discussion leader, make sure that everyone contributes, keep the discussion to the point, and summarize the group's conclusions at the end of the discussion.**
5. **Whatever your role is in the group, do your part to help the group stay on task. Do not let the discussion degenerate into a social exchange.**

The more involved you are in your classes, the more you will feel at home in the learning community. Sharpening your classroom skills will make you a more confident student.

CONFIDENCE BUILDER

Interpersonal Skills for College and Career

When you interact with others in class, especially in small group activities and on collaborative projects, you are building interpersonal skills that will give you an edge in the workplace. The days of isolated workers sitting in their cubicles are giving way to work teams in which work is shared by a group of colleagues, each contributing his or her expertise. At companies such as AT&T and Lockheed Martin much of the work is done in teams, and employees are expected to have the necessary interpersonal qualities and leadership skills. In many ways, today's collaborative classroom shadows the already emerging workplace of the twenty-first century.

In 1991, The U.S. Department of Labor, through the Secretary's Commission on Achieving Necessary Skills (SCANS), issued a report on the skills students need to succeed in the high-performance workplace of the twenty-first century. The Department of Labor calls these skills, collectively, "workplace know-how." One of the skill areas cited as being necessary for solid job performance is *interpersonal skills*.

Participating in class and working collaboratively on projects in and out of the classroom have the potential of helping you develop two of the SCANS' interpersonal skills: *working as a member of a team* and *exercising leadership*. According to the report, there are several things teachers can encourage students to do that will help them be successful team members in the workplace. Interestingly, these are the same things you should do to be a successful group member in class:

- Share the work.
- Encourage others by listening and responding appropriately to their contributions.
- Recognize each other's strengths and build on them.
- Settle differences for the benefit of the group.
- Take responsibility for achieving goals.
- Challenge existing procedures, policies, or authorities, but do so in a responsible way.

How do you exercise leadership within a group? The SCANS report says that competent leaders do the following:

- They make positive use of the rules and values followed by others.
- They justify their positions logically and appropriately.
- They establish their credibility through competence and integrity.
- They take minority opinion contributions into consideration.

In plain language, what do these competencies for participating and leading mean? Simply put, if you are the leader of a group discussion in class, you can make "positive use of rules and values" by making sure your group follows the guidelines your instructor has given for completing the assignment. As a leader, you "justify" your position "logically and appropriately" by not monopolizing the discussion and by keeping order when things get out of hand. You "establish credibility" by doing your share of the work, and you show "integrity" by seeing that the work gets done. If someone in the group expresses an opinion different from that of the majority of group members, you treat that "minority contribution" fairly and do not dismiss it out of hand. Suppose that you do not understand the instructions or that you see an easier, better way to accomplish the task than to follow the guidelines you've been given. How do you "challenge existing procedures" responsibly? Discuss your concerns with your instructor, asking in a polite way whether the guidelines can be modified, being willing to proceed as instructed if necessary.

Respect for others and their opinions is the key to effective participation in groups, whether in class or at work.

EXERCISE 3.4

How well do you participate in your classes? Read about three members of a sociology class, and see if you find yourself mirrored in their profiles. Then answer the questions that follow.

Bob always sits at the back of the classroom so that he can nap quietly if he has stayed out late the night before. He rarely makes a comment or asks a question. If he doesn't understand something the instructor says, he forgets about it. He's sure that he'll figure the problem out when he does the reading just before the final exam. He would probably forget about it anyway before the exam rolled around.

Sam can't wait to get to class. He has done all the reading, and he has millions of questions to ask. Sam's voice is always the first one heard. His hand is raised many times each class hour, whether there's a lecture or a discussion. Often frustrated, Sam does not listen to either his peers or his instructor. If he did listen, he'd realize that many of his questions had already been addressed. Sometimes Sam is so interested in speaking aloud that he interrupts his classmates' remarks or he attacks them for challenging his views.

Carmen loves sociology class. She enjoys listening to the lecture, but she also enjoys the give-and-take of class discussions. At first, she was hesitant to speak out, but once she became convinced that she could learn a great deal from the questions and comments of her peers, she tried participating. When she leads a discussion, Carmen makes sure that everyone has a chance to contribute, keeps the discussion focused, and summarizes the discussion at its close.

1. List three negative behaviors that Bob exhibits in class. ______

______

______

______

2. How could Bob change his behavior so that he could participate more fully in class? ______

______

______

3. Why is Sam's behavior negative? How might he change his behavior to participate in a more positive fashion? ______

______

______

4. How does Carmen play an active role in class? ______

______

______

5. Why is Carmen a good discussion leader? ______________________________

____

____

6. Which of the students has an internal locus of control, and how can you tell? ______________________________

____

____

CRITICAL THINKING APPLICATION

How does your learning style affect your listening and note taking? For example, suppose you know that one of your instructors will be giving a lecture in tomorrow's class. Think about your body's reactions and your preferred learning environment. What will you do to make yourself comfortable so that you can concentrate? How will you motivate yourself to pay attention and stay interested in the lecture? What will you do to listen actively? What note-taking system will you use, and how does your learning style affect your choice? Write an essay in which you answer these questions. Include anything else you want to discuss about the topic. Give your essay a title.

SUMMARY

*An **information map** is a visual representation of how ideas relate to one another. If your learning style preference is visual, then you may prefer information maps to outlines as a way of organizing information. The summary below is followed by an information map that has been partially filled in. After reading the summary, complete the map.*

The five essentials of successful classroom performance are *prepare for class, become an active listener, develop a personal note-taking system, make effective oral presentations, and participate in class and group activities.*

To prepare for class, do the following. Attend regularly and arrive on time. Use your syllabus to keep up with assignments, and bring textbooks and other supplies to class every day. Do all homework assignments and anticipate the next lesson or assignment. Improve your listening skills by becoming an active listener. Listen with a positive frame of mind, focus your attention on the speaker, encourage the speaker, take notes, and decide what is important in a lecture by listening for signal words and phrases.

To take notes effectively, you need a personal note-taking system. There are many such systems with which students have been successful. For example, you can use the informal outline/key words system, the Cornell method, or the clustering technique discussed in this chapter. Any of these systems or one that you adapt from them will work.

To make an effective oral presentation, have a *purpose* for speaking on the topic you have chosen. Then *plan* and *organize* your presentation by using this three-part development: *Tell listeners what you are going to say, say it, and tell them what you have just said.*

Take part in group activities and discussions, and ask questions as needed. Do your share of the work, and don't monopolize the discussion. Your involvement in class helps you add to your background of knowledge, which is the framework on which you can build effective listening and note-taking skills.

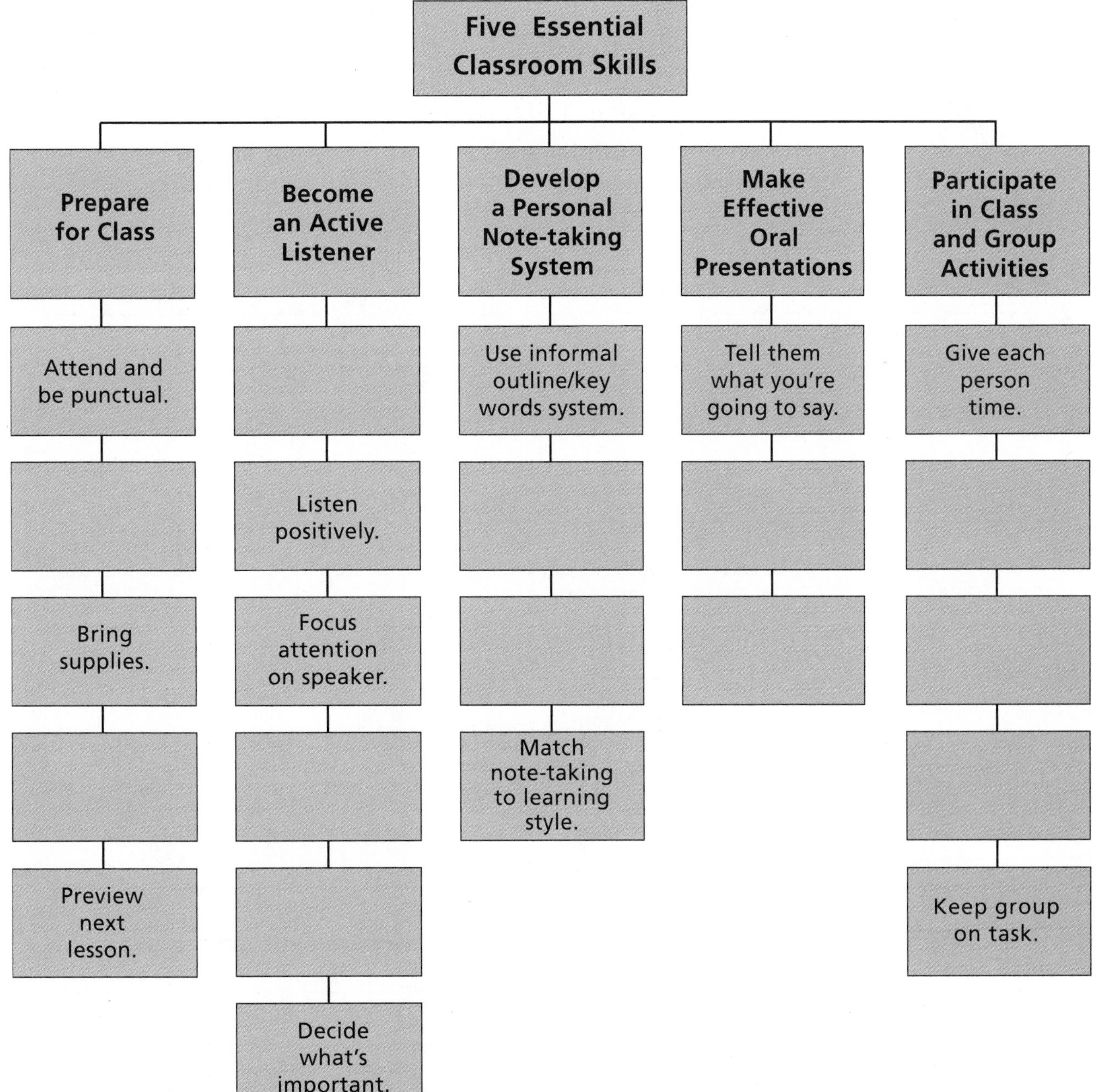

YOUR REFLECTIONS

Reflect on what you have learned about classroom skills and how you can best apply that information. Use the following list of questions to stimulate your thinking, and then write your reflections. Your response may include answers to one or more of the questions. Incorporate in your writing specific information from this chapter.

- Of the five essential classroom skills listed on page 45, which is your strongest? On what do you base this conclusion?
- Which of your classroom skills needs improvement? What have you learned from this chapter that will help you make needed changes?
- What relationship do you see between attendance and punctuality in the classroom and in the workplace?
- How has your preparation for classes either led to or prevented your success?
- Which of the strategies explained in this chapter do you plan to try, and how?

Date ______________________________

CHAPTER 4

Making the Most of Your Time

Much of Lewis Carroll's *Through The Looking Glass* takes place on a giant chessboard. As a pawn on this chessboard, Alice wants to win the game and become a queen. But when she tries to move, she can't, and when she tries to stay on her square, she finds herself on the other side of the board. Finally, the Red Queen explains the rules of the game to Alice: "Here," she says, "it takes all the running you can do to keep in the same place." Do you sometimes feel, like Alice, that you are running furiously in place—and getting nowhere—simply to survive? What are the factors that make it difficult for you to manage your time?

The demands of work, family responsibilities, personal needs, and course requirements all compete for your time. Nevertheless, time is a resource you can learn to manage. By taking control of your time now, you will establish efficient work habits that lead to success in college and career. You already possess several keys to effective time management. Use your assessment skills to identify your time-management strengths and weaknesses. Your understanding of learning styles opens the door to your and others' time-management styles. Finally, your knowledge of critical thinking and study skills provides access to the strategies explained in this chapter that can help you manage your time instead of letting time manage you:

- Use the GRAB method to take control.
- Make and follow schedules.
- Avoid procrastination.

HOW TO GRAB SOME TIME

To take control of your time, you must be aggressive, especially if you are a chronic procrastinator: one who consistently puts off doing difficult, boring, or time-consuming tasks. Unless you live alone, you may have to fight for some time by yourself to study. Be willing to talk honestly with family members about your goals. Sit down with them and discuss how they can help you by taking on more responsibilities around the house. Ask for their suggestions. Make clear that their support, cooperation, and encouragement will increase your chances for success. Be willing to talk plainly to a roommate who is making too much noise, not sharing the responsibility of keeping up your room or apartment, keeping late hours, or inviting friends in to party when you should both be studying. You may find time slipping away from you unless you GRAB it and hold tight (see Figure 4.1).

FIGURE 4.1 How to GRAB Some Time

G	GOAL	Set a goal.
R	RESPONSIBILITIES	Determine your responsibilities.
A	ANALYSIS	Analyze where your time goes.
B	BALANCE	Balance work, class, study, and leisure time.

Goal

To GRAB study time, **set a goal.** What do you want to do? Would you like to set aside a block of time each day for completing all your assignments? Would you like to have two hours free on Tuesday and Thursday evenings to complete your algebra assignments? Do you want to set aside one afternoon a week, in the library, to write drafts of essays for your composition class? The goal is up to you; it should be a reachable goal, one you can reasonably expect to achieve. The time limit you set should be one you can live with. For more information on how to set reachable goals, see Chapter 2, pages 24–44.

Responsibilities

Determine your responsibilities. Do you live alone? If not, then you may have responsibilities to the person or people with whom you live. You will have greater success setting goals and reaching them if you involve these people in your plans. For example, if you have children and you need time in the evenings for studying, you will need to see that your children are occupied. Convince family members that if they will help more with the household chores, then you will have more time for studying and they will be helping you reach your educational goals. If you share an apartment or live in a dorm with a roommate, then you both

Your fixed times may include special activities or classes that meet during the same hours each week.

© Jean Claude Lejeune

need to compare schedules and arrange times for studying that will allow you plenty of quiet time for concentrated work. Taking others' needs into consideration helps you set goals that are fair to all concerned. At the same time you must be assertive about *your* needs.

Analysis

Analyze where your time goes, and you may be able to find a more efficient way to use your time. What are the **fixed times** in a typical day for you? Fixed times include the hours you spend at work, in classes, and traveling to and from each. These are the time slots that may be difficult or impossible to change. For example, if you are an athlete, then your fixed times will include hours you spend practicing and participating in games or events. If you are a parent, then your fixed times may include driving children to and from school and to other regularly scheduled activities. If you are working full time and attending college part time, then your fixed times include the time you spend at college and at work. **Flexible times** include the hours you spend doing such things as sleeping, eating, watching television, and studying. You can choose when you do these activities and how much time you spend on each.

Balance

To manage your time more effectively, **balance work, class, study, and leisure time** through scheduling. *A schedule is a structure you impose on the events of one day, week, semester, quarter, or any other block of time you choose.* A schedule is a plan for getting things done; it is a commitment you make that reminds you of your goals and helps you stay on track. Since it is *your* commitment, you are free to revise, change, or terminate your schedule at any time. In order to achieve balance among work, class, study, and leisure, you must first determine how much time you presently spend on these activities. Complete the Awareness Check to assess your use of time.

AWARENESS CHECK #8

Where Does Your Time Go?

Estimate the number of hours you spend each week on the following activities. When you are finished, subtract your total hours from 168, the number of hours in a week. How much time is left? How can you use this time to reach your goals?

Activity	Hours per Week
1. Attending classes	______
2. Working	______
3. Sleeping	______
4. Dressing, showering, etc.	______
5. Traveling to and from work, college, etc.	______
6. Studying	______
7. Eating	______
8. Watching television	______
9. Engaging in leisure activities	______
10. Caring for family	______
11. Cleaning and doing laundry	______
12. Socializing	______
13. Attending athletic practice	______
14. Other	______
Total =	______
168 Hours Minus Total =	______

Now answer the following questions:

1. On what activity do you spend the least amount of time?

 ____

2. On what activity do you spend the most time? ______________

3. Is the amount of time you spend studying producing the grades you want? ______________________

4. Overall, are you satisfied with the way you spend your time? Why or why not? ______________________

 ____

5. If you could make some changes, what would they be? __________

 ____

After completing the Awareness Check, you may find that you have some surplus time during the week. You might use this **free time** either for scheduling additional study hours as needed, for setting aside a block of regular, consistent study time, or for completing a task or activity you did not think you had time to do. Schedules can make your life easier, not harder, because they help you organize your time.

SCHEDULING YOUR TIME

Schedules put you in control of your time and your life. Your schedule is the result of the inward decision you make to control events instead of letting external circumstances control you. **Semester** or **quarter calendars**, **weekly schedules**, and **daily lists** are three time-honored plans that have helped thousands of students become better time managers. Build confidence in your ability to manage your time by trying out each of these plans.

The Semester or Quarter Calendar

A calendar for the current semester or quarter allows you to see at a glance what you need to accomplish each month in order to complete your course requirements. A semester is about sixteen weeks long, a quarter about ten weeks long. If your college is on a semester system, you probably attend different classes on alternate days: Monday, Wednesday, and Friday or Tuesday and Thursday. On the quarter system, however, you may attend some classes every day. The system your college uses will determine what your calendar will look like and how you will be able to schedule the rest of your time around your classes. To make a complete semester or quarter calendar, you need the following three items:

- **Your college calendar,** printed in the college catalog.
- **A syllabus,** or instructor's outline, for each course.
- **A calendar,** one you either buy or make yourself, that contains squares big enough for you to write in the information you want to remember.

Use your semester or quarter calendar as a quick reference to remind you of such things as upcoming tests and the due dates of important assignments. Keep the calendar on your desk, on a wall above your desk, or on a bulletin board where you will see it every day when you sit down to study. Follow these steps to make your calendar:

1. Enter the following information in the appropriate squares: when classes begin and end, holidays, registration and final exam times, and any other dates or deadlines you must remember, such as midterm exams or application for a degree. You can find most of this information in your college catalog.
2. Review the instructor's **syllabus** you received for each course. The syllabus, or course information sheet, may list test dates and major assignments such as essays, research papers, or projects that are due throughout the term. Some instructors do not plan very far ahead. They may wait to announce test dates several days beforehand. If that is the case, you will want to update your calendar as you get this information.
3. Enter any other information, event, or activity you want to include. For example, if you plan to attend football games or concerts, enter those on the calendar. If you take part in any regularly scheduled activities such as football practice or debate team, also add them to your calendar.
4. Be sure to leave enough space in each square. You may have to list more than one item under each date.

Be creative with your calendar. Make planning your semester or quarter an enjoyable activity. Either purchase a calendar that you find attractive or make your own. Use different colored inks or marking pens for each kind of information you enter. Figure 4.2 shows one month from a student's calendar for a typical semester or quarter.

Your Weekly Schedule

The main purpose of the weekly schedule is to help you plan your study time. Scheduling your study time and making a commitment to stick to your schedule help you give studying the same importance that you give to going to work or attending classes. Without a schedule, you may begin to study only when there is nothing else to do, at the last minute before a test, or late at night when you are too tired. If you are a procrastinator, a weekly schedule may provide the extra motivation you need to get your work done. Your schedule is your commitment to learn. Figure 4.4 on page 77 is an example of a student's weekly schedule.

This student, Lloyd, has fixed times for classes and church attendance. He has flexible times for his other regular activities. In the time remaining, he has allotted the same block of time each day for studying. He has made a commitment to treat studying like a job. If Lloyd sticks to his schedule,

FIGURE 4.2 One Month in a Student's Semester or Quarter

November						
Sunday	**Monday**	**Tuesday**	**Wednesday**	**Thursday**	**Friday**	**Saturday**
			1	2	3 Essay for Comp.	4
5	6 Psych. test	7	8 Algebra test	9	10	11 Golf tournament
12 Golf tournament	13	14 Concert 8:00 P.M.	15	16	17 Essay for Comp.	18
19	20 Dentist 4:00 P.M.	21	22 Algebra test	23 Thanksgiving Holidays	24 Thanksgiving Holidays	25
26	27 Psych. paper due	28	29	30		

then, over a period of time, studying will become a habit for him. When he sits down to study at his regular time, he will be able to get to work quickly and give his assignments maximum concentration. Some weeks Lloyd may require additional time to study for a test or to complete an especially lengthy assignment. On these occasions he can use some of his "free" hours for more studying. What if Lloyd decides to take a part-time job? Then he will have to make some adjustments in his fixed, flexible, and free times. Lloyd's schedule puts *Lloyd* in control of his time and his life.

As you experiment with making schedules, keep in mind that for maximum performance, many experts recommend at least two hours of study time for every hour spent in class. For a class that meets three times a week, this would mean six hours of study per week. Thus, if you are taking five three-hour courses and you want to do your best, you would need to schedule thirty hours a week study time. If you are a working student, you may have difficulty finding that much time to study. To reach your goals, you may be forced either to take fewer courses or to reduce your working hours.

If the ratio of study time to class time seems high, remember that it takes a lot of time and effort to acquire knowledge and learn skills. However, you may spend less time studying subjects that are easy for you than on those that are difficult to master.

EXERCISE 4.1

Make a semester or quarter calendar. Either buy a calendar or make copies of the template in Figure 4.3 for each month in your semester or quarter. Write in the month, days of the week, and each day's date on each calendar page, then staple them together. Look again at Figure 4.2, and then enter the following information:

1. When classes begin and end, holidays, final exam dates
2. Registration date for the following semester or quarter
3. Test dates and dates when major assignments are due
4. Dates of activities or events you want to participate in or attend
5. Any other dates or deadlines you want to remember

FIGURE 4.3 Calendar Template

Sunday	Monday	Tuesday	Wednesday	Thursday	Friday	Saturday

FIGURE 4.4 **Lloyd's Weekly Schedule**

	Sunday	Monday	Tuesday	Wednesday	Thursday	Friday	Saturday
6:00 – 7:00	Sleep	Run Dress Eat	→	→	→	→	Sleep
7:00 – 8:00	Sleep	← Transportation to Class →					Sleep
8:00 – 9:00	Sleep	Algebra Class	Study in Library	Algebra Class	Study in Library	Algebra Class	Eat Run
9:00 – 10:00	Run Dress	Comp. 1	French 1	Comp. 1	French 1	Comp. 1	Study
10:00 – 11:00	Eat Trans. to church	Biology Class	Biology	Biology Class	French	Biology Class	Study
11:00 – 12:00	Church	Lunch/ Trans.	Lab	Lunch/ Trans.	Lab	Lunch/ Trans.	Lunch
12:00 – 1:00	Trans. Church to home	Home		Home		Home	
1:00 – 2:00	Lunch Clean	Study	Study	Study	Study	Study	
2:00 – 3:00	Apart-ment						
3:00 – 4:00	Free	Laundry, other chores →					Leisure or study
4:00 – 5:00	Free	→					
5:00 – 6:00	Free	→					May Go
6:00 – 7:00	Dinner	→					Out
7:00 – 8:00	↑	→					Later ↓
8:00 – 9:00	Study	→					
9:00 – 10:00	or Watch	→					
10:00 – 11:00	TV	→					
11:00 – 12:00	↓	→					↓
12:00 – 1:00	Sleep	→					

FIGURE 4.5 Weekly Schedule Template

	Sunday	Monday	Tuesday	Wednesday	Thursday	Friday	Saturday
6:00 – 7:00							
7:00 – 8:00							
8:00 – 9:00							
9:00 – 10:00							
10:00 – 11:00							
11:00 – 12:00							
12:00 – 1:00							
1:00 – 2:00							
2:00 – 3:00							
3:00 – 4:00							
4:00 – 5:00							
5:00 – 6:00							
6:00 – 7:00							
7:00 – 8:00							
8:00 – 9:00							
9:00 – 10:00							
10:00 – 11:00							
11:00 – 12:00							
12:00 – 1:00							

EXERCISE 4.2

Make a weekly schedule (see Figure 4.5 for the template that accompanies this exercise). To make out your schedule, follow the directions below.

1. Fill in your fixed-time activities. These are the things you must do at scheduled times—for example, working and attending classes.
2. Fill in your flexible-time activities. These are things you need or want to do that you can schedule at your own discretion.
3. The squares remaining are your free times. Schedule a regular time each day for studying.
4. Be sure to schedule some time for leisure activities.
5. Fill in every square.

A Daily List

Keep a daily list of things to do and appointments to keep. Nearly everyone makes lists: grocery lists, appointment lists, errand lists. As a student, you need to make lists, too: when to return library books, specific study tasks you must complete, counseling appointments, and so on.

Some people make lists on little scraps of paper. Others use fancy notepads, small spiral-bound notebooks, daily planners, or appointment books that they buy in bookstores or office supply stores. (If you buy a daily planner or appointment book, be sure to get one with squares big enough to hold several items or one that includes a separate notepad.) Whatever you use for making your daily lists, make sure it is a convenient size, and keep it handy.

EXERCISE 4.3

Review the Awareness Check you took near the beginning of this chapter. Notice how many hours per week you estimated that you spend for each of the activities listed. For one week, keep track of the actual hours you spend on those activities. Write down the *actual* amounts of time as you spend them (*not* later that day, or you could easily end up estimating your time again). At the end of the week, write your original estimates and the exact hours below; then complete the following items.

Activity	Estimated Time	Actual Time
1. Attending classes	________	________
2. Working	________	________
3. Sleeping	________	________
4. Dressing, showering, etc.	________	________

Activity	Estimated Time	Actual Time
5. Traveling to and from work, college, etc.	______	______
6. Studying	______	______
7. Eating	______	______
8. Watching television	______	______
9. Engaging in leisure activities	______	______
10. Caring for family	______	______
11. Cleaning and doing laundry	______	______
12. Socializing	______	______
13. Attending athletic practice	______	______
14. Other	______	______

1. List the activities in which you spent more time than you had estimated.

____

____

____

2. List the activities in which you spent less time than you had estimated.

____

____

____

3. How can you use this new information to revise your weekly schedule?

____

____

____

If you have a personal computer, you might want to invest in an electronic calendar. Several programs allow you to keep records of important dates and appointments on your computer and set up your calendar in a variety of formats. When you turn on your computer, for example, the calendar could tell you the day's date and list your schedule for the day. In some programs, you can instruct the computer to beep as a reminder that you have an appointment.

Keeping a daily list can be a quick and easy way to start planning your time effectively. Your daily lists should include whatever you want to do or whatever you need to remember that you might otherwise forget. Figure 4.6 shows a student's list for one day.

FIGURE 4.6 A List for One Day

Things To Do

1. Read chapter 7 for psych.
2. Do outline for essay.
3. Finish algebra homework.
4. Review for algebra test.
5. Pick up tickets for game.
6. Call Mom.

EXERCISE 4.4

Apply what you have learned about schedules by doing this exercise with group members. Remember to follow the guidelines for group discussion explained in Chapter 1, pages 12–13. Discuss the questions below. When you reach consensus, record your answers on the lines provided. Then evaluate your work.

1. What are your experiences with making and following schedules? Which group members have used schedules, and which have not?

___

___

___

2. What are the advantages and disadvantages of making daily, weekly, and semester or quarter schedules?

___

___

___

3. Which type of schedule do you find most useful, and why?

____

____

____

4. Discuss a specific problem you have had with time management. How could you use schedules to overcome this problem?

____

____

____

Evaluate your discussion. Did everyone contribute? Did you accomplish your task successfully? What additional questions do you have about making and following schedules? How will you find answers to your questions?

____

____

____

Special Challenges for Commuters

Unlike the resident student, you have to build travel time into your schedule. The time you spend traveling to and from campus or from campus to work to home leaves less time for studying and other activities. You may also have to take your children to their school before you can go to yours, and you may also have to finish in time to pick them up. Because it is easy to underestimate the time it takes you to get from place to place, you must give special consideration to travel time as you plan your schedule and select courses.

Adding college courses and study time to an already busy schedule is another challenge. You may be tempted to meet it by scheduling all your classes on one or two days. Although this may seem like a good idea at the time, you may encounter one or more common problems. Suppose you schedule all your classes on one day. If you have to be absent, then you will miss *all* your classes for the whole week. Also, papers, tests, and other assignments for those classes will always be due on the same day. Instead of having a paper due on Monday, several math problems due on Wednesday, and a test due on Thursday or Friday, you will have to turn in the paper and the problems and take the test all in one day. Spreading your classes over two days is not much better; you still may have several assignments or tests due on the same day.

What happens at the end of the one or two days you attend class? For one thing, you are probably exhausted and have so many other things to do that you don't or can't take time to review your notes from each class or begin doing the assignments. Also, you may postpone the work until the night before your classes meet, leaving you only enough time to do a portion of the work. You may even skip one or two assignments, thinking you'll catch up later. This almost never happens.

One- or two-day schedules often lead to scheduling classes back to back, which may seem like another good way to save time. Unfortunately, when you attend one class right after another, you don't have time to absorb and process the information covered in the previous class. You set yourself up for *information overload,* a condition in which the material explained in one class gets confused with that covered in another.

Ideal schedules are those that spread classes and study times over the whole week and that alternate class periods with free periods. During your free periods, you can either review notes from your previous class or do some last-minute review for a test you must take in the next class. Because you have free time between classes, you must remain on campus. This puts you in a good position to form a study group that you meet with at a regular time or to set up a standing appointment with a tutor if you are having difficulty in one of your classes. You may find that by scheduling classes over the whole week, you are actually *saving* time, because it is easier to schedule study time around one or two classes a day and still meet your other obligations than it is to try to pack in some study time after having attended four or five classes. However, if you absolutely have to attend class on a two-day schedule because of work or other obligations, at least try to schedule a free hour between classes.

Time Management and Learning Style

Chapter 1 explains that your body's reactions affect your learning style. For example, you probably have an optimum time of day when your concentration seems to be at its highest and you are most productive. But being a morning person or a night person isn't just a preference, nor do you have a choice about it.

You have a biological clock that regulates your internal rhythms, telling you when to eat, when to sleep, and when to get up and get moving. The time of day that your temperature is highest is what determines whether you are an early bird or a night owl. Since you can't control fluctuations in your body's temperature, you may as well take advantage of it. Do important activities that require thinking and concentration at your optimum time of day. Try to schedule your classes, especially ones that you expect to be difficult, at the time of day when you are most alert. If you have to take a class at a time when you know you will be working at a disadvantage, try these suggestions:

- When you feel yourself getting drowsy, take a few deep breaths.
- Change your position every few minutes: cross and uncross your legs, sit up straight, make other adjustments in the way you are sitting.
- Eat a snack, such as a handful of raisins or a piece of fruit, before you go into class. This will raise your blood sugar level and your body temperature, making you feel more alert.
- Take deep, rhythmic breaths to get more oxygen into your bloodstream.

EXERCISE 4.5

Write a short essay in which you explain how your present schedule of classes and study times either does or does not conflict with your learning style. Consider which classes require the most work, which assignments need greater concentration, your optimum time of day, whether your schedule permits you to eat regularly and get enough rest. What are your schedule's strengths and weaknesses? How can you improve your schedule next semester or quarter? Give your essay a title.

Try these same suggestions whenever you must study at a time when you are tired. In addition, when you are at home, prop up your feet to increase the blood flow to your brain.

Time Management and Reading

One of the big differences between high school and college is the amount of reading assigned. Whether you are a recent graduate or an older student, you may have been frustrated by the number of pages per week that each instructor assigns. A common complaint you will hear from students of all ages is "Each of my instructors must think his or her class is the only one I have."

Nevertheless, the reading has to be done. Are there any short cuts? No. Reading takes time. The more difficult the reading, the more time it takes. However, you can learn to read more efficiently. Try these strategies:

- Determine the time you need for reading.
- Schedule your reading time.
- Develop active reading habits and study skills so that you do not waste time.

To calculate your reading time, follow the steps given in Figure 4.7. For example, suppose you have been assigned a fifty-page chapter from your biology text. The assignment is due at the next class meeting. You have determined that it takes you two hours to read twenty-five pages from this book. Sometime between now and the next class meeting, you should schedule four hours of reading time for biology.

Active reading habits include underlining, making notes in the margins, outlining, making study guides, and other activities explained in Chapter 14. SQ3R, explained in Chapter 7, is a time-honored reading/study system you can use that has helped many students read efficiently. Chapter 8 explains different ways to organize information into study guides that are easier to study and take less time to review than re-reading chapters. In fact, re-reading is an inefficient way to study and one you should avoid. If you take the time to read, mark your text, and make notes in the first place, you may be able to shorten your review time. If you feel that you have missed something, you can always re-read just those sections of a chapter that contain the information needed.

FIGURE 4.7 Calculate Your Reading Time

1. Choose three consecutive textbook pages that contain mostly print.
2. Time yourself on the reading of these three pages.
3. Jot down your starting time in minutes and seconds. When you have read three pages, jot down the time and subtract your starting time to get the total reading time. Divide total time by 3 to get the time it takes you to read one page.
4. To get the time needed to complete a reading assignment, multiply the number of pages by your time per page. Divide by 60 to get the number of hours and minutes it will take you to finish your reading.

Example: You have twenty pages to read. How long will it take you? Here are the results of your initial calculation:

Starting time: 3:00
Finishing time: 3:18

Subtract starting time from finishing time:

 3:18
−3:00
 0:18 ÷ 3 = 6 minutes per page

Multiply the number of minutes per page times the number of pages in the assignment, and divide by 60:

6 × 20 = 120 ÷ 60 = 2 hours (time needed to read twenty pages)

PROCRASTINATION

Procrastination means needlessly postponing tasks until some future time. Although procrastinating once in a while may not hurt you, if you delay studying and put off doing important assignments too often, you will sabotage your efforts to succeed. Complete Awareness Check 9 to gauge your tendency to put off tasks.

Four Reasons for Procrastination

Ann has to write a research paper for her composition course. The paper is due in six weeks. She thinks she has plenty of time, so for the first two weeks she doesn't even think about the project. That leaves her only a month to choose a topic, do her research in the library, make an outline, and write the paper. It takes her another week to select a topic, but when she gets to the library she finds that several of the books she wants have been checked out. By the time Ann decides on another topic and compiles her research materials, she has only a week left to complete the paper. She *does* hand it in on time, but she knows it is not her best effort. She doesn't like to write anyway and is not expecting to receive a very good grade. "Next time," she

AWARENESS CHECK #9

Are You a Procrastinator?

To find out whether procrastination is keeping you from getting your work done, put a check beside the statements that apply to you.

- ☐ 1. I put off doing an assignment if it seems too difficult.
- ☐ 2. I put off doing an assignment if completing it will take a lot of time.
- ☐ 3. I put off studying if I don't like the subject.
- ☐ 4. I put off studying if I'm not in the mood.
- ☐ 5. I put off writing an essay if I don't know how to begin.
- ☐ 6. I put off studying for a test if I don't know what the test will cover.
- ☐ 7. I put off studying if I get hungry.
- ☐ 8. I put off studying if I am too tired.
- ☐ 9. I put off studying if I don't feel well.
- ☐ 10. I put off studying if there is something else I'd rather do.

All the items of the Awareness Check describe common tactics students use to avoid studying. To build confidence, you need to understand when and why you procrastinate and fight your tendency to delay getting started.

swears, "I'll get started sooner." But next time Ann will probably procrastinate again because that is her pattern of behavior. Ann doesn't like to do difficult or lengthy assignments and will put them off until the last minute. Like many students, Ann procrastinates for one of four common reasons. Perhaps you procrastinate for one of these reasons also:

- Your tasks seem difficult or time consuming.
- You have trouble getting started.
- You lack motivation to do the work.
- You are afraid of failing.

Putting off difficult or time-consuming assignments makes them even harder to do when you actually do get started and further ensures that you won't be able to do your best because you will not have enough time. However, a task may be less difficult than you think if you break it down into segments that you can handle in short periods of time. If you have trouble getting started on an assignment, or if you waste a lot of time before sitting down to study, then you may be using avoidance tactics.

If you budget your studying time wisely, you will have more time for leisure activities.

© D. Young-Wolff/PhotoEdit

Why are you avoiding what you have to do? Perhaps you lack interest in the subject, or perhaps you'd simply prefer to be doing something else. You may be insufficiently motivated to perform the work. You may not see a direct connection between the assignment and your goals or your overall grade in the course. Or you may be afraid of failure. If you believe that you will not get a good grade whatever you do, you may delay getting started on an assignment. Complete the next Awareness Check for more insight into why you procrastinate.

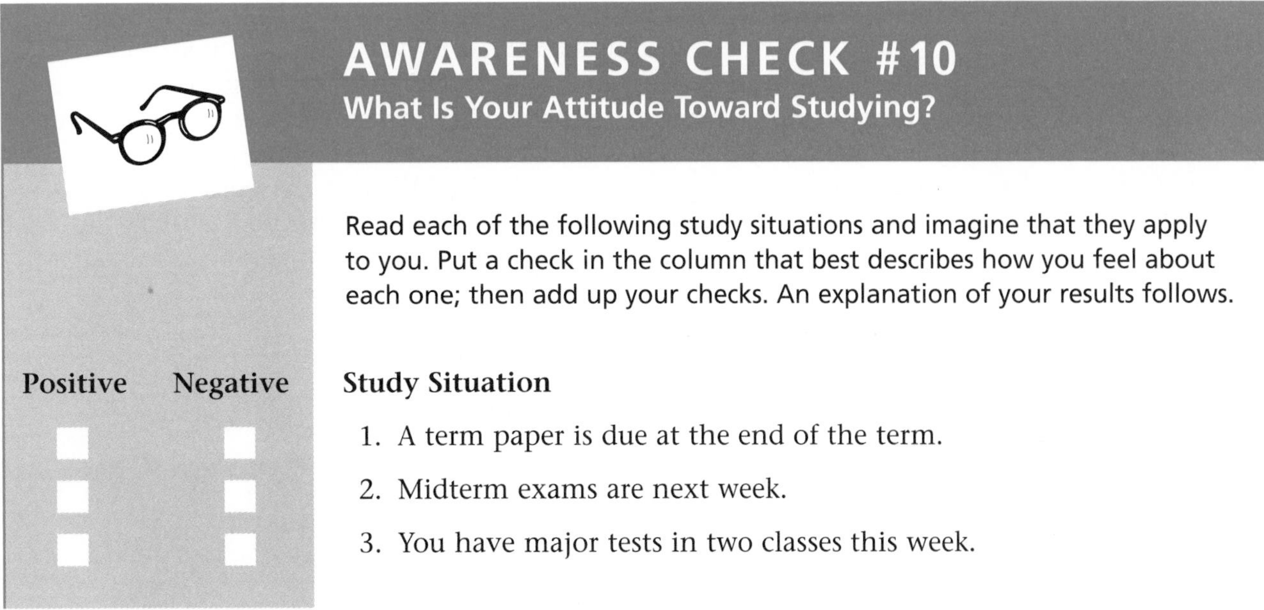

AWARENESS CHECK #10

What Is Your Attitude Toward Studying?

Read each of the following study situations and imagine that they apply to you. Put a check in the column that best describes how you feel about each one; then add up your checks. An explanation of your results follows.

Positive	Negative	Study Situation
☐	☐	1. A term paper is due at the end of the term.
☐	☐	2. Midterm exams are next week.
☐	☐	3. You have major tests in two classes this week.

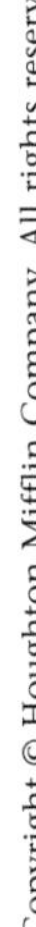

Positive	Negative	Study Situation
☐	☐	4. In one of your classes, the final exam will determine whether you pass or fail.
☐	☐	5. You are in a self-paced math course. You have a list of assignments and several tests to complete by semester's end.
☐	☐	6. You have a sixty-page chapter to read in your psychology text for tomorrow's class.
☐	☐	7. You have a speech to prepare for your speech class.
☐	☐	8. You have a 500-word essay to write for your composition class.
☐	☐	9. You have final exams to study for in all of your classes.
☐	☐	10. You are taking an anatomy course. You must learn the names of all the bones in the body.

Totals: Positive _____ Negative _____

All of these study situations represent tasks that are difficult or time consuming. Look at your totals in each column. In general, based on this exercise, how do you feel about difficult or lengthy assignments? Specifically, if you checked negative for items 1 and 8, perhaps writing is difficult for you and you avoid getting started for that reason. If you checked negative for items 2, 3, 4, and 9, perhaps you avoid studying for tests because you have test anxiety or are afraid that you will fail. If you checked negative for item 5, maybe the self-paced learning situation seems overwhelming and you need the structure of a classroom setting, in which the instructor sets the pace for you. If you checked negative for item 6, it could be that the length of a reading assignment affects how you feel about it. Perhaps you'd be more motivated to start sooner if you divided up the reading assignment into smaller segments with breaks in between. If you checked negative for item 7, perhaps you don't like giving speeches, can't think of what to say, or are afraid you will get nervous and do a poor job. The sooner you start writing your speech and the more time you give yourself to practice it, the more confident you will feel in your ability to do a good job. If you checked negative for item 10, perhaps you avoid starting assignments like this one because the number of items you have to learn and remember seems more than you can handle. One of the memory techniques suggested in Chapter 11 may make it easier for you to get started.

COMPUTER CONFIDENCE

Use the Computer to Save Time

Effective time management is crucial to success in college, especially when it comes to writing papers. For many students, writing papers is the most time-consuming part of any course. How about you? Does the process of planning, researching, drafting, revising, editing, and rewriting seem endless? Is just the thought of selecting a topic, gathering information, and organizing it into a research paper or essay overwhelming? Do you find yourself waiting until the last minute to get started? If so, try using a computer. You'll be surprised at how much more efficient your planning and writing will become and how much better your results will be.

There are several reasons for using a computer for your writing assignments. A computer lets you make changes almost instantly. You can change or move words, sentences, and even whole paragraphs just by hitting one or two keys on the keyboard. That saves you time—you don't need to retype or cut and paste. A computer gives you a neatly printed draft whenever you want one, quickly and painlessly. Some word-processing programs check your spelling, grammar, and writing style. A computer simplifies the mechanics of writing and lets you concentrate on expressing your ideas.

Before you start writing, a computer can help you organize your notes. Suppose you have taken notes from several books and magazines. If you enter those notes into a computer, integrating them into a coherent outline will be easy, and your outline may help you write a logically organized paper. (See Computer Confidence: Chapter 3, page 58 for more information about outlining.)

Whenever you use a computer to write a paper, follow these steps to make sure that you don't accidentally "lose" your work:

1. Use the "save" command frequently. Save every five or ten minutes. Save every time you complete a page. And save whenever you leave the computer, even if you will be away for only a few minutes. Remember: Save it; don't lose it!

2. Give your files easily recognizable names that clearly indicate the project and its stage of development—for example, the file name ENG2DR1 might stand for English class, paper number two, first draft. Date each file so that you can quickly and easily find the most recent one. Write the file name and date on a label you attach to your disk.

3. Before you revise a draft, copy it in case you want to refer to your original version. Renaming each draft automatically saves both in separate files. At the end of every writing session, print out a paper copy of your new work. This "hard copy" is always useful for revisions. If you have a hard copy and if something goes wrong with your disk, then you will still have your work.

4. Keep a backup disk of all of your work. At the end of every writing session, copy your completed work onto the backup disk. Store your disks carefully.

How to Beat Procrastination

To avoid being a procrastinator, change your behavior. If you procrastinate when assignments are too difficult or too long, if you have trouble getting started or lack motivation to do the work, then instead of focusing on your feelings about the assignment, focus on the advantages of completing it on time. If you get started right away, you will have the advantage of enough time to do your best; you may complete the assignment with time left over to do something else. If you wait too long to begin, then you won't be able to do your best or you may not finish at all. Fear of failure is sometimes the result of not knowing what to do. If you are not sure what is expected of you, then you may not know how to begin the assignment. To help you overcome the fear of failure and get started, try these tips that have worked for many students:

1. Break a large assignment or project into smaller units of work that you can complete in one sitting.
2. Plan rewards for yourself for completing each part of the assignment. Take a break or do something you enjoy.
3. Make a schedule for completing a long assignment. Set a goal to spend a certain amount of time working each day until the assignment is finished.
4. Get organized. Your attitude toward studying will improve if you have an orderly work area with everything you need at your fingertips—books, pens and pencils, paper—so that you are ready to begin the moment you sit down.
5. If you put off assignments because you don't know where to start or aren't sure how to do the work, find out what you need to know. Make an appointment with your instructor. Explain the difficulty you are having, and ask for advice. If you have started the assignment, show your instructor where you are having trouble. Talk to someone in the class. If you missed a lecture or have gaps in your notes, your friend might be able to fill you in.
6. Assume an attitude of confidence and you will *be* confident. Instead of thinking "This is too difficult" or "I'll never finish this," think "I *can* do this, if I get started right now" and "There's a lot of work to do, but if I can do a little bit at a time I'll be finished before I know it."

Learning to manage time and avoiding procrastination require some effort. Do not be discouraged if your first efforts are unsuccessful. Try to pinpoint your reasons for procrastinating. Identify your avoidance tactics and try to eliminate them. Experiment with schedules until you come up with a plan that works for you. With determination, you will take control of your time and your life—and you will reach your goals.

Your Study Place

Managing your time well also means choosing a quiet place to study. If you are a resident student, you probably do most of your studying in your room or in the library. If you are a commuter, chances are you do the

CONFIDENCE BUILDER

Time Management, Your Goals, and Your Career

Time management helps you attain your goals, big or small, which can lead to a rewarding and enjoyable career.

Much of the work conducted in businesses today is done as team projects. A project manager oversees the work, breaking it down into segments for which each member of the project group is responsible. A successful project begins with setting goals both for its achievement of purpose and for its completion on time. People who come into the workplace lacking goal-setting and time-management skills are at a disadvantage. J. C. Penney, the founder of the retail chain of stores by the same name, said, "Give me a stock clerk with a goal, and I will give you a man who will make history. Give me a man without a goal, and I will give you a stock clerk." He recognized that through goal-setting, people can direct and change the courses of their lives—and they get the job done, whatever the task.

Goal-setting and time management are linked, because to set a reachable goal, as explained in Chapter 2, you must determine a reasonable time for its completion. A goal that has no foreseeable end is a goal you will never reach. Setting a time limit, one you *can* reach, keeps you focused and on task. Whether you are planning your course schedule for your next term or making a study schedule for this semester or quarter, you are gaining practice in goal-setting and time management—two valuable career skills.

One test of your ability to manage your time is whether you are able to follow through with your plan to achieve a goal within the time limit you have set. Of course, there will be setbacks, but you should be able to recover and continue making progress. Goal-setting and time management have several advantages:

- They lead to self-improvement.
- They help you make and keep commitments.
- They lead to greater self-control.
- They enable you to accept responsibility.
- They improve your overall effectiveness in all your relationships.

It may take a while for you to see these advantages, particularly if setting goals and managing your time are skills you are just beginning to acquire. It takes hard work to follow through with a schedule or to take each step necessary to reach a goal, but the effort is worth it. The skills you are gaining will make your life more rewarding and improve your prospects for the future.

Your study place should be comfortable, quiet, well-lighted, and supplied with everything you need for study. © Tony Freeman/PhotoEdit

majority of your studying at home. In either case, you probably have to fight distractions, and the best way to do that is to schedule your study time when and where you are least likely to be disturbed.

If you are a commuter, set up a study area in a quiet part of your home. Your study place doesn't have to be elaborate. A desk or small table in your bedroom or in a guest room will do. Avoid studying in bed because you will probably fall asleep. Avoid places in high-traffic areas such as the kitchen or family room. Not only will you be distracted, but your family may conclude that the study is not serious business and that you won't mind being interrupted. A study area away from the family and the noise of TV and children's play—a place where you do nothing but study—sends a subtle message that you are treating studying like a job and do not want to be distracted.

Let your family know that you need quiet time to do your work. Schedule a regular time for studying at home, and make it a routine. Soon your family will get used to the idea that when you are in your study place you are unavailable except in case of emergency. If you can arrange to study at a time when your children are asleep or when no one else is in the house, so much the better.

To help fight procrastination, outfit your study place with everything you might need to get the job done: pens, pencils, paper, dictionary, a good desk lamp, and whatever other supplies you need. When you come in from

class, go immediately to your study place and unload your books. Then they will already be there waiting for you when you are ready to study.

If you are a resident student, set up a study area in your part of the room. Put your desk against a wall, away from a window or door if possible, and keep the door closed when you are studying. Then you won't be tempted away from your books by what is going on outside the window or in the hallway. Like the commuter, you should avoid studying in bed. Like the commuter's family, your roommate and friends across the hall are your temporary "family" and a source of distractions. Make a deal with your roommate early in the term that you will not disturb each other while studying. Try to work out mutually agreeable study times. For example, one of you might study while the other is in class. On the other hand, you may want to schedule some of your study time so that you can work together.

CRITICAL THINKING APPLICATION

If you procrastinate only now and then, it may not hurt you, but if you regularly put off tasks that you know you should be doing, you are in for trouble. Chronic procrastinators make excuses for their procrastination that are really cop-outs, or evasive tactics that they use to deflect responsibility for the procrastination from themselves. Following is a list of the top ten excuses students make for not studying or for not completing assignments. The list is adapted from Edwin C. Bliss's list of top forty cop-outs in *Doing It Now,* a book that explains why people procrastinate and how to avoid it.

Read the list. How many of these cop-outs have you used? How many have you heard other students use? Choose three of them and explain why they are invalid. What advice would you give to students who use these excuses? What suggestions can you make to help them avoid procrastination?

1. It's not due yet.
2. I work better under pressure.
3. I don't feel like doing it now.
4. It's too difficult.
5. I really mean to do it, but I keep forgetting.
6. I don't know where to begin.
7. It's boring.
8. I don't really know how to do it.
9. I don't have all the materials I need.
10. I probably wouldn't do a very good job anyway.

SUMMARY

As you read the following summary, note how the first paragraph is highlighted and marked. As part of your review, highlight and mark the rest of the summary, using the first paragraph as a guide.

Time management and procrastination pose major problems for many students. Managing your time effectively and beating procrastination call for aggressive action. You can GRAB time by following four steps.① First, set *goals* and give yourself a time limit to reach them.② Second, determine your *responsibilities* to the important people in your life and find ways to involve them in your plans to reach your goals.③ Third, *analyze* where your time goes so that you can find more efficient ways to use it. ④Finally, *balance* your fixed, flexible, free, and study times by making and following schedules.

Semester and quarter calendars, weekly schedules, and daily lists can help you remember important dates, deadlines, assignments, events, and appointments. Make out a semester or quarter calendar early in the term so that you can see at a glance what you have to accomplish each month. Use your weekly schedule to help you keep up with weekly assignments and plan reviews for tests. Your daily list can be a reminder of all the things you need to do during a day that you might forget: phone calls you need to make or appointments you must keep, for example. Schedules help keep you organized and on track.

Though you may procrastinate for many reasons, four common ones may apply to you. Your tasks seem difficult and time consuming; you have trouble getting started; you lack motivation to do the work; you are afraid of failing. Avoid procrastination by understanding the reasons you delay performing required tasks and by changing the behaviors that may contribute to the problem.

YOUR REFLECTIONS

Reflect on what you have learned about making the most of your time and how you can best apply that information. Use the following list of questions to stimulate your thinking; then write your reflections. Your response may include answers to one or more of the questions. Incorporate in your writing specific information from this chapter.

- What are some of the obligations and responsibilities that compete for your time?
- Are you able to manage your time effectively? Why or why not?
- Do you procrastinate? If so, what are your reasons? What can you do to keep from procrastinating?
- What relationship do you see between managing your study time and managing time in other situations?
- Which of the time-management strategies explained in this chapter do you plan to try, and how?

Date ______________________________

CHAPTER 5

Adapting to College Life

Getting along in college and being able to take advantage of everything it has to offer depend on how well you can adapt to change. If this is your first semester or quarter in college, it has probably taken you some time to find your way around campus, make new friends, and begin to feel comfortable in your new learning community. Even if you are a returning student, there is still a period of adjustment to go through each term during which you orient yourself to a new schedule of classes, new instructors, and a different set of requirements and expectations.

The key to getting along in college is to get involved so that you can enjoy the many benefits of using your college's resources. This chapter explains several ways you can make adapting to college life easier:

- Become familiar with your diverse campus.
- Know the people on campus who can help you.
- Know the places to go to for help.
- Read the publications that can help.
- Find out what resources are available for commuters.

YOUR DIVERSE CAMPUS

Before the 1960s, college students in the United States typically were white males who had similar social and economic backgrounds. Their readiness for college was generally assured, since many of them either had attended prep schools or had been on a college-prep track, rather than a vocational or business track, throughout high school. However, the number of women attending college has been increasing since the 1960s;

AWARENESS CHECK #11

Do You Know Your Campus Culture and Its Resources?

Put a check beside the statements below that describe you or your behavior.

☐ 1. I know what courses are required for graduation from my college.

☐ 2. I know what my instructors' attendance and grading policies are.

☐ 3. I believe that my attitudes and values reflect those of many of the students who attend my college.

☐ 4. I am aware of some of the problems that minorities may face as they pursue their educational goals.

☐ 5. I know what services are available to all students at my college.

☐ 6. If I should happen to be in academic difficulty, I know what services are available to help me and where to go to get them.

☐ 7. I know where to go to apply for campus employment.

☐ 8. I know where to go on campus to apply for a grant or scholarship.

☐ 9. I have a college catalog or know where to get one.

☐ 10. I know what other college publications are available to students and how they can help.

If you checked 8 or more of the statements above, you may already be making a successful adjustment to your campus culture. If you checked fewer items, you may need to develop or improve your adaptive strategies.

women now constitute about 54 percent of the college population. The student body has also become increasingly diverse. Students come from a variety of backgrounds. They differ in age, race, socio-economic level, and learning ability. Many are international students, and some are disabled. Some grew up in urban neighborhoods; others are from rural communities. Today, there is no typical college student.

Although the dominant culture on many campuses is still white, the college culture may include some or all of the following minority groups: African Americans, Asians, Hispanics, Europeans, Native Americans, and others. Older students and disabled students are also considered minorities. A *minority* is any group of people whose differences from the dominant culture or group may cause them to be discriminated against. Women have also been considered a minority. Even though they make up half the population, they have been discriminated against. It is estimated that by the year 2080, non-whites will become the dominant culture. Because everyone must learn to live and work together, college provides the place and the opportunities for you to reach out to others in a spirit of friendship and community. Despite your differences, you may find you have much in common. Moreover, being able to work with people from culturally diverse backgrounds is an interpersonal skill essential to success at work.

Racial, Ethnic, and Cultural Minorities

Because colleges value diversity, there are probably a number of programs, services, and interest groups on your campus that can help minority students get involved. The Black History Association is a group found on many campuses; there are also religious groups and groups for women, international students, lesbians, and gay men. Although having a support group of others like yourself is important, it is equally important to make an effort to reach out to those who differ. College isn't only classrooms, studying, and testing. Getting involved in extracurricular activities can help you find friends who share one of your interests. Join a group that appeals to an interest such as art, drama, or music, a career such as engineering, or an issue such as SADD (Students Against Driving Drunk). Become involved in student government or a service organization on campus. You will meet people from diverse cultures and backgrounds with whom you have something in common.

Adult Learners

If you are an older returning student, or one who never had the opportunity to go to college and are attending for the first time, you have probably given considerable thought to continuing your education and are committed to learning. Getting an education is *your* goal and *your* desire; no one is making you do it. Also, you are probably the one paying for your education, so you want good value for your money. At the same time, you, like many older students, may be aware of weaknesses in reading, writing, or math that held you back in the past. Find out what "refresher" or skill-development courses in these areas your college offers—courses that may not carry any credit but that may help you fill in gaps in your skills before you tackle more challenging courses.

You also may feel a pressure to perform, especially if family members have not been supportive or if you are having to use family savings to pay for your education. This, in turn, can cause stress, making it hard for you to succeed. Trying to juggle college, career, and family responsibilities can also create stress. Realize this, and don't try to take on too much. Go slowly. You've waited this long to get an education; take one or two courses at a time until you feel comfortable with an increased load. Find out what services are available on campus to help older students, such as day care, financial aid, and counseling. As difficulties arise, you need to know where you can go to find help.

Learning Disabled and Physically Disabled

Most colleges have special services for the disabled, such as note takers for blind students or extra testing and writing time for the learning disabled (students who have dyslexia, for example). Providers of these services usually won't seek you out. You may have to ask your advisor or counselor if such services exist, and then take advantage of them.

Non-Native Speakers of English

If English is your second language, it may be tempting to spend most of your out-of-class time on campus with those who speak your native language. If you are a commuter, you may go home to family members who do not speak English. This gives you little opportunity to practice your new language. If you plan to continue your education and to live and work in the United States, you will need to become proficient in English as soon as possible. Even if you don't plan to remain in this country after you complete your education, you should know that English is the language of international business, so it is still to your advantage to improve your English skills, especially if a career in business is one of your aspirations. Take every opportunity you can to meet and interact with students and others who speak English.

If you have difficulty understanding English in class or if you don't know how or what to study, observe what successful students do and copy their behavior. Join a study group that includes native speakers of English. Listen to the radio, watch TV, and read American newspapers and magazines to immerse yourself in American speech and culture.

CONFIDENCE BUILDER

How Flexible Are You?

Learning to be flexible in your daily activities prepares you for life's greater challenges and changes.

Do you hold on to cherished opinions even in the face of conflicting evidence? Do your first impressions about people remain largely unchanged even after you get to know them? How do you handle broken relationships, changes in plans, personal and financial setbacks? If you have difficulty adapting to change, then much of your life, whether at college, at work, or at home, is probably filled with stress. Change, according to many experts, is one of life's greatest stressors. People who are inflexible in their beliefs, attitudes, and plans set themselves up for disappointment, discomfort, and distress.

The way to adapt to change is to be flexible. Flexibility is a trait employers often cite as being a valuable personal skill, and it is one you can develop. What are some of the situations at college that call for flexibility? You painstakingly make out a schedule only to find out that one of your courses is closed. Your roommate is a day person; you are a night person. You spend hours studying for a test, you are motivated and ready to perform, and your instructor postpones the exam until next week. How can you adapt to the day-to-day changes such as these that can make life miserable if you let them? How can you become more flexible? Three tips may help:

- **Watch your attitude.** Remember that you are not perfect, and neither is anyone else. Life does not always proceed according to schedule. It isn't the end of the world if things don't go as planned. Learn to shrug instead of vent.
- **Have a contingency plan.** You can't plan for all emergencies or temporary setbacks, but you can anticipate some changes. For example, have alternates in mind when you select courses. Expect that in any situation where two people live together conflicts will arise. Remind yourself to stay calm, talk it over, and be willing to compromise. Whenever you make a schedule, set a goal, or plan for a future event, try to build into your plans some alternatives in case things don't work out.
- **Keep an open mind.** Change has its good points. Change keeps you from getting in a rut. Change opens up possibilities you may not have had a reason to consider. Above all, adapting to change successfully makes you grow and makes it easier for you to accept the next change that comes along.

College is a great place to loosen up rigid ways of thinking and behaving in order to become a more flexible person. The challenges that a college education offers, the diverse learning environment, and the opportunity to expand your mind will enable you to meet the even greater challenges that lie ahead. For more help in accepting the need for change, and in coping with the stress that results from life's major changes, see Chapter 6, pages 132 and 144.

EXERCISE 5.1

Form a small group with three other class members. Using the guidelines for group discussion explained in Chapter 1, page 12, determine the ethnic mix of your college's student population: how many racial, cultural, and international minorities are represented and what percentage of the student body belongs to each of these groups. In addition, find out what services or special programs your college provides to meet the needs of these minorities.

PEOPLE WHO CAN HELP

If the college atmosphere seems intimidating to you at first, it's helpful to remember that in a community of learners the primary function of each faculty member, administrator, employee, department, and resource is *to help you reach your goals.* Although college requirements may seem like obstacles at times, they are actually bridges carefully placed to aid your progress. Everyone in your college community hopes that you will succeed. Therefore, your college is rich in resources to guide your learning and help you solve your problems. One of these resources is people. If you have not already done so, you need to form a personal network of "helpful others": people who can answer questions, offer advice, and boost your confidence.

Faculty

The instructors of your courses are in the best position to advise you concerning all matters related to their classes. If you want to know what material will be covered on a test, if you have a question about an assignment, if you missed something on a test and you don't understand why, ask the instructor. Instructors want you to ask questions.

Most instructors are very well informed about their college and its requirements. They can usually answer any question you may have, or they can direct you to another person or office where you can find the help you need. If you have an instructor you feel especially comfortable with, you can turn to this person when you need advice or have a question about an assignment.

If you begin to experience difficulty in one of your courses, don't wait until midterm; make an appointment to see the instructor as soon as you can.

Advisors and Counselors

Academic advisors and guidance and career counselors are among the most helpful people on campus. These professionals handle academic and personal problems of every kind all day long, so they can understand what you are going through. If you need help preparing a schedule, an academic advisor will show you how to select the courses you need. If you want help deciding on a major or choosing a career, a career counselor can provide valuable assistance, both in determining where your interests lie and in assessing employment opportunities. If you have a problem you don't know how to handle, such as test anxiety, a guidance counselor may talk this over with you or refer you to someone else.

Counselors and advisors know your college's rules and requirements. They may offer such services as keeping you informed of important dates and deadlines, explaining your assessment-test scores, and informing you of any skill-development courses or programs you may need. Some advisors, either through the guidance office or another department, may work only with students having unique needs, such as the learning or physically disabled, international students, adult learners, or minority students.

At some colleges you may be assigned to an advisor in your first semester or quarter. The advisor tracks your progress throughout your academic career. If you plan to transfer from a two-year college to a university, an advisor can help you select courses that will meet the university's requirements so that you won't lose credits. Therefore, it is important to meet with an advisor as soon as you know that you intend to transfer. If you need academic advice or career or personal counseling, find the office or

Your instructors want you to succeed in their courses. They can answer questions about class material, assignments, and tests, and give you sound advice about where to seek extra help if you need it.

© Bonnie Kamen/PhotoEdit

department on your campus where these services are available. Since the names of these departments may differ from campus to campus, check the college catalog or inquire at your admissions office.

Mentors

A *mentor* is an ally, a friend, someone who takes a personal and professional interest in you. On many college campuses today, instructors may serve as mentors to students in special programs funded by federal grants or other sources. Students are assigned to mentors in their first term. They meet regularly with their mentors, usually four or more times during the term, to talk about their progress and any problems they may be having in reaching their goals. Mentors may offer helpful tips on how to study, take tests, and reduce test anxiety. They may help students plan their schedules for the following term.

The relationship between student and mentor serves several purposes. It gives the student a contact person on campus to turn to for advice, help in solving a problem, or specific suggestions on how to meet course requirements. If you begin to experience academic difficulty, for example, the mentor may help you find a tutor. Mentors stay in contact with their students' instructors throughout the term, and they often work together to help these students be successful.

In adjusting to college, many students have complained that the close relationships they enjoyed with faculty in high school are not available in college. Mentoring programs may be one way to close this gap. They may operate differently from campus to campus, but the goal of any mentoring program is the same: to help students succeed. To find out whether there is a mentoring program on your campus, call the admissions office.

More Helpful People

Each subject area department, such as English or math, may have special requirements and services that pertain only to that department and the courses it offers. On some campuses, the heads of departments handle students seeking permission to enroll in courses that are already filled. If you have a question or a problem related to enrollment in a course, it is best to start by seeing the head of the department. He or she will either answer your questions and help you solve the problems or refer you to someone who can.

EXERCISE 5.2

Select a course in which you really want to make your best effort this term. Make an appointment with the instructor to interview him or her for your study skills or orientation course. Tell the instructor this interview will help you determine what you can do to succeed in his or her course. Ask the instructor the following questions.

1. What is the best way to prepare for your class? ____________________

____

____

2. What special study or reading techniques do you think I should use to get the most out of my textbook? ____________________

____

____

3. Do your test questions come mainly from lectures, reading assignments, or both? ____________________

____

____

4. What is the best way to study for one of your tests? ____________________

____

____

5. How would you describe your teaching style? ____________________

____

____

6. Is there anything else you can recommend that I do to succeed in your class? ____________________

____

____

Other students might be the most helpful people in your college life. Exchange phone numbers with a friend in each of your courses who can help you catch up on classes you may have to miss.

© Jean Claude Lejeune

Departmental secretaries can be very helpful, too. They can answer questions about departmental requirements and course offerings. They can tell you who is teaching each section of a course. They can also tell you where an instructor's office is and give you the instructor's campus telephone number, or they can leave a message for an instructor you have been unable to reach.

If you live in a residence hall on campus, your resident advisor, or RA, can be a person to turn to when you need advice about campus services or student affairs. RAs are easy to talk to because they are usually students like you. They have lived through some of the same problems you have, and they have asked and found answers to some of the same questions. An RA can usually point you in the direction of a helpful person, department, or office.

If you are involved in athletics, your coach can be an ally. Your coach wants you to remain eligible to participate in sports. Coaches are well aware of grade requirements, and they keep track of your progress in your courses. Your coach wants you to do your best in class and on the team. He or she is someone you should find easy to talk to if you need advice.

Club and organization sponsors are people who tend to take an active part in campus life. Like coaches, they share an interest of yours, and they may know you as a person in a way that your instructors or advisors may not. Although a club sponsor may not be able to answer some of your questions, he or she will probably know someone on campus who can.

Don't underestimate the value of making friends with other students. Exchanging phone numbers with a student in each class gives you someone to call when you are absent so you can find out what you missed. Having friends in each class may allow you to form a study group or find a ride to campus if you need one.

Your network of helpful others might include an advisor, an instructor, a departmental head or secretary, a coach or club sponsor, and a friend in each class. In a community of learners, you need never be alone.

EXERCISE 5.3

Select five people on your campus whom you would be willing to talk to if you needed advice, had a question, or wanted some help solving a problem. Write the names, titles, office locations, and phone numbers of these people in the spaces provided. Post this list on your bulletin board, refrigerator, or other handy place so you can refer to it easily.

Helpful People on Campus

Name and title: ______________________________

Office: ______________________________

Phone: ______________________________

Name and title: ______________________________

Office: ______________________________

Phone: ______________________________

Name and title: ______________________________

Office: ______________________________

Phone: ______________________________

Name and title: ______________________________

Office: ______________________________

Phone: ______________________________

Name and title: ______________________________

Office: ______________________________

Phone: ______________________________

PLACES TO GO FOR HELP

Suppose you have a question or a problem that you do not think any of the people in your network can resolve with you. Where are you most likely to find assistance? The following is a list of typical campus offices and centers and the services they provide. Your college catalog, campus directory, or telephone book listing under your college's name can direct you to the office you seek.

Registrar's Office. This office keeps records of students' grades and issues transcripts. If you have a question about graduation requirements, application for a degree, dropping or adding a course, transferring credits, or changing majors, see someone in this office.

Career Center. If you are having trouble setting career goals or deciding on a major, someone in this office can help. In addition to having a staff of helpful persons, these centers display pamphlets and brochures that contain information about occupations and careers. Either at no charge or for a small fee, you can take one or more tests that will assess your interests, personality, and skills. Through these tests you might discover the job or career that is right for you. Some career centers provide a job placement service for graduates. If you want this service, all you have to do is file a résumé. Your career center may also invite prospective employers to recruit on campus. Meeting these visitors is a good way to decide whether the business or profession they represent is something that would interest you.

Guidance Office. The name this office is called varies from campus to campus, but it may offer two kinds of services: academic advising to help you with course selection and planning and counseling to help you with personal or other problems that affect your adjustment to college. Some campuses may have separate offices or departments for academic advisement and personal counseling. Since you may need these services, find out the name and location of the office or offices that provide them.

Financial Aid Office. Go to this office to apply for scholarships, loans, and work-study grants. People in this office are best qualified to answer your questions about financial matters including special financial aid options such as scholarships and loans for which you may be eligible. If you want a campus job, your application process begins here. For some jobs, you may have to meet special requirements or demonstrate financial need.

If you have a fee or a fine to pay, or if you need to pick up a paycheck for work done on campus, the financial aid office may also handle those transactions. On the other hand, your campus may have a separate office—the *bursar's office,* for example—that collects fees and fines and issues checks.

Student Health Services. What happens if you get sick or have an accident on campus? If your college provides health services to students, you can get medical assistance from a campus nurse or physician. Some may provide mental health services as well. If you have a chronic health problem such

Your library or media center may offer a tour that you can take to learn about all its resources. It's a good idea to get an overview before you begin your first research project.

© Dana White/PhotoEdit

as diabetes or epilepsy, you should make sure that your instructors know about it so that if you become ill in class they can call someone to help you.

Learning Labs and Centers. Do you need to develop your reading, writing, math, or study skills? If your college has a learning lab or center, you can find help there. In the lab you will probably work independently on programs or materials that either you select yourself or that are selected for you, based on your needs and level of ability. Some labs are voluntary, but at some colleges time in a learning lab may be one of a student's course requirements. If you are required to attend a reading, writing, or math lab, think of it as a great opportunity to strengthen your skills so that you will be successful in courses that are going to become increasingly more difficult.

Library. Your campus library contains all the resources you need for research and recreational reading, such as books, magazines, newspapers, journals, reference books, documents, and microfilms or microfiche. It may also have audiovisual holdings, such as tapes and videos. Most libraries have information retrieval systems that are networked with other libraries and document centers. If you have never done any research, a librarian or library assistant can show you how. Most libraries provide an orientation to their holdings and the services they offer.

Tutorial Center. If you are having trouble in a course, your instructor may suggest that you spend some time with a tutor. A tutor is often a student who has taken the course you are taking and made an A in it. This student tutor probably has been through a training program and knows how to explain the material to you. Working with a tutor can sometimes be easier than working with an instructor because the tutor is your peer, and you can talk to him or her as you would to a friend. You may or may not have to pay a fee for the tutor's services. To find out whether tutorial services are available on your campus, ask your instructor or academic advisor.

EXERCISE 5.4

Take a walking tour of your campus. Your college may not have all the places listed here, but find as many of them as you can and write down their building and office or room numbers. If an office on the list is not on your campus, write *none* in the space provided. Post this list in a handy place.

Important Campus Locations

Registrar's office ____________________

Student health service ____________________

Career center ____________________

Guidance center ____________________

Athletic Director's office ____________________

Learning labs and centers ____________________

Financial aid office ____________________

English department office ____________________

Library ____________________

Tutorial center ____________________

Veterans office ____________________

Minority affairs office ____________________

Housing office ____________________

EXERCISE 5.5

Apply what you have learned about places on campus to go for help by completing this exercise with group members. Remember to follow the guidelines for group discussion explained in Chapter 1, page 12. Discuss and answer the questions below, doing any research that may be needed. Resources to consider are your college catalog and any materials that may be available in your admissions or guidance office. When you have finished, evaluate your work.

1. Adult Learners

   a. What special services or programs exist on your campus for adult learners?

   ____

   b. Where is the service or program offered (office or other location)?

   ____

   c. Give the name of a contact person to ask for information.

   ____

2. Women

   a. What special services or programs exist on your campus for women?

   ____

   b. Where is the service or program offered (office or other location)?

   ____

   c. Give the name of a contact person to ask for information.

   ____

3. Learning Disabled and Physically Disabled

   a. What special services or programs exist on your campus for the learning disabled and physically disabled?

   ____

   ____

   b. Where is the service or program offered (office or other location)?

   ____

   c. Give the name of a contact person to ask for information.

   ____

4. Does your campus provide help for students who need to reduce stress? Where is the service offered, and who is a person to contact for information?

   ____

   ____

5. Does your campus provide help for students who need a tutor? Where is the service offered, and who is a person to contact for information?

____

____

Evaluate your discussion. Did everyone contribute? Did you accomplish your task successfully? What additional questions do you have about places on campus to go for help? How will you find answers to your questions?

____

____

____

PUBLICATIONS THAT HELP

When you have a question about some aspect of college life—whether there is a chess club on campus, for example, or how many credit hours it takes to graduate—you can probably find the answers in one of your college's publications. One way to become a more confident and self-sufficient student is by familiarizing yourself with the kind of information contained in these sources:

- The college catalog
- The college newspaper
- The student bulletin
- The student handbook
- Informational flyers and posters

Frequent reference to these materials will make you a more informed member of your college community.

The College Catalog

Your *college catalog* contains a wealth of information about your college's programs, policies, requirements, and services. The *calendar* in your catalog is one of the items you will use most frequently. The college calendar lists dates, deadlines, and a fee payment schedule for which you are responsible. The calendar is usually among the first few pages of your catalog. It shows when classes begin and end, when holidays occur, when the drop and add period is over, when final exams are scheduled, and when you should make an application for a degree. The catalog will also tell you whether a fee is involved in applying for a degree and under what conditions you can get your money back if you withdraw from a course.

To save time, many students like to prepare a schedule in advance. To do this, you need to know what courses are available, how many credits each course is worth, and the names and numbers of courses. You will find courses listed in the catalog under department or subject area names. There is a complete description of every course including any fees or prerequisites required.

At the end of each semester, you will get a computer printout of your grades. The printout will show a grade for each course, your average for the semester, and a *cumulative GPA,* which is the average of all grades earned from the time of your enrollment. The GPA is stated as a number from 1.00 to 4.00. Your catalog explains, using examples, how to calculate your GPA.

Have you ever wondered what an instructor's full name is, what degrees he or she holds, or what college he or she attended? Look in your catalog. Toward the end, you may find an alphabetical list of instructors and their degrees and colleges attended.

Your library or media center will have copies of the catalog available for use as a reference. Furthermore, there may be a shelf or more devoted to the catalogs of many other colleges. If you are attending a two-year college and plan to continue your education after graduation, one good way to learn more about a college you are interested in is to look through its catalog.

EXERCISE 5.6

Use your college catalog to find the answers to the following questions, noting the page number where you found each answer. *Hint:* Use the contents and index to help you find the topics each question covers.

1. How many credits are required for graduation?____________________

2. What degrees are offered? ____________________

3. What GPA must you maintain in order to avoid being placed on probation? ____________________

4. Does your college offer a grade of I, or incomplete? ____________________

5. What happens if you don't make up an incomplete grade?____________________

6. Is class attendance required? Is there an attendance policy stated in the catalog? What page?____________________

7. What are the degrees held and colleges attended of one of your instructors? ____________________

8. Where do you go to get a campus parking permit? ____________________

9. What courses are all students required to take? ______________________________

____

10. On what dates are final exams given? ______________________________

____

11. When does the next registration period begin? ______________________________

____

12. What is the number and title of a reading course offered? ______________________________

____

13. How many math courses are required of all students? ______________________________

____

14. What are two clubs or organizations you can join? ______________________________

____

15. What is the college president's name? ______________________________

____

More Publications

Your *college newspaper* is written and published by students. Students who work as reporters, photographers, and editors are usually pursuing careers in journalism and receive some credit toward their degrees by working on the newspaper staff. The college newspaper is a mirror of campus culture, and it contains information of interest to the college community along with articles that report on local and world events from a student's point of view. The newspaper is published several times a semester or quarter, and reading it is an excellent way for you to keep up with what is happening on campus.

Your college may have a *student bulletin* or other weekly publication that keeps you informed of campus activities and events, and contains additional items of general interest. The bulletin is usually sponsored by the student government association, which may also publish a *student handbook*. The handbook condenses and summarizes information contained in the catalog concerning the college's policies and regulations, but is usually written in a way that is more appealing to students.

Throughout your campus—on bulletin boards and kiosks, in the cafeteria, bookstore, and student union, in the library and learning labs, and in some classrooms—you will find various informational flyers about services and events, printed by the people or departments who are sponsoring the events. These flyers contain just the essentials about the service or event: the time, place, and whether it costs anything. All these publications and materials are additional means by which people at your college express their interest in you, your needs, and your continued success as a student.

Most campuses have numerous kiosks and bulletin boards for posting important academic and social events. You can easily check for new listings on your way to and from classes.

© Bob Daemmrich/TSW

COMMUTER INVOLVEMENT IN CAMPUS CULTURE

If you commute to college, you may be at a disadvantage in one respect. It may be less convenient for you to become involved in activities and events than it would be if you lived on or near campus. But there are ways you can take a more active part in campus life. Consider your interests. What are your career aspirations? Is there an activity you would like to try but have not had an opportunity to pursue? There are many clubs and organizations on your campus. If you join one of these groups, you will meet people who share your interests, and you may learn even more about an activity you already enjoy. You may also meet people with whom you can share transportation to and from campus activities and events. Your catalog and student handbook contain a list of campus organizations, or you could drop by your student government office and introduce yourself. Someone there will be happy to tell you about the many activities and upcoming events in which you can take part. Forming a study group that meets on campus or scheduling yourself some on-campus study time is another way to remain on campus and stay involved.

CRITICAL THINKING APPLICATION

Living in a diverse nation, we must increase our awareness of the many contributions minorities have made to American culture. Identify a minority person in each of the following fields who has achieved recognition and success. What are his or her contributions to the field? Use your library as a resource. Ask a librarian to help you find the appropriate index or other source that contains the information you need.

Politics

Literature

Art

Music/entertainment

Mass communications (a news anchor or syndicated columnist, for example)

Education

Invention/discovery

SUMMARY

To review the chapter's important points, read the summary. Then complete the partially filled-in information map that follows.

To become more involved in campus life, use your college's resources, which include *people who can help, places to go for help, and publications that help.*

Your instructors, academic advisors, counselors, department heads, resident advisors, coaches, and club sponsors are among the people you can ask for help.

Become familiar with the services your college provides and know where to get them. The *registrar's office* answers all questions about records and grades. The *career center* can help assess your interests and skills. The *guidance office* offers help with course selection and scheduling and may offer personal counseling as well. *Learning labs and libraries* provide equipment and learning resources to help you improve your skills and meet course requirements. The *financial aid office* handles questions about fee payment, scholarships, loans, grants, and jobs available on campus. If you need more instruction than you are getting in the classroom, your college may provide a tutor.

Use your *college catalog* as a reference to keep up with dates, deadlines, degree and program requirements, and course offerings. Read the *college newspaper, student bulletin,* and the various flyers and posters displayed on campus. The *student handbook* is another helpful source that summarizes college rules and requirements.

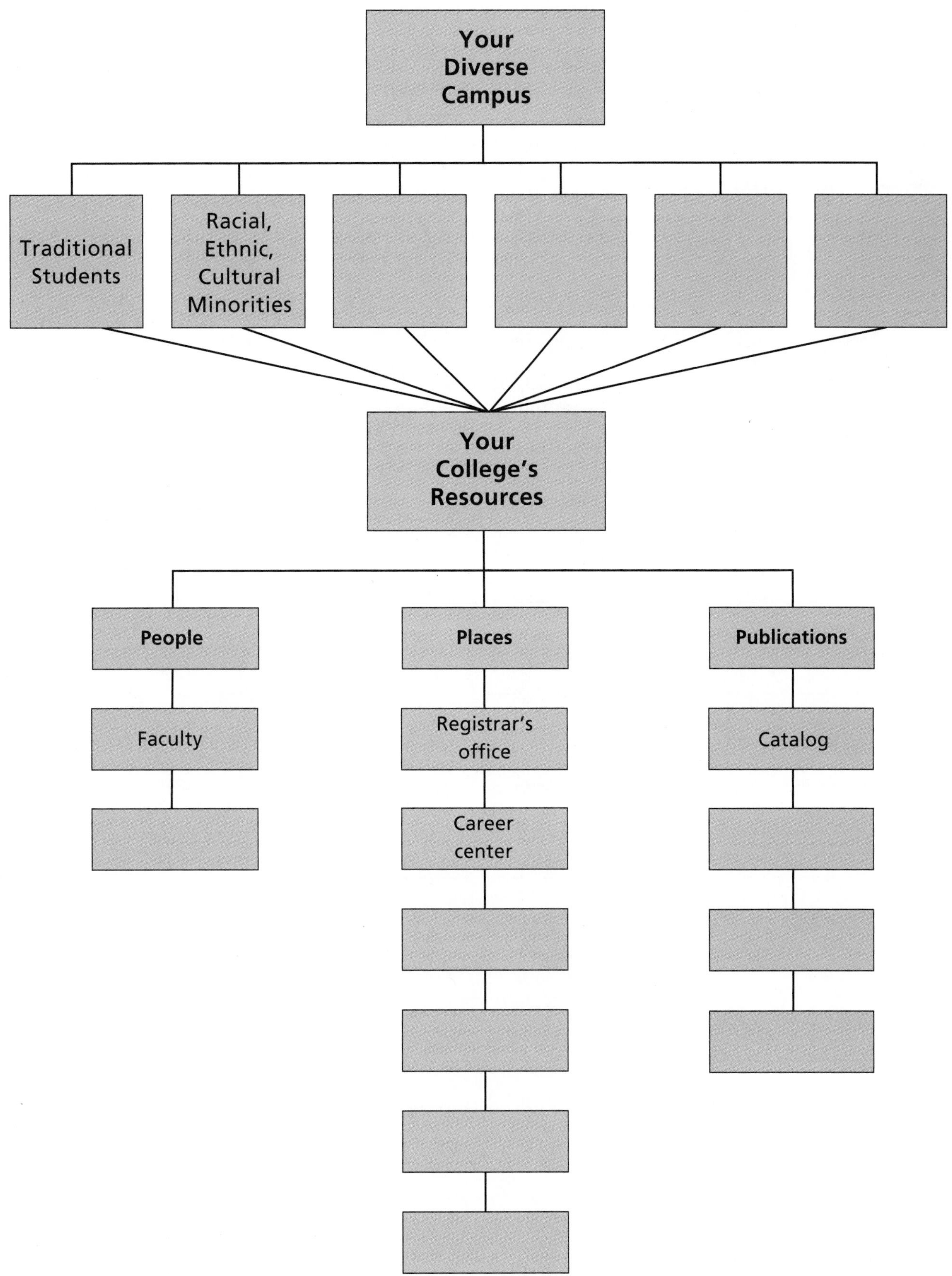
Your Diverse Campus
Traditional Students
Racial, Ethnic, Cultural Minorities
Your College's Resources
People
Faculty
Places
Registrar's office
Career center
Publications
Catalog

YOUR REFLECTIONS

Reflect on what you have learned about adapting to college life and how you can best apply that information. Use the following list of questions to stimulate your thinking; then write your reflections. Your response may include answers to one or more of the questions. Incorporate in your writing specific information from this chapter.

- Have you found adapting to college life easy or difficult? Explain what has made it easy or difficult for you.
- Would you describe yourself as a flexible person? Why or why not?
- What campus resources have been most helpful to you?
- If you were assigned the task of helping a new student get adjusted to campus life, what advice would you give?
- Are you familiar with all the resources explained in this chapter? Which ones are new to you? Are there any not included that should be?

Date ______________________________

CHAPTER 6

Maintaining Your Health and Well-Being

One of the values of a college education is that it exposes you to new people and new ideas. It offers you a chance to develop socially, culturally, and intellectually—to become a well-adjusted person. *A well-adjusted person is one who has achieved a balance among his or her physical, emotional, and social needs.* Some students are not managing their lives as well as they could. Other students' emotional and physical well-being are out of balance. Some may place excessive emphasis on their friends' and family's needs and neglect their studies. Still others may be a little too conscientious, neglecting the importance of social relationships and leisure-time pursuits.

Your physical self is linked with health, diet, fitness, and stress management. Your emotional self involves your feelings, your amount of satisfaction in life, and your locus of control—all keys to success in college. Your social self derives from your relationships and your behavior. This chapter explains what you can do to meet your physical, emotional, and social needs:

- Stay healthy.
- Control your emotions and adapt to change.
- Improve your interpersonal skills.
- Manage your sex life.

AWARENESS CHECK #12

Are You Leading a Balanced Life?

Check the statements in each part that describe you.

Part I: Your Physical Self

1. I exercise regularly, three times a week or more.
2. I feel that I am getting enough sleep most nights.
3. As far as I know, I eat a balanced diet.
4. I limit my intake of foods high in fat, salt, and sugar.
5. I feel well most of the time.
6. I believe that I am not under a great deal of stress.
7. When I do have stress, I am able to manage it.
8. I am neither overweight nor underweight.
9. I do not smoke.
10. I do not abuse alcohol, caffeine, or other drugs.

Part II: Your Emotional Self

1. Basically, I am a very confident person.
2. Generally speaking, I am happy.
3. When I do feel angry or depressed, I can get over it quickly and go on with my life.
4. My outlook for the future is good.
5. I am rarely, if ever, overcome by nervousness, stress, or anxiety.
6. Overall, my self-esteem is high.
7. For the most part, I believe that I am in control of what happens to me.
8. I am not a fearful person by nature.
9. I am able to take criticism.
10. I can cope with change.

Part III: Your Social Self

1. It is fairly easy for me to make friends.
2. I have several friendships that mean a lot to me.

Check the statements in each part that describe you.

3. I am not uncomfortable if I am at a party where I don't know many people.
4. People would probably not describe me as shy.
5. I welcome opportunities to meet new people.
6. I am a good listener.
7. I can also contribute to a conversation.
8. Most of the time I get along well with significant people in my life.
9. I understand and accept my responsibilities in a sexual relationship.
10. I believe I am assertive about what I want without being overbearing.
11. If a friend points out a fault that I have, I do not take offense; I try to change my behavior if I agree with my friend.

All these statements are positive ones, and if you have checked most of them you may be managing your life successfully. Of course, the Awareness Check is an informal survey that does not begin to cover all possible aspects of adjustment, but your responses should give you a starting point for improving your health and well-being.

HEALTH, WELL-BEING, AND SUCCESS IN COLLEGE

Health and well-being can affect your ability to do well in college. If your health is poor, if you have troubled relationships, if you lack confidence and self-esteem, then your mind will be occupied with these problems and you will not be able to give studying and classes your full attention. If you are excessively preoccupied with doing well in college and neglect your health, then again you may create problems for yourself that will eventually affect your ability to succeed.

Getting an education is not all tests, lectures, and assignments. If you are a young college student, you are also learning how to live effectively for the rest of your life, and you can take advantage of unique opportunities for establishing good health habits, building self-esteem, and forming close friendships. If you are an adult learner, college is another responsibility you are adding to the ones you already have. Your health, relationships, and self-esteem may be put to the test as you struggle to cope with the challenges of being a student.

When you are young and strong, it is easy to believe you can eat and drink whatever you want, as much as you want, or even experiment with dangerous drugs or unprotected sexual intercourse, yet somehow manage

Your social well-being and physical well-being are just as significant as your academic abilities in leading a successful life. College provides unique opportunities for enjoying recreational activities and making lasting friendships.

© Judy S. Gelles/Stock Boston

to emerge from these abuses healthy and unscathed. Even when you are well into middle age, it is easy to think that illness and death happen only to other people. The older you get, however, the more you may begin to understand your body's needs and the need to improve your health. At the same time, the older you get, the harder it becomes to make the changes that are necessary. The longer a person smokes, for example, and the more he or she smokes, the harder it is to quit.

College is the place, and now is the time for you—no matter what your age—to break any habits that may be ruining your health or affecting your performance, and to establish new habits that may prolong your life. Your doctor is the first person you should talk to if you have any questions or problems related to your health or if you want to start a fitness program. In addition, your college may offer a course in fitness and health. For one or more of your electives you could take courses in aerobic dancing or in weight training, using fitness machines and equipment. Consult your catalog, course bulletin, or athletic director.

STAYING HEALTHY

Health is a basic need. If your body doesn't work, your mind can't function. Health, good or bad, is rarely something that just happens; it is partly the result of a person's choices and actions. If your health is good, then you want to keep it that way; if your health is poor, then you must do all you can to improve it. The four questions that follow embody four goals of healthful living that can lead to improved brain functioning. Think

about your life and your habits; then mentally answer the questions *yes* or *no*.

1. **Do you eat nutritionally sound, balanced meals?**
2. **Are you physically fit?**
3. **Are you able to manage stress?**
4. **Do you avoid the use of harmful substances?**

In this chapter you will get a brief overview of some ways to maintain good health.

Eating Sensibly

A nutritionally sound, balanced diet is one that includes more fish and poultry than red meat, plenty of fruits and vegetables, whole grains in the form of bread or cereal, and dairy products. A balanced diet contains a variety of foods. It also contains more carbohydrates (starches and sugars) than protein and less fat than either carbohydrates or protein. A fast-food meal of a hamburger, french fries, and a soft drink, for example, is not a balanced meal because it contains too much fat. A more balanced meal would consist of broiled lean meat, chicken or fish, two cooked vegetables or a cooked vegetable and a salad, rice or other carbohydrates, and a piece of fruit for dessert (see Figure 6.1).

Not only should you eat balanced meals, but you should also eat at regular intervals spaced throughout the day so that your brain is continually supplied with the nutrients it needs to function properly. Skipping

FIGURE 6.1 Nutrition Chart: Guidelines for Good Eating

GUIDELINES	FOODS	REASONS
Eat some of these foods every day.	Fruits, vegetables, whole grains, bread, cereal, dairy products (low-fat milk, cheese, yogurt)	To achieve a varied, balanced diet that supplies enough energy and essential nutrients for optimum brain functioning
Increase carbohydrate intake to 67% of your total daily calories.	Fruits, vegetables—especially starchy vegetables such as broccoli, corn, and cauliflower—nuts, whole grains	For maintaining energy throughout the day
Reduce protein intake to 8% of your total daily calories.	Lean meat, fish, chicken, eggs, peas, and beans	For the growth and repair of tissue and to help fight infections
Limit fats to no more than 25% of your total daily intake.	Butter, mayonnaise, other fats and oils, eggs, rich desserts, fatty meats, whole milk and milk products	To reduce risk of high blood pressure, heart disease, and diabetes

breakfast, for example, or going into an exam hungry can interfere with concentration and memory function and make you feel drowsy and less alert. Your brain responds to highs and lows in your blood sugar levels. When you haven't eaten, the level of glucose in your blood is low, and your mental alertness is diminished.

Glucose is a sugar best synthesized from proteins and fats. Eating a candy bar before a test will temporarily raise the level of glucose in your blood, but the burst of energy you get from it will be short lived and leave you feeling sluggish. Instead, eat balanced meals three times a day with snacks in between. A protein snack such as a piece of fruit, which is high in fructose (another sugar), or a cup of yogurt, is a good high-energy snack.

What can you do to maintain a healthful diet while in college? Try these suggestions:

1. Schedule your classes and other activities so that you have time for three meals a day.

2. Eat balanced meals. You may be able to get a nutritious meal in your college's cafeteria. A variety of vegetables is usually available, and you can select your own combination of foods. If you live off campus, select foods according to the guidelines in Figure 6.1.

3. Avoid rich, high-calorie snacks. If you get hungry between meals, eat an apple or other fruit, carrot or celery sticks, or unbuttered, unsalted popcorn. For an energy boost, try lowfat yogurt or a few unsalted nuts instead of sugary or salty snacks.

4. If you live off campus, go home for lunch or bring your lunch. Be in control of what you eat.

5. If you go to parties, go easy on the snacks and alcoholic drinks. You may not know this, but alcohol converts to sugar in the bloodstream and is stored as fat. Apart from the other dangers of too much drinking, it can make you gain weight, and it can interfere with your body's absorption of essential nutrients.

6. Don't make a habit of skipping meals. Fatigue, fuzzy thinking, and diminished concentration are among the problems this habit can cause.

7. If you are overweight and would like to reduce, see your doctor. He or she will help you select an appropriate weight-loss program.

8. Exercise regularly; it will increase your level of fitness, make you feel positive and energetic, and help reduce stress. If you are trying to lose weight, combining a sensible diet with exercise will speed up the process and keep the weight off.

9. Put food in perspective. Eat for good health. Don't eat because you feel depressed, because you want to celebrate, or as a social event.

10. Drink eight to ten glasses of water a day to aid the digestive process, help eliminate wastes and toxins from your body, and supply needed moisture to the tissues.

EXERCISE 6.1

Find out what you eat and whether your diet is as balanced and healthful as it could be. Keep a record of what you eat for one week; then determine ways to eat more sensibly if necessary. For example, if you discover that most of your calories are coming from fats, decrease your intake of fatty foods such as butter, cheese, ice cream, margarine, salad dressings, luncheon meats, or other meats rich in fat, and increase your intake of whole grains, fruits, vegetables, lean meats, fish, and poultry. Keep recording your meals and attempting to adjust what you eat until you achieve a balanced diet.

	Sunday	Monday	Tuesday	Wednesday	Thursday	Friday	Saturday
Breakfast							
Lunch							
Dinner							
Snacks							

Make copies of this chart and keep it handy so that you can record what you eat throughout the day. If you wait until evening, you may forget what you've eaten.

Improving Fitness

Exercise has many benefits; fitness is just one of them. Regular exercise strengthens your heart, improves circulation, and helps lessen your risk of cardiovascular illness and death from a heart attack or stroke. Exercise can make you strong and able to withstand other diseases, and it can relieve stress. It helps you lose weight and improves your appearance.

The best exercise is aerobic. *An aerobic exercise is one that lasts for a minimum of 20 minutes during which your heart rate is elevated and your muscular activity is continuous.* You should not do aerobic exercises without checking your pulse frequently and without first receiving instructions on how to perform the activity. Overstressing your heart can have serious, even fatal, effects. "No pain, no gain" is a dangerous myth. "FIT" is a much better guideline.

F = Frequency	How often you exercise—three times a week is the generally recommended starting frequency
I = Intensity	Your target heart rate, based on your age and present level of fitness
T = Time	The amount of time you spend exercising—start with 15 minutes or less, depending on your age and condition, and then gradually increase the time as you are able

Exercise is great for you if you do it correctly. If you think you would benefit from regular exercise, an excellent place to start is in your college's athletic department. Courses and individual counseling may be available at a lower cost than you are likely to find at one of the commercial health clubs or spas, and may even be offered free of charge. If you feel you don't have time for exercise that requires a change of clothes or a special place or type of equipment, try walking. You can walk anywhere; one half-hour a day of brisk, uninterrupted walking greatly reduces your risk of heart problems and improves your overall level of fitness. Here is a list of aerobic activities, some of which you may already do:

Aerobic dancing

Rowing

Swimming

Bicycling

Running

Walking

Jumping rope

Walking is one of the simplest forms of aerobic exercise. Just one half-hour of brisk walking every day can make a significant difference in your fitness level.

© David Madison/TSW

Managing Stress

Some stress won't hurt you. In fact, you should expect to experience stress now and then. For example, it is normal to feel a little anxious before getting up in front of a group to speak. You want to do your best, and you are wondering whether you will be able to remember everything you want to say. Once you get started, this anxiety should quickly pass as you begin to focus your attention on giving the speech. It is also normal to feel a little anxiety on the day of an exam. But once you have the exam in front of you and get down to the business of taking the test, the anxiety should pass. *Real stress is unrelieved anxiety that persists over a long period of time.* Stress is especially harmful if you are unable to manage it. Unrelieved stress can weaken you physically so that you become vulnerable to disease, and it can impair your ability to think clearly so that your performance in class and at work suffers.

There are many warning signs that stress is getting out of control. Look at the brief list that follows and see whether you have any of these common symptoms of stress. The more of these symptoms you have, the more likely it is that you need to learn some strategies for coping with stress.

Depression
Difficulty falling asleep
Extreme tiredness, fatigue
Feelings of anger or resentment
Frequent absence from work or classes
Impatience
Inability to concentrate
Loss of pleasure in life
Increase or decrease in appetite
Muscular aches for no apparent reason
Stomach or intestinal disturbances
Sweaty palms
Tension headaches
Test anxiety

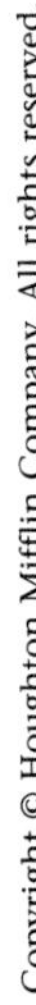

Many students find adjusting to college and meeting course requirements extremely stressful, especially when they are also working or raising a family. Some students are chronically anxious about tests, and their nervousness before and during tests may make it impossible for them to do their best. Test anxiety is a special kind of stress related to testing situations. Chapter 17 explains test anxiety and how to overcome it. It is important that you find ways to manage stress so that you can reach your goals and enjoy yourself in the process. Try these tips for managing stress:

EXERCISE 6.2

If you want an exercise program that works, choose a form of exercise that you enjoy and can easily fit into your schedule. Try out some of the forms of aerobic exercise listed on page 124; then use the chart below to summarize and comment on your experiences. The chart will help you determine the form of exercise that works best for you and why.

Type of exercise	Aerobic dancing					
Time of day	7:00 p.m.					
Amount of time spent	1 hour					
Reaction	I went to an aerobics class with a friend, and I liked it so much I decided to join too.					

Ten Stress Beaters

1. **Be realistic.** You know what you can and cannot do, what is within your power to change and what you can't do anything about. Try not to waste energy worrying about matters that are out of your control. Instead, use your energy to change those situations that you have the power to change. Unrealistic goals, perfectionism, and believing you have to do everything right the first time will set you up for failure. Be reasonable in what you expect of yourself, and don't be afraid to make mistakes.

2. **Exercise tensions away.** When you are under stress, your muscles tense involuntarily. You may have noticed the tightness in the back of your neck and across your shoulders that often precedes a headache. Exercise has a natural calming effect that is accompanied by a positive feeling. For example, you may have heard about or experienced "runner's high," the feeling of euphoria and sudden burst of energy runners get after they have been running a long time.

Find a way to take a break and lose yourself when you are experiencing a great deal of stress. Hobbies, sports, and friendly conversations can provide relief from pressure or worries.

© John Boykin/PhotoEdit

To help you relax, try the desktop relaxation technique explained on page 219, Chapter 10; the chair-seat relaxation technique discussed on page 200, Chapter 10; and this simple deep-breathing technique for calming yourself in any situation: Breathe slowly through your nose, filling your lungs. Then slowly exhale through your mouth. As you take ten deep breaths in this manner, think to yourself: "I am relaxed; I am calm."

3. **Learn to say no.** For whatever reason, many of us have difficulty saying no when someone asks us to do something, even if we don't have the time or desire to do it. When you are under stress because of work, family, and course obligations, the last thing you need is to take on more responsibilities. When someone makes demands on your dwindling time, think carefully about how you feel. Ask yourself, "Do I really want or need to do this?" If the answer is "No," don't be afraid to say so. If you have trouble saying no, you may need to become more assertive, as explained on pages 136–137 of this chapter. If you are interested in assertiveness training, consult your counseling department. Check the newspaper for an announcement of a workshop, or request one through your student activities office. You could also check your campus bookstore or the library for a book on the topic.

4. **Ask for help.** Some problems may be more than you can handle by yourself, and you may need to seek financial, medical, or some other type of help or advice. Some problems may look a lot worse than they are until you talk to someone about them and get a different perspective. If you are the kind of person who hates to ask for help, try to get over this attitude. Many times we worry needlessly and cause ourselves even more stress by living with problems we think are unsolvable, when asking for help and getting it might bring immediate relief.

5. **Learn to deal with negative people.** People who display negative attitudes, a pessimistic outlook on life, and a constant state of nervousness can make you experience negative feelings that add to your stress. If you can eliminate negative people from your life, do so. If they are friends or family members, try to counter their negative remarks with positive ones of your own. When they do behave in a more positive way, comment on what you like about their behavior, thereby positively reinforcing a behavior that you want them to continue.

6. **Lose yourself in activity.** When you are under stress, engage in some activity that causes you to lose all track of time. During those moments, you can forget your worries and experience happy, calming feelings. Reading, playing golf or tennis, and spending time pursuing a hobby or special interest are all activities in which you can lose yourself.

7. **Treat yourself.** Do something nice for yourself, especially when you are under stress. Buy yourself a present. Go out to dinner or see a movie you've been meaning to see with a friend whose outlook is positive.

8. **Get your life in order.** You've probably been meaning to do this anyway. If you are off schedule or behind in your courses, if your room or your house is a mess, and you keep postponing a trip to the dentist, then it is no wonder you are feeling stressed out. Resolve to get organized. Make out a new study schedule that includes time to catch up on work you've missed. Make a list of all the other tasks that need doing;

then tackle them one at a time. Don't worry if it takes you a while to get organized. After all, it took a while to get off schedule.

9. **Make a wish list.** We all have a tendency to say to ourselves, "If only I had the time, I'd do ________." How would you complete this sentence? Make a list of all the things you'd do if you had the time. When stress has become more than you can handle and you have to get away for a while, do one of your wish-list activities.

10. **Help someone else.** It is no secret that doing something for someone else can make you feel good and take your mind off what is worrying you. Take the opportunity to help a friend who has a problem. Helping your friend find a solution may give you ideas for ways to solve one of *your* problems. If you know someone who is having trouble in a course you are taking, offer to study with him or her. There are many things you can do for others that not only help them but also have a positive effect on you.

EXERCISE 6.3

If you smoke or drink and would like to quit or cut down, first try examining the reasons why you smoke or drink and determine the conditions or situations that trigger that response. use this chart to keep a record of your smoking or drinking behavior for one day. Each time you light a cigarette or take a drink, put a check in the smoke/drink column, record the time of day, and state your reason for wanting to smoke or drink.

Smoke/drink	Time of day	Reason
☐	________	________________
☐	________	________________
☐	________	________________
☐	________	________________
☐	________	________________
☐	________	________________
☐	________	________________
☐	________	________________
☐	________	________________
☐	________	________________

Think of ways to modify your behavior to eliminate reasons for smoking or drinking. If you find that you do most of your smoking when you are nervous, try to find out what makes you nervous and avoid it. If you are serious about breaking either habit, ask your doctor to recommend an effective program.

Avoiding Harmful Substances

"Just say no to drugs" is a good idea, but it is an oversimplification of a problem that remains a complex issue. The Surgeon General's office has found convincing evidence that alcohol and tobacco addiction are no different from drug addiction. What compounds the problem of convincing people to "say no" is that one group of addicting substances is legal and another group is not. Like everything else, the substance abuse issue is something you will eventually have to deal with on your own terms. It is better to avoid something that is potentially addictive than to form a habit that will be difficult to break. Consider some of the reasons people abuse drugs, alcohol, caffeine, and tobacco. Then consider the decisions you either have made or intend to make about using these substances.

According to psychologists and other professionals, some reasons for substance use and abuse are low self-esteem, lack of confidence, desire to be *in* or *with it,* craving for excitement, desire to rebel or to do something forbidden, desire to punish parents or other authority figures, the need to escape problems, and the desire to find relaxation. Drugs, alcohol, and tobacco provide temporary relief from stress. The lift you get from caffeine quickly wears off. These substances create illusions of confidence, superior mental ability, acceptance, and happiness, all of which fade when the effect of the substance wears off. There are many more positive ways to find escape, relaxation, excitement. For example, plan activities with your friends that involve physical and mental stimulation. Attend sports events, take bicycle or hiking trips, go to the beach for a day of surfing and sunning, go to a movie, go out to dinner once in a while to a different restaurant. Solitary pursuits that provide escape, adventure, and excitement include reading, writing poems, essays, and stories, and learning a new hobby, craft, or sport. For example, you might enjoy a course in creative writing, sculpture, or tennis.

YOUR EMOTIONS

Although you may be faced with a situation you cannot change, you *can* change how you feel about it. For example, if you are having trouble getting along with a roommate, you may be losing study time because of arguing or worrying about the problem. Soon your grades will suffer if you can't resolve your differences and get back on schedule. Obviously, you can't change your roommate's behavior, but you can change your feelings about that behavior. You can decide not to let it get to you. Focus your attention on doing well in your courses. Concentrate on meeting every requirement, completing every assignment, preparing for every test. Do most of your studying in the library or some other place away from your roommate. Try to resolve your differences, but if you cannot, make the best of the situation until you can make other living arrangements. Avoid getting into arguments and say to yourself, "I am in charge of my feelings, and I will not let my conflict with my roommate interfere with my success in my courses."

Similarly, if you are an older student who lives off campus, you may have a family member or friend who tries to undermine your efforts to be successful, making such comments as "You'll never make it" or "You shouldn't put yourself through this." Negative comments like these don't have to upset you. Your emotions belong to you. People cannot control how you feel unless you give them that power.

Understanding Your Feelings

One way to begin taking control of your emotions is to understand what causes you to feel one way or another. Begin by listening to yourself think and talk. Are your thoughts and words dominated by statements that begin with *they, he, she,* or *you?* You may often think or say such things as the following:

> *You* make me angry because you don't listen to what I say.
>
> *She* doesn't care how I feel.
>
> *He* really hurt my feelings.
>
> *They* make it hard for me to get the schedule I want.
>
> *She* gave me a D on that paper, and I deserved better.

When you make statements like these, you place all the blame for your feelings on someone else. You place yourself at the mercy of others' whims. If they choose to, they can make you feel great. If they choose to, they can make you feel awful. You never know where you stand with people.

Chapter 1 explains locus of control as a factor that influences your motivation. If your locus of control is *external,* you expect someone or something to motivate you. If your locus of control is *internal,* you are more self-motivated. Locus of control may also explain, in part, what controls your feelings. Externally motivated students tend to blame others for the way they feel. Internally motivated students are more likely to examine their own behavior to find the source of their feelings.

One way to take control of your emotions is to replace any statements of feeling that begin with *they, he, she,* or *you* with statements that begin with *I.* You will then be able to determine what actually caused the feeling. For example, here are the same statements you read before, but *I* has replaced the first word, and the statement has been altered to shift the cause of the feeling to the person making the statement:

> *I* get angry when I think you're not listening to what I say.
>
> *I* believe she doesn't care how I feel.
>
> *I* feel hurt by some of the things he does.
>
> *I* find it hard to get the schedule I want.
>
> *I* made a D on that paper, and I could have done better.

Pretend for a moment that you made these statements. Notice how you have accepted responsibility for the feeling. For example, by accepting that the D is what you earned, you are likely to do better next time. But if you blame someone else for the D, then you are off the hook and have no control over your future in the course. Similarly, if "they" are not responsible for your schedule, then you are free to determine why you are having such a hard time making one. This kind of thinking can lead you to do something to correct the situation.

In the first three statements, you accept responsibility for your feelings that seem to result from others' actions. The value of doing this is that it opens a discussion about behavior you don't like without blaming the other person. For example, if it turns out that your friend really doesn't listen, doesn't care how you feel, or does things that hurt you, then you must decide what *you* are going to do about that. *You* have to decide whether it is worth it to try to improve the relationship or to end it. In either case, you open the way for communication rather than for more arguments and bad feelings.

Leading a Purposeful Life

When you control your emotions and accept responsibility for your feelings, you increase your chances for happiness and decrease your chances for disappointment. A sense of well-being results from having goals to reach and making plans for achieving them. As explained on pages 26–31 in Chapter 2, setting reachable long-term and short-term goals will give you a purpose for attending college, completing your tasks at work, and realizing family dreams and plans.

When your life seems to lack purpose, examine what you are doing in your courses, at work, or at home. Ask yourself, "Why am I doing this?" Answers may not come right away, but when they do, they may remind you of your goals or indicate a need to make some changes in your life. This will give you a renewed sense of purpose.

Accepting the Need for Change

Negative feelings and a sense of helplessness result when something you are doing isn't working out but you are afraid to make a change. An unhappy wife or husband may continue without help in a relationship that is making both partners miserable because one or the other is afraid of the changes that counseling might require. A person who has been offered a new and better job or a transfer to a higher-paying job out of state may turn down the offer because he or she fears change. You may keep working on a research paper even though you realize you have chosen an unworkable topic, because you don't want to start over. If you are "test anxious," you may avoid seeking help, believing that the problem will go away or that there is nothing you can do about it. Trying to avoid change by ignoring a problem can be very self-destructive. Negative feelings breed more negative feelings and encourage the belief that a bad situation can only get worse.

Accept the need for change when it becomes clear that you have done all you can do in a situation that is not working. Acceptance is the hard part. Once you're committed to making a change in your life, exploring your options and deciding what to do next can be fun and challenging.

EXERCISE 6.4

In the following statements, the pronouns *they, he, she,* and *you* suggest that the people making the statements are not taking responsibility for their feelings and behavior. Rewrite each statement so that the focus is on the person making the statement. Replace any pronouns with the first-person pronoun *I,* and change any other wording as needed.

1. You didn't tell us we had to do the exercises.

____

____

2. Why can't I have an override? They told me the department chairman would let me in the course even though it was full.

____

____

3. You are not paying attention to me.

____

____

4. She gets on my nerves.

____

____

5. He is never in his office when I come to see him.

____

____

EXERCISE 6.5

Like most people, you probably have times in your life when you feel disappointed, depressed, angry, frustrated, lonely, incompetent, or unloved. Like many people, you may tend to blame others for making you feel this way. In fact, no one needs to have that much power over you if you assume responsibility for your well-being. Complete the statements that follow to remind yourself of what you have and the things that make you feel good. Think about these positive qualities and accomplishments whenever you are feeling a lack of confidence.

1. My best physical feature is ______________________________
2. My finest character trait is ______________________________

3. My favorite possession is ______
4. My closest friend is ______
5. I am proud of myself for ______
6. I feel happiest at home when I ______
7. I feel most comfortable at work when I ______
8. The course in which I am doing my best is ______
9. Something I enjoy doing by myself is ______
10. A skill I mastered very quickly is ______
11. One thing I can really do well is ______
12. On my next vacation I will ______
13. One of my plans for the future is ______

CONFIDENCE BUILDER

Emotional Intelligence—Another Way of Being Smart

Why do some highly intelligent people fail? Why do some whose IQs are not so high still manage to do well?

Emotional intelligence, or EQ, may be the answer. Daniel Goleman, author of *Emotional Intelligence,* draws on Howard Gardner's theory of "personal intelligences," Peter Salovey's definition of "emotional intelligence," and the research of many others to explain why your EQ may be more important than your IQ.

According to Goleman, "IQ contributes about 20 percent to the factors that determine life success, which leaves 80 percent to other factors." One of those factors is emotional intelligence: the qualities that enable you to control your emotions instead of letting them control you. For example, you could have the IQ of an Einstein and still find yourself on academic probation if you could not control the emotions that make you want to party instead of study. What exactly is emotional intelligence, and can it be developed? Goleman says it can. Emotional intelligence adds up to *character,* and it includes these qualities:

- **Self-motivation.** You alone are responsible for paying attention, maintaining concentration, and relieving yourself of boredom.
- **Persistence.** Following through on schedules and commitments, living up to obligations, and continuing to make progress despite temporary setbacks will help you achieve your goals.

- **The ability to control impulses and delay gratification.** Now and then we all do things on a whim or "in the heat of the moment." But some people let passion rule with disastrous results: the student who drinks too much, has unprotected sex, or acts first and thinks later. To control your impulses, you have to think ahead to the consequences and ask yourself "Is it worth it?"
- **The ability to regulate moods.** How fast can you bounce back from disappointment and frustration? Do you allow yourself to be overcome by sadness, anxiety, or anger? Constantly giving in to your emotions produces stress that has harmful physical and mental effects. If your inclination is to say "But I can't help how I feel," think again. The answer is to know yourself. Learn to recognize what your feelings are and what causes them. When you know *why* you are depressed, for example, you can figure out what it will take to eliminate the cause.
- **Empathy.** *Empathy* is another word for *caring,* and it is a valuable interpersonal skill. People who are empathetic have a high degree of self-awareness that enables them to sense the feelings of others. They are able to put themselves in another's place so that they can tell what he or she wants or needs.
- **Hope.** You have to believe that things will get better, that life is basically good, and that with hard work and persistence you will achieve your goals. Without hope, it is unlikely that you will have either the will or self-discipline to make a plan and follow it through.

Can you see a connection between Goleman's emotional intelligence and the internal locus of control? Remember that internally motivated people take responsibility for their own successes and failures. They manage their lives, as opposed to allowing life's circumstances to manage them. It is probably true that the more internal your locus of control is, the more emotional intelligence you have.

YOUR INTERPERSONAL SKILLS

The most influential people in your life may include your parents, your spouse or other intimate partner, your children, your roommate and your friends. You depend on these people for many things, and they depend on you. Your relationships with these people can span the entire range of emotions, from great happiness to extreme disappointment. What makes a relationship succeed or fail? Educators, philosophers, psychologists, writers, and many others have explored this question. Perhaps you have explored it also. Though each relationship is based on a complex system of need satisfaction, though each type of relationship has characteristics that distinguish it from other types, there are five interpersonal skills you can improve that will lead to more satisfying relationships:

Listen. Give all your attention to the people you are with. Spend an equal amount of time listening and talking. In this way you are sharing your ideas, but you are also giving others an opportunity to share theirs. Listen actively and make eye contact. Show interest by asking questions and commenting on what is said. Encourage people to explain how they feel; then listen without judging. Respond by giving your opinions. When you are not sure what the other person means, paraphrase (restate) and preface your remarks with "Did I hear you say . . . ?" or "Did you mean that . . . ?"

Converse. Don't "hold forth," don't deliver long, rambling monologues, and don't interrupt. A conversation is an interchange of ideas and opinions. Remember to listen 50 percent of the time and talk 50 percent of the time. Avoid making critical or judgmental remarks. If talking with you is unpleasant, people will avoid conversation, believing that they won't be understood or appreciated. A breakdown in communication is the first sign that a relationship is in trouble. When people are asked what they like most in a relationship, a frequent answer is "Someone I can really talk to."

Have Fun. Create opportunities to have fun together. Make a mental list of interests you have in common with each of your relatives and friends, and plan trips or outings that focus on those interests. Or plan an adventure with someone. Go someplace new or try out a sport or activity together that neither of you has ever done before. When you discover a new activity that you both enjoy, set aside time to pursue it together. Make sure you do not change or cancel plans at the last moment.

Be Supportive. You know how you feel when you have a problem and the person you turn to for help lets you down. You know how you feel when you come home from work excited about some small but important accomplishment and the person you were hoping would share this excitement acts uninterested. Don't be that kind of person. Encourage another person's dreams. Share his or her triumphs and disappointments as if they were your own. Don't assume someone you love knows you care; let your feelings show.

Be Assertive. Being assertive means being able to ask for what you want. It also means not giving in to people who try to make you do something you don't want to do. But don't confuse assertiveness with aggressiveness. *Aggressive behavior* is rude, domineering, intimidating. *Assertive behavior* is polite but strong and independent. Being assertive means *standing up for your rights without denying the rights of others*. As an assertive person, you have the right to express your feelings and opinions, to ask for what you want, and to say no. At the same time, you must respect the fact that others have the same rights.

Few college students are truly aggressive, and far more students are passive than assertive. Being passive is taking the easy way out by letting other people make decisions for you. If you're at a party and someone pushes another beer on you when you don't want it, do you take the beer so you won't rock the boat? If you don't want another beer, say so assertively and mean it: "No thanks, I've had enough." If you're a mother who comes in from classes to find dishes stacked in the sink and laundry piled up by the washer, do you start rinsing the dishes and sorting the clothes? Only if that's what you want to do. You should make clear to your family that you need some help. Getting them to share the problem and its solution rather than demanding their help increases your chances of success.

Assertive behavior is responsible behavior. When you are assertive, you accept responsibility for what you will or will not do and for the consequences of your actions. Aggressive people, on the other hand, are irresponsible because they attempt to get what they want by intimidation. This may lead to outright refusal or a fight, a consequence the aggressor may not have intended. People who are aggressive are less likely to predict or control the outcome of events than are people who are assertive, because they don't take into account others' feelings or reactions. Passive people are also irresponsible because they give other people control over their lives or expect others to guess what they want, rather than telling them.

As a college student, the more assertive you become, the more likely you are to be successful. As an assertive person, you will ask questions, seek out information, and be able to express clearly to your instructors what you do not understand and what help you need from them.

EXERCISE 6.6

Apply what you have learned about interpersonal skills by completing this exercise with group members. Remember to follow the guidelines for group discussion explained in Chapter 1, page 12. Read the following scenario and, using the questions as a guide, discuss how Jack and Becky could improve their relationship. When you arrive at consensus, record your answers on the lines provided. Then evaluate your work.

Jack was exhausted. He had three college courses on Mondays and worked the lunch shift at the cafeteria. Then he had to rush to pick up his girlfriend Becky at her part-time nursing job. Today Becky seemed particularly disgruntled. "I hate the hospital. I hate my supervisors," she said. "I just want to be home practicing my guitar."

"Your supervisors work hard all day, too," Jack snapped.

"Why don't we stop for an ice cream on the way home?" asked Becky.

Jack sighed. "Not today. I have a paper to finish. And maybe you should spend some time on those job applications."

Becky turned her back and looked out the window.

1. At what point could Jack have listened more actively to what Becky was saying?

____

____

2. What could Jack have said to start a positive conversation with Becky?

____

____

3. How could Becky have been supportive of her boyfriend?

4. How could Jack and Becky have had fun together before they went home to do their work?

Evaluate your discussion. Did everyone contribute? Did you accomplish your task successfully? What additional questions do you have about interpersonal relationships? How will you find answers to your questions?

EXERCISE 6.7

Following is a list of behaviors typical of assertive people. Put a check beside those that are typical of you. For any behaviors you did not check, summarize on the lines below why you would or would not feel comfortable engaging in those behaviors.

Assertive people:

- ☐ 1. Turn down invitations without feeling guilty
- ☐ 2. Politely refuse offers of food or drink if they don't want it
- ☐ 3. Do not let themselves be talked into doing something that goes against their values
- ☐ 4. Make choices and decisions based on what they think is right to do
- ☐ 5. Have little difficulty saying *no*
- ☐ 6. Reserve the right to express their opinions while respecting others' rights to do the same
- ☐ 7. Reserve the right to change their opinions
- ☐ 8. Are not afraid to speak up, ask questions, seek information
- ☐ 9. Are not afraid to make mistakes or take action to correct them
- ☐ 10. Do not feel compelled to share others' feelings, beliefs, or values that go against their own

© Gary A. Conner/PhotoEdit

MAKING FRIENDS

College offers the opportunity to build new relationships and test old ones. Your well-being depends, in part, on the relationships you are able to establish and maintain. When you are new in college, it may seem difficult to meet people at first, but don't be discouraged. Many students are in the same situation you are, and they are just as eager to make friends. In the student center or cafeteria, resist the temptation to sit by yourself. Join a group at a table and introduce yourself. Offer to exchange phone numbers with one or two people in each of your classes so that you can compare notes if one of you should be absent. Participate in as many campus activities as you can. You will meet people who share your interests, which is the basis of any long-lasting relationship. If you live in a dorm, introduce yourself to the students living on either side of you and across the hall. Invite someone to go home with you one weekend. As you extend these offers of friendship to others, you will find them responding to you with similar offers of their own.

EXERCISE 6.8

College offers a variety of situations and settings for meeting new people. But college students often spend hours in solitary studying and miss out or ignore opportunities for socializing. Imagine you are a new transfer student at your college and don't know a soul. How would you go about meeting new people? Using your student handbook, college newspaper, student bulletin, and posted flyers as resources, list places and situations for meeting new people. Find examples in the following three categories.

1. Academic activities

____

____

____

2. Social events

____

____

____

3. Recreational activities

____

____

____

Are you the kind of person who meets new people easily, or do you take a long time to "warm up" to someone? Think about the three newest friends in your life. Describe where and how you met these people. Can you draw a conclusion about what kinds of situations you find most conducive to meeting new friends? Write your conclusion in one or two sentences.

Friend 1: ______________________________

____

Friend 2: ______________________________

____

Friend 3: ______________________________

____

Conclusion: ______________________________

____

____

SEX AND THE COLLEGE STUDENT

Sex is one of the most powerful of all human needs. In a purely biological sense, your reason for living is to reproduce, and the purpose of life is the continuation of your species. However, sex and life are not that simple. Unfortunately, sex is implicated in other issues such as AIDS, date rape, sexual harassment, and unwanted pregnancy. These tragedies can prevent you from reaching your goals.

Practicing Safe Sex

The AIDS epidemic has heightened our awareness of the dangers of unprotected sexual intercourse, of the risks we take in having sex with a partner whose sexual history we do not know. On many campuses, AIDS counseling and courses about AIDS are available. Student groups dispense free information about AIDS, birth control, and abortion. Your library is another place to go for information.

If you engage in sex, be prepared to protect yourself. Use condoms or provide them for your partner, but also understand that condoms don't *guarantee* protection from AIDS. Remember, too, that AIDS is not the only *STD* (sexually transmitted disease) that should concern you. Syphilis, gonorrhea, herpes, venereal warts, and other diseases and infections are all transmitted through sexual intercourse. The more partners you have, the greater is your exposure to STDs.

Before entering into a sexual relationship, take into account your own sexual history and that of your potential partner. AIDS and other STDs pose threats to your life as well as to your academic future. Become aware of the risks involved and eliminate them by becoming informed and by protecting yourself.

Understanding Date Rape

Date rape, forced sexual intercourse involving acquaintances, has plagued colleges and universities in recent years. Studies done on campuses place the percentage of women who may become the victims of rape or attempted rape before they graduate at anywhere from 15 to 35 percent. During the past few years, newspapers and magazines have regularly carried stories about date rape among college students.

In any discussion of date rape, there are three things to keep in mind. Rape is is a crime, no matter whether the people involved know each other. A person who forces sexual intercourse on an acquaintance is just as guilty of a crime as someone who sexually assaults a stranger. Secondly, a person has a right to say no to sex at any point during a date or in a relationship, regardless of any previous sexual activity that may have occurred. Finally, because alcohol lowers inhibitions, date rape may be more likely to occur in situations where one or both parties involved have had too much to drink.

Exactly what are your responsibilities to your partner in a relationship or on a date? The following guidelines should serve as a first step toward date rape prevention:

© Tony Freeman/PhotoEdit

- **Set standards for sexual conduct.** Decide how far you want to go both physically and emotionally before getting involved with someone.
- **Communicate with each other.** Talk with each other about your expectations. Don't expect your partner to read your mind. Sex is too important to leave to chance.
- **Stand your ground.** If you do not want to respond to someone's sexual advances, your responsibility is to be assertive. Say no and mean it. Don't be hesitant, and don't back down. Even if you do want to have sex, your responsibility is to listen when your date says no and to believe that no means *no* even if your date's nonverbal signals seem to say yes.
- **Treat each other with respect.** You have a right to your opinions and should trust your feelings. When something feels wrong, it probably is. Demand respect from your partner. At the same time, respect his or her choices as well. Don't let sexist notions or social pressures determine your behavior. Stick to your standards.

If you are a victim of rape, realize that you are not at fault and that you have options. Seek help immediately. Get medical attention. Do not shower, douche, or change clothes. Then call the police. To help you cope with the aftereffects of sexual assault, which may include nightmares, depression, mood swings, feelings of guilt or shame, and various physical symptoms, call a rape crisis center.

Dealing with Sexual Harassment

Sexual harassment is any kind of unwanted teasing, touching, or inappropriate remarks. Sexist jokes, sexist remarks, an unwanted pat on the behind, or an unwelcome request for sexual favors are forms of sexual harassment and are inappropriate behaviors in any relationship. Your college probably has a policy on sexual harassment, which may be stated in a pamphlet or handbook. There may be a designated counselor or college official on your campus who deals with sexual harassment issues and complaints.

Once sexual harassment starts, it will probably continue until you demand that it stop. Dropping a course to get away from an offending professor or changing your major because you are the recipient of sexist remarks and behaviors are ineffective ways of coping with sexual harassment. Instead, you should speak up at the first sign of sexism and confront the harasser by making it clear that you want the behavior to stop. Don't keep sexual harassment to yourself. Talk to a counselor or report the behavior to the person at your college who handles complaints of sexual harassment. Make sure you have kept a record of the date, time, and place the harassment occurred and of those present who can act as witnesses.

Sexual harassment is everybody's problem, and creating a friendly, nonsexist environment is everyone's responsibility. Speaking out against sexism is one way students let professors and each other know that sexism has no place in the classroom or on the campus.

Avoiding Unwanted Pregnancy

If you are an older student and either married or living with someone in a long-term monogamous relationship, sex and pregnancy may be issues that you have resolved. If you are a young student who is either sexually active or plans to be, there are a few things you should know. We are living in an era of sexual freedom, when you might expect most recent high school graduates to be well-informed about the risk of unwanted pregnancy and the contraceptive methods they can use to prevent it. However, each year a large number of college students have their academic careers interrupted or terminated by pregnancy. If you intend to have sex and do not want to become pregnant or cause someone else to become pregnant, choose a reliable method of contraception and use it *every time* you have sexual intercourse. Although no contraceptive method short of abstinence is 100 percent effective, some methods are more effective than others, as indicated in Figure 6.2. Keep in mind that the effectiveness rate listed for each method is true only if you use the contraceptive consistently and as directed.

Some contraceptives require a prescription; others you can buy over the counter. Natural family planning and coitus interruptus require neither a prescription nor a device, but they are only 80 percent effective. Before choosing any method, talk it over with your partner, and seek the advice of your doctor, pharmacist, family planning clinic, health department, or someone at your campus health center. If you are a woman who wants to try natural family planning, a doctor can tell you how to determine when you are ovulating.

FIGURE 6.2 Contraceptive Methods and Their Effectiveness Rates

METHOD	EFFECTIVENESS RATE
Oral contraceptive	97–99%
Intrauterine device (IUD)	94–98
Condom	90
Diaphragm	80–95
Contraceptive cap	80–90
Spermicidal creams, foams, jellies	75–80
Natural family planning (refraining from sexual intercourse during a woman's periods of ovulation)	80
Coitus interruptus (withdrawal before ejaculation)	80

CRITICAL THINKING APPLICATION

As explained on page 132, accepting the need for change is one way to control the emotional feeling of helplessness you get when something isn't going well. When you accept the need for change, you make a positive choice either to act or feel differently about a situation. But what about the *unwelcome* event in your life that forces a change upon you that you did not choose? The result is stress, and unless you can adapt to the desired and undesired changes in your life, the stress will go unmitigated and become a threat to your health and well-being.

Listed below are some stress-producing changes that can upset the balance of health and well-being. How many of these changes have affected you within the last year or six months? Write about what you are doing to adapt to these changes, or write about another change or event that may be the source of stress in your life. Explain what you are doing to cope with the change.

Death of a husband or wife
Death of a parent
Death of other close family member
Divorce

Unwanted pregnancy
Major injury or illness (self)
Major injury or illness (family member)
Loss of job or financial support
Breakup of a relationship other than marriage
Serious argument with someone
Legal problem
Academic difficulties, probation
Relocation of residence

SUMMARY

In the first paragraph of the following chapter summary, key ideas are highlighted. Read the summary. Then, using the first paragraph as a model, highlight the rest of the summary.

Your health and well-being are within your power to control, and they affect your ability to do well in college. Successful adjustment depends on achieving a balance among your physical, emotional, and social needs. This chapter suggests ways to maintain good health and increase your well-being. To become healthy and stay healthy, choose a balanced diet that includes a variety of foods and is low in fat. Become physically fit by choosing and following an aerobic exercise program you can live with. Learn to manage stress by first determining what circumstances and conditions make you feel stressed, then by trying out the stress beaters suggested in this chapter. Avoid harmful substances such as illegal drugs, alcohol, nicotine, and caffeine.

To increase your well-being, learn to take control of your emotions by understanding your feelings, leading a purposeful life, and accepting the need for change. To improve your relationships, try five strategies:

1. Listen to your friends and important others.
2. Converse and have fun with them.
3. Be supportive of them.
4. Take advantage of the opportunity college offers for making new friends.
5. Be assertive about what you want.

Protect yourself by making good decisions about sexual behavior. Practice safe sex, reduce your risk of date rape, deal assertively with sexual harassment, and avoid unwanted pregnancy.

YOUR REFLECTIONS

Reflect on what you have learned about maintaining your health and well-being and how you can best apply that information. use the following list of questions to stimulate your thinking; then write your reflections. Your response may include answers to one or more of the questions. Incorporate in your writing specific information from this chapter.

- Are you leading a balanced life? Are your physical, emotional, and social selves in balance? Explain.
- Do you have any harmful habits that need changing? If so, what self-improvement goals will you set?
- Of the interpersonal skills listed on pages 135–137, which is your strongest? Which needs work?
- What relationship do you see between your EQ, as explained on pages 134–135, and your locus of control?
- What is the most helpful piece of advice you have learned from this chapter, and how will you use it? What can you add to the information given on health and well-being?

Date ______________________________

CHAPTER 7

Creating Your Study System

The keys to creating your study system are twofold: You need to develop appropriate study skills and use your learning style. If you have trouble getting started when you sit down to study, or trouble staying with it once you have started, you may not have a reliable *study system* that you consistently apply to the tasks of reading and studying from textbooks. Studying with a system can transform a burdensome chore into a pleasant task. You can adopt a proven system such as SQ3R, which is explained in this chapter, or you can devise one to fit your learning style and the courses you are taking.

As explained in Chapter 1, not everyone learns in exactly the same way. As you experiment with study systems, remember that you may prefer a certain learning mode, such as *visual, auditory,* or *tactile,* and your study system should allow you to use your favorite mode. If you see yourself as a visual learner, for example, your study system may include making diagrams or charts of information you want to remember. Also, your system will work best if you study at the time of day when you are most alert and if you study in your preferred learning environment.

A system that you use for college reading and study can be adapted to any workplace learning situation that requires you to read, remember, and use information to develop reports or complete projects.

This chapter explains several strategies that will help you create your study system:

- Identify and use the common parts of textbooks and chapters as convenient study aids.
- Experiment with proven study systems such as SQ3R and PREP.
- Devise your own system to meet course requirements or specific learning tasks.

AWARENESS CHECK #13

Are You Using Your Textbooks Efficiently?

Part 1

Can you identify and use the parts of a textbook? Match the textbook parts in Column A to their functions in Column B.

Column A	Column B
1. _____ title page	A. contains supplementary material
2. _____ copyright page	B. lists topics, terms, names of people, and their page numbers
3. _____ contents	C. tells when a book was published
4. _____ introduction	D. lists chapter titles, main headings, and page numbers
5. _____ glossary	E. lists author's sources or references
6. _____ index	F. tells author's purpose for writing the book
7. _____ appendix	G. identifies title, author, and publisher
8. _____ bibliography	H. contains terms and definitions

Part 2

Can you identify and use the common parts of most textbook chapters? Match the chapter parts in Column A to their functions in Column B.

Column A	Column B
1. _____ title	A. restates and condenses author's points
2. _____ introduction	B. help explain or illustrate
3. _____ headings	C. identifies overall topic covered
4. _____ visual aids	D. provide review or skill practice
5. _____ summary	E. identify topics covered in each section
6. _____ questions and exercises	F. states author's purpose and gives overview

Part 3

Yes No

Do you have a study system? Respond *yes* or *no* to the following statements.

☐ ☐ 1. When I sit down to read or study, I often have trouble getting started.

☐ ☐ 2. My studying is "hit or miss." I don't have any set way to study; I do it when and if I have time.

☐ ☐ 3. I underline or highlight when I read.

☐ ☐ 4. I know how to tell what is important in a chapter.

Check your answers to Part I: 1. G, 2. C, 3. D, 4. F, 5. H, 6. B, 7. A, 8. E. The answers to Part II are 1. C, 2. F, 3. E, 4. B, 5. A, 6. D. In Part III, if you checked yes for statement 1 or 2, and *no* for statements 3 and 4, you will benefit from learning how to use a study system.

SQ3R: THE BASIC SYSTEM

It's easy to see why students who don't read textbook assignments make poor grades. It may be a little harder to see why students who do read all assigned material may still not make the grades they want. There is a big difference between reading and studying. You can't merely read a chapter from first word to last and expect to retain the information. You must do something active as you read: underline, make notes, formulate questions in your mind, and then follow the author's ideas to find the answers. Studying with a system guides your reading so that you can find the information you need to complete assignments and prepare for tests.

Perhaps you've heard of SQ3R. Developed by Francis P. Robinson in 1941, SQ3R is an old system that still works. Millions of students have successfully used this system's five steps, or a variation of them, to improve their reading and studying. Before reading the detailed explanation of each step, see Figure 7.1 on p. 150 for an overview of the whole system.

Survey

A *survey* is a quick preview or brief overview of an entire textbook or a single chapter. You need to survey textbooks and chapters for different reasons.

When to Survey a Textbook. Survey a textbook once, as soon as you can before your class meets for the first time. When you are trying to decide which courses to take, spend a few minutes in your campus bookstore surveying textbooks to get an idea of the topics that will be covered in the courses in which the books will be used. This may save you some time in the long run. For example, you might think you want to take a course and

FIGURE 7.1 SQ3R—An Overview

S—Survey:	Preview textbooks and chapters to get an idea of their content and organization.
Q—Question:	Turn chapter headings into questions that you can answer as you read.
1R—Read:	Read slowly and carefully, one section at a time, to find answers to the questions in your mind. Then make marginal notes, underline or highlight important parts, and construct study guides.
2R—Recite:	Stop at the end of each section to repeat, silently or aloud, the main points covered in the section. Recite from your marginal notes or from the information you have underlined.
3R—Review:	Review the chapter immediately after reading it. Review it again before a test. Review as many times as needed to keep the information fresh in your mind.

discover, after surveying the textbook, that the course does not cover what you thought it would or is either too advanced or too basic for you.

Why Survey a Textbook? If you survey your textbook before you attend class, you will walk into the classroom with an advantage. You will already know what topics the course is likely to cover. You will also have determined which of the eight common parts your textbook has and how they may be useful to you. For example, if you are taking a biology course and you find out, by surveying your textbook, that the book has a glossary, then you know that you will be able to save time when you are studying. It is much quicker and easier to look up specialized terms in a glossary than in a dictionary. Also, glossary definitions fit the writer's use of terms within the context of the book's subject matter.

Surveying has a practical advantage beyond the classroom. You can survey *any* book that you are thinking of buying. To survey a work of fiction, read the title to get an idea of what it will be about. Then read the plot summary on the back of a paperback book or on the jacket of a hardcover book. Read any comments from reviewers to find out what they think about the book. Read the first paragraph to see if the writer's style and subject matter grab your attention and make you want to read more. Your survey will help you decide whether the book is one you will like.

Surveying also has practical application in the workplace where a significant amount of information processing occurs. Surveying articles and other printed matter is a quick way to assess their importance or usefulness.

How to Survey a Textbook. To survey a textbook, examine its parts in the order in which they appear as you leaf through the book from beginning to end. Look first at the *title page;* there you will find the title, author, and publisher (see Figure 7.2 on page 151). In addition to identifying the

FIGURE 7.2 Sample Title Page

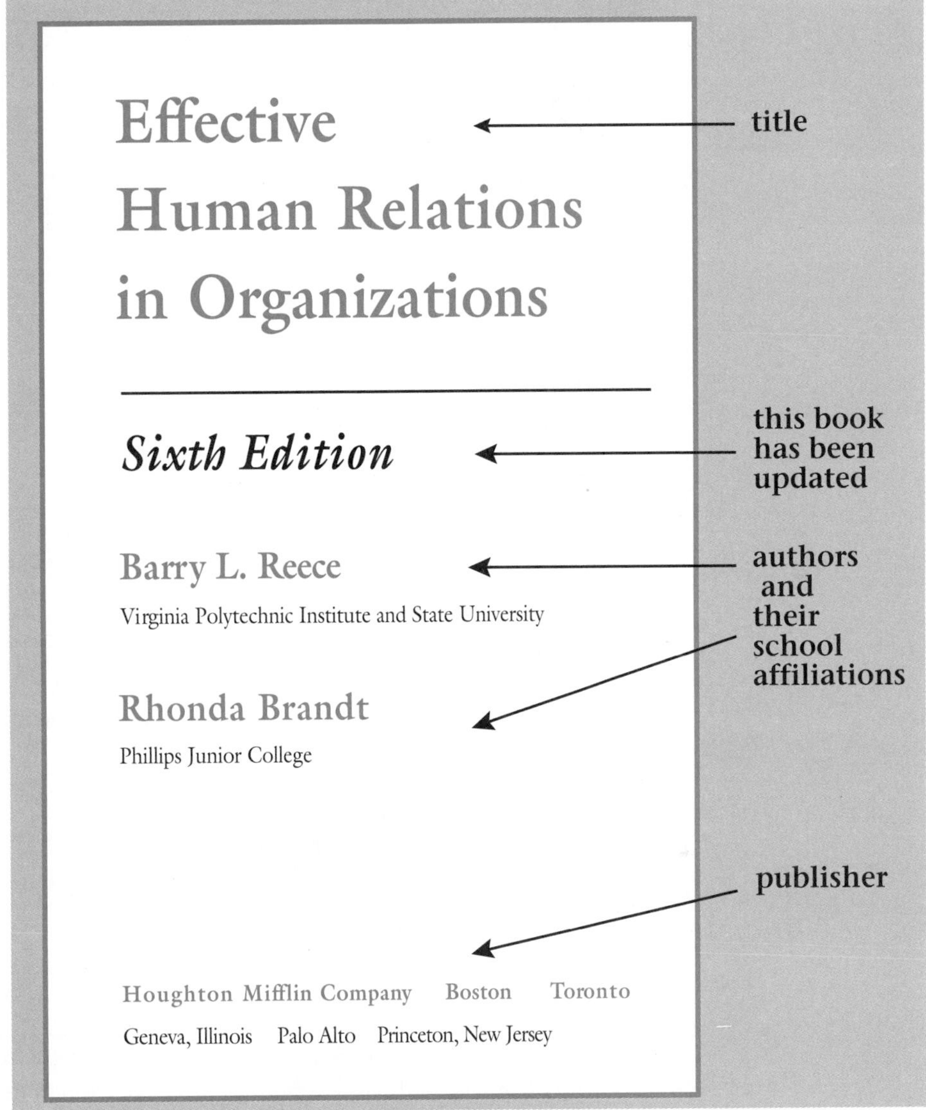

Barry L. Reece and Rhonda Brandt, *Effective Human Relations in Organizations,* Sixth Edition. Copyright © 1996 by Houghton Mifflin Company. Reprinted by permission.

book's topic, the title may also indicate the book's type and the level for which it is intended. For example, a book titled *Psychology* is likely to be a general introductory text for a first course in psychology. A book titled *Adolescent Psychology* is likely to be a more advanced text, dealing with one aspect of psychology. The writer assumes that you have taken an introductory course before enrolling in a course that uses *Adolescent Psychology.*

Beneath the author's name on the title page might be his or her college affiliation and perhaps a title or degree. This information suggests the writer's background and qualifications.

Next, look at the *copyright page* to find out when the book was published (see Figure 7.3 on page 152). Your instructors generally select recently published texts so that the information you read is current. Timeliness is especially important in the sciences and other subjects in

FIGURE 7.3 Sample Copyright Page

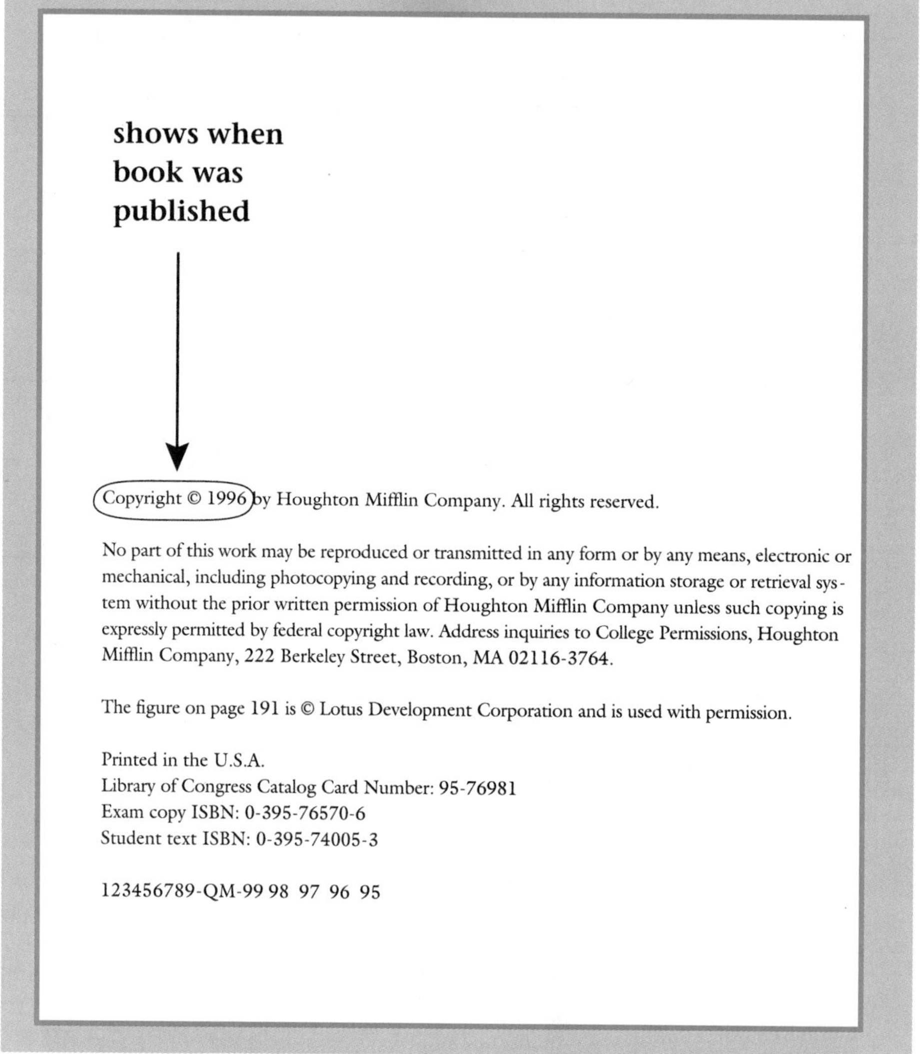

Copyright © 1996 by Houghton Mifflin Company. All rights reserved.

No part of this work may be reproduced or transmitted in any form or by any means, electronic or mechanical, including photocopying and recording, or by any information storage or retrieval system without the prior written permission of Houghton Mifflin Company unless such copying is expressly permitted by federal copyright law. Address inquiries to College Permissions, Houghton Mifflin Company, 222 Berkeley Street, Boston, MA 02116-3764.

The figure on page 191 is © Lotus Development Corporation and is used with permission.

Printed in the U.S.A.
Library of Congress Catalog Card Number: 95-76981
Exam copy ISBN: 0-395-76570-6
Student text ISBN: 0-395-74005-3

123456789-QM-99 98 97 96 95

Barry L. Reece and Rhonda Brandt, *Effective Human Relations in Organizations,* Sixth Edition. Copyright © 1996 by Houghton Mifflin Company. Reprinted by permission.

which new information may cause a book to be out-of-date soon after it is published. Books are revised often to update information. The edition number appears on the title page, usually following the title. If a book is a second edition, it has been revised once.

Read the *introduction* to determine the writer's purpose and his or her intended audience. The introduction may also tell you how to use the book or explain its special features. Some books also have a *preface* or "To the Student" section (see Figure 7.4 on page 153). Alone or in combination, all these sections provide a brief overview of the book's content, purpose, audience, and use.

Scan the *table of contents,* which is a listing of parts and chapters by title and often includes the major headings and features that appear within each chapter (see Figure 7.5 on page 154). When you are surveying a textbook, scanning the contents will tell you what topics will be covered in the course as well as in the book.

FIGURE 7.4 Sample Preface

TO THE STUDENT

The purpose of this textbook is to introduce you to the basic facts and principles of chemistry. Chemistry is a vital and dynamic science. It is of fundamental importance not only to all the other sciences and modern technology but also to any explanation of the material things around us. Consider these diverse questions. What is the environmental role of ozone in the earth's atmosphere? What is responsible for the red color of Io, one of Jupiter's moons? And finally, how can we see inside the brain of a patient without doing harm? All of these questions involve chemistry, and they are just some of the questions you will explore in your reading of this text. I hope I have piqued your curiosity. In your study of general chemistry, you will discover many things, but ultimately you will find that there is so much more to learn and that it is exciting to discover and to question.

The challenge to any author of a general chemistry text is to present a solid understanding of the basic facts and principles of chemistry while retaining the excitement of the subject. I feel strongly that the way to do this is by constantly relating the subject matter to real substances and problems in the real world. We begin the study of chemistry with the discovery of the anticancer activity of a bright yellow substance called cisplatin. We use this discovery to illustrate the introductory ideas presented. In Chapter 2, we start by looking at sodium (a soft, reactive metal) and chlorine (a pale green gas) and the reaction between them to produce sodium chloride (ordinary table salt). Each of these substances is quite different, and the reaction, which is shown in an accompanying photograph, is a dramatic example of the transformation that occurs when substances react. With this vivid picture in mind, we go on to explain substances and chemical reactions in terms of atomic theory. In each chapter, wherever we introduce basic principles of chemistry, we keep close contact with the world of real chemical substances and their everyday applications.

Darrell Ebbing, *General Chemistry,* Fifth Edition. Copyright © 1993 by Houghton Mifflin Company. Used with permission.

Look for a *glossary.* This is a comprehensive listing of special terms and definitions used in the text; it is usually found near the end of the book. Special terms are also highlighted within chapters. Sometimes they are grouped together in a list at either the beginning or end of each chapter. Typically they appear in **boldface** or *italics* within paragraphs (see Figure 7.6 on page 155). If your book does not have a glossary, you may want to keep a list of special terms as they occur in each chapter.

Some books have an *appendix* and/or a *bibliography.* The appendix usually precedes the bibliography. An appendix contains supplementary material of interest to readers who seek additional information: charts, articles, exercise sheets. A bibliography lists references or sources that the writer consulted to research and write the text. Suppose you are taking an economics course. You have to write a research paper, but you don't know where to begin or you can't think of a topic. If your textbook has a

FIGURE 7.5 Sample Table of Contents

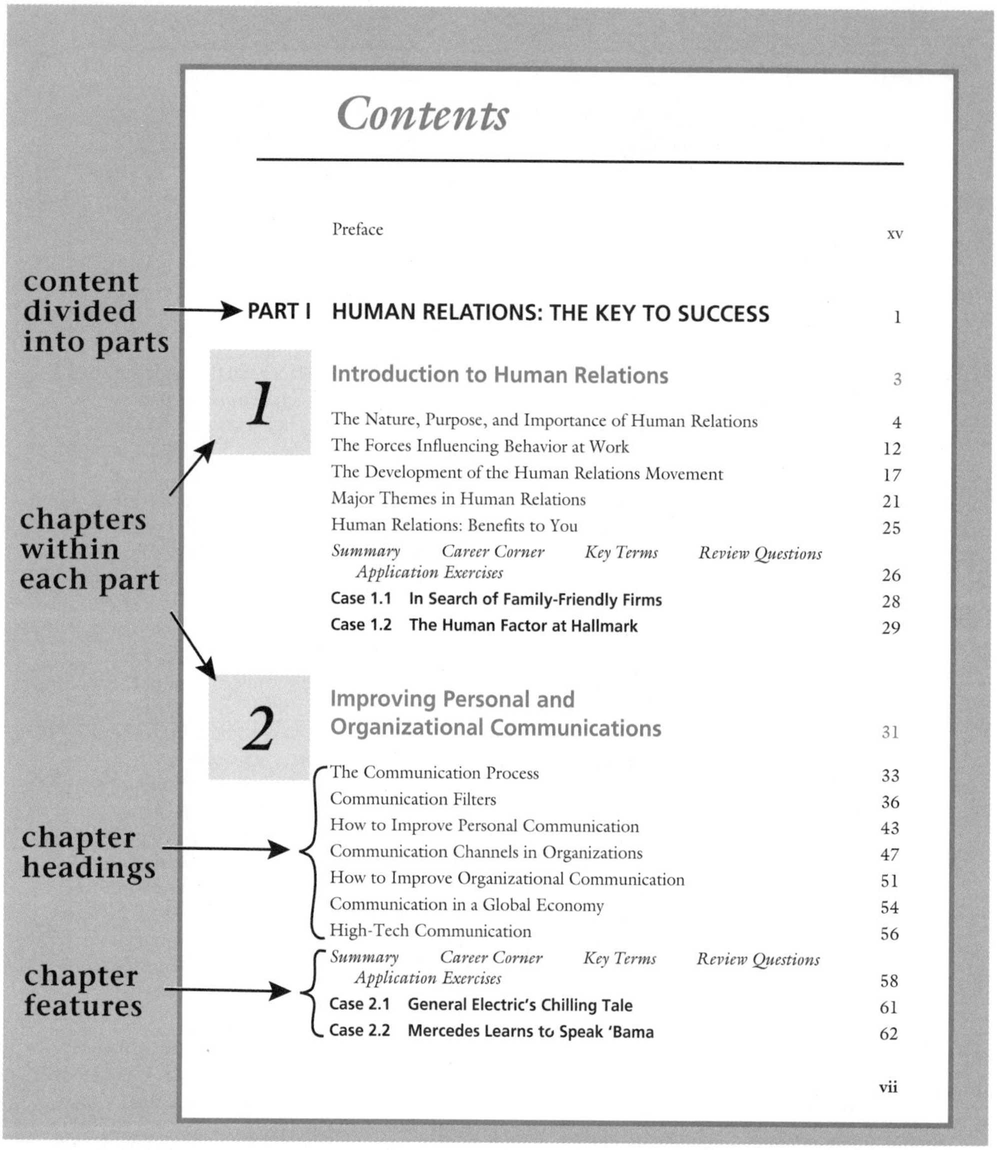

content divided into parts

chapters within each part

chapter headings

chapter features

Contents

vii

Barry L. Reece and Rhonda Brandt, *Effective Human Relations in Organizations,* Sixth Edition. Copyright © 1996 by Houghton Mifflin Company. Reprinted by permission.

bibliography, reading the titles of the writer's sources might give you an idea for a topic.

The last section in most textbooks is the *index*. When you want to review a topic, look it up in the index. Entries are listed alphabetically and include page numbers for each topic. Certain books may also include a special index to help you locate information in the form in which you might recall it. For example, a poetry book may contain an index of first lines, or a physics textbook may include an index of key formulas.

You can survey a textbook in about ten minutes, and you need do it only once to know what your book covers and what helpful aids it contains. This knowledge will help you enter class with confidence on the first day.

When to Survey a Chapter. You should survey a chapter before you read it for the first time. You should resurvey chapters that you are reviewing

FIGURE 7.6 Where to Look for Key Terms

at the beginning of a chapter →

Vocabulaire: *Salutations (Greetings)*

Formal		*Informal*	
Bonjour, Monsieur.	*Hello (Sir).*		
Bonjour, Madame.	*Hello (Ma'am).*	**Salut!**	*Hi!*
Bonjour, Mademoiselle.	*Hello (Miss).*		
Comment allez-vous?	*How are you?*	**Ça va?**	*How are you?*
Et vous?	*And you?*	**Et toi?**	*Et toi?*
Je vais...	*I am...*	**Ça va...**	*Things are going...*

IMPORTANT TERMS FOR REVIEW

ethical issue
conflict of interest
honesty
fairness
communication
organizational relationships

← at the end of a chapter

within paragraphs →

3.3 PRECIPITATION REACTIONS

In the previous section, we used a precipitation reaction to illustrate how to convert a molecular equation to an ionic equation. A precipitation reaction occurs in aqueous solution because one product is insoluble; that is, it does not dissolve readily in water. Now we will look at some simple solubility rules for ionic compounds. Then we will see how to use these rules to predict whether mixing two ionic compounds together will result in a precipitation reaction.

G-8 GLOSSARY

Gravimetric analysis a type of quantitative analysis in which the amount of a species in a material is determined by converting the species to a product that can be isolated completely and weighed. **(4.11)**

← in the glossary

Jean Paul Valette and Rebecca M. Valette, *Contacts,* Fifth Edition. Copyright © 1993 by Houghton Mifflin Company. Used with permission. O. C. Ferrell and John Fraedrich, *Business Ethics,* Second Edition. Copyright © 1996 by Houghton Mifflin Company. Reprinted by permission. Darrell Ebbing, *General Chemistry,* Fifth Edition. Copyright © by Houghton Mifflin Company. Used with permission.

for a major exam. Resurveying material that you have not read for a while will refresh your memory.

Why Survey a Chapter? Surveying helps you make assumptions about what a chapter covers. It is a prereading activity that focuses your attention on a topic. By relating the topic to what you already know, you prepare yourself for the next step in the SQ3R system: forming questions in your mind.

Surveying tells you how long a chapter is. After surveying, you can decide whether to read a chapter at one sitting or in two or three sittings with breaks in between. Resurveying a chapter activates your long-term memory. If, after resurveying, you think you remember a chapter very well, you may decide to spend less time reviewing that chapter and more time reviewing chapters with which you are not as familiar.

How to Survey a Chapter. To survey a chapter, examine its parts in the order in which they appear. Figure 7.7 lists the parts of most chapters and a purpose for surveying each one.

Your chapter survey will not take long, and it will focus your attention and give you a purpose for reading. It is worth your time and effort. For more detailed information on how to read graphics such as tables, charts, and diagrams, see Chapter 13, pages 285–288.

EXERCISE 7.1

Borrow a textbook from a friend who is taking a course that you plan to take. Survey the textbook from beginning to end, and then respond to the following items.

Book Title: ______________________________

Name of Course: ______________________________

1. Can you tell from the title whether the book is an introductory text or an advanced text? Explain your answer.

____

____

2. How current is the information in the text? In what part of the book did you find your answer?

____

____

3. What is the author's purpose? In what part of the book did you find your answer?

____

____

4. Where are chapters listed? Write the title of a chapter whose topic interests you.

____

____

5. Does the book contain a glossary? If so, on what page does it begin?

____

____

6. Does the book contain a bibliography? If so, on what page does it begin?

____

____

FIGURE 7.7 How to Survey a Chapter

PARTS TO SURVEY	HOW TO SURVEY	PURPOSE
Title	Read title.	to determine what you already know about the subject and to find out what the chapter is about
Objectives or goals	Read chapter objectives or goals if any are listed.	to determine what points the author will cover and what you are expected to learn
Introductory material	Read introductory section, paragraph or sentence.	to determine the author's purpose and thesis; to determine what the author wants you to understand or be able to do after you read the chapter
Major headings and subheadings	Read headings and subheadings.	to reveal the author's organization and content—how he or she organizes the chapter and develops the topic
Graphic aids	Look over charts, diagrams, photos, illustrations, and other aids.	to see what points or topics the author felt needed further explanation or clarification
Key words and terms	Note whether key words or terms are italic, boldface, defined within context, or listed at the end or beginning of the chapter.	to find out how the author calls attention to key words and terms; also to find out what the key words or terms are
Summary	Read summary if there is one.	to get an overview of the author's key ideas—what he or she thinks is important
Questions for discussion or problems for practice	Briefly read over any questions or problems.	to determine which concepts the author wants you to apply; to establish a context for reading

Question

During your chapter survey, as you read each heading, try to turn it into a question. The heading of a section identifies the major point of that section. For example, three questions you could ask about the heading "Concentration" are "What is concentration?" "How can I improve my concentration?" and "Why is concentration important?" The "what" question asks you to read for a definition. The "how" and "why" questions stimulate you to think critically about concentration—its value and what you can do about it.

Turning headings into questions directs your reading so that you can find the details and examples that support major points. Later, as you read each section carefully, try to find the answers to the questions you formed from the headings. You may discover that some of your questions are beside the point; but even if they are, you still win. Right or wrong, your questions can help you follow the writer's ideas and help you correct errors in your comprehension.

EXERCISE 7.2

The purpose of this exercise is for you to practice surveying a textbook chapter with the members of your group. Remember to follow the guidelines for group discussion explained in Chapter 1, page 12. Your tasks are as follows: Select a chapter to survey from Part 3 of this book. Each person must survey the chapter and write answers to items 1–7 within a time limit of ten minutes. Discuss your answers, resolving any differences of opinion to arrive at consensus. Your best answers should be recorded on a separate sheet of paper to be handed in along with the group evaluation.

Chapter Title: ____________________

1. What are the chapter goals or objectives? ____________________

2. According to the introductory section or paragraph, how will the information contained in this chapter help you? ____________________

3. List three major headings and turn each one into a question to guide your reading.

Headings	**Questions**
____________	____________
____________	____________
____________	____________

4. How many visual aids are there and what kind?

____

____

5. List two key words or terms you should remember. ______________________________

____

____

6. List a major point that is emphasized in the summary. ______________________________

____

7. What skill or topic is covered in the first exercise? ______________________________

____

Group Evaluation:

What have you learned about surveying? Is surveying a strategy that you will use? Why or why not? Did your group complete its tasks successfully? What improvements can you suggest? How will you find answers to your questions?

____

____

____

Before you sign up for a course, visit the campus bookstore to survey the text the instructor has chosen. This will enable you to see what the course will cover and whether the level of the material is suited to your background and skills.

© Bob Kramer Studio/Stock Boston

Read

Read slowly and carefully, concentrating on one section at a time. Don't worry about how long you take. You may wish you could read faster. But console yourself with the thought that it takes time to absorb ideas, especially if the information is new to you and there is little in your experience to which you can relate it. Do not skip unfamiliar words or technical terms. If you can't infer their meanings from context, look them up in the book's glossary or in a dictionary. Then be sure to reread the sentence in which each new word appears to make sure you understand it. Carefully examine each diagram, chart, illustration, table, or other visual aid. Often, ideas that are hard to understand when you read them are easy to comprehend in a diagram or other graphic.

After reading, try to determine the main point of the section. Summarize this point in a marginal note that will aid your recall when you review. Read through the section again, and underline the main idea and key details or examples. If you have difficulty deciding what is important, see pages 314–317 in Chapter 14 for a complete explanation of how and what to underline or highlight.

If a section seems particularly technical or complex, you may have to read it more than once. You may also have to restate the writer's ideas in your own words to get the information into your long-term memory. Chapter 8 shows you how to make study guides to aid your recall.

Making notes, underlining or highlighting, and constructing study guides are essential steps of active reading. They help you think critically about what you read, they make studying a productive activity, and they help you remember what you read.

Recite

Recitation is an essential aid to memory. After reading a section, try to state, aloud or silently, the important points covered in that section. If you find this hard to do, you probably have not understood the section and need to reread it. However, if the central idea comes easily to mind, then you can be confident that you understand it. Try to state the points that support or develop the central idea before you go on to the next section. Reciting not only increases your memory's power; it also helps you monitor your comprehension.

Review

Review a chapter immediately after you finish reading it. One quick way to review is by resurveying the chapter. Go over any notes you made in the margins, and see if they still make sense to you. Reread any passages that you underlined or highlighted. Also, review a chapter before you take a test. It is a good idea to review a chapter at least once between your first reading of it and your last pre-test review. With practice, you will determine how many times you need to review a chapter in order to keep the information in your long-term memory.

DEVISING YOUR STUDY SYSTEM

There is no one best way to learn, no system that works for everyone all the time. What is best for you, what helps you read, study, and remember information, depends on your learning style. Commitment and consistency lead to success in college. Finding a study system that works, making a commitment to learn, and using your system consistently are much more important than *which* system you use.

Most study systems are variations on the basic one, SQ3R. Try SQ3R first and see if it works for you. Or use it as a starting point to create your own study system by varying the steps to fit your preferred way to learn and the material that you need to study.

For Mathematics Courses

Add a *practice* step for solving problems. In math courses you learn mathematical operations and procedures. To master them you must practice, so doing the practice exercises in your math textbook is an essential part of studying for the course. Before you start a new assignment, review the previous one since every assignment builds on the preceding lesson. Do not attempt to do the exercises in a new chapter until you have read the chapter and studied the example problems.

Your *review* step in a math course should include a review of mathematical terms. Math has a specialized vocabulary. Every chapter in a math textbook is filled with new terms to learn. In fact, terms and definitions often appear in bold type, italics, or a special color. As you read a chapter, make a list of terms and definitions. When you study, review your list. Many students who do well in math courses say that learning the language of math is an important key to their success.

Your studying for a math class will be most productive if you do it as soon after the class meets as possible, while explanations are still fresh in your mind. For more tips on how to improve your performance in math courses, see Chapter 16.

For Science Courses

Add a *draw* step to supply a visual mode for getting information into your long-term memory. Make your own diagrams of processes and concepts such as reproduction and food chains. Draw organisms and label their parts. Your diagram of a complex process may be easier for you to remember than a verbal list of the steps. When you recite, describe processes and state principles in your own words. If your preferred mode of learning is auditory, recitation is an important step for you. Your own words are easier to retrieve from memory during an exam than someone else's words that you memorized. Make flash cards of specialized terms to recite from and review. For more tips on how to succeed in science courses, see Chapter 17.

For Literature Courses

Expand the recite and review steps of SQ3R to include *interpret, evaluate,* and *write*. In a literature course you must interpret the theme of a story, the meaning of a poem, or the development of a character, and you must evaluate the worth or literary merit of what you read. Put your thoughts in writing to prepare for papers and essay exams. Underlining and marking your book can help you remember the characters and events of a story or a novel. Mark words and phrases that identify characters or suggest a theme. Write plot summaries of stories. Make flash cards of important literary terms. Write a brief statement of your interpretation of a poem's meaning. When reading literary criticism, summarize in your own words the critic's evaluation of the story, poem, or novel. Then write your own evaluation of the significance of the literary work you are studying.

For Foreign Language Courses

As in math courses, practice exercises are an essential part of studying a foreign language. Exercises help you learn new words, verb conjugations, and parts of speech. They also provide practice in using words in different contexts so that you can develop your skill in forming sentences and translating from one language to another. Follow a regular study routine. Review the previous chapter, read the new chapter, and then do the practice exercises as soon as possible after your class meets. Spend a lot of time reciting new words and meanings and drilling yourself on verb conjugations through all the tenses. To the *review* step of SQ3R, add making flash cards of terms and conjugation charts for verbs. Recite from these and use them to review for tests.

For Social Science Courses

When you underline and mark during the *read* step, focus on theories and principles of behavior and research findings that support a certain theory. Make charts to compare theories and recite from your charts.

Other ways to vary SQ3R may take into account whether you prefer to study alone or with someone and whether you prefer visual, verbal, auditory, or tactile modes of learning. For example, if you prefer to study with someone, do your surveying, questioning, and reading on your own, but recite and review with a study partner. If you prefer auditory modes of instruction, tape the material you want to review—a list of vocabulary words and definitions, for example—and listen to the tape. If you prefer visual modes of learning, make charts, diagrams, and illustrations to look at and review. If taking notes from textbooks and outlining information you need to remember are strategies that work for you, by all means, use them. You will have to resort to these strategies if you are studying from library books or materials your professor has put on reserve.

When you have settled on a study system that works, use it consistently. Knowing that you have a study system will make you feel confident that you can learn and remember. Also, if you are like many students and have trouble getting started when you try to study, a study system will provide the starting point you need. Figure 7.8 is a summary of ways

FIGURE 7.8 How to Vary the SQ3R Study System

COURSE	WHAT TO STUDY	YOUR SYSTEM
Math	Sample problems and exercises	Add a *practice* step for solving problems.
Literature	Elements of fiction: plot, characters, point of view, theme, style, and tone	Expand *recite* and *review* to include *interpret, evaluate,* and *write.*
Science	Facts, processes, and principles	Add a *draw* step to illustrate principles and processes.
Foreign languages	Words, meanings, pronunciations, and tenses	Add flash cards and conjugation charts to your *review* step.
Social sciences	Theories and principles of behavior and the people who developed them	Add underlining and marking to the *read* step; make charts to compare theories and record data.

EXERCISE 7.3

Do you know what to study for your courses? List the courses you are taking and the kinds of information you are expected to know. To help yourself with this exercise, look at the assignments you have been doing for these courses and at your old tests.

Course	Information
__________	__________
	__________
__________	__________
	__________
__________	__________
	__________
__________	__________
	__________
__________	__________
	__________

Now find the types of information you listed in the "What to Study" column in Figure 7.8. Look at the "Your System" column for ways to build the best study system for you.

to vary the SQ3R study system to meet specific course needs. It shows that surveying, questioning, and reading, reciting, and reviewing are essential for studying every subject. Variations in the system can be made in the way you apply the steps or in the addition of a step. As you become more comfortable using a study system, you will think of many more variations. Some of them may be better for you than those suggested in this chapter because they will be based on your own learning style.

EXERCISE 7.4

Read the next assigned chapter in one of your textbooks, and try out the SQ3R study system. When you have finished, answer these questions.

Yes	No	
☐	☐	1. Did surveying the chapter before reading give you an idea of what the chapter covers?
☐	☐	2. Were you able to formulate questions from the headings to guide your reading?
☐	☐	3. Did you find answers to most of your questions as you read each section?
☐	☐	4. After reading, did you know what to underline?
☐	☐	5. Did you make any marginal notes?
☐	☐	6. Did you find any material that would be easier to understand if you were to diagram it to make it more visual?
☐	☐	7. After reciting and reviewing, did you feel you had a good understanding of the information contained in the chapter?
☐	☐	8. Given your learning style, is SQ3R an effective system for you? Why or why not? ____________________ ____________________
☐	☐	9. How can you adapt SQ3R to fit your learning style? ____________________ ____________________

CONFIDENCE BUILDER

The PREP Study System

Use this system to prepare for classes and tests in skill-development courses such as algebra and foreign languages. The PREP system integrates two of the critical thinking strategies explained in detail in Chapter 13, *predict* and *evaluate,* with the steps of SQ3R.

P = Predict
R = Read
E = Evaluate
P = Practice

Predict Predict or anticipate what a reading assignment will cover. Monitor your comprehension as you read by surveying the chapter to get an overview and by formulating questions to guide your reading and predict outcomes.

Read Use RMO, a three-step process of *read, mark,* and *organize. Read* carefully, one section at a time. *Mark* your textbook by underlining important information and summarizing key ideas or concepts in the margin. For example, in a math chapter you could briefly list the steps for solving a problem, or you could restate a rule or principle in your own words. To *organize* information that you want to remember, make notes or study guides. Make lists or note cards of vocabulary words or verb conjugations for a language class. These activities help you to read actively and retain information.

Evaluate As you recite and review, apply the standard of usefulness to evaluate your progress by making connections between newly acquired knowledge or skills and what you already know. For a math course, whenever you review, distinguish the principles, rules, and types of problems that you understand from those that need more review. Spend most of your time reviewing material that you have not learned sufficiently.

Practice The most important step in studying for a skill-development course is the practice of new skills. For a math course, do exercises and solve example problems. For a language course, complete exercises that require you to speak, write, and translate in your new language. By attempting to do exercises and problems, you learn whether you are able to apply your knowledge to new situations and you discover your strengths and weaknesses. To ensure that you get enough practice, always complete all exercises in a math or language chapter.

CRITICAL THINKING APPLICATION

Think about the courses you are taking, the difficulty level of the textbooks, the types of tests and assignments required, and the problems and successes you have had in meeting the objectives of the courses. Then select one course you are taking or will take. Come up with a plan that will help you learn the kinds of information taught in that course. Summarize your results in writing.

SUMMARY

The following summary includes a partially filled-in information map of the SQ3R and PREP study systems. Read the summary; then complete the chart.

Making graphic aids of material you want to remember is especially helpful if your preferred learning style is visual. Remember, too, that the best study system is one you create that takes into account the

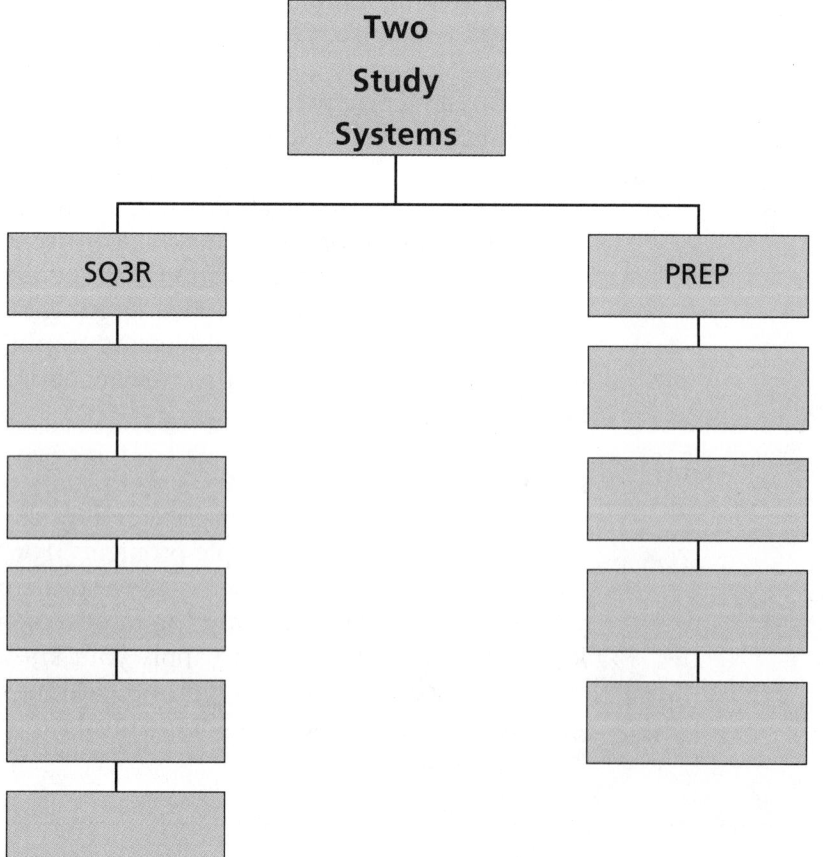

characteristics of your learning style and the kind of information you need to remember.

Depending on how you use them, your textbooks can be either indispensable tools or dead weight in your backpack. To get the most out of your textbooks and individual chapters, become familiar with their common parts, and survey them before you begin to study.

Use textbook parts to help you find information you need. For example, look up a topic in the index quickly and easily instead of wasting time flipping through pages of text to find it. Use the parts of a chapter to form questions in your mind to guide your reading.

In addition to knowing how to use your books and how the information contained within them is organized, you need a study system to help you understand and remember what you read. SQ3R and PREP are two of several systems. The best system for you is one that works, whether you adopt someone else's or create your own. To vary SQ3R to fit your needs, take into account the characteristics of your learning style and the kind of information you need to remember. Try the PREP system if you are taking a skill-development course.

YOUR REFLECTIONS

Reflect on what you have learned about study systems and how you can best apply that information. Use the following list of questions to stimulate your thinking; then write your reflections. Your response may include answers to one or more of the questions. Incorporate in your writing specific information from this chapter.

- Evaluate the study system you now use. What works, what doesn't work, and why?
- How do time management and learning style affect the way you study?
- What is your most demanding course? What have you learned from this chapter that will help you improve the way you study for this course?
- Are you taking a course that is *not* covered on pages 161–162? How can you adapt SQ3R to meet the needs of this course?
- How do you plan to use this chapter's information to create your most effective study system.

Date ______________________________

CHAPTER 8

Organizing Information For Study

Trying to memorize facts, concepts, and other important information is an ineffective way to study—particularly when the information may not be clear to you. It is better to take as much time as necessary to understand what you read and then try to organize or restructure the information into a format—such as a diagram or chart—that makes it meaningful to you.

Diagrams, charts, and other such organizers have three advantages. First, they condense information into smaller, meaningful chunks that are easier to remember than an author's exact words. Second, they help you visualize relationships among ideas. Third, the process of deciding what is important, choosing the best organizer for the purpose, and constructing your study guide helps you build organizational and decision-making skills essential in college and the workplace. These critical thinking skills are your key to efficient study and review.

This chapter explains how to make six types of organizers that you can use as study guides:

- Concept or information maps
- Comparison charts
- Time lines
- Process diagrams
- Informal outlines
- Branching diagrams

AWARENESS CHECK #14

How Well Do You Organize Information for Study?

The following Awareness Check will help you determine whether you are getting all the information you can out of your textbooks and using it effectively for studying, remembering, and recalling what you have learned. Check the statements that apply to you.

1. Part of my textbook study includes making some type of study guide to help me remember important information.
2. I rarely, if ever, outline chapters or make study guides.
3. When I make notes from textbooks, I don't copy the information directly; I put it in my own words.
4. If I make notes, I usually copy directly from the text.
5. I have tried, or heard about, information maps and other ways of organizing information.
6. I am not aware of ways to organize information. I study by rereading textbook chapters or reviewing my lecture notes.
7. I can usually decide what is important in a chapter, and that is what I study.
8. I have difficulty deciding what is important in a chapter, so I try to study all of it.
9. Overall, I would say that my method of studying from textbooks is effective.
10. Overall, I feel that my method of studying from textbooks needs improvement.

If you checked mostly odd-numbered statements, you probably are already using an effective method of organizing information from textbooks. If you checked mostly even-numbered statements, you may want to try some of the helpful organizers suggested in this chapter. Although none of them is necessarily better than the others, you may discover one that works best for you.

CONCEPT OR INFORMATION MAPS

Unlike an outline, which is a *linear,* or sequential, listing of main ideas and supporting details, a concept or information map is a *spatial,* or visual, breakdown of a topic that may not be sequential. But like an outline, a map breaks down the information from general to specific concepts or ideas. If your learning style is visual, you may prefer information maps to outlines. To construct an information map, first identify the topic and write it in a box. Identify the ideas that relate to the topic, and write them in connecting boxes to show their relationship to the topic.

Read the following paragraph. Then study the concept map shown in Figure 8.1.

Television advertisers use five common fallacies, among others, to manipulate viewers' attitudes toward their products and get them to buy. ***Glittering generalities*** *are words and phrases that make viewers respond favorably to a product. Phrases such as "no preservatives," "low fat and cholesterol," or "97% fat free" associated with food products make people believe they're getting something that is healthful.* ***Transfer*** *is a fallacious type of reasoning whereby a product is related to an idea or activity with which the reader is likely to identify. Restaurant commercials are a good example of transfer. Families are shown having a good time in a restaurant, or a young couple is depicted in a romantic cafe. Viewers are supposed to get the idea that if they eat at the restaurants, they will become like the happy families and couples in these ads. Many advertisers use* ***testimonials*** *of famous people to endorse their products. A film star advocates the use of one brand of shampoo. A sports celebrity endorses a company's athletic shoes. Some advertisers use* ***plain folks,*** *people the audience can identify with, to sell products; others encourage viewers to jump on the* ***bandwagon*** *and buy a product because "everybody does it." Viewers need to pay attention to ads and sift the hype from the facts. Of course, they can always press the mute button on their remote control unit.*

The map shown in Figure 8.1 is very simple. It breaks down the topic *Five Common Fallacies* into its five supporting details, providing the key term for each one. For a more detailed map, you could attach two more boxes to each of the five detail boxes. In one you could write a definition of the term; in the other you could write an example of your own that is similar to one given in the paragraph. Concept maps can break down ideas as far as you need to in order to show how they relate.

FIGURE 8.1 Concept Map

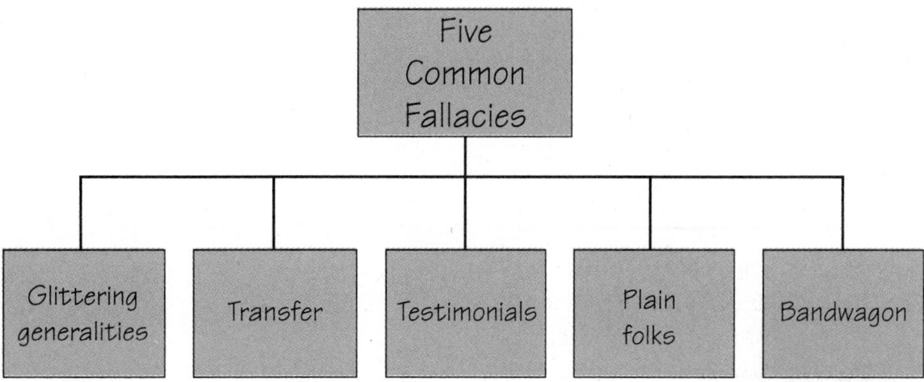

In some material, an order of importance, or *hierarchy,* is stated or implied. When that is the case, your map must show that one concept is more important than another or that one stage precedes another.

Read the next paragraph. Then look at Figure 8.2 for two ways to map the information.

Abraham Maslow was a psychologist who believed that five basic needs motivate human behavior. In Maslow's view, low-level needs have to be at least partially satisfied before higher-level needs can be met. At the bottom of Maslow's hierarchy are **biological** *needs for food, oxygen, water, and sleep. At the next level are* **safety** *needs: the need for shelter and clothing and the need to protect oneself from harm. Working to satisfy safety needs consumes the energy of many people. When safety needs are met, the need for* **belongingness and love***—the desire for affection and the need to feel part of a group or society—asserts itself. At the next-to-highest level is the need for* **esteem,** *or recognition by others of one's self-worth and achievements. At the top of Maslow's hierarchy is* **self-actualization,** *the need to achieve one's fullest potential. Maslow believed that only a few people, such as Jesus or Gandhi, have ever achieved self-actualization, though everyone has the potential to do so.*

Notice how the pyramid and the staircase shown in Figure 8.2 effectively illustrate the hierarchy of needs described by Maslow. The staircase and pyramid are common patterns that you can use to represent any hierarchical arrangement of ideas.

To use an information map as a study guide, look it over a few times. Read the information you have diagrammed. Then close your eyes and try to picture the diagram. If you were studying the staircase of Maslow's needs, for example, you would picture the staircase and visualize each need falling into place on the appropriate stair. During a test, you would visualize your map to recall the information.

FIGURE 8.2 Two Ways to Map Maslow's Hierarchy of Needs

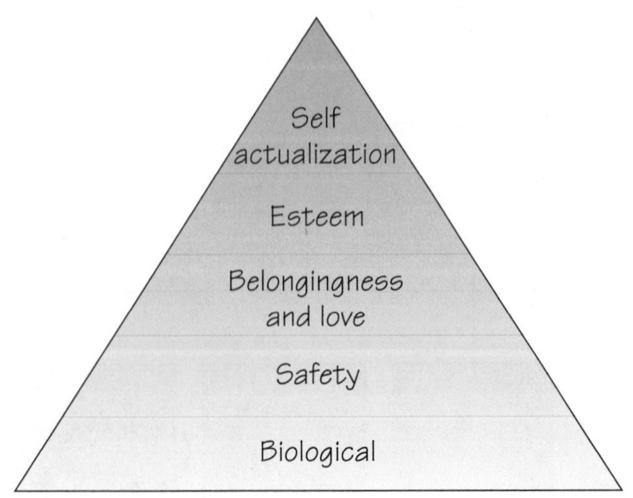

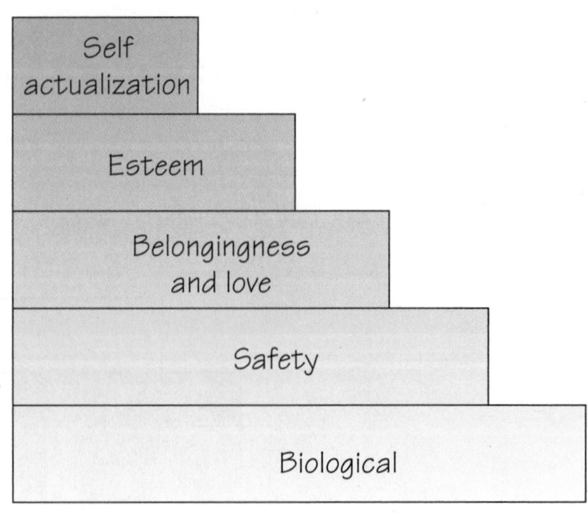

EXERCISE 8.1

From one of your textbooks, select some material that is hierarchically arranged—that is, arranged in a certain order from lowest to highest or most important to least important. Map this information to clearly show the hierarchy. Use the pyramid or staircase pattern illustrated in Figure 8.2 on page 172, or devise a pattern of your own. Then share your map with the rest of the class.

COMPARISON CHARTS

Comparison charts let you organize facts and other information into categories according to similarities and differences or group characteristics. A comparison chart enables you to take information out of context and reorganize it in a way that makes sense to you. Furthermore, a comparison chart arranges information visually, allowing you to *see* relationships among categories and to compare information that is sorted into each category. If your learning style is visual, you may enjoy making and using comparison charts as study guides. Read the annotated paragraph below and examine the comparison chart shown in Figure 8.3. The annotations show how one student thought through the information explained in the paragraph before making a comparison chart.

Main idea: 3 purposes for writing

1st: inform

2nd: entertain

3rd: persuade

Purpose determines language, goals, type of material

A writer may have one of three major purposes for writing. Writers who want to inform the reader present facts in an objective way and cover all sides of a topic. Their language is usually formal, and their goal is to explain or instruct. Informational writing is characteristic of textbooks, periodicals, and scholarly journals. Writers whose purpose is to entertain are, primarily, storytellers. Their language may be formal or informal, but it is always descriptive. To amuse, delight, and engage the reader's imagination are goals of writers who want to entertain. They write short stories, novels, essays, and poems. Writers whose purpose is to persuade have taken a stand on an issue of importance to their readers. These writers may attempt to inflame their readers with emotional language. Their prose is a mix of fact and opinion, and they may slant evidence in their favor. Their goal is to change readers' minds; they speak out from books, from the editorial pages of newspapers, and from popular magazines. Writers' purposes may determine what they write, how they write, and for whom they write.

Figure 8.3 shows the relationship among three purposes for writing and compares their similarities and differences in three categories: the language, goals, and type of material best suited to each purpose. Read down the chart for purposes; read across for a comparison of similarities and differences. For another example of a comparison chart, see Figure 10.3 in Chapter 10; it compares the stages and functions of memory.

FIGURE 8.3 Comparison Chart

A Writer's Three Purposes

	Inform	Entertain	Persuade
Language	Usually formal	Formal or informal; descriptive	May be emotional, slanted
Goals	To explain or instruct	To amuse, delight, engage imagination	To change reader's mind
Type of Material	Textbooks, periodicals, journals	Short stories, novels, poems, essays	Books, editorials, magazine articles

EXERCISE 8.2

Read the passage that follows. Then organize the important information on the comparison chart, which is partially filled in. Give the chart a title that indicates what the paragraph is about.

There are several types of social groups, and they play a very important role in our lives. Sociologists study two major types of social groups. ***Primary groups*** *are small, and people's relationships within these groups are intimate and personal. Examples of primary groups include families, teams, friends, and lovers. The function of these groups is to act as a buffer against the larger society. You can always come back to these groups and find security and acceptance.* ***Secondary groups*** *may be either small or large. They are usually organized around a task or a goal, and relationships within them are usually impersonal. Examples of secondary groups include the military, businesses, colleges, and universities. The purpose of these groups is to help you reach a goal or accomplish some type of work. These groups remain fairly impersonal in order to get their work done, but it is possible to develop close relationships with members of your secondary group.*

Title: ______________________________

TYPE	SIZE	RELATIONSHIPS		
Primary groups				Families, teams
		Usually impersonal		

A comparison chart lets you organize a lot of information into a relatively small and compact format that you can put in a notebook for frequent review. You may be able to draw comparison charts on 5″ × 7″ note cards, which are even easier to carry with you.

TIME LINES

Time lines are effective organizers for material that is presented chronologically. They are especially useful for visualizing a historical development or a sequence of events. Review a time line by looking at it and reciting the events in order. Then close your eyes and try to visualize the events as positions on the line.

To make a time line, draw a vertical or horizontal line. Divide the line into sections. On one side of the line, write dates; on the other side, write events that correspond to the dates, and give your time line a title that indicates what it covers.

Read the following paragraph and follow the sequence of events. Then examine the time line shown in Figure 8.4 on page 176.

> *Except for variety shows and a few programs such as* American Bandstand, *which in the 1950s became one of television's first hits, and* Your Hit Parade, *which aired from 1950–1974, television paid little attention to popular music. That changed in 1981 with the formation of the Music Television (MTV) cable network. . . . MTV quickly became a 24-hour-rock-video powerhouse that targets teens and young adults aged 12 to 24. A co-owned network, Video Hits One, programs to attract 25–34-year-olds.*
>
> *Originally intended to promote record sales, music videos became a television genre in their own right. Performers act out song lyrics, interpret them, or otherwise create imaginative visual images for songs. As promotional tools, videos came free of charge to stations and networks. But MTV changed the ground rules in 1984 by* paying *for exclusive rights to Michael Jackson's much-publicized* Thriller *video. MTV now contracts for exclusive early* windows *(periods of availability) for some videos. These strategies essentially demolished music videos as a source of free program material. . . .*

From *Broadcasting in America,* 2nd ed., Sydney W. Head, Christopher H. Sterling, and Lemuel B. Schofield, Houghton Mifflin Co., 1996.

FIGURE 8.4 Time Line

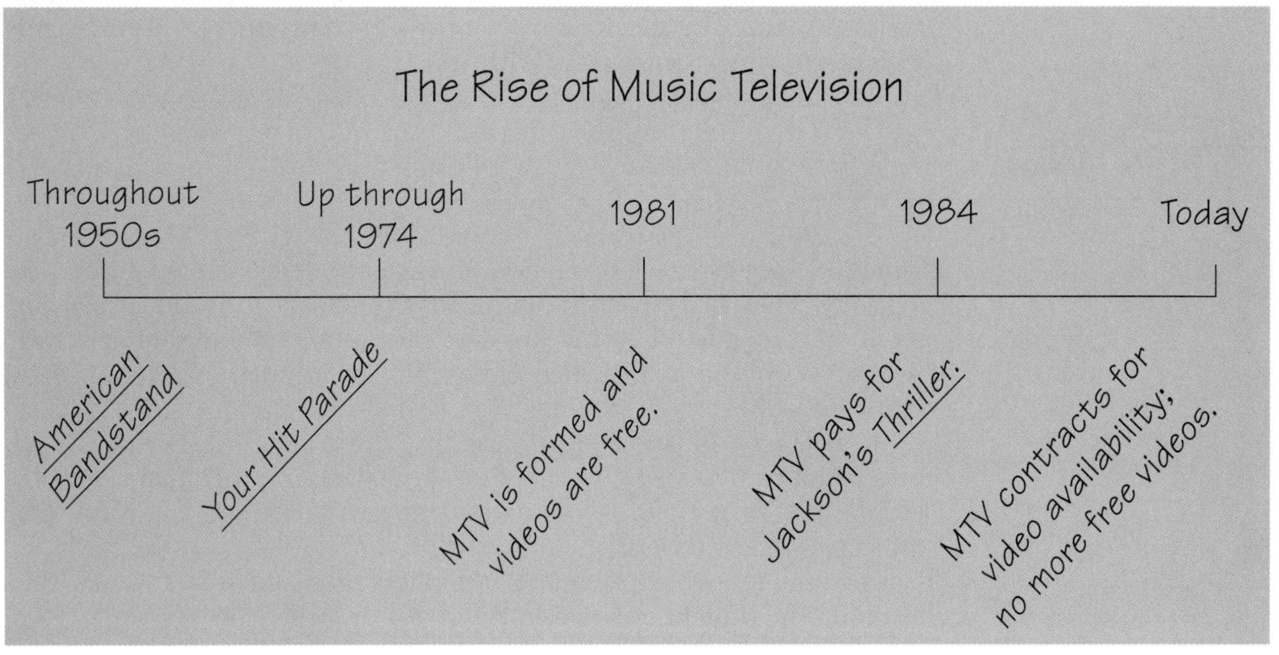

FIGURE 8.5 Process Diagram

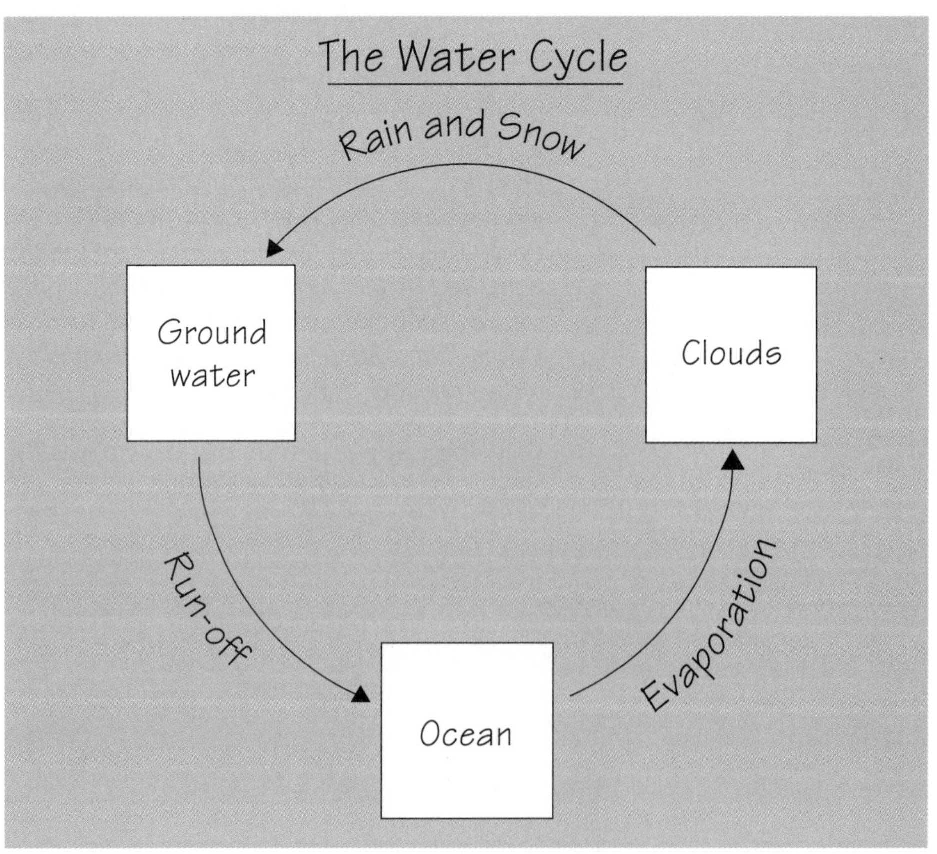

PROCESS DIAGRAMS

Processes are methods, steps, and stages that describe how events occur. They are an essential part of most courses. In a biology class, you learn how diseases are transmitted or how food is processed in the human body. In a political science class, you learn how a bill becomes a law. In an economics class, you learn how periods of inflation and recession develop. In a social science or psychology class, you read about experiments that explain certain aspects of human behavior. A chart that visually represents a complicated process may make it easier for you to learn and remember each step or stage. The process diagram shown in Figure 8.5 on page 176 illustrates the natural movement of water from the ocean to freshwater sources and back to the ocean.

EXERCISE 8.3

In this exercise you practice identifying and reading a process diagram with the members of your group. Remember to follow the guidelines for group discussion explained in Chapter 1, page 12. Your tasks are as follows: Search through your textbooks to find a good example of a process diagram. These diagrams are typical of science and social science textbooks but may also appear in other types.

Process diagrams are easy to recognize. Look for drawings connected by arrows to show the direction of the process. Look for stages illustrated by connected boxes or circles, as in the diagram of the water cycle (Figure 8.5) on page 176. When you have found a process diagram, examine it carefully and read the textbook explanation that accompanies it. Use the following questions to guide your discussion. Record the group's answers to the questions and the group's evaluation.

1. What process does the diagram illustrate?

____

2. How many stages or steps are in the process, and what are they?

____

____

3. Which seems easier to understand, the textbook explanation or the process diagram, and why?

____

____

4. Does the answer to question 3 depend on your learning style? How?

____

____

Group Evaluation:

How will you use what you have learned about process diagrams? Did your group complete its tasks successfully? What improvements can you suggest? How will you find answers to your questions?

INFORMAL OUTLINES

You have already learned one use of outlines. In Chapter 3, you learned that you can use the informal outline/key words system to take notes from lectures. Chapter 15 explains how to make an outline to organize your ideas for an essay. Outlines of important information are also useful as study guides.

FIGURE 8.6 Study Guide for Maslow's Hierarchy of Needs

Maslow's Hierarchy

1. Originator: Abraham Maslow

2. Theory: Five basic needs motivate human behavior and form a hierarchy from lowest to highest. Lower-level needs have to be met first.
   * Biological, physiological needs (lowest level)
   * Safety
   * Belongingness and love
   * Esteem
   * Self-actualization (highest level)

3. Weakness of theory: People don't always act according to the hierarchy.
   * A higher-level need might be satisfied before a lower-level need.

4. Researchers agree theory useful because it describes motivation in general.

Suppose that you are taking a psychology course. You have just finished reading a chapter on motivation and listening to a lecture in class on theories of motivation. Your instructor listed some theories on the board and said, "This is important." You have a test in a few days, and you know what you should study: theories of motivation. Your study guide for Maslow's theory might look like the outline shown in Figure 8.6 on the previous page. The outline has four major details, indicated by the numbers 1, 2, 3, and 4. Stars and indentations signal material that supports or explains each of the four major details.

You could write the outline on a 5″ × 7″ note card. You could make outlines on note cards for all the theories and cover the same four points: the name of the originator, the gist of the theory, a weakness, and what makes the theory useful. How would you study from your guides? You could read and recite the information written on your cards. You could mentally try to fill in details. For example, can you explain each level of need in Maslow's hierarchy without looking back at the chapter? Suppose you get to esteem needs and draw a blank. Suppose you can't even

FIGURE 8.7 Outline of a Chapter's Title and Headings

Social Responsibility

The Economic Dimension
* The Economy
* Competition
* Technological Concerns

The Legal Dimension
* Laws Regulating Competition
* Laws Protecting Consumers
* Laws Protecting the Environment
* Laws Promoting Equity and Safety

The Ethical Dimension
* Ethics As a Force in Social Responsibility
* Organizational Direction for Ethics and Social Responsibility
* Future Issues

The Philanthropic Dimension
* Quality-of-Life Issues
* Philanthropic Issues

O. C. Ferrell and John Fraedrich, *Business Ethics,* Second Edition. Copyright © 1996 by Houghton Mifflin Company. Reprinted by permission.

remember what *esteem* means. The value of your study guide becomes clear: It tells you what information you need to review or re-read.

An outline serves the same purpose as any other type of organizer. It shows how ideas relate to one another and to the topic, and it indicates the relative importance of ideas. Outlines use a listing and indentation system that makes clear which ideas support one another.

A study guide that is easy to make is an outline of a chapter's title and headings. For an example, see Figure 8.7 on page 179. By making the guide, you not only reveal the writer's outline, but you also condense the major points of the chapter down to one review sheet. Instead of re-reading a chapter before a test, or flipping through all the pages to read the headings, simply read the outline on your review sheet. As you read a heading, try to recite the major points covered in that section. If you can recall the important points, then you know the material. If you cannot remember some of the information under a certain heading, then you know exactly which section of the chapter you should study some more. If you like to study with a partner, take turns quizzing each other from your review sheets.

FIGURE 8.8 Branching Diagram

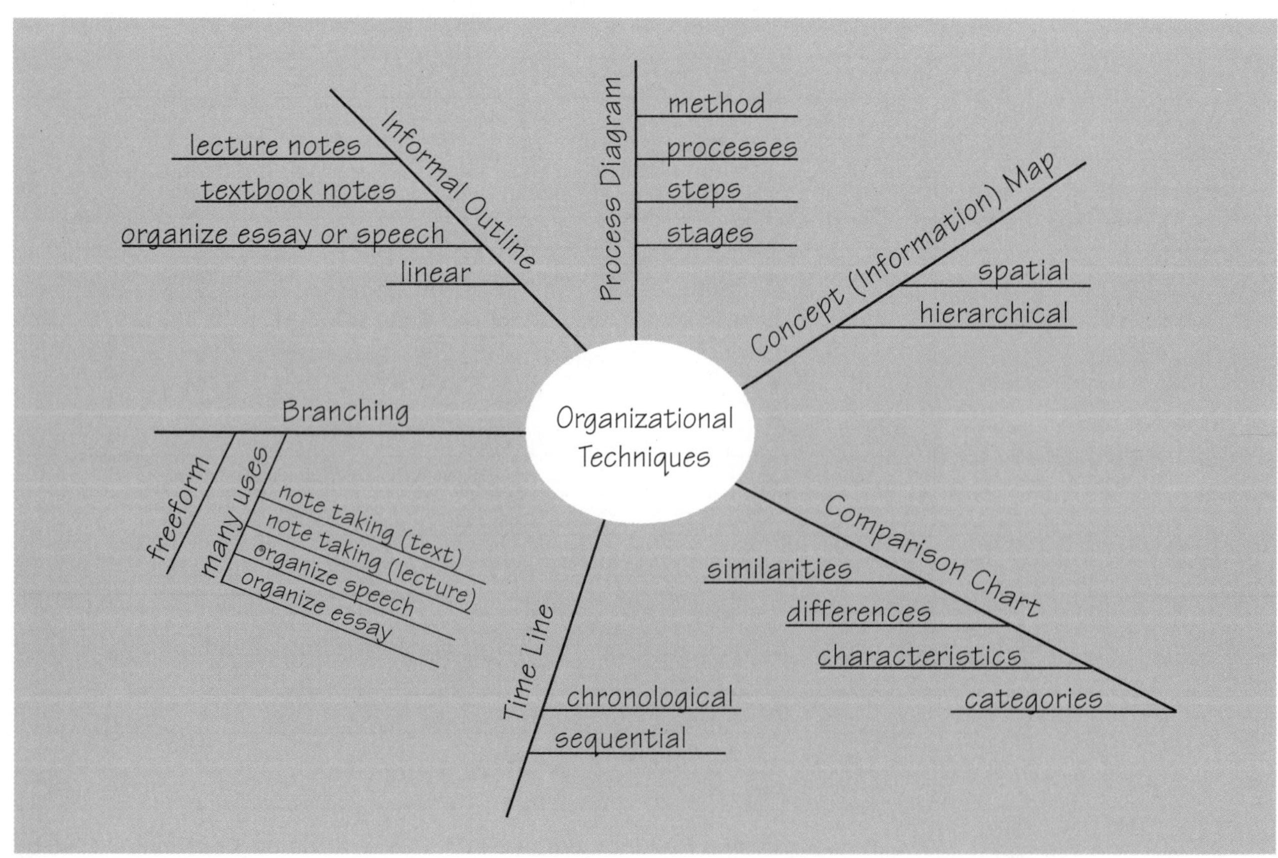

BRANCHING DIAGRAMS

Branching is a less formal, less structured technique than outlining or other techniques for creating study guides. In a branching diagram, ideas radiate outward from a central point instead of following in a sequence, one after the other. To branch out from a topic, draw a circle in the middle of your page. Inside the circle, write the point of the information about which you are constructing the study guide. Draw lines from the circle like the spokes of a wheel, but don't put them too close together. On these lines, write the major details that support the point. Draw more lines coming off these lines, and write in additional examples that support each of the details. Figure 8.8 shows a branching diagram of the five organizational techniques described in this chapter.

CONFIDENCE BUILDER
Branching: The All-Purpose Organizer

Branching appeals to some people because their thinking can proceed from a central point and branch out in all directions. They can write ideas all over the page as they occur instead of being forced to follow a logical order. Making study guides is one use of branching. Try these others:

Writing When you are planning an essay, do you get stuck on one point, unable to go any further? Do you know your last point but can't write it down because you don't know what the points before it will be? Instead of writing an outline, write your thesis in a circle in the middle of your paper. *As ideas occur to you, branch out from the circle.* As you think of more details to support a point on one of your branches, draw lines from that branch and write them in. Branching approximates the way you actually think, which is not always orderly. When you have branched out from the topic as far as you can, look at your diagram. Then decide the order in which you will develop your points in the essay. You are then ready to write your first draft.

Speaking Are you most comfortable holding something in your hands when you get up in front of an audience? But do you worry that you will get nervous and drop your note cards or that your hands will shake and your papers will rattle? Instead of outlining your topic, branch out from it. You can easily diagram a whole speech on one side of a 5″ × 7″ card. If memory fails, just glance at your card.

Taking Notes from Lectures Do you have trouble with most conventional note-taking techniques because some speakers don't move sequentially from one topic to the next? Do you write down a point, think the speaker is through, write something else on the next line, then hear the speaker returning to the previous point? Branching may solve your problem. Draw a circle in the middle of your paper before the speaker starts. As soon as you know the lecture topic, write it in the circle. When the speaker makes the first point, draw a branch from the circle and write in the point. If the speaker gives an example, extend a line from the branch and fill in the example. When the speaker makes another point, draw another branch. If the speaker returns to the first point with an additional example, just add another line to the branch.

Reviewing for an Exam Do you have trouble remembering sequential information for an exam? Try branching to aid your recall. Let's say you know there will be a question on advertising techniques on your next psychology exam. Write "advertising techniques" in a circle; then write on branches the techniques and descriptive details as you remember them. Compare the diagram to your notes to be sure you've remembered everything important.

EXERCISE 8.4

Read the following passage and complete the branching diagram that accompanies it, adding branches as needed. The diagram illustrates the relationship between the main idea of the passage and the details that support it.

For most people, effective financial planning takes into account five lifetime objectives. Making money *is a goal that can be reached either through employment or investments.* Managing money *so that there is some left over for savings after spending is a goal people can reach by becoming effective consumers. Preparing and following a budget, using credit wisely, choosing good investments, buying economical insurance, establishing inexpensive bank accounts, and keeping accurate records of all transactions are all part of being an effective consumer.*

Living well *is a goal many people strive for, in part, by trying to achieve financial success. Personal achievement, a challenging career, good health, satisfying relationships, community service, and material comforts are among some of the factors most people equate with living well. The decisions a person makes about all these factors determine the level of income and savings needed to achieve the quality of life he or she desires.*

Becoming financially secure *is a goal best achieved through effective money management. People who are financially secure are free from debt and concerns about money. They have enough to buy the things they need plus occasional luxuries. They have savings, investments, and insurance to maintain their quality of life in the future.*

Planning for the future *is a primary reason for saving money and making investments. It is a goal of many people who want to save money for their children's education, to live well in retirement, and leave an estate for their heirs. This objective, like the other four, is a lifetime one.*

Making money, managing money, living well, becoming financially secure, and planning for the future are related goals in the sense that achieving one usually requires achieving the others.

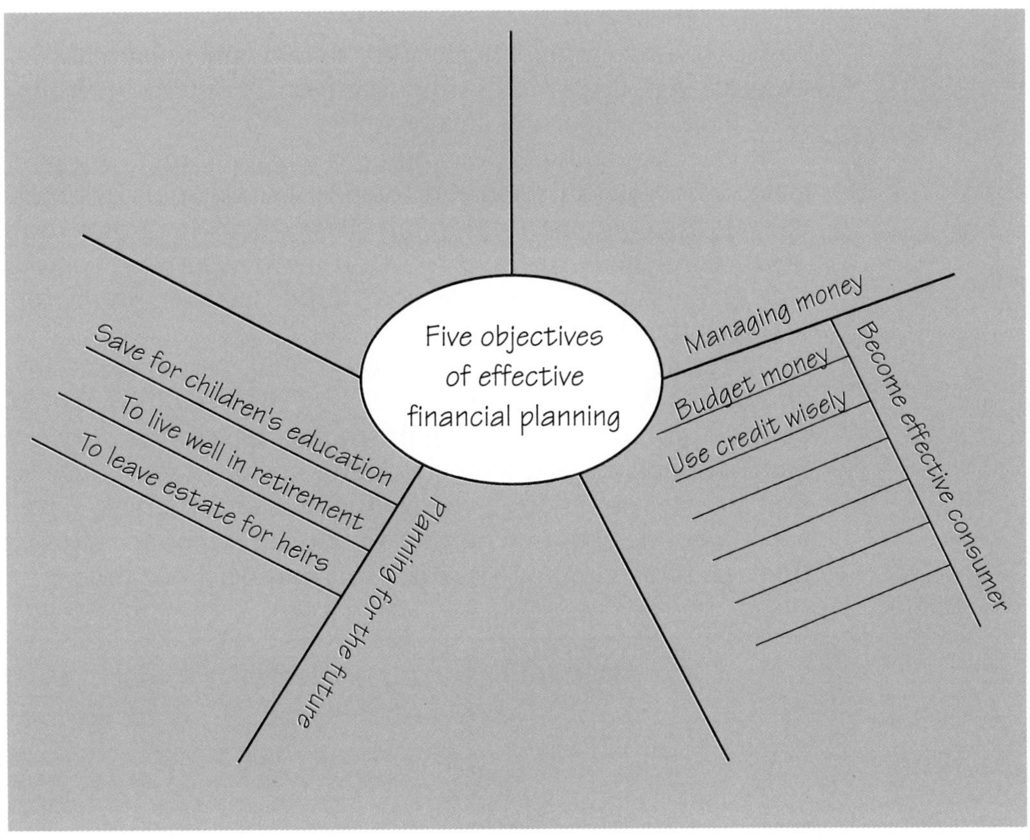

COMPUTER CONFIDENCE

Using a Computer to Make Study Guides

Once you become comfortable using your computer to organize notes, you can use it to create study guides as well. If you like concept or information maps, experiment with ways to arrange your notes on the screen. Some software programs allow you to place boxes and circles around type. You can also use your tabs and margins to set off words or blocks of type in an ordered way, then pencil in boxes or circles on the hard copy.

If you want a map that shows a hierarchy, your program may allow you to use various type sizes to represent levels. Start with the largest type for the most important concept and reduce the type size for each step, ending with the least important stage in the smallest type. You can also use type style functions to diagram differences. Use capitals, boldface, italics, underlines, double underlines, and plain text to make up your own hierarchy, selecting a different style for each idea on your map. Write a key to remember your choices. For example, ALL CAPS = most important idea; **boldface** = secondary idea; *italics* = supporting detail.

If you already use the computer to make informal outlines from class notes, you can begin constructing a study guide by inputting chapter titles and headings from your textbook in outline form. Then, using the "copy" and "move" functions on your computer, pick up portions of your class notes and insert them in appropriate places in the chapter outline.

Try using numbers for major points and asterisks (stars) for details. Or make up your own symbols to set off major and supporting points. You can also use different spacing, type styles, or type sizes to make distinctions. Some programs give you a choice of typeface or font so that you can even change the look of the letters. Have fun experimenting with different treatments for important ideas until you find one that helps you visualize your outline at test time.

EXERCISE 8.5

Read this excerpt from a psychology textbook; then underline and mark it to make the important information stand out. Using an organizer that best supports your learning style, make a study guide.

Freud's Structure of Personality. *Have you ever had a burning urge to kiss or embrace someone you're attracted to, or to hit someone who has angered you, only to hear the haunting voice of your conscience? How do you resolve these dilemmas? Based on his clinical experiences, Freud believed that people are driven by inner conflicts (conscious vs. unconscious, free association vs. resistance, life vs. death)—and that compromise is a necessary solution. Freud thus divided the human personality into three interacting parts: the id, ego, and superego.*

The ***id*** *is the most primitive part of personality. Present at birth, it is a reservoir of instincts and biological drives that energize us. According to Freud, the id operates according to the* ***pleasure principle,*** *motivating us to seek immediate and total gratification of all desires. When a person is deprived of food, water, air, or sex, a state of tension builds until the need is satisfied. The id is thus a blind, pleasure-seeking part of us that aims for the reduction of all tension. If the impulsive, id-dominated infant could speak, it would scream: "I want it, and I want it* now!"

The ***superego*** *is a socially developed aspect of personality that motivates us to behave in ways that are moral, ideal, even perfect. Whereas the id pushes us to seek immediate gratification, the superego is a prude, a moralist, a part of us that shuns sex, aggression, and other innate sources of pleasure. Where does the superego come from? According to Freud, children learn society's* *values from their parents. Through repeated experiences with reward for good behavior and punishment for bad, children eventually develop internal standards of what's right and wrong. There are two components to the superego. One is the* ego-ideal, *an image of the ideals we should strive for. The other is* conscience, *a set of prohibitions that define how we should not behave. Once the superego is developed, people reward themselves internally for moral acts by feeling pride, and they punish themselves for immoral acts by suffering pangs of guilt.*

The third aspect of personality is the **ego,** *which mediates the conflict between the "wants" of the id and the "shoulds" of the superego. According to Freud, the ego is a pragmatic offshoot of the id, the part of personality that helps us achieve realistic forms of gratification. In contrast to the id (which strives for immediate gratification) and the superego (which seeks to inhibit the same impulses), the ego operates according to the* **reality principle**—*the goal being to reduce one's tensions, but only at the right time, in the right place, and in a socially appropriate manner. The ego is thus a master of compromise, the part of us that tries to satisfy our needs without offending our morals. The ego, said Freud, is the executive officer of the personality, the part that controls our behavior. . . .*

Saul Kassin, *Psychology.* Copyright © 1995 by Houghton Mifflin Company. Reprinted by permission.

CRITICAL THINKING APPLICATION

Form a group with two other people in your class who are taking one of the same courses as you. Talk about a chapter that has been assigned. Decide what in the chapter is important to remember and what your instructor is likely to test. Compare what each of you has underlined or made notes on so far. Then, working together, construct a study guide using one or more of the organizers explained in this chapter. Make copies of the guide for each member of the group, and share your results with the rest of the class.

SUMMARY

After reading the summary, fill in the partially completed comparison chart that follows.

This chapter explains how to organize information and make several types of study guides.

Outlines and *time lines* are linear because they arrange information sequentially according to what comes first, next, and so on. These organizers appeal to your sense of order. *Maps* and other types of visual organizers such as *comparison charts* and *process* and *branching diagrams* are useful for non-linear thinkers because they arrange information in ways that are logical but not necessarily sequential. The organizers explained in this chapter share one thing in common: They help you see the relationships among ideas. All of these organizers are effective although some may work better than others for some kinds of information.

There are several good reasons to organize information into outlines, maps, or charts that you can use as study guides. For one thing, the process of making a study guide forces you to think about ideas and how they relate. Also, arranging the information in a format that appeals to you makes it easier to remember. Finally, it is easier to remember information you have thought about and summarized on a study guide using your own words than it is to memorize the author's words.

Organizers to Use as Study Guides

Type of organizer	What it does	Useful for
Concept or Information Map	Provides spatial, visual breakdown of topic	Relating ideas from general to specific or in order of importance
Comparison Chart	Organizes information into categories	Comparing similarities and differences
		Tracing historical developments or sequence of events
	Describes how things happen or get done	

YOUR REFLECTIONS

Reflect on what you have learned about the ways to organize information for study and how you can best apply that information. Use the following list of questions to stimulate your thinking; then write your reflections. Your response may include answers to one or more of the questions. Incorporate in your writing specific information from this chapter on previous chapters as needed.

- Of the types of organizers explained in this chapter, which ones have you tried?
- Are you satisfied with the ways you have found to organize information for study? Why or why not?
- Do you think making study guides is an essential part of any study system?
- Which step or steps in the SQ3R system could be strengthened by the use of study guides?
- How do you plan to use this chapter's information?

Date ______________________________

CHAPTER 9

Controlling Your Concentration

To concentrate means *to pay attention by focusing your thinking on what you are doing*. Whether listening to a lecture, writing a paper or report, participating in a group discussion, or studying for an exam, you must be able to concentrate on the task at hand. The reason is clear: Concentration and memory are linked. In fact, they are essential aspects of your information-processing system, which also includes active reading and critical thinking—topics covered in later chapters. By becoming aware of the ways you process information and by choosing strategies that aid the process, you can take control of your learning.

Self-assessment and learning style are your keys to managing concentration. Through self-assessment you can find and eliminate your distractions. A familiarity with your learning style will help you make the choices that put you in control of where and how you study. Whether you are working independently or with others, being able to maintain concentration is an academic and career asset.

This chapter explains what you must do to take control of your concentration:

- Know what causes you to lose concentration.
- Identify your distractions and eliminate them.
- Find or create your best study environment.
- Study with a system that helps you concentrate.

AWARENESS CHECK #15

What Causes Poor Concentration?

Check the statements that apply to you. If you can think of another cause of poor concentration, write it in the space provided at the end of the list.

- [ ] 1. I am easily distracted when I study.
- [ ] 2. My mind wanders when I read.
- [ ] 3. I can't seem to find time to study.
- [ ] 4. I have a tendency to procrastinate and put off studying to do something else.
- [ ] 5. My mind goes blank on a test.
- [ ] 6. If I don't like the instructor, I lose interest and don't pay attention.
- [ ] 7. If the subject doesn't relate to my job or career choice, I have a hard time concentrating on it.
- [ ] 8. If an assignment takes too long or if it's difficult, I may not stick with it.
- [ ] 9. I don't have a career goal or a reason to study.
- [ ] 10. It's hard for me to listen and take notes at the same time.
- [ ] 11. I also have trouble concentrating when ______________________

____

Now that you have identified reasons for your inability to concentrate, read the rest of the chapter. The next section suggests ways to eliminate distractions. Subsequent sections discuss ways to eliminate other causes of poor concentration. Be sure to read the sections referred to in other chapters if the cause is a significant problem for you.

ELIMINATE DISTRACTIONS

First, you need to identify *what* is distracting you so that you can eliminate its source. You may need to change your home study environment or your daily habits. The following discussion and Figure 9.1 will give you some guidelines.

Distractions can have internal or external causes. *Internal distractions* originate within you. They include feelings of hunger, tiredness, and discomfort that you can control. *External distractions* originate outside you.

They include noise, temperature, and interruptions. You may not be able to eliminate all external distractions, but you can change the way you respond to them so that they don't keep you from concentrating. Figure 9.1 below lists some common internal and external distractions. Put a check next to those that trouble you. If you are often distracted by something that is not listed in the figure, write it in under the appropriate column.

You can eliminate some internal distractions if you *anticipate your needs*. For example, study when you have eaten and are rested. Study in a comfortable place. Make sure you understand how to do an assignment before you begin. If you are not feeling well, postpone studying until you feel better. Worrying about grades, dwelling on job-related or personal problems, and having negative feelings about courses and instructors cause stress and distracting thoughts. When you have distracting or negative thoughts, stop studying for a moment and remind yourself of what you are trying to accomplish. Focus your attention on completing the task. If you lack interest in what you are studying, or if you don't have the motivation to do the work, studying with a partner might help. Choose someone who *is* interested and motivated. Studying will be more enjoyable, and the time will seem to pass quickly.

You can eliminate most external distractions by creating a study place where *you* may be able to control the lighting, temperature, noise level, and the availability of materials needed for study. Say *no* to friends who

FIGURE 9.1 What Distracts You from Studying?

INTERNAL DISTRACTIONS	EXTERNAL DISTRACTIONS
☐ Hunger	☐ People talking to each other
☐ Tiredness	☐ Telephones ringing
☐ Illness	☐ Music or television playing
☐ Thinking about work or personal problems	☐ Noise or activity going on outside
☐ Worrying about grades, personal matters, etc.	☐ Lighting too bright or too dim
☐ Stress	☐ Temperature too high or low
☐ Physical discomfort	☐ Lack of proper materials
☐ Not knowing how to do an assignment	☐ Party or other activity that you want to take part in
☐ Negative feelings about courses or instructors	☐ Family members asking you to do something
☐ Lack of interest or motivation	☐ Friends wanting to talk
☐ Other internal distraction? ______________	☐ Other external distraction? ______________
______________	______________
______________	______________

distract you from studying by tempting you with invitations to go out and have fun. If you save the fun as a reward for studying, you'll have a better time.

EXERCISE 9.1

The purpose of this exercise is for you and the members of your group to gain experience identifying internal and external distractions and ways to eliminate them. Remember to follow the guidelines for group discussion explained in Chapter 1, page 12. Your tasks are as follows: Read and discuss the following scenario about a student who has trouble concentrating. Use the questions as a guide. Then record the group's answers to the questions and the group's evaluation.

Yesterday afternoon I had some time between classes, so I went to the library, found a comfortable couch in the reading section, and began reading a chapter in my psychology book. Two students came in, sat on the couch next to me, and began talking about their dates from the night before. Their evenings sounded pretty funny. I didn't mean to eavesdrop, but I was sitting right there! Suddenly I realized I was shivering. Why had I forgotten to bring a sweater? I knew the library's temperature was kept at energy-efficient levels. Not only was I cold, but the light cast a glare on my book. I moved to a warm spot near the window where the sun was coming in and decided to take notes for the upcoming test. I looked all through my backpack for the pen I was sure I had packed. By the time I had borrowed a pen and sat down to take notes, it was time for my next class. I like psychology. Why was I unable to complete my reading assignment? I felt as though I was struggling with an unknown language.

1. What is the first distraction the student encounters? Is it an internal or external distraction?

____

____

2. What should the student have done immediately?

____

____

3. What are the student's other distractions? Are they internal or external?

____

____

4. Why is the student unable to complete the reading assignment?

____

____

5. What behavioral changes would help the student eliminate distractions?

____

____

Group Evaluation:

What have you learned about internal and external distractions? Do you think some distractions cannot be eliminated? Why or why not? Did your group complete its tasks successfully? What improvements can you suggest? What additional questions do you have about concentration, and how will you find answers to your questions?

Find Your Best Study Environment

Do you do most of your studying at home, in the library, or in some other place? Where you study is not as important as whether you are able to concentrate on studying when you are there. If you have a lot of distractions at home—small children who need attention, other family members who make demands on your time, noise from the television, the stereo, or ringing telephones—you may find it more pleasant and productive to study on campus. But many students find they can't concentrate in the library or other places on campus, so they set aside a place to study at home.

If you prefer to do most of your studying at home, use your learning style as explained in Chapter 1 to help you create a home study place that meets your needs. Try to manage your time so that you do most of your studying when your concentration is greatest. To adapt your study place to your learning style, try these suggestions:

- **Visual learners.** Make your place visually appealing. Display calendars, lists, and study aids where you can see and use them.
- **Auditory learners.** Keep a cassette recorder in your study place. Some instructors or departments tape lectures to supplement classroom activities, and they make these available through the library. If you are studying a foreign language, you probably attend a language lab. Find out if lab tapes may be checked out for use at home. You can also tape your notes, vocabulary words, and other practice material. Turn on the recorder and recite along with your tape.
- **Tactile learners.** If you have a personal computer, use a word-processing program to make your own study guides. Get a program that lets you create a calendar on which you can record important dates and assignments. Using a computer will also activate your visual sense.

You don't have to spend a lot of money to set up an efficient and convenient workplace in your house, apartment, or dorm room. Consider the following six factors when you plan your study environment: location, lighting, temperature, furniture, supplies, and motivational aids.

Location. You need a study place where you feel comfortable and where you are likely to have few distractions. Ideally, you should do all your studying in the same place, and you should not use your study place for anything but studying. For example, if you get sleepy while studying, don't nap at your desk. Leave your study area and return after you have rested. If you get hungry, don't eat at your desk. Take a break, have something to eat, and then return to finish studying. In this way, studying will become a habitual response triggered by your study place, and you will be able to maintain concentration.

If you have a spare room in your house, turn it into a home office, a workplace where you can shut the door and shut out distractions. If space is limited, turn a corner of your bedroom into a study area. If you must share space with someone—in a dorm room, for example—arrange the furniture, if possible, so that your desks are on opposite sides of the room facing a wall. When you sit at your desk, you will have the illusion of privacy. Plan or negotiate your time so that each of you can study when you are most alert, in a room free of noise and distracting activity.

Lighting. Too much studying in too little light causes eyestrain. Keeping your eyes focused for too long on the pages of your textbook or on a computer screen, especially in poor light, can make you feel tired and tense. Study in a well-lighted place and look up from your work occasionally. Rest your eyes by looking off in the distance without focusing on anything or by closing them for a few seconds.

Overhead lighting that illuminates your whole study area without casting glare or creating shadows is best. If you do not have an overhead light, use a lamp that can handle a 250-watt bulb and position it close to your work so that you are not reading or writing in glare or shadows. Two lamps, one on each side of your desk, will achieve the same effect if you put a 150-watt bulb in each. There is no need to buy new lamps if you can't afford them. Make the best use of whatever lamps are available by placing them properly and by choosing the right bulbs.

Temperature. The right temperature for studying is the one at which you feel most comfortable. A room that is too hot will make you feel drowsy and sluggish. Cooler temperatures raise your energy level and keep you alert. Your body is a gauge that registers changes in climate and temperature. Extreme changes affect your ability to concentrate because they cause you to focus your attention on your body's discomfort. Optimum temperatures for most people are between 68 and 70 degrees Fahrenheit. In your study area, you may be able to control the temperature and keep it at the level at which you feel most energetic.

Temperatures in public buildings may vary greatly from room to room, and they are usually controlled automatically. If one of your classrooms stays uncomfortably cold, pack a sweater or light jacket in your book bag when you go to that class because it is unlikely that your instructor will be able to adjust the temperature. You are probably aware of the hot and cold spots on your campus, so if you prefer to study there, find a comfortable place.

Furniture. To save money, use furniture that you have on hand, or pick up what you need at a used-furniture store or garage sale. You'll need a desk or sturdy table big enough to hold a computer (if you have one), with space left over for reading a book, writing a paper, or studying from notes.

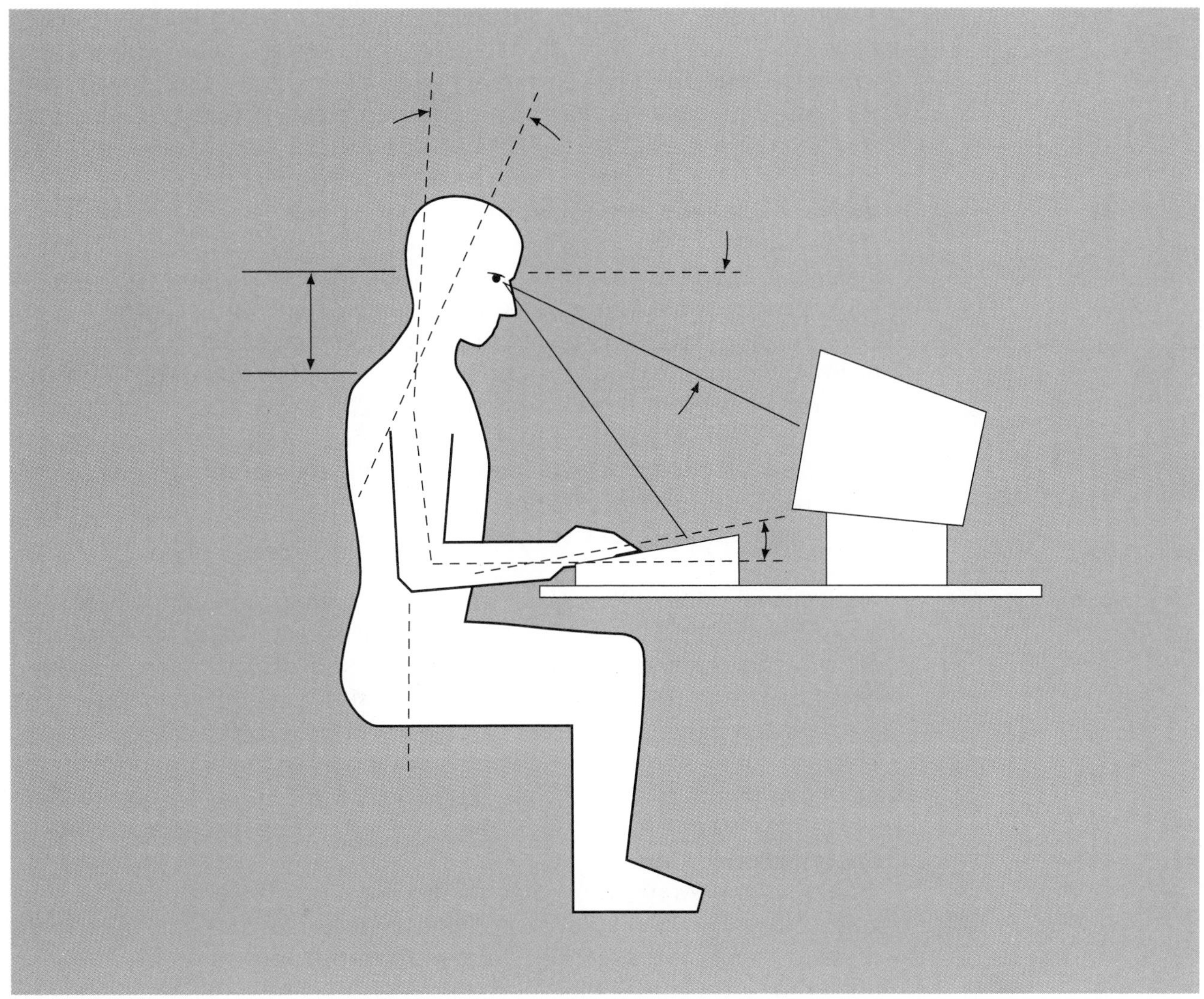

The science of ergonomics studies the conditions under which people work most comfortably and efficiently. The design of some office furniture is based on information about the way the human body is structured and best supported.

If you can afford to buy a new desk, get one with drawers for storing paper, pens, and other supplies. If you have a computer, you might want to invest in a desk or table made especially to hold a computer, printer, disks, manuals, and other supplies.

Don't underestimate the importance of a comfortable chair that provides adequate support for your back and is not too low or too high for the table or desk you are using. Studies have shown that many employees who work at computers all day suffer from chronic pain in their necks, arms, and backs. Such discomfort is the result of sitting in one position for long periods of time in a chair that doesn't provide enough support. Your arms or neck may become sore if your elbows and wrists are not supported as you type or if your computer screen is not at eye level. If you cannot buy or do not own a chair that provides enough back support, experiment with placing a pillow behind your lower back until you feel comfortable.

Whenever you have been sitting at your desk for a while and are beginning to feel tired or uncomfortable, try this exercise. Look up from your writing or away from your computer screen. Look to the right or left without focusing your eyes on anything in particular. Lower your shoulders, and let your arms hang limp at your sides. Shake your hands. Push back from your desk, and stretch your legs. If you still feel tired or stiff, take a short walk before returning to work.

Supplies. Keep your supplies handy and replenished. Most students use pens, pencils, lined and unlined paper, paper clips, a stapler and staples, note cards, and markers or highlighters in several colors. Whatever you need, including textbooks, make sure your supplies are available so that you don't have to interrupt studying to look for them.

Using a cardboard file box is a convenient and inexpensive way to organize your papers, returned tests, and materials from previous courses that you want to keep for future reference. You can buy a file box at your campus bookstore or office supply store.

Motivational Aids. Personalize your study environment. Be creative. Make it *your* place. Keep a calendar that lists exam dates, due dates for papers, and other important information, and display it on a bulletin board or tack it to the wall above your desk. Check off the days as you progress through the semester or quarter. Keep a record of your grades. This will help you see whether your studying is paying off, and it will signal when you need to make an extra effort. Tack up papers and tests on which you make good grades. When you are feeling discouraged, look at the evidence of your success.

If studying away from home or the dorm is a better option for you, your college library may be a good choice. It usually has quiet areas with desks or small tables that are away from traffic and noise. Explore your library to find a corner that meets your lighting and temperature requirements. Also, visit the library at different times of the day to find the time when it is most distraction-free.

Make studying in your place a habit so that it becomes your trigger for concentrated study. Research has shown that studying at the same time every day reinforces the habit. Although your present schedule may not permit a set study time, this is a goal you can work toward.

An added advantage of finding or creating your best study environment is that you can transfer what you have learned in the process to your workplace environment. The same conditions will apply: location, lighting, temperature, furniture, supplies within reach, and motivational aids. You might not have control of all these conditions, but you may be able to make some changes in the environment that will help you increase your productivity.

EXERCISE 9.2

Your body's reactions and your preferred learning environment are aspects of your learning style that affect both concentration and your choice of a study place. To review these aspects of learning style before completing this exercise, see Chapter 1, pages 5–10.

1. Based on your responses to Figure 9.1, are your distractions mostly internal or external?

2. What seems to be your greatest distraction, and why?

3. What relationship do you see between your answers to Awareness Check 3 on page 9 and the distractions you checked in Figure 9.1?

4. What is your preferred learning environment, as explained in Chapter 1, pages 10–13?

5. Based on your body's reactions and your learning environment preference, describe your ideal study place and explain what you will do to achieve it.

Use a Study System

Another way to eliminate distractions and maintain concentration is to study with a focused, consistent approach such as SQ3R or a system of your own. For additional strategies, try these six suggestions:

- **Break large assignments, such as research papers, into smaller tasks.** Schedule those tasks over several days or weeks, depending on when the completed assignment is due.
- **Study difficult subjects first.** Tackle your toughest or most unpleasant assignments when you are alert and can give them your full attention. Study easier subjects later. Even if you are tired, you can complete the work if it is not too difficult for you.
- **Separate similar subjects.** Suppose you are taking a history course, a math course, and an accounting course. Study history between math and accounting so that you won't confuse the two courses that require you to use computational skills.

Most people cannot concentrate for more than an hour without becoming distracted. Take short breaks away from your desk or study area to refresh your mind and body.

© Jean Claude Lejeune

- **Take breaks.** Do not try to study for several hours straight. You'll become distracted, tired, and cranky. Take a short break every hour. Get up, move around, or relax away from your desk. Look out the window to rest your eyes and to relieve tension.
- **Reward yourself.** When you complete a difficult or unpleasant task, have a nutritious snack, listen to some music, or call a friend. Then get back to work.
- **Study from your own textbooks.** Do not share books with a friend, and do not buy underlined textbooks. It may cost more to buy new or nearly new books, but they're worth the price because you will have to do your own thinking and make your own decisions about what is important and what should be underlined.

ELIMINATE OTHER CAUSES OF POOR CONCENTRATION

Perhaps you have eliminated distractions but your concentration remains poor because of test anxiety, ineffective note-taking skills, or a tendency to procrastinate. Throughout this book, you will find solutions to these

and other problems. Be sure to read the chapters or pages referred to in the following discussions if the problem applies to you.

Mind Wanders While Reading

If your mind wanders when you read, you may be losing concentration because the material is unfamiliar, technical, or too difficult. You will learn in Chapter 10 that you can't remember what you don't understand. It is also true that you can't concentrate on what you don't comprehend. To comprehend more, become actively involved in the process of reading by following the suggestions in Chapters 7 and 14, including the following:

- **Formulate a purpose for reading.**
- **Turn headings and subheadings into questions to answer as you read.**
- **Underline main ideas and key words or phrases.**
- **Summarize key ideas in the margins.**
- **Look up any words you do not understand.**
- **Read one section at a time.**

EXERCISE 9.3

Set a goal for completing assignments. Choose a block of time, during the day or in the evening, during which you will study or complete assignments for the following day's classes. Decide on the order in which you will complete your tasks, and estimate the amount of time you will need to finish each one. Then write them in below. Check off each assignment as you complete it, noting the actual time it took. This exercise will help you determine whether you are allowing enough time to complete your work.

Task	Estimated Time	Actual Time
1. ______	______	______
2. ______	______	______
3. ______	______	______
4. ______	______	______
5. ______	______	______
6. ______	______	______
7. ______	______	______

Can't Find Time to Study

If your concentration is poor because you can't seem to find time to study, then you are not managing your time effectively. You may be trying to do too many things at once. Try taking fewer courses next term, adjusting your hours at work, getting family members or roommates to share more of the housekeeping responsibilities, or participating in fewer extracurricular activities. If studying is a low-priority item on your list of things to do, review your goals and reasons for coming to college. You can improve your concentration by focusing your attention on a positive goal. If you have trouble managing time, try the suggestions in Chapter 4 for scheduling your time to allow for consistent, concentrated study.

Tendency to Procrastinate

If you often put off studying to do other things, then you are procrastinating. You are probably concentrating on something other than studying, and that interferes with your ability to concentrate on tasks at hand. If you need help beating procrastination, review the suggestions on pages 90–93 of Chapter 4.

Mind Goes Blank on Tests

If your mind goes blank during a test, you may have test anxiety. Test anxiety causes you to lose concentration and interferes with your ability to recall the information you have studied. Adequate preparation for tests will reduce mild anxiety. Severe anxiety may have causes that good preparation alone will not overcome, and you must work to eliminate them.

If test anxiety interferes with your ability to concentrate, try the technique in the Confidence Builder on page 201. Also, Chapter 12 suggests many other ways to deal with this problem.

Feelings About Instructors

If you lose interest in a course because you don't like the instructor, you may have an external locus of control. Re-read the discussion on locus of control on pages 14–16 in Chapter 1 and remember that you can control your interest level. Accept your lack of interest and loss of concentration as your own and say to yourself, "Okay, I'm bored. Now what am I going to do about it?"

During your college career you will encounter a number of instructors who are lively, entertaining lecturers. But unfortunately, some of the most knowledgeable people are not excellent speakers. Try to accept your instructor's limitations, and don't let your feelings about him or her keep you from doing well in the course. Instead, focus your attention on the material, and try to make connections between the new information and what you already know. Remind yourself that doing well in the course will help you reach your goals, and keep them in mind as you go about the daily business of attending classes and studying.

Controlling your feelings about instructors also has applications in the workplace. Negative feelings about employers, supervisors, or coworkers may distract you. Learn to control these feelings by focusing your attention on your goals and the task at hand.

CONFIDENCE BUILDER

A Desktop Relaxation Technique

When you are taking a test and your mind goes blank because you are nervous, this simple technique will calm you down so that you can finish the test.

1. Relax your shoulders and sit comfortably with both feet on the floor.
2. Place your elbows on the desktop, lower your head, close your eyes, and gently cup the palms of your hands over your eyes. Your fingers should be curled over the top of your head, and you should see no light coming in around your hands.
3. In this position, slowly count to ten while you breathe deeply.
4. Empty your mind of all negative thoughts by concentrating on feeling calm and relaxed.
5. When you are feeling calm, lower your hands and open your eyes.
6. You should feel relaxed enough to continue taking the test.

This technique works because you can't feel relaxed and anxious at the same time. As you concentrate on becoming calm, you forget about your test anxiety. When you return to the test calmly, the information you had blanked out because of nervousness will come back to you. And other students will not know what you are doing. They may think you are just resting your eyes.

EXERCISE 9.4

Attitude and behavior affect concentration. Your attitude and behavior in a class are related to your locus of control and the degree of responsibility you take for your performance in a course. Select as a target a course in which you would like to do better. Complete the analysis that follows; then decide what you can do to become a more internally controlled student.

1. Write the name and number of the course. ______________________________

____

2. Is there anything about the course that you don't like or that you think is difficult? __________

____

____

____

3. What are your distractions in this class? ______________________________

____

____

4. Are the distractions internal or external? ______________________________

____

____

5. What is your attitude toward this class? Answer *yes* or *no* to the following statements.

	Yes	No
I enjoy coming to this class.	☐	☐
I like the instructor's teaching style.	☐	☐
I feel confident in this class.	☐	☐
I am not afraid to ask questions in this class.	☐	☐
I am learning something in this course.	☐	☐
I see a relationship between this course and my goals.	☐	☐
I am interested in the subject taught in this course.	☐	☐

6. Make a plan to improve your concentration in this course by selecting a behavior or attitude that you will try to change. Describe what you will do. ______________________________

____

____

____

____

Try out your plan long enough to receive two or more test or assignment grades. If you are satisfied with the results, continue with your plan. If not, examine this analysis again to see if there is something else you can do to improve your performance in this course.

Subject Doesn't Relate to Job, Major, Career Goal

If you can't put your mind to a subject that doesn't seem to relate to your job, major, or career goal, then you are missing one of the great opportunities of a college education: to learn something new, to become exposed to different ideas. Research shows that most people change careers two or more times during their lives. If you take only courses that relate to your chosen career, you will be handicapped if you ever change jobs. Not only that, you may be missing an opportunity to broaden your mind and discover new interests.

Moreover, whatever career you have chosen for now may require skills of which you are currently unaware. Courses that seem unrelated may teach you skills that you *can* use in the workplace or in other life experiences. Chapter 2 includes a discussion on setting reachable goals that allow room for flexibility and new learning opportunities. If you have trouble concentrating in courses that don't seem to have an immediate or practical use, see pages 30–31 and Chapter 5, pages 99–100.

Long and Difficult Assignments

If you feel like giving up when you encounter a very long or hard assignment, you probably have a low tolerance for unpleasant tasks. You can change your attitude toward unpleasant tasks so that you can concentrate and get them done. First, remind yourself that the sooner you start, the sooner you will finish. Next, remind yourself that your attitude toward studying may be causing you to lose concentration and may be keeping you from doing your work as well as you can. Third, make long or difficult assignments easier to handle by following the suggestions on pages 86–87 of Chapter 4.

Lack of Goals or Reason to Study

If you don't have a goal or if you can't find a reason to study, perhaps you don't know yet why you're in college or what you want out of life. You may be attending college at your parents' request. Or you may want a college education but don't know how you plan to use it. Before you make serious career plans, you may need to explore possibilities for a term or two, taking required courses and electives until you get a feel for college life and being on your own.

Eventually you must decide what you want to do and get on with it. A visit to your college's career center or to a counselor might be helpful. Without a goal or a clear purpose for studying, it is difficult to concentrate. For suggestions on how to set and reach long-term goals, see pages 28–30 in Chapter 2.

Can't Listen and Take Notes

Listening to a lecture while taking notes is a new experience for many students, and it may seem impossible at first. Usually when you concentrate, you are focusing attention on one of many things that are happening around you. You remain aware of all that is going on at a sensory level, but you concentrate on that one thing. In a classroom lecture, you must focus attention on *two* things: listening and taking notes. In a sense, this is no different from eating an apple while reading a book, watching a TV program while carrying on a conversation, or driving a car while looking for an address. Your attention shifts rapidly back and forth between the two activities on which you are concentrating.

Taking notes during a lecture actually improves your concentration because you must make an extra effort to follow the speaker's ideas and get them down on paper. If you can't listen and take notes at the same time, then your note-taking skills probably need improvement. Try these suggestions:

- Sit near the front of the room.
- Focus attention on the speaker.

FIGURE 9.2 **Strategies to Improve Concentration**

CAUSES OF POOR CONCENTRATION	STRATEGIES
1. I am easily distracted.	**Eliminate your distractions:** • Create a good study place; do all your studying there. • Get enough sleep. • Study when rested. • Eat well so that you won't be hungry. • Study with a partner to increase motivation.
2. My mind wanders when I read.	**Become an active reader:** • Have a purpose for reading. • Turn headings into questions. • Underline main ideas. • Summarize key ideas in margins. • Look up unfamiliar words.
3. I can't find time to study.	**Learn to manage your time:** • Make a study schedule. • Use a calendar and daily lists. • Take fewer courses. • Adjust work hours. • Ask family members to help out with chores.
4. I procrastinate.	**Follow a six-step plan:** • Schedule time for long assignments. • Break long assignments into smaller parts. • Assemble your materials. • Think positively about your ability to complete assignments. • Get help if you need it. • Reward yourself for completing work.
5. My mind goes blank on tests.	**Reduce test anxiety:** • Prepare adequately for tests. • Learn how to practice a relaxation technique.
6. I don't like my instructor.	**Develop an internal locus of control:** • Accept your instructor's limitations. • Accept your responsibility to raise your interest level. • Accept the course as a step you must take to reach your goals.

FIGURE 9.2 **Strategies to Improve Concentration *(continued)***

CAUSES OF POOR CONCENTRATION	STRATEGIES
7. The course doesn't relate to my job, major, or career goal.	**Look to the future:** • Welcome new learning opportunities. • Set realistic and flexible goals.
8. The assignment is too hard.	**Make assignments easier:** • Be sure you know what to do. • Break long assignments into smaller parts. • Allow plenty of time. • Ask your instructor for help.
9. I don't have a goal.	**Decide what you want to do:** • Get a feel for college life. • Visit the career center or see a counselor. • Choose a major; make career plans.
10. I can't listen and take notes at the same time.	**Learn how to take notes:** • Sit up front. • Watch the speaker's gestures and expressions. • Listen for key words. • Copy information from the board. • Skip lines between main ideas.

CRITICAL THINKING APPLICATION

Think about this statement: "Concentration may be linked to motivation." Do you think the statement is true? Write a short paper in which you explain your answer.

As you think about what to write, remember what you have learned about *locus of control*—people are motivated in one of two ways, either *externally* or *internally*. Do you think that locus of control has anything to do with concentration? For example, is an externally motivated person more subject to internal and external distractions than an internally motivated person? Who is more likely to accept control for his or her level of concentration, an externally or an internally motivated person? What about your own locus of control and the kinds of distractions that affect you? You may want to review the section on locus of control in Chapter 1, pages 15–18.

It may take time and practice to become an effective note taker. Keeping your attention focused on the speaker is a basic step toward understanding what is important in a lecture.

© Bob Daemmrich

- Watch for gestures or facial expressions that signal important points.
- Watch your body language. Maintain the posture of concentration by sitting up straight, making eye contact with the speaker, and looking interested. These simple actions promote concentration by forcing you to involve yourself in what is going on. They have a positive effect on the speaker as well.
- Listen for key expressions such as "Now this is something you need to remember."
- Copy in your notes whatever the speaker writes on the board.
- Skip several lines between main points, leaving room to write in details and examples.

See pages 52–61 of Chapter 3 for a more detailed discussion of how to take notes.

Now help yourself by reviewing the strategies summarized in Figure 9.2 to combat the causes of poor concentration.

SUMMARY

Following this summary is a branching diagram—one of the common methods of organizing information explained in Chapter 8. After reading the summary, complete the partially filled in diagram.

You can improve your concentration by identifying and eliminating internal and external distractions. Internal distractions are physical feelings that you can take control of since they originate within you. External distractions may be beyond your control, but you can learn to control your reactions to them. To minimize internal and external distractions, take care of your physical needs before beginning a task, maintain a positive attitude towards studying, and work to solve problems that you know cause worry and stress.

You can improve your concentration by having a good place to study. The ideal home or dorm study environment is as distraction-free as you can make it. Choose a quiet location with adequate lighting. Select comfortable furniture suited to your needs. Keep your books and supplies readily available so you don't have to interrupt your studying to find them. Prominently display motivational aids, such as a calendar, weekly and semester or quarter plans, or assignments on which you have made good grades. If studying away from home or dorm works best for you, find a study place that has as many of the characteristics of a good study environment as possible.

How you study can also affect your concentration. Use your time efficiently. Break large tasks into smaller ones. Study similar subjects at different times. Take frequent breaks. Reward yourself for work accomplished. Use your own textbooks so that you are not influenced by what another student thought should be underlined or highlighted.

You can improve your concentration in other ways by applying the strategies listed in Figure 9.2 on pages 204–205.

How to Improve Concentration
Try additional strategies.
Become an active reader.
Manage your time.
Learn how to take notes.
Minimize internal and external distractions.
Attend to physical needs.
Study efficiently.
Break up large tasks.
Study similar subjects at different times.
Quiet location.
Adequate lighting.

YOUR REFLECTIONS

Reflect on what you have learned about controlling your concentration and how you can best apply that information. Use the following list of questions to stimulate your thinking; then write your reflections. Your response may include answers to one or more of the questions. Incorporate in your writing specific information from this chapter or previous chapters as needed.

- How are motivation and concentration linked?
- Which distractions have you been able to overcome?
- Which distractions are still causing you to lose concentration, and what do you plan to do about them?
- Based on what you have learned from this chapter and from Chapter 1, how does your learning style affect your ability to concentrate?
- How will you use this chapter's information now and in the future?

Date ________________________________

CHAPTER 10

Improving Learning and Memory

Your memory is an information-processing system. All learning takes place through this system. By concentrating, you can control or manage the system. By making changes in the way you learn, you can regulate the flow of information through the system, combat forgetting, and build a powerful memory.

Becoming aware of and taking control of the way you process information can lead to lifelong learning. A college degree does not represent knowledge gained, or skills learned, once and for all. On the contrary, a degree merely represents where you stand academically at a given time. In your career, as in life, you will be faced with tasks, problems, and decisions that require you to apply your knowledge in new ways and to develop new skills. One of the best things you can do for yourself while in college is to learn how to learn. Critical thinking and study skills are your key.

This chapter will help you understand the stages and functions of memory so that you can improve the way you learn. As you read the chapter, keep in mind these simple truths about memory:

- It is normal to forget.
- You can probably remember more and retain more for a longer period of time than you think you can.
- A few memory aids that many students have found useful may work for you.
- The best memory techniques may be those that you create or adapt for yourself and that correspond to your learning style.

HOW MEMORY WORKS

When you were a child, your teacher explained the multiplication tables and wrote them on the chalkboard. While you were listening to the teacher and looking at the board, you were *receiving* information about the tables through your senses of sight and sound. Then, to help you learn them, your teacher asked you to write them out on paper, and that activity engaged your sense of touch. You also recited the tables aloud. Those practices in the classroom helped you to *retain* the tables. Finally, the teacher told you to practice your tables at home because you would be tested on them. You would have to *recall* them. If your practice and memory techniques have served you well, then you have retained the tables and can recall them even now.

Memory is a three-stage process by which your mind receives information and either discards it or stores it for later use. Memory involves *reception* of information, *retention* of information that has been received, and *recollection* of information that has been retained. (Researchers also refer to these activities as *encoding, storage,* and *retrieval.*) Figure 10.1 suggests a convenient way to remember the stages.

FIGURE 10.1 The Three R's of Memory

Reception

Retention

Recollection

Reception

Your mind receives, takes in, or processes information through your five senses. It is important for you to understand the information you receive because you can't retain or recall material that you don't understand.

Relating new information to something familiar can aid understanding and reception because it either adds to or changes what you already know. As you connect new information with what you already know, you start thinking critically about it. The information now has a *context* and is easier to remember. Suppose you have been assigned a chapter on stress in your psychology text. Before beginning, assess your prior knowledge. Ask yourself what stress means to you. Imagine yourself in stressful situations, and recall what you have done to overcome stress. If you have not successfully managed stress in the past, the chapter may suggest a new method to try. Read to find out whether the author's points about stress confirm what you already know or give you new information.

Here are some more tips to improve your reception:

- **Become more attentive and observant.** If you stay alert in class and keep your attention focused, you will be a better receiver.
- **Engage as many of your senses as possible when receiving information.** In a lecture, *look* at the speaker. *Listen* attentively to what he or she says. *Take notes* to help you remember. If you do these things, you will be making full use of your visual, auditory, and tactile senses.
- **Ask questions, as needed, to aid understanding.** Remember: *You can't recall what you don't understand.* Make sure you understand the information you receive.
- **Before you read a textbook chapter, *survey* it** to get an overview of its content and to establish a purpose for reading. This step is especially helpful when the chapter covers a topic that is new to you. Surveying is the first step in the SQ3R study system. Chapter surveys are discussed on pages 145–154 of Chapter 7.

Retention

Your mind stores and retains, for varying lengths of time, the information it receives. Some information—your name, your birth place, your birthday—you remember for life. Such information is part of you, although you may not remember when you first learned it. You retain other information—the multiplication tables, how to ride a bicycle—through use or practice. Was it difficult for you to learn to drive a car? You probably had trouble at first, but eventually you were able to get into a car and drive without mentally reviewing each step. When you reached that point, you had *internalized* the process of driving. You do not easily forget information you have internalized. Like your name, it has become part of you.

Anything you really want to learn is going to stay with you because you are motivated to remember it. The key to retaining academic information is to *make a conscious effort to remember.* Here are some ways to make retention an active and effective process:

- **Become an active reader.** Underline and mark your textbook while you are reading. See pages 317–318 in Chapter 14 for suggestions on how and what to underline and mark.
- **Review frequently.** The more often you review information that you hope to learn and remember, the longer it will stay in your memory.
- **Recite to improve retention.** When you repeat information to yourself that you want to remember, you are activating your auditory sense and opening another pathway into your brain. You can recite information from note cards and study guides that you make. See Chapter 8 for instructions on how to make a variety of maps and study guides.
- **Do all homework assignments.** Homework provides practice in using new information or procedures. Frequent practice helps you internalize information.

If you make reception an *active* process by looking at the speaker, listening attentively, and taking notes, then you are more likely to understand the information you receive and be able to remember it later.

© Cindy Charles/PhotoEdit

- **Find a reason to remember.** Motivating yourself to learn because you want better grades is a start, but try to get beyond grades. Think about what you are learning and how it relates to your goals and your hopes.

Recollection

Problems with Recollection. Your mind enables you to recall information you have retained. Sometimes recollection is difficult. When you are taking a test, you might know one of the answers but be unable to remember it. Later, after the test is over, you remember the elusive answer. Or perhaps you have gotten confused because two similar kinds of information were competing for your attention. That was the problem plaguing a student named Otis.

Otis decided to take trigonometry and statistics in the same semester. Because his grades had been consistently high in math courses, he didn't anticipate any difficulty. Unfortunately, his first grades in both courses were not as good as he had expected: an F on his trig test and a D on his statistics test.

With an instructor's help, Otis realized that he had been confusing the information from one course with the other because the two courses both dealt with numbers and mathematical procedures. Since the classes met one after the other, he had no time to absorb information from one before going to the other.

Otis realized that he should have taken the courses at different times or on different days. He also realized that he should study the subjects at different times or at least take breaks between them.

Otis knew it would be hard to maintain his current average without withdrawing from one of the courses. He decided to remain in statistics, and because of the time he then had available for study, he passed the course with a B.

Improving Recollection. Otis had problems with recollection because he was confusing one course's information with the other's. If you have this problem, or if you need to improve your recollection for other reasons, try one or more of these suggestions:

- **Before a test, organize the information you want to study** in a way that is meaningful to you. Make summaries or set up categories in which you group similar items. See pages 231–238 of Chapter 11 for suggestions on how to organize information as you prepare for a test.
- **Use your preferred sensory mode.** If you learn best visually, make diagrams, charts, or information maps of material you want to remember. Picture these in your mind when you are studying and when you are responding to test questions. See Chapter 8 for detailed information on mapping and other visual organizational techniques. If auditory modes work best for you, try reciting aloud information you want to remember. Or you could study with a partner and quiz each other orally. If you are a tactile learner, try combining recitation with a physical activity such as walking or jogging. In this way, you are engaging both your auditory sense and your tactile sense.
- **Give yourself practice tests.** Try to anticipate test questions and write some of your own. Answer them; then check yourself against your textbook and your notes.
- **Go over old tests.** Review material that gave you trouble in the past. Your mistakes are clues to information that you haven't retained.

EXERCISE 10.1

Imagine that you will be tested on the part of this chapter that you have read so far. You need to practice organizing the information in a way that will help you study for the test. Fill in the following outline by answering the questions with information from this chapter.

1. What are four simple truths about memory?

   a. ______________________________

   b. ______________________________

   c. ______________________________

   d. ______________________________

2. What are the three R's of memory?

   a. ______________________________

   b. ______________________________

   c. ______________________________

3. What are some tips for improving memory?

   ____

   ____

   a. How can you improve reception?

      1. ______________________________

      2. ______________________________

      3. ______________________________

      4. ______________________________

   b. How can you improve retention?

      1. ______________________________

      2. ______________________________

      3. ______________________________

      4. ______________________________

      5. ______________________________

   c. How can you improve recollection?

      1. ______________________________

      2. ______________________________

      3. ______________________________

      4. ______________________________

WHY YOU FORGET

Do you ever wish you could read something once and remember it? Unfortunately, the mind doesn't work that way. One reading of textbook material is seldom enough. Much of the information printed in textbooks is new to you, and you may need several readings to understand and absorb it. Also, you forget most of what you read soon after reading it unless you make a conscious effort to remember it. Finally, if you want to retain information, you must periodically review what you have read.

Forgetting is not only normal, but necessary. If you never forgot anything, your mind would be so crammed with useless information that you wouldn't be able to think. Do you remember what your phone number was in every place you have lived? You probably don't. Information that you cease to use soon passes out of your memory unless it has special significance. *Your mind remembers only what you need and discards the rest.* In fact, when you learn something new, forgetting starts within an hour. After several days, you remember very little of the new information unless you take action to prevent forgetting.

The stages of memory—reception, retention, and recollection—work because of three functions. Your *sensory memory, short-term memory,* and *long-term memory* determine what you remember and for how long. You have some control over each of these functions. Together, the stages and functions of memory make it possible for you to process information. Figure 10.2 illustrates the process.

Sensory Memory

Your five senses—sight, hearing, taste, smell, and touch—are the media through which you experience the world. Everything that is happening around you is conveyed to you by your senses. Your mind takes in all this information and, through a process called *selective attention,* sorts the important from the insignificant.

FIGURE 10.2 How You Process Information

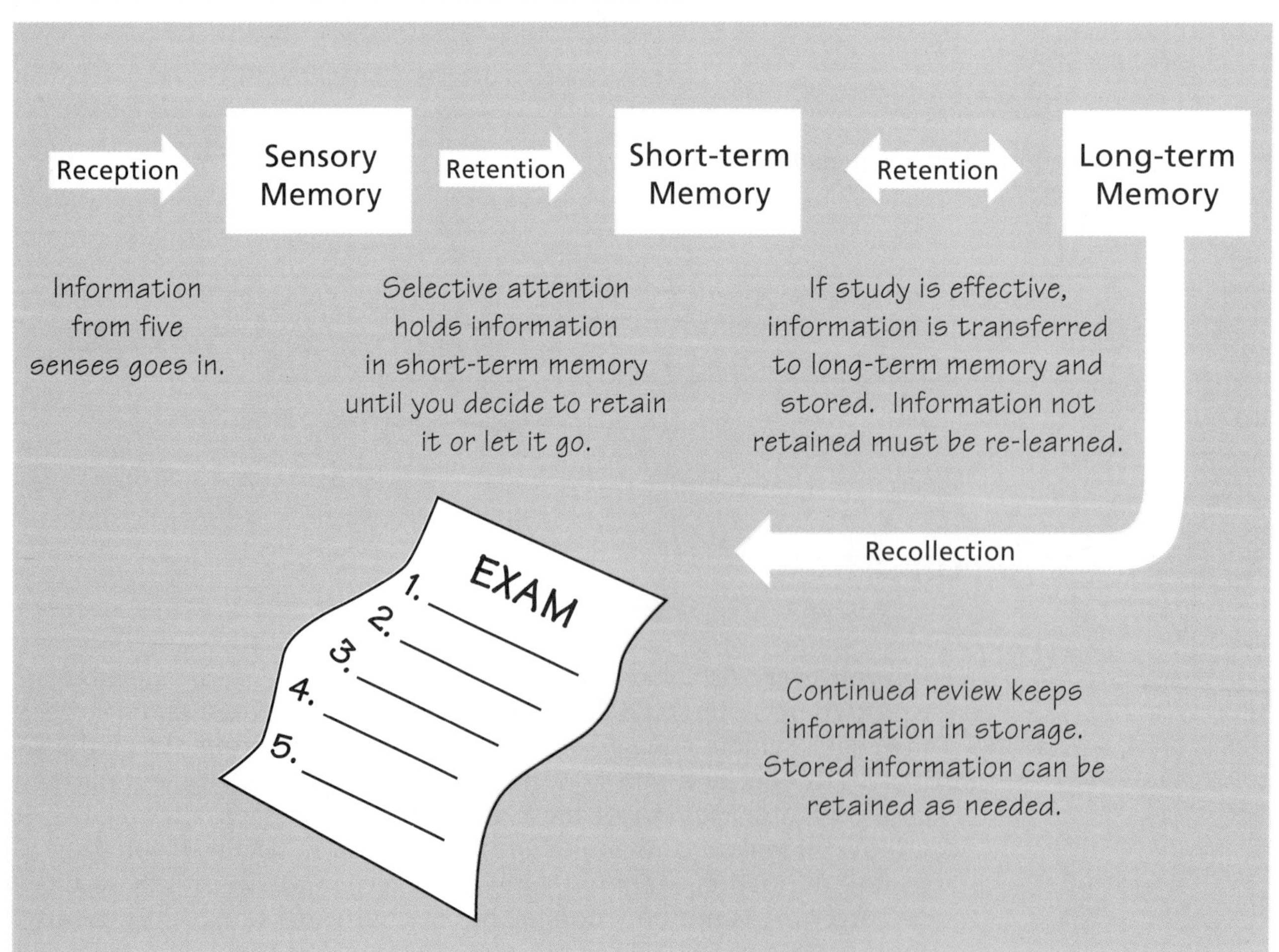

You've felt this process at work whenever you've been so caught up in watching a television program that you didn't hear someone speak to you. Your mind screened out the interfering sound of the person's voice. Had you lost interest in the show, you would have found yourself suddenly aware of other things going on around you, and, your attention would have shifted to those things.

In class, when you are listening to a lecture, your task is to concentrate on the speaker's words and take notes on the important points. Although everything the speaker says registers on your sensory memory, you may have to work at maintaining concentration and ignoring external stimuli, such as a conversation between two students who are sitting near you.

Everything registers on your sensory memory but only for a few seconds. By concentrating on a certain idea, image, or piece of information, you transfer it to your short-term memory, where you can retain it for a while longer.

Short-Term Memory

You can hold information in your short-term memory for a little under a minute. For example, you meet someone at a party. He tells you his name, and you strike up a conversation. A few minutes later, you see a friend you want to introduce to the person you just met, but you can't remember his name. Or you're in a phone booth, and you look up a telephone number. You close the directory and start to dial; you reach in your pocket for some change, and you realize that you've forgotten the number. Most people have had such experiences, but there is something you can do about them. You will remember names, phone numbers, and other bits of information longer if you recite them. Reciting activates your short-term memory by engaging another of your senses. Every time you look up a phone number, repeat it to yourself; you may be able to dial it from memory.

Research has shown that short-term memory has a limited capacity. You can hold only about five to nine numbers at a time in your short-term memory. Seven is average for most people. A phone number has seven digits. You might have difficulty remembering your nine-digit driver's license number or credit card number unless you make a point of transferring it into your long-term memory. You won't remember lectures or chapters you read either unless you review them enough to transfer them into long-term memory. Using a study system such as those described in Chapter 7 aids the transfer of information from short-term memory to long-term memory.

Long-Term Memory

Your long-term memory is more or less permanent and can hold a vast amount of information—everything from names, dates, facts, and images to learned skills and personal experiences. Stored information falls into three categories. *Verbal information* comes from books and other printed sources. Verbal information that is oral, such as music or a lecture, is transmitted through your auditory sense. To improve retention of verbal information, become an active reader and listener. *Visual information* includes everything you see—paintings and other artwork, photographs, dance, the world around you. To improve retention of visual information,

EXERCISE 10.2

How good is your short-term memory? Imagine you are at a party full of strangers By the end of the evening you have met many people and learned a great deal about them. How much can you remember? Study the facts about these people for three or four minutes. Then cover up the facts and try to answer the questions.

Name:	Matt	Claudia	Bill
Age	34	29	23
Eye color:	Brown	Blue	Brown
Favorite book:	*War and Peace*	*The Wind in the Willows*	*Great Fly-Fishing Tales*
Favorite place:	Disney World	The Grand Canyon	The Wind River
Favorite film:	*The Quiet Man*	*Casablanca*	*The Wizard of Oz*
Favorite activity:	Traveling	Hiking	Fishing
Favorite color:	Purple	Red	Sky Blue

1. Whose favorite activity is hiking? ______
2. How old is Matt? ______
3. Who has blue eyes? ______
4. Who loves to travel? ______
5. Who would love to hike in the Grand Canyon? ______
6. Who is the youngest? ______

Now uncover the facts and check your answers. How accurate was your short-term memory? If you got fewer than three answers right, you probably did not use a memory aid such as recitation or grouping of similar items. For example, did you notice that Claudia's favorite activity, hiking, could be done at her favorite place, the Grand Canyon? Bill's favorite book, place, and activity are all related, too.

become more observant, attentive, and involved in what you are learning. *Physical and motor information* includes things you learn by doing: writing, drawing, participating in sports, and operating machines, for example. To improve retention of physical and motor information, you must practice new skills or activities until they become automatic.

Do you see a relationship between the categories of stored information and learning style? Which kind of information is easiest for you to remember? Which is the hardest? For example, some visual learners may find it easier to remember visual information than physical or motor information. Imagine a person who is learning to drive a vehicle with a standard transmission. Whereas a strongly tactile/kinesthetic learner would be able to feel or sense where the gears are, a strongly visual learner would do better with a diagram that illustrates the positions of the gears. You can see in this example that the diagram enables the visual learner to adapt to a physical learning task. Similarly, you must find effective ways to learn any kind of information no matter what your learning style.

In conclusion, getting and keeping information in your long-term memory requires conscious activity, a desire to remember, and practice. Actions such as using study systems, reciting and reviewing, and making study guides all aid retention.

Try Awareness Check 16 to see more examples of the information stored in your long-term memory.

AWARENESS CHECK #16

What's in Your Long-Term Memory?

Write your answers on the lines provided.

1. Write your zip code here. ______
2. Describe the contents of your medicine cabinet. ______
3. Describe how to start a dishwasher. ______
4. Multiply 5 times 9. ______
5. Write the capital of your home state. ______
6. Think of someone you know well. What color is this person's hair? ______
7. Describe in detail a piece of furniture in your home or in your room. ______
8. Describe how to pedal a ten-speed up a steep hill. ______
9. Write the names of any three United States presidents. ______
10. How many ounces are in a pound? ______

Items 1, 4, 5, 9, and 10 call for verbal information. Items 2, 6, and 7 call for visual information. Items 3 and 8 call for physical or motor information.

INCREASE YOUR MEMORY POWER

The strategies that follow have worked for many students. Perhaps you already use some of them, or maybe you'll discover a new technique to try.

- **Decide to remember.** Resist passivity. Become an active learner by making a conscious, deliberate decision to remember. Follow through on this decision. This is the most important step you can take. Unless you *decide* to remember, none of the other techniques will work.
- **Try relaxed review.** Don't wait until the last minute before a test to do your reviewing. Review regularly, and do it in a relaxed way. When you are tense, you cannot concentrate. Try the chair-seat relaxation technique described below and shown in Figure 10.3.

1. **Start off in a positive frame of mind. Believe that you can and will remember.**
2. **Sit in a straight-backed chair with your feet together, flat on the floor.**
3. **Close your eyes; grasp the chair seat with both hands.**
4. **Pull up on the chair seat as hard as you can.**
5. **While you are pulling up with your hands, press your feet firmly to the floor.**
6. **Hold that position and count slowly to ten. Feel how tense all the muscles of your body are becoming.**
7. **Now relax completely. Settle down into the chair and feel how calm you've become.**
8. **With your eyes still closed, visualize yourself being successful. Experience how success feels.**
9. **Slowly open your eyes and, in this calm state, begin to review your study material.**
10. **If you feel yourself becoming tense again, repeat steps 1–9.**

This relaxation technique is a variation of anxiety-reduction techniques used by professionals in fields such as psychology, medicine, education, and sports.

- **Combine review with a physical activity.** Each sense that you use while reviewing provides another pathway for information to reach your brain. Recite, either silently or aloud, while riding a bicycle, while doing aerobics or calisthenics (floor exercises like sit-ups and jumping jacks), and while walking and running. Feel good about yourself for keeping fit *and* for exercising your mind.
- **Use mnemonics.** Mnemonics are tricks, games, or rhymes that help you remember things. You learned some as a child—for example, "In 1492, Columbus sailed the ocean blue." Also, you may have learned the rhyme that begins "Thirty days hath September"; it helps you

FIGURE 10.3 **The Chair-Seat Relaxation Method**

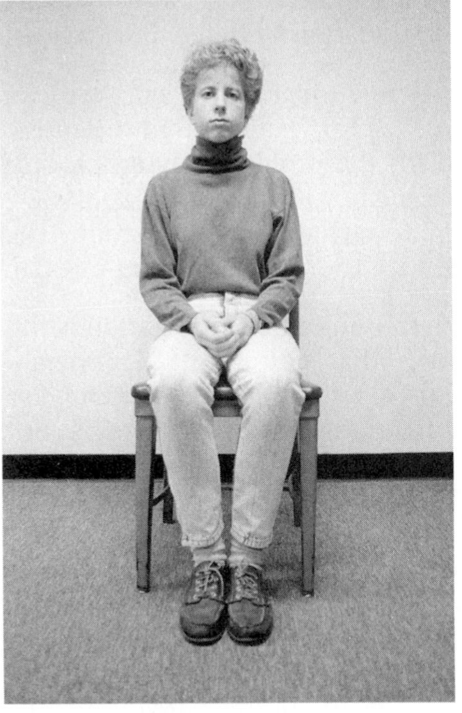

Steps 1 and 2

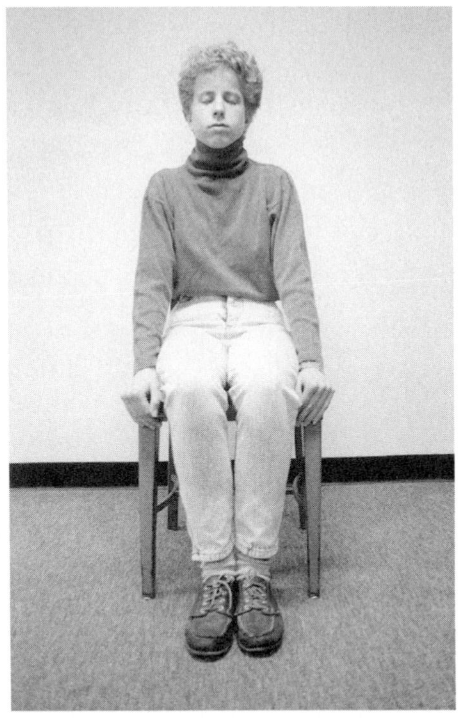

Steps 3 and 4

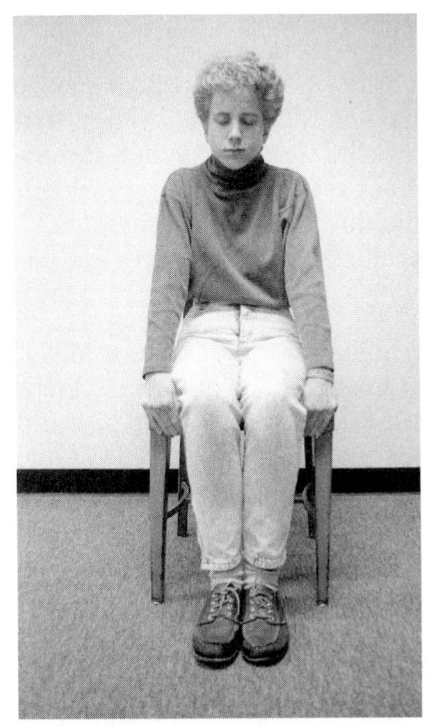

Steps 5 and 6

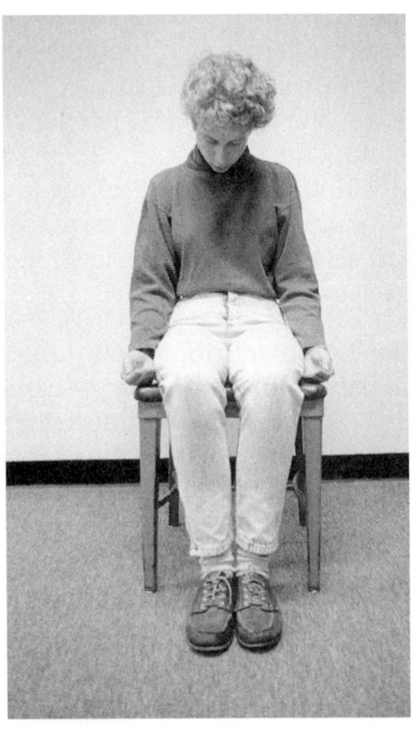

Steps 7 and 8

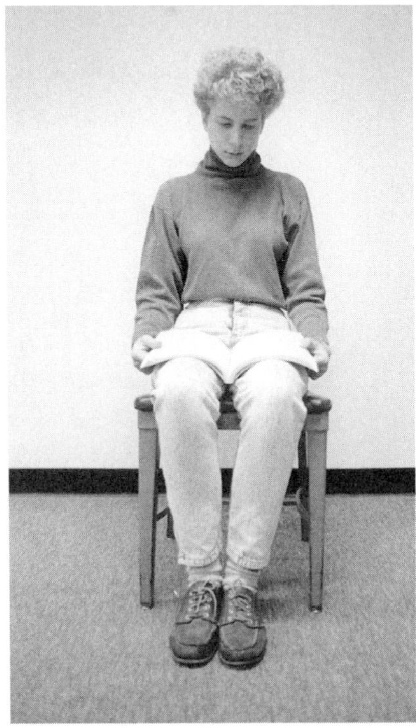

Step 9

© Jeffrey Holland

remember the number of days in each month. Here is one that you probably haven't heard: "Tyranny nixed in '76." This rhyme recalls the year the Declaration of Independence was signed.

- **Use acronyms.** An *acronym* is a word formed by the first letters of other words. For example, in Chapter 2 you learned COPE, an acronym for the problem-solving process explained in that chapter. Test your memory now. What does COPE stand for? Turn back to Chapter 2 to review this information. Then test your memory again, this time with the GRAB acronym in Chapter 4.

- **Associate to remember.** Association is the process of connecting new information that you want to remember to something that you already know. An association is often personal. For example, a student who wanted to remember the particles of the atom—proton, electron, and neutron—associated the names of the particles with the names of her brothers—Paul, Eric, and Norman. Her brothers' names and the particle names begin with the same letters, and they form the acronym PEN.

  To help yourself remember the three stages of memory, you could associate the mind with a computer, and memory's three stages (reception, retention, and recollection) with three computer processes (input, storage, and output). If your instructor asks you to describe the three stages of memory, think of how a computer works and you will be able to recall the three stages.

- **Visualize.** Form an image, or picture, in your mind of something that you want to remember. Visualization is an especially good way to link names with places or parts with locations. In geography, visualize places on a map. In physical science, draw an idealized continent that could stand for any continent, and fill in climate zones. When reviewing this information or recalling it during a test, picture the continent and visualize the zones. In anatomy, label the bones on a drawing of a human skeleton. When reviewing or recalling, close your eyes and see the skeleton with your labels.

- **Use an organizational technique.** Organize information in a meaningful pattern that shows how each item relates to the others. List steps in a process. Outline complex material. Make charts, diagrams, and information maps that show the relationship of parts to a whole or one part to another. Figure 10.4 is a comparison chart showing the memory functions and stages discussed in this chapter. The chart condenses the information into one page that you can use for quick reference. Read the chart across the rows *and* down the columns. As you can see, the stages and functions are related: Your sensory, short-term, and long-term memory process information throughout the three stages.

- **Sleep on it.** Reviewing before sleep helps you retain information. Because you are relaxed, concentration is focused. The information stays in your mind while you are sleeping, and interference from conflicting sounds, images, or ideas is minimal. When you wake, try to recall what you reviewed the night before. Chances are, you will remember.

FIGURE 10.4 Your Memory Box

STAGES AND FUNCTIONS OF MEMORY	RECEPTION: GETTING INFORMATION	RETENTION: STORING INFORMATION	RECOLLECTION: RECALLING INFORMATION
Sensory Memory	Registers perceptions	Quickly lost without selective attention	Automatic from second to second
Short-Term Memory	Focuses on facts and details	Quickly lost unless recited or reviewed	Possible for short time only until information is lost
Long-Term Memory	Forms general ideas, images, and meanings	Integrates information transferred from short-term memory for storage	Possible for long periods of time or a lifetime

- **Remember key words.** Sometimes you have to remember a series of connected ideas and explanations, such as the chair-seat relaxation technique described on pages 220–221. To recall items stated in phrases or sentences, select one or more key words in each item that sum up the phrase or sentence. Recalling key words will help you recall the whole item.

- **Memorize.** Some people have reservations about memorization. They say memorization is not learning because it is usually done out of context. Students may not be able to recall items memorized in a certain order if the instructor puts them in a different order on a test. Critics also say that memorization is an inefficient technique and that memorized items are difficult to recall. Yet memorization does work. What is 9 times 9? You probably know the answer.

  Memorization can be a useful technique for recalling certain kinds of information, especially if it is combined with another memory strategy and is not the only technique you know how to use. Of course, you cannot expect yourself to remember anything that you do not understand. First, make sure you comprehend any new information well enough to link it to knowledge you have already acquired. Memorization works best on information such as the spelling and definition of words, math and chemical formulas, poetry, and facts that belong in a certain order, such as historical events or life cycles and food chains.

  To use memorization effectively for recalling the life cycle of a parasitic organism, for example, try this: Combine memorization with the use of key words to remind you of each stage in the cycle. Learn the stages in order, but also be able to recall *any* stage in the cycle and what stages come before and after it. Figure 10.5 shows the stages in the life cycle of a malaria-causing parasite and key words you could use to recall them.

FIGURE 10.5 Life Cycle of *Plasmodium Vivax*

STAGES IN THE LIFE CYCLE	KEY WORDS
1. Female Anopheles mosquito bites someone who has malaria.	Mosquito, bites
2. Mosquito sucks up gametes of the parasite with the victim's blood.	Gametes
3. Gametes form a zygote in the mosquito's digestive tract.	Zygote
4. Oocysts develop from the zygote.	Oocysts
5. Oocysts divide into spindle-shaped cells called *sporozoites,* which migrate to the mosquito's salivary glands.	Sporozoites, salivary glands
6. Mosquito bites a new person and infects him or her with the sporozoites.	Mosquito, infects
7. Sporozoites enter person's liver cells and divide.	Sporozoites, liver
8. Merozoites, formed from the sporozoites, enter red blood cells and divide.	Merozoites, blood cells
9. Merozoites break out of blood cells about every 48 hours and produce fever	Merozoites, fever
10. Parasites produce gametes through asexual reproduction, and cycle begins again if the parasites are ingested by a mosquito.	Parasites

EXERCISE 10.3

This exercise asks you to work with group members to practice selecting appropriate memory strategies. Remember to follow the guidelines for group discussion explained in Chapter 1, page 12. Your tasks are as follows: From the list below, choose a learning activity that you think may be difficult for some students. Then review the memory strategies explained in this chapter. Using the questions as a guide, discuss which strategy would best help students complete the activity. Then record the group's answers to the questions and the group's evaluation.

- Reading a chapter from a biology textbook
- Listening to a lecture
- Taking notes from a lecture
- Learning the bones of the human body
- Remembering how to do a math problem
- Matching the names of artists with examples of their work

1. Which learning activity did your group choose, and why do you think it may be difficult for some students? ______________________________

____

2. Does the activity require students to process verbal, visual, or physical motor information?

____

____

3. Which memory strategy would improve students' *reception* of the information? How?

____

____

4. Which memory strategy would improve students' *retention* of the information? How?

____

____

5. Which memory strategy would improve students' *recollection* of the information? How?

____

____

Group Evaluation:

What have you learned about memory strategies? Which ones do you currently use, and which ones will you try? Did your group complete its tasks successfully? What improvements can you make? What additional questions do you have about memory, and how will you find the answers to your questions?

____

____

____

____

____

CONFIDENCE BUILDER

Do Something Weird to Jog Your Memory

Your best memory tricks are those you invent. Here are some suggestions to build on.

An old-fashioned memory trick is to tie a string around your finger to remind you of something important you don't want to forget. Although some people still use this trick, two present-day variations are a rubber band around the wrist and a paper clip on the cuff of a blouse or shirt sleeve. These tricks work because they call attention to something you've placed on your body or clothing that doesn't belong there. Seeing the string, clip, or rubber band reminds you of why you put it there. In the same way, doing almost anything that is a little weird can help you remember. Try out these three ideas; then adapt them to suit your personal style.

The Car Key Technique Do you forget to take your umbrella or books to class? As you're walking out the door do you forget to pick up a stack of letters you need to mail? Try putting your car keys on or beside anything you want to take with you. Since you can't drive anywhere without your car keys, you will also be reminded of the books, letters, or other things you need to take along.

The Fence-Post System If your learning style is visual, this memory technique may appeal to you. Imagine that you have several items you need to remember. They might be things you want to take on a trip, a few purchases you need to make at the supermarket, or some materials you need to take to class tomorrow. First, visualize a row of fence posts. Then picture each item on a different fence post. Fix in your mind the order of the items. When this image is clear, picture again the empty fence posts. Then try to make each item appear, one at a time, on its appropriate post. Repeat these steps as many times as needed to recall all the items.

The Odd Object Method One student puts a large, empty cardboard box in front of the door when he wants to remember to make a phone call or do something important. Each time he starts toward the door he wonders why the box is there; then he remembers what he has to do. Another student has a pewter dinosaur she received as a birthday gift that she places beside her purse to remind her of something she needs to do. When she starts to pick up her purse, she sees the dinosaur and remembers. Any odd object placed somewhere you don't expect it can serve as a memory cue.

EXERCISE 10.4

Sometime soon you will face midterm or final exams. Understanding your personal learning style and using the appropriate memory strategies suggested in this chapter will help you prepare effectively. Answer the following questions about strategies you plan to try.

1. Underline your preferred learning style: visual, auditory, tactile. How have you determined that this is your preferred learning style?

   ____

   ____

2. List three memory strategies from this chapter that seem best suited to your learning style. Write one sentence about each strategy to explain why you believe it is appropriate for you.

   a. ______________________________

   ____

   b. ______________________________

   ____

   c. ______________________________

   ____

3. List two memory strategies that do not fit your learning style but that you are willing to try. Write a sentence about each to explain why you would like to try it.

   a. ______________________________

   ____

   b. ______________________________

   ____

4. What relationship do you see between the type of information to be learned (verbal, visual, or physical motor) and your learning style preference (visual, auditory, or tactile/kinesthetic)?

   ____

   ____

   ____

   ____

   ____

CRITICAL THINKING APPLICATION

Using the guidelines for group discussion explained in Chapter 1, form a small group. Or you may prefer to do the application on your own. Reread and discuss Otis's dilemma explained on pages 213–214. Otis decided to withdraw from his trig class so he could concentrate on raising his grade in statistics. Some might think this was not such a good idea. They might feel that Otis had wasted his time and money. Also, if statistics is required for his program, he will have to take the course again, which will cost more money. Do you think these are valid criticisms? Why or why not? Suppose withdrawing from the course is not an option. What else could Otis do to solve his problem? Talk it over; then write down your suggestions to share with the rest of the class.

SUMMARY

The summary is followed by a partially filled-in information map. Read the summary; then complete the map.

The three R's of memory are *reception, retention,* and *recollection.* In every waking moment, you are receiving information about the world around you through your five senses. This information is stored, or retained, for varying lengths of time so that you can recall it as needed. All the information you receive from the environment stays briefly in your *sensory memory.* Through *selective attention,* important information is separated from the insignificant and is stored in *short-term memory.* Short-term memory, like sensory memory, is brief, enabling you, for example, to hold a phone number in your mind long enough to dial it. If you are reading a textbook passage or listening to a lecture, the information that you receive from these sources must be stored in *long-term memory* and reviewed frequently if you want to retain it. *Verbal, visual,* and *physical* or *motor memories* are stored in *long-term memory.* Some things you have learned, such as how to drive a car, stay with you all your life. Memories that become permanent have been *internalized* and are part of you.

Forgetting occurs because of the brevity of sensory and short-term memory. To combat forgetting, you must transfer information from short-term to long-term memory. Transference is a process you influence by employing various aids to strengthen your memory, the most important of which is *decide to remember.* Information is more likely to stay in long-term memory if you relate it to your existing knowledge.

As you try the memory suggestions in this chapter and in other sources, keep in mind that they may or may not work for you. In the end, your best memory strategy will be one that corresponds to your learning style. If your preferred style is visual, try visualization. If you prefer an auditory learning mode, recite. If you think of yourself as a tactile or physical person, combine reviewing with a physical activity. Also, experiment with varying your style. Though you may *prefer* one mode of learning, it is not the *only* mode you can learn to use.

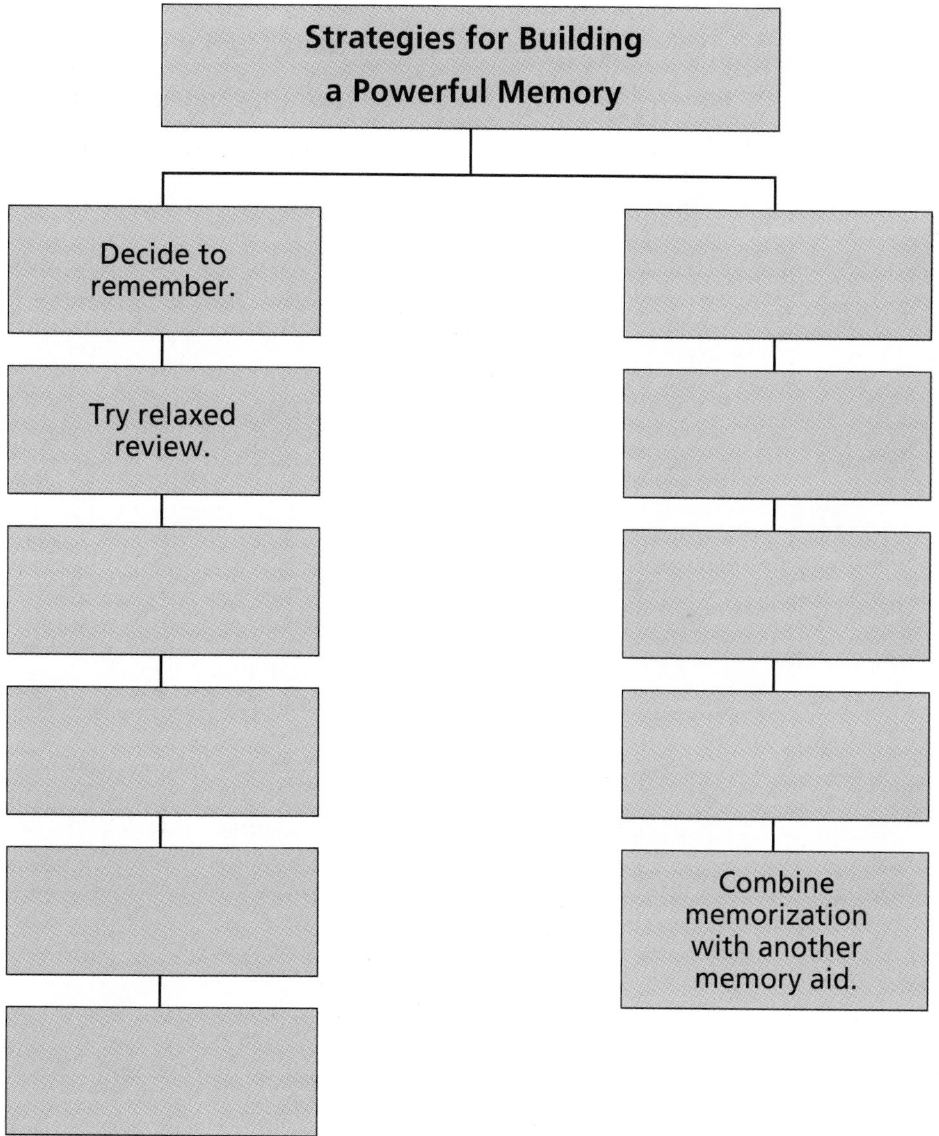

YOUR REFLECTIONS

Reflect on what you have learned about information processing and memory and how you can best apply that information. Use the following list of questions to stimulate your thinking; then write your reflections. Your response may include answers to one or more of the questions. Incorporate in your writing specific information from this chapter or previous chapters as needed.

- How are concentration and memory linked?
- What are some learning strategies that have worked for you?
- Is memory automatic, or can you control it? How?
- What kinds of information are easy for you to learn? What kinds give you difficulty?
- How will you use what you have learned from this chapter to improve the way you process information?

Date ______________________________

CHAPTER 11

Preparing for Tests

If you ask college students what their most persistent academic worry is, many will say "Grades." Like most college students, you may be looking for ways to improve your grades and may even wish there were a secret formula or short cut to success. Although there are no short cuts, there *is* a key to good grades, and it's no secret: preparation.

Time management, planning, and the use of appropriate study skills are your keys to preparing for tests. Individual responsibility and self-management keep you motivated and on task. Being responsible means accepting that grades are the direct result of your effort. Being a good self-manager means having the self-discipline to put study first.

As you can see, preparing for tests requires the interaction of several skills and personal qualities that not only lead to good grades but have an added benefit. Planning, managing your time, being responsible, and choosing appropriate strategies are marketable workplace competencies you can carry into the future.

Do you need to improve the way you prepare for tests? Find out by taking Awareness Check 17. The strategies explained in this chapter can help you prepare for tests with confidence:

- Decide what, when, and how to study.
- Have a test-taking routine and use it consistently.
- Know how to prepare for any kind of test.

AWARENESS CHECK #17

How Do You Study for Tests?

Yes No

Answer *yes* or *no* to the following questions.

1. Do you allow sufficient time to prepare for tests?
2. Do you usually know what to study?
3. Do you use a study method such as SQ3R?
4. Are you satisfied with the grades you make on tests?
5. Do you know what kinds of errors you make?
6. Do you often become distracted during tests?
7. Do you enter a testing situation feeling mentally and physically prepared?
8. Do you have a test-taking routine that you follow?
9. Do you know how to take multiple-choice, true-false, and fill-in-the-blank tests?
10. Do you know how to plan and write an essay for an exam?

If you answered *no* to any of these questions, you will benefit from this chapter, which shows you how to prepare for tests and what to do in a testing situation to improve your performance.

HOW TO PREPARE FOR TESTS: THREE STEPS

If you walk into a test knowing that you are well prepared, you will feel confident that you can succeed. If you do not prepare sufficiently, you will probably feel a lack of confidence, maybe even some anxiety that you will not make a good grade. To ensure that you will be prepared for every test, follow these three essential steps:

1. Make a study schedule.
2. Decide what to study.
3. Use your study system.

These steps are the answers to three common questions students ask about studying for tests: When should I study? What should I study? How should I study?

Relaxing and talking with others for a few moments is a good way to break from an exam review.

© Lee Snider/The Image Works

Make a Study Schedule

The purpose of making a study schedule is to establish fixed times for review so that review becomes a habit. You should allow time in your schedule for daily, weekly, and exam reviews.

Daily Reviews. Take five to ten minutes per day to review each course. Begin by reviewing your notes and assignments for the previous class. Immediately or as soon as possible after class, review new material and try to relate it to what you have learned in the course so far. In doing this, you will make connections among topics and gain a broad perspective on the course.

Weekly Reviews. In addition to the time you spend doing assignments, spend about an hour a week reviewing each subject. Review lecture notes, textbook notes, and your study guides, and try to anticipate test questions. A weekly review is an in-depth look at what you have covered in a course during one week. Relate the week's work to the previous week's work, and determine how the new material fits into the course.

Exam Reviews. About one week before a test, conduct a major review. Exam reviews will take longer than weekly reviews because they may cover several weeks' material. To prepare for exams, review lecture notes, textbook notes, study guides, note cards, instructors' handouts, and previous tests, papers, or graded assignments. Your daily and weekly reviews will make the material seem familiar so that you may see a pattern in the topics you are studying and may think of possible test questions.

Your study schedule should allow five to ten minutes a day per course for daily reviews, an hour per course for weekly reviews, and two hours or more for a specific exam review. Enter times for review on your schedule, and make a commitment to follow it.

Exam reviews are the hardest because they take the longest and cover the most material. Try these tips for improving concentration when you have to study for two or more hours:

- Review at the time of day when you are most alert.
- Study for your hardest exam first.
- About once every hour, take a break. Get up and walk around; do something unrelated to studying.
- Reward yourself for getting the job done. Plan to go out with friends or do something fun when you have finished your review.

Decide What to Study

Test questions can come from a variety of sources. When you study for a major test, you should review lecture notes, textbook chapters, textbook notes and study guides, previous tests, papers, homework, and instructors' handouts. Don't waste time reviewing information you already know; study material you have not fully grasped. Study the most difficult material first. If you study the easiest topics first, then by the time you get to the hard ones, you will probably be tired and unable to give them your best effort. Study the most complex or technical concepts when you are most alert; be willing to look up definitions and re-read sentences until you grasp their meaning. Later, when you are tired, take a short break and then study less challenging material. Your understanding of the subject will lead to improved confidence and productivity.

Lecture Notes. Lectures often supplement information presented in textbooks. They are usually organized around a major topic in the course outline. If your instructor gives weekly lectures, the lecture topics probably build upon weekly assigned chapters and the week's topic listed in your syllabus.

Textbook Chapters. Review your underlining and marginal notes. If you have underlined or annotated important material, your review will cover essential information.

Textbook Notes and Study Guides. Review any additional notes, maps, outlines, note cards, or other study materials you have made. Since your own notes and guides are summaries of textbook material written in your own words, they are easiest for you to remember.

Previous Tests, Papers, Homework, and Other Assignments for Which You Received Grades. Your previous tests are useful for two reasons. First, you can determine from these tests the kinds of questions your instructor asks. Second, you can learn from your mistakes. Questions that you missed enable you to spot weak points in your studying—information that you

EXERCISE 11.1

Make out a new week's schedule. Include time for daily reviews and for one weekly review. After you have completed this schedule, update your semester or quarter calendar. Schedule times for major exam reviews one week before each test date.

	Sunday	Monday	Tuesday	Wednesday	Thursday	Friday	Saturday
6:00 – 7:00							
7:00 – 8:00							
8:00 – 9:00							
9:00 – 10:00							
10:00 – 11:00							
11:00 – 12:00							
12:00 – 1:00							
1:00 – 2:00							
2:00 – 3:00							
3:00 – 4:00							
4:00 – 5:00							
5:00 – 6:00							
6:00 – 7:00							
7:00 – 8:00							
8:00 – 9:00							
9:00 – 10:00							
10:00 – 11:00							
11:00 – 12:00							
12:00 – 1:00							

Outdoor exercise is a great reward for completing your review. It can help to relieve pre-exam stress and ensure a good night's rest as well.

© Bob Daemmrich

forgot, ignored, or didn't understand. Instructors' comments on papers and other graded assignments may also point out strengths and weaknesses and provide clues about what you should study.

Instructors' Handouts. Anything your instructor hands out is bound to be important. Instructors frequently summarize information on handouts. Don't overlook these important study aids when you review for a major test.

You may benefit from studying with another student. Comparing your notes with someone else's can help both of you. What one of you misses the other may have in his or her notes. Also, students vary in their understanding of lectures and textbook chapters. A topic that gave you trouble may have been easy for a friend. Talking it over gives you another perspective on the subject.

Use Your Study System

Once you have decided *what* to study, *how* you study will determine the effectiveness of your review. Don't study in a hit-or-miss fashion, and don't re-read chapters. Instead, use a system. By now you may have tried the suggestions in Chapter 7 for using SQ3R or PREP or for adapting a system to your own learning style. If your system is working, use it. If you would like to try a different strategy, follow these steps to prepare for a major test in one of your courses:

1. One week before the test, schedule two or more hours of time to review all chapters and topics that the test will cover. Do not attempt to study for two hours straight without taking a break because you will lose interest and concentration. Instead, plan your study time to review specific material in several short sessions, taking a break in between.
2. Organize your materials. Sort lecture notes, textbook notes, study guides, handouts, and previously graded tests and assignments by chapter or topic; then make a list of the important topics, kinds of problems, or other specific information you think will be on a test.
3. If you must review a lot of facts, terms, formulas, steps in a process, or similar material, put the information on 3″ x 5″ note cards to carry in your pocket or purse. Recite from these cards, silently or aloud, at every opportunity. Look at the sample note cards in Figure 11.1 below for examples of the kind of information to include and how much to write. Keep your cards simple; write just enough to serve as a memory cue.

FIGURE 11.1 Note Cards for Review

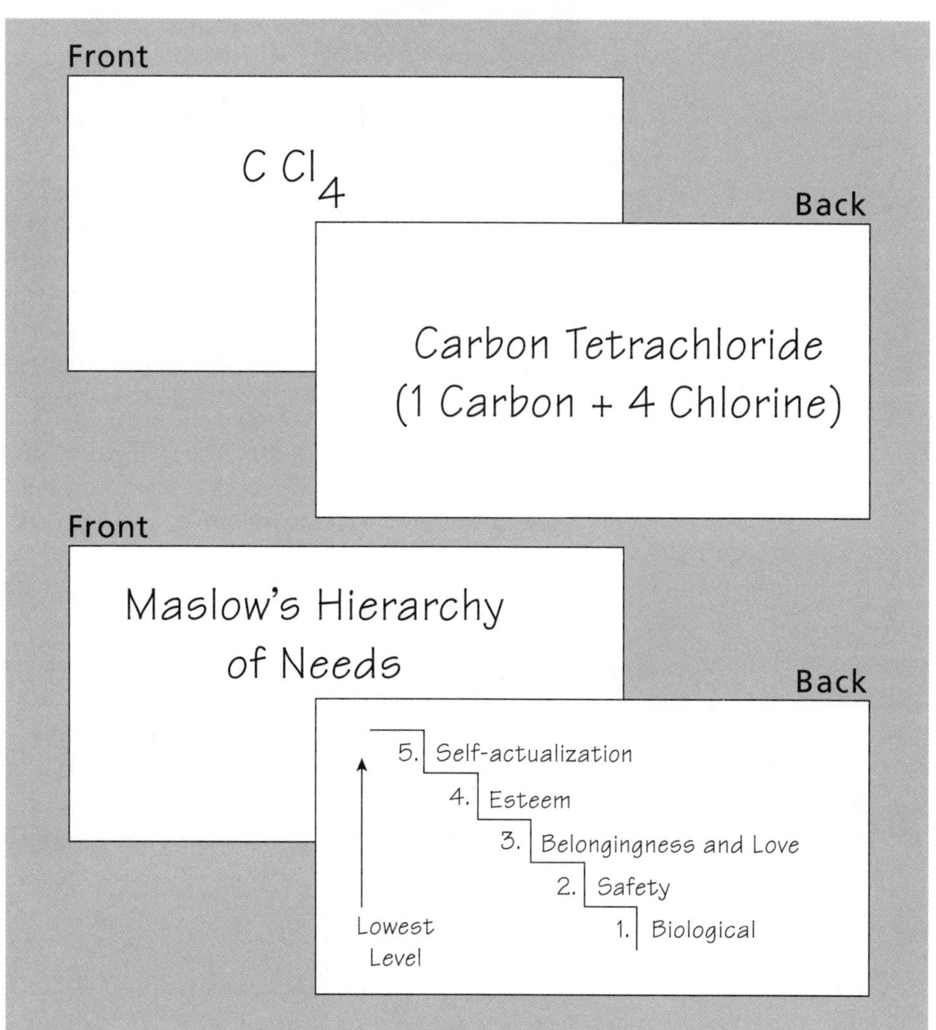

FIGURE 11.2 A Concept Map for Review

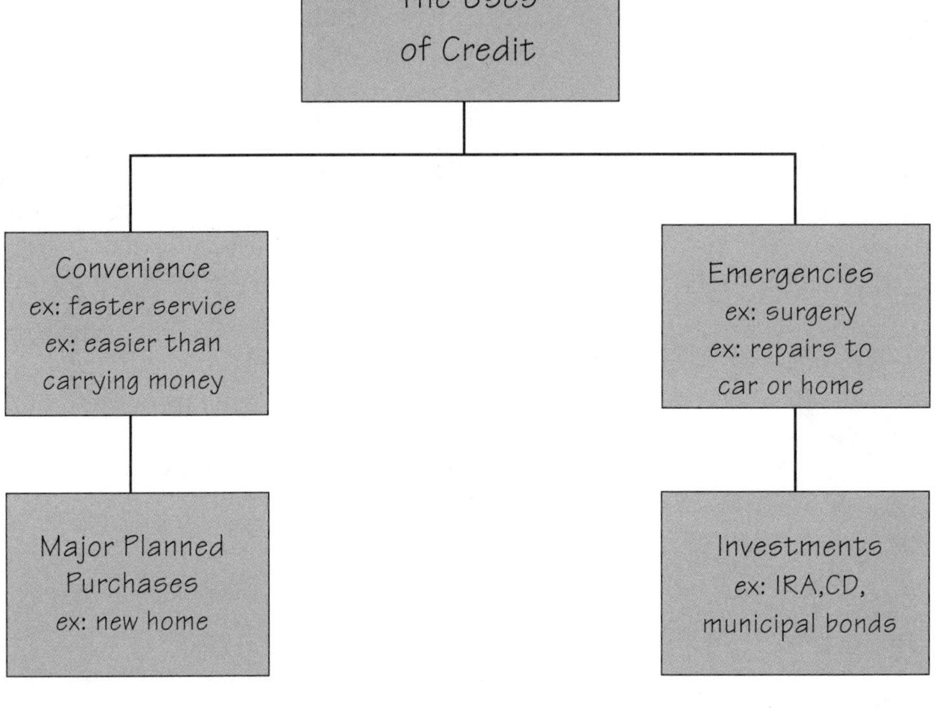

4. Map or diagram any information that you think will be difficult to remember. Maps, as explained in Chapter 8, are visual representations of relationships among ideas. Maps are convenient; they summarize a lot of information in a little space. When studying for a test, try to redraw your maps from memory. When taking a test, close your eyes and visualize your maps. Reconstruct them in your mind and try to "see" what you have written in each square or circle. See Figure 11.2 above for an example of a concept map to be used as a study guide.

5. Once a day until you take the test, review your maps and other materials. Review them again the night before the test, just before you go to sleep. Research shows that studying before sleeping improves retention. Review once more the day of the test.

EXERCISE 11.2

Discover your own best way to prepare for a test by answering the following questions about test preparation and your learning style. As you are working through the questions, see Chapter 1 to review the components of learning style as needed.

1. Based on your answers to Awareness Check 17, what are your strengths and weaknesses in preparing for tests?

____

____

____

2. What relationship do you see between your body's reactions and the way you prepare for tests? For example, when is your best time to study, and how do you accommodate your body's reactions when preparing for tests.

____

____

____

3. What is your preferred learning style (visual, auditory, tactile/kinesthetic), and how does it affect the way you prepare for tests.

____

____

____

4. Is your locus of control internal or external, and how does it affect your motivation to study for tests?

____

____

____

5. What changes can you make in the way you prepare for tests that will help you take advantage of your learning style preference?

____

____

____

DEVELOP A TEST-TAKING ROUTINE

You can improve your scores on tests by developing a routine to follow that helps you stay calm, avoid distractions, and demonstrate your knowledge. Your test-taking routine should include most or all of the following steps.

Arrive on Time

If hearing other students discuss the test makes you nervous and distracted, don't arrive early. Arrive on time, and try to sit near the front of the room, where you are less likely to be distracted. If you feel a little nervous, close your eyes, take a few deep breaths, and think positive thoughts. If anxiety either before or during tests is a problem for you, see Chapter 12 for an explanation of how to reduce test anxiety.

Jot Down Memory Cues

If there are facts, formulas, dates, names, terms, or other items that you might forget, write them in the margin or on the back of the test as soon as you get it. For example, math students tend to get nervous when they are working on a difficult problem or can't remember the next step in a process. This anxiety can cause them to forget other concepts and applications. The facts, formulas, and other items that you jot down on your test are memory cues. Knowing that the cues are there will boost your confidence. You won't be worried that you will forget the information, and you can concentrate on taking the test.

Survey the Test

As soon as you receive your test and after you have jotted down your memory cues, survey the test to determine how many questions there are, how many points each is worth, and what kinds of questions you must answer: true-false, multiple-choice, fill-in, or essay. If it's not clear from the test how many points each question is worth, ask your instructor. A quick survey of the test will let you know what you must accomplish within the time limit so that you can plan your test-taking time.

Plan and Use All Your Time

Plan to spend the most time answering the questions that are worth the most points. If there are twenty-five multiple-choice questions worth one point each and two essay questions worth twenty-five points each and you have 50 minutes to complete the test, answer as many of the multiple-choice questions as you can in 10 minutes. That will leave you 40 minutes to complete the two essay questions. Spend 15 minutes answering the first question; then stop and go on to the next one even if you have not finished. Spend 15 minutes on the second question. You will now have 10 minutes left. Use the 10 minutes as needed. You can return to the multiple-choice questions if the essays are done, or you can work more on your essays if you finished the multiple-choice questions earlier. Try to save a few minutes to proofread the whole test and answer any multiple-choice questions that you may have skipped.

Although there are many ways to plan your time, the one suggested here will help you gain some points for each part of the test even if you are unable to finish all of the questions. If you plan your time and stick to your plan, you will not have to rush. Use all of your time, even if you don't need it. The extra care you take may help you spot mistakes or think of a better way to state an answer.

Read Directions

It may seem obvious that you should read test directions before beginning, but a surprising number of students do not do so. Perhaps they think that it wastes time or that they already know what to do. To avoid needless mistakes, always read directions and ask the instructor to explain anything that you do not understand.

Do Easy Questions First

When you survey the test, you will probably spot questions that will be easy for you to answer. Do those first, since you have a good chance of getting the answers right. In addition, doing the easy questions first will raise your confidence in your ability to answer the rest of the questions.

Skip and Return to Difficult Questions

Don't spend too much time on a difficult question. Skip it and return to it later. If something you read or recall as you answer the other questions triggers your memory, you can go back to the one you didn't answer and then resume the test where you left off.

Guess (If There Is No Penalty)

If there is a penalty for wrong answers, the test directions will probably say so. If you are in doubt, ask the instructor. If there is no penalty, guess. Don't leave questions blank; even if you don't think you know the answer, write something anyway. You may pick up a few points. If you guess the answer to a multiple-choice question that has four choices, chances are one out of four that you will get the right answer. If you don't answer, your chances are zero.

Control Your Feelings and Attention

Remain in control of your feelings and attention throughout the test. To avoid becoming distracted, focus your attention on the test. Keep your eyes on the test and don't look up or around. If you don't know what other students are doing, you're not likely to be disturbed by them. You won't notice what page someone else is on or whether someone finishes early.

Maintain a positive attitude. If you feel negative thoughts creeping in, don't let them undermine your work. Counteract them with positive ones. Say to yourself, "I have studied and I am doing fine." If you become anxious, close your eyes, breathe deeply, and relax. When you feel calm, return to the test and give it your full attention. See Chapter 12 for more suggestions on how to reduce test anxiety.

Check Your Work

Always save time to proofread your test for careless errors and for questions you skipped or forgot to answer. Change answers only if you're absolutely sure your first answer was wrong. First choices are usually correct, so if you have doubts about one of your answers, don't change it.

Learn from Your Mistakes

The next time your instructor returns a graded test, determine what kinds of mistakes you made. Look for a pattern. If you are like many students, you make the same mistakes over and over again. If you can prevent these errors, you will improve your test scores.

MASTER OBJECTIVE TESTS

If you are well prepared for a test, you should be able to answer the questions whether they are true-false, multiple-choice, fill-in-the-blank, or essay. But when confronted with questions you cannot answer, try to gain points by making informed guesses.

True-False Tests

Since there are only two possible answers to a true-false question, you have a 50 percent chance of choosing the right answer if you guess. Use these strategies for guessing the answer to a true-false question when you are sure that you don't know the answer:

1. **Mark a statement true unless you know it is false because true-false tests often contain more true answers than false ones.**
2. **Assume a statement is false if it contains absolute words.**
3. **Assume a statement is false if any part of it is false.**

Mark a statement false if it contains absolute words such as *always, never, invariably, none, no one, all,* and *everyone.* Absolute words tend to make statements false because they do not allow for exceptions. For example, you should mark the statement "It never gets cold in Florida" false because the word *never* means "never in the history of the world." It is highly unlikely that there is a place on Earth where it has never gotten cold even once. Is this statement true or false? "A statement that contains an absolute word is always false." The statement is false. Remember, absolute words *usually* make statements false, but not always.

Mark a statement false if any part of it is false. If part of a statement is untrue, then the whole statement is untrue. For example, the statement "*Hamlet, Macbeth* and *The Dream Merchant* are three of Shakespeare's most famous tragedies" is false. Although Shakespeare did write *Hamlet* and *Macbeth,* he did not write *The Dream Merchant.* If you don't know whether a statement is true or false, but you're certain that part of it is untrue, mark it false.

EXERCISE 11.3

Use the guessing strategies you just learned to mark the statements *T* for true and *F* for false. Work with a partner, or complete the exercise on your own.

	T	F
1. The heart contains a left and right ventricle.	☐	☐
2. You can look up the meaning of a word in a glossary, index, or dictionary.	☐	☐
3. All fears are learned at an early age.	☐	☐

	T	F
4. Making note cards is the only way to study vocabulary.	☐	☐
5. Whenever there is a fatal accident on the highway, drinking is invariably involved.	☐	☐
6. It is doubtful whether there is human life on other planets.	☐	☐
7. College graduates will always be able to find good jobs.	☐	☐
8. Most violent crime today is drug-related.	☐	☐
9. Carl Jung has been called "the father of modern psychology."	☐	☐
10. The numbers 1, 3, 5, and 9 are prime numbers.	☐	☐

Multiple-Choice Tests

The part of a multiple-choice item that asks the question is called the *stem*. The answer choices are called *options*. The incorrect options are called *distractors* because they distract your attention away from the correct option. Usually there are four options, though there might be three or five. Your job is to identify the one correct option. You can do this in several ways:

- If you know the material, first answer the question in your mind, and then read all the options and choose the correct one.
- If you know the material but cannot answer the question in your mind, read the options, eliminate those you know are incorrect, and choose the answer from those remaining. The more options you eliminate, the more likely your choice will be correct.
- If you do not know the material, or if you cannot figure out the answer, guess.

Options that contain the phrases "all of the above" or "none of the above" are frequently the correct choices. If two options are similar—for example, "Northern Hemisphere" and "Southern Hemisphere"—one of the options is probably the correct answer. Finally, if one option is more complete or contains more information than the others, it may be the correct one.

An option that contains an absolute word such as *all, always,* or *never* is probably a distractor, an incorrect answer. An option that contains an unfamiliar word may also be a distractor. Many students assume that an unfamiliar term is probably the correct answer, but it is more often a wrong answer. When you are guessing, you are more likely to choose the right answer if you choose an option that is familiar to you. Finally, if the list of options is a list of numbers, middle numbers tend to be correct answers, and the highest and lowest numbers in the list tend to be distractors. These strategies are not foolproof, but they are useful as a last resort if you must guess the answer to a question.

EXERCISE 11.4

This exercise asks you and the members of your group to practice the guessing strategies that are appropriate to use when you do not know the answer to a multiple-choice item. Remember to follow the guidelines for group discussion explained in Chapter 1, page 12. Your tasks are as follows: First, each person should answer questions 1–10. Next, discuss your answers and come to a consensus about the best answer choice for each question. Be able to explain why you think your answer is correct, and the strategy you used to arrive at it. Review the guessing strategies explained on page 243 as needed. Finally, summarize your answers and explanations on a separate sheet of paper to be handed in along with the group evaluation.

1. A marriage may have a better chance of succeeding if the wife and husband have which characteristic in common?
   a. a similar level of education
   b. similar social and economic backgrounds
   c. shared interests and goals
   d. all of the above
2. Most of the assignments college students are asked to do require them to use
   a. left-brain capacities.
   b. right-brain capacities.
   c. learning styles.
   d. visualization.
3. Which of the following are examples of fallacious reasoning?
   a. glittering generalities
   b. plain folks
   c. bandwagon
   d. glittering generalities, plain folks, and bandwagon
4. A balanced diet should include
   a. milk, cheese, and fruit.
   b. bread, cereal, and whole grains.
   c. milk, fruit, vegetables, meat, and whole grains.
   d. vegetables, fruit, and meat.
5. Most of the world's population is situated
   a. in the Pacific islands.
   b. in the Northern Hemisphere.
   c. in the Southern Hemisphere.
   d. near the equator.
6. Approximately what percentage of immigrants to the United States between 1971 and 1984 came from Asia?
   a. 60 percent
   b. 30 percent
   c. 40 percent
   d. 15 percent
7. Which of these words is a synonym for *intractable?*
   a. synergistic
   b. acerbic
   c. exacerbating
   d. stubborn
8. Television commercials
   a. always attempt to deceive viewers.
   b. are sometimes interesting to viewers.
   c. are never in the public interest.
   d. influence only people who listen to them.
9. The first quiz programs were televised
   a. in the 1970s.
   b. in the 1950s.
   c. in the 1940s.
   d. before 1920.
10. A smile
    a. may mean different things in different societies.
    b. always signifies happiness.
    c. occurs among the people of only some societies.
    d. never occurs involuntarily.

Group Evaluation:

What advantage do guessing strategies offer? What is the best way to avoid having to guess? Did your group complete its tasks successfully? What improvements can you suggest? What additional questions do you have about taking multiple-choice tests, and how will you find answers to your questions?

____

____

____

Fill-in-the-Blank Tests

A fill-in test may require you to recall an answer from memory or choose an answer from a list of options. Choosing an answer from a list is easier than recalling an answer from memory. In either case, the information given in the incomplete statement may provide clues that will help you decide what to write in the blanks. There are three strategies that can help you fill in the blanks correctly.

First, decide what kind of answer the statement requires. Read the statement carefully and decide whether you are supposed to supply a name, a date, a place, or some other kind of information. Knowing what the question asks will help you recall or select the right answer.

Second, the way a statement is expressed may help you decide how to complete it. Your answer should complete the statement logically and grammatically. For example, if you are asked to choose options from a list to fill in the blanks and the statement you are working on requires a verb to complete it, scan the list for verbs and choose among them.

Third, key words in statements may help you determine what topic the question covers. Knowing the topic will help you recall information needed to complete the statement. For example, if a question asks you to briefly describe Piaget's third stage of development, the key words *Piaget* and *third stage of development* let you know that the topic is Piaget's stages. If you can't recall the third stage, reconstructing the other stages in your mind may jog your memory.

EXERCISE 11.5

The following fill-in-the-blank test covers the preceding section, "Master Objective Tests." Review the section; then complete the test for practice without looking back at the book. When you have finished, look back to check your answers. Any questions that you missed indicate material you need to review.

1. Three common types of objective tests are __________, __________, and __________.
2. Words such as *always, never,* and *only* are called ____________________.

3. These words generally indicate a wrong answer because ______________________________

____.

4. A statement is false if any part of it is ______________________________.
5. True-false tests often contain more __________ answers.
6. The question part of a multiple-choice item is called the ____________________.
7. __________ are the possible answers to a multiple-choice question.
8. Incorrect answer choices to a multiple-choice question are called ____________________.
9. Three strategies to use when taking fill-in-the-blank tests are __________, __________, and __________.

KNOW HOW TO ANSWER ESSAY QUESTIONS

You can expect to see two kinds of essay questions—those that require a short answer and those that require a longer, more developed answer. You can often tell how much you are expected to write by the number of points a question is worth or the amount of space left between questions. Sometimes the directions will be specific: "Answer any two of the five questions that follow, and devote no more than a page to each." If you are not sure how much you should write or how detailed your instructor expects your answer to be, ask. In general, follow these guidelines for composing answers to essay questions of the short-answer type:

- Read the question carefully, and make sure you understand what the question asks.
- Watch for instruction words. Short-answer questions often ask you to supply definitions, examples, or other specific pieces of information.
- Concentrate on answering the question briefly and precisely.
- Stay on the topic, and avoid stating your opinion or making judgments unless the question asks you to do so.
- Be sure to restate the question in your answer. This makes it easier for your instructor to read and follow your explanation.

If you do not know the answer to a question, go on to another part of the test and return to it later. Information you read in another question may jog your memory. In any case, don't leave a question unanswered. Try to write something. Essay questions are often worth several points, and you have nothing to lose by trying to answer. Read the following sample test question and its answer:

Question: Define *memory* and illustrate your definition with examples.

Answer: *Memory is a mental process that occurs in three stages: reception, retention, and recollection. In the reception stage you take in information through your senses. Most of this information you will forget unless you store it during the retention stage in your short-term or long-term memory. Short-term memory is fleeting. It enables you to remember a phone number you have looked up long enough to dial it, or the name of someone you met at a party long enough to introduce him or her to someone else. Long-term memory can be permanent. For example, you never forget your birthday. In the recollection stage you retrieve information you have stored much as you would retrieve a file from a computer's directory.*

This answer responds to both instruction words in the question: *define* and *illustrate*. The student defines memory as a three-stage process, names and explains each stage, and gives examples of each. Figure 11.3 contains a list of instruction words that are frequently used in essay questions and their meanings.

Some essay questions require a longer answer that may cover several points. You will stand a better chance of getting a good grade if your answer is detailed but not rambling, if you stick to facts and information and avoid opinions and judgments, if your answer follows a logical plan of development, and if you state your ideas clearly in error-free sentences. In general, apply the same skills you use for writing essays in your composition class to composing answers to essay questions. Be sure to look for

FIGURE 11.3 Instruction Words Used in Essay Questions

INSTRUCTION WORDS	MEANINGS
Compare	Explain similarities and differences.
Contrast	Explain differences only.
Criticize or evaluate	Make a judgment about strengths and weaknesses, worth or merit, positive or negative aspects.
Define	Give a precise and accurate meaning.
Describe	Give a mental impression, a detailed account.
Discuss or explain	Give reasons, facts, details that show you understand.
Enumerate or list	State points one by one and briefly explain.
Illustrate	Explain by using examples.
Interpret	Explain in your own words and discuss significance.
Justify or prove	Construct an argument for or against and support with evidence.
Outline	Describe in general and cover main points.
Relate	Show a connection among ideas.
Summarize	Condense main ideas; state briefly.
Trace	Describe a series of steps, stages, or events.

instruction words in each question that tell you what kind of answer to write.

The following general guidelines will help you compose good answers to longer essay test questions:

- Read the question carefully. Watch for instruction words, and make sure you understand what the question asks you to do. Ask the instructor for an explanation if necessary.
- Think about what you will write. Plan your answer, and allow yourself enough time to write thoughtfully.
- Jot down a scratch outline of the major points you will cover so that you don't forget them.
- Incorporate the question into your first sentence, and briefly state your answer to the question.
- In the rest of your essay, develop the points that explain your answer, and provide enough details to show that you know the material well.
- Save time at the end of the exam to proofread your essay and correct errors.

The essay question and list below show how to plan an effective answer by adapting the five-paragraph plan described on pages 312–321 of Chapter 15. Instruction words and topics are in italics.

Question	How can a student learn to improve *time management?* Discuss the effective use of a *semester schedule, weekly schedule,* and *daily list.*
Paragraph 1:	Briefly introduce and restate the question, and briefly state your answer.
Paragraph 2:	Discuss semester schedule.
Paragraph 3:	Discuss weekly schedule.
Paragraph 4:	Discuss daily list.
Paragraph 5:	Summarize what you have said.

Time management is the topic, and it is broken down into three types of schedules. The instruction word *discuss* tells you to supply reasons, facts, or details to explain the schedules.

When your test paper is returned to you, read over your answers to the essay questions. Notice how many points you gained, how many you lost, and the reasons for each. Check for these three common mistakes: First, did you read directions carefully? If not, your answer may be off the topic. Second, did you cover all parts of the question to receive full credit? Third, did you include enough details? If not, you may have lost points. Read your instructor's comments to determine what you need to do to improve your grade on the next test. If you scored poorly on the essay portion of the test and you do not understand why, make an appointment with your instructor to discuss your grade. Be sure to ask your instructor what you can do to improve.

EXERCISE 11.6 Use the five-paragraph format described on page 248 to write an essay answering the question about time management. If you need to review a semester schedule, weekly schedule, or daily list, see Chapter 4.

CONFIDENCE BUILDER

How to Raise Scores on Standardized Tests

You can't study for a standardized test, but try these ways to prepare yourself for success.

Check your campus or local bookstore to see if you can purchase a study guide for the test you need to take. Find out if your college offers a prep course or review session that will help you get ready for the test. In addition, try these suggestions:

- Know how many sections there are on the test and what each section covers. Find out whether you will be required to write one or more essays.
- Find out whether the test will be timed, how long it will last, and how much time you will have to complete each section. If the test will last longer than two hours, take a snack that you can eat during a break for a quick energy boost.
- If you must write an essay as part of the test, practice writing in a timed situation. Choose a topic, set a timer or alarm clock, and write your essay. If you practice writing within a time limit, you are less likely to become anxious when taking a timed test.
- Find out if you will be allowed to use a dictionary, calculator, or other aids during the test.
- Purchase any special materials you will need, such as number two pencils or examination booklets.
- Get a good night's sleep, eat a nourishing breakfast, and arrive at the testing site on time, rested and in a positive frame of mind.
- To increase your chances of getting a good score, apply the strategies you have learned from this chapter about how to take tests. Use guessing strategies if there is no penalty for guessing and you do not know the answer.
- During breaks between sections of the test, get up and move around to increase circulation. This little bit of exercise will make you feel more alert when you return to the test.

- Check over your answer sheet to erase any stray marks and to make sure you did not leave blank any questions that you meant to answer.

Don't worry if you are unable to complete a section of the test. On some standardized tests, hardly anyone finishes. Also, you can miss many of the items and still make a passing score. Finally, even if you score below a cutoff on a standardized test, you may be allowed to retake the part of the test on which you scored low.

CRITICAL THINKING APPLICATION

Choose a partner or form a small group of students who are taking the same course, whether psychology, biology, algebra, economics, this course, or another. Discuss what your class has covered recently and when your next test will be. Then write at least five test questions that you think your instructor is likely to ask. Your questions can be true-false, multiple-choice, fill-ins, or essay. Write the answers to your questions and determine what the most effective way to study for this test would be. Share your results with the rest of the class.

SUMMARY

This chapter's important points are summarized below and followed by a partially filled-in cluster diagram. After reading the summary, complete the diagram.

Sufficient preparation for tests involves three steps: First, make a study schedule that allows time for daily, weekly, and exam reviews for each course. Next, decide what topics or specific information to study by reviewing your lecture notes, textbook notes and study guides, previous tests, papers, homework, other graded assignments, and instructors' handouts. Finally, use SQ3R, PREP, or a study system you have devised to help you make efficient use of your study time.

To improve your grades on tests, develop a test-taking routine that includes these steps: arrive on time, jot down memory cues, survey the test, plan and use all your time, read directions, do easy questions first, skip and return to difficult questions, guess if there is no penalty, control your feelings and attention, check your work, and learn from your mistakes. Your test-taking routine should also include strategies for taking true-false, multiple-choice, fill-in, and essay exams, as well as strategies for taking standardized tests.

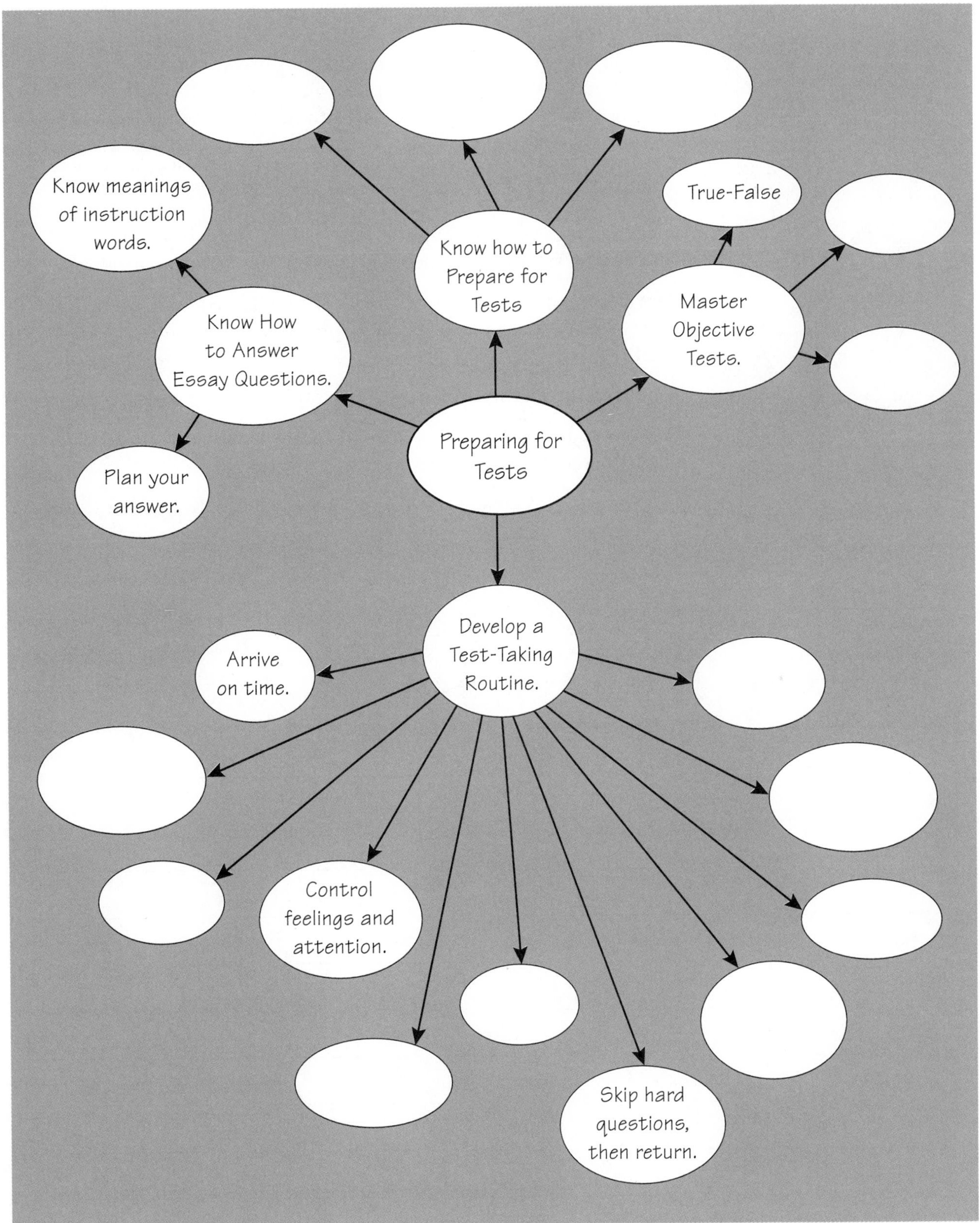
Know meanings of instruction words.
Know how to Prepare for Tests
True-False
Know How to Answer Essay Questions.
Master Objective Tests.
Preparing for Tests
Plan your answer.
Develop a Test-Taking Routine.
Arrive on time.
Control feelings and attention.
Skip hard questions, then return.

YOUR REFLECTIONS

Reflect on what you have learned about preparing for tests and how you can best apply that information. Use the following list of questions to stimulate your thinking; then write your reflections. Your response may include answers to one or more of the questions. Incorporate in your writing specific information from this chapter or previous chapters as needed.

- What are your grades in your courses so far, and are you satisfied with them? Why or why not?
- To what extent has each of the following affected your grades on tests: anxiety, amount and kind of preparation, attitude, and health?
- Which of the factors affecting your grades can you control? How?
- How good are you at taking tests? What routine do you use, and does it need improvement?
- Of the strategies covered in this chapter, which one do you think will be most helpful to you? Why?

Date ______________________

CHAPTER 12

Reducing Test Anxiety

Testing is stressful. Poor test scores may lower a grade average. In some courses, a final exam may determine whether you pass or fail. Scholarships, admittance to graduate school or a profession, entry to some job markets or careers, and even a promotion within a company may, in part, depend on test scores. It is no wonder that you may feel some anxiety when faced with a test. In fact, it would be unusual if you didn't.

Test anxiety is stress that is related to a testing situation, and it may affect students in different ways. Bonnie's test anxiety causes her to have various physical and mental reactions. Before she takes a test, her palms sweat, her head aches, or her stomach may be upset. During the test she tries to calm herself, but her anxiety increases. She reads a question, and her mind goes blank even through she may have known the answer before the test began. Her inner voice says, "I'm going to fail." Bonnie's reactions are triggered by any test, whether she is prepared for it or not. However, Jerome has reactions like Bonnie's only when he is not well prepared. Although there may be questions on the test for which he has studied and should be able to answer, he may miss some of them because his anxiety blocks his recall. As soon as the test is over, he remembers what he should have written.

Jerome's test anxiety results from lack of preparation. Effective study skills and a test-taking routine, as explained in Chapter 11, are his keys to anxiety relief. However, Bonnie's anxiety may be the result of causes that are not so easily or quickly resolved. Self-assessment is Bonnie's key to what causes her anxiety. Eliminating the causes will bring relief.

The good thing about test anxiety is that it is a *learned response;* therefore, it can be unlearned. This chapter explains what you can do to reduce test anxiety:

- Determine what causes your test anxiety.
- Eliminate the causes.
- Choose a strategy that works for you.

AWARENESS CHECK #18

Do You Have Test Anxiety?

Never	Sometimes	Usually	Check the response that seems most characteristic of you.
☐	☐	☐	1. I have trouble sleeping the night before a test.
☐	☐	☐	2. During a test, my palms sweat.
☐	☐	☐	3. Before a test, I get a headache.
☐	☐	☐	4. During a test, I become nauseated.
☐	☐	☐	5. Because of panic, I sometimes cut class on a test day.
☐	☐	☐	6. I have pains in my neck, back, or legs during a test.
☐	☐	☐	7. My heart pounds just before or during a test.
☐	☐	☐	8. I feel nervous and jittery when I am taking a test.
☐	☐	☐	9. During a test, I have trouble remembering.
☐	☐	☐	10. I lose my appetite before a test.
☐	☐	☐	11. I make careless errors on tests.
☐	☐	☐	12. My mind goes blank during tests.
☐	☐	☐	13. I worry when other students are finished before I am.
☐	☐	☐	14. I feel pushed for time when I am taking a test.
☐	☐	☐	15. I worry that I may be doing poorly on a test but that everyone else is doing all right.
☐	☐	☐	16. When I am taking a test, I think about my past failures.
☐	☐	☐	17. During a test, I feel as if I studied all the wrong things.
☐	☐	☐	18. I can't think clearly during tests.
☐	☐	☐	19. I have a hard time understanding and remembering directions when I am taking a test.
☐	☐	☐	20. After a test, I remember answers to questions I either left blank or answered incorrectly.

Items 1–10 on the Awareness Check refer to physical symptoms of text anxiety, and items 11–20 refer to mental symptoms. If you checked "sometimes" or "usually" ten or more times, you may have some test anxiety. To be sure, you might want to visit a counselor and talk to him or her about how you feel before, during, and after taking tests.

ELIMINATE THE CAUSES OF TEST ANXIETY

What causes your test anxiety? If you are like many test-anxious students, your anxiety may result from one or more of these common causes:

- Being afraid that you won't live up to the expectations of important people in your life, worrying that you will lose the affection of people you care about if you don't succeed
- Believing grades are a measure of self-worth
- Giving in to guilt feelings that result from inadequate preparation for tests
- Feeling helpless, believing that you have no control over your performance or grades

Expectations

Many students' *perceptions* of what their parents or important others expect may be inaccurate. If you worry that you may alienate people you care about unless you do well in college, you may become fearful and anxious that you will disappoint them or make them angry. If you believe that you can't live up to the expectations of others, tests may make you especially anxious. Suppose your parents or important others become angry if you make any grade lower than A or B. You need to talk this over with them to determine the source of their anger. Perhaps they feel that a grade lower than A or B means that you aren't trying hard enough or that you aren't committed to getting an education. But there may be other reasons why you are not performing as expected in a course. You may have been unprepared for the level of the course, or illness or other hardships may have affected your level of performance. It is unreasonable to expect a student to achieve someone else's ideal grade, but it is not unreasonable to expect a student to do his or her best. If a C represents a student's best effort, then it is a good grade. Try to separate yourself from others' expectations. Focus instead on what *you* expect from yourself and work hard to achieve it.

Grades and Self-Esteem

Much test anxiety results from placing too great an emphasis on grades. A low grade for some students translates into "I don't measure up." The result is a loss of self-esteem. One way to reduce test anxiety is to emphasize *performance* instead of grades. Rather than let grades control your feelings, take control of your performance.

Turn each testing situation into an opportunity for self-assessment. Use tests to track your performance in a course. Keep a record of the number and type of items missed, your level of anxiety during the test, your level of preparation, and what you need to review. Over a period of time, you may see a pattern in your study and testing behavior. For example, if you consistently miss the same type of question or if your level of anxiety goes up when you haven't prepared sufficiently, then you will know what and how much to study for the next test.

FIGURE 12.1 A Chart for Tracking Performance on Tests

Test/ Course	Items Missed	Type of Item	Anxiety Level	Preparation Level	To Do
Math chapter quiz	# 3 # 6, # 7 # 10	Avagadro's Law ratio of effusion ratio of gasses partial pressures and mole fractions	high	low (1 hr.)	1. Review laws. 2. Do more practice problems.

When you emphasize performance over grades, a test becomes a personal challenge, a chance for you to apply your knowledge and skill to new problems and tasks, an opportunity for you to discover your strengths and weaknesses. Improved performance is the goal. Grades are not a measure of self-worth. They are just a way to keep score. To track your performance on tests, make a chart like the one illustrated in Figure 12.1, or devise one of your own. The chart is filled in as an example.

Feelings of Helplessness

As explained in Chapter 1, if you have an external locus of control, you may not see the connection between study and grades. You may become anxious because you cannot predict the outcome of a test. Even if your locus of control is internal, you may feel temporarily helpless in a testing situation when you know you have not studied enough. Feeling guilty for not meeting your responsibilities may cause you to experience test anxiety.

If you can identify the cause of your test anxiety, you can do what is necessary to eliminate it. Figure 12.2 on page 257 shows you how.

LEARN TO RELAX

A proven way to reduce the physical and mental discomfort caused by test anxiety is to learn how to relax. You can't be relaxed and anxious at the same time. When you feel nervous before or during a test, you need to be able to relax so that you become calm enough to focus your attention on the task of taking the test.

Muscle relaxation exercises help you control the physical symptoms of test anxiety. Become aware of the sixteen muscle groups of your body (see

FIGURE 12.2 Text Anxiety: Causes and Eliminators

CAUSES	ELIMINATORS
1. Trying to meet others' expectations	Decide whether living up to these expectations is something you want to do for yourself. Set your own goals and live up to your own expectations.
2. Letting grades determine your self-worth	Emphasize performance over grades. Take control by tracking performance to overcome weaknesses.
3. Inadequate preparation and guilt	So you weren't prepared this time. Keep your goal in sight and resolve to do better.
4. Feeling helpless, with no control over what happens	The way to take control is to develop an internal locus of control. Improve your study habits. Prepare for your next test, and observe the connection between the amount and quality of your studying and the grade you make.

Figure 12.3), and practice a technique that will help you relax each group. When you are relaxed, you can program yourself for success.

Some people don't even know when they are tense. As you locate each of the sixteen muscle groups in Figure 12.3, try to sense whether you are holding any tension in your own muscles at each location. Try this exercise: Close your eyes and search for the tension in your body. Are you clenching your teeth? If so, open your mouth slightly and relax your jaw. Are your shoulders hunched? Lower your shoulders and feel an immediate sense of relief. Now breathe deeply. Uncross your legs if they are crossed, and press your feet flat on the floor. Do not tense your leg muscles. Settle comfortably into your chair and enjoy how good you feel when your muscles are relaxed. Imagine taking a test when you are this calm.

To feel the difference between tension and relaxation even more, try this exercise: Clench your hand into a fist. Squeeze as tightly as you can until you feel your fingers pressing uncomfortably into your palm. Hold that position a few seconds. Feel your pulse pounding in your fingertips. Very slowly, open your hand. Uncurl your fingers and let go of the tension. When you are experiencing test anxiety, your mind is like your clenched fist. When you relax, your mind is like your hand opening and letting go of the tension.

Here is another relaxation exercise you can do the evening or morning before a test. Either sit or lie down comfortably; close your eyes and breathe deeply for a few seconds. Beginning with your feet, focus on each muscle group, one at a time; tense and then relax the muscles so there is a sharp difference between tensing and letting go. While you are relaxed, visualize a pleasant scene. For example, imagine yourself lying on a beach

FIGURE 12.3 Sixteen Muscle Groups

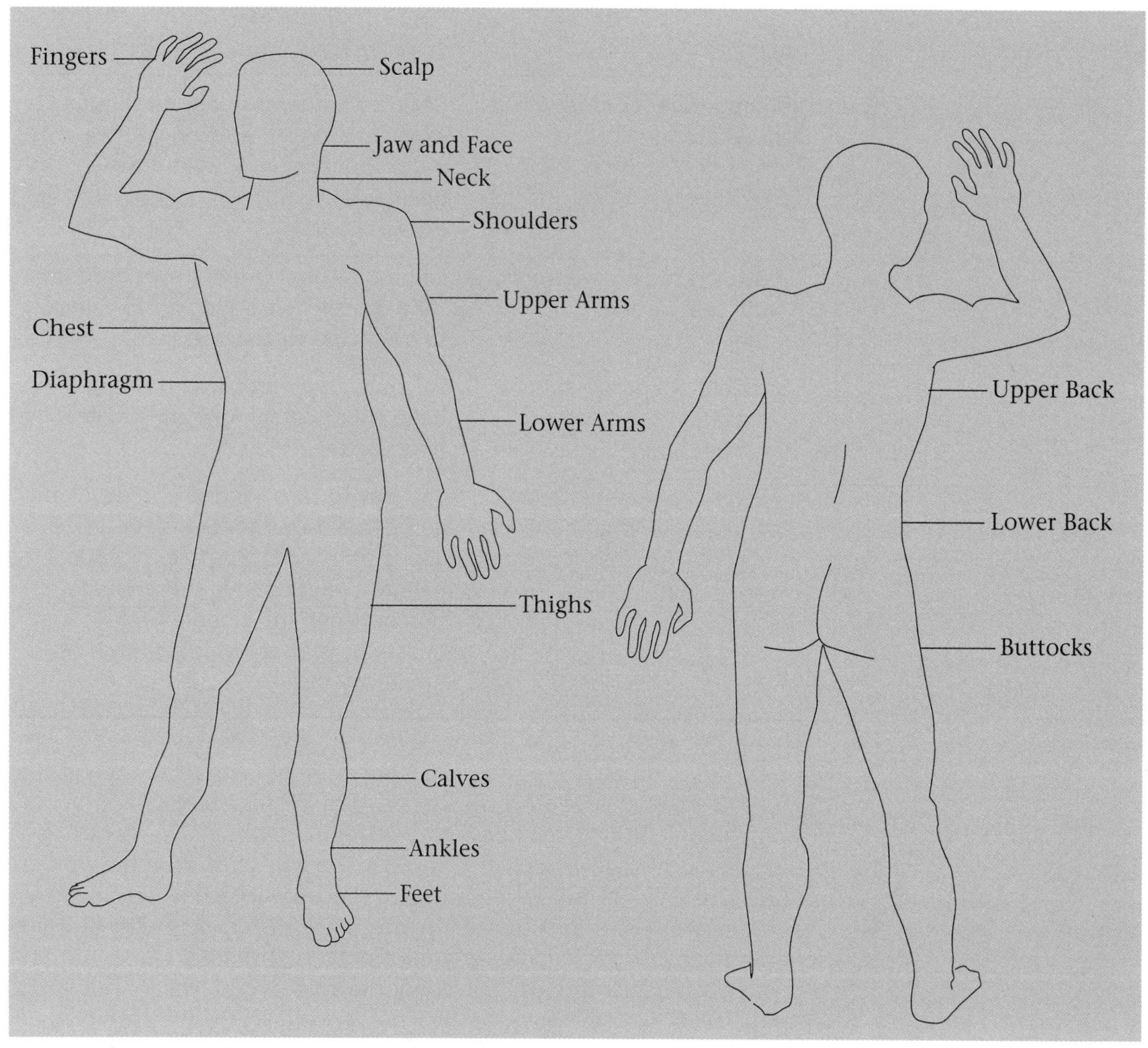

in the warm sun. Hear the waves washing up on the shore. Enjoy this scene for a few seconds; then let it fade. Concentrate on relaxing your body even more. Breathe slowly and deeply for a few more minutes; then open your eyes.

To relax yourself in a classroom situation, try these two simple but effective exercises. No one will know you are doing them. You will look as if you are concentrating or taking a moment to relax.

1. Take a deep breath and drop your shoulders. Put your hands in your lap and clench your fists to feel the tension. Slowly open your hands and let them drop down at your sides, letting go of the tension.
2. With your elbows on the desk, bow your head over your open book or test paper while resting your forehead on top of your hands. Either close your eyes or leave them open but unfocused. Breathe slowly and deeply until you feel calm.

FACE YOUR FEARS

Students who have severe test anxiety are anxious and fearful not only while taking a test but also while they are studying for tests. As Bonnie said, "I can be taking notes in a class and doing all right until the instructor says that we are going to have a test the following week; then I freeze up." If you are this anxious, you may be spending more time worrying about tests than preparing for them.

To face your fear, accept the fact that you have a problem. Facing the fear puts *you* in charge so that you can eliminate the cause of your anxiety. Any positive step you take toward overcoming your anxiety is another way of facing your fear. Define your fear and determine its origin. For example, a fear of failure may have its origin in past experiences. If you have a history of failure in a certain subject, you may fear that you will fail again. But if you can discover and eliminate the cause of those past failures so that you are less likely to repeat them, then you may overcome the fear.

Test anxiety is like any bad habit. The longer you practice it without any attempt to control it, the more ingrained it becomes. When you learn to relax, you are replacing an old, destructive habit with a new, productive one. Eventually, relaxation may become as natural to you as anxiety is now.

FIGHT DISTRACTIONS

Another way to relieve test anxiety is to become task-oriented. Give all your attention to the test. While sitting at your desk before a test and while papers are being passed out, silently review what you have studied. When you get the test, read each question carefully so that you know what you are being asked to do. Look only at the test. If you need to relax a few minutes or think over an answer, close your eyes so that you will not notice what is going on around you. Test-anxious students tend to become distracted by other students. Their anxiety increases as other students begin handing in their papers. If you do not look at other students, you are less likely to start worrying about how you are doing in comparison to them.

Avoid self-preoccupation. For example, if you start focusing on your physical discomfort or on the likelihood that you will fail, then these thoughts will distract your attention from the test. Fight distracting thoughts and focus your attention on the test in front of you. Re-read the question you are on. Mentally review everything you studied that is related to that question. Underline or circle key words in questions to increase your concentration. Read questions slowly; move your lips to involve your tactile and auditory senses. If oral distractions such as gum smacking, whispering, or paper shuffling bother you, try distancing yourself from them either physically or mentally. Choose a seat away from those who tend to create these distractions. If that is not possible, distance yourself mentally by focusing attention on the task. Silently re-read the question or the words of your answer as you write. Your own inner dialogue may drown out the distractions.

© Bob Daemmrich

TALK POSITIVELY TO YOURSELF

Although you may sometimes feel that your mind is blank, it really is not. You keep up a running conversation with yourself no matter what else you are doing. While you are listening to a lecture, you are also thinking ahead to what you will do when class is over, or recalling something that happened earlier, or thinking about a problem that has been on your mind. When you have a conversation with someone, while you are listening you are also thinking about what you will say next. Your inner voice is talking to you, and it is extremely persistent.

Take a few minutes right now to listen to that inner voice. Try this simple exercise: Sit or lie down comfortably; close your eyes and breathe deeply. Concentrate on making your mind go blank. You probably find it very hard to think about nothing because your inner voice keeps interrupting. What are your thoughts? Are they positive or negative? Do you praise or belittle yourself? Students who have test anxiety are frequently troubled by negative thoughts such as these:

"I'm going to fail this test."

"I hate this class."

"This course is doing nothing for me."

"The instructor doesn't care whether I pass or fail."

"Everybody in this class is doing better than I am."

Examine each negative thought and see how it hurts you. If you think and believe "I am going to fail this test," then you probably will because you will become more anxious and less able to focus your attention on the test. If you say to yourself "I hate this class" and "This course is doing nothing for me," you are wasting time indulging thoughts that keep you from concentrating on recalling information you need to answer questions. Saying to yourself "The instructor doesn't care whether I pass or fail" or "Everybody in this class is doing better than I am" causes you to focus attention on other people instead of the test. To combat negative thoughts, become task-oriented. Block out all but positive thoughts specifically related to the task of taking and passing the test. Negative thinking can become a habit. To break the habit and program yourself for success, do three things:

1. Become aware of all the negative messages you may be sending yourself.
2. Replace negative thoughts with positive ones such as these:

   "I'll pass this test."

   "I'm learning something in this class."

   "The instructor wants me to succeed."

   "This course is a step toward my goals."

   "I am well prepared, and I will do my best."
3. Change your inner voice into one that is calm and confident.

You may have to apply conscious effort for a long time before you learn to control your inner voice. Chances are that your negative thoughts about yourself go way back to your early childhood; they are probably so automatic that you hardly even notice them when you are involved in an activity such as taking a test. But learning to silence those thoughts and to replace them with positive, supportive ones will have a positive effect on other areas of your life besides test taking. You may find yourself having more fun in your classes and outside activities such as sports, hobbies, and work if you aren't so critical about your performance. Studying will become easier too, and your chances for success in college will improve. Thinking positively about yourself can even change the expression on your face. If you look and feel confident, people will have a higher opinion of you.

You can relieve test anxiety by focusing all your attention on the test. Try to avoid thinking about what other students are doing and try to fight internal distractions such as minor physical discomfort or negative thoughts.

© Jean Claude Lejeune

Once you have learned to focus all of your attention on taking a test, to speak positively to yourself, and to feel confident that you will be able to demonstrate your knowledge, test taking may become an enjoyable intellectual challenge for you.

EXERCISE 12.1

Practice positive thinking. Listen to your inner voice. In the first column, list any negative thoughts. Then, in the second column, rewrite them as positive self-directions. For example, the negative thought "I'm going to fail this test" becomes the positive direction "I'm well prepared for this test, so I will expect a good grade."

Negative Thoughts	Positive Thoughts
1. ______	1. ______
2. ______	2. ______
3. ______	3. ______
4. ______	4. ______
5. ______	5. ______

CONFIDENCE BUILDER

A Meditation Exercise

To meditate is to think deeply and continuously about something during a time you have set aside for that purpose. When you combine meditation with muscle relaxation, the result is a deep level of mental and physical calm, which may be accompanied by a heightened level of awareness. During meditation, many people become very receptive to self-directions for making positive changes in their lives. The following meditation exercise will help you practice the kind of positive thinking that can lead to success. Follow these steps to complete the exercise.

1. Select a time of day or night when you are alone and won't be disturbed.
2. Find a quiet, comfortable place such as your bedroom; go in and shut the door.
3. Lie flat on the floor, on your back.
4. Put a pillow under your head if you need one.

5. Place your arms down at your sides with your palms open and the backs of your hands resting on the floor.
6. Breathe slowly and deeply through your nostrils; exhale through your mouth.
7. If you feel any tension in any part of your body, release it.
8. Concentrate on becoming calm and relaxed. Empty your mind of all other thoughts.
9. When you feel completely calm, speak positively to yourself with your inner voice. Say the words that you alone know will make you feel confident and capable of doing your best.
10. Open your eyes. Remain lying down for a few minutes to enjoy feeling confident and calm. Then get up and resume your day's or night's activities.

© T. Michaels/The Image Works

EXERCISE 12.2

Claudia is overwhelmed with text anxiety when she thinks about her statistics midterm. Read about her attempt to overcome this problem; then answer the questions.

Even though the exam is more than three weeks away, Claudia is already waking up at night, panicked by the thought of her statistics midterm. She knows that she is always well prepared for class. She does all the reading. Why does she feel so anxious about the exam? *In desperation, she decides to try a visualization technique that her psychology teacher explained to her. Here is what she does.*

Each day for about 20 minutes she sits alone in her room. Closing her eyes, she begins to breathe deeply and then, through a process of tensing and relaxing each muscle individually, she relaxes her entire body. When she feels totally relaxed, she imagines herself sinking into the overstuffed pillows of a lovely old chair in a beautiful garden. Feeling the warmth of the sun on her face, she breathes in the fragrances that surround her. She enjoys this imaginary scene for a few long seconds, then lets the scene slowly fade and replaces it with another scene. She is sitting in her statistics class about to begin taking her exam. She feels totally relaxed and prepared for the test. Calmly, she takes the test booklet and begins to write. Again, she imagines how prepared she is, how good she feels at that moment. She knows she can pass the exam. She feels confidence flow through her body. After lingering for a few moments on this image, Claudia imagines one last scene. Her professor is handing back the test booklets. Confidently accepting hers, Claudia opens the cover and reads the handwritten note at the top of the page: "Great work. You should be proud of your success on this exam." Claudia concentrates on her intense feelings of success and then allows the scene to fade. She breathes deeply for a few more moments, then slowly opens her eyes.

1. How does Claudia begin her visualization technique? ______________________

____

2. Why does she imagine a beautiful garden? ______________________

____

3. What other scenes might she imagine? ______________________

____

4. Why do you think she visualizes the garden scene before the classroom scene? ______________________

____

5. What is the final image that Claudia visualizes? ______________________

____

6. Why is it important for Claudia to visualize this final scene? ______________________

____

____

7. How might this visualization exercise help reduce Claudia's test anxiety? ____________________

____

____

8. Based on your learning style, what changes would you make in Claudia's visualization if you were to try this technique yourself? ____________________

____

____

FIND YOUR BEST SOLUTION

Test anxiety is an individual problem. Anxiety differs in degree and kind from student to student. It is important to remember two things. First, a little anxiety won't hurt you and may be the incentive you need to do your best. Second, even if you have a great deal of anxiety that causes you considerable discomfort, you are not a hopeless case. Furthermore, you have a lot of company. For many students, test anxiety has become a way of life, but it doesn't have to remain so.

The coping strategies discussed in this chapter have worked for many students. Here are six more tips for reducing test anxiety:

- Improve the way you prepare for tests by following the suggestions offered in Chapter 11. Most test anxiety is the result of irrational fears. The only real cause for fear is insufficient preparation for a test, which almost always *does* result in a poor grade. If you know you are not prepared, then you must expect to have some anxiety. Calm yourself by using one of the relaxation techniques explained in this chapter; then do your best on the questions you are able to answer.

- Your body will tell you when you are becoming anxious during a test. Learn to recognize the signals that may be signs of stress: increased pulse rate, excessive perspiration, shallow breathing, sweaty palms, upset stomach, and headache.

- Dress comfortably for tests. Wear loose-fitting clothes and comfortable shoes. Dress in layers so that you can put something on or take something off if the temperature in the room is too cold or too hot.

- Arrive at the testing site on time. Don't be too early. If you have time on your hands before the test, waiting may make you nervous. Also, you may get into conversations with other students who will shake your confidence by reminding you of material you haven't studied.

- Develop a test-day tradition. Viana wears a pair of "good luck" jeans on test days. For reasons only she knows, these jeans have pleasant associations and make her feel successful. Another student, Nguyen, plays the *1812 Overture* to get himself ready for a test. Maybe you have a lucky pen or some other talisman that can serve as a confidence builder.

- See test anxiety for what it is—a learned response that you can unlearn, a habit that you can break.

EXERCISE 12.3

Apply what you have learned about test anxiety by completing this exercise with group members. Remember to follow the guidelines for group discussion explained in Chapter 1, pages 12–13. Review the COPE method of problem solving in Chapter 2. Discuss how a student could use COPE to solve a test-anxiety problem. Then work through COPE's steps to illustrate the solution. You can make up a hypothetical student with a problem, or you can use a real test-anxiety problem contributed by one of your group members. When you arrive at consensus, record your answers on the lines provided. Then evaluate your work.

1. **Challenge:** State the problem, its causes, and the result you want.

____

____

____

2. **Options:** List possible options to reduce anxiety.

____

____

____

3. **Plan:** Choose an option, write your plan, and set a time limit for reaching your goal.

____

____

____

4. **Evaluation:** How will you evaluate your plan? How will you know it has worked? What will you do if it doesn't?

____

____

____

Group Evaluation:

Evaluate your discussion. Did everyone contribute? Did you accomplish your task successfully? What additional questions do you have about test anxiety, and how will you find answers to your questions?

____

____

____

CRITICAL THINKING APPLICATION

What have you learned about test anxiety and your experiences with it? Relate the anxiety you may feel in a testing situation to the stress or anxiety you may feel in other situations. For example, does having to give a speech make you nervous? Does a trip to the dentist provoke anxiety? Do you feel stress when something goes wrong at work or when your child is sick or has a problem at school? What are the similarities and differences between these real-life stressors and test anxiety? Write about the ways you have found to cope with stress in your daily life. Which of these strategies might also help you to reduce test anxiety?

SUMMARY

In the following summary, part of the first paragraph is highlighted and annotated to make important points stand out. After reading the summary, continue highlighting and annotating on your own.

definition →

causes →

Test anxiety is stress that is related to a testing situation. It may be caused by your inability to cope with the expectations of important people in your life, a belief that grades are a reflection of your self-worth, or feelings of helplessness resulting from past failures. If you have test anxiety, you may suffer from physical symptoms such as headaches and nausea, and mental symptoms such as a lack of confidence and negative thoughts and feelings. Test anxiety can keep you from demonstrating your knowledge on tests, but since it is a learned response, it can be unlearned.

Being prepared for tests and feeling confident about your abilities may reduce some of your anxiety. Or you may need to develop coping strategies such as learning to relax, facing and dealing with your fears, fighting distractions, and programming yourself for success by replacing negative thoughts with positive ones. If your anxiety is extremely severe, you might want to talk over your problem with your instructor or a counselor.

YOUR REFLECTIONS

Reflect on what you have learned about test anxiety and how you can best apply that information. Use the following list of questions to stimulate your thinking; then write your reflections. Your response may include answers to one or more of the questions. Incorporate in your writing specific information from this chapter or previous chapters as needed.

- How do you feel about taking tests in general?
- Do you have physical or mental reactions to tests that are similar to Bonnie's and Jerome's, as explained on page 252? What are your reactions?
- Do you do better on some kinds of tests than others? Which ones, and why?
- Relate the information from Chapter 11 about preparing for tests to what this chapter says about test anxiety. What conclusions can you draw?
- What have you learned from this chapter that you can apply to reduce test anxiety or other types of stress?

Date ______________________________

CHAPTER 13

Using Critical Thinking Strategies

Critical thinking is the process of constructing and evaluating meaning. Thinking critically helps you make sense of the world. Critical thinking is also a process of self-reflection, whereby you examine your actions and their consequences and determine what to do next. Finally, critical thinking is conscious and purposeful. When you are thinking critically, you are conscious, or aware, that you *are* thinking. At the same time, you have a reason for thinking, whether it is for solving a personal or job-related problem, understanding a complex social issue, or working your way through a difficult assignment.

To make decisions, solve problems, find and organize information, and complete other important tasks, you must be able to think critically. This chapter explains four strategies that are the keys to thinking critically and confidently both now and throughout your life. Flow charts in each of the next four sections show how each strategy is linked to different skill areas. If you begin using these strategies, consciously at first, they will soon become second nature, and your whole approach to learning may change for the better. Note that the first letter of each boldfaced word in the list below makes the acronym **A PIE.** Use the acronym to help you remember the strategies.

- Examine your **assumptions.**
- Make **predictions.**
- Sharpen your **interpretations.**
- **Evaluate** what you learn.

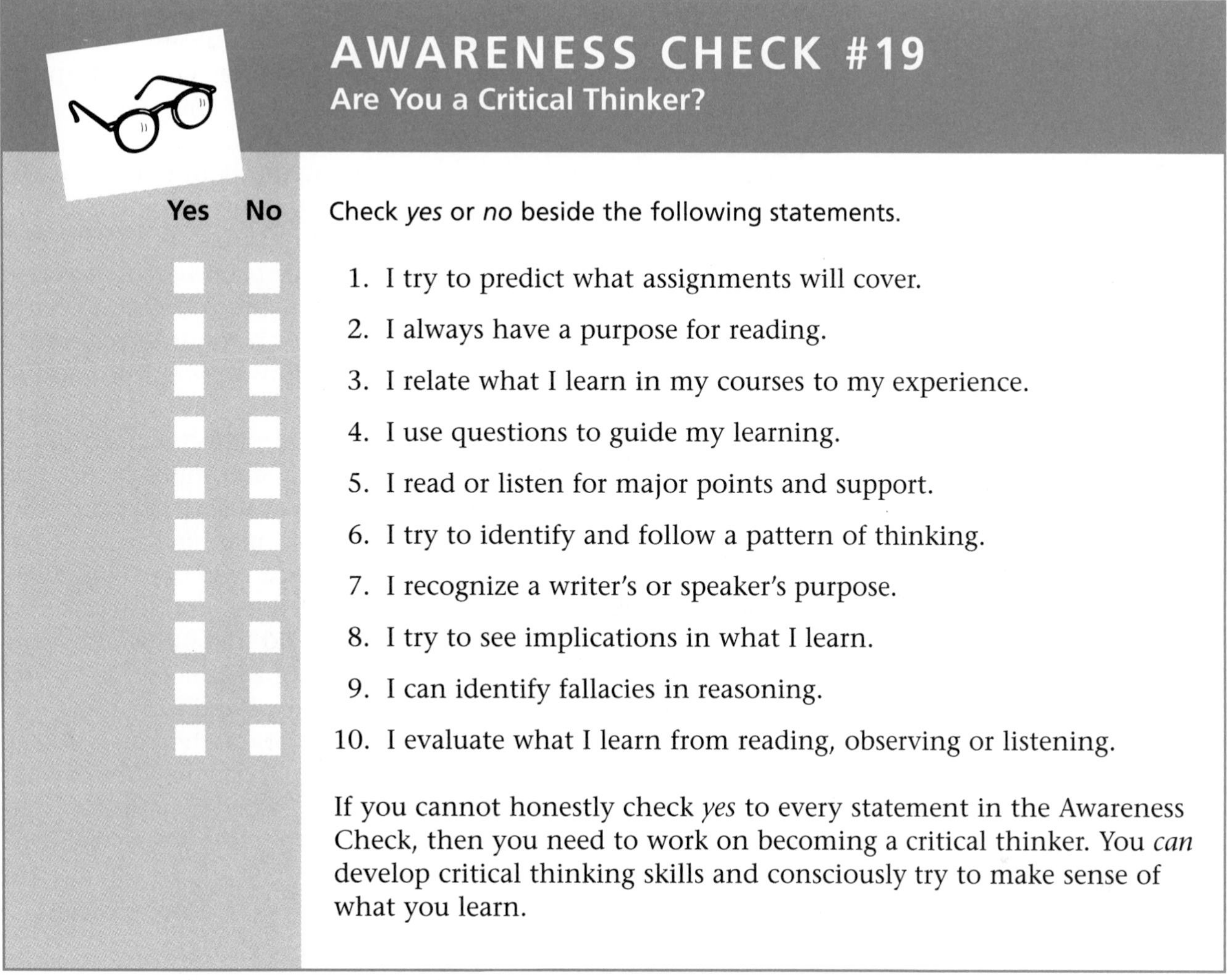

AWARENESS CHECK #19

Are You a Critical Thinker?

Yes	No	Check *yes* or *no* beside the following statements.
☐	☐	1. I try to predict what assignments will cover.
☐	☐	2. I always have a purpose for reading.
☐	☐	3. I relate what I learn in my courses to my experience.
☐	☐	4. I use questions to guide my learning.
☐	☐	5. I read or listen for major points and support.
☐	☐	6. I try to identify and follow a pattern of thinking.
☐	☐	7. I recognize a writer's or speaker's purpose.
☐	☐	8. I try to see implications in what I learn.
☐	☐	9. I can identify fallacies in reasoning.
☐	☐	10. I evaluate what I learn from reading, observing or listening.

If you cannot honestly check *yes* to every statement in the Awareness Check, then you need to work on becoming a critical thinker. You *can* develop critical thinking skills and consciously try to make sense of what you learn.

EXAMINE YOUR ASSUMPTIONS

An *assumption* is an idea or belief that you take for granted without necessarily having proof that it is true. For example, when you sign up for a course, you probably assume that you will be able to pass it. Most people enter into marriage assuming that it will last. As time passes, experience proves assumptions true or false.

Similarly, when you think about and discuss current issues, you probably make certain assumptions based on what you have learned from your reading or from other sources. For example, health care is an issue that concerns everyone. Most people agree that some health care reform is needed, but opinions differ as to what should be changed and how. Those who support a national health care plan assume that under such a system health care would cost less, but the quality of service would remain high. Those who oppose a national health care plan base their thinking on different assumptions. For example, they may assume that fewer qualified people would choose medicine as a career or that consumers of medical services might lose their freedom to choose their physicians.

Either set of assumptions may be correct; only time will tell. Often you have to act on your assumptions, knowing that you can't necessarily predict the consequences of your choices. Therefore, critical thinkers inform themselves and change their assumptions as they receive new information.

Politicians and many others who speak and write about political issues know how compelling assumptions can be. They know that people who don't think critically tend to hold onto their assumptions even in the face of conflicting evidence. Even so, writers and speakers on both sides of an issue try to determine what your assumptions are and to select evidence to invalidate opponents' assumptions. The first step toward becoming a critical thinker is to examine your own assumptions as you learn and to be open to change.

The assumptions you bring to whatever you learn affect your ability to construct meaning. For example, examine your assumptions before you begin to read. Do a quick survey of a chapter, skimming over the title, headings, summary, illustrations, and other visual materials to see what the chapter covers. Determine how much you already know about a lecture topic, and identify your assumptions about it. As you listen, try to relate what you are learning to your experience, and find out whether the assumptions you began with need changing. Figure 13.1 below shows you how making assumptions extends to other skill areas and activities.

Suppose you have decided that next semester or quarter you will take your first college writing course. As you anticipate this, you wonder what it will be like and whether you will be successful. What assumptions can you make about the course? What experiences with writing have you had?

FIGURE 13.1 **Examine Your Assumptions: How You Can Use This Critical Thinking Strategy**

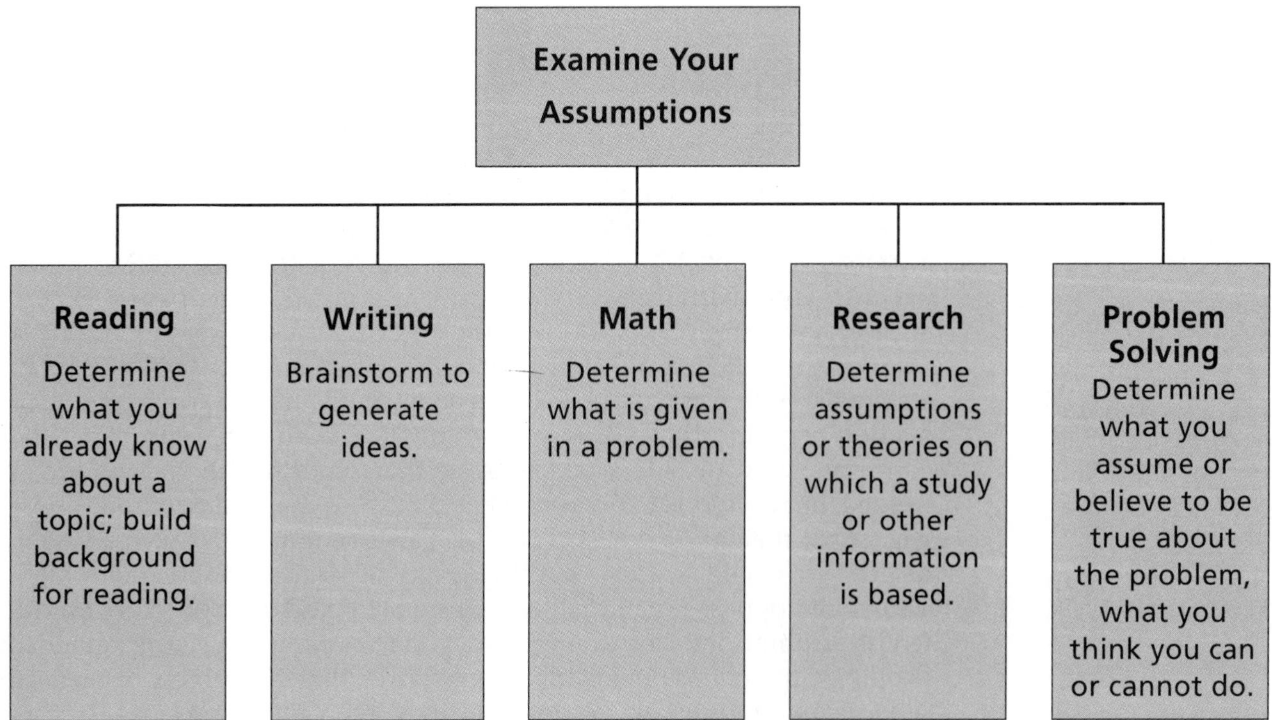

Do you like to write, or do you stare with dread at the blank page in front of you? Do you believe writing takes talent that only a few people possess, or do you believe that you or anyone else can learn to write effectively? Do you brainstorm, or do some other thinking activity, before you begin to write? Does it work for you? Asking yourself questions like these will help you determine what assumptions you bring to the task of learning to write.

Writers also make assumptions—about their readers' background knowledge. They assume that you already know such things as the names of important or famous people, the dates of events that have historical significance, the meaning of figures of speech such as *to strike out* or *to string along,* and the ideas or experiences that most people have in common. Often, writers mention such culturally shared information without explaining it, assuming that readers will know what they mean.

EXERCISE 13.1

It is important to recognize and analyze the assumptions that you bring to everyday interactions with people as well as to the subjects you study.

To examine some of your assumptions about other people, look at the group in the photograph below, and then answer the questions.

© Peter Chapman

1. Who are these people? What assumptions can you make based on their clothing or on other details in the photograph?

___

___

2. Where are they, and what do they seem to be doing? What details in the photograph help you make your assumptions?

___

___

3. Based on their expressions, what do these people seem to be thinking or feeling?

___

___

4. How do your assumptions about the people in the photograph relate to your experience?

___

___

5. Has your learning style either helped or interfered with your ability to complete this exercise? Explain your answer.

___

MAKE PREDICTIONS

A *prediction* is a decision made beforehand about the outcome of an event. Predictions are based on assumptions. Because you believe that certain things are true, you expect or believe that certain things will happen. If you believe, for example, that you are good at math, then you can predict that you will do well in a math course. If you have a favorite author who has just published a new book, you can predict that you will probably like it. Your prediction is based on the assumption that the new book will be similar to others by this author that you have read and enjoyed.

Predictions are often the result of asking yourself questions and looking for answers. When you wake up in the morning, you may wonder, "What will the weather be like today? What should I wear?" You look out the window at a sunny, cloudless sky. You step outside, and it is breezy and cool enough for a sweater. You remember that yesterday's weather started out like this, but by noon the temperature had risen to eighty degrees. Predicting that today's weather will be the same, you dress in layers so that you can remove some of your clothing as the temperature warms. By lunchtime, however, clouds have begun to form. Friends tell you that rain is forecast. You run out to your car to grab an umbrella from the trunk. In doing so, you have acted on the prediction that it will rain. Based on new information, the clouds, and your friends' comments, you think the outcome is likely. Figure 13.2 gives some possible tips on making predictions.

FIGURE 13.2 Make Predictions: How You Can Use This Critical Thinking Strategy

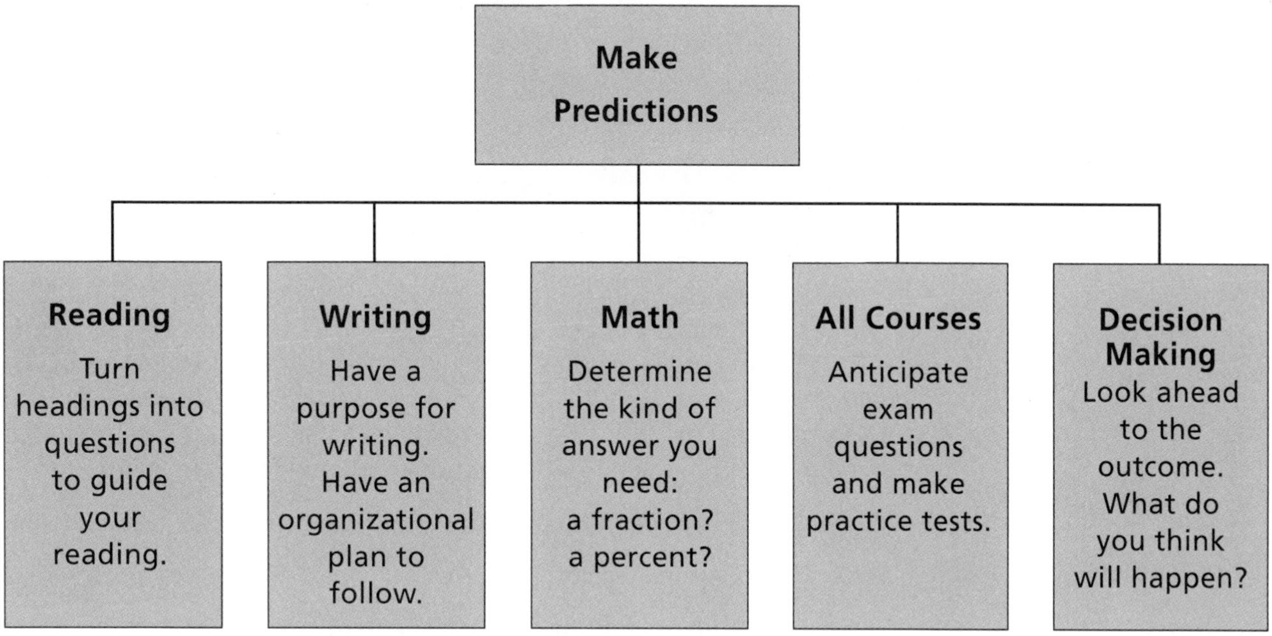

Understand Lectures

Your predictions, if they are flexible, can help you understand the information you are trying to take in. Suppose you are listening to a lecture on the topic *Five Strategies for Improving Your Memory.* You have confidence in your ability to take good notes, and so far you have been able to follow the speaker's ideas, successfully predicting that the speaker would explain the five strategies and how to use them. This prediction has caused you to listen for cues such as a *number* to indicate where in the series of five strategies the speaker is and *names or other identifying words* to indicate *what* the strategies are. The speaker says, "Acronyms are another helpful memory aid," and writes *acronym* on the board. As you're copying this term into your notes, you're thinking, "Is the speaker explaining a new strategy, or is this another example of the use of mnemonic devices, which is the third strategy mentioned so far?" Now you raise your hand to ask a question to clarify the point. Based on the speaker's answer that acronyms are indeed a mnemonic device, you predict that following the explanation of acronyms, the speaker will either provide an additional example of mnemonics or will proceed to the fourth strategy. In either case, your questions and predictions have helped you understand and follow the speaker's ideas.

Read with a Purpose

Predictions are useful for reading your textbooks as well as understanding a lecture. To see how this critical thinking strategy applies to reading textbooks, look at the following chapter title and headings from *Personal Finance,* by E. Thomas Garman and Raymond E. Forgue.

Title:	**The Importance of Personal Finance**
Headings:	Reasons for Studying Personal Finance
	Goals of Effective Personal Financial Management
	Factors That Affect Personal Income
	Steps in Personal Financial Management

What predictions can you make about the chapter's content? Notice how the writers of *Personal Finance* try to help you. They begin each heading with a key word that tells you exactly what to look for in each part of the chapter: *reasons, goals, factors,* and *steps*. Here are some guide questions you could formulate from the title and headings to start you thinking about personal finance in general—and your own attempts to manage money:

- What does this writer think is important about personal finance?
- Why should I study personal finance?
- What are the goals of financial management?
- Which factors affect personal income, and what is their effect?
- How many factors are there?

Constructing guide questions such as these and making predictions about content enable you to read with a *purpose*. There are three main purposes for reading informational material (such as that found in most textbooks) and three strategies best suited to each purpose. Figure 13.3 on page 276 shows these relationships among the different purposes and strategies.

When you read a chapter for the first time, you should use the first strategy. Read every word so that you will understand ideas and comprehend the author's meaning. Read actively, turning headings into questions and trying to anticipate the answers.

After you have read a chapter, you may need to search for a fact or the answer to a question you missed on a test. To do this, use the second strategy. Decide what kind of fact you're looking for: a number, name, or place, for example. Then skim over the chapter section that is likely to contain the fact. If you're looking for a date, ignore everything else and read only the dates until you find the right one.

If a passage is difficult, use the third strategy. Read it again slowly and carefully. If you still don't understand the passage, read one sentence at a time. If sentences are long, break them down into parts and restate them in your own words. Read aloud. Sometimes hearing yourself read a difficult passage helps you make sense of it, especially if your preferred learning style is auditory.

The first purpose and strategy will help you understand how the writer constructed the arguments or discussions in the text. Reading with the second purpose in mind will help you make predictions and discover the author's purpose (see page 280). The third purpose and strategy will help when you read complex or technical material as well as literature. Chapter 14 contains more information on these purposes.

FIGURE 13.3 Purposes and Strategies for Informational Reading

PURPOSE	STRATEGY	WHEN TO USE
Reading to understand ideas and construct meaning	Read carefully at normal speed; slow down for difficult parts; try to relate ideas; ask guide questions.	The first time you read a chapter
Reading to find facts	Scan-read for dates, names, places, lists of steps, or other factual material. (*Scan* means to glance rapidly over a page, looking for specific information or the answer to a question.)	To look for an answer to a question missed on a test; to look for information you know will be on a test; to look for answers to questions covering a chapter; to verify information in your notes; to survey and review chapters
Reading to analyze difficult or complex passages	Read slowly; pay attention to every word; break sentences into parts, and express the parts in your own words; summarize difficult passages.	To read a sentence or passage that you don't understand; to analyze a complex or difficult section that you want to understand more fully; to read literature, especially poetry

EXERCISE 13.2

Before reading the passage, test your assumptions about homosexuals on campus by answering questions 1 and 2. Then read the following passage below and answer the questions that come after it.

1. Do you think that most students support equal rights for homosexuals? On what do you base this assumption?

____

____

2. Do you think most students' attitudes towards homosexuals on campus are positive or negative? On what do you base this assumption?

____

____

Several years ago, a group of gay students at a large state university picked a date and announced, "If you are gay, wear blue jeans today." Nobody sought to quantify the result, but can you guess what may have happened? (Fewer students than usual wore blue jeans.) Studies show that although most Americans support equal rights, attitudes toward gay men and lesbians are generally negative (Herek, 1988). Based on a recent poll, Time *magazine found that 53 percent of American adults believe that homosexual relationships between consenting adults are morally wrong, and 64 percent believe that marriage between homosexuals should not be recognized by law (Henry, 1994).*

Not everyone harbors anti-gay prejudice, of course, and there is a wide range of individual differences of opinion. The problem is that people with negative attitudes toward homosexuals may also discriminate in important matters. In one study, Geoffrey Haddock and his colleagues (1993) told student subjects that their university's student government had to cut funding to campus-wide organizations by 20 percent—and that they wanted to hear student opinions on where to make these cuts (two weeks earlier, each subject's attitude toward homosexuals had been assessed). Subjects were then given a list of ten campus organizations, including one for gays and lesbians. As you might expect, negative attitudes were linked to discriminatory decisions. Those with the most anti-gay sentiment proposed an average budget cut of 45 percent, compared to 26 percent among subjects with the least negative attitudes. Discrimination can take on many forms. In a recent survey of 800 American adults, 75 percent said they would vote for a homosexual political candidate and only 39 percent said they would see a homosexual doctor (Henry, 1994).

1. What is the passage about?

___

___

___

2. What evidence from paragraph 1 does the author provide to support the opinion that Americans' attitudes toward homosexuals are generally negative?

___

___

3. What seems to be the relationship between attitudes toward homosexuals and discrimination? Use evidence from paragraph 2 to support your answer.

___

___

4. If an announcement were to appear in your college newspaper saying "If you are not gay, wear red next Friday," how do you think students would respond, and why?

___

___

5. Define the words *sought* (paragraph 1, sentence 2) and *harbors* (paragraph 2, sentence 1).

___

___

Now look at your answers to Exercise 13.2. Did you write them in your own words, or did you copy directly from the passage? Often the wording of a test question is different from the wording that appears in your textbook. When information in your textbook is complex or unfamiliar, be sure you understand it first; then summarize it in your own words so that you can remember it and recognize it on a test.

Predict Test Questions

Predicting test questions is another way you can use critical thinking. When you study for a test, try to predict the questions your instructor will ask. This is a good activity for a study group. Each member of the group may have different assumptions about what is important. By pooling your information gathered from lecture notes and other sources, you may be able to determine the essential concepts or skills your instructor expects you to have learned. Based on those assumptions, you should be able to predict the questions he or she might ask. Then make up your own questions and answer them. First, find out what kind of questions will be on the test—essay or multiple-choice, for example—so you can construct questions of the same type.

SHARPEN YOUR INTERPRETATIONS

To interpret what you read or hear, you must be able to follow ideas on two levels. The *literal level* is the stated meaning, the writer's or speaker's points. The *implied level* is the suggested meaning, or what you can infer, conclude, or guess from what is said or deliberately left unsaid. An *inference* is an informed guess based on experience and available information. Figure 13.4 on page 280 shows how sharpening your interpretations extends to other skill areas and activities. Read the following poem.

On Reading a Favorite Book

Carol Kanar

Deep in the Maine woods,
On a starless September night,
Lights flicker, then go out.
Miles from any incandescence,
I sit in the middle of fear,
Black, thorough,
And mourn the sudden loss of sight
As if it were not temporary.
The mind adjusts, takes its measure
Of eternity.
My book lies open in the dark;
I read by lights I cannot see.

On a literal level, you know that the events described in this poem take place in September in the woods of Maine on a night when no stars are out. You also know that the lights go out. Specific words in the poem tell you these facts.

On an implied level, what more can you figure out from these lines? Because the night is starless, you could infer that it is cloudy, maybe even stormy. Perhaps a utility line is down—that would explain why the lights go out. Also, you could infer that the person in the poem is isolated in the

FIGURE 13.4 Sharpen Your Interpretations: How You Can Use This Critical Thinking Strategy

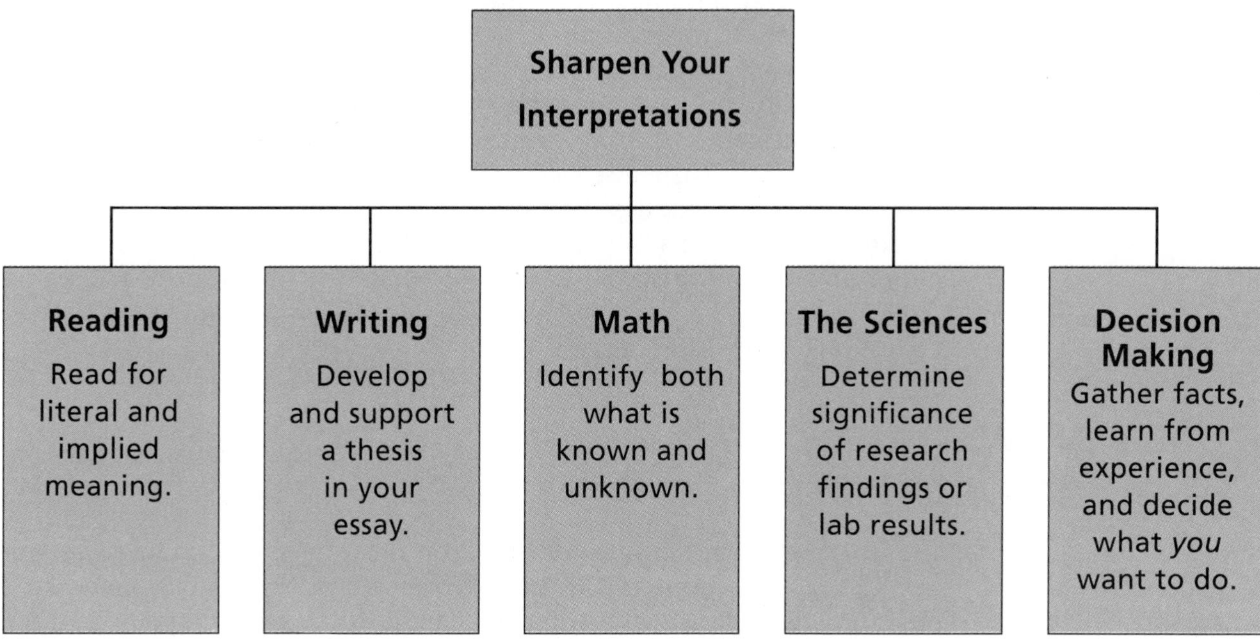

deep woods, far from neighbors or a town. Your experience helps you make more inferences. If you have ever been in the woods at night, you know how dark it gets, especially if you can't see the moon and stars. If you have ever lived in New England, you know that by September the weather is starting to get cold and it is not unusual for a frontal storm to pass through at night, causing a power outage.

Your interpretation of anything you read, see, or hear is your construction of meaning on two levels: the literal level and the implied level. Your interpretations are affected by the experience you bring to whatever you are trying to understand or learn.

You must understand informational material—the kind found in most college textbooks—on two levels as well. At the literal level, you must try to understand what the writer says. At the implied level, you must try to figure out how to apply in a different context the knowledge and skills you are gaining. In other words, you must make inferences, or see the *implications* in what you read. For example, when you read a chapter in an algebra textbook, you must first understand the rules and steps involved in solving a certain kind of problem. Then you must be able to apply the rules and steps to similar problems in the chapter. The three-step process explained in Chapter 14, pages 303–314, will help you improve your textbook reading comprehension.

Sharpening your interpretations also means making useful inferences outside of your studies. If you have children, you have had to learn to tell whether your child has a harmless cold, has a bad case of the flu, or is pretending to be sick to get attention or to get out of doing an unpleasant task. Cold and flu symptoms are similar, but with the flu they are more pronounced and last longer. A child may have a fever with either a cold or the flu, but if the child is faking, there is no fever. Mothers and fathers are good at making inferences about the severity and meaning of their children's symptoms based on experience. No matter what the situation, the more facts you have and the more experience you have had in similar situations, the better will be your inferences.

Here is a six-step approach to sharpening your ability to interpret information on two levels. Chapter 14 contains more detailed information on how to adapt these six steps to reading specific kinds of textbook and study materials.

- Understand the writer's or speaker's purpose.
- Read or listen for the point and proof.
- Read or listen for an organizational pattern.
- Find implications in what you learn.
- Define new or unfamiliar terms.
- Read and understand graphics.

Understand the Writer's or Speaker's Purpose

The textbook writer's purpose is to inform, provide information, and impart knowledge. Textbook writers use various devices to make information accessible to students. For example, the writer of an introductory biology text uses formal language, but defines technical terms in context as they occur within chapters and also includes a glossary of terms at the end of the book. The preface of a textbook provides clues to the author's structure and emphasis, and may explain how to use the book and its features.

Because textbook writers know that much of the information will be new to you, each chapter contains illustrations, charts, tables, and other visual materials that help summarize and clarify complex ideas. Often, writers use a standard format and structure in every chapter so that you can follow the development of ideas. Once you become familiar with a writer's format, you will be able to predict a great deal about each chapter. Survey to get a feel for important topics, and see what your assumptions are about each topic before you begin your careful reading. For more information on chapter organization and how to use it to guide your reading and studying, see Chapter 7, page 157.

Instructors who lecture also use various methods to make information accessible. They may use visuals such as overhead transparencies and illustrations on the board. They may give verbal cues, numbering their examples or singling out a point for emphasis, saying "this is important" or using other emphatic expressions. Their language may be formal or informal depending on their personalities and teaching styles. As you listen to a lecture, try to determine a purpose for listening by asking yourself questions such as "Why is this important?" or "What concept or skill am I supposed to learn?" Listen carefully for any clues the instructor may give you about his or her purpose.

EXERCISE 13.3

Apply what you have learned so far about making inferences from facts given by completing this exercise with group members. Remember to follow the guidelines for group discussion explained in Chapter 1, pages 14–15. Read the paragraph below and determine whether you can make the inferences that follow it. Discuss each inference, arrive at consensus, and then check *yes* or *no* for each statement. Then evaluate your work.

Susan is not doing well in her composition course. She missed the first two days of class because she was dropping and adding other courses. She missed the introduction to the course and the instructor's description of the course requirements. Her instructor gave her a syllabus, but she didn't read it. As a result, she was not prepared for the first grammar test, and she made a D on it. She decided that the instructor was too demanding, and she tried to get into another section. Unfortunately, the drop-add period was over. Susan's counselor convinced her to stay in the course and suggested that she make an appointment with the instructor to see what she can do to catch up. The counselor believes that if Susan begins right now to take a serious interest in the course, do the assignments, and keep up with the syllabus, she can still do well in the course because it is early in the semester.

Yes	No	
☐	☐	1. Susan will fail the course.
☐	☐	2. The instructor is too demanding.
☐	☐	3. If Susan had read the syllabus, she might have known that a test was scheduled.
☐	☐	4. The instructor may be willing to let Susan make up what she missed on the first two days of class.
☐	☐	5. It is important to attend the first few days of class.

Group Evaluation:

Evaluate your discussion. Did everyone contribute? Did you accomplish your task successfully? What additional questions do you have about making inferences from facts? How will you find answers to your questions?

____

____

____

____

____

____

Read or Listen for the Point and Proof

Many writers and speakers develop ideas by making and supporting points. The *controlling idea,* or *thesis,* is stated in an introduction or near the beginning of a chapter. Each heading within a chapter summarizes a point that helps explain the writer's thesis, and subheadings may summarize additional points. Within each section following a heading or subheading, each paragraph also makes a point or continues the development of a point made in a previous paragraph. From the beginning of a chapter to the end, the writer's thesis is systematically broken down into individual units of thought and explained by details and examples, which are the writer's proof or support. In the chapter summary (if there is one), the writer restates the thesis and major points. Before you begin to study a chapter, do a brief survey of the author's main points. Read all of the major headings, subheadings, and first sentences of paragraphs. This survey will give you a very good idea of what a chapter covers. Busy people also use this technique to get through the morning newspaper or a magazine. After their survey, they decide which articles to read more thoroughly.

Many students have difficulty keeping main points and examples separate in their lecture notes. Instructors don't always lecture from an outline. An instructor may make a point, give an example or two, make another point, then come back to the first point. As you're taking notes, you may think the speaker is making a new point when he or she is actually giving an example of a previous point. You might have to draw an arrow in your notes from the example to the point it supports or make some other changes to keep information in the right sequence. This is why it is advisable to skip lines between points so you can fill in details and examples as the speaker gives them. It may be useful also to reorganize your notes following a lecture to get points and proof in order.

Finding and following the writer's or speaker's points is not always easy, and you may have difficulty distinguishing a main idea from a supporting detail or example. Therefore, when you begin to study, read your book or notes carefully and ask guide questions as you go.

EXERCISE 13.4

Each group of sentences contains one sentence that expresses the main idea and three sentences that present supporting details. Working with a partner or on your own, underline the main idea.

1 a. Many parents support sex education courses and programs in the public schools.
b. Students should have access to accurate information about sexually transmitted diseases.
c. Some birth control methods are more effective than others, and students should know what their options are.
d. It is easier for students to talk about sex with peers and teachers than with parents.

2 a. Take your car to a commercial car wash instead of washing it at home.
b. Don't leave the water running while brushing and flossing your teeth.
c. A few simple guidelines can help you save money while conserving water.
d. Take baths or limit your showers to no more than two minutes.

3 a. Sanibel Island is known for the variety of shells that wash up on its shores.
b. Daytona Beach is one of the few beaches in the world where you can drive your car on the sand.
c. The white sand and turquoise water draw tourists to Florida's Gulf Coast.
d. Florida's beaches have many features that make them attractive to visitors.

4 a. The sticker price may be only a fraction of the real price you pay to own a car.
b. The costs of maintenance and repairs vary with the make and model of car you buy.
c. Gas mileage and insurance premiums are additional factors that may increase your cost of operating a car.
d. If you finance your car, interest rates may make it cost twice as much by the time you pay off the loan.

Read or Listen for an Organizational Pattern

Common organizational patterns link points and support. If you can spot the pattern early in a chapter or lecture, you can use it as a guide to predict what will follow. Key words may suggest how ideas are organized. For example, if the writer's or speaker's point is that memory is a three-stage process that you can improve, then the key words *three-stage process* alert you to the **process** pattern of organization. Read or listen to find out what the three stages are, what happens at each stage, and how you can improve the functioning of the process.

There are six other common organizational patterns to identify as you listen to a lecture or as you read:

1. If two things are being compared, the pattern is **comparison and contrast.** Read or listen for similarities and differences.

2. If the writer or speaker explains why something happens, the pattern is **cause and effect.** Read or listen for reasons and results.

3. If the writer or speaker groups items into categories, the pattern is **classification.** Determine how many categories there are, and identify the characteristics of each category.

4. If the writer or speaker develops a point by giving examples, the pattern is **example.** Read or listen for key phrases such as *for example* and *for instance.*

5. If the writer's or speaker's details follow a certain order, the pattern is **sequence.** Read or listen for numbers in a sequence or for events explained according to time periods. A sequence is often part of a process, especially when the stages of a process occur in a certain order or at specific times. Processes explain *how* things happen. Sequences explain *when* things happen.

6. If the writer or speaker provides an extended meaning of a word or a concept, the pattern is **definition.** Read or listen for words and phrases such as *the meaning is* and *can be defined as.*

EXERCISE 13.5 The following statements might begin sections of a textbook chapter or an article. Read each statement to predict which organizational pattern the writer will follow. Write the letter of your answer in the space provided.

A. cause and effect C. sequence E. classification G. process
B. example D. comparison and contrast F. definition

1. ______ A computer is an information-processing system that, in some ways, works much like your brain.
2. ______ Numbering consecutive pages in a document is easy if you follow these steps.
3. ______ A computer has five major units: input, control, storage, retrieval, and output.
4. ______ Computer-managed inventory control systems have proven beneficial to small businesses for a number of reasons.
5. ______ In the following section, we will examine two data-processing programs and their advantages and disadvantages.
6. ______ The ability to move sentences and paragraphs around is but one example of the features of a word processor that make writing easier.
7. ______ People who have never used computers can be grouped into three general categories: those who are afraid learning will be time consuming and difficult, those who resist learning for personal or other reasons, and those who want to learn but have neither the means nor the opportunity to do so.
8. ______ What does it mean to be computer literate?
9. ______ The next section traces the development of the computer from a crude piece of equipment that was little more than a calculator to the complex information processor it has become.
10. ______ Learning how to use a word-processing program can be easy if you follow these steps.

A writer or speaker who brings together more than one organizational pattern in a single explanation is using **mixed patterns.** For example, someone might use classification to describe the kinds of students who attend a certain college and then use comparison and contrast to describe the similarities and differences among them. Identifying organizational patterns requires very slow reading. You may need to translate the writer's words into your own. Similarly, careful listening may help you identify key words that are clues to the speaker's pattern.

Find Implications in What You Learn

To see the implications or understand the significance of what you are learning, try to see the big picture. If you are taking a writing class, you know that one of the course objectives is to help you develop skills that will improve your writing. As you learn each new skill, determine its significance by asking questions such as "How will this improve my writing?" and "What should I be able to do when I have mastered this skill?"

Once you have the big picture, find the details. Read instructors' comments on your returned papers, and determine why you have missed certain items on tests. What do the comments tell you about your writing—the way you have expressed yourself or your level of skill mastery? What can you learn from your mistakes so that you will be less likely to repeat them?

Finally, try to relate what you learn in college to other areas of your life. Your psychology class may give you a better understanding of your own motives and behavior. What you learn about art, music, and literature in a humanities class may lead you to new interests in these areas. Examine the ways you are changing as the information you absorb tests your assumptions and challenges your beliefs.

Being able to see implications in what you read is another important application of this critical thinking skill. For an explanation of how to use this strategy in your reading, see Chapter 14, pages 311–314.

Define New or Unfamiliar Terms

Most academic disciplines use special terminology to describe theories, concepts, and principles. You may have encountered the terms *id, ego,* and *superego* in a psychology class, *photosynthesis* in a biology class, *integer, binomial,* and *polynomial* in a math class. In order to understand the information presented in each course, you must know the meaning of special terms related to each discipline. Get a college-level dictionary if you don't already have one, and get into the habit of using it. An excellent way to develop your vocabulary is by reading. The more you read, the more you are exposed to new words and ideas that increase your background knowledge.

Read and Understand Graphics

Textbooks and other printed sources of information are filled with graphics that are essential to your understanding of what you read. Graphics condense and summarize a great deal of information. Graphics illustrate relationships among ideas, and they provide a visual supplement to the text they accompany. You should always make reading graphics an important part of your study. Following are five common types of graphics you should recognize. Refer to Figure 13.5 on pages 287–288 for examples.

Circle or "Pie" Charts. Pie charts illustrate part-to-whole relationships. Slices of the pie represent amounts and percentages. The size of each slice in relation to the other slices and to the whole pie indicates its significance. For example, where a student's monthly income goes could be illustrated on a pie chart, with each slice representing a different expenditure.

Bar Graphs. Bar graphs illustrate relationships between *variables,* or quantities, such as time and amount. They also show trends such as an increase or decrease in amount over a period of time. One variable is measured on a vertical axis; the other variable is measured on the horizontal axis.

FIGURE 13.5 Textbook Graphics: Some Common Types

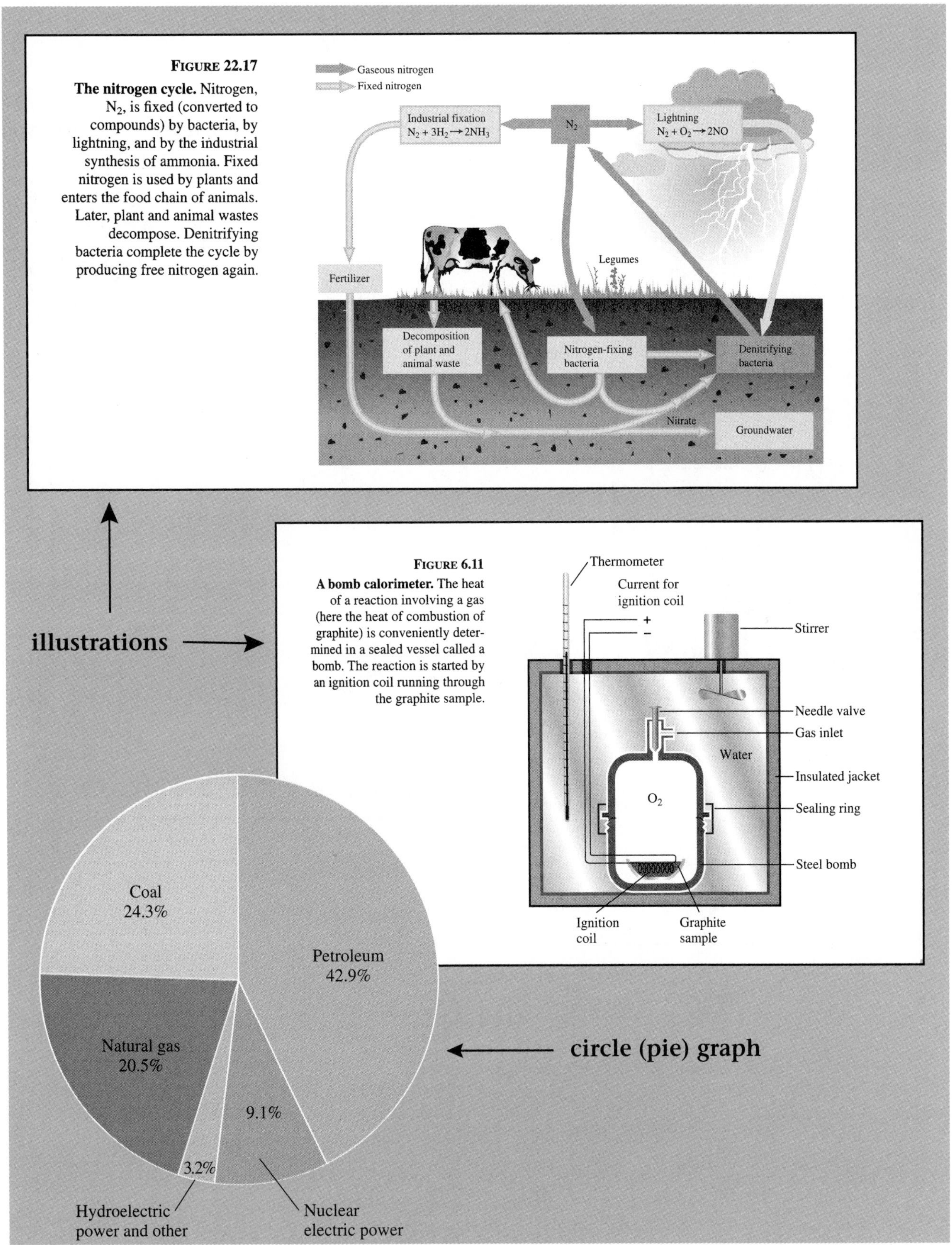

Figs. 22.17, 6.11, 6.14, Darrell Ebbing, *General Chemistry,* Fifth Edition. Copyright © by Houghton Mifflin Company. Used with permission.

FIGURE 13.5 Textbook Graphics: Some Common Types *(continued)*

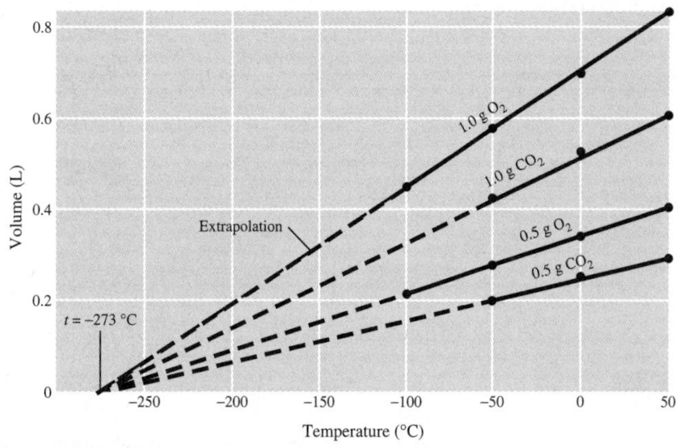

FIGURE 5.8
Linear relationship of gas volume and temperature at constant pressure

line graph

Figure 12.3
Relative Size of the Federal Bureaucracy

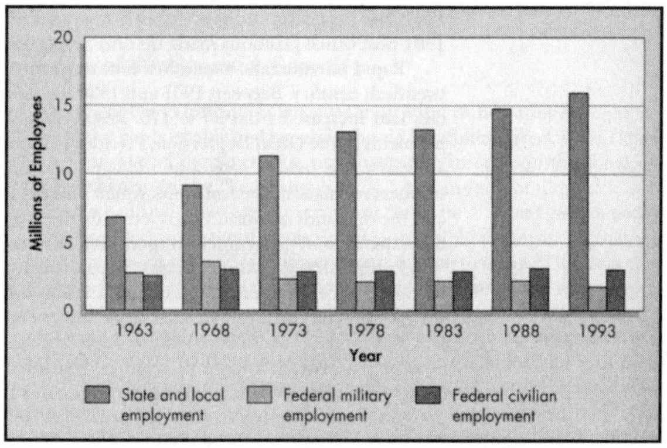

bar graph

tables

TABLE 5.1
Properties of Selected Gases

Name	Formula	Color	Odor	Toxicity
Ammonia	NH_3	Colorless	Penetrating	Toxic
Carbon dioxide	CO_2	Colorless	Odorless	Nontoxic
Carbon monoxide	CO	Colorless	Odorless	Very toxic
Chlorine	Cl_2	Pale green	Irritating	Very toxic
Helium	He	Colorless	Odorless	Nontoxic
Hydrogen	H_2	Colorless	Odorless	Nontoxic
Hydrogen chloride	HCl	Colorless	Irritating	Corrosive
Hydrogen sulfide	H_2S	Colorless	Foul	Very toxic
Methane	CH_4	Colorless	Odorless	Nontoxic
Neon	Ne	Colorless	Odorless	Nontoxic
Nitrogen	N_2	Colorless	Odorless	Nontoxic
Nitrogen dioxide	NO_2	Red–brown	Irritating	Very toxic
Oxygen	O_2	Colorless	Odorless	Nontoxic
Sulfur dioxide	SO_2	Colorless	Choking	Toxic

Table 3.3 BALANCE SHEET FOR A COLLEGE STUDENT (BILL SOSHNIK), JANUARY 1, 1994

Assets	Dollars		Percent
Cash on hand	$ 85.00		1.4
Checking account	335.00		5.5
Savings account	800.00		13.2
Personal property*	1,240.00		20.5
Automobile	3,600.00		59.4
Total assets		$6,060.00	100.0
Liabilities			
Utilities	$ 30.00		.5
Telephone	70.00		1.0
Bank loan — automobile	3,100.00		51.2
College loan	1,000.00		16.5
Government educational loan	2,500.00		41.3
Total liabilities		$6,700.00	110.6
Net worth		($640.00)	(10.6)
Total liabilities and net worth		$6,060.00	100.0

*Schedule includes clothes, $800; dresser, $50; television, $150; chair, $30; table, $40; desk, $120; and dishes/tableware, $50.

Fig. 5.8 and Table 5.1 from Darrell Ebbing, *General Chemistry,* Fifth Edition. Copyright © by Houghton Mifflin Company. Used with permission. Fig. 12.3 from Alan R. Gitelson et. al., *American Government,* Fourth Edition. Copyright © 1996 by Houghton Mifflin Company. Used with permission. Table 3.3 from Thomas E. Garman and Raymond E. Forgue, *Personal Finance,* Fourth Edition. Copyright © 1994 by Houghton Mifflin Company. Used with permission.

Line Graphs. Like bar graphs, line graphs illustrate relationships between variables. Trends are represented by lines instead of bars or columns. Voter turnout among different age groups over several presidential elections could be illustrated by either a line graph or a bar graph.

Diagrams. Diagrams are drawings that illustrate functions or processes. A *process diagram* may illustrate the steps and stages of a process or trace a sequence of events. The stages of pregnancy and the events that occur during cell division are two examples. *Function diagrams* illustrate parts of a whole, such as the separate bones of a skeleton.

Tables. Tables are organized lists or rows of numbers or text. They classify and compare large amounts of information or statistical data. A table that lists contraceptive methods and their rates of effectiveness is one example.

To read a graphic with understanding, determine its *purpose;* discover what *relationship* it illustrates; and find the connection between the graphic and the *narrative,* or text, that accompanies it. To help you recall these steps, remember the acronym **PRN:**

1. To determine the **purpose,** read the title of the graphic and its caption for any clues they may provide.
2. To help you discover the **relationship,** determine the graphic's type. If you know the type, then you know what to look for. If you have identified a graphic as a process diagram, for example, then you know that you must determine what process is illustrated, be able to trace the steps, and understand what happens at each stage.
3. To find the **narrative** connection, read the text that accompanies the graphic. Look back and forth, if necessary. For each part of the explanation in the text, find its counterpart in the graphic. To test yourself, try to reconstruct the explanation in your own words while looking at the graphic.

EXERCISE 13.6

Choose a graphic from one of your textbooks. Using *PRN,* read the graphic and interpret it by answering the following questions.

1. What is the graphic's title?

   ____

2. Is there a caption? If so, summarize what it says.

   ____

3. Based on your answers to 1 and 2, what is the graphic's purpose?

   ____

4. What type of graphic is it?

   ____

5. Based on your answer to question 4, what relationship does the graphic illustrate?

____

____

6. What is the narrative connection between your graphic and the text that accompanies it?

____

____

____

EVALUATE WHAT YOU LEARN

To *evaluate* means to determine worth or value. To evaluate also means *to judge,* that is, to make decisions about whether something is right or wrong, good or bad, fair or unfair. If you decide to withdraw from a course, you must evaluate that decision on the basis of whether it is good or bad for you. On the one hand, withdrawing from a course may have a negative effect on your grade point average. But a positive effect might be that it will leave you more time to devote to your remaining courses. Evaluating your progress in a course means checking yourself for improvement. What skills have you mastered since the beginning of the term, and what effect has the application of these skills had on your grades?

Making evaluations is a critical thinking strategy you use in other areas of your life besides college. Deciding whether to take a job, quit a job, marry, divorce, or buy a home all depend on making judgments about these important decisions. At work, you may be asked to judge which machines, tools, or procedures produce the desired outcomes.

An evaluation is a *measurement* of worth. "How much will this help or hurt me?" and "How important is this to me?" are questions you can ask when making evaluations. To make evaluations, you need a standard to go by. To evaluate the worth of continuing a relationship that has proved unsatisfying, your standards might be the expectations you have for a relationship. To evaluate the purchase of a car, your standards might include its being safe, dependable, and affordable. There are many criteria, or standards, by which you can make sound evaluations. As a college student, you can evaluate what you learn by applying three basic standards: *reliability, objectivity,* and *usefulness*. Figure 13.6 on page 291 shows how making evaluations extends to several skill areas and activities.

Reliability

A good way to check for reliability is to ask yourself three questions:

- Who says so?
- What are his or her credentials?
- How does he or she know?

FIGURE 13.6 **Evaluate What You Are Learning: How You Can Use This Critical Thinking Strategy**

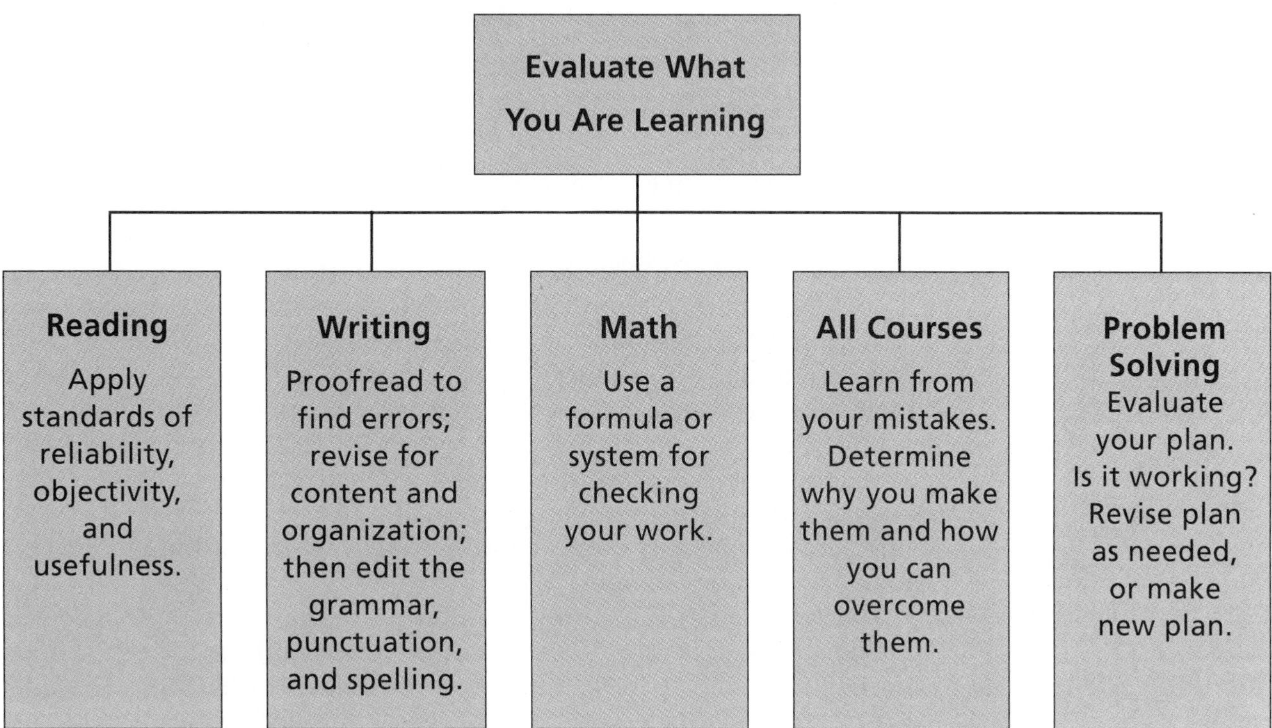

As you read, research, and listen to lectures, remember that primary sources are more reliable than secondary sources. A *primary source* is a first-hand or direct source of information. A *secondary source* is an interpretation of a primary source. For example, if the president addresses the nation on television, the text of his speech is a primary source. If a newscaster summarizes what the president said, the summary is a secondary source. A newspaper account of the president's speech is also a secondary source, unless the newspaper reprints the entire text of the speech. Have you ever listened to a newscaster's summary of a speech you just heard and wondered whether the newscaster heard the same speech you heard? A secondary source is only as reliable as the person who interprets the primary source.

Sometimes you may have difficulty in determining whether a source is primary or secondary. When you are doing research on a topic, look at the bibliographies at the ends of books and articles you read. If the same titles and authors appear over and over again, chances are that they represent either primary sources or reliable secondary sources of information. If you are just beginning to do research, your instructor or a librarian can help you select sources and evaluate their reliability.

Another way to evaluate reliability is to look at an author's background or credentials. If you are doing research on a scientific topic such as the greenhouse effect, a research scientist with a Ph.D. who is on the faculty at a major university is a more reliable source than a concerned political activist who writes letters on the subject to his or her local newspaper. Instructors try to select textbooks that are reliable sources of information, written by experts who may be instructors themselves. The title page of a textbook usually includes a college affiliation underneath the writer's name.

Objectivity

To determine whether a writer's presentation is objective, ask yourself three questions as you read:

- What is the writer's or speaker's purpose?
- Are all sides of the issue presented or acknowledged?
- Is the language free of slanted or manipulative words and phrases?

If the writer's or speaker's purpose is to inform, then you should expect the development of the topic to be mainly factual. Opinions should be supported by sound reasons and identified as opinions with introductory or interruptive phrases such as *it seems* or *it appears that.* Writers such as textbook authors, whose purpose is to inform or increase your knowledge, should give fair treatment to differing viewpoints so that you can make a reasoned decision concerning what to believe or how to act. Their language should be free of words and phrases that provoke emotional reactions that could cloud your judgment. Although most of them do try to be objective, some may have a motive or viewpoint that influences their choice of words or examples.

A writer who has something to gain by a change in readers' beliefs or behaviors will not be as objective as one who has nothing to gain. Writers whose purpose is to persuade may write forcefully in favor of one viewpoint. If they persuade fairly, they will acknowledge other viewpoints. Writers who persuade unfairly are likely to distort facts, leave out facts, state opinions as if they were facts, and use manipulative language. Usually they have something to gain by an appeal to your emotions or a change in your beliefs or behavior. Advertisers want your money. The proponents of various interest groups want you on their side. Politicians want your vote. Apply your critical thinking skills as you read or listen to their material and evaluate their ideas for objectivity.

Can you spot the manipulative language in these two examples?

- An animal rights activist says, "We must stop the needless torture of animals in medical experiments that serve only to provide researchers on college campuses with lucrative grants."
- A medical researcher says, "No one in our profession sets out to torture animals in painful experiments, but some pain and even death may be necessary if, through these experiments, we can effect cures that will prevent the loss of human life."

In the first example, the activist tries to manipulate your feelings by suggesting that research is an excuse to get grant money, that animals in experiments are always tortured, and that the experiments are needless. In the second example, the researcher denies that anyone in his or her profession would be so callous as to deliberately cause an animal pain. At the same time, the researcher suggests that some pain or death is acceptable if it will save human lives. In this example, the researcher manipulates your thinking so that you must make a choice: your life or an animal's life.

Manipulative language is characterized by simple arguments that seek to explain complex issues. Read the next two examples.

Passage A

It is becoming impossible to find good candidates willing to run for public office. A politician's life is an open book. The would-be candidate for office must dodge photographers and news reporters lurking in the bushes around his house, eavesdropping on his conversations in restaurants, and spying on him through binoculars when he is on his boat supposedly away from their prying eyes. If a person has ever taken a drink, smoked a marijuana cigarette, had a meaningless affair, or cheated on an exam, his chances for winning an election are ruined. Journalists and photographers have gone too far. Everyone, even a political candidate, is entitled to a private life.

Passage B

As soon as someone runs for election, it is understood that she gives up her right to privacy. Indeed, there is some question as to whether the Constitution guarantees a right to privacy to anyone. We the public have the right to know whether we can trust the people we elect to office. Cheating on one's husband or on an exam isn't the issue. The real issue is dishonesty. Most people think that someone who would cheat in one situation would probably cheat in another. Also, drinking to excess, using drugs, engaging in illicit sex, and dishonest behavior of any kind show poor judgment. People want elected officials to be responsible. Therefore, journalists and photographers perform a great public service when they expose the indiscretions of candidates.

Both passages oversimplify the issues raised by their proponents. Both writers attempt to manipulate the reader's thinking with an appeal to emotions instead of an appeal to reason. The writer of the first passage blames journalists and photographers for making people afraid to run for office. The writer of the second passage praises journalists and photographers for exposing the weaknesses of potential candidates. The first writer tries to make you identify with the candidate whose privacy has been

EXERCISE 13.7

Identify words or phrases in each of the passages above that appeal to readers' emotions and manipulate their feelings.

Passage A: ____________________

____

____

____

Passage B: ____________________

____

____

____

FIGURE 13.7 Standards of Evaluation: Questions to Ask

Reliability	• Who says so? • What are his or her qualifications? • How does he or she know?
Objectivity	• What is the purpose? • Are all sides of the issue presented? • Is the language free of slanted or manipulative words and phrases?
Usefulness	• What have I learned? • Will I use what I have learned either now or in the future? • Does the new knowledge relate to my courses? • Having learned the material, am I more interested in the topic?

violated. The second writer appeals to your right as a citizen to know as much as you can about the person you will elect to office. Are journalists and photographers scandalmongers or public servants? Neither passage offers convincing evidence.

Usefulness

To evaluate the usefulness of what you learn, consider what you have gained from it. Does it improve your understanding of the subject? Have you gained a skill or knowledge that you can use now or in the future? Can you relate the knowledge or skill to your course objectives? Has the information made you more interested in the topic it covers? If you answer *no* to all of these questions, then try to figure out what is missing and what you might need to learn next. Figure 13.7 above lists the questions you can ask to evaluate information.

CONFIDENCE BUILDER

Thinking Creatively

Creative thinking is a skill you can develop.

How does creative thinking differ from critical thinking? The tool of the critical thinker is *analysis*. The tool of the creative thinker is *invention*. Analysis is the procress of logical reasoning. When you think through the steps of a process or consider all sides of an issue or argument, you are using analysis. When you come up with a solution to a problem, or when you use what you know to discover what you don't know, you are using invention.

Critical thinking and creative thinking work together. The COPE problem-solving method provides a good example. The COPE method defines a problem as a *challenge,* which is a positive way of looking at a difficult situation. Your first step is an analytical one: to clearly identify your challenge. Suppose your challenge is "I have gained 10 pounds," and the result you want is "I want to lose the extra weight." To add a creative thinking step, ask yourself, "What is in conflict with the result I want?" You might say, "My conflicts are that I hate diets and I don't have time for exercise." Now you have a clue that will help you work through COPE's second step, considering your *options*. Since any effective weight-loss program involves a combination of diet and exercise, you must choose among the possible options one that will help you overcome your conflicts. Analysis helps you determine what the options are. Invention helps you arrive at a *plan,* the third step of COPE. Your plan will be one you create that chooses a diet you can live with and an exercise program you can follow in the time you have available.

The last step of COPE, *evaluate,* works by both analysis and invention. Suppose that after five weeks, you have lost only two pounds. Now you must analyze what has happened. Did you stick to your diet? Did you make time for exercise? What has gone wrong? More importantly, what can you do about it? Again, thinking creatively about your challenge will help you discover ways to modify your weight-loss plan and get you back on track.

No matter what your challenge, a valuable question to ask that starts the creative thinking process is "What if?" This question takes you beyond what you know to imagine what could be. The members of a work team in a large company were having trouble using the company's new computer operating system. Some members resisted learning the program because it was too difficult. Others were angry because they liked the old program better. A major problem was that help was not immediately available as problems arose. The supervisor wondered, "What if help were more readily available? Would team members be more willing to work with the program?" Team members were involved in finding a solution. Working with a technical writer, they produced an in-house manual that simplified the program.

By using a combination of critical and creative thinking, you also can meet any challenge. Invention and analysis are your tools.

CRITICAL THINKING APPLICATION

Many large corporations spend millions of dollars a year on magazine advertising. They must believe that people respond to magazine ads, or they wouldn't pay for full-page ads in magazines such as *Time* or *Newsweek*. Advertisers profit by researching and appealing to the market for their products or services. Thinking critically about the ads will prevent your being manipulated.

Working with a group according to the guidelines explained in Chapter 1 or working on your own, examine the Federal Express ad on page 297. Then answer the questions below.

1. To whom does the ad appeal? Who uses FedEx and other express delivery services?
2. To what consumer need does the ad appeal?
3. Who are some of FedEx's competitors?
4. How many European business centers can FedEx ship to by 10:30 A.M. of the second business day?
5. Why do you think the ad doesn't specify the cost of the service?
6. According to the ad, your FedEx packages now arrive "a little earlier than they used to." What is the advantage of faster service?
7. What is FedEx's guarantee if the shipment doesn't arrive on time?
8. What is the relationship between the picture and the printed message (ad copy)?
9. What inferences can you make from FedEx's slogan: "The Way The World Works"?
10. Evaluate the ad for usefulness: What is its purpose? Does it accomplish the purpose? How?

Hold on to your hats. FedEx announces delivery to 17 major business centers in Europe by 10:30 a.m. Which means your letters and packages arrive a little earlier than they used to. Europe wasn't always this close, but today, it's the way the world works.SM

The Way The World Works.SM

©1996 Federal Express Corporation. Call 1-800-247-4747 for details. TDD: 1-800-238-4461. http://www.fedex.com
Check service guide and addenda for details on European cities and money-back guarantee.

SUMMARY

The summary is followed by a partially filled-in chart. Read the summary; then complete the chart.

Critical thinking is the process of constructing and evaluating meaning from the world around you as revealed through your five senses. Four strategies can help you think critically: Examine your *assumptions,* make *predictions,* sharpen your *interpretations,* and *evaluate* what you learn.

Your assumptions are your beliefs, what you take for granted. To examine your assumptions, you must first determine what they are. Make an effort to relate new information to prior knowledge and experience. Always be willing to change your assumptions when new information proves them wrong.

Your predictions are what you think may happen, or what you can anticipate based on the information you have. To make predictions, have a purpose for reading and listening. Try to anticipate what follows in your reading or in a lecture. Ask questions to guide your thinking.

Your interpretations are the meanings you get from what you read or hear. To sharpen your interpretations, determine a writer's or speaker's purpose. Read or listen for point, proof, and organizational patterns. Define terms and look for implications in what you read.

Your evaluation of what you learn is the worth or significance you see in it. To evaluate what you read or hear, ask questions that help you assess the reliability, objectivity, and usefulness of the information.

Critical Thinking Strategies	Definitions	Ways to Develop
Assumptions	Beliefs Things taken for granted	Determine assumptions. Relate new info. to old. Change if necessary.
	What you can anticipate	
		Determine purpose. Listen for point, proof, pattern. Define terms and see implications.
Evaluations		

YOUR REFLECTIONS

Reflect on what you have learned about critical thinking and how you can best apply that information. Use the following list of questions to stimulate your thinking; then write your reflections. Your response may include answers to one or more of the questions. Incorporate in your writing specific information from this chapter or previous chapters as needed.

- Would you describe yourself as a critical thinker? Why or why not?
- Of the strategies explained in this chapter, which ones are new to you? Which ones have you already used, and how?
- What else do you do, or have done, that you would call "critical thinking"?
- Why is critical thinking an important skill? Explain how you use critical thinking at work or in your personal life.
- What have you learned from this chapter that you can apply to improve the way you think and learn?

Date ______________________________

CHAPTER 14

Becoming an Active Reader

Reading is a lifelong skill and a key to success in college and career. As a college student, you must read, understand, and remember information not only from textbooks, but also from journals, periodicals, and other sources. As an employee in tomorrow's workplace, you will have to be able to read well enough to understand correspondence, manuals, graphics, and specifications.

Reading is also a necessary part of any study system. You can gain essential information from your textbooks by employing these three strategies to improve your application of the *read* step of SQ3R, explained in Chapter 7, or whatever system you use:

- Take control of your reading process by becoming an active reader.
- Find the writer's point and proof, and look for implications in what you read.
- Use underlining and marking systems to focus your attention and identify information to recite and review.

To find out whether you are an active reader, complete Awareness Check 20.

AWARENESS CHECK #20

Are You an Active Reader?

To determine how actively you read, check the following statements that apply to you.

1. I usually read straight through a textbook chapter from beginning to end without stopping.
2. I stop frequently to re-read difficult parts or to check my comprehension by asking myself questions about what I have read.
3. If I don't understand something I have read, I wait to hear the instructor's explanation in class.
4. When I hit a rough spot, I make a note to remind myself to ask about it in class.
5. I usually have trouble deciding what is important in a chapter; often I'm not sure what the writer's point is.
6. I can usually find the writer's point, and I rarely have trouble determining what is important.
7. I often have a hard time relating information covered in a chapter to my life or to the course as a whole.
8. I can often see a connection between something I've read in a chapter and my life or the course.
9. I rarely underline, mark, highlight, or make notes in my textbooks.
10. I usually mark, underline, highlight, or make notes in my textbooks.
11. I have difficulty deciding what to mark or underline.
12. I can usually tell what to mark or underline.
13. I have to be interested in what I am reading to get anything out of it.
14. Even if a subject covered in a textbook doesn't interest me, I can still determine what I should learn and remember from it.
15. I think I should be able to read something once and remember the information covered in it.
16. I know that I may have to read something several times before the information sinks in.

If you checked mostly even-numbered statements, you are probably already an active reader. If you checked mostly odd-numbered statements, you may be a passive reader who would benefit from developing active reading strategies.

BE AN ACTIVE READER

If you are an *active reader,* you are in control of your reading process and know how to direct your attention. In addition, you have a purpose for reading; you know what information to look for and why. You constantly question what you read and try to make sense of the information as it unfolds. If you are a *passive reader,* you are not in control, but are like television watchers who expect their attention to be engaged. As a result, they are often distracted. As their minds wander from what they are reading, they may "wake up" in the middle of a paragraph, wondering what they have read. Instead of trying to make sense of what they read, passive readers wait for the moment when everything falls into place. Unfortunately, that rarely happens.

As an active reader, you think about what you read as you are reading—perhaps underlining or marking as you go. Then, when you return to a section to find specific information or the answer to a question, you have a good idea of where to look. You also set realistic goals: If you have sixty pages to read, you don't try to do it at one sitting. Instead, you break the reading assignment into smaller chunks so that your level of interest remains high and your attention stays focused. As an active reader, you are also a critical thinker. Remember that critical thinking, as explained in Chapter 13, is the process of constructing meaning. *You* are the one who either makes sense or doesn't make sense of what you read; comprehension doesn't happen automatically.

Active reading, therefore, is a constructive process that requires critical thinking. The critical thinking strategies *assume, predict, interpret,* and *evaluate,* explained in Chapter 13, are part of the active reading process. As you use them, you are interacting with the text actively rather than passively. Another active reading strategy is setting realistic reading goals based on what research tells us about concentration, memory, and reading comprehension. You can't remember what you don't understand, and you will have trouble understanding unless you keep your attention focused on the task of reading. Moreover, as an active reader you must accept responsibility for keeping yourself motivated and for not giving in to feelings of boredom. Thus, becoming an active reader is also a way of developing an internal locus of control. To develop active reading strategies, follow these suggestions:

- **Set a realistic reading goal.** Don't try to read sixty pages all at once. Break up the assignment into two or three sessions—whatever amount of time you think you can maintain optimum concentration. If you feel your concentration slipping before your time is up, stop, take a break, and then refocus your attention.

- **Read with a purpose.** Know what you are expected to get out of the assignment. Perhaps you will be tested on the material, you may be asked to summarize the information or perhaps you have several questions in mind that you expect the assignment to answer. Having specific information to look for may help you keep your attention focused on your reading and should give you a reason to talk yourself out of any boredom or lack of interest.

- **Read with a pen or highlighter** so you can mark parts of the chapter that answer your questions, suggest possible test questions, explain concepts, or expand on topics covered in class lectures. If you are reading from a library book or other source that you cannot mark, make notes on note cards or in a notebook, making sure to label them with the source's title, page number, or any other identifying information you may need later. For more information on marking textbooks, see pages 315–318 of this chapter.
- **Review and recite from your notes or marking.** Reviewing helps reinforce your learning so that it stays in your memory. Reciting from notes or textbook markings provides another pathway into your memory: the auditory sense. Reciting is especially helpful for those who have an auditory learning preference, but anyone can benefit from it.

The more active you become in taking control of your reading process, the less likely you will be to lapse into passive reading habits. As an active reader, you are *doing something* throughout the process, whether it be marking the text, stopping to think about what you have read, re-reading difficult passages, formulating questions and looking for answers, or reciting from your notes and markings. These activities aid in the transfer of information from your short-term memory to your long-term memory. For more on how the memory process works and is enhanced by the way you study, see Chapter 10.

You can become aware of the times you are either comprehending well or poorly. To read actively and consciously, you must be able to follow the development of ideas as they occur in a chapter or other source. One way you can do this is by reading to find the writer's point, proof, and implications.

EXERCISE 14.1

Write an evaluation of yourself as an active or passive reader. Describe your study system for reading a textbook chapter or other assigned reading material. Be specific. What type of learning style is dominant in the way you read? If possible, describe the study system you used for an assigned reading in one of your classes and any difficulties you had. Also, take into consideration your results of Awareness Check 20 as you complete this exercise.

FIND THE POINT, PROOF, AND IMPLICATIONS

Paragraphs, as indicated in Figure 14.1, are the third ring in a widening circle of meaning that begins with words. Each paragraph within a chapter may provide information that is essential to your understanding of the whole chapter.

FIGURE 14.1 The Widening Circle of Meaning

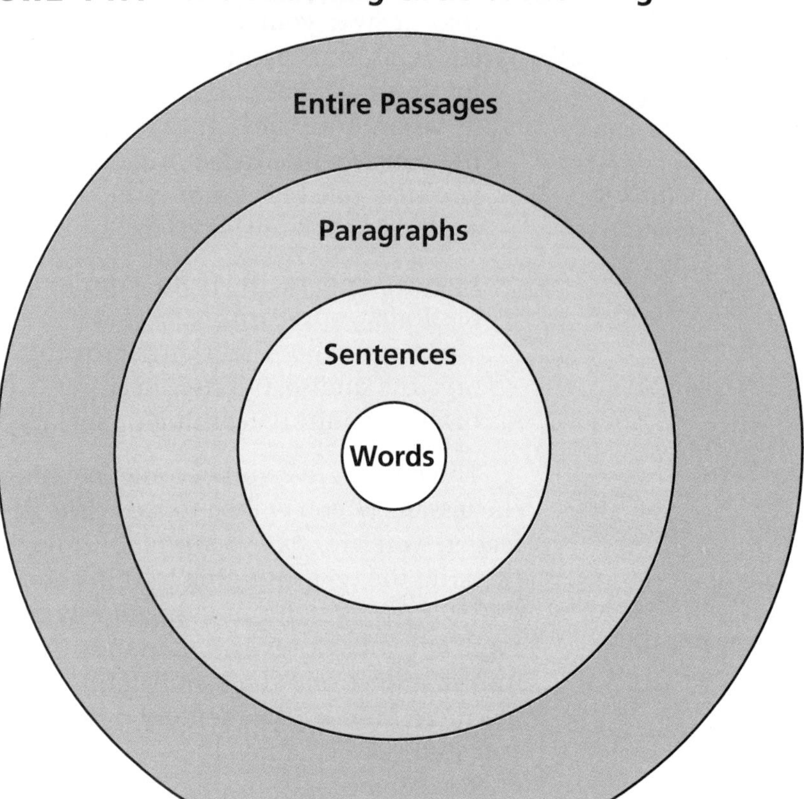

You can begin right away to improve your textbook reading by learning how to find the point in a paragraph. A paragraph is usually several sentences long, and it may contain three types of sentences:

1. The **topic sentence** is a direct statement of the writer's point, or main idea.
2. The **support sentences** contain major or minor details that develop, or prove, the writer's point.
3. The **concluding sentence** may restate the writer's point, introduce a new but related idea, make an inference about the writer's point, end the paragraph with another detail, or provide a transition to the next paragraph.

For examples of these three kinds of sentences, read the next paragraph and the explanation that follows it.

Topic sentence: Point

Adjusting to college can be difficult for students because of the pressures they face from family, teachers, and friends. *Family members, for example, may expect a student to add studying and attending classes to his or her other responsibilities. They may resent being asked to take on more chores or spending time alone while the student studies. A student who faces this kind of pressure from family may have difficulty reaching desired goals. Another pressure students face is from teachers. From the student's point of view, each instructor acts as if the*

Support sentences: Proof

student had no other courses to take. Add to this the necessity to get to every class on time, to attend class regularly, and to keep up with all assignments. Friends too can make a student's adjustment difficult. For one thing, they may pressure a student to put off studying to engage in leisure-time activities. Friends who are not attending college feel threatened and, without meaning to, may do or say things that make a student wonder if college is worth it. ***To overcome these pressures, a college student must have a strong desire to succeed.***

Concluding sentence

The first sentence of this paragraph is the **topic sentence**, which states the writer's point: Pressures from family, instructors, and friends can make students' adjustment to college difficult. The last sentence of the paragraph is the **concluding sentence.** In between are the **support sentences**, which give examples of three kinds of pressures and explain how these pressures can make it difficult for a student to adjust to college. The concluding sentence then introduces a new but related idea: Students can overcome these pressures.

Finding the Point

In a paragraph, the writer may make his or her point in one of two ways: (1) by stating it directly in a topic sentence, as in the example paragraph about pressures students face, or (2) by leaving it unstated and letting the reader infer the point from the proof.

Now read another paragraph about students' pressures:

Some parents may insist that a student carry a full-time load and maintain an A or B average while working part time and sharing household tasks. A student who has too many things to do may not be able to do any one of them very well. Another pressure students face is from instructors' expectations. Instructors expect students to arrive on time, to attend class regularly, and to keep up with all assignments. They also expect students to participate in class, ask questions, and do extra work or get help outside of class if they are having trouble meeting course objectives. Friends too can make a student's adjustment difficult. For one thing, they may pressure a student to put off studying in order to party or to engage in some other leisure-time activity. Friends who choose not to attend college may try to make a student feel guilty for leaving them behind. To overcome these pressures, a college student must have a strong desire to succeed.

This paragraph has no topic sentence, but several clues help you infer the writer's point. From the third sentence, which begins, "Another pressure," you can infer that the first two sentences are talking about one kind of pressure and that now you are reading about another kind. The sixth sentence, which begins, "Friends too," introduces a third pressure students face. In the last sentence, the phrase "these pressures" is the strongest clue that the paragraph is about the effects of the three kinds of pressure.

When a paragraph has no topic sentence, the writer's point is implied by the proof, or detailed support sentences. Once you identify the idea or topic that all the details support, you should be able to state the writer's point in your own words.

© Chip Henderson/TSW

To find the writer's point, read a paragraph carefully and then follow these steps:

1. Look for the **topic sentence.** It can be anywhere in the paragraph, but it is often the first sentence. The topic sentence is the most general sentence in the paragraph. It combines the writer's topic and comment and summarizes *all* the information presented in the support sentences. The topic sentence expresses the writer's point.

2. If the writer's point is not stated in a topic sentence, identify the **topic** by inferring the point from the details. Ask yourself, "What one idea do all the sentences in the paragraph support?" Look for signal words that introduce major details.

3. Find the writer's **comment.** In general, what does the writer say to expand your knowledge about the topic? Does the writer *explain how* to do something? Does the writer *compare two things?* Does the writer *explain why* something exists or *give reasons* as to why something happens in a certain way? Does the writer *argue for or against* a particular idea?

EXERCISE 14.2

Find the writer's point in each paragraph. If the point is stated, underline it. If the point is implied, write a sentence that expresses the main idea.

1. *Increases in the number of college-level jobs depend generally on the overall rate of economic and employment growth in the United States, but more specifically on employment growth in occupations that typically require college graduates. Additional college-level jobs open up in occupations when skill requirements or business practices change, resulting in employers hiring college graduates to fill positions formerly held by less educated workers, a phenomenon known as educational upgrading. A significant number of openings for college graduates will also arise as workers holding existing college-level jobs leave the labor force and need to be replaced. . . .*

From "1994–2005: Lots of College-Level Jobs—But Not for All Graduates," Kristina J. Shelley, *Occupational Outlook Quarterly,* Summer 1996, Vol. 40, No. 2, Office of Employment Projections, Bureau of Labor Statistics, U.S. Department of Labor.

____

____

2. *You may frequently hear the terms* drug abuse *and* drug addiction *in certain college classes. Although all forms of drug addiction are classified as drug abuse, not all drug abuse is considered addictive. Drug abuse may be only an occasional indiscretion with a chemical substance, whereas addiction suggests a regular, dependent pattern of substance abuse. The individual who likes to get intoxicated for the weekend game may simply be abusing alcohol, but the person who makes drinking a dominant part of each day's activities is addicted to alcohol.*

From *Toward a Self-Managed Life Style,* 3rd ed., Robert L. Williams and James D. Long, Houghton Mifflin Co., 1988

____

____

3. *Some carcinogens in the environment are present in such low concentrations that their effects can scarcely be noted. But one carcinogenic agent has an effect so strong that it cannot be ignored: cigarette smoking. Lung cancers, nearly 90 percent of which are caused by smoking, are now the leading cause of death from cancer among men and women in the United States. A decision to avoid smoking virtually ensures that an individual will not suffer from this disease.*

From *Biology,* Joseph S. Levine and Kenneth R. Miller, D. C. Heath and Company, 1991.

____

____

Finding the Proof

To find the writer's proof in a paragraph, identify the details that support the point. Writers frequently use three types of details:

- Facts
- Reasons
- Examples

Facts. A fact is an observation, quotation, statistic, date, number, report of an event, or expert testimony that can be verified. For example, if a movie critic says there are twelve shootings within the first seven minutes of a new action film, you can verify this information by seeing the movie and counting the shootings that occur within the first seven minutes.

The writers of the following paragraph use facts to support the point:

Most children receive the news of their parents' divorce as a shock, followed by depression, denial, anger, and low self-esteem. Fantasies of parental reconciliation are almost universal. The adjustment period for children varies according to their age and emotional maturity, but usually children resume normal development within a year or two. Judith Wallerstein and Joan Kelly (1980) found that five years after a divorce 34 percent of children were resilient and happy, 29 percent were doing reasonably well, and 37 percent were depressed, looking back toward life before the divorce with longing. These researchers have noted age differences in their studies of children of divorce. Very young children and older adolescents seem to handle the situation best; adjustment appears most difficult for children ages seven to eleven.

From *Toward a Self-Managed Life Style,* 3rd ed., Robert L. Williams and James D. Long, Houghton Mifflin Co., 1988.

The writers' point is that the time it takes for children to adjust to their parents' divorce varies with the age and maturity of the children. The point is clearly stated in the third sentence. The writers' proof is their summary of the findings of the researchers Wallerstein and Kelly. To verify the writers' proof, you could read the book or periodical in which Wallerstein and Kelly reported their findings.

Reasons. Writers use reasons to support a point when their purpose is to explain *why* something happens, *why* something is important, *why* one thing is better than another, or *why* they feel or think as they do. Think of reasons as the *causes* that are responsible for producing certain effects, results, or outcomes. For example, a sportswriter may use reasons to explain why a basketball team lost an important game it was favored to win. Or a political commentator might write an article explaining reasons for a presidential candidate's popularity among a certain group of voters.

In the following paragraph, reasons support the writer's point:

One of the most important goals that a college student can aim for is an expanded vocabulary. One reason this goal is so important is that an expanded vocabulary can improve students' writing. With sufficient words and definitions at their command, students will have less difficulty writing what they mean. Also, increased reading improves vocabulary, which leads to greater comprehension. A third reason for improving vocabulary is the confidence students feel when they use words accurately. Students are less afraid to speak out in class discussions or to give reports and speeches when they know they are not going to mispronounce or misuse words. Increasing the vocabulary is a worthwhile goal for students who also want to improve their speaking, reading, and writing.

The writer's point in this paragraph is that an expanded vocabulary is an important goal that students should try to reach. The point is stated in a topic sentence, which is the first sentence of the paragraph. The writer supports the point by stating three reasons students should increase their vocabularies:

1. An expanded vocabulary improves writing.
2. An increased vocabulary improves reading.
3. An improved vocabulary results in confidence.

The *signal phrases* "one reason" and "third reason" help you locate the writer's proof. The second reason follows the signal word "also." Chapters 3 and 15 explain ways that writers and speakers use signal words to help you follow their ideas.

Examples. Examples are situations, instances, or even people that writers use to illustrate, support, or clarify a point. Writers may use one extended example or several short ones. Or they may support a point with an example, then use facts or reasons as additional proof. Some use examples as minor details to explain and clarify major details.

Notice how the writers use examples in the next paragraph:

Many legends were based on bizarre possibilities of matings between individuals of different species. The wife of Minos, according to Greek mythology, mated with a bull and produced the Minotaur. Folk heroes of Russia and Scandinavia were traditionally the sons of women who had been captured by bears, from which these men derived their great strength and so enriched the national stock. The camel and the leopard also mated from time to time, according to the early naturalists, who were otherwise unable—and it is hard to blame them—to explain an animal as improbable as the giraffe (the common giraffe still bears the scientific name of Giraffa camelopardalis). Thus folklore reflected early and imperfect glimpses into the nature of hereditary relationships.

From Helena Curtis and N. Sue Barnes, *Biology,* 5th ed., Worth Publishers Inc., 1989.

In the first sentence of this paragraph, the writers make the point that many legends are based on strange matings between members of different species. Examples of three legends support the point:

1. The Minotaur was a legendary being born of Minos's wife, who mated with a bull.

2. Russian and Scandinavian folk heroes were believed to have great strength because they were the sons of women who had mated with bears.

3. Because the giraffe was such an odd-looking creature, a legend developed that giraffes were the offspring of camels and leopards.

These examples, or major details, are easy to understand. The writers add a minor detail that makes the giraffe example even more interesting. The animal's scientific name reflects earlier scientists' beliefs about its heredity.

EXERCISE 14.3

Read each passage and check whether the writer's proof is based mainly on facts, reasons, or examples.

1. No two people spend their money in exactly the same way because personal values influence financial decisions. Our values shape our standard of what we want our lives to be. ***Values*** *are fundamental beliefs of what is important, desirable, and worthwhile that serve as the basis for goals. Each of us is different from others in the ways we value education, spiritual life, health, employment, credit use, family life, and many other factors. Values change little over a lifetime. Personal financial goals grow out of our values because we consider some things more important or desirable than others. We express our values, in part, by the ways in which we spend our money. Thus our personal values dictate our financial plans.*

From *Personal Finance,* 4th ed., E. Thomas Garman and Raymond E. Forgue, Houghton Mifflin Co., 1994.

☐ **Facts** ☐ **Reasons** ☐ **Examples**

2. Memo to All Employees
From J. Todd, Manager

It is with deep regret that I inform you of the passing of one whose life has been an example to all of us. Spot was the mainstay of Curtis Nursery and Landscaping. The first to arrive and the last to leave, he greeted everyone warmly. He was a friend to all and discriminated against none. Who among us has not sought Spot's company when in need of a little cheering up? Spot has never been one to miss a day at work. This morning, we knew something was wrong when he was not waiting for us in the back of the truck. Instead, we found him in his favorite place under the house, where he had died peacefully during the night. A gentleman among dalmations, he will be missed.

☐ **Facts** ☐ **Reasons** ☐ **Examples**

3. Although projections indicate there will be more openings over the 1994–2005 period than there were during the 1983–94 period, even more entrants are expected, making for somewhat increased competition in the job market for future college graduates. . . . Between 1994 and 2005, job openings will average 1,040,000 annually, while college graduates joining the labor force are expected to average 1,340,000 each year. During the earlier 11-year period, openings averaged 970,000, while entrants averaged 1,180,000. Since the number of college graduate jobseekers will grow more quickly than the number of college-level jobs, the proportion of college graduate entrants expected to end up in noncollege jobs or unemployed will grow from 19 percent to over 22 percent.

From "1994–2005: Lots of College-Level Jobs—But Not for All Graduates," Kristina J. Shelley, *Occupational Outlook Quarterly,* Summer 1996, Vol. 40, No. 2, Office of Employment Projections, Bureau of Labor Statistics, U.S. Department of Labor.

☐ **Facts** ☐ **Reasons** ☐ **Examples**

Seeing Implications

To see an implication means to infer information that is implied, not stated. When the writer's point is unstated, you must infer the point from the details that are given. You might see many implications in a writer's point and proof, but most can be classified into one of two categories. *Personal implications* are those you can see by relating information you have read to what you know and have experienced. *Inferential implications* are educated guesses or conclusions you can draw about what the writer means based on stated information. The ability to see implications enables you to use the information you gain from your reading to understand or learn something else.

Personal Implications. You probably see some personal implications in every day's events because your experience tells you what to expect or what seems likely. Suppose you are absent from several classes, and the next time you attend there is no one in the classroom. You wait ten minutes, and still no one shows up. You conclude that class must not be meeting for some reason that was announced during your absence.

A good friend of yours is suddenly uncommunicative. When you try to start a conversation, you receive a sharp reply. You conclude that your friend is either preoccupied with a personal problem or that perhaps you have done something to offend him or her.

The manager of the company where you are employed needs someone to work overtime. You assume she will ask you because she knows you need the extra money and because you have helped out before.

Earlier in this chapter you found point and proof in a paragraph about the pressures students face from instructors, family, and friends. Now read a paragraph about another common source of pressure:

> *Stress is one pressure you bring on yourself when you go to class unprepared or when you don't manage your time effectively. Poor preparation*

results in inattention and that "lost" feeling. When you haven't read the assignment, you can't enter into the class discussion. If you haven't studied for a test, you are not likely to do well. In either situation, knowing your performance is not at its best creates stress. Being unprepared is almost always the result of poor time management. If you are like many students, you have more to do than you can possibly get done unless you schedule your time. Time management also involves setting priorities. You have to decide which is more important, seeing that new movie with a friend tonight or getting those algebra problems done for tomorrow's class. If you consistently put off doing things you need to do so that you can do what you want to do, the stress will eventually catch up with you. Make a decision now to improve your time management and to become better prepared for class, and you will have taken the first step toward reducing some of your stress.

One student who read this paragraph said, "Boy, that's me; I can always find something else to do besides algebra." This student related a detail from the paragraph to his own experience: "It's not that I don't want to do the work or that I don't realize I'm undermining my chances for success in the course. It's just that algebra is so hard. I know I'm going to get frustrated, so I dread getting started. As a result, I wait until the last minute, and that stresses me out." Relating the idea that you can bring stress on yourself to what she had read about locus of control in Chapter 1, another student said, "Since this kind of stress is the result of your own behavior, you can get rid of it by changing your behavior. In a way, this is easier to deal with than the stress that comes from the pressures you get from family, teachers, and friends. Those pressures are outside you, so they're harder to control."

Inferential Implications. What you read in your college textbooks will be more meaningful to you if you relate it to your experience with and knowledge of the writer's subject. Just as you can see personal implications in what you read, you can make *inferences,* or base informed guesses, on stated information. A valid inference is one that can be supported by a writer's points and proof.

Read the following paragraph:

Styles in cars, dress, furniture, and architecture come and go. Some styles become outdated or may disappear. Others never really go away but reassert themselves, with some changes, over many years. A ***fad*** *is a style of short duration. A* ***fashion*** *is a more lasting style. Both fads and fashions are engaged in by large groups of people. Fads of recent times include the hula hoop, hot pants, love beads, disco dancing, automobile "tail fins," and Klick-Klack Blocks. You may be thinking "I've never heard of some of these fads" and for good reason: They have come and gone. Fashions stay with us. Mini-skirts—once considered a fad—have enjoyed several revivals. Columns, a feature of ancient Greek architecture, have never gone out of style. You see them on public buildings and private homes—wherever a "classic" look is desired. Because fashions are more lasting than fads, they tend to be more socially acceptable. What is the difference between a fashionable person and a faddist? One is selective about which trends and behaviors to embrace, developing his or her own personal style. The other is* *swept along by each new fad that enjoys a brief popularity and seems to have no recognizable style.*

According to this paragraph, both fads and fashions are forms of collective behavior, but they differ in duration. You can use this information to make inferences about other behaviors. For example, a few years ago, many people displayed this sign in their cars' rear windows. Now you rarely see the sign. Was it a fad or a fashion?

The "baby on board" sign was probably a fad because of its relatively short duration. Bumper stickers, which may have started as a fad, have become a trend of longer duration and are, therefore, fashionable.

EXERCISE 14.4

Apply what you have learned about point, proof, and implications by completing this exercise with group members. Remember to follow the guidelines for group discussion explained in Chapter 1, pages 14–15. Read the following paragraph. Discuss the point, identify the proof, and decide whether you can see the implications. If you can, check *yes.* If not, check *no.* In either case, be able to explain why. When you reach consensus, record your conclusions on the lines below. Then evaluate your work.

If you want to expand your vocabulary, there are two methods you might want to try. The first method involves making note cards and using them for recitation and review of words that you want to learn. Prepare each note card by writing the word on one side of the card and its definition on the other side. Recite to learn by pronouncing the word and saying its definition. Then turn the card over and check yourself. Do this with each card until you can recite all the definitions from memory. Review the words by repeating these steps once a week, or as often as needed, to keep the words in your memory. The second method for learning words involves keeping a word list as you read. As you are reading an assigned chapter in one of your textbooks, jot down in a notebook any unfamiliar words you encounter. Look up these words and write the definitions that fit the contexts in which the words appear. The next time you read a chapter from the same textbook, keep your word list handy. You can add to the list or use it to review definitions of your words when they appear in new contexts. These two methods have worked for many students.

Point: If you want to expand your vocabulary, there are two methods you might want to try.

Proof:

a. ______________________________

____

____

b. ______________________________

____

____

Implications: **Yes** **No**

a. These vocabulary building methods may work for you. ☐ ☐

Explain your answer. ______________________________

____

____

____

Yes **No**

b. Using one of these two methods is the only way to expand your vocabulary. ☐ ☐

Explain your answer. ______________________________

____

____

____

Group Evaluation:

Evaluate your discussion. Did everyone contribute? Did you accomplish your task successfully? What additional questions do you have about point, proof, and implications? How will you find answers to your questions?

____

____

____

CONFIDENCE BUILDER
Calculate Your Reading Rate

Does Speed Reading Really Work?

You may have read accounts of people who can "read" 1,700 words per minute, and you may have wished you could read that fast. Speed reading is a controversial issue. Although you may want to increase your reading rate in order to save time or improve your chances of answering all the items on a timed reading test, you may lose comprehension as you gain reading speed if you try to read *too* fast.

Efficient reading, not speed reading, should be your goal. To read efficiently, adjust your reading rate to the *type of material* and your *purpose* for reading. You can skim a news or magazine article that you read for personal interest, but when you read textbooks and other materials to gain and retain knowledge, you must read slowly and carefully for maximum comprehension.

Do you read everything at the same rate? If you do, then you are not reading as efficiently as you could. Use this formula to calculate your reading rate; then experiment with adjusting your rate to the type of material and your purpose for reading it.

$$\frac{\text{No. of words in passage}}{\text{Reading time}} = \text{Reading rate in words per minute (wpm)}$$

To estimate the number of words in a passage, find the average number of words per line and multiply that number by the number of lines in the whole passage (if the passage is less than one page) or by the number of lines on one page (if the passage is several pages). Then use a stopwatch, digital watch, or clock with a second hand to time yourself, in minutes and seconds, as you read. Finally, round off to the nearest minute to use the formula.

USE A TEXTBOOK MARKING SYSTEM

Marking your textbooks by *underlining* or *highlighting* and by *annotating,* or making notes, improves your concentration because it focuses your attention on the task of reading. You must think critically about what you read so that you can make decisions about what to underline, highlight, or annotate. When done well, marking your textbook can save you time by providing you with specific information to review so that you do not have to re-read a whole chapter in order to study for a test. Whether you underline or highlight is a matter of personal preference. Highlighting pens come in a variety of colors, and the type of ink they contain may vary. Experiment with highlighters to find one that won't bleed through your pages. Underlining is best done with a fine-line ballpoint pen or felt-tip marker. Again, choose one that doesn't bleed through. A pencil may not be as good a choice for underlining. A sharp point may tear the paper; also, pencil smudges and fades and doesn't show up nearly as well.

Marking your textbook is an essential part of any study system because it improves your reception and retention of information. In the next paragraph a student, Alex, describes the system he worked out for underlining and marking his textbook:

> *I read one section at a time. After I read the section, I draw a bracket, [ ], around the main idea and put a star beside it in the margin. I underline the major details, and I put a number in a circle next to each detail. That way I can see how many details there are when I review the section for a test. If a word I don't know is defined in a section, I underline it and write "def." in the margin. If I have to look up a word that is not defined, I circle it and write my definition in the margin. Also, I don't underline everything in a sentence. I underline just key words. Before I did this, I used to underline too much; then I would end up having to re-read almost the whole chapter when I reviewed instead of studying just the important parts.*

Alex makes a good point: Underlining too much is not useful (nor is underlining too little). The purpose of marking textbooks is to make the important information stand out and to provide memory cues. Then you can determine what you need to study in depth and what you can skip when you review. Here is what one of Alex's underlined passages looks like. Notice the way he has annotated the passage in the margins.

[Two types of evidence indicate that, as Darwin proposed, the basic facial expressions of emotions are innate.] ★

(def.) grimace= expression of pain

Studies of infants show expressions are inborn.

One source of evidence comes from infants. They do not need to be taught to (grimace) in pain or to smile in pleasure; they exhibit facial movements that are appropriately correlated with their well-being. Even blind infants, who cannot see adults in order to imitate them, show the same emotional expressions as do sighted infants (Goodenough, 1932).

People of all cultures react the same to same stimuli.

similar facial responses: 4 examples

A second line of evidence for innate facial expressions comes from research showing that, for the most basic emotions, people of all cultures show similar facial responses to similar emotional stimuli (Ekman, 1984, 1993; Ekman & Friesen, 1986). Studies that demonstrate the universality of emotional expressions ask people to look at photographs of faces and then pick what emotion the person in the photo is feeling. The pattern of facial movements we call a ①smile, for example, is universally related to positive emotions. ②Sadness is almost always accompanied by slackened muscle tone and a "long" face. Likewise, in almost all cultures, people ③contort their faces in a similar way when presented with something disgusting. And a ④furrowed brow is frequently associated with frustration or unpleasantness (Smith, 1989).

Douglas Bernstein, et. al., *Psychology,* First Edition. Copyright © 1988 by Houghton Mifflin Company. Used with permission.

Marking your textbooks focuses your attention on the task of reading and helps you think critically about what you read.

© Dion Ogust/The Image Works

Here are some guidelines for effective textbook marking. Try them out; then, like Alex, develop a system that works for you and use it consistently.

What to Mark in Textbooks

Deciding what to mark is the same as deciding what is important. *Definitions of terms* are important. Even if they are already italicized or printed in boldface, mark them anyway if you do not already know them. *Examples* used to illustrate theories are important; so are *experiments,* including who conducted them, what happened, and what they proved. *Names, dates,* and *events* are important. *Principles, rules,* and *characteristics* are additional examples of the kinds of information that may be important within the context of what you are reading.

How to Mark Your Textbooks

1. It is usually better to read before you underline, and to read one section at a time. You may not be able to tell what is important until you have read a whole section to see how the ideas relate.

2. In the margin, write key words or symbols that will serve as memory cues to call your attention to words, names, dates, and other important information.
3. Use your own words when you make notes in your textbook. Putting the author's ideas into your own words will help you test your understanding, and you will be more likely to retain them.
4. Decide on some symbols to indicate certain kinds of information, and use these symbols consistently. Here are some common symbols students use. You probably use some of them already.

   def. = definition

   ex. = example

   T = possible test item

   * = an important point

   1., 2., 3., etc. = used when sequence matters.
5. Underline or highlight words and phrases only, not entire sentences, unless you are marking a topic sentence or thesis statement.

Review for a test or prepare for class by reciting from what you have marked or annotated in the margin. Use your underlining and marking to identify sections of a chapter that need to be reorganized to make them easier for you to remember. Chapter 8 shows you how to make study guides to organize information into patterns that are more meaningful to you.

EXERCISE 14.5

Apply the guidelines for underlining and marking textbooks to this excerpt from a textbook chapter. Read and mark the passage. Then answer the questions that follow to help you determine whether you correctly identified the important information.

Guidelines for Wise Buying Over the Life Cycle

Examples of ways that people waste money could fill the pages of dozens of books. Fortunately, a few simple guidelines can yield savings of 10 to 20 percent during a year, equivalent to a sharp increase in income. Suggestions follow.

Control Buying on Impulse *Simple restraint will help avoid **impulse buying,** which is nothing more than buying without fully considering need and alternatives. Say, for example, you have shopped carefully by comparing various microwave ovens and have selected one at a discount store with the lowest price of $200. While at the store, you impulsively pick up some microwave cookware and a cookbook that you really don't need. The extra $45 spent on impulse ruined some of the benefits of the comparison shopping for the oven itself.*

Pay Cash *Paying cash whenever possible can help save money in two ways. First, it helps control impulse buying that is made easy by using credit cards to make purchases that one really can't afford. Second, use of credit can make financial planning more difficult by taking away financial flexibility and by adding to the cost of items. You may pay 12, 18, or even 24 percent more for your credit purchases, because you pay that much more in interest.*

Buy at the Right Time *Paying attention to sales and looking for the right time to buy will save money. As you probably know, 30 to 60 percent can be saved on telephone charges just by making calls in the evenings and on weekends. Many items, such as sporting goods and clothing, are marked down near certain holidays and at the end of each climate season. Also, $5 or $10 weekly can be saved on food simply by stocking up on advertised specials. Make sure that what you buy on sale is something you will really use, however.*

Don't Pay Extra for a "Name" *Some people have an "Excedrin headache" for 30 cents a dosage or an "Anacin Headache" for 25 cents a dosage, and others have a plain aspirin headache for 2 cents a dosage. Scientific research (not the advertiser's research) consistently shows that the effectiveness of all over-the-counter pain relievers is about the same. This why the ads say "none better" rather than "we're the best." Gasoline, vitamins, laundry and other soaps, and many grocery items are all products with minor quality differences. Buying generic products is a good way to save money.* ***Generic products*** *are sold under a general commodity name such as "whole kernel corn" rather than a brand name such as Del Monte. Savings can be especially significant for prescription drugs. Many states allow consumers to request that the pharmacist use a generic equivalent even if the physician writes the prescription under a brand name. In other states consumers can ask the physician to write the prescription generically. Also note that many less expensive, store-brand products (such as appliances sold at Sears and J. C. Penney) are actually made by the brand-name manufacturers. . . .*

The High Price of Convenience Shopping *A bottle of ketchup or jar of peanut butter bought at a supermarket probably costs 50 cents less than at a nearby convenience store, whereas bread and milk may be priced about the same. Buying a few items daily at a convenience store or neighborhood market rather than making a planned weekly visit to a grocery store can raise food bills 30 percent or more through higher prices and the more frequent temptation of impulse purchases. Also, although it may be convenient to shop for furniture and appliances in the local community, better prices on the same items may be found in larger, more competitive shopping areas, such as outlet shopping malls.*

Life-Cycle Planning for Major Purchases *"You can't have everything," as the old saying goes, but many young Americans certainly try. This is one of the reasons why the average household headed by someone under age 25 spends 17 percent more than its disposable income. (How? By using credit, of course.) What is important to realize is that although one cannot have everything right now, planning will help keep things in perspective. Comparing what one has to parents or older relatives and friends is fine. But recognize that it takes a lot of time to build up the quantity and quality of possessions that they may have. Intelligently setting short- and long-term goals and recognizing budget limitations will enable you to reach goals for major purchases but not at the expense of financial security. . . .*

From Thomas E. Garman and Raymond E. Forgue, *Personal Finance,* Fourth Edition. Copyright © 1994 by Houghton Mifflin Company. Used with permission.

1. What is the point, or central idea, of this passage?

2. How many guidelines for buying are explained in the passage? Briefly list them on the lines below.

3. How much can you save by stocking up on advertised specials at the grocery store?

4. What is a good way to avoid impulse buying?

5. Why is it not a good idea to shop at convenience stores?

6. What is the advantage of paying cash for purchases?

7. Define *disposable income* as used in the last paragraph, second sentence.

8. **Personal implication:** Which of the suggested guidelines for buying do you use?

9. **Personal implication:** What is one way you could save money that you haven't tried?

10. **Inference:** Why do you suppose so many young people try to have everything now, as the authors suggest?

CRITICAL THINKING APPLICATION

Examples A and B below show the same passage as marked by two different students. Evaluate each student's marking for usefulness. Determine which student has successfully applied the suggestions for marking textbooks that are explained in this chapter. Summarize your findings in writing.

Example A

Stress shows in your face, voice, actions, posture.

Behavioral Stress Responses. Clues about people's physical and emotional stress reactions come from changes in how they look, act, or talk. Strained facial expressions, a shaky voice, tremors or spasms, and jumpiness are common behavioral stress responses. Posture can also convey information about stress, a fact observed by skilled interviewers.

Cooper et al.: avoidance tactics keep you from dealing with stress

Even more obvious behavioral stress responses appear as people attempt to escape or avoid stressors. Some people quit their jobs, drop out of school, turn to alcohol, or even attempt suicide. Unfortunately, as discussed in the chapter on learning, escape and avoidance tactics deprive people of the opportunity to learn more adaptive ways of coping with stressful environments, including college (Cooper et al., 1992).

avoidance tactics

Aggression often directed at family

Aggression is another common behavioral response to stressors. All too often . . . this aggressiveness is directed at members of one's own family (Hepworth & West, 1988; MacEwan & Barling, 1988). In the months after Hurricane Andrew hit south Florida in 1992, for example, the rate of domestic violence reports in the devastated area doubled. . . .

Example B

Behavioral Stress Responses. Clues about people's physical and emotional stress reactions come from changes in how they look, act, or talk. Strained facial expressions, a shaky voice, tremors or spasms, and jumpiness are common behavioral stress responses. Posture can also convey information about stress, a fact observed by skilled interviewers.

Avoidance tactics

Even more obvious behavioral stress responses appear as people attempt to escape or avoid stressors. Some people quit their jobs, drop out of school, turn to alcohol, or even attempt suicide. Unfortunately, as discussed in the chapter on learning, escape and avoidance tactics deprive people of the opportunity to learn more adaptive ways of coping with stressful environments, including college (Cooper et al., 1992).

Hepworth, West, MacEwan, Barling

Aggression is another common behavioral response to stressors. All too often . . . this aggressiveness is directed at members of one's own family (Hepworth & West, 1988; MacEwan & Barling, 1988). In the months after Hurricane Andrew hit south Florida in 1992, for example, the rate of domestic violence reports in the devastated area doubled. . . .

Excerpts from Bernstein, Clarke-Stewart, Roy, Srull, and Wickens, *Psychology,* Third Edition. Copyright © 1994 by Houghton Mifflin Company. Reprinted by permission.

SUMMARY

The first two paragraphs of the following summary have been highlighted and annotated as an additional example of how to mark your textbook. Read the summary and mark the rest of it on your own.

Two strategies to improve textbook reading and study

Reading is an essential step in any study system. Improve this step in your system by applying two strategies: (1) read for point, proof, and implications; (2) Mark your textbook by underlining or highlighting and by annotating.

Marking helps you follow a writer's ideas.

Follow the development of an idea by reading to find the writer's point, proof, and implications. To find the *point,* look for a *topic sentence* or *thesis statement* if there is one. If the point is implied, not stated, you must infer it from the *proof,* or supporting details. Proof consists of facts, reasons, and examples that help support, or explain, the writer's point. *Implications* may be personal or inferential. Personal implications are those you discover when you relate the writer's point and proof to your own experience. Inferences are implications based on your understanding of the writer's point and proof.

Marking focuses your attention on the task of reading and improves your retention by helping you isolate important information for study and review. Underline or highlight and make notes in the margin to create memory cues for definitions, examples, details about experiments, names, dates, events, rules, lists, characteristics, causes and effects, and similarities and differences. To mark and annotate effectively, use a ballpoint pen or a highlighter and write key words and phrases or summaries in the margin. Devise symbols for annotation that you use consistently. Use your own words for making notes and summaries; you are more likely to remember your own words than the writer's. Either mark or bracket topic sentences and thesis statements. Then mark other words and phrases in the rest of the passage.

YOUR REFLECTIONS

Reflect on what you have learned about active reading and how you can best apply that information. Use the following list of questions to stimulate your thinking; then write your reflections. Your response may include answers to one or more of the questions. Incorporate in your writing specific information from this chapter or previous chapters as needed.

- Would you describe yourself as an active reader? Why or why not?
- Of the strategies explained in this chapter, which ones are new to you? Which ones have you already used, and how?
- What kinds of reading activities do you do well? What gives you trouble?
- Why is reading an important skill? Explain how you use reading at work or in your personal life.
- What have you learned from this chapter that you can use to improve the way you read?

Date ______________________________

CHAPTER 15

Becoming a Confident Writer

Probably nothing you do in a college course demands more focused attention and critical thinking than writing. Developing your writing skills will give you the confidence to tackle whatever college writing task is asked of you, whether it be an essay for your composition class, a report for a science class, a research paper for any class, or a test that requires you to respond by writing an essay.

Writing is an essential communication skill. Being able to communicate effectively in writing gives you an edge in the workplace. The writing skills you develop in college will help you write letters and produce reports and documents that express clearly and concisely what you mean. Your writing is a reflection of you. By improving your writing skills, you can ensure that your writing reflects you in the best light possible.

This chapter explains two things you can do to become a confident writer:

- Apply critical thinking strategies to the writing process.
- Use a five-paragraph plan as a starting point.

What experience do you bring to college writing? Find out by taking Awareness Check 21.

AWARENESS CHECK #21
What Is Your Writing History?

Write short answers to the questions that follow.

1. Do you have a positive or negative attitude toward writing? Why?

____

____

____

2. What kinds of writing have you done in the past—in high school, in college, or at work?

____

____

3. Has your writing generally been evaluated favorably or unfavorably?

____

4. In which of your college courses do you have to write? What kind of writing do you do, papers or essay tests?

____

____

____

5. Which aspects of the writing process do you find difficult or easy? Check the appropriate column. If you haven't done much writing, make educated guesses about these aspects of the writing process.

Difficult	Easy	
☐	☐	Choosing a topic
☐	☐	Organizing ideas
☐	☐	Thinking of what to say
☐	☐	Writing a thesis (central idea statement) and introduction
☐	☐	Making points in paragraphs
☐	☐	Coming up with examples
☐	☐	Writing a conclusion
☐	☐	Choosing the right words
☐	☐	Using correct grammar
☐	☐	Spelling and punctuating correctly

6. How much time do you spend writing a paper?________________

7. How far ahead do you begin planning and writing before a paper is due?________________

8. When you finish writing, do you usually feel positive or negative about the result?

9. What is your strongest point as a writer?

____

____

10. What is your weakest point as a writer?

____

____

If your responses to the Awareness Check are mostly negative, then you are missing out on the pleasures of writing. Building your skills will lead to improved performance and a more positive, confident attitude about writing.

THINKING CRITICALLY ABOUT WRITING

Use the critical thinking strategies explained in Chapter 13—*assume, predict, interpret,* and *evaluate*—to help you become a confident writer who thinks clearly and carefully about what you want to say and why. The characteristics you look for in someone else's writing should appear in your own writing:

- A purpose
- A controlling idea or thesis
- A pattern of thought or logical development of an idea
- Points and support in paragraphs
- Implications for the reader

In addition, you must choose words carefully. Make sure that your *diction,* or choice of words, is appropriate to your purpose, your development of the topic, and your intended reader. As you would expect of other writers, you must also define in context any technical or specialized terms that you use.

The following list shows the relationship between critical thinking and confident writing:

- **Assume**

  Brainstorm to determine your assumptions about a topic and generate ideas.

Assume that your reader is uninformed: someone for whom you must define terms and explain ideas clearly and completely.

- **Predict**

  Have a purpose for writing.

  Have an organizational plan that helps readers anticipate and follow your ideas.

- **Interpret**

  Explain ideas by stating topic, purpose, and pattern in a thesis.

  Develop the thesis with points and support.

  Conclude with implications for the reader.

- **Evaluate**

  Write from knowledge and experience for reliability.

  Revise for completeness of ideas and for objectivity.

  Edit for clarity and usefulness.

Assumptions

Active writers ask themselves what they already know or take for granted about their topics. To help themselves answer this question and identify their assumptions, they may use a prewriting technique such as *brainstorming.*

To brainstorm, make a list of everything you know about a topic or everything that comes to mind when you think about a topic. Don't stop until you have twenty or more items on your list. Then look at your list, and try to see ways to connect the items. For example, could several be grouped under one heading? Your list of items and the connections you make among them may become points and support in your essay.

Active writers also make assumptions about their audiences. In a college writing class, you should assume that your audience will be composed of your peers, or classmates, and your instructor. You should assume that they do *not* know as much about your topic as you do. This assumption is especially important when you are writing on a technical topic that you know a lot about. You must be careful not to take for granted that your readers will understand what you mean. Go out of your way to clarify and explain your ideas. Write as if you were writing to an uninformed reader.

Keeping a *journal* is another way to get in touch with what you know or think about a subject. *Your Reflections* might be a source of information for future essays, or you might want to keep another journal for your writing class in which you explore your ideas about reading assignments or topics covered in class. In your journal, jot down ideas for essay topics or your thoughts about a political or social issue that you've been following in the news.

Brainstorming and journal writing help you build a context for your ideas. When you build context, you enlarge your background of experiences and add to your framework of knowledge on a topic. Moreover, these skills can help you generate ideas not only for college writing but for other types of writing as well.

Keeping a journal is a good way to remember what you think or know about a subject. If you jot down your thoughts about political or social issues, your journal can be an excellent resource for essay topics.

© Bob Daemmrich/The Image Works

Predictions

As an active reader, you try to predict what an assignment will cover so that you can ask questions to guide your reading. As a confident writer, you should decide beforehand what your paper will cover so that you can make plans to guide your writing. A plan may be a formal or an informal outline of points and support. Keep it flexible because as you are writing, ideas may come to you that you hadn't previously considered. Predicting or planning the outcome of an essay will also help you discover your *purpose* for writing, if you have not already thought of one.

When you write an essay, is your major purpose to *entertain, inform,* or *persuade* the reader? It may be any one of these three, or it may be more than one of them. For example, you may want to inform *and* persuade.

Entertain. If your purpose is to entertain, then your goal is to give your readers a pleasant experience. Choose words and examples that will produce the response you want from readers.

Inform. If your purpose is to inform, then your goal is to explain an idea that your readers may not understand. For example, you may be telling readers how to study more effectively, how having your own apartment compares to living at home, or why you find your part-time job rewarding. To inform effectively, you need to choose examples carefully and organize your essay so that readers have no trouble following your ideas.

Persuade. If your purpose is to persuade readers, then your goal is to influence them to support your point of view. To be fair, examine both sides of an issue. Explain your position, illustrate your reasons for holding it, and answer opposing claims. Convince readers by using sound reasoning. Avoid appeals to emotions and the use of manipulative language.

Interpretations

As an active reader, you try to determine the writer's purpose, follow his or her points and support, discover a pattern of thought, and see implications in what you read. As a confident writer, you must consider your readers when you organize your essay. Make your purpose clear in the introduction and *thesis*—the central idea statement that controls the development of your essay. Make points stand out in topic sentences of paragraphs, and support them with details and examples.

Confident writers set up a pattern of thought for readers to follow. For example, a writer who wants to compare and contrast high school and college might write a thesis like this for the introductory paragraph of an essay.

> *Recognizing the similarities and differences between campus and workplace, classmates and coworkers, course requirements and job responsibilities may help students make the transition from college to work.*

This thesis statement gives the writer a plan to follow, and it gives the reader an idea to follow. The writer's purpose is to inform readers by suggesting a way they can help themselves make the transition from college to work. The writer's organizational pattern is comparison and contrast. College and work are the two items being compared; they will be compared and contrasted on the bases of campus and workplace, classmates and coworkers, course requirements and job responsibilities. The thesis sets the stage for the writer and reader, both partners in learning, to communicate with each other.

As an active reader, you must look beyond the writer's literal meaning to the world beyond the essay. Relate what you learn to your own life and to what other writers have said on the same topic. As a confident writer, you may conclude an essay by restating your thesis in a new way to give readers a different perspective on the same idea. Or you may challenge readers to take action or change their opinions based on what you have written. Your essay isn't finished until you pull your ideas together into a conclusion that inspires further thinking. A good essay stays in the minds of readers and continues to affect their lives.

EXERCISE 15.1

Does the ever-expanding time that Americans spend watching television take away from the time they might otherwise spend reading for pleasure? Imagine that you have been assigned to write an essay about this topic. Answer the following questions to think critically about it and to brainstorm ideas for writing. State all of your answers in complete sentences. When you have finished, you will have constructed an outline for a possible essay.

Assume

1. Do you believe people read less than they used to because they are watching television instead?

____

2. What assumptions can you make about the average number of hours a week that most Americans spend watching television? ______________________________

____

3. Estimate how many hours a week you and your friends spend reading for pleasure.

____

4. Who do you assume your audience for this essay will be? ______________________________

____

Predict

1. What is your purpose in writing the essay—to entertain, to inform, or to persuade?

____

2. Will you use humor, examples, or two points of view to reach your audience?

____

3. What points will the essay cover? ______________________________

____

____

Interpret

1. State the thesis, or controlling idea, of your essay. ______________________________

____

____

2. List three details to support your thesis. ______________________________

____

____

____

Evaluations

As a writer, you need to be concerned with two kinds of evaluation: your own evaluation of your essay and readers' evaluations of your essay's reliability, objectivity, usefulness, and readability.

As you review what you have written, remember that evaluation results in *revision,* the continuing search for a better way to express your ideas. Some experts feel that real writing begins with the revision process. In a writing class, your instructor may require you to write one or more rough drafts before you hand in a final paper. What the instructor is looking for is not merely your correction of grammatical and spelling errors, but better word choices, tighter sentence construction, and more and better details and examples. Figure 15.1 is a checklist for revision that you can use to evaluate an essay in progress for content and organization. The checklist will help you focus your attention on each part of your essay so that you can determine what needs to be added, left out, or revised.

Readers of your essays—in a class this would mean your instructor and classmates—evaluate your reliability as a writer on the basis of whether you grasp your topic well enough to explain it clearly. This is why most instructors will advise you to choose topics that you know something about and to write from your own experience. Readers evaluate your

FIGURE 15.1 Checklist for Revision

1. Does your introduction

☐ Build readers' interest?

☐ State or suggest your purpose? (to entertain, inform, or persuade)

☐ Make clear what your topic is?

☐ **2.** Does your essay have a clear thesis statement? (central idea)

3. Do you have enough support for your thesis?

☐ Do your paragraphs have topic sentences?

☐ Do the topic sentences relate clearly to your thesis?

☐ Does each paragraph contain concrete details (facts, reasons, examples) that support the topic sentence?

4. Is your essay well organized?

☐ Do the ideas flow smoothly and follow a plan, such as comparison and contrast, process, or cause and effect? (see Chapter 13.)

☐ Have you used effective signal words and phrases to connect ideas? (*for example, one reason is, another reason, first, next, also, in addition, most important,* and *finally* or *in conclusion*)

☐ Do all of your sentences stay on topic?

☐ **5.** Does your essay have a conclusion?

☐ **6.** Do you have any sentence errors that need correcting?

objectivity, especially if you are writing persuasively, by checking to see whether you consider other points of view fairly. They will evaluate the usefulness of your ideas by determining whether you have presented them in a clear and understandable way, whether they have learned anything, and whether they can apply your information to their lives.

Readers will have a better chance of understanding your essay if it is clearly written, and you will communicate better as a writer if you try to write error-free papers. To do this, you need to *edit* your drafts by looking for and correcting errors. When papers are returned to you, don't look at the grade only. Read your instructor's comments, and note the errors that are marked. Look up the rules for correcting these errors. More likely than not, your writing or composition textbook is a handbook of standard English usage.

If you frequently make grammatical errors that lower your grades, start a self-improvement program. Use the editing chart in Figure 15.2 below to analyze the errors you make. As you write each paper, try to make fewer and fewer of these errors. To use the chart, enter the due date and number of the writing assignment in the square provided. Then count the

FIGURE 15.2 Self-Improvement Editing Chart

Errors	Assignment No. and Date Due						
	NO.	NO.	NO.	NO.	NO.	NO.	NO.
Fragment							
Verb Tense							
Subject–Verb Agreement							
Pronoun–Antecedent Agreement							
Misplaced or Dangling Modifier							
Confused Sentence Structure							
Word Choice							
Punctuation							
Spelling							
Other Error ____________							

number of times you make each error that is listed. Record the number of errors in the appropriate squares underneath your assignment date or number. By the time you have analyzed four papers, you may see a pattern developing. You may find that you consistently make the same kinds of errors. This should alert you to a need for help. See your instructor or visit the writing lab or skills center to see what additional help may be available. As you continue to analyze your papers and record errors on your chart, you will be able to see whether you are improving.

EXERCISE 15.2

Do you approach a writing assignment eagerly or reluctantly? Perhaps you could make better use of your learning style by creating a writing environment that is comfortable for you. Analyze your current environment by answering these questions.

1. Where do you do your writing? ______________________

2. Do you prefer to write in longhand or on a computer? ______________________

3. What kinds of materials do you need to have on hand to write? ______________________

   Are these readily available in your writing area? ______________________

4. Does your ease in writing depend on how you feel about the assignment or the instructor? ______________________

5. What internal distractions affect your ability to write—hunger, lack of sleep, worries about personal problems? ______________________

6. What external distractions, such as noise or friends' interruptions, disturb your concentration while you are writing? ______________________

7. Your writing will improve if you choose the time and place where you can concentrate best. When and where would that be? ______________________

8. Analyze your responses to 1–7 above and write a plan for improving your writing environment. ______________________

COMPUTER CONFIDENCE

Use a Computer as a Writing Tool

The computer can be an extremely powerful thinking and writing tool because it allows you to move, add, and delete sentences or paragraphs quickly and easily. The computer eliminates some of the physical labor involved in writing so that you can focus your attention on thinking about and organizing your ideas. Remember that to use a computer for writing, you must have a word-processing program. Following are some ways you can use your word-processing program for prewriting, drafting, revising, and editing.

Prewriting

Brainstorming. One of the best ways to start thinking about a topic is to brainstorm. Open up a file for the subject you want to brainstorm. List everything you can think of about your subject. The computer allows you to discard one idea and add another in seconds.

Freewriting. Another way to get started writing is to freewrite. Dim the computer screen and start to type. For about five minutes, write whatever comes to mind about your subject. The dark screen frees you from the need to stop, change your words, or tinker with your ideas. When you finally finish, you'll be surprised at how much you've written. Freewriting allows you to jump into your writing without worrying about how difficult a task it might be.

Planning. Besides brainstorming and freewriting, there are many other prewriting strategies you can try. Open a file to plan. Make a list of questions about your topic. Create some categories for classifying information about the topic. Type in your key concepts or ideas, or make an informal outline of what you want to say. Type a more formal outline if you wish. Many word-processing programs include outlining features. Type a first attempt at a thesis statement. Then use the appropriate commands to copy the thesis statement several spaces below. Leaving the original version in place, write a second and then a third version of your statement so that you can choose the strongest thesis for your paper.

Drafting

Using the ideas you generated during the prewriting stage, begin writing a rough *draft,* or copy, of your paper. With the help of commands that add, delete, move, and reformat, you can make all kinds of changes in your draft without substantial retyping. Until you have completed your final draft, save your material instead of deleting it.

Insert a page break at the end of your draft and title a new page "Scrap." Hold any scrapped material on this page, where it may be retrieved in seconds if you decide you really do need it in your paper.

Revising and Editing

Hard Copy Revisions. If you are a beginner on a computer, try the "hard copy" approach to revision. Triple-space your draft, leave extra-wide margins, and print out your draft. Make all revision notes on the hard copy, or printout, of your draft, and then type the changes onto your draft in the computer file.

On-Screen Revisions. Once you become comfortable working on a computer, you can try on-screen revisions. These work best for simple changes—additions, deletions, and mechanical changes.

Final Draft

Once you have made final changes, insert your name and paging codes, print a draft-quality copy for yourself, and print a high-quality copy to submit. Be proud of your accomplishment!

For more information on using the computer for writing, see Robert Perrin, *The Beacon Handbook,* 4th ed. (Boston: Houghton Mifflin, 1997).

THE FIVE-PARAGRAPH PLAN

Getting started is the hardest part of writing an essay. Suppose you had a fairly simple formula to follow—a plan for writing an essay that tells you how to begin and end the essay and what to include in each paragraph. Then you could focus your attention on developing your ideas with vivid details and examples instead of suffering over how to structure, or organize, your essay. There is such a formula: the *five-paragraph plan.* As an added advantage, this plan provides a reliable structure for developing ideas in a timed situation such as an essay exam.

Think of the five-paragraph plan as a starting point. When you gain confidence as a writer, you will want to venture beyond it to try more challenging and creative ways to structure your essays so that you can vary your writing style. But if you are new at writing or if your attempts at writing essays for assignments or tests have been disappointing, try the five-paragraph plan as illustrated in Figure 15.3. Introduce a *three-part thesis* in the first paragraph; include *points and support* for each part of the thesis in the three body paragraphs; state a *conclusion* in the last paragraph.

If you examine the structure of textbook chapters and essays, as well as articles by professional writers, you will find that authors develop their ideas within a structure that is usually greater in length and complexity than the five-paragraph plan. For example, there may be several paragraphs of introduction before you get to the writer's thesis. In a textbook,

FIGURE 15.3 The Five-Paragraph Plan

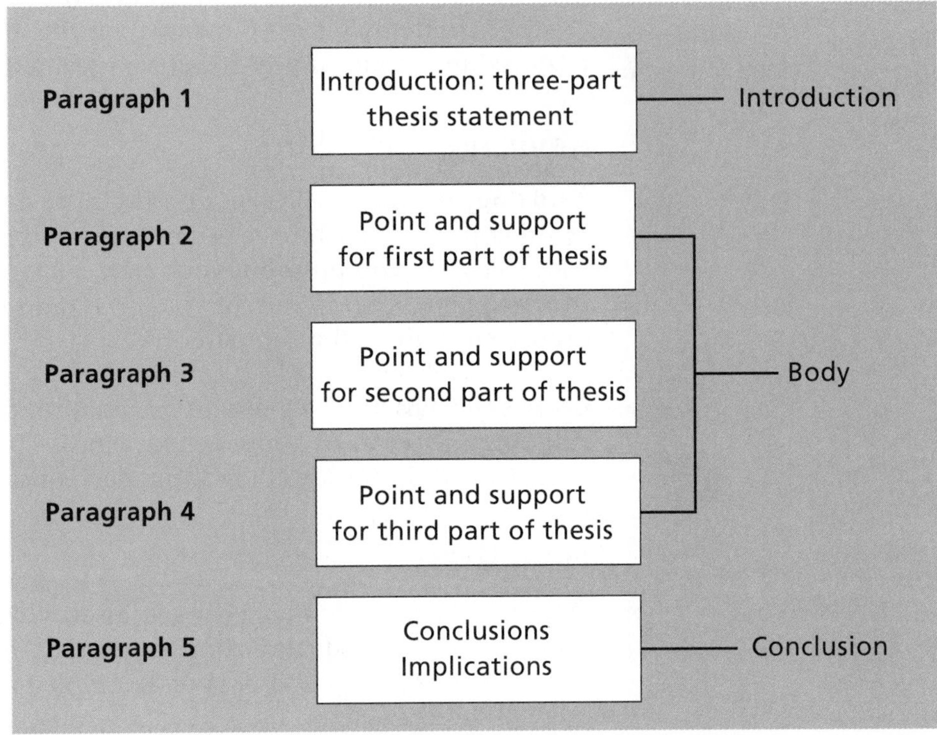

the writer's concluding points may be in a separate section, the summary, which also may be several paragraphs long. Moreover, a writer may use more than one paragraph to develop a single point, or main idea, if the point is complex and needs a lot of explaining or breaking down into parts. Still, almost any informational chapter, essay, or article will have three identifiable parts: introduction, body, and conclusion. This chapter, for example, begins with a short introductory paragraph and an Awareness Check. The two sections "Thinking Critically About Writing" and "The Five-Paragraph Plan" make up the body, and the chapter concludes with the Summary and Your Reflections. Professional writers develop their ideas in a variety of ways by manipulating the three parts.

Thesis and Introduction

Your essay will be most effective if you introduce, or lead up to, your thesis statement with a few sentences calculated to interest readers, get their attention, and make them want to read further. There are a number of ways to introduce your thesis. You might begin with an *anecdote,* a short story or account of events, that makes a point related to your thesis. Or you can introduce your thesis with an appropriate quotation and explanation. You might begin your essay with a surprising remark, a way of looking at the issue that your readers might not have considered. The introductory paragraph sets the stage on which your ideas will be displayed for your readers.

The thesis statement is your essay's controlling idea. It is a single sentence that reveals three things:

- A topic, or what your essay is about

- Your opinion about the topic
- The organizational pattern, or division of the topic, that you will use

Can you identify the topic, opinion, and organizational pattern in the following thesis statement?

Students can improve their time management by making and following daily, weekly, and semester plans.

The topic is *time management.* The writer's opinion is that students can *improve* their time management by making and following plans. The writer's organizational pattern classifies the topic into three parts—*daily plan, weekly plan,* and *semester plan*—each of which can be explained in a separate paragraph.

Here is another thesis statement:

In order to reach your goals, you must eliminate several common causes of difficulty.

The topic is *how you can reach your goals.* The writer's opinion is that you can reach your goals if you can *eliminate the causes of difficulty.* The writer's organizational pattern, *cause and effect,* allows the writer to develop the topic by explaining in a separate paragraph each cause and its effect on students.

Body Paragraphs

If you classify the topic of your thesis into three parts as in the example above, you have a plan for three body paragraphs in your essay. Compose a *topic sentence,* or main idea statement, for each part of your thesis. Begin each body paragraph with one of your topic sentences. All the other sentences in a paragraph should support the topic sentence by explaining it in detail.

Read the following thesis statements and topic sentences that follow. Do you see how they form an outline for the writer to follow?

THESIS:	**Students Can Improve Time Management by Making and Following Daily, Weekly, and Semester Plans.**
Topic Sentence #1:	One way to improve time management is by making and following a daily plan.
Topic Sentence #2:	Students can improve their time management by following a weekly plan as well.
Topic Sentence #3:	Making and following a semester plan is another way students can improve their time management.
THESIS:	**In Order to Reach Your Goals, You Must Eliminate Several Common Causes of Difficulty.**
Topic Sentence #1:	Procrastination is one common cause of difficulty that you must eliminate.
Topic Sentence #2:	Another cause of difficulty you must eliminate is the fear of failure.
Topic Sentence #3:	Finally, you must find ways to reduce stress, another common cause of difficulty.

EXERCISE 15.3

Review the "time management" and "causes of difficulty" examples on page 337, and then compose a thesis statement and topic sentences for any two of the topics below.

1. Memory improvement techniques
2. College requirements
3. Adjusting to college
4. Setting goals
5. How to solve problems
6. Your college's resources
7. Active reading strategies
8. Critical thinking strategies
9. Learning style
10. How to take notes
11. Procrastination
12. The importance of listening

Now choose one of your thesis statements and its supporting topic sentences from Exercise 15.3. Using these as a starting point, write a five-paragraph essay. After you have written a rough draft, evaluate it using the checklist for revision in Figure 15.1; then write another draft. Proofread and edit this draft before writing your final copy.

Your thesis statement and topic sentences should make very clear to readers what you are going to say. Suppose you are given a test in your study skills class, and your instructor asks you to write an essay explaining how students can improve their time management. If you use the thesis and topic sentences in the first example, if your paragraphs sufficiently explain each part of your thesis, and if your essay is reasonably free of errors, there is no doubt that you will make a good grade.

Notice the signal words in the topic sentences of both examples: *one, as well, another, finally.* Using signal words in your topic sentences can help you make a smooth transition from one paragraph to another. In longer essays that develop more than three points, signal words help the reader keep track of which point is being explained.

Concluding Paragraph

The last paragraph of your essay should leave the reader with a feeling of completion because your points have been thoroughly explained. You can conclude your essay in several ways: by restating your thesis and summarizing major points, by ending with a related idea that challenges readers' thinking, or by explaining how the information you provide may affect their lives. For example, a student writing an essay about time management could conclude by challenging readers to find ways to manage their time more effectively, or by explaining how managing their time may help them reduce stress. In other words, your conclusion should help readers see implications in what you have written.

Now read the following essay written by Robin Simmons; she has used the five-paragraph plan. As you read, look for her thesis and topic sentences, and follow her organizational pattern. Notice the kinds of details she uses. Notice also that she has chosen words carefully to appeal to readers' five senses. Finally, notice how Simmons concludes her essay.

Give Mine to the Birds

I realize that worms are a very available food source, that if I dig up rich, damp earth, I can harvest many of these squirming creatures free. Since ground beef goes for $2.49 a pound, worms would be a considerable savings. I also know that worms are very high in protein and that some cultures consider worms a delicacy. Still, I would never eat worms because they are unappetizing, difficult to prepare, and unpopular with other people.

Initially, I would be repelled by the worms' unappetizing characteristics. I am not used to seeing my pork chops writhing on my plate, so wiggling worms would make me queasy. Moreover, I would gag if I stabbed a worm with my fork and it started to squirm wildly. Because they are mucous-coated on the outside, they would slip around in my mouth, sliming my tongue. On the inside, worms are gritty from all the dirt in their digestive tract, so my teeth would grind annoyingly as I chewed. Furthermore, worms are usually bluish-grey and tipped with pink. These colors remind me of chewing gum stuck to the undersides of school desks, a rather distasteful association.

Even if I could stomach their unpalatable features, I would not know how to prepare worms. The last time I perused the meat section of Winn-Dixie, there were no cellophane-packaged worms snuggled between the chicken legs and cube steaks. Nor can I buy prepared worms at a deli as I do chicken salad and baked beans. Even if I had a supply of fresh worms, I would not know how to filet the critters because they are so thin and easily punctured. Furthermore, no cookbook has worm recipes. Are worms most tasty scrambled with eggs for breakfast, chopped and sprinkled over ice cream, served as an appetizer on Hi-Ho crackers, or heaped like fried onions on hot sandwiches?

The most important reason I would never eat worms is that everyone would think I was crazy. Dad, in anger and disappointment, would disinherit me while Mom would wring her hands and ask over and over, "What did we do wrong?" Next, my friends would no longer accept my dinner invitations or invite me to potluck suppers if they knew I was preparing a worm dish. I would similarly be shunned by my coworkers. Everyone would steer clear of me in the cafeteria because no one wants to sit next to a person slurping up worms Alfredo.

It is too much trouble learning to stomach the many unappetizing characteristics of worms. I also do not have time to find delicious recipes for cooking these slimy creatures. Nor do I wish to live with the ostracism that eating worms would win me. So until McDonald's creates a McWorm item for its menu, I will leave worms for early birds.

The five-paragraph plan has several important advantages. First, it is reliable. Because you know what to include in your five paragraphs, you can start planning your essay as soon as you have a topic. Second, having a plan for writing frees you to think of other important things such as choosing the most appropriate example, finding the right word, and saying something no one else has said in quite the same way. Third, if you are following a plan you are less likely to leave out an essential part of your essay such as the introduction, conclusion, or development of one of your points in a body paragraph. The five-paragraph plan is also a great help when you write essay exams. You can concentrate on covering all parts of the question because you won't have to struggle with how to structure your essay. Finally, the plan is easy to adapt. If you can think of more than three points to develop in support of your thesis, simply increase the number of body paragraphs.

EXERCISE 15.4

Apply what you have learned about the five-paragraph plan by completing this exercise with group members. Remember to follow the guidelines for group discussion explained in Chapter 1, page 12. Review and discuss "Give Mine to the Birds." The following questions will help you analyze the essay's structure and effectiveness. When you arrive at consensus, record your answers to the questions. Then evaluate your worth.

1. Is the writer's purpose to entertain, inform, or persuade? How do you know?

___

___

___

2. Where is the thesis statement? Write it below.

___

___

3. Does the writer introduce her thesis with a question, quotation, or surprising remark? Explain your answer.

___

___

4. What is the topic sentence of the second paragraph?

5. What is the topic sentence of the third paragraph?

6. What is the topic sentence of the fourth paragraph?

7. What signal words does the writer use to make a smooth transition between the third and fourth paragraphs?

8. Circle the writer's organizational pattern.
   a. comparison and contrast
   b. cause and effect
   c. sequence
   d. process

9. What word in the thesis statement alerts you to the pattern?

10. Circle the letter of the statement that most accurately describes the writer's conclusion.
    a. The writer restates the thesis in different words.
    b. The writer summarizes and concludes the essay with a surprising idea.
    c. The writer summarizes points made in the topic sentences.

11. Do you think the title of the essay is effective? Why or why not?

12. Which words in the essay appeal to your five senses?

Group Evaluation:

Evaluate your discussion. Did everyone contribute? Did you accomplish your task successfully? What additional questions do you have about the five-paragraph plan, and how will you find answers to your questions?

____

____

____

____

____

CONFIDENCE BUILDER

A Writer's Tools

When you sit down to write, have one or more of these helpful tools available. You may already be using a dictionary or a thesaurus, but have you ever used a spelling dictionary or a book of quotations?

College-Level Desk Dictionary. This basic reference defines words and traces their origins, and provides pronunciation spellings, synonyms, and examples of usage. Be sure to keep one in your study area to look up unfamiliar words and check spellings.

Pocket Dictionary. Carry this dictionary with you to classes and when you study in the library. Although it is not as complete as your desk dictionary, it is a useful resource for quick reference.

Thesaurus. A book of synonyms is just the thing you need when you can't find the right word to create the effect you want.

Spelling Aids. If you are a poor speller, you may need a spelling dictionary to carry with you. You can look up words phonetically or by their common misspellings. If you use a computer, the spell check feature of your word-processing program is a helpful editing tool.

Book of Quotations. *Simpson's Contemporary Quotations* by James Simpson is just one of many good collections of quotations. Use it when you need an attention-getting quote or when you are browsing for ideas. The following web sites also are sources for Quotations:

Quotation Resources, htt://www.walrus.com/~johnnonyc/cgibin/quotes. cgi, and *Bartlett's Familiar Quotations,* http://www/columbia. edu/acis/bartlby/bartlett. Dozens of Quotations and resources are available through these sites.

Handbook of Grammar and Rhetoric. Most writing instructors require students to buy a handbook. If you don't have one, it would be a good investment. When in doubt about a grammar rule, check your handbook. You'll use it throughout college and, if you plan to continue writing, later on.

Guide to Writing Research Papers. Most handbooks contain a guide, or you can buy one at your campus bookstore. Some instructors prefer that you use a certain guide. Other standard style manuals are the APA *(Publication Manual of the American Psychological Association); CBE Style Manual: A Guide for Authors, Editors, and Publishers in the Biological Sciences*; and the *MLA Handbook for Writers of Research Papers.* Ask your instructor for advice before you purchase one.

Journal or Idea Book. If you are ever at a loss for topics, this tool may be just what you need. Carry a small notebook in your backpack or purse to jot down ideas on current events, books or articles you have read—*anything* that you could explore in an essay.

CRITICAL THINKING APPLICATION

Evaluate your writing skills using the information you have learned in this chapter. Select a paper that has been graded and returned to you. It might be an essay you wrote for a composition class or an essay test you wrote for another course. What comments has your instructor written on the paper? What errors have been marked? Does the paper make a point? Do you develop the point with enough evidence? Do you have an effective introduction and conclusion? Use the checklist for revision in Figure 15.1 and the self-improvement editing chart in Figure 15.2 to evaluate your paper for content and grammar.

When you have completed your evaluation, write a paragraph or short essay in which you explain your findings and suggest one or more ways you can improve your writing skills.

SUMMARY

Read the summary and complete the partially filled-in map that follows:

The critical thinking strategies that you apply to active reading you can also apply to writing.

As an active writer, you make *assumptions* about your readers and about your knowledge of a topic. You *predict* how your essay will develop by having a *purpose* for writing and by structuring your essay—that is, by following an organizational plan. You *interpret* your ideas clearly to readers: you relate each point you make in a paragraph to your essay's thesis, you introduce your thesis, and you bring your ideas to a satisfying conclusion. You *evaluate* what you write by examining your essays for errors and revising for completeness and clarity. You should also keep in mind that readers will evaluate your essays for reliability, objectivity, and usefulness.

One way to begin thinking and writing more effectively right away is to use a formula for writing that can be adapted to a variety of writing tasks such as writing papers for courses or composing answers to questions on essay tests. *The five-paragraph plan* helps you construct an essay that has an introduction, a three-part thesis statement, three body paragraphs that move from topic to examples with smooth transitions, and a conclusion that leaves the reader with some implications to consider. The five-paragraph plan frees you to do creative thinking about your thesis, your examples, and your choice of words because you know the plan you are going to follow.

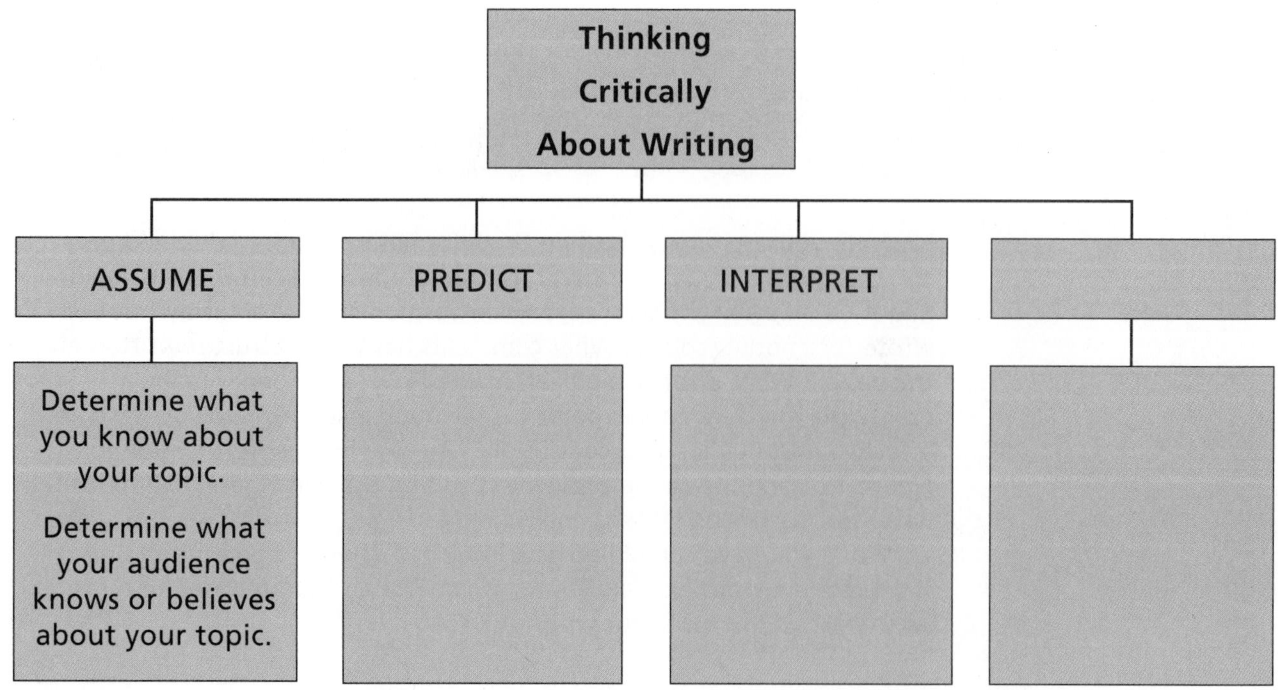

YOUR REFLECTIONS

Reflect on what you have learned about confident writing and how you can best apply that information. Use the following list of questions to stimulate your thinking; then write your reflections. Your response may include answers to one or more of the questions. Incorporate in your writing specific information from this chapter or previous chapters as needed.

- Would you describe yourself as a confident writer? Why or why not?
- What kinds of writing do you do well? What kinds give you trouble?
- Why is writing an important skill? Explain how you use writing in your courses, at work, or in your personal life.
- What strategies have helped you write successfully in the past?
- How do you plan to use the strategies explained in this chapter?

Date ______________________________

Gaining Math Confidence

Why take math courses, you may have wondered, especially if the field you plan to major in doesn't seem to require math? The fact is, some mathematical ability or knowledge may be essential to any field and an important workplace skill. Engineering, marketing, drafting and design, architecture—all require practical application of mathematical concepts. Dosage calculation is one of the skills nursing students must learn. Statistical analysis is a skill many people in fields such as the biological and social sciences and education apply either to conduct research or to analyze research findings.

Math has practical value in your daily life. Someday you may buy a home, apply for a loan or mortgage, make investments, or buy insurance. Certainly you will buy various consumer goods throughout your lifetime, and you will need to compare prices to determine whether you are getting a good deal. What happens to your investments as interest rates vary? Is it better to pay the balance on your credit card each month or pay the minimum rate plus interest? To answer these questions and others like them, you need a knowledge of math.

Apart from its practical applications, a knowledge of math is valuable for its own sake. For example, algebra teaches you a thought process, a discipline of the mind that builds critical thinking skills such as problem solving, analysis, and logical reasoning—all keys to success.

Whatever your math history has been, your future can be better. Begin by taking Awareness Check 22. In addition, this chapter explains numerous strategies that can help you gain math confidence:

- Overcome math anxiety.
- Learn how to read and study math textbooks.
- Keep a math notebook.
- Use WHISK for solving word problems.

- Learn from your mistakes.
- Know how to choose an instructor.
- Know when to ask for help.
- Know when to take math courses.

AWARENESS CHECK #22

How Are You Doing in Math?

Check *yes* if a statement applies to you, *no* if it does not.

Yes	No	
☐	☐	1. My grades in math are not as good as I would like them to be.
☐	☐	2. I believe I have math anxiety.
☐	☐	3. My basic skills (addition, subtraction, multiplication, division) need strengthening.
☐	☐	4. Regular attendance is a problem for me in math courses.
☐	☐	5. I have a tendency to procrastinate on math assignments.
☐	☐	6. I may put off getting help if I have trouble in a math class.
☐	☐	7. I have difficulty reading and understanding my math textbook.
☐	☐	8. I am frequently unprepared for math tests.
☐	☐	9. I don't know what kinds of errors I make or how to correct them.
☐	☐	10. I don't have a math study partner.

Yes answers to any of these questions may indicate behaviors or skill weaknesses that are keeping you from doing your best. Math anxiety can interfere with recall and cause you to perform poorly on tests even though you study. Basic arithmetic skills are a prerequisite for any college-level math course. If your skills are weak, strengthening them will help you meet the challenge of these courses. Poor attendance, procrastination, and not getting help when you know you need it will keep you from developing skills in the sequential way that is important in math courses. By learning a few math study strategies, you can overcome difficulties in reading your textbook, preparing for tests, and spotting and correcting a pattern of errors.

Finding a study partner is a simple first step you can take toward improving your performance in a math course. Select someone like yourself who is determined to succeed and will contribute his or her share as you discuss assignments, work out problems, or prepare for tests. Studying with a partner can also have a calming effect if you suffer from math anxiety.

The work of artist Jasper Johns reflects his intense fascination with numbers and mathematical symbols.

"0–9." U.L.A.E., 1960. Lithograph by Jasper Johns. 29⅞" × 22½". The Museum of Modern Art, New York, Gift of Mr. and Mrs. Armand P. Bartos.

OVERCOME MATH ANXIETY

Math anxiety is mental disorganization, fear, or panic associated with math courses and other math-related situations. The *fear* or *panic* you feel may be mental, such as a fear that you will fail, or physical, such as the sweaty palms, nausea, headaches, and jittery feelings that are symptoms of anxiety. You experience *mental disorganization* whenever you confuse one concept with another, forget what you have studied, or write down one answer when you really mean to write down another. Like general test anxiety (see Chapter 12), math anxiety is a learned response that you can overcome by improving your study habits and by using relaxation techniques. When you are overly anxious about math in general or about a math test in particular, you are focusing attention on yourself and your uncomfortable feelings instead of directing your attention to completing the course or taking the test. For some students, overcoming math anxiety is as simple as making a commitment to succeed and doing everything that promotes success. For others, reducing math anxiety may take a while and may require the intervention of a counselor, psychologist, or other professional. If you believe you have math anxiety, first review Chapter 12, especially the Awareness Check, and then visit your math department office, counseling department, or learning center. Ask whether help is available to reduce math anxiety.

In addition to following the suggestions offered in Chapter 11 for preparing yourself to take tests, try these two strategies if you become anxious, "freeze up," or "go blank" during a math test:

- As soon as you receive your test, jot down formulas or rules that you know you will need to use but are likely to forget. If you become nervous later on and do forget this information, you have only to read the memory cues you have written down.

- Use this simple relaxation technique to calm yourself during tests without calling attention to what you are doing. Stretch your feet out in front of you and let your arms hang limply at your sides. Relax your shoulders, lower your head, close your eyes, and breathe deeply and slowly for a count of ten or until you feel calm enough to return to the test. For more relaxation techniques, see Chapter 12. The chair-seat technique explained on pages 220–221 of Chapter 10 is also good for relaxing yourself during testing situations.

LEARN HOW TO READ AND STUDY MATH TEXTBOOKS

Your math textbook contains fewer words and more graphic materials than your other textbooks. Much of what you "read" in a math book is sample problems and illustrations of mathematical concepts in the form of charts, graphs, and diagrams. To read your textbook effectively and make the best use of your study time, use a study system such as SQ3R or PREP, explained in Chapter 7, or use a system you have developed. The system you use should include these steps, which work especially well for learning math:

1. **Preview, or survey, before reading.** Survey a chapter to note new terms or rules that are introduced. Read the summary, look at the exercises, and review the previous assignment. Since each new chapter develops sequentially from the last, a review of the previous chapter will refresh your memory and establish a background for the material that you will read in the new chapter.

2. **Learn mathematical terms.** Numbers, symbols, and formulas stand for ideas and relationships in math. You must be able to translate mathematical language into everyday language. Make note cards for terms, symbols, and formulas that you don't know. Include a definition, sample problem, and answer. Review your cards as often as necessary to retain the terms. See Figure 16.1 for examples of note cards for mathematical terms.

3. **Read for explanation, problem, and illustration.** Analyzing these three essential elements of a math discussion will make it possible for you to understand the principles or processes covered in the chapter so that you can apply them as you solve problems in homework assignments and tests. It is essential that you understand *how* to work a problem and *why* a process works rather than memorizing sample problems. First, read the *explanation*. Next, follow the sample *problem* step by step. If you have trouble understanding it, re-read the explanation and try again. Study any *illustration* of the process or principle until you think you can recall it from memory. Then cover up the

FIGURE 16.1 Sample Note Cards for Mathematical Terms

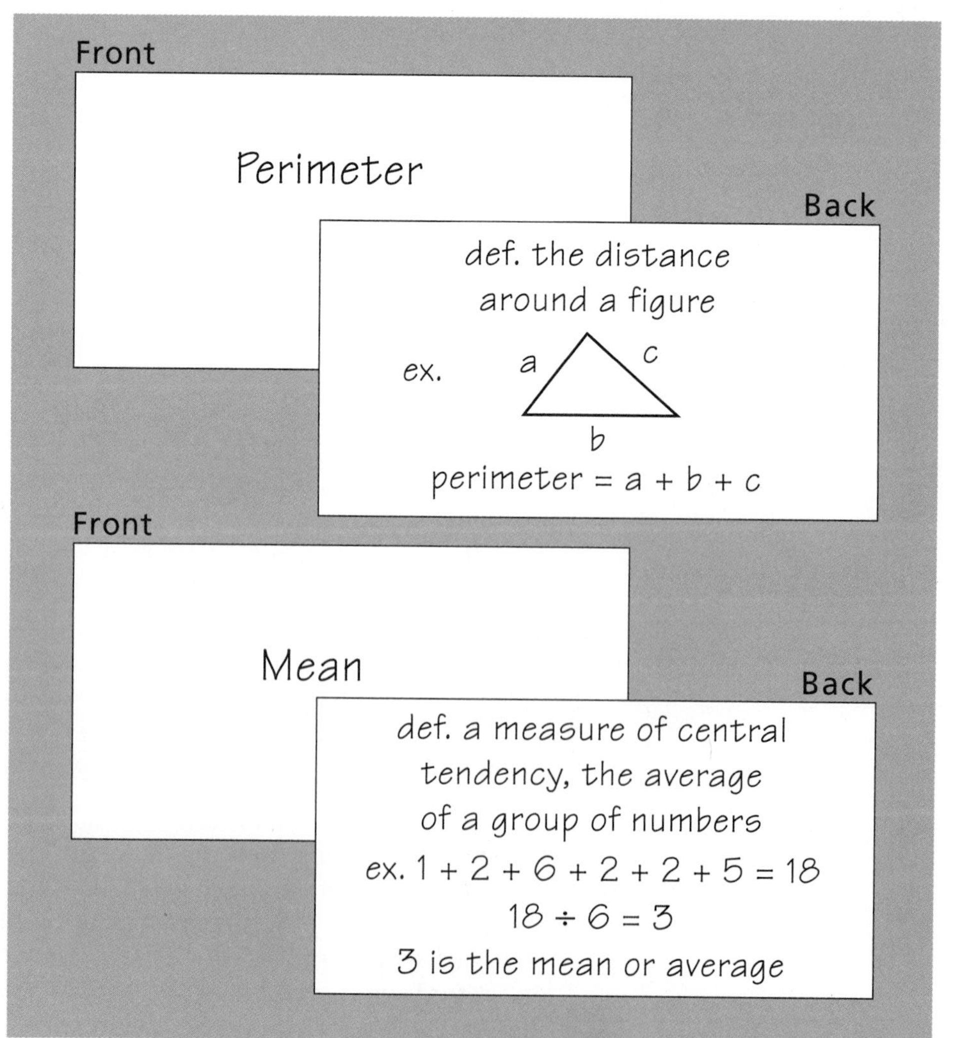

Architects must have a full range of mathematical skills at their disposal in order to calculate angles, tolerances, and other factors that make a structure safe, strong, and practical as well as attractive.

© Bob Daemmrich/The Image Works

solution to the sample problem and try to work out the problem on your own. Check your work against the text. Proceed in this manner, section by section, until you have completed the chapter. See Figure 16.2 on page 352 for an example of these three essential elements in a math textbook discussion.

4. **Practice the principle or process.** To get the practice you need applying new skills, always do all the problems at the end of a chapter even if your instructor does not assign them. The more problems you do, the more confident you will become in your ability to do math and perform well on tests. First, try to solve each problem without looking back at the examples in the text. If you are unable to do so, then review the example and try again. Keep trying until you are able to complete each problem successfully.

   When doing math homework, do not give in to frustration. To maintain a positive, hopeful outlook, stop working if you feel yourself becoming frustrated or anxious because you are having difficulty solving the problems. Put your math aside for a half-hour or so and do something else. Then come back to it with a fresh start.

FIGURE 16.2 Three Essential Elements in a Math Textbook Discussion

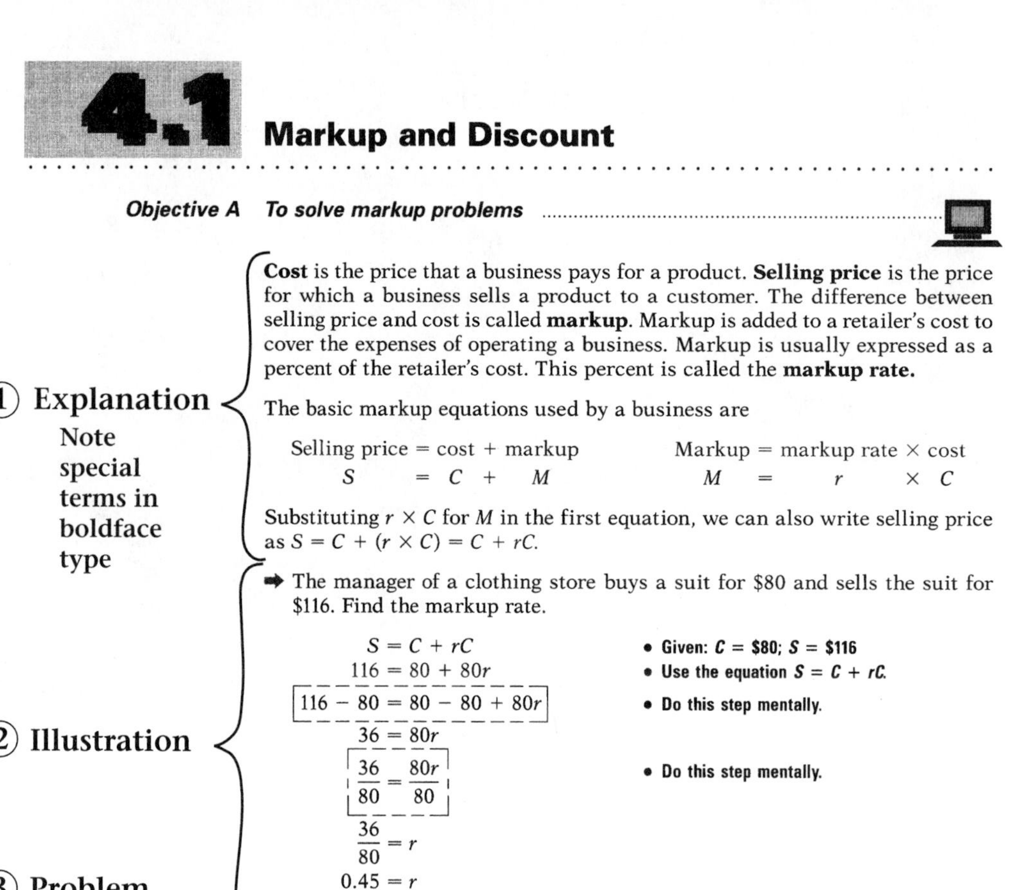

4.1 Markup and Discount

Objective A To solve markup problems

① Explanation
Note special terms in boldface type

Cost is the price that a business pays for a product. **Selling price** is the price for which a business sells a product to a customer. The difference between selling price and cost is called **markup**. Markup is added to a retailer's cost to cover the expenses of operating a business. Markup is usually expressed as a percent of the retailer's cost. This percent is called the **markup rate.**

The basic markup equations used by a business are

Selling price = cost + markup	Markup = markup rate × cost
$S = C + M$	$M = r \times C$

Substituting $r \times C$ for M in the first equation, we can also write selling price as $S = C + (r \times C) = C + rC$.

② Illustration

➡ The manager of a clothing store buys a suit for \$80 and sells the suit for \$116. Find the markup rate.

$$S = C + rC$$
$$116 = 80 + 80r$$
$$116 - 80 = 80 - 80 + 80r$$
$$36 = 80r$$
$$\frac{36}{80} = \frac{80r}{80}$$
$$\frac{36}{80} = r$$
$$0.45 = r$$

- **Given: C = \$80; S = \$116**
- **Use the equation $S = C + rC$.**
- **Do this step mentally.**
- **Do this step mentally.**

The markup rate is 45%.

③ Problem

Example 1
A hardware store manager uses a markup rate of 40% on all items. The selling price of a lawn mower is \$105. Find the cost.

Strategy
Given: $r = 40\% = 0.40$ $S = \$105$
Unknown: C
Use the equation $S = C + rC$.

Solution
$$S = C + rC$$
$$105 = C + 0.40C$$
$$105 = 1.40C$$
$$75 = C$$
The cost is \$75.

You Try It 1
The cost to the manager of a sporting goods store for a tennis racket is \$40. The selling price of the racket is \$60. Find the markup rate.

Your strategy

Your solution
50%

Richard N. Aufmann and Vernon C. Barker, *Introductory Algebra: An Applied Approach,* Fourth Edition. Copyright © by Houghton Mifflin Company. Used with permission.

5. **Recite and review.** As with any course, recitation and review should be an essential part of your study system. When preparing for a test, you should understand the example problems in your textbook well enough so that you can apply your skill to solving similar problems on the test. Make note cards of example problems to use as study guides. Write the problem on one side of the card and its solution on the back. To review, work out the problem on scratch paper; then check your solution by looking on the back of the card. See Figure 16.3 for an example of problem–solution note cards.

FIGURE 16.3 Sample Problem–Solution Note Cards

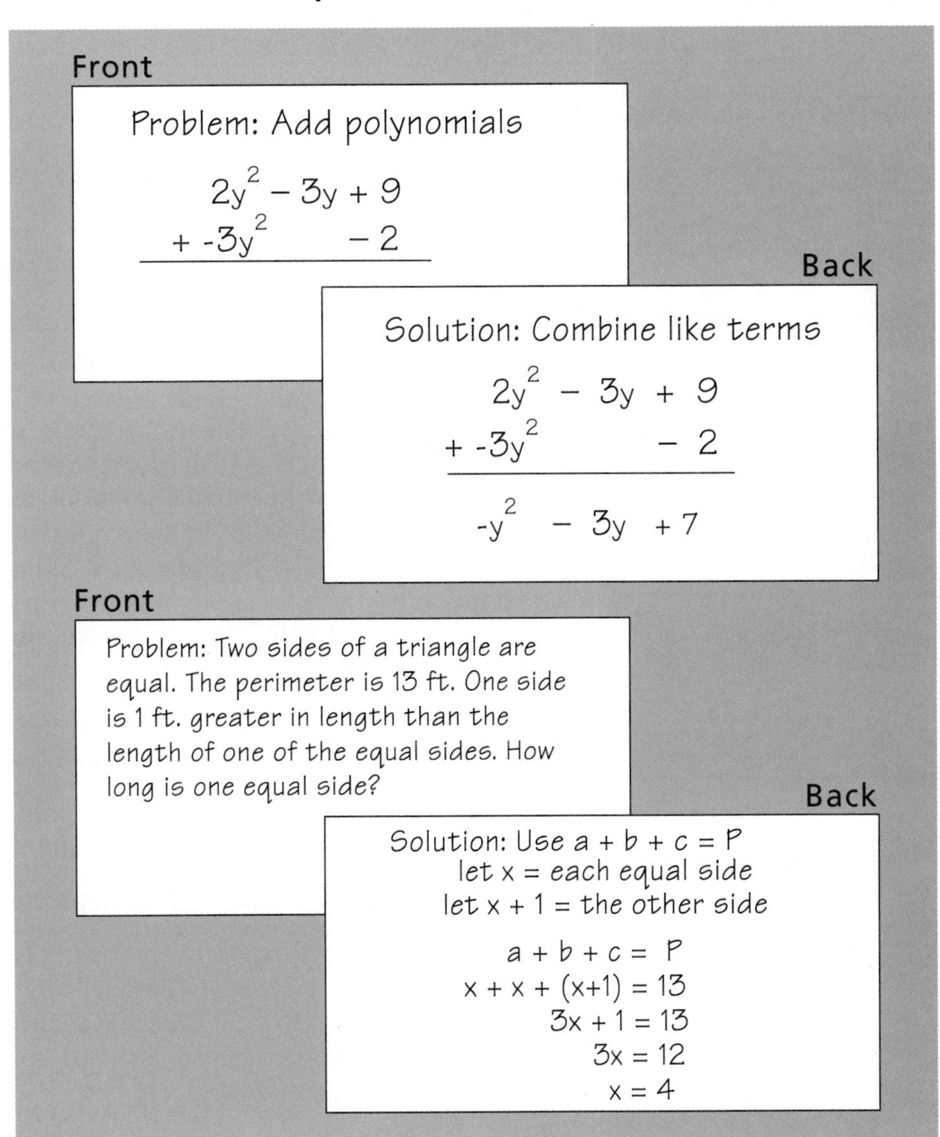

EXERCISE 16.1

Try out the note-card system for learning new terms and reviewing examples. Choose one unfamiliar term, symbol, or formula from your math textbook. Fill in the blanks below to show how you would make a complete note card to help yourself review. If you do not have a math book, do the exercise with someone who does.

Side 1: term, symbol, or formula: ______________________________

Side 2: definition: ______________________________

example: ______________________________

answer: ______________________________

Now search through your textbook to find an example problem that has been giving you difficulty or a new problem from a chapter you have yet to cover. Use the space below to jot down what you would write on both sides of a problem–solution note card for the example.

Side 1: problem: ______________________________

____

Side 2: solution: ______________________________

____

KEEP A MATH NOTEBOOK

Good organization is essential in a math course so that you do not fall behind and so that when you sit down to study you have everything you need at your fingertips. Keeping a notebook of lecture and textbook notes will help you see relationships between classroom lectures and discussions and the topics covered in your textbook. Skip several pages between each set of lecture notes. Use these pages to take notes from chapters or to make study guides that cover the same topic. Follow these additional guidelines for keeping a notebook:

- Head each set of notes with the date and topic of the lecture or the page number and topic covered in the chapter.
- Write explanations in your own words, not just numbers, because later on you will forget what the numbers stand for.
- Write step-by-step instructions for all processes; illustrate or map them.
- If you have difficulty listening and taking notes, tape the lecture. If you do tape a lecture, take notes too; writing will help you concentrate. Later, you can listen to your tape and fill in any gaps. Before taping any lecture, however, remember to ask your instructor for permission.
- Find a spiral notebook that has pockets or use a loose-leaf notebook so that you can keep handouts and graded tests with your notes.

USE *WHISK* FOR SOLVING WORD PROBLEMS

Word problems tell a story. Like all stories, they contain some information that is essential and some that is not. Word problems test your skill in translating everyday English into mathematical expressions. To solve word problems, you may have to translate the essential information into formulas or equations.

Think of a word problem as a puzzle. Some of the pieces don't belong; one or more pieces are missing. Your job is to find the right pieces and put them together. To do this, you need a reliable system. WHISK is a five-step method that works. Follow these steps; then with time, concentration, and practice you may be able to whisk through a problem to a solution.

W = **What?**
H = **How?**
I = **Illustrate**
S = **Solve**
K = **Key**

1. Determine **what** the problem is asking you to find. Read the problem through to get an overview of the situation; then identify and underline only the information that will help you solve the problem. Ignore irrelevant information.

2. Decide **how** you will solve the problem—whether you will add, subtract, multiply, divide, or use some other mathematical procedure. Use key words or symbols to guide you. For example, you may be able to use the formula $d = rt$ (distance equals rate multiplied by time) if a problem asks you to determine "how far" something or someone has traveled.

3. **Illustrate** the problem so that you can visualize the situation that is being described and make it seem real. Draw a picture; make a diagram, table, or graph.

4. **Solve** the problem. Perform the mathematical calculations needed to arrive at the answer.

5. Use two **keys** to check your answer. The first key is *common sense*. Is the answer reasonable or logical? Does your final number seem too great or too small? Verify your common-sense response with the second key, *computation,* or a mathematical check of the answer. For example, if you set up an equation to solve the problem, put your answer in the equation. If both sides of the equation come out equal, your answer is correct; if they do not, work the problem again. Sometimes you can check an answer by using the opposite mathematical procedure. For example, if you used subtraction to solve the problem, you can check your answer by using addition.

Problem and solution: 308 – 25 = 283
Check for the answer: 283 + 25 = 308

Now study this example problem, which illustrates each step in the WHISK method.

Problem: Susan bought six quarts of lime sherbet at the grocery store for the punch she wanted to make for her party. Her bill was $11.58. All she had was a fifty-dollar bill, so the cashier had to give her a lot of ones in change. How much did each quart of sherbet cost?

Step 1: What does the problem ask you to find? Look at the question at the end of the paragraph. The key words are *how much* and *cost.* They tell you that the answer will be an amount in dollars and cents. The fact that Susan is going to make punch for a party and that she paid for the sherbet with a fifty-dollar bill and got a lot of ones in change is irrelevant information—you can ignore it.

Step 2: How are you going to solve this problem? *Each quart* is a key phrase that tells you to find out how much *one* quart costs. You already know that six quarts cost $11.58. The process to use is division. Divide six quarts into $11.58 to find out how much one quart costs.

Step 3: Illustrate the problem.

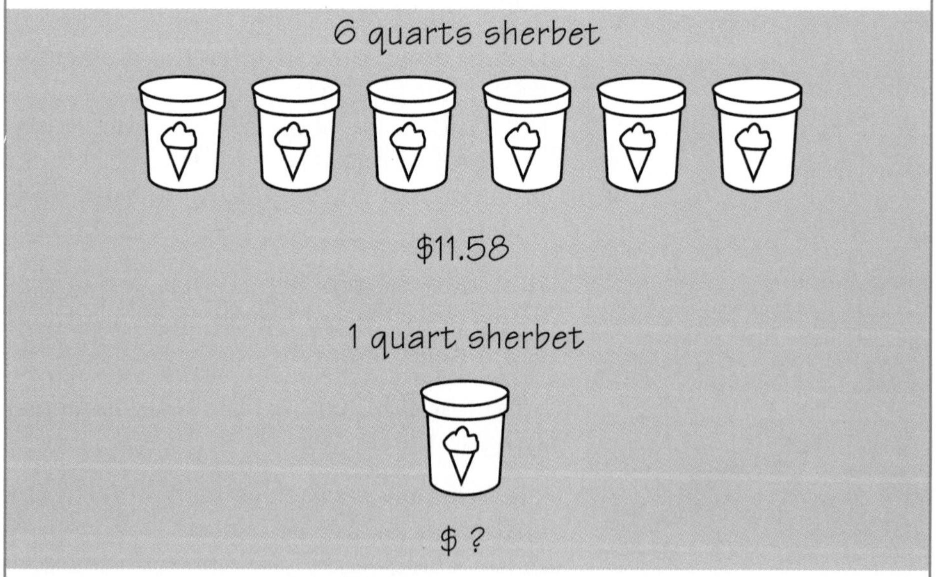

Step 4: Now solve the problem.

```
      1.93
6 )$11.58
    6
    55
    54
     18
     18
```

Step 5: Use the keys to check your answer. You want to know how much one quart of sherbet costs. If your answer is a number larger than $11.58, the cost of six quarts, then the common-sense key tells you that your answer is wrong. To check with the second key, multiply your answer by 6. Multiplication is the computation key to use when checking a division problem.

The computation key verifies your answer.

```
     1.93
6 )$11.58          $1.93
   6                 x 6
   55              $11.58
   54
    18
    18
```

EXERCISE 16.2

You have learned that WHISK is a five-step system designed to help you solve word problems correctly. Read the following word problems; then use the WHISK method to help you solve each problem. Use a separate sheet of paper to follow the steps.

W = **What?**
H = **How?**
I = **Illustrate**
S = **Solve**
K = **Key**

1. Sam is a member of a work team charged with the task of preparing a brochure to advertise his company's product. The brochure consists of four pages. At 5 cents a page, how much will it cost to print 5,000 brochures?

2. Sally and Emi toured Canada on bicycles last summer. They practiced biking all last year in preparation for the trip. As planned, they rode fifty miles a day. The distance between Toronto, where they began, and Montreal, where they went camping with friends, is 477 miles. Sometimes they stopped for a picnic lunch or did some sightseeing along their route; then they pedaled faster than their usual ten miles an hour. How many days of biking did it take for Sally and Emi to reach their Montreal destination?

3. Joan is in charge of the annual walk to collect money for the neighborhood scholarship fund. She needs to make $500 to cover her expenses. Three hundred volunteers have signed up to walk the ten-mile course. The volunteers range in age from eight to seventy-five years. Each volunteer has pledges worth one dollar for every mile walked. Assuming that each volunteer walks the entire course, how much money will be collected?

Engineers who build and repair suspension bridges rely on their knowledge of math and physics to determine where to place the towers and cables, as well as how much to tighten the vertical supports that hold the structure together.

© Peter Menzel

LEARN FROM YOUR MISTAKES

Determining the kinds of errors you make in math courses will give you something specific to discuss with your instructor or tutor when you ask for help. Many students make the same kinds of errors over and over again. Discovering and eliminating a pattern of errors is the only way to break the cycle. Three common kinds of errors are the following:

- Concept errors
- Application errors
- Careless errors

Analyze returned tests to identify the kinds of errors you make. Then apply appropriate strategies for eliminating them.

Concept Errors

A *concept error* is a mistake you make when you do not understand or know what principle or rule to use. If you make concept errors, review the sections of chapters in which the kinds of problems you missed are explained. Do practice problems until you understand the concept. Write the concept, its explanation, and a sample problem on a note card. Write the solution on the back of the card. When you review your concept cards, try to work the problems. Then turn the cards over and check your work by looking at your solutions.

Suppose, for example, that you analyze the errors on three or four tests and find that you missed every problem that required you to factor. When you realize which factoring concepts you haven't mastered, review them and work as many practice problems as you need to until you are sure you can factor. If necessary, hire a tutor to help you.

It is not unusual to forget concepts and rules that you learned in previous math courses. Save your books so that you will have them as references for future courses.

Application Errors

An *application error* is a mistake you make when you know what concept applies to a problem but you are unable to apply it correctly. You may make application errors when trying to solve word problems that require you to derive a formula such as $r = d/t$ (rate equals distance divided by time). Although you may understand the formula and have applied it successfully to other problems, you may be unable to do so for a test problem. Application errors are frustrating because you know *what* to do but are unable to make it work. To eliminate application errors, improve your understanding of concepts. Anticipate which formulas you will be asked to use on a test; then practice solving those kinds of problems until you can apply the formula in any situation.

Careless Errors

Careless errors are needless mistakes you make when you do not proofread your work before handing it in. For example, do you often drop the plus or minus sign when you write your answer, as in this example?

$$-2x(2x) = 4x^2$$

The correct answer is $-4x^2$.

To reduce your chances of making careless errors, plan your test-taking time to include five or more minutes at the end to check for mistakes such as forgetting a sign, not reducing to lowest terms, or adding or subtracting incorrectly. Try to determine what kind of careless error you make most often so that you will be conscious of it when you proofread your homework and tests.

EXERCISE 16.3

Apply what you have learned about spotting careless errors by doing this exercise with group members. Remember to follow the guidelines for group discussion explained in Chapter 1, page 12. Imagine that you have completed the following problems on a test. Each one contains a careless error. Proofread the problems to find the errors. When you arrive at consensus, write your answers or explanations on the lines provided. Then evaluate your work.

1. $\frac{1}{6} + \frac{1}{2} = \frac{1}{8}$ ____________________
2. $-4x + (3x - 2x) = 3x$ ____________________
3. $3x - (3x - 2x) - \frac{1}{2} \times 4 = 2x - \frac{4}{2}$ ____________________
4. $\frac{3}{4} - \frac{1}{4} = \frac{2}{0}$ ____________________

Group Evaluation:

Evaluate your discussion. Did everyone contribute? Did you accomplish your task successfully? What additional questions do you have about finding careless errors, and how will you find answers to your questions?

____

____

____

KNOW HOW TO CHOOSE AN INSTRUCTOR

Although other factors are more influential in determining whether you will learn, a good instructor with whom you feel comfortable *can* make a difference. If relationships with instructors are very important to you, it may be helpful to choose a math instructor whose teaching style is compatible with your learning style.

Students seek out instructors who have a reputation for making the material understandable, for being approachable, and for making themselves available to answer questions and provide help. Find out who these instructors are and register early to get into their classes. Department chairpersons and counselors can tell you whose classes fill first. Also ask other students which math instructors helped them the most.

Generally, when you are selecting courses, it is a good idea to try different instructors so that you get exposure to a variety of personalities, viewpoints, and teaching styles. However, if you know that math is your problem area and you find an instructor who makes it easy and pleasant for you to learn, then you may want to choose that instructor for the next course in sequence.

Of course, these suggestions apply only in situations where you *are* free to choose your instructor. It may be that only one instructor is teaching a math course that you need for your major. Because of scheduling problems, you may have to take the only section available at the time you need it. In either case, perhaps the instructor will be someone with whom you develop rapport and whose teaching style is compatible with your learning style. If not, make the best of the situation by doing all you can to meet the instructor's requirements and by adapting to whatever teaching methods he or she uses. Find a study partner or form a study group for additional support, and seek a tutor at the first sign of difficulty.

CONFIDENCE BUILDER
Writing to Learn Mathematics

How can writing help you learn mathematics?

Researchers in all academic disciplines, including mathematics, have discovered the value of *writing to learn.* Writing requires critical thinking. Also, the physical act of writing engages your tactile sense, providing another pathway to the brain and improving your chances of retaining information and transferring it to your long-term memory.

Because explanations in math textbooks are often complicated and because everything seems important, many students say "I don't know what to highlight or mark." If you find yourself agreeing with this statement, writing to learn may be a strategy you'll want to try. Highlighting and marking math concepts and procedures are usually not enough to help you learn them. Instead, try reading a concept, then writing it in your own words. Check your textbook explanation and rewrite it until your explanation is a good paraphrase of the text. Writing about math concepts and procedures causes you to translate the language of math into words that make sense to you. As you do this, you will quickly find out how much of the textbook explanation you understand. This, in turn, may help you think of questions to ask to improve your understanding of the information covered. What other ways can you use writing to learn mathematics? Following are a few suggestions:

Explain processes. Write out the steps for solving problems. Include reasons and explanations.

Rewrite lecture notes. Rewriting your notes is useful, both as a way to review lectures and to add details, reasons, and explanations where needed. Chances are, you use your own kind of shorthand for taking notes. Rewriting allows you to fill in gaps and reconstruct the lecture.

Write questions. As you are listening to lectures, reviewing your notes, studying for a test, or completing an assignment, questions may arise that you can't answer. Keep a list of these questions; then try to answer them with the help of your textbook, instructor, study group, or a classmate.

Keep a math journal. At the end of a class, summarize what the lesson has covered, and comment on anything you had trouble understanding. Your journal will be both a record of topics covered and your progress in the course. Review your journal entries as part of your review before an exam or as a basis for discussing with your instructor any difficulties you are having.

Write possible test questions and problems. This is an effective way to prepare for a test because it forces you to review material that has been covered. Share test questions and answers with study group members. Someone is sure to come up with a kind of question or problem that the others have overlooked.

EXERCISE 16.4

Experiment with *writing to learn* as explained in the Confidence Builder above. Select an activity below that appeals to your learning style. Use the activity to help you with a math course or other course you are taking.

1. Select a type of math problem that has given you difficulty and write out the steps for solving the problem. Include an example problem that illustrates the steps. Write your steps and problem on a 3 × 5 card so you will have it for review.
2. Select a set of notes that seem messy or incomplete. Rewrite them to make them more useful. You may need to meet with a classmate and compare notes to fill in gaps before you begin.
3. As you do your next homework assignment, jot down questions that occur to you either about the assignment or about a concept or process it is based on. Answer your questions either by referring to your textbook or by asking your instructor or a classmate.
4. Start a math journal. For the next week, as soon as possible after each class, summarize what the class covered. Comment on whether you understood it. Make a point to ask the instructor to clarify what you did not understand. Then revise your journal entry accordingly.
5. Determine when your next test will be and what it will cover. Then write five or six possible test questions and answer them. A good way to do this is to write the question on one side of a 3 × 5 card and the answer on the other side. Then you can use the cards for review.

COMPUTER CONFIDENCE

Use the Computer for Math Applications

Computers were originally designed to solve complex mathematical, scientific, and business-related problems. If you are already consistently using your computer as a study tool, then there are a number of ways you can use it to help you with complicated computations and math problems.

First, many computer programs allow you to use the numerical keypad on your keyboard as a calculator. Find out if your system has this application. When you are calculating answers, always remember to use the "key" steps from the WHISK system. You should not assume that the answer blinking on the screen is always correct. Use your common sense to determine if you have come up with an answer that is either too large or too small. Students often input too many or too few digits by mistake. For example, you might easily punch in 500 instead of 50, or 500,000 instead of 50,000. Double check the number of digits and the placement of decimal points in every part of a problem. Always try to check your solutions by performing another computational step; either place your answer in the equation or use the opposite mathematical procedure.

Second, use your computer to reinforce what you are learning in math class. Use whatever study-guide technique you have chosen for your other courses (see Computer Confidence, Chapter 8, page 183) to make a study guide of important concepts from your math textbook and lecture notes. Leave spaces under any concepts in which you need extra practice by pushing the Return key. Then, each time you print out your notes, you will have space to solve example problems. Keep a list of all the specialized terms, symbols, and formulas.

Third, use your computer to prepare for tests. Analyze your previous math tests to see if your most common errors are mistakes in concept, application, or carelessness. Then check with the math or learning lab to see if there are *tutorial* or *drill and practice* programs that are appropriate for your math course. *Tutorial* programs teach concepts and information. The lesson often starts with a presentation of information followed by a series of questions. If you answer the questions correctly, more information is presented. If you type incorrect answers, the program provides a hint or a review of the information. *Drill and practice* programs will help if you understand the concepts but make errors in application. These programs present sets of problems that gradually increase in difficulty. The drills proceed through a sequence of skills until you have mastered that particular area of math through repeated practice. Both kinds of programs will give you the understanding and practice you need to avoid careless mistakes.

KNOW WHEN TO ASK FOR HELP

Get help at the first sign of trouble. The first time you make a low score on a test, analyze your errors and make an appointment to discuss the test with your instructor. As soon as you start to fall behind in your assignments, make out a new study schedule that adds catch-up time to your regular study time for math.

If you are going to have difficulties in a math course, it is very likely that they will begin to surface within the first three weeks. As soon as you realize that you are not understanding concepts or cannot work the problems, make an appointment with a tutor. Most colleges offer low-cost tutorial assistance, and appointments with tutors can be arranged at your convenience. Many students who have started out slowly in a math course are able to overcome their difficulties and start building skills if they get help right away.

Your college may also have a learning center or math lab where you can get help. This center or lab may provide workbooks, computer programs, and other materials that you can use on your own. It may offer some free tutorial assistance as well.

KNOW WHEN TO TAKE MATH COURSES

Whether your college divides the year into quarters, semesters, or other time periods, you probably have a choice of attending full-length terms of ten to sixteen weeks or shorter terms of five to eight weeks. In addition, your college may offer mini-courses that begin a few weeks into a term and end a few weeks before the term is over. *Do not take a math course in a short term.* There is simply not enough time to absorb the material from one chapter before you move on to the next.

Take math courses during the longer terms and take them one right after the other. In any course that is sequentially based, there will be some loss of skill after the course unless you immediately begin taking the next course in the sequence. It is also a good idea to take your first math course as soon as possible. Take additional courses in consecutive longer terms until you complete your math requirement. Before you sign up for a math course, examine the textbook to be sure your previous courses have given you enough background knowledge to understand the new material. Before a fall term begins and between semester or quarter breaks, review the material from your previous math courses so that the information will remain in your long-term memory. If you take good class notes, mark your textbooks, make note cards and study guides, and keep your old tests, you'll have a set of study materials to review before taking your next math course.

If you must take a competency test as part of your graduation requirement, attend a math review session to refresh your skills, especially if it has been a while since you took your last math course.

CRITICAL THINKING APPLICATION

One of the quickest ways to build math confidence is to determine what kinds of errors you make so that you can catch these mistakes and correct them before handing in assignments and tests.

Analyze several returned tests or graded homework assignments. Decide whether you are making *concept, application,* or *careless errors,* as explained on pages 358–359. You may find that you make more than one type of error. Determine how you can avoid making these errors. Make a written report of your results, giving examples of the types of errors you make and explaining your plan for avoiding them in the future.

SUMMARY

The summary is followed by a partially filled-in list of math study strategies. Read the summary and complete the list.

To build confidence and improve your future math performance, use the math study strategies discussed in this chapter. If you have math anxiety, you may be able to overcome it by preparing well for tests, learning how to relax when you become anxious, and writing down memory cues on tests before you begin.

If you find math textbooks difficult to understand, use a study system that includes these steps: *preview; learn mathematical terms; read for explanation, problem, and illustration; practice processes and principles* by working out the end-of-chapter problems; and *recite* and *review* to improve your retention of new concepts. Keeping a math notebook will help you relate concepts explained in the textbook to lectures and also help you organize materials for study. Use WHISK for solving word problems: Determine **what** the problem is asking you to find; decide **how** you will solve the problem; **illustrate** the problem; **solve** the problem; and use the **keys** of common sense and computation to check your answer. Learn from your mistakes, and ask for help when you need it. If possible, choose an instructor whose teaching style matches your learning style.

Take math courses during full quarters or semesters and in consecutive terms so that your new skills are fresh in your mind. The purpose behind all the strategies explained in this chapter is to give you positive steps you can take to become a more confident and successful math student. Believe that you *can* do it.

MATH STUDY STRATEGIES

1. Reduce math anxiety by being well prepared, by learning to relax, and by jotting down memory cues on tests.
2. Use a study system such as ________________ or ________________.
3. Read math textbooks for three essential elements: ________________, ________________, and ________________.
4. Keep a math notebook because ________________.
5. WHISK is a system for ________________.
6. The letters of WHISK stand for ________________, ________________, ________________, ________________, and ________________.
7. Learn from your ________________, ________________, and ________________ errors.
8. Choose a math instructor by ________________.
9. The time to get help is ________________.
10. The best time to take a math course is ________________.

YOUR REFLECTIONS

Reflect on what you have learned about gaining math confidence and how you can best apply that information. Use the following list of questions to stimulate your thinking; then write your reflections. Your response may include answers to one or more of the questions. Incorporate in your writing specific information from this chapter or previous chapters as needed.

- Is your attitude toward math courses positive or negative? What has caused you to have this attitude?
- Describe your performance in math courses. What has led to or prevented your success?
- Do you have math anxiety? What have you learned from this chapter that will help you overcome it?
- Have you ever worked with a math study partner or group? Do you think this is a good idea? Why or why not?
- Which strategy explained in this chapter will be the most helpful to you, and how do you plan to use it?

Date ______________________________

CHAPTER 17

Developing Science Strategies

You may have heard someone say "If we can put a person on the moon, why can't we find a cure for AIDS?" For one thing, space technology and medicine are two different disciplines within the sciences. Also, scientists don't claim to have all the answers. In fact, the "answers" they give us are always changing. For example, we thought that long ago the structure of the atom had been determined, yet during the past decade a new atomic particle was discovered. This event led to much scientific speculation and modification of existing theories. Scientists in all fields continually test and modify their conclusions as they acquire new information. Moreover, scientists are persistent, so one day we probably will have a cure for AIDS.

The key to succeeding in a science course is to enter the dialogue of the discipline by learning its terms, methods, and theories and how to apply them. You must also learn to think like a scientist. The discoveries and inventions of science are the result of critical and creative thinking. Scientists analyze what is known and imagine what is possible. As a critical thinker, you must ask "What?" and "How?" As a creative thinker, you must ask "Why?" and "What if?" Your science course can help you develop your critical and creative thinking skills, and these will ensure your inclusion in the workplace of the twenty-first century.

This chapter explains the strategies that can lead to successful performance in science courses:

- Accept the challenge of science courses.
- Know the divisions of science and how they differ.
- Understand and apply the scientific method.
- Overcome science anxiety.
- Know how to prepare for your science class.
- Use specific strategies for the biological and behavioral sciences.

THE CHALLENGE OF SCIENCE COURSES

There are many reasons for taking science courses. You may need them to prepare for a career in nursing, medicine, psychology, engineering, forestry, nutrition, pest control, agriculture, or meteorology. In fact, a basic knowledge of science is vital for many careers and helpful in all of them.

Science courses are challenging and different from other courses in several ways.

- They place more emphasis on *facts* and *theories, principles* and *rules* that you must learn and be able to apply.
- Each division of science has its own specialized terminology.
- Most of the reading focuses on research findings and experiments.
- Courses in the biological and physical sciences may include a lab in which *you* conduct experiments and write reports explaining *your* findings.
- Most of what you learn in a science class will be new to you.

Although science courses can be exciting and challenging, absorbing new material and learning to apply it take time. To meet these challenges, work on motivating yourself to improve your preparation for classes. Take Awareness Check 23 to see how motivated you are.

AWARENESS CHECK #23
How Motivated Are You?

Place a check next to the statement that best describes your feelings about your science course.

☐ 1. I am taking a science course as an elective or because I must in order to graduate.

☐ 2. I am taking a science course as an elective or because I must in order to graduate, and I need it for my major.

☐ 3. I am taking a science course as an elective or because I must in order to graduate; I need it for my major, and it is essential to my career.

☐ 4. I am taking a science course as an elective or because I must in order to graduate. I need it for my major, it is essential to my career, and I want to increase my knowledge of science.

☐ 5. I am taking a science course as an elective or because I must in order to graduate. I need it for my major, it is essential to my

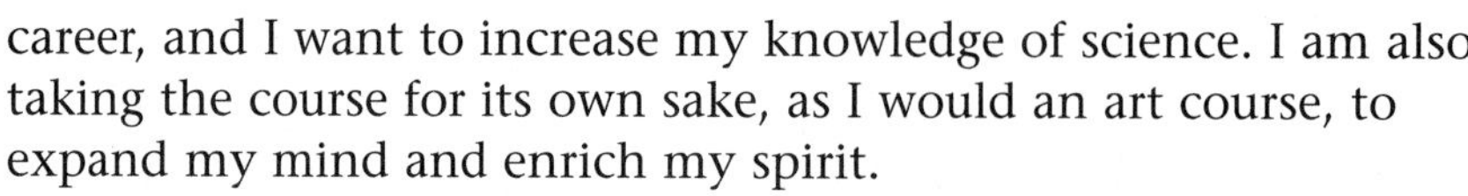

career, and I want to increase my knowledge of science. I am also taking the course for its own sake, as I would an art course, to expand my mind and enrich my spirit.

The first statement expresses the lowest level of motivation; the fifth statement expresses the highest level. The higher your level of motivation for taking a science course, the more likely you are to be successful and to benefit from the course after college. Thus, it is to your advantage to increase your level of motivation if it is not as high as it could be.

THE DIVISIONS OF SCIENCE

In an academic context, the term *science* usually refers to disciplines within the biological and physical sciences. Other disciplines draw on knowledge from these sciences and put it into practice. These disciplines are called *applied sciences.* In the twentieth century, another area of scientific inquiry came into its own, the *social and behavioral sciences.* Because they are based primarily on observations of human behavior, theories within these disciplines change very rapidly and are difficult to test or confirm. The following list identifies some of the disciplines within each division.

BIOLOGICAL AND PHYSICAL SCIENCES

DISCIPLINE	CONTENT
Biology	The life processes of all living things
Botany	The life processes of plants
Ecology	The relationship between living things and their environment
Microbiology	The effects of microorganisms, bacteria, etc. on other life forms
Zoology	The life processes of animals
Astronomy	The origin and structure of the universe and the celestial bodies
Chemistry	Matter and its atomic or molecular properties
Geography	Features of Earth such as soil and mountains and the distribution of life on Earth
Geology	The origin and structure of Earth
Meteorology	The atmosphere, especially the weather
Physics	The interaction of matter and energy

SOCIAL AND BEHAVIORAL SCIENCES

DISCIPLINE	CONTENT
Anthropology	The origin of human development, society, and culture
Psychology	Mental processes and behaviors
Sociology	Behavior of individuals within groups and how they affect one another

APPLIED SCIENCES

DISCIPLINE	CONTENT
Agriculture	Applies the sciences of botany, zoology, and chemistry to the raising of crops and animals
Engineering	Applies various biological and physical sciences to fields such as architecture, electronics, and aerospace technology
Industrial psychology	Applies the sciences of psychology and sociology to business and industry
Medicine	Applies the sciences of biology and chemistry to the study and treatment of disease

THE SCIENTIFIC METHOD

As a first step toward becoming well prepared for your science class, you need to understand scientific concepts and methods. Scientists study the natural world to discover unifying principles, or laws, that control or explain everything from how a black hole is formed to why people behave as they do. They begin with the assumption that the universe and every known part of it are understandable according to certain principles or laws. Scientists follow five basic steps to investigate problems, test theories, and define principles:

1. **Scientists ask questions.** For example, it is now common knowledge that cigarette smoking causes some kinds of cancer, but what are the effects of second-hand smoke on non-smokers?
2. **Scientists make careful observations.** For example, they may note that some non-smokers who develop certain kinds of cancer are, or were, repeatedly exposed to second-hand smoke. They may also note that more of these people develop cancer than do non-smokers not exposed.
3. **Scientists formulate a hypothesis based on their observations.** A hypothesis is a statement that can be tested. "Non-smokers who are repeatedly exposed to second-hand smoke are more likely to develop cancer than those who are not" is a hypothesis that can be tested.
4. **Scientists do research and conduct experiments to test the hypothesis.** For example, to test a hypothesis about the link between second-hand smoke inhalation and cancer, a scientist might expose a number of animals to cigarette smoke, then observe and record the

Professionals draw upon their knowledge of science to perform tasks in a wide-ranging variety of careers, such as archaeology (a social/behavioral science), botanical research (a biological science), and medical research (an applied science).

© Michael Rosenfeld/TSW

effect on their health over a long period of time. Another scientist might study a large group of non-smokers, those who are regularly exposed to second-hand smoke and those who are not, over a period of years to see which non-smokers develop cancer. Scientists pay close attention to other scientists' findings and continue to test a hypothesis many times to make sure their own results are consistent.

5. **Scientists analyze their data, then either accept or reject the hypothesis.** They publish their findings so that other scientists can *replicate,* or reproduce, their research and either affirm or find flaws in the hypothesis. The hypothesis that second-hand smoke causes cancer in non-smokers has been tested and affirmed by enough studies to cause concern that has resulted in legislation requiring the separation of smokers from non-smokers in public places such as offices and restaurants. Some states have proposed laws that would ban any smoking in public places. But agreement as to the effects of second-hand smoke remains a controversy to some, and thus the testing of the hypothesis continues.

When experiments conducted by various scientists produce the same results, a hypothesis becomes a theory. Eventually the theory may become a law or a unifying principle. For example, Sir Isaac Newton, a seventeenth-century scientist, tested his theory of gravity many times by dropping objects off tall towers. We now refer to Newton's theory as the "law of gravity" because so many scientists have retested and confirmed Newton's findings. But Darwin's theory of evolution, although it is almost 140 years old, is still not accepted as a law by many religious groups, and modern scientists continue to make observations and discoveries that modify Darwin's theory.

© Alan Levenson/TSW

To help yourself recall the steps of the scientific method, remember these five words:

Question
Observe
Hypothesize
Research
Analyze

EXERCISE 17.1

How many phone calls come into your home on any given evening? Do you think the number of calls is fairly constant, or do you think the number varies? Try this experiment to find out.

1. Count the number of phone calls that come in one evening between the hours of 5 P.M. and 11 P.M. (or during some other convenient time period). Write your answer on the line below.

   ____

2. Formulate a hypothesis about the approximate number of phone calls that will come in during the same period in each of the next three evenings. Write the number.

   ____

3. Test your hypothesis by counting the number of phone calls that actually come in on those three evenings. Write down your results.

   Evening 1: ________

   Evening 2: ________

   Evening 3: ________

4. What hypothesis can you formulate about the number of phone calls that will come in on the next evening? On any evening?

____

____

____

OVERCOME SCIENCE ANXIETY

Are you a nursing student who hyperventilates at the thought of an upcoming exam? Are you a biology student who is all thumbs in lab? Do you have a sinking feeling before you open your chemistry text to complete the homework for the next day's class? These examples illustrate the more blatant forms of science anxiety, but the signs of stress can be subtle as well.

While sitting in class, you may notice a student smoothing her skirt although there are no wrinkles in the material. Someone may be fiddling with his hair or tugging at a collar or shirt sleeve. You may see students rubbing their necks, hands, or arms. All these motions are *self-grooming gestures,* and they may signal that a person is anxious. When you are under stress, touching yourself or your clothes is reassuring. It's a symbolic way of saying "I'm okay; I'm still here." Moreover, these self-grooming gestures have a positive, calming effect. Studies have shown that they actually do relieve feelings of anxiety.

Have you ever noticed someone rolling a pen or pencil back and forth between the palms of his hands or drumming on the desktop with his fingers? Have you noticed a student tapping her foot or shifting around in her seat? These students may not even be aware of their actions. Often a foot tapper is startled when asked to be quiet. Do you recognize yourself in any of the students described so far? Once you become aware of your body's subtle signs of stress, you may begin to wonder what you can or should do about them.

First of all, accept them for what they are—your body's natural way to alert you to your anxiety and to calm you. Secondly, choose an object to act as an "anxiety reliever" and absorb your stress. Any small object will do. It might be a pen that you roll between your fingers whenever you feel nervous, a large eraser that you can squeeze in the palm of your hand, or whatever you can find in your pocket or purse at the time: a coin, a tube of lip balm. As you hold your stress reliever, say to yourself, "I'm transferring my anxiety to this object so that I will feel calm." Students who have tried this say it helps. Some say that after a while, all they have to do is lay the stress reliever on the desk. Having it in view is enough to evoke the calming response.

Ultimately, you need to discover the source of your anxiety and eliminate it either by becoming better prepared or by using relaxation techniques. For short-term relief, become aware of your self-grooming or self-calming gestures. Give in to them, and take advantage of whatever calming effect they have.

PREPARATION FOR YOUR SCIENCE CLASS

You have learned in previous chapters that you can do certain basic things to prepare for *any* course in which you want to do your best: attend regularly, keep up with assigned reading, use effective note-taking procedures, do the homework, use a study system, and learn specialized terms. These preparations are especially important for science courses because they often have unique requirements and your instructors may assume that you have background in specialized areas. Follow these strategies to help you prepare for your science courses.

Strategies for Social and Behavioral Sciences

In a psychology or sociology class, the emphasis is on three things: establishing a **background** or perspective from which to view the discipline, understanding the **research** that has led to the acceptance of theories, and comparing the **theories** of major scientists in the field. As you study, try these strategies.

Establish Background. In your textbook and in your lecture notes, emphasize established facts, rules, and principles to expand your background in the discipline. When your instructor discusses a principle, write it down along with any examples he or she uses to explain it. Underline facts as you encounter them in your reading. Develop a code such as a star or other symbol that you can write in the margin to indicate where a rule or principle is explained. Summarize rules and principles on note cards, and review them frequently. Keep your cards organized, and identify them by course, chapter, or both. Note cards come in several colors; you might want to use a different color for each course. For examples of science note cards, see Figure 17.1.

You will use the background you are building to help yourself understand new theories or current research into new but related problems. For example, in a psychology course you learn, just as you learned in Chapter 10, that there are three kinds of memory: sensory, short-term, and long-term memory. Understanding these three kinds of memory and how they work will give you information on which to build as you learn about current research and new findings about memory and other brain functions.

Understand the Research. Science textbooks provide summaries or descriptions of research studies to support facts and theories. Read for *point, proof,* and *implications,* as explained in Chapter 14. Ask yourself these questions and either underline the answers or summarize them in the margin as you find them in your textbook:

FIGURE 17.1 Note Cards for Science Courses

Front	Back
Chapter 1 psych. correlation coefficient	"r" for short A statistic used to calculate strength and duration of correlations r varies from 0 – + 1.00 or –1.00
Chapter 5 biology Metabolism	All chemical reactions that occur within cells or organisms
Chapter 2 chemistry $C_2H_3O_2^-$	Acetate (an ionic compound)

- **What was the *point* of the research, the question, or the problem?**
- **Who conducted the research and when?**
- **How many people or groups were involved? Who were they?**
- **What *proof,* or data, was collected?**
- **What was the outcome of the research, and what were its *implications?***

Now read the following excerpt from a chapter in a psychology textbook that describes a research study, and notice how it is annotated:

*By **rehearsing** information, repeating it to yourself, you can maintain it in short-term memory for as long as you want. But people usually forget*

information in short-term memory quickly unless they continue to rehearse it. You have undoubtedly experienced this yourself in order to hold a telephone number in short-term memory while you walk across the room to dial the phone. You must rehearse the number over and over. If a friend comes in and interrupts you, even for a few seconds, you may forget the number but this limitation of short-term memory is actually useful. Imagine what life would be like if you kept remembering every phone number you ever dialed or every conversation you ever heard.

Research question

Brown-Peterson procedure prevents rehearsal.

Data: subjects got 3 letters to learn. Counted backward by 3's until signal, then tried to recall letters.

How long does unrehearsed information stay in short-term memory? To answer this question, researchers needed a way to prevent rehearsal. In two famous experiments published almost simultaneously, John Brown (1958) in England and Lloyd and Margaret Peterson (1959) in the United States devised a method for doing so, which is called the ***Brown-Peterson procedure.*** *A subject is presented with a group of three letters, such as GRB. Then the subject counts backward by threes from an arbitrarily selected number until a signal is given. Counting prevents the subject from rehearsing the letters. On the signal, the subject stops counting and tries to recall the letters. By varying the number of seconds the subject counts backward, the experimenter can determine how much forgetting takes place over a given amount of time.*

Outcome: information stays in short-term memory about 20 sec. without rehearsal.

ex. air-traffic controller almost causes accident because of memory lapse.

Implication: recitation (rehearsal) improves memory.

Forgetting of information in short-term memory happens gradually but quite rapidly; after eighteen seconds, subjects can remember almost nothing (Peterson & Peterson, 1959). This is a striking demonstration of the importance of rehearsal for keeping information in short-term memory. Evidence from these and other experiments suggests that unrehearsed *information can be maintained in short-term memory for no more than about twenty seconds. As noted earlier, although this can be a blessing, it can sometimes be dangerous. For example, on May 17, 1986, an air traffic controller at Chicago's O'Hare Field forgot that he had just instructed an aircraft to land on one runway and allowed another plane to take off on an intersecting runway. The two aircraft missed each other by only twenty feet.*

The underlining and marginal notes summarize important information that you would want to review in preparation for a test on the chapter from which this excerpt is taken.

Compare Theories. In a social science course you should pay particular attention to theories and the scientists who developed them, noting similarities and differences among theories that explain the same phenomenon or behavior. When reading about or listening to a lecture that explains a theory, ask yourself these questions and annotate your text, or take lecture notes to emphasize the answers:

- **What is the theory?**
- **Who proposed it and when?**
- **What phenomenon or behavior does it explain?**
- **What proves the theory?**
- **What are its implications?**

Comparison charts (discussed on pages 173–174 in Chapter 8) are useful for comparing theories. Figure 17.2 is a chart one student made to compare three theories of personality in order to review for a psychology exam.

FIGURE 17.2 Comparison Chart: Three Theories of Personality

Three Theories of Personality

Who and When	Components of Personality	Development of Personality
Sigmund Freud (c. 1890)	Id – unconscious Ego – self Superego – conscience and ego-ideal	5 psychosexual stages 1. oral 2. anal 3. phallic 4. latency 5. genital
Carl Jung (1916)	Personal unconscious (memories and impulses) Collective unconscious (shared "archetypes" like "Mother")	Development is through degrees of: Introversion – (self focus) or Extraversion – (social interest).
Alfred Adler (1927)	Feelings of: Inferiority (from infant dependency) Superiority (need for personal fulfillment)	Personality develops as a "style of life" as a person strives to reach goals and self-fulfillment.

EXERCISE 17.2

Read, underline, and make notes on a section of a chapter in one of your social science textbooks that explains some important research; then answer these questions.

1. What was the point of the research, the question, or the problem that was posed?

___

___

2. Who conducted the research and when?

___

___

3. What proof or data was collected? (Briefly describe the study or experiment.)

___

___

___

4. What are the implications of the experiment?

___

___

___

5. Imagine that you will be tested on the research. Based on your learning style, how will you study the information?

___

___

___

Strategies for Biological and Physical Sciences

Scientists use the scientific method to help them explain and control natural phenomena. Among other things, scientists are currently investigating causes and cures for cancer and AIDS. They are also investigating ways to prevent further damage to Earth's atmosphere and natural resources.

In a biology, chemistry, or physics class, the emphasis is on observation, experimentation, and the explanation of scientific principles and processes. To prepare for your science courses, use the PREP study system (review the Confidence Builder in Chapter 7), diagram or illustrate processes and other information you need to study, and follow a routine to ensure success in science lab.

Use PREP or Another Study System. PREP will help you get as much out of your science textbooks as you get from your math or language textbooks. Follow these steps:

1. **Predict:** Before reading, predict what topics are covered by surveying the chapter as explained in Chapter 7, pages 149–156. Most of what you read will be new to you, and surveying will give you an overview that will help you build a context for the unfamiliar material. As you survey, look at the questions at the end of the chapter and read the summary; they emphasize the principles explained in the chapter.
2. **Read:** Read one section at a time, slowly and carefully, paying attention to every detail. Underline and mark the section *after* reading and before going on to the next section. Mark theories and the names of the scientists who originated them; point, proof, and implications of research experiments; and explanations of rules, formulas, principles, and processes.

   Pay particular attention to graphic aids, especially if your learning style is more visual than verbal. Studying charts, tables, graphs, diagrams, illustrations, and photographs will help you understand information that may not have been clear to you on the first reading.

   Use your book's glossary (if there is one) to quickly find the meaning of unfamiliar terms. A dictionary will give you all the definitions of a word, but a glossary gives you only the definition of the word that pertains to the science you are studying.
3. **Evaluate:** Try to anticipate test questions. Use the end-of-chapter questions as a guide. Decide what material is important, then restate it in your own words in an informal outline or study guide.
4. **Practice:** In a chemistry, physics, or biology course there will be end-of-chapter exercises and problems that require math. These exercises will show you how to apply scientific concepts to real-life situations. Always do all of them as part of your preparation for class, and be sure to discuss with your instructor any difficulties you have.

Make Diagrams and Other Study Guides. Diagrams help simplify complex material so that you can learn and remember it. In a biology class, for example, you will learn parts of different organisms and stages in their life cycles. On a test, you may be asked to draw parts and label them, illustrate stages from memory, or label parts on a diagram provided by your instructor. Make diagrams like the one in Figure 17.3 on page 381, and make copies of it. Label one to study from, and use the others as practice tests, labeling parts or stages from memory. Then recite aloud from your diagrams as you study.

Establish and Follow a Lab Routine. To be successful in your science lab, you need to establish and follow a routine that will enable you to get your work done and understand how your work in the lab relates to the rest of the course. Follow these four steps or adapt them to suit the needs of your lab situation:

1. Prepare for each lab by reading, underlining, and making notes on the experiment beforehand to understand its purpose and what you are supposed to do.

FIGURE 17.3 Sample Study Guide: Parts of a Paramecium

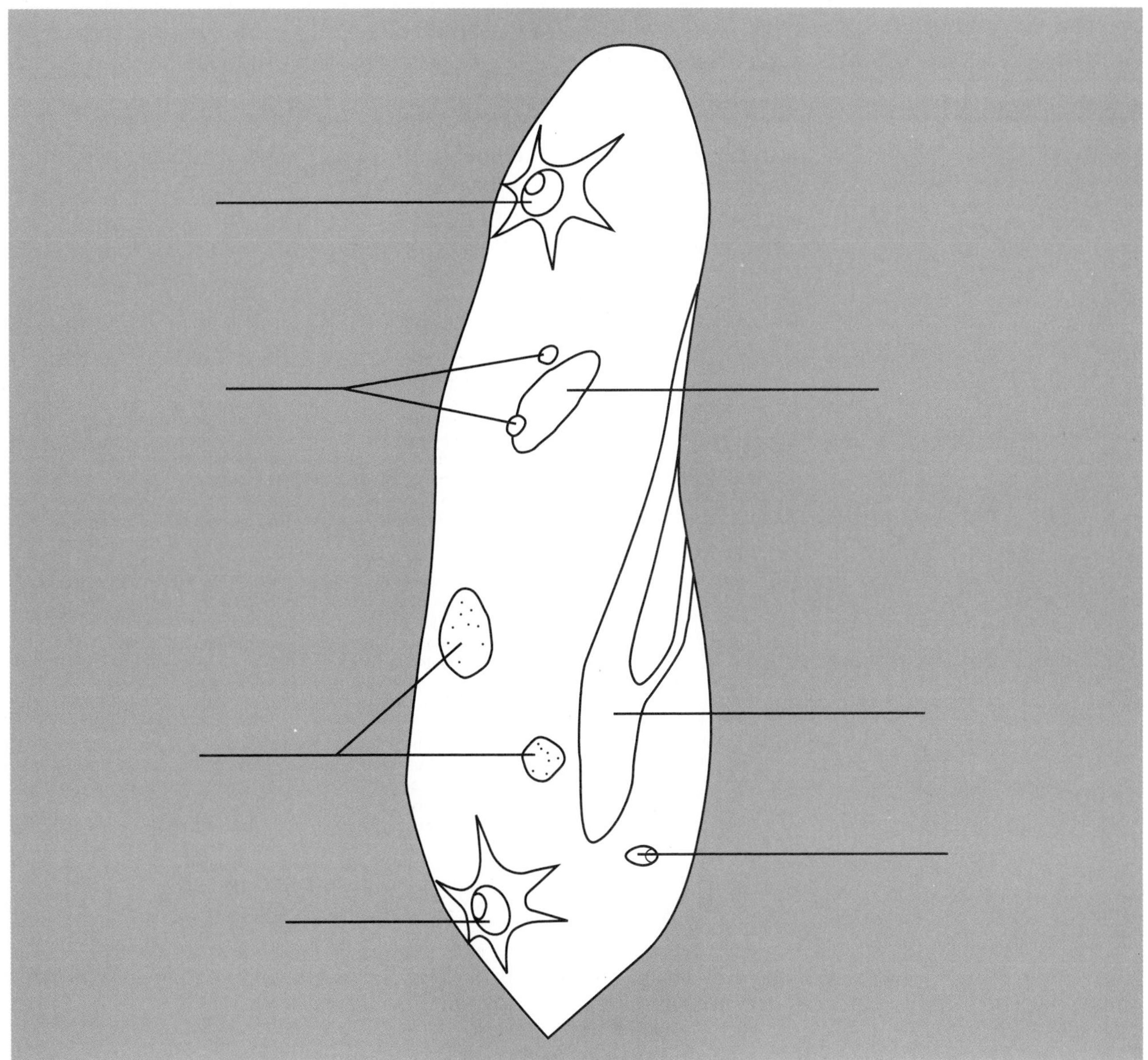

2. Ask questions before you begin so that you will understand the purpose of each step and avoid making mistakes. This may prevent you from hurting yourself or from having to repeat lengthy procedures. If your experiment involves one or more formulas, try to memorize these so that you will not have to break your concentration while you are pouring chemicals or preparing other materials for the experiment.
3. Write up your results as soon as possible—before you leave the lab if you can—while they are still fresh in your mind. You can discuss them later with other students and your instructor.
4. Whenever you do an experiment in lab, try to see its relationship to similar material presented in the textbook and lectures. Experiments conducted in the lab often illustrate important principles or concepts discussed in lectures or assigned readings.

EXERCISE 17.3

Apply what you have learned about study strategies for the sciences by completing this exercise with group members. Remember to follow the guidelines for group discussion explained in Chapter 1, pages 14–15. Read and discuss the following excerpt, which describes three different temperature scales. Decide what information should be underlined in the passage. On the lines provided, briefly summarize what you think is important to know about the three scales, emphasizing their differences. Then evaluate your work.

2.8 Temperature Scales and Heat

When we heat a substance, we add a quantity of heat to that substance. We can then use a thermometer to measure the temperature of the substance. The thermometer measures the *intensity* of the heat; it tells us nothing about the quantity of heat that has entered the substance. (We shall discuss heat quantity in Chapter 10.)

Three different temperature scales are commonly used in measuring heat intensity. Two of these—the Fahrenheit and Celsius scales—are in general use. The third, the Kelvin scale, is used mainly by scientists.

The Fahrenheit scale was devised by Gabriel Daniel Fahrenheit, a German scientist, in 1724. On this scale (Figure 2.5), the freezing point of pure water is at 32 degrees (32°F), and the boiling point of water is at 212 degrees (212°F). There are thus 180 Fahrenheit degrees between the freezing point and the boiling point of water.

The Celsius scale was devised in 1742 by Anders Celsius, a Swedish astronomer. His objective was to develop an easier-to-use temperature scale; he did so by assigning a nice, round 100 Celsius degrees between the freezing and boiling points of pure water. On the Celsius scale (Figure 2.5), the freezing point of water is at zero degrees (0°C), and the boiling point of water is at 100 degrees (100°C). (The Celsius scale is also sometimes referred to as the centigrade scale.)

The Kelvin scale is an *absolute* temperature scale. That is, its zero point (0 K) is at absolute zero, the lowest possible temperature theoretically attainable. The divisions of the Kelvin scale are the same size as Celsius degrees, but they are called kelvins (abbreviated K) rather than degrees. Chapter 11 discusses the Kelvin scale in more detail.

Figure 2.5
A comparison of Fahrenheit and Celsius scales

Alan Sherman, et. al., *Basic Concepts of Chemistry,* Fourth Edition. Copyright © 1988 by Houghton Mifflin Company. Used with permission.

1. Fahrenheit scale:

___

___

2. Celsius scale:

___

___

3. Kelvin scale:

___

___

Group Evaluation:

Evaluate your discussion. Did everyone contribute? Did you accomplish your task successfully? What additional questions do you have about strategies for the sciences, and how will you find answers to your questions.

____

____

____

CONFIDENCE BUILDER

Learning Scientific Terms

Prefixes, roots, and suffixes are your key to scientific terms.

Learning scientific terms and being able to use them are necessary for effective class and test preparation. Keep a terms list for every chapter. Write terms and definitions on note cards for review. Use your textbook glossary, if there is one. As you read, pay attention to words or terms that are either printed in bold type or highlighted in some other way. In addition to these basic strategies, a knowledge of the parts that make up a word is a key that unlocks the meaning of scientific terms and many other words as well.

Words are made up of parts called *prefixes, roots,* and *suffixes.* The word *root* suggests origin or foundation. A *root* is a base word or word stem. For example, *affect* is a base word, or root, that means "to cause." A *suffix* is a word part added to the end of a root, and it may change the root's grammatical form or expand its meaning. For example, *-ed* is a suffix that indicates past tense. The suffix *-ion* means "state or condition." The words *affected* and *affection* result when these parts are added. A *prefix* is a word part attached to the beginning of a root, and it usually changes the root's meaning. The prefix *un-* means "not." By adding this prefix to *affected* you get a word that means just the opposite: *unaffected.* If you know the meaning of one word part, you have a key to the meaning of many other words containing that part.

Now look what happens when you apply the analysis of word parts to a scientific term, *microbiology.* In this word, the root *micro* means "very small," the prefix *bio-* means "life," and the suffix *-logy* means "study of." Putting these parts together, you can see that *microbiology* means "the study of living things that are very small." The smallest living things are called *microorganisms,* and they must be viewed through a *microscope.* The root *scope* means "look." Here are some more words that contain some of the parts found in *microbiology:*

micro	**bio-**	**-logy**
microfilm	biotic	genealogy
micrometer	bionic	paleontology
microwave	biosphere	chronology

The following chart contains a few prefixes, roots, and suffixes that commonly occur in scientific terms and words describing health and the body. If you plan a career in science or any of the health-related services, these word parts will give you a jump start on learning the vocabulary of your chosen field. Remember, a word part is a key to the meaning of any word in which it appears. As you examine the chart, try to think of as many other words as you can that contain each prefix, root, and suffix.

Prefix	Meaning	Example Words
bene-	good, well	benign, beneficial
chem-, chemo-	chemical	chemistry, chemist
geo-	earth	geography, geology
mal-	bad, harmful	malady, malignant
physio-	nature, physical	physics, physician
psycho-	mind, mental	psychology, psychiatrist
socio-	society, companion	sociology, social
Root	**Meaning**	**Example Words**
anthrop	human	anthropology
audi	hear, hearing	auditory, inaudible
hepat	liver	hepatitis
patho, pathy	feeling, disease	pathology, sympathy
ped, pod	foot	podiatrist
phobia	fear of	claustrophobia
Suffix	**Meaning**	**Example Words**
-logy	study of	oncology, physiology
-ist	one who	radiologist, optometrist
-itis	inflammation	tonsillitis, appendicitis
-oid	like, resembling	rheumatoid arthritis
-osis	condition, process	mitosis, diagnosis

CRITICAL THINKING APPLICATION

Apply the writing-to-learn technique explained in the Chapter 16 Confidence Builder to your science class. Use writing to learn to prepare for an upcoming test. Write out any principles, formulas, or rules you need to remember. Make note cards for special terms. If you will be tested on one or more experiments that verified certain theories, summarize each experiment. Include who conducted it, why, who or what was tested, and what the experiment proved. Work on your own or with a partner; then share your results with the rest of the class.

SUMMARY

Read the following summary and complete the partially filled-in outline of its important points.

You learn scientific concepts and theories by reading about research that led to their formation and following the steps of the scientific method: *question, observe, hypothesize, research, analyze.* In the science lab, you observe, form hypotheses, and conduct experiments. Through these studies you will learn two things: how to solve scientific problems and a basic method that you can apply to other problem situations. Science courses can be challenging. To prepare for a science class, do all the things you would normally do to be successful in any course, but be sure to take special requirements into account. For social science courses, establish a background, understand the research, and compare theories. For natural science courses, use the PREP study system, make diagrams, and establish and follow a lab routine.

I. The divisions of science
   A. Biological and physical sciences
   B.
   C.

II. The scientific method
   A. Question
   B.
   C.
   D.
   E.

III. Preparing for science classes
   A. Strategies for social and behavioral sciences
      1.
      2.
      3.
   B. Strategies for biological and physical sciences
      1.
      2.
      3.

YOUR REFLECTIONS

Reflect on what you have learned about strategies for the sciences and how you can best apply that information. Use the following list of questions to stimulate your thinking; then write your reflections. Your response may include answers to one or more of the questions. Incorporate in your writing specific information from this chapter or previous chapters as needed.

- What is your level of motivation in science courses as compared to other courses?
- Describe your performance in science courses. What has led to or prevented your success?
- Do you have science anxiety? What have you learned from this chapter or others that will help you overcome it?
- Think about a science course you are taking or have taken in the past. What application does this course have in your life or career?
- Which strategy explained in this chapter will be the most helpful to you, and how do you plan to use it?

Date ______________________________

Index

Credits

Richard N. Aufmann and Vernon C. Barker INTRODUCTORY ALGEBRA: AN APPLIED APPROACH, Fourth Edition. Copyright © by Houghton Mifflin Company. Used with permission.

Douglas Bernstein, et al., PSYCHOLOGY, First Edition. Copyright © 1988 by Houghton Mifflin Company. Used with permission.

Excerpts from Bernstein, Clarke-Stewart, Roy, Srull, and Wickens, PSYCHOLOGY, Third Edition. Copyright © 1994 by Houghton Mifflin Company. Reprinted by permission.

Adapted with the permission of Scribner, a division of Simon & Schuster from DOING IT NOW by Edwin C. Bliss. Copyright © 1983 by Edwin C. Bliss.

Darrell Ebbing, GENERAL CHEMISTRY, Fifth Edition. Copyright © by Houghton Mifflin Company. Used with permission.

O. C. Ferrell and John Fraedrich, BUSINESS ETHICS, Second Edition. Copyright © 1996 by Houghton Mifflin Company. Reprinted by permission.

Thomas E. Garman and Raymond E. Forgue, PERSONAL FINANCE, Fourth Edition. Copyright © 1994 by Houghton Mifflin Company. Used with permission.

Adapted with permission from USING YOUR HEAD: THE MANY WAYS OF BEING SMART (Macmillan 1984) by Sara Gilbert.

From Alan R. Gitelson et al., AMERICAN GOVERNMENT, Fourth Edition. Copyright © 1996 by Houghton Mifflin Company. Reprinted by permission.

Saul Kassin, PSYCHOLOGY. Copyright © 1995 by Houghton Mifflin Company. Reprinted with permission.

Walter Pauk, HOW TO STUDY IN COLLEGE, Fifth Edition. Copyright © 1993 by Houghton Mifflin Company. Used with permission.

Barry L. Reece and Rhonda Brandt, EFFECTIVE HUMAN RELATIONS IN ORGANIZATIONS, Sixth Edition. Copyright © 1996 by Houghton Mifflin Company. Reprinted by permission.

Alan Sherman, et. al., BASIC CONCEPTS OF CHEMISTRY, Fourth Edition. Copyright © 1988 by Houghton Mifflin Company. Used with permission.

Jean Paul Valette and Rebecca M. Valette, CONTACTS, Fifth Edition. Copyright © 1993 by Houghton Mifflin Company. Used with permission.

Instructor's Resource Manual

The Confident Student

Third Edition

Carol C. Kanar
Valencia Community College

HOUGHTON MIFFLIN COMPANY • BOSTON NEW YORK

As part of Houghton Mifflin's ongoing commitment to the environment, this text has been printed on recycled paper.

Assistant Editor: Melissa Plumb
Associate Project Editor: Gabrielle Stone
Manufacturing Coordinator: Priscilla J. Bailey

Printed in the U.S.A.

ISBN: 0-395-88644-9

123456789-WC-01 00 99 98 97

Contents

Introduction

The Confident Student Third Edition is a student-oriented text. Its tone is friendly and direct as it speaks to students about their study problems and suggests strategies for coping with the demands of college life and work.

Adjusting to college can be a traumatic experience for those students who do not realize that there is more to getting a college education than signing up for and attending classes. Recent high school graduates must make the transition from high school to college and adjust to the greater difficulty and number of assignments. At the same time, they must learn to seek help, for college instructors may not give them the degree of personal attention they were used to receiving from their high school teachers.

Older students who have postponed college to raise families because of insufficient funds or for other reasons must learn all over again how to study. Especially if these students have held responsible jobs, they may find some of their college requirements demeaning and meaningless unless they receive proper counseling from understanding instructors and other interested campus professionals. All students who need skill development may be ill-equipped to succeed in their courses without the help that a study skills or orientation course can provide. Students need to develop confidence in themselves and their abilities so that they can reach their goals.

Keeping students in college has been and remains one of our biggest academic problems. If they do not get off to a good start in the first few courses they take, many students lose heart and give up, particularly if they are struggling with financial and family demands in order to attend college. As an instructor of a study skills, orientation, student success, or other course for which you have chosen this book, you are faced with a most rewarding job. Students come to your classes hoping that you have something to tell them that will make their lives as students easier. They are eager to learn the strategies that will help them solve their most pressing problems, such as managing time, dealing with test anxiety, learning how to read and think critically, study, take notes, concentrate, remember, and much more.

With *The Confident Student* Third Edition as a guide, you can show your students how to be successful. You can create a learning experience for them that they will never forget because the strategies you will teach them have applications beyond the classroom. This *Instructor's Resource Manual* will show you how to use the textbook to help make every student a confident student.

I welcome your comments and suggestions. Please write and tell me what works or does not work for you and your students as you use *The Confident Student* Third Edition. If you have an idea for an exercise or other activity, please share it with me. Should I use your idea in a future edition of this text, I will acknowledge your contribution in the book's credits. Write to me at this address:

Carol C. Kanar
c/o Student Success Programs
222 Berkeley Street
Boston, MA 02116

Course	Instructor	Tests (Percentages)	Projects/ Other (Percentages)	Attendance	Late Work	Makeup Policy
English	Ames	Midterm 25% Final 25%	Weekly essays 50%	Withdrawal after three absences	Grade on work lowered one letter for each day late	Midterm: before next class meeting; no others

Organization and Content

The Confident Student Third Edition is divided into three parts. Its seventeen chapters progress logically from topics related to adjusting to the demands of college to the specific strategies needed to master every course. Because the chapters are each self-contained, you can assign them in any order that seems reasonable; you can also skip chapters that do not seem appropriate for your students. A consistent system of cross-referencing throughout the text directs readers to chapters in which a topic is either introduced or explained in more detail.

You will find in *The Confident Student* Third Edition complete coverage of all the traditional study skills, including how to improve concentration and memory, how to read better and study more efficiently, how to listen and take effective notes, and how to prepare for tests and study specific subject areas. The orientation material suggests ways to solve problems, set goals, use college resources, maintain health and well-being, and manage time. In addition, there is unique material on relaxation techniques for reducing stress and test anxiety, on determining learning style preferences and developing an internal locus of control, and on critical thinking strategies that can be applied across the curriculum. New to the third edition is a more pronounced focus in every chapter on workplace skills: specifically the foundation skills and workplace competencies identified by SCANS (the Secretary's Commission on Achieving Necessary Skills). See the end of this section for more information.

The Three Parts of *The Confident Student*

Each of the three parts covers a topic that can be a potential problem for students, causing them to lose confidence. **Part One,** "Becoming a Confident Student," is designed to help a diverse population of students conceptualize college as a community of learners in which they must take an active part in order to be successful. Returning students who enter your class after one or more unsuccessful semesters, intending to improve their skills, can also benefit from the reorientation to college they will get by completing the chapters in **Part One.**

This part stresses the importance of developing an internal locus of control. It provides strategies for strengthening motivation as well as for developing goal-setting and problem-solving abilities.

It also guides students through campus resources, suggests ways to get help with specific problems, and emphasizes the importance of maintaining health and well-being, to ensure good performance.

If there is one problem that all students seem to have, it is time management. It is the rare college student who has no obligations other than attending classes. Most students today also work, have families to care for, or both. Many are surprised to find out how much study time is needed to get the grades they want; indeed, juggling work, family, and school responsibilities can be overwhelming. Such students may also exhibit the natural human tendency to procrastinate when tasks are difficult or unpleasant. For those who lack appropriate learning strategies, studying *is* difficult and unpleasant, and they will often procrastinate until it is too late to do their best. In **Part One**, students learn how to manage time effectively. They also learn strategies for effective listening and note taking, for participating in group activities, and for making oral presentations. These strategies can help them become active and confident learners who are involved in what goes on in their classes, their communities, and at work.

To study with power and confidence, students need to develop textbook reading strategies and effective study systems such as SQ3R, the classic system, and PREP, a system that is especially effective when used in conjunction with math, language, and science texts. Students also need to know how to organize information and make useful study guides, such as concept maps, comparison charts, outlines, and diagrams. These graphic organizers enable students to recast information from textbooks and other sources into a format that not only helps them to remember it but also appeals to their learning styles. In addition to these essential skills, **Part Two** shows students how to improve their concentration and strengthen their memory through the use of proven memory aids and techniques. **Part Two** also covers another topic that many students say is a problem for them: preparing for and taking tests. Most students want to know how to make better grades. Usually they are hoping for short cuts, but there is no substitute for being thoroughly prepared—whatever it takes. In this part of the text, students are encouraged to discover how much studying it takes to do their best on tests, to make a study schedule that will allow sufficient time for that study, and to develop a test-taking routine that will enable them to enter a test situation with confidence, believing they will succeed. In addition, **Part Two** shows students how to reduce test anxiety—first, by being well prepared, and then, by using relaxation techniques when anxiety overcomes preparation.

A common complaint of many instructors is that students do not know how to think; they seem to take little responsibility for their own learning, expecting someone to *give* them an education rather than doing what is necessary to *get* an education. In recent years, critical thinking has been proposed as an antidote to this problem. Many instructors believe that, by teaching certain processes such as how to write an essay or how to solve a word problem, they are automatically teaching students to think. Writing *is* thinking, some instructors say, and they are right. Studying is a concentrated kind of thinking, too—as is active reading. But learning to think critically doesn't happen automatically; you have to reveal the process to your students and help them become aware that they are thinking. **Part Three** defines critical thinking as a process of four essential analytical strategies—assuming, predicting, interpreting, and evaluating. **Part Three** also shows students how to develop their reading and writing, for these are the principal strategies they will use to gather and interpret information and to apply what they have learned.

To master every course, students need to understand the assumptions on which various academic disciplines are based and the kinds of information to look for as they are reading assigned chapters. **Part Three** covers two subject areas that are often the most difficult for students—math and science—and suggests strategies to apply when studying each subject.

Chapter Content and Features

The chapters of *The Confident Student* Third Edition are designed to have a strong visual appeal, since the predominant learning style of many students is visual. Concepts are illustrated with photographs, diagrams, and figures, and exercises are integrated with text material to promote greater understanding. Included in each chapter is at least one exercise that can be used for collaborative learning. Carried over from the second edition, the collaborative exercises have been re-formatted to make students' collaborations more focused and fruitful.

The instructional approach is a step-by-step one; students are guided through difficult concepts by textual aids such as bulleted or numbered lists and concept maps. Chapters 7, 8, 13, and 14 teach students specific methods for reading and studying actively, and for finding the underlying structure in what they read. The structure of each chapter of *The Confident Student* Third Edition is carefully designed to be clearly visible to readers so that they can follow and remember ideas.

The Third Edition's instructional method is also a very personal approach that encourages students to try all the study strategies and suggestions presented in each chapter and to choose the ones that work best to create their own study systems. The scenario, or student example, is a device that grounds concepts in the reality of students' lives and their experiences in college. In many of the chapters, these stories about students who are building their skills and trying out the techniques suggested in the text help readers relate text material to their own lives. Many of the exercises ask readers to help hypothetical students solve their study problems; in so doing, they may learn ways to solve their own.

Strengthening self-awareness and confidence are underlying themes of *The Confident Student* Third Edition. Independence in learning comes from self-knowledge and the acquisition of skills that build confidence in one's ability to succeed. Many students do not know what strengths they possess and what weaknesses are holding them back. Two features that encourage self-examination are the **Awareness Checks** that appear in all chapters and the **Your Reflections** at the end of every chapter.

The Awareness Checks help students find out what they already know about a topic and what more they need to learn, whereas Your Reflections provides an opportunity for students to self-reflect on their progress. Students' reflections and Awareness Check results can also inspire class activities and discussion.

The text features **Confidence Builders** as well, which broaden the scope of topics covered in each chapter by providing information on current research or additional strategies for students to try. For example, the Confidence Builder for Chapter 11, "How to Raise Scores on Standardized Tests," suggests ways to prepare for these types of exams. The one for Chapter 16, "Writing to Learn Mathematics," explains how to use writing to learn mathematics, a strategy many math instructors report as being helpful to their students. Again, you can develop discussions and activities around the material presented in Confidence Builders.

Yet another feature in six of the chapters is **Computer Confidence,** a feature unique to *The Confident Student* Third Edition that explains how to use a computer to enhance study skills. Computers are a fact of life; many of your students are not only interested in computers but may also have experience using them. Students do not have to own computers in order to have access to them. Many colleges have computer labs staffed with technicians who will teach students to use word processing and other programs. If you have a computer lab at your school, a worthwhile activity would be to take your students on a tour and have lab technicians explain the services that are available.

Summaries at the end of each chapter have been revised as interactive exercises. For example, students complete a partially filled-in outline or concept map as a chapter review. Encourage your students to read the Summaries as part of their preliminary survey of each chapter. Knowing in advance what the chapter covers helps students formulate questions to guide their reading and encourages them to follow the development of concepts. Rereading the Summaries is also an excellent way for students to review chapters before taking a test. If a topic they read about in the Summary doesn't cue their memories, then they know they should reread that section of the chapter.

The **Critical Thinking Application** comes near the end of the chapter, just before the Summary. This feature is an exercise that requires students to use critical thinking skills to apply a concept or knowledge gained from the chapter to a practical situation or academic scenario. The Critical Thinking Applications can be equally effective as individual or collaborative exercises.

Transparency Masters

The transparency masters are on pages 88–112 of this manual. Use them to supplement instruction and build interest in a topic. The transparencies will appeal to your visual learners who need to have something to look at while you are giving a lecture or an explanation. Specific ideas regarding the use of these chapter-related transparencies follow in the section titled "Suggestions for Each Chapter."

Tests for *The Confident Student* Third Edition

This manual contains 17 chapter tests and one comprehensive final test with an answer key. All of the tests are primarily short-answer/essay-type exams, and all are self-reflective in nature. They have been field tested by instructors in several states.

Collaborative Learning: Method and Exercises

This manual contains a listing of all the collaborative exercises that have been updated and where to find them. The section also includes additional exercises, which have been modified to address SCANS competencies, and a brief explanation of the methodology and benefits of collaborative learning activities.

Supplementary Chapters

In response to colleagues, some of whom wanted a shorter textbook and some of whom still wanted to address vocabulary development and research methods in their student success courses, we have moved Chapters 9 ("Developing Your Vocabulary") and 15 ("Using Your Library, Doing Research") from the Second Edition to the Instructor's Resource Manual for the Third Edition. You can photocopy these chapters and distribute them to your entire class or to selected students.

"Roundtable Discussion" Videotapes Activities

The "Roundtable Discussions" videotapes were created for use in any course on study skills and techniques for success in college. *Study Strategies* covers the four primary proficiencies (note taking, reading, memory, and test taking) and introduces specific tools and techniques for mastering each set of skills. The *Life Skills* videotape addresses three areas that help to ensure success (goal-setting, time management, and stress management).

This supplement is intended to help you integrate the *Study Strategies* and *Life Skills* videotapes with the textbook and other materials you use. In addition, you will find suggested activities and summary exercises for linking specific topics with students' experiences both inside and outside the classroom.

For information on ordering the "Roundtable Discussion" videotapes, please contact your Houghton Mifflin representative or telephone 1-800-733-1717.

Focus on Workplace Skills

The third edition of *The Confident Student* adds a new dimension to student success: a focus on workplace skills. Instructors have always known that a way to grab students' attention is to demonstrate that the skills they are learning in the classroom have a practical application outside the classroom. Lifelong learning is a goal every instructor encourages.

In 1991, the Secretary's Commission on Achieving Necessary Skills (SCANS) published *What Work Requires of Schools: A SCANS Report for America 2000.* Former Secretary of Labor, Elizabeth Dole, created the Commission which included members from industry, labor, education, and government. The report, which is the culmination of the Commission's work, identifies the skills students need to succeed in the workplace. The following chart summarizes the skills.

Workplace Skills

The skills and personal qualities needed for success at work make up the foundation on which the five SCANS competencies are based.

The Foundation

Basic Skills	reading, writing, arithmetic and mathematics, speaking, and listening
Thinking Skills	thinking creatively, making decisions, solving problems, reasoning, knowing how to learn, and seeing things in the mind's eye
Personal Qualities	individual responsibility, self-esteem, sociability, self-management, and integrity

The Competencies

Resources	allocating time, money, materials, space, and staff
Interpersonal Skills	working on teams, teaching others, serving customers, leading, negotiating, working with others from culturally diverse backgrounds
Information	acquiring and evaluating data, organizing and maintaining files, interpreting and communicating, and using computers
Systems	understanding social, organizational, and technological systems, monitoring and correcting performance, and designing or improving systems
Technology	selecting equipment and tools, applying technology to specific tasks, and maintaining and troubleshooting technologies

Chart adapted from "Workplace Know-How" on page vii of *What Work Requires of Schools: A SCANS Report for America 2000;* the Secretary's Commission on Achieving Necessary Skills; U.S. Department of Labor; June, 1991.

Although it is not possible to address all of these skills in your student success course, it is easy to integrate many of them with your course objectives. For example, if you do collaborative learning activities in your class, you are addressing the SCANS interpersonal skill of "working on teams." To help students see the value of collaborative learning, point out that team work is expected of graduates entering the workplace and that your class is providing experience and practice in that essential skill. Similarly, everything you do to help students improve reading and studying from textbooks addresses the SCANS basic skills of "reading," "reasoning," and "knowing how to learn," and the SCANS information competency of "acquiring," "evaluating," and "organizing" data.

No doubt you are already making a connection between today's classroom and the workplace of the future. The new SCANS material in *The Confident Student* Third Edition can help you give greater emphasis to workplace competencies in three ways:

1. The first page of every chapter lists objectives and states the workplace competencies addressed.
2. A chart at the end of this section lists objectives and competencies by chapter. Use this chart for your own convenience or feel free to make copies of it to share with your students.
3. The exercises for collaborative learning at the end of this manual have been revised to reflect both chapter objectives and SCANS workplace competencies.

The focus on workplace skills both in chapter introductions and throughout the chapters is subtle so that the instructor who does not wish to make an issue of SCANS need not do so. However, instructors who are interested will find the text supportive of their efforts to make a SCANS connection.

The following chart correlates the four keys to success explained in Chapter 1 with each chapter's objectives and the workplace skills they address. To read the chart, read across from left to right. The first column lists chapters by number and title. The second column lists chapter objectives and the success key emphasized. The third column lists workplace skills or subskills that correspond to chapter objectives. Beside each subskill in parentheses is the abbreviation of the workplace skill it falls under. Refer to the following list of skills and abbreviations as you read the chart.

The Foundation

- Basic Skills (BS)
- Thinking Skills (TS)
- Personal Qualities (PQ)

The Competencies

- Resources (R)
- Interpersonal Skills (IP)
- Information (I)
- Systems (S)
- Technology (T)

Correlation Chart for Success Keys, Chapter Objectives, and Workplace Skills*

Chapter	Success Keys/ Chapter Objectives	Workplace Skills/ Competencies Addressed
1 Motivating Yourself to Learn	Use **four keys** to success in college: **1. Assess your strengths and weaknesses.** **2. Discover and use your learning style.** **3. Develop critical thinking and study skills.** **4. Adapt to others' styles.**	Individual responsibility (PQ) Self-management (PQ) Reasons, knows how to learn (TS) Works with others (IP)
2 Setting Goals and Solving Problems	Use **the third key** (critical thinking) to: Set goals for success. Set long-term and short-term goals. Solve problems.	Acts responsibly (PS) Acquires and organizes information (I) Makes decisions, thinks creatively (TS)
3 Sharpening Your Classroom Skills	Use **the third key** (study skills), **the second key** (learning style), and **the fourth key** (adapt) to: Prepare for class. Become an active listener. Develop a personal note-taking system. Make effective oral presentations. Participate in class and group activities.	Acts responsibly (PS) Basic skill (BS) Knows how to learn (TS) Teaches others (IP) Participates as team member (IP)
4 Making the Most of Your Time	Use **the first key** (assess), **the second key** (learning style), and **the third key** (study skills) to: Take control of your time. Make and follow schedules. Avoid procrastination.	Acts responsibily, self-manages (PQ) Allocates time and space (for study) (R) Exercises leadership (IP) Monitors/corrects performance (S)
5 Adapting to College Life	Use **the third key** (critical thinking) and **the fourth key** (adapt) to: Become familiar with your diverse campus. Find helpful people, places, and publications. Find resources for commuters.	Self-esteem, sociability (PQ) Works with cultural diversity (IP) Acquires information (I)

*Technology is also addressed in Computer Confidence (Chapters 3, 8, and 15); *working on teams* is addressed in collaborative exercises that appear in every chapter. You may find other SCANS connections in addition to those charted here.

Chapter	Success Keys/ Chapter Objectives	Workplace Skills/ Competencies Addressed
6 Maintaining Your Health and Well-Being	Use **the first key** (assess) and **the third key** (critical thinking) to:	
	Stay healthy.	Self-management (PQ)
	Control your emotions and adapt to change.	Integrity, honesty (PQ)
	Improve your interpersonal skills.	Sociability (PQ)
	Manage your sex life.	Integrity, self-esteem (PQ)
7 Creating Your Study System	Use **the third key** (thinking and study skills) to:	
	Identify and use textbook study aids.	Acquires and evaluates information (I)
	Experiment with proven study systems.	Reasons, knows how to learn (TS)
	Devise your own study/learning system.	Designs and improves systems (S)
8 Organizing Information and Making Study Guides	Use **the second key** (learning style) and **the third key** (thinking and study skills) to:	
	Try out different types of organizers.	Reasons, knows how to learn (TS)
	Choose the ones that work best for you.	Monitors/corrects performance (S)
9 Controlling Your Concentration	Use **the first key** (assess) and **the second key** (learning style) to:	
	Find out why you lose concentration.	Self-management (PQ)
	Identify and eliminate distractions.	Solves problems (TS)
	Find or create your best study environment.	Allocates time and space (R)
	Study with a system that helps concentration.	Knows how to learn (TS)
10 Improving Learning and Memory	Use **the second key** (learning style) and **the third key** (thinking and study skills) to:	
	Understand stages and functions of memory.	Knows how to learn (TS)
	Learn to combat forgetting.	Self-management (PQ)
	Improve the way you process information.	Monitors/corrects performance (S)
11 Preparing for Tests	Use **the third key** (study skills) to:	
	Decide what, when, and how to study.	Self-manage (PQ), allocate time (R)
	Follow a test-taking routine.	Reasons, makes decisions (TS)
	Know how to prepare for any kind of test.	Knows how to learn (TS)

Chapter	Success Keys/ Chapter Objectives	Workplace Skills/ Competencies Addressed
12 Reducing Test Anxiety	Use **the first key** (assess) to:	
	Determine what causes your test anxiety.	Self-manage, self-esteem (PQ)
	Eliminate the causes.	Solves problems (TS)
	Choose a strategy that works for you.	Reasons, thinks creatively (TS)
13 Using Critical Thinking Strategies	Use **the third key** (critical thinking) to:	
	Examine your assumptions.	Reading (BS), thinks creatively (TS)
	Make predictions.	Makes decisions (TS)
	Sharpen your interpretations.	Sees things in mind's eye (TS)
	Evaluate what you learn.	Acquires and evaluates data (I)
14 Becoming an Active Reader	Use **the first key** (assess basic skills) and **the third key** (thinking and study skills) to:	
	Take control of your reading process.	Monitors/corrects performance (S)
	Read for point, proof, and implications.	Reading (BS), sees in mind's eye (TS)
	Use underlining and marking systems.	Knows how to learn (TS)
15 Becoming a Confident Writer	Use **the first key** (assess basic skills), **the second key** (learning styles), and **the third key** (critical thinking skills) to:	
	Take control of your writing process.	Monitors/corrects performance (S)
	Apply critical thinking skills to writing.	Reasons, thinks creatively (TS)
	Use a five-paragraph plan as a starting point.	Writing (BS), knows how to learn (TS)
16 Gaining Math Confidence	Use **the first key** (assess basic skills), **the second key** (learning styles), and **the third key** (thinking and study skills) to:	
	Overcome math anxiety.	Self-manage, self-esteem (PQ)
	Develop math study strategies.	Knows how to learn (TS)
	Learn from your mistakes.	Monitors/corrects performance (S)
17 Developing Science Strategies	Use **the third key** (thinking and study skills) to:	
	Accept the challenge of science courses.	Self-manage (PQ)
	Learn the divisions of science.	Acquires data (PQ)
	Understand and apply the scientific method.	Knows how to learn (TS)
	Overcome science anxiety.	Self-esteem (PQ)
	Learn how to prepare for your science class.	Individual responsibility (PQ)
	Use specific strategies for the sciences.	Reasons (TS)

How to Use The Confident Student *Third Edition*

In building your course around the textbook, take into consideration the following elements of instruction: motivation; assessment of students' strengths, weaknesses, and needs; assignments and class activities; and evaluation of students' progress.

Most instructors would agree that selecting assignments and devising ways to evaluate students' progress are essential parts of course planning, even though the need for motivating students and assessing their strengths and weaknesses may vary from course to course. In study skills and orientation classes, however, motivation and assessment play key roles. Many students take study skills classes precisely because they are not motivated to study and want to learn how to increase their motivation. Whenever an orientation course is required of entering freshmen, some are likely to feel that the course is a waste of their time. You will have to convince these students that what they learn will help them become more successful so that they will be motivated to try out the learning strategies you suggest.

Assessment is especially important in a study skills or orientation course because your students probably will be a diverse group having a wide range of ability and skill levels. To plan effectively and cover the skills most of your students need, you must assess their strengths and weaknesses. Use the Skill Finder on pages xx–xxii of the text and the Awareness Checks in Chapter 1 for this purpose, and add to them any assessment measures you are already using.

Motivation

You can use students' Awareness Checks and the student examples in the text as a means of initiating discussions about what works and what does not work as your class tries out the strategies offered in each chapter. Keep the discussion focused on learning style so that students begin to see that creating a study system is a personal matter related to their preferences and the ways in which they believe they learn best. Throughout the course, review the Chapter 1 discussion about locus of control; students need to be reminded that *they* are responsible for motivating themselves.

To help students become more internally motivated, refuse to accept excuses. When students make excuses for poor performance or lack of preparation, say, "That's interesting, but what will you do now?" Treat lack of motivation as a problem your students can solve by setting goals, as explained in Chapter 2. The COPE problem-solving method, also explained in Chapter 2, can be the focus of a class activity on finding motivation to study. Work through COPE's four steps with your students to help them come up with ways to increase motivation.

Early in the semester, invite an expert to talk to your class about motivation and ways to increase it. Someone from your psychology department, learning center, or career center may be willing to give a brief lecture and lead a discussion. Time this activity to coincide with your assignment of Chapter 5, and then point out that the speaker is an important resource to whom your students can turn if they need additional help with motivation.

The great reward in teaching study skills is that, as students try out their new strategies in other classes, they see immediate, positive results. Once this happens, they will come back to your class motivated to learn more. Turn students' positive experiences into learning activities that can motivate the whole class. Also, develop class discussions around students' success in other classes; for example, when you are teaching Chapters 11 and 12, ask students to explain what they did to prepare for a test on which they received an A, or how they managed to overcome test anxiety.

Keep the tone of your class positive. Don't let discussions degenerate into gripe sessions. Encourage students to let go of the past and look ahead to a more successful future. Ideally, motivation should come from within, but initially it may have to come from you.

As an additional motivator, make practical connections between strategies for success in college and their application in the workplace. Use the SCANS chart on page 6 as a quick reference to the competencies addressed in each chapter.

Assessment

Many students will enter your class knowing they need to improve their study habits, but they will not be able to tell you exactly why they have a problem or what they need to improve. Early in the term you will want to help them assess their strengths and weaknesses. You will find out that most of them need to improve their time management and learn how to study. A few will have special problems such as test anxiety. If you have prepared a syllabus in advance, it should be flexible enough to account for individual needs.

At the beginning of the course, use the Skill Finder on pages xx–xxii of the text and the four Awareness Checks in Chapter 1 to help you assess students' strengths, weaknesses, and needs. At the same time, determine what you might want to emphasize in the text. Plan discussions around Skill Finder and Awareness Check results to assist students both in identifying their learning style preferences and determining which study skills they need to develop or improve. In subsequent chapters, you can use the Awareness Check results to help students establish a context for understanding the topics covered and to build their confidence in what they already know.

Assignments and Activities

In planning activities and assignments for your students, appeal to their learning styles by varying the ways that you present material. To reach auditory learners, lecture. To reach visual learners, demonstrate and illustrate. To reach tactile learners, plan hands-on activities such as an orientation trip to the library, where students must use the computerized card catalog, vertical file, and other resources to find information on a list you have compiled.

Some researchers suggest that each time you introduce a new skill or concept, you should use a visual, auditory, and tactile mode in your presentation if possible. To introduce the topic of test anxiety in Chapter 12, for example, you can appeal to auditory learners by giving a brief lecture on the use of relaxation techniques to reduce test anxiety. To involve visual learners, have students look at the illustration on page 258 of the sixteen muscle groups that are tensed and relaxed during the relaxation process. To hold tactile learners' attention, demonstrate a relaxation technique and ask your students to follow along with you.

Since many students have short attention spans, you may want to break up an hour of instruction into three or four different activities. For example, give a brief lecture followed by a class discussion and a related activity that students can engage in singly or in groups. Guest speakers add variety to your class and introduce students to helpful people and services on your campus. Invite someone from the appropriate department or office to speak to your students on the following subjects or others you may think of that are related to topics covered in *The Confident Student* Third Edition.

Financial Aid

Managing Money

Career Development

How to Manage Stress

Health and Fitness

Drug and Alcohol Use and Abuse

Sexual Harassment

Computer Lab Services

Learning Lab and Reading, Writing, or Math Center

Student Government/Activities

Learning Styles

Memory Techniques

If you decide to invite guest speakers, be sure to tell them exactly what you want them to talk about and how long you want them to speak. Use the Speaker Evaluation Form, a reproducible master on page 72 of this manual, to help you decide whether to invite the speaker again and to help students focus their attention on the speaker.

Evaluation

The Skill Finder and the Midterm Awareness Check in this manual (reproducible masters on pages 65–68 and 71, respectively) are informal measures of student progress. The Midterm Awareness Check can alert students to areas they still need to work on. The Skill Finder, used as a post-test near the end of the term, can help you and your students see what skills they have mastered.

I do not recommend that you give letter grades for the Midterm Awareness Check, Skill Finder, or Awareness Checks throughout the chapters. Since the purpose of these instruments is to encourage self-evaluation, students should not approach them as "tests" because of all the negative connotations of tests and the anxiety-arousing feelings they sometimes provoke.

To determine grades for your students, in addition to whatever other means of evaluation you use, you might want to give quizzes at the end of each chapter. Or you may wish to give three or four unit tests covering the chapters discussed throughout the term. A comprehensive final exam is optional. See pages 113–133 for tests covering Chapters 1–17 and a comprehensive final exam.

The new Critical Thinking Application feature can be used as an evaluative tool. Since this exercise requires students to apply their knowledge, their performance will indicate how well they have mastered chapter content and the critical thinking skills they must use to complete the exercise. In addition, their performance may indicate to you what skills or concepts need further explanation.

Portfolio Assessment and Student Success

New to this edition is a guide to the use of portfolios in your student success class. If you have used portfolio assessment in other courses, or even if you have never used it but would like to, this section explains how.

According to many instructors who use portfolios, the advantages are threefold: (1) They ease the transition from a teacher-centered classroom to a student-centered learning environment, (2) They promote independence in learning by making students responsible for their performance, grades, and maintenance of the work to be included in their portfolios; (3) They relieve instructors of some of the burden of grading.

Portfolio assessment also lends itself to collaborative activities that require students to work in teams. The teacher's role shifts from leader to manager. Some instructors believe that the resulting learning environment reflects today's workplace in a way that the traditional classroom does not, thereby preparing students for the move from college to job or career.

If you think portfolios would supplement your instruction in a useful way, read on. However, if this instructional tool/approach does not appeal to you, skip this section and resume with the next section's suggestions for each chapter.

What Is a Portfolio?

A **portfolio** is a folder, binder, accordion file, or other holder in which students collect their work over time. The samples of work contained in the portfolio provide a record of students' growth and skill development throughout the term. Some or all of the work can be used as alternative achievement measures. Portfolios allow for the assessment of work products that require the integration of reading and writing (Fernan & Kelly, 1991). Also, a review of the entire collection of work makes clear the relationship among the variables of instruction, student performance, and assessment.

Who Is Responsible for Keeping the Portfolio?

Opinions vary as to whether students should be entirely responsible for managing the portfolio. Instructors will surely want to specify the kinds of assignments that are to be collected but may leave it up to students as to which samples will be graded. Some instructors may require students to keep their portfolios at home; others may insist that students store them in the classroom; still others may keep the portfolios, or copies of the work, in their office.

What Kind of Work Is Collected in the Portfolio?

Again, instructors are free to decide what kinds of work products they want to see in the portfolios. Some possibilities include but are not limited to: tests, surveys, journal activities, essays and other written materials, students' reflections.

How Is the Work Evaluated?

Generally speaking, there are three types of evaluations that lend themselves to portfolio assessment: instructor evaluations, self-assessment, and peer evaluations.

How Can I Implement Portfolio Assessment?

As with any other teaching approach, you need to think carefully about what you want to do before, during, and after instruction. *Before instruction,* do some diagnostic testing. Use the Skill Finder at the beginning of *The Confident Student* Third Edition, to assess students' skills. Any other measures you want to use at this point can flesh out what you and your students learn from the Skill Finder. Guide your students through a discussion of their pre-assessment results, course expectations, and the outcomes they expect. Introduce the course syllabus—your plan for the term—after having made whatever adjustments are needed based on the results of your diagnostic testing.

During instruction focus on skills and outcomes. Have students work collaboratively and individually on skill development. Make sure students know what the expected outcome of any activity/task is, and teach them how to self-monitor and check for progress. For example, Your Reflections at the end of each chapter is a performance-based self-monitoring activity. Consistently read and respond to students' self-reflective writing and adjust instruction accordingly.

After instruction review expectations and outcomes. Ask "What did you need to learn? Did you learn it? How do you know?" Have students reflect orally or in writing, on their strengths, weaknesses, and their intellectual and personal growth. At the end of each chapter, unit, or designated period of work, have students choose work products/samples that best represent their achievement. These items can be collected in their portfolios. Have them write a summary of what they have learned, organize their work, and turn in the portfolio for assessment. Some instructors develop an assessment form that can be added to the portfolio before returning it to the student.

The portfolios should contain items from all three phases of instruction, organized in whatever way you determine. You may want to develop a handout that lists what goes in the portfolio. Many instructors find portfolio assessment an inspiration to their own creativity and are able to design many useful activities and forms to meet a variety of instructional/assessment needs.

The following outline lists items from each chapter of *The Confident Student* Third Edition that are appropriate for portfolio inclusion. The list is comprehensive to allow for flexibility in your choice of items to be included.

Chapter 1
Awareness Checks (summary of results)
Collaborative Exercise 1.4
Your Learning Profile (Critical Thinking Application)
Your Reflections

Chapter 2
Awareness Check (summary of results)
An essay about goals developed from Exercise 2.2
Collaborative Exercise 2.1
Critical Thinking Application (CTA)
Your Reflections

Chapter 3
Awareness Checks (summary of results)
An essay on learning style, listening, and note-taking (CTA)
Collaborative Exercise 3.1
Your Reflections

Chapter 4
Awareness Checks (summary of results)
Exercise 4.3 (with summary paragraph)
Collaborative Exercise 4.4
Your Reflections

Chapter 5
Awareness Check (summary of results)
Collaborative Exercise 5.5
Your Reflections

Chapter 6
Awareness Check (summary of results)
An evaluation of student's Emotional Intelligence based on the Confidence Builder
Collaborative Exercise 6.7
Your Reflections

Chapter 7	Awareness Check (summary of results) Collaborative Exercise 7.2 Your Plan for Learning (CTA) Your Reflections
Chapter 8	Awareness Check (summary of results) Collaborative Exercise 8.3 or CTA Have students experiment with making study guides and select the best one to include in the portfolio with an evaluation of its usefulness. Your Reflections
Chapter 9	Awareness Check (summary of results) Collaborative Exercise 9.2 An essay that compiles information gained from the exercise and CTA Your Reflections
Chapter 10	Awareness Check (summary of results) Collaborative Exercise 10.3 or CTA Your Reflections
Chapter 11	Awareness Check (summary of results) Collaborative Exercise 11.4 or CTA Exercise 11.2 with summary of results Your Reflections
Chapter 12	Awareness Check (summary of results) Collaborative Exercise 12.3 Student essay (CTA) Your Reflections
Chapter 13	Awareness Check (summary of results) Collaborative Exercise 13.3 or CTA Your Reflections
Chapter 14	Awareness Check (summary of results) Collaborative Exercise 14.3 or CTA Your Reflections
Chapter 15	Awareness Check (summary of results) Learning Styles Exercise 15.2 Collaborative Exercise 15.4 Student essay (CTA) Your Reflections

Chapter 16 Awareness Check (summary of results)
Collaborative Exercise 16.3
Student report (CTA)
Your Reflections

Chapter 17 Awareness Check (summary of results)
Collaborative Exercise 17.3
CTA with evaluation of usefulness
Your Reflections

An item should not be added to the portfolio without some explanation or justification for its inclusion. If you use portfolios, you may have already worked out a way to handle this. If not, feel free to duplicate or modify the suggested form that follows. This form can accompany any item on the above list that calls for a summary of results.

Portfolio Summary Sheet

Name: ______________________________

Course: ______________________ Date: ______________

1. What is the title or description of your item?

____

2. What was your objective in completing the item?

____

____

3. Was the item an individual or collaborative effort?

____

4. What skills did you use in completing the item?

____

____

5. What new skills did you learn?

____

____

6. How can you apply these skills to other courses?

____

____

7. How can you apply these skills to a job or career you seek?

____

____

Your comments

____

____

Instructor's comments

____

____

Suggestions for Each Chapter

This section describes various ways to use the chapters, the transparency masters, and the reproducible masters in this *Instructor's Resource Manual*. I have used these methods in my own student success classes, and you will undoubtedly think of additional ones. I have also included speaker suggestions and ideas for portfolios for instructors who are interested in those types of instruction. Answers to exercises begin on page 51.

Chapter 1: Motivating Yourself to Learn

Chapter 1 is very important because it introduces the concepts of learning style and locus of control, which are reinforced throughout subsequent chapters. The chapter also focuses on four keys to success that build confidence:

1. Assess your strengths and weaknesses.
2. Discover and use your learning style.
3. Develop critical thinking and study skills.
4. Adapt to others' styles.

The four keys represent areas of life and learning that students *can* control. Using these keys will help them become independent learners. The four keys are a thread that runs through all the chapters. The keys unlock chapter objectives and workplace skills. (See chart on pages 8–10 of this manual.)

You may have some diagnostic reading or study skills tests or a learning style inventory you like to use. If not, use the Skill Finder and the Awareness Checks in Chapter 1 as your diagnostic instruments. Allow class time to go over the results with your students, pointing out that all of the information in the first chapter is designed to help them assess their strengths and weaknesses and discover how they learn. You can assign the Skill Finder as homework and discuss the results in class, or you can have students complete it as an in-class assignment. If you can't be certain that all of the students will have their textbooks during the first week, use the Skill Finder master on pages

65–68 of this manual to make copies. A discussion of Skill Finder results can also serve as an introduction to the text. The Confidence Builder, "Your Kind of Intelligence," explains five kinds of intelligence and demonstrates the value of each. Since being book smart is only one way that people are intelligent, students who think of themselves as not very gifted academically may discover that they are smart in other ways. Not only will this boost their self-confidence, but it will also give them an additional strength to consider as they assess their strengths and weaknesses as students.

Transparency #1 (Four Keys to Success in College) and Transparency #2 (What Affects Your Grade?) are a good introduction to the chapter; you might want to use them as discussion-openers before students read the chapter. Introduce the concept of locus of control by using the master on page 73 (How Much Control Do You Have?) to initiate a discussion about the amount of control students believe they have over the circumstances of their lives.

A point I have always emphasized is that to be successful in college, students must accept responsibility for their own learning; they must develop or strengthen an internal locus of control and realize it is *their* effort that results in good grades. I also believe that my role is to teach learning and study strategies that will benefit the students only if they *use* them and make them their own.

Exercises

Exercise 1.1 is especially useful for helping tactile learners understand the concept of learning style. You might want to lead your students through this exercise in class as an introduction to a lecture or discussion on learning style. Exercise 1.2 helps students apply what they have learned about their bodies' reactions to the classroom environment. Exercise 1.3 introduces students to an effective method for working collaboratively. There is at least one collaborative exercise in every chapter, and each is cross-referenced to Exercise 1.3 as the model for group activity. Exercise 1.4 can be assigned as homework and discussed in class. The Critical Thinking Application asks students to write a learning profile based on their strengths, weaknesses, learning style, and locus of control.

Speaker Suggestions

Invite someone from the counseling department or learning center to speak on learning style or locus of control. See if this person can lead the class through a short, informal test or activity.

Portfolio Highlight

The learning profile essay from the Critical Thinking Application is a good portfolio entry.

Chapter 2: Setting Goals and Solving Problems

This chapter explains how to set short- and long-term goals; it also introduces COPE, a four-step problem-solving method. Students who have an external locus of control will often let things happen to them rather than try to control events. Setting goals is one way to take control. By setting goals and working to achieve them, students can develop an internal locus of control.

Many students are overwhelmed by problems they believe they are powerless to solve. Inability to solve a problem may be the result of not clearly defining the problem or not knowing what options are available to solve it. The COPE method empowers students to face their problems and find solutions. In short, COPE is another means by which students can develop an internal locus of control.

I am always interested in knowing why my students are in college. Early in the term we discuss how college fits into their future plans. Use Awareness Check #5 (What Are Your Reasons for Attending College?) and a discussion of the results as an introduction to the chapter. The master on pages 74–75 (Goals) can be used to supplement the section on goals if you feel students need additional practice.

Use Transparency #3 (The COPE Problem-Solving Method) to introduce the section on problem solving. The master on page 76 (Questions for Problem Solvers) is a good review sheet; alternatively, students can use it to accompany Exercises 2.3 and 2.4.

Exercises

Exercises 2.1 and 2.2 can be done in class or as homework assignments followed by discussion. Exercise 2.3 is designated collaborative, and Exercise 2.4 addresses learning styles. The Critical Thinking Application contains three scenarios that illustrate common problems students face. Students must apply COPE to come up with solutions.

Speaker Suggestions

Invite someone from the counseling department to speak on goals or problem solving. Take an informal survey in your class to find out what career possibilities students might be interested in knowing more about, and invite someone from the career development center to discuss them. You might also invite a professor of an academic discipline to discuss job opportunities in his or her field.

Portfolio Highlight

From Exercise 2.2 students can develop an essay about goals to add to their portfolios.

Chapter 3: Sharpening Your Classroom Skills

Chapter 3 covers five essentials of successful classroom performance:

1. Prepare for class.
2. Become an active listener.
3. Develop a personal note-taking system.
4. Learn to make effective oral presentations.
5. Participate in class and group activities.

To introduce the chapter, have students complete Awareness Check #6 and discuss their results in class. Students with an internal locus of control tend to engage in the behaviors explained in the section titled "Preparing for Class," whereas students with an external locus of control tend *not* to and often fail to understand why they make poor grades. These students need to be reminded that it is their responsibility to attend class regularly, arrive on time, read and follow the syllabus, and do all the other things mentioned in this section.

Call students' attention to Figure 3.1 (Traits of Passive and Active Listeners); to the new Confidence Builder on pages 63–64 (Interpersonal Skills for College and Career); and to Figure 3.2 (Signal Words and Phrases). Build a class activity and discussion around these three features. For example, prepare and give a short lecture on good listening, and ask students to practice active listening techniques as they listen to your lecture and take notes. Evaluate the effectiveness of their listening by having them compare their lecture notes to an outline of your lecture that you have either duplicated on a handout or copied onto a transparency. This activity, along with Awareness Check #7, can also serve as an introduction to the guidelines for note taking.

When discussing note taking, emphasize the importance of developing a method of one's own that corresponds to learning style preferences. Encourage students to try out all three methods explained in the chapter—the outline/key words system, the Cornell method, and clustering—and either adopt one of them or adapt it to suit individual preferences. Have students practice note taking by listening to and taking notes on another of your lectures, and then comparing their notes to yours. Or invite a guest speaker to lecture on a topic you think will interest students, and ask them to take notes. Again, evaluate their notes by comparing them to your own or to the notes supplied by the speaker. Transparency #4 illustrates the informal outline/key words system, which you can use to begin a discussion on note-taking methods.

How much emphasis you give to the section on oral presentations depends upon whether your students need this information now. You may want to assign the section for reading and discussion only, or you may want to follow it up with an activity you devise that requires students to plan and give a short speech using the three-step method explained in the chapter.

The section on group discussion techniques and the Critical Thinking Application, which reviews group members' roles and tasks as initially explained in Chapter 1, are especially useful if you plan for students to do much collaborative work in your class.

Exercises

Exercise 3.1 is designated collaborative. Exercises 3.2 and 3.3 can be assigned for homework or used as in-class activities. Exercise 3.4 addresses learning styles.

Speaker Suggestions

Invite someone from the psychology, speech, or communications department to speak on listening, note taking, body language, or related topics.

Portfolio Highlight

The Critical Thinking Application essay on learning style, listening, and note taking can be added to the portfolio.

Chapter 4: Making the Most of Your Time

For many students, managing time is the most difficult problem of all. This chapter is packed with information tied together by GRAB, a four-step time-management system. GRAB stands for *Goals, Responsibilities, Analysis,* and *Balance.* The first step—setting goals—recalls material in Chapter 2, suggesting that students need to set goals for studying by deciding what to study and how much time they are going to spend. The second step—determining responsibilities to others—helps students take into account their family and work obligations, and encourages them to enlist the help and cooperation of important others as they strive to reach their goals. The third step—analyzing where their time goes—helps students see how much time is available for studying so that they can make adjustments in their other activities as necessary. The fourth step—balancing work, class, study, and leisure time—suggests the need for scheduling these activities in order to avoid procrastination and to get things done.

Introduce this chapter by engaging students in a discussion about the difficulties they have finding time to do everything they want to do. Talk about priorities; ask them what *they* think is most important and what they are willing to put off in order to do something else. Find out how many of your students procrastinate and under what conditions. Encourage them to be completely honest with themselves and each other. Then use Transparency #5 (The GRAB Time-Management System) to illustrate how they can take control of their time and their lives before someone or something else does.

Ask students to complete Awareness Check #8 either in class or as homework prior to reading the chapter; then assign the chapter itself, or a portion of it, as homework. Before students complete Exercises 4.1 and 4.2, you may want to have them summarize their requirements for every course. Make copies of the master (Course Requirements) on page 79 for your students to fill in, and use Transparency #7 (Sample Course Requirements) to show them how. Ask volunteers from the class to explain how they would fill in the blank spaces on the transparency. You might even write in the spaces as students tell you what to record. Have students bring to class syllabi from other courses so they can determine, for example, how many math tests they are going to have.

Many students enjoy making out a weekly schedule and will want to continue doing so throughout the term. You might find it helpful to make copies of the weekly schedule grid and have them available for students. If this idea appeals to you, use the master (Weekly Schedule) on page 81. Similarly, if you decide to make blank calendars to give to your students at the beginning of the term, use the calendar grid master on page 80. Smaller calendar and schedule forms are available in the textbook, but if the students fill these in during class, they may want additional copies for home use.

Awareness Check #9, which introduces the section on procrastination, forms the basis for a good class discussion on this topic. Supplement this section with Transparency #6 (Reasons for Procrastination). The Awareness Check suggests that students' attitudes toward studying affect time management and procrastination. Discuss students' responses to Awareness Check #9, and talk about ways to build a more positive attitude—for example, by following the suggestions on page 90 for beating procrastination as well as the tips in the Confidence Builder on page 91.

Although many of your students do not own computers, they may have access to them through a computer lab if your college has one. If so, they might want to try out the time-saving suggestions in the Computer Confidence box on page 89. A worthwhile activity would be a group visit to the computer lab. Arrange ahead of time to have someone demonstrate some of the programs that are available for student use.

Exercises

Exercises 4.1–4.3 can be completed in class or as homework. Exercise 4.4 is designated collaborative, and Exercise 4.5 addresses learning styles. The Critical Thinking Application is an effective group activity when followed by discussion.

Speaker Suggestions

Invite someone from the psychology department to talk about time management or procrastination. Unless you plan a visit to the computer lab, invite someone to speak to your class about lab programs that are available for student use.

Portfolio Highlight

Students can add their essays from Exercise 4.5 to their portfolios.

Chapter 5: Adapting to College Life

If you are teaching an orientation course to incoming freshmen, you can use this chapter both to acquaint them with college personnel and resources that can make their lives as students easier, and to help them adjust to the diversity of campus life. The section that begins this chapter and Awareness Check #11 are designed to increase multicultural awareness and understanding. If most of the students in your class are not first-timers, you may want to give the chapter a brief overview, emphasizing the importance of knowing where to find help when it is needed.

Tactile learners learn best by doing. To involve them, and to help your auditory and visual learners make use of their tactile senses, take a campus field trip as a supplement to this chapter. All your students will benefit from a trip to the library, media center, career development center, learning lab, or computer center. Arrange to have someone give them a tour of the facility and answer their questions. If there are some hands-on activities they can do while there, so much the better. Emphasize how this campus resource and its services will assist students in their studying.

I find that even students who have attended college for a semester or two still don't know about some of the services that are available, and most of them seem to be unclear about such matters as withdrawal policy, probation, and dates on which to apply for and take statewide competency exams. Students frequently ask me when midterm is, when Christmas or Spring vacation begins and ends, where the lost and found is, and how they can get a part-time job on campus. All this information is available in the college catalog. Even when I teach a class of mostly older returning students, I give them a short quiz (such as the one in Exercise 5.4) to find out how much they know about our college's resources. I also ask everyone to get a college catalog and bring it to class. Either I take them through it, pointing out details I think they may have forgotten or overlooked, or I compile a list of dates and other information for them to look up as a small-group activity.

Students are concerned about their grades, and many of them do not understand how the GPA is derived or what the cumulative GPA entails. Occasionally, students will bring their grade reports to me for an explanation. If you want to spend some time helping your students understand GPA, use Transparencies #8 and #9 as well as the master on page 65 (How to Calculate GPA [System 2]) to supplement the chapter explanation.

Exercises

Most of the exercises in this chapter can be assigned as homework followed by discussion. Exercise 5.1 can be used as an in-class assignment to introduce the chapter. Exercise 5.2 addresses learning styles. Exercise 5.5 is designated collaborative. Exercises 5.3, 5.4, 5.6, and the Critical Thinking Application can be used individually or collaboratively.

Speaker Suggestions

If any new regulation or requirement has been enacted on your campus, invite someone from the appropriate office or department to talk to your students about it. If you have a tutorial center on campus, invite someone to explain what kind of help is available, how much it costs, what hours the center is open, and how students can arrange for a tutor. Many students want this help but don't know how to go about getting it. Ask your students which of the campus services they would like to know more about, and invite a speaker to give a short presentation.

Portfolio Highlight

Have students select an exercise from this chapter to include in their portfolios. Have them write a paragraph explaining why they chose the exercise and what they learned from it.

Chapter 6: Maintaining Your Health and Well-Being

This chapter discusses health and well-being in terms of leading a balanced life, which involves giving equal importance to the physical self, the emotional self, and the social self. Use Transparency #10 (Leading a Balanced Life) to introduce this chapter. The transparency is a map of the chapter that shows how the topics covered relate to each other. Awareness Check #12 is also a good introductory exercise that encourages students to examine their physical, emotional, and social behavior and to determine how it affects their health and well-being. If your students want additional copies of the nutrition record in Exercise 6.1 on page 123, use the Nutrition Record master on page 78 of this manual.

Health and well-being are two areas of life over which students have control—whether they realize it or not. In this chapter students will learn strategies for improving health and fitness, managing stress, controlling emotions, and improving relationships. Many issues discussed in this chapter can lead to productive discussion. If you do not feel comfortable dealing with the more complex issues of nutrition, drugs, and sex, you may want to invite guest speakers to address these topics. Find out if any person or group on your campus deals with students' problems related to drugs and alcohol, or dispenses information about sex issues, AIDS, and other sexually transmitted diseases. Make sure your students know where to go for help.

Exercises

When the time comes to discuss fitness in your class, ask your students to complete Exercise 6.2 as homework and to share their charts at the next class meeting. You might also have the students find out what courses for improving fitness are available through the physical education department and either share that information with the class or describe courses they have taken that they think other students might enjoy.

Because some students may consider it an invasion of their privacy to discuss their smoking and drinking behavior in class, you may want to make Exercise 6.3 an optional one. Encourage students to complete it on their own and to make an appointment with you to discuss their results if they want to. Conversely, if you sense that your students *can* be open about these topics, discuss them in class. The results of such an exercise, seen in comparison to someone else's results, might be just the incentive a student needs to stop smoking or to modify drinking behavior. If no one objects to sharing his or her chart, you can build a class or small-group activity around the comparison of students' charts.

Exercises 6.1 through 6.3 can be completed as homework and discussed in class. Exercise 6.4 addresses learning styles. Exercise 6.7 is designated collaborative, but Exercise 6.5 is also an effective group exercise. The Critical Thinking Application in this chapter works best as an individual exercise.

Speaker Suggestions

Invite someone from the physical education department, the counseling office, or a campus organization to speak on health, stress, or any of the other topics discussed in this chapter. Find out from your students what they would like to know more about.

Portfolio Highlight

The Critical Thinking Application is a good portfolio entry. You could also have students write an essay in which they evaluate their "EQ" based on Goleman's definition of emotional intelligence as briefly explained in the Confidence Builder on pages 134–135.

Chapter 7: Creating Your Study System

To use textbooks effectively, students need to use a study system that combines active reading and memory techniques. Two systems are described in this chapter: SQ3R, the classic system on which all the others are based; and PREP, a new system (original to *The Confident Student*) that is especially adapted to skill-development texts such as math and language books. Students can also use PREP for math-based science courses such as chemistry and physics. The point you want to emphasize in this chapter is that study systems save time and that if students use them they will understand and remember more. When students read the expanded explanations of the steps involved in a study system, or when you explain these steps, their first response may be "I don't have time to do all that." However, the steps take longer to explain than to do.

An assumption that informs this chapter is that the best study system is the one a student devises for himself or herself, through trial and error—one that is compatible with the student's learning style. If you agree with this assumption, introduce SQ3R and PREP as systems that students can try out and adopt as their own, if they work. If they don't work, the students should try to adapt these systems to their needs or create a new system that does work. The important point is that students come up with a consistent, effective way to read and study.

Two transparencies are useful both for explaining the topics covered in the chapter and for generating discussion. Transparency #11 (The PREP Study System) and Transparency #12 (The SQ3R Study System) are useful for introducing and reviewing the systems. Use Awareness Check #13 to introduce the chapter; then start a discussion on how your students study and the difficulties they have in reading and understanding their textbooks.

In the process of explaining SQ3R and PREP, have your students go through the steps with you in class, using *The Confident Student* Third Edition or some other textbook they have brought with them. Such an activity involves students both visually and tactilely. SQ3R is covered on pages 149–160; PREP is explained in the Confidence Builder on page 165.

Exercises

Exercises 7.1 and 7.3 work well as in-class activities. If you assign Exercise 7.3 in class, have students who are taking the same courses compare the lists that they generate. Exercise 7.2 is designated collaborative, and Exercise 7.4 addresses learning styles. The Critical Thinking Application is an individual exercise.

Speaker Suggestions

This chapter provides an opportunity for student speakers to discuss the success they have had using study systems or to explain how they earned an A in a course.

Portfolio Highlight

Have students write a plan for learning as explained in the Critical Thinking Application, or have them evaluate their current study methods and suggest ways to improve.

Chapter 8: Organizing Information and Making Study Guides

Throughout *The Confident Student* Third Edition I emphasize (as you probably do in class) that reading, by itself, is not enough. Nor is it productive for students to try to memorize a lot of information that they do not understand. Students best remember what they understand and can state in their own words. The purpose of this chapter is to impart some strategies that will help them organize textbook information into other formats that make it easier for them to remember. The chapter describes several kinds of maps and outlines that make useful study guides; it also invites students to try them all and to decide which ones work best for them.

You may want to emphasize that, in creating maps, students are making their own visual aids. Remind them that visualization is a powerful memory technique. Also point out that mapping will naturally appeal to visual learners, but students who react more favorably to other modes can benefit as well because mapping requires them to use another of their senses.

One way to introduce this chapter is by having students turn to the figures that illustrate each type of study guide and then asking them to describe their immediate reaction—which ones appeal to them and which ones do not. Students whose learning style is more verbal than visual will prefer the linear arrangement of outlines. Students who are more visual in their preferences may prefer a branching diagram, or the staircase or pyramid. A discussion based on their responses will increase their awareness of their learning preferences.

You might also introduce Chapter 8 with Transparency #13, which is a map of the chapter, or you could save it to use as a review.

Exercises

Exercises 8.1 and 8.2 can be assigned as homework. Exercise 8.3 is designated collaborative, and Exercise 8.5 addresses learning styles. Exercises 8.4 and 8.5 can be done as homework, but you will need to go over them in class or collect them and write comments on students' papers, suggesting ways to improve their branching and underlining. The Critical Thinking Application works well as a group exercise but can also be done individually.

Speaker Suggestions

If you have a computer lab, take your students there and have someone explain how to make study guides (as explained in the Computer Confidence box on pages 183–184), using whatever programs are available. You might also ask someone from the English department to demonstrate branching as a prewriting activity.

Portfolio Highlight

Students can make and evaluate study guides, selecting the best one or two to add to their portfolios.

Chapter 9: Controlling Your Concentration

Concentration and memory are linked. To remember what they read in a textbook or hear in a lecture, students must be able to focus and maintain their attention. This chapter deals with the causes of poor concentration and the means of eliminating them—for example, by finding or creating a good study environment and by using a study strategy. Introduce the chapter by asking your students to complete Awareness Check #15 and Figure 9.1. Discuss how the body's reactions, a component of learning style, should be taken into account when creating a home study environment or finding a study place away from home.

The causes of poor concentration discussed in this chapter are the ones students mention most. Although they may think they have no control over these distractions, the power to eliminate them is within their reach. In particular, students can develop an internal locus of control by accepting responsibility for making or finding a distraction-free study environment and by using a study strategy such as the six-step method described on pages 197–198.

Test anxiety, explained in Chapter 12, can interfere with concentration. That is why the desktop relaxation technique is included as a Confidence Builder on page 201. Demonstrate this technique to your students and have them try it out.

Exercises

Use Exercises 9.3–9.4 in class, or assign them as homework; then follow up with a class discussion. Exercise 9.1 is designated collaborative, and 9.2 addresses learning styles. The Critical Thinking Application works well as either an individual exercise or one that partners can do.

Speaker Suggestions

If there is someone at your school who has done research on concentration and memory, invite him or her to speak to your class. Ask someone in your psychology department to speak on the ways in which characteristics of the study or work environment affect concentration and productivity.

Portfolio Highlight

Students can compile data from all exercises and the Critical Thinking Application to write about their distractions and suggest a plan for eliminating them.

Chapter 10: Improving Learning and Memory

From this chapter students learn that merely reading a selection is not enough. They must use other sensory modes such as writing and reciting in order to remember the information. This point is explained in detail in Chapter 14 in the context of active reading, in Chapter 7 as a function of using a study system, and in Chapter 8 in relation to organizing information to make study guides.

Chapter 10 explains the complex process of memory in jargon-free terminology. Use Transparency #15 (The Three Stages of Memory) to introduce the chapter. Use Awareness Check #16 and Exercise 10.2 to help students understand the differences between long- and short-term memory. Exercise 10.2 can also serve as a class activity in the following way. Ask students to cover up the questions. Tell them you are going to time them (for 2 or 3 minutes) while they study the facts listed in the top half of the exercise; then quiz them to see how much they remember about each person. When the time is up, have the students close their books; then ask them the questions. A related activity is to ask students to write a list of facts about themselves similar to those in Exercise 10.2, exchange lists with someone, study the facts, and see how much they are able to remember about the person.

In discussing the eleven memory techniques on pages 220–223, and the Confidence Builder on page 226, ask students which techniques they generally use and how effective they are. Encourage students to describe other effective memory techniques that are not explained in the chapter.

Demonstrate the chair-seat relaxation technique by going through the steps with your students. Sit in a chair in front of the room so they can watch you. Explain that they can use this technique to relieve tension before they begin to study for an important exam, or they can use it in class, during an exam, to reduce test anxiety.

Exercises

Assign Exercise 10.1 as homework, as a group activity in class, or as an oral activity for review. If you want students to write out their answers, ask them not to copy directly from the text but to restate the information in their own words. (This is a memory technique discussed in the chapter.) As described above, Exercise 10.2 can be done as homework or as a class activity. Exercise 10.3 is designated collaborative, and Exercise 10.4 addresses learning styles. The Critical Thinking Application can be used as either an individual exercise or a group activity.

Speaker Suggestions

Invite someone from your psychology department or learning center to speak on the memory process and memory techniques, or to discuss left- and right-brain capacities as they relate to learning and memory. The talk will be especially interesting and helpful if the speaker is able to bring in an informal test or plan an activity in which students can participate.

Portfolio Highlight

Have students write an essay on one of the questions from Your Reflections to add to their portfolios.

Chapter 11: Preparing for Tests

Many students are interested in becoming "test wise." Test-wise students look for short cuts and tricks. But I prefer to encourage students to become "test confident." Confident test takers are well prepared; they have developed a reliable test-taking routine; they know how to apply guessing strategies when they don't know the answer; and they know how to take different kinds of tests, including standardized tests.

Use this chapter to help your students become test confident. Encourage discussion about their grades on tests, the kinds of mistakes they make, and what they can do to become better prepared. Offer to look at their returned tests from other classes, and show them how to analyze their errors.

A discussion of the results of Awareness Check #17 (How Do You Study for Tests?) would be a good introduction to the chapter. Use the master on page 82 (Extreme Modifiers and Qualifying Words) to supplement the sections on how to take true-false and multiple-choice tests. Transparency #16 (Exam Checklist) is a list of the things students should do to prepare for an exam. Use the transparency as a visual aid to a lecture on this topic, as a review of the section on how to prepare for tests, or as a reminder to students before midterm and final exams of what they should do to get ready. Use the master on page 83 (Final Exam Schedule) as a class activity. Have your students make out a schedule of all the exams they must take, and use it to plan their reviews.

The Confidence Builder titled "How to Raise Scores on Standardized Tests" will be useful to many students who must take statewide competency exams, reading tests, or other standardized tests. Many students are very nervous about taking standardized tests because such tests are timed. Encourage your students to attend exam review sessions and to take practice exams to help them prepare for these tests.

Exercises

Exercise 11.4 is designated collaborative, and Exercise 11.2 addresses learning styles. Exercises 11.1, 11.3, and 11.5 can be done as class activities or as homework. The Critical Thinking Application is a good group exercise but can also be done individually.

Speaker Suggestions

If your students must take a state-level competency test, invite someone from your campus who is involved in the administration of this exam to speak to your students and answer their questions.

You might also invite someone from the counseling department or learning lab to speak to students about courses or materials that may be available to help students prepare for the test. Ask your students which course gives them the most difficulty. Invite an instructor who teaches a section of that course to speak to your students on the kinds of information, concepts, or rules they should study to successfully prepare for tests in that course.

Portfolio Highlight

Exercise 11.2, accompanied by a paragraph explaining what students have learned and how they will apply the information, can be added to their portfolios.

Chapter 12: Reducing Test Anxiety

Some test anxiety is the result of inadequate preparation and is to be expected. This may be thought of as situational test anxiety, and students who experience it may be perfectly calm in testing situations for which they *are* prepared. For other students, test anxiety is a more complex problem evoked by deeply rooted emotional and psychological states rather than by a simple lack of preparation. Severely test-anxious students may be very well prepared as they walk into an exam, but anxiety soon overcomes them and their minds go blank. Afterward, they suddenly remember answers to questions they could not recall during the test. For anyone who has experienced it, test anxiety is indeed frustrating.

This chapter stresses adequate preparation as the answer to situational anxiety. For students who have severe anxiety, preparation is also important but may not be sufficient to relieve it. Chapter 12 explains the causes of test anxiety and how to eliminate them. It also explains relaxation procedures and visualization as two proven techniques for overcoming test anxiety.

Although test anxiety is a learned response that students can unlearn, they need to understand that this process will take some time. Once they learn the relaxation procedures and understand the other strategies explained in this chapter, they must practice them at home until they begin to see results.

Use Transparency #17 to introduce the topic of test anxiety. This transparency is a list of statements that students can read and compare to their own feelings about taking tests. The more statements they agree with, the greater their anxiety may be. Awareness Check #18 is also a good introduction to the chapter. You might have students complete the Check and discuss it in class; then assign the chapter and one or more of the exercises as homework.

The relaxation techniques described on pages 256–258 are most effective if you can demonstrate them and have students follow along with you. When students experience a relaxed state, they will be convinced that, with practice, they can learn to control their anxiety. If you do not feel confident about demonstrating these techniques, someone at your college, perhaps in the psychology department, may be willing to visit your class and take your students through the relaxation procedure. Also available are many good relaxation tapes; your library or learning center may have them for students to check out or use on the premises.

Call your students' attention to the meditation technique described in the Confidence Builder, and review the desktop and chair-seat techniques explained in Chapters 9 and 10, respectively.

Exercises

Completion of Exercise 12.1 takes some time and should be done as homework. You can have a productive class discussion by comparing responses to this exercise. Exercise 12.2 addresses learning styles, and it can be done as homework or as an in-class activity. In Exercise 12.3, which is designated collaborative, students apply the COPE problem-solving method explained in Chapter 2 to solve their test anxiety problems. (A review of the COPE method should precede this exercise.) Also use Transparency #3 (The COPE Problem-Solving Method). The Critical Thinking Application works well as a group activity but can also be done individually.

Speaker Suggestions

Invite someone from the psychology department or learning center to speak to your students about test anxiety and to demonstrate relaxation techniques.

Portfolio Highlight

The essay from the Critical Thinking Application can be added to students' portfolios.

Chapter 13: Using Critical Thinking Strategies

Chapter 13 may be difficult for students because it introduces a topic with which they may be unfamiliar: critical thinking. Critical thinking is defined as a process involving four strategies:

1. Assume
2. Predict
3. Interpret
4. Evaluate

This chapter shows students how to use the four strategies to think critically; it is also a very important chapter because critical thinking strategies are integral to skills introduced in other chapters. They are part of the study systems that students learn to apply or create in Chapter 7. In Chapter 14, two more strategies—finding the point, proof, and implications, as well as underlining and marking textbooks—are part of the critical thinking process that enhances the SQ3R and PREP study systems. Finally, critical thinking is a necessary part of deciding what information to include on a concept map or other study guide, as explained in Chapter 8.

Use Awareness Check #19 to introduce the chapter and initiate a discussion of critical thinking. Make the Confidence Builder on pages 294–295 (How to Read Graphic Materials) and Figure 13.5 the basis of a class activity in which you discuss types of graphs and how to read them; then have your students examine the graphic materials in the textbooks they have with them. Before assigning Exercise 13.6, you might find it helpful to devote a class session to the section titled "Look for a Pattern of Thinking." Use Transparency #18 (Signal Words) to emphasize the point that students can look for signal words to help them identify the writer's thought pattern. Figure 13.7 (Standards of Evaluation: Questions to Ask) can be the basis of a class activity after the section titled "Evaluate What You Learn" has been read and discussed. You might also bring in additional examples of persuasive writing and have your students apply the standards.

Exercises

All of the exercises, including the Critical Thinking Application, in this chapter work well as in-class, homework, or small-group assignments. Exercise 13.1 addresses learning styles, and Exercise 13.3 is designated collaborative.

Speaker Suggestions

Invite someone from the psychology department to speak on cognitive processing. Many students are interested in learning more about how the mind works and how thinking can be improved. If someone you know has done research on this topic, invite him or her to talk to your students.

Portfolio Highlight

Have students select their best exercise to add to their portfolios along with a paragraph explaining why they chose it and what they learned.

Chapter 14: Becoming an Active Reader

This chapter introduces two additional reading strategies that students can use to enhance the reading step of SQ3R, PREP, or any other study system. The first strategy—*find the point, proof,* and *implications*—will help students read actively to find the writer's thesis and support, and interpret both of these elements. This three-part strategy is an integrative strategy rather than a breaking down of the reading process into separate skills. The second strategy—*underline* and *mark* textbooks—will help students decide what to underline and mark based on the subject areas of their textbooks. To introduce the chapter, begin with Awareness Check #20 to help your students understand the difference between active and passive reading. Emphasize the importance of reading actively—that is, making an effort to do more than just read. Students need to underline, highlight, or mark text; make notes; and monitor their comprehension as they read. Exercise 14.1 asks students to evaluate themselves as active or passive readers and is a good follow-up to the Awareness Check and the section on active reading.

To help students make the transition from simulated reading experiences in *The Confident Student* Third Edition to actual reading experiences, have them work individually or in small groups to find paragraphs in their own textbooks in which topic sentences are supported by facts, reasons, or examples. Or have them look for facts, reasons, and examples in an article you bring to class.

To introduce the section on underlining and marking textbooks, and before your students complete Exercise 14.5, try this group activity. Have students who are taking the same course compare their textbook underlining and marking. Conduct a discussion on what they underlined and why. As a review, use Transparencies #20 and #21 (Underlining and Marking Textbooks), which summarize the kinds of information to underline and mark in various subject-area texts.

Many students are concerned about their reading speed, believing that their reading problems stem from being unable to read fast enough. But for most students, comprehension—not speed—is the problem. Still, students tend to be interested in "speed reading," and the Confidence Builder (Calculate Your Reading Rate) will appeal to them. If you think your students would benefit from a discussion and activity on reading rate, discuss the Confidence Builder with them. Choose a reading assignment—either something you bring into class or a passage from *The Confident Student*—and take them through the steps of rate calculation. Try to convince them that increasing their comprehension is the way to improve reading rate: It is better to be an efficient reader—one who applies appropriate strategies to reading tasks—than a fast reader.

Exercises

All the exercises, including the Critical Thinking Application, can either be assigned as homework or completed in class as group activities. Exercise 14.5 is especially effective for generating a discussion about attitudes toward homosexuals and for helping students see the implications of what they read. Moreover, they can compare their underlining and marking of the excerpt among themselves. To make a visual aid of the excerpt, underline and mark a copy of it to show students what you think is important. Or project the excerpt on a screen, using an opaque projector. Exercise 14.1 addresses learning styles, and Exercise 14.3 is designated collaborative.

Speaker Suggestions

A point made in this chapter is that, when taking a variety of courses, students must remember different kinds of information. What they decide is important to underline depends, to some extent, on the kind of material they are reading. Invite a professor from an academic discipline such as biology, math, or sociology to speak to students about what they should underline in their textbooks and what kinds of information the students are expected to remember.

Portfolio Highlight

Have students evaluate their own underlining and marking systems and explain, in writing, their strengths, weaknesses, and suggestions/plans for improvement.

Chapter 15: Becoming a Confident Writer

Students can apply the four critical thinking strategies—assume, predict, interpret, evaluate—to become more actively involved in the writing process and to produce logical, clearly written essays either for a composition course or as responses to essay exam questions.

This chapter explains the connection between reading and writing; it also introduces the five-paragraph plan for writing essays. It emphasizes use of the plan in a strategic way, as a guide to writing a fully developed essay that follows a simple, logical pattern of organization. Because the plan specifies what should go into an essay, it works well not only for beginning writers but also for those students who have trouble deciding what to write. As writers mature, they will want to experiment with more innovative and sophisticated ways of constructing an essay. But the purpose of this chapter is to build students' confidence *now* in their ability to write and to provide them with a few tools and strategies that will dispel some of the anxiety or dread they may have about writing.

Awareness Check #21 asks students to describe their writing histories. Use their responses to help you decide how best to present this chapter to meet their needs. The Computer Confidence box on page 334 and the Confidence Builder on pages 342–343 explain how a word processor and other helpful tools can make the writing process easier and more fun. The essay titled "Give Mine to the Birds" is useful as a class activity to illustrate the five-paragraph plan. The essay demonstrates to students that it is possible to be extremely creative within what some may consider a rigid format. You may want to read the essay aloud so that students can enjoy the humor and choice of words. And you can use Transparency #22 (How to Begin an Essay) as the basis for a discussion on how to write a good introductory paragraph.

Exercises

Assign Exercise 15.1 as homework, or have students do it in class and use it as the basis of a class discussion. If some students' answers do not form the outline of a potential essay as the exercise directions suggest they should, construct the outline on the board with the help of student volunteers whose answers do form an outline. With help from the whole class, revise the outline until all are satisfied that it is a good one. This exercise will take students through the process of thinking about what they write.

Exercise 15.2 is a self-assessment activity that helps students examine the writing process in terms of learning style preferences. Use this exercise as the basis of a class discussion and review of the characteristics of a good study/writing environment, as explained in Chapter 9. In Exercise 15.3, students construct a thesis statement and topic sentences similar to the examples in the chapter. You can either assign the exercise for homework or have students do it in class while you monitor their writing and offer help. Exercise 15.4 is designated collaborative, and Exercise 15.5 works well as a small-group activity following reading and discussion of "Give Mine to the Birds." The Critical Thinking Application asks students to apply their newly acquired skills to the process of writing an essay.

Speaker Suggestions

In choosing a speaker, focus on making writing enjoyable. Invite someone who teaches a creative writing course to talk about the course and read samples of student writing. Also ask someone on your campus who has had a book or articles published to talk about what he or she does to make writing easier or to come up with ideas.

Portfolio Highlight

Have students add the Critical Thinking Application essay or Your Reflections to their portfolios.

Chapter 16: Gaining Math Confidence

It is estimated that about 50 percent of all students fail college algebra at least once. Math anxiety (test anxiety related to math situations in particular) plagues many students. Two things we can do to help students succeed in math are (1) encourage them to develop a more positive attitude toward math and (2) teach them strategies for coping with math courses. This chapter explains how to reduce math anxiety, how to read and study math textbooks, how to analyze errors and learn from mistakes, when to ask for help, when is the best time to take a math course, how to choose an instructor, and how to solve word problems using WHISK—a method first explained in *The Confident Student.*

Use the photographs of people engaged in math-related careers and the Confidence Builder as interest-building devices to promote a more positive attitude toward math. Discussion of answers to Awareness Check #22 will help students determine why they might not be doing well in math and what they can do to improve.

In discussing the Computer Confidence box (Use the Computer for Math Applications), stress the importance of practice in developing skills. Also suggest to your students that they visit the learning center or math lab to find out what practice materials are available.

Introduce WHISK by referring to Transparency #23 (The WHISK Problem-Solving Method). Encourage students to use this system to solve math word problems that are assigned for homework.

Exercises

Exercises 16.1 and 16.2 work best as homework assignments, but allow some time to go over them in class. Exercise 16.3 is designated collaborative, and Exercise 16.4 addresses learning styles. The Critical Thinking Application can be used as either an individual exercise or a small-group activity.

Speaker Suggestions

Invite someone from the math department to speak to your class about what help is available (in the form of math labs, tutors, etc.) to students who are having trouble. You might also invite someone to talk in a positive way about math, to discuss career opportunities for math majors, or to describe new math-related discoveries.

Portfolio Highlight

Students' Critical Thinking Application reports can be added to their portfolios.

Chapter 17: Developing Science Strategies

Because courses in science (particularly the natural sciences) are difficult, students tend to procrastinate instead of doing assignments on time and studying for tests in an orderly fashion.

The first task to accomplish in covering this chapter is to help students increase their motivation for studying science. Motivation is often a problem for students taking science courses if they believe the course is unrelated to their major or to anything they plan to do in life. As I always tell my classes, however, the typical college student switches majors two or more times before graduating and changes jobs or careers at least as often during a lifetime. How, then, can one make a judgment now that a course is not relevant?

Awareness Check #23 prompts students to determine how motivated they are, and the section following explains the divisions of science and summarizes each discipline's concerns. Starting with a discussion of the Awareness Check results and the divisions of science, lead into an analysis of the differences between the natural and social sciences and the strategies that students should use for success in each.

From this chapter students learn how to prepare for science classes, including procedures for getting more out of the labs that often accompany courses in the natural sciences. As you discuss this topic, review the instructions in Chapter 14 for determining what to underline or mark in science textbooks. Point out to your students that the PREP study system is especially useful when reading chemistry or physics textbooks. Use Transparency #24 to introduce the scientific method prior to assigning Exercise 17.1.

Exercises

Exercises 17.1 and 17.2 can be assigned either as homework or for in-class activities. Exercise 17.2 addresses learning styles, and Exercise 17.3 is designated collaborative. The Critical Thinking Application probably works best as an individual exercise since it asks students to practice the writing-to-learn technique.

Speaker Suggestions

Invite someone from the career development center to speak on career possibilities in the sciences. Or invite colleagues to speak about particularly interesting aspects of their work. For example, ask a psychology professor to talk about the use of subliminals in advertising, or ask a biology professor to give a brief slide presentation on protective coloration. Both of these topics are very popular with students.

Portfolio Highlight

The Critical Thinking Application exercise can be added to the portfolios along with an explanation of its usefulness.

Preparing Your Syllabus

As Chapter 1 explains, students who have an external locus of control will expect you to keep them informed of class procedures instead of informing themselves. Insisting that they use the syllabus is one way to help your students develop responsibility for their progress in the class. As discussed in Chapter 4, the syllabi for their other courses are important references that students can use in preparing a study schedule. A worthwhile activity is to have your students bring their syllabi to class and to summarize their course requirements on a course requirement form. A reproducible master of this form is on page 79 of this guide. You can lead students through the activity by using Transparency #7, which demonstrates how to fill out the form.

A common complaint of many students is that some instructors either do not provide a syllabus or are late in getting it out. Don't allow these students to believe that they are off the hook under these circumstances. It is still *their* responsibility to find out when tests will be given and when assignments are due. Encourage them to visit instructors in their offices whenever they are in doubt as to what they are supposed to be doing in class. This will serve two purposes: Students will demonstrate independence by seeking out answers to their questions, and they will interact with their instructors (something they are often reluctant to do).

In compiling a syllabus for *The Confident Student* Third Edition, keep two points in mind: You do not have to cover everything in the book, and you do not have to maintain the order suggested in the Table of Contents. The order I chose in writing this book reflects the way I structured my course. I began by assessing students' skills, acquainting them with the concept of learning style, and orienting them to college life. But you may prefer to introduce study systems much earlier or to skip one or more chapters. *The Confident Student* Third Edition is a comprehensive text covering all the traditional study skills as well as orientation material and specific strategies for successful completion of math and science courses. Because every college and class is a little different, you will want to choose among the topics covered to tailor your course to your students' needs.

The first sample syllabus below is intended for a sixteen-week course. It is designed for maximum flexibility and does not specify which exercises students must do. This syllabus is a general guideline that allows you to decide how much to cover in a class period and to assign exercises accordingly. Each week, one or two chapters are covered, and the focus is on a major topic dealt with in one of the chapters. This syllabus is suitable for an orientation course because it schedules guest speakers from around the college to give a presentation about every other week. To adapt the syllabus to a traditional study skills class, you might want to skip Chapters 4 and 6 and focus more on the reading and study chapters. You might also want to invite fewer speakers or none at all.

Sixteen-Week Course

Week 1 Topic: Keys to Success in College
Reading Assignment:
Chapter 1: Motivating Yourself to Learn

Week 2 Topic: Taking Control
Reading Assignment:
Chapter 2: Setting Goals and Solving Problems
Chapter 4: Making the Most of Your Time
Guest Speaker and Topic:
Professor Choice, Reading Department, "Beating Procrastination"

Week 3 Topic: Listening and Taking Notes
Reading Assignment:
Chapter 3: Sharpening Your Classroom Skills

Week 4 Topic: Getting Involved
Reading Assignment:
Chapter 5: Adapting to College Life
Guest Speaker and Topic:
Kate Singleton, Student Services, "What College Has to Offer You"

Week 5 Topic: How to Study, Part 1
Reading Assignment:
Chapter 7: Creating Your Study System

Week 6 Topic: How to Study, Part 2
Reading Assignment:
Chapter 8: Organizing Information and Making Study Guides

Week 7 Topic: Learning and Memory, Part 1
Reading Assignment:
Chapter 10: Improving Your Concentration

Week 8 Topic: Learning and Memory, Part 2
Reading Assignment:
Chapter 11: Improving Learning and Memory

Guest Speaker and Topic:
Professor Johnson, Psychology Department, "Why Do We Forget?"

Week 9 Topic: Preparing for Exams
Reading Assignment:
Chapter 11: Preparing for Tests

Week 10 Topic: Managing Stress
Reading Assignment:
Chapter 6: Maintaining Your Health and Well-Being
Chapter 12: Reducing Test Anxiety
Guest Speaker and Topic:
Dr. Holbrook, Learning Specialist, "How to Manage Test Anxiety"

Week 11 Topic: Critical Thinking
Reading Assignment:
Chapter 13: Using Critical Thinking Strategies

Week 12 Topic: Active Reading, a Critical Skill
Reading Assignment:
Chapter 14: Becoming an Active Reader

Week 13 Topic: Confident Writing, a Critical Skill
Reading Assignment:
Chapter 15: Becoming a Confident Writer

Week 14 Topic: Reducing Math Anxiety
Reading Assignment:
Chapter 16: Gaining Math Confidence

Week 15 Topic: Succeeding in Science Courses
Reading Assignment:
Chapter 17: Developing Science Strategies
Guest Speaker and Topic:
Professor Glover, Science Department, "Careers in the Sciences"

Week 16 Topics: Review
Self-Assessment (Skill Finder)
Course Evaluation
Final Exam

The following sample syllabus is intended for a ten-week skills-focused course and is more structured than the first one. This syllabus specifies which exercises students will do in class and as homework. It covers all seventeen chapters in order, whereas the first one organized them according to each week's topic. To adapt this syllabus to the specific needs of your class, you can leave out some of the chapters and extend the time you spend on the ones you do select. To add flexibility, write "Subject to Change" at the top of the list of assignments and tell students that depending on how the class progresses you may need to add, delete, or change the exercises listed. If you have time for a guest lecture, you can try one of the suggestions in the previous syllabus.

Ten-Week Course

Week 1 Topics: Self-Assessment, Introduction to Course
Chapter 1: Motivating Yourself to Learn
Exercises 1.1, 1.4, and CTA (Critical Thinking Application) in class
Exercises 1.2 and 1.3 as homework

Week 2 Topic: Goals and Classroom Skills
Chapter 2: Setting Goals and Solving Problems
Exercises 2.3, 2.4, and CTA in class
Exercises 2.1 and 2.2 as homework
Chapter 3: Sharpening Your Classroom Skills
Exercises 3.1 and 3.3 in class
Exercise 3.2 as homework

Week 3 Topic: Time Management
Chapter 4: Making the Most of Your Time
Exercise 4.4 and CTA in class
Exercises 4.1 through 4.3 as homework

Week 4 Topic: Health and Resources
Chapter 5: Adapting to College Life
Exercises 5.1, 5.5, and CTA in class
Exercises 5.2–5.4 and 5.6 as homework
Chapter 6: Maintaining Your Health and Well-Being
Exercises 6.4 and 6.7 in class
Exercises 6.1–6.3, 6.8 and CTA as homework

Week 5 Topic: Study Systems and Study Guides
Chapter 7: Creating Your Study System
Exercise 7.2 and CTA in class
Exercises 7.1, 7.3, and 7.4 as homework
Chapter 8: Organizing Information and Making Study Guides
Exercise 8.3 and CTA in class
Exercises 8.1, 8.2, 8.4, and 8.5 as homework

Week 6 Topic: Concentration and Memory
Chapter 9: Controlling Your Concentration
Exercise 9.2 and CTA in class

	Exercises 9.1–9.4 as homework Chapter 10: Improving Learning and Memory Exercise 10.3 and CTA in class Exercises 10.1, 10.2, and 10.4 as homework
Week 7	Topic: Tests and Test Anxiety Chapter 11: Preparing for Tests Exercises 11.3, 11.5, and CTA in class Exercises 11.1, 11.2, and 11.4 as homework Chapter 12: Reducing Test Anxiety Exercise 12.2 and CTA in class Exercises 12.1 and 12.3 as homework
Week 8	Topic: Thinking Critically Chapter 13: Using Critical Thinking Strategies Exercises 13.1, 13.3, and CTA in class Exercises 13.2 and 13.4–13.6 as homework
Week 9	Topic: Reading and Writing with Confidence Chapter 14: Becoming an Active Reader Exercises 14.1–14.3 in class Exercise 14.4 and CTA as homework Chapter 15: Becoming a Confident Writer Exercises 15.1 and 15.5 in class Exercises 15.2 and 15.3 as homework
Week 10	Topic: Strategies for Special Courses Chapter 16: Gaining Math Confidence Exercise 16.3 and CTA in class Exercises 16.1 and 16.2 as homework Chapter 17: Developing Science Strategies Exercises 17.1–17.3 in class

Both of these syllabi are assignment schedules only. Your complete syllabus may include test dates and any other general information for which you want your students to be responsible.

You may have selected *The Confident Student* Third Edition to use in an individualized lab course, in which students work on their own according to a program you have prepared for them, then confer with you individually or in small groups about their progress. In that case, your syllabus may be a general information sheet rather than a list of assignments. You can either allow students to choose which chapters they cover or assign them the chapters you think they need, based on the Skill Finder and whatever other assessment measures you use. You can also coordinate lab materials such as cassette tapes, videocassettes, and workbooks with chapters in *The Confident Student* Third Edition. For example, you could develop a unit on time management that would include reading Chapter 4 and doing the exercises, listening to a cassette tape on how to manage time, and reading a handout you have written on procrastination.

In a lab course, students generally work at a slower pace because they don't have the benefit of lectures and class activities to supplement their reading of the text. Therefore, I would suggest that you don't require your students to complete the whole book. Instead, set a minimum number of chapters for them to finish by the end of the term. They can practice making schedules and managing time if you have them select the chapters they will complete, determine the order in which they will complete them, and make out a semester or quarter schedule. Give them a syllabus that spells out your lab requirements, lists course objectives, and briefly summarizes each chapter. You may also want to write handouts that explain how to complete each chapter. For my own lab courses, I color-coded all handouts so that as I walked around the lab I could see at a glance what each student was working on. Following is a sample syllabus for the first four chapters of *The Confident Student* Third Edition as well as a handout for Chapter 5.

Sample Lab Syllabus

Chapter 1: Motivating Yourself to Learn

This chapter shows you how to use four keys to success that will unlock the confident student within you. You will learn how to assess your strengths and weaknesses, discover and use your learning style, sharpen your thinking and study skills, and adapt to others' styles.

Chapter 2: Setting Goals and Solving Problems

In this chapter you will learn how to set goals that allow you to make a flexible plan for achieving success in college and throughout life. You will also learn how to use the COPE method for solving problems that might otherwise cause delays in reaching your goals.

Chapter 3: Sharpening Your Classroom Skills

Chapter 3 explains how to become a better listener and note taker, and it provides additional strategies for being successful in class.

Chapter 4: Making the Most of Your Time

This chapter provides tips for beating procrastination and shows you how to manage your time by making three types of schedules.

Sample Handout for Chapter 5

Chapter 5
Adapting to College Life

Materials: *The Confident Student* Third Edition, college catalog

What You Will Do:

Read Chapter 5, pp. 92–111; complete assignments listed below.

Course Objectives to Be Met:

You will learn what resources are available and how to use them.
You will broaden your understanding and appreciation for the diversity of campus culture.

Purpose:

The purpose of this chapter is to help you become a more confident and successful college student by showing you how to make use of the resources that are available to assist you in reaching your goals and by helping you adapt to your diverse campus.

Assignments:

		Date completed	Check or grade
1.	Read pp. 93–95; do Exercise 5.1.	____________	____________
2.	Read pp. 96–99; do Exercises 5.2 and 5.3.	____________	____________
3.	Have a conference with your instructor.	____________	____________
4.	Read pp. 101–104; do Exercise 5.4.	____________	____________
5.	Read pp. 104–105; do Exercise 5.6.	____________	____________
6.	Have a conference with your instructor.	____________	____________
7.	Read the rest of the chapter and complete Your Reflections.	____________	____________
8.	Visit the Career Development Center; write a short summary of the services available.	____________	____________
9.	Have a conference with your instructor.	____________	____________

Answer Key

Chapter 1: Motivating Yourself to Learn

Exercise 1.1 This is a tactile exercise that does not call for a written response.
Exercise 1.2 Answers vary.
Exercise 1.3 Answers vary.
Exercise 1.4 Answers vary.
Exercise 1.5 Answers vary.
Critical Thinking Application Answers vary.

Chapter 2: Setting Goals and Solving Problems

Exercise 2.1 Answers vary.
Exercise 2.2 Answers vary.
Exercise 2.3 Answers vary.
Exercise 2.4 Answers vary.
Critical Thinking Application Answers vary.

Chapter 3: Sharpening Your Classroom Skills

Exercise 3.1

1. The signal words *for example* indicate that an example follows. The example is this: "A good listener is not reading the newspaper or watching television while listening to a friend talk about a problem."
2. The word *characteristics* indicates categories or divisions.
3. *First, second,* and *most important* indicate sequence.
4. The most important characteristic is a genuine interest in the speaker and what he or she is saying.

5. The writer's concluding idea is that listening, a lifelong skill, improves with practice and hard work.

Exercise 3.2

1. One blank circle should be filled in with "Informal Outline/Key Words System." The small circles students attach to this circle should contain phrases that resemble the following.
   A) 2½" column on right (key words); 6" column on left (notes)
   B) Take notes/leave margin blank
   C) review/rewrite key words
2. Another blank circle should be filled in with "Cornell Method." The small circles students attach to this circle should contain phrases that resemble the following.
   A) 2½" margin on left (questions), 6" column on right (notes), 2" space at bottom (summary)
   B) Record: notes in wide column
   C) Question: write in left margin
   D) Recite: key word/question, then fact/idea
   E) Reflect: apply to real life
   F) Review: to begin daily study
   G) Recapitulate: summarize at bottom
3. Another blank circle should be filled in with "Clustering." The small circles students attach to this circle should contain phrases that resemble the following.
   A) First major point in circle—middle of page
   B) Arrows and circles for examples
   C) New major point starting new cluster

Exercise 3.3 Answers vary.

Exercise 3.4 Answers vary but should resemble the following.

1. Bob's negative behaviors are as follows: taking naps in class; rarely commenting or asking questions; and, when he doesn't understand something, forgetting about it.
2. Bob could change his behavior by sitting near the front of the room so he won't fall asleep, by participating in class, and by asking the instructor to explain anything he doesn't understand.
3. Sam's behavior is negative because he does not pay attention and monopolizes class time. He can improve by practicing good listening techniques.
4. Carmen plays an active role by participating in class.
5. Carmen is a good discussion leader because she takes notes, gives everyone a chance to contribute, focuses, and summarizes the discussion.
6. Carmen has an internal locus of control because she takes responsibility for her own learning.

Critical Thinking Application Answers vary.

Chapter 4: Making the Most of Your Time

Exercise 4.1 Calendars will vary but should resemble the textbook example in Figure 4.2.
Exercise 4.2 Schedules will vary but should resemble the example in Figure 4.5.
Exercise 4.3 Answers vary.
Exercise 4.4 Answers vary.
Critical Thinking Application Answers vary.

Chapter 5: Adapting to College Life

Exercise 5.1 Answers can be verified by college catalog or college official such as the registrar.
Exercise 5.2 Answers vary.
Exercise 5.3 Answers can be verified by college catalog or directory.
Exercise 5.4 Answers can be verified by college catalog or directory.
Exercise 5.5 Answers can be verified by college catalog.
Exercise 5.6 Answers can be verified by college catalog or directory.
Critical Thinking Application Answers vary.

Chapter 6: Maintaining Your Health and Well-Being

Exercise 6.1 Chart responses vary.
Exercise 6.2 Chart responses vary.
Exercise 6.3 Chart responses vary.
Exercise 6.4 Answers vary but should resemble the following.

1. I didn't find out whether we had to do the exercises.
2. Replace "They told me" with "I thought."
3. I feel that you are not paying attention to me.
4. I feel nervous when I am around you.
5. I never come to see you when you are in your office.

Exercise 6.5 Answers vary.
Exercise 6.6 Answers vary but should resemble the following.

1. Jack could have listened more actively when Becky said, "I hate the hospital."
2. Jack could have said, "I'm sorry you had a bad day. What could we do together that would make you feel better?"
3. Becky could have been more supportive of Jack by offering to help him with his paper.
4. Stopping for ice cream on the way home is one way Jack and Becky could have had fun.

Exercise 6.7 Answers vary.
Exercise 6.8 Answers vary.
Critical Thinking Application Answers vary.

Chapter 7: Creating Your Study System

Exercise 7.1 Answers vary.
Exercise 7.2 Answers vary.
Exercise 7.3 Answers vary.
Exercise 7.4 Answers vary.
Critical Thinking Application Answers vary.

Chapter 8: Organizing Information and Making Study Guides

Exercise 8.1 Maps vary.
Exercise 8.2

Title: Two Types of Social Groups				
	Size	**Relationships**	**Function**	**Examples**
Primary Groups	Small	Intimate, personal	Act as a buffer	Families Teams
Secondary Groups	Small or large	Usually impersonal	Help you reach a goal or get work done	Military Businesses Colleges

Exercise 8.3 Process diagrams vary.
Exercise 8.4 Branching diagrams vary.
Exercise 8.5 Study guides vary.

Chapter 9: Controlling Your Concentration

Exercise 9.1
1. The first distraction Roberta encountered was the conversation between two students about their dates.
2. Roberta should have moved to a quieter part of the library.
3. Other distractions were the temperature, the lighting, and being without a pen.
4. Roberta couldn't complete her reading assignment because she used up her study time dealing with distractions.
5. Roberta can avoid distractions either by studying at home or by finding a quiet place on campus. She should sit where the temperature is comfortable and the light is adequate. She should also bring a sweater and any supplies she needs.

Exercise 9.2 Answers vary.
Exercise 9.3 Chart responses vary.
Exercise 9.4 Answers vary.
Critical Thinking Application Answers vary.

Chapter 10: Improved Learning and Memory

Exercise 10.1
1. a. It is normal to forget.
   b. You can remember more and retain it longer than you think.
   c. There are memory aids that may work for you.
   d. The best memory techniques are those you create.
2. a. reception
   b. retention
   c. recollection
3. a. 1. Become attentive and observant.
      2. Use as many of your senses as possible when receiving information.
      3. Ask questions to aid understanding.
      4. Survey before reading.
   b. 1. Underline and make notes when reading.
      2. Review frequently.
      3. Recite when you review.
      4. Do all homework.
      5. Motivate yourself to remember.
   c. 1. Organize information to prepare for tests.
      2. Use your sensory preference.
      3. Make and take practice tests.
      4. Review old tests and learn from mistakes.

Exercise 10.2
1. Claudia
2. 34
3. Claudia
4. Matt
5. Claudia
6. Bill

Exercise 10.3 Answers vary.
Exercise 10.4 Answers vary.
Critical Thinking Application Answers vary.

Chapter 11: Preparing for Tests

Exercise 11.1 Schedules vary.
Exercise 11.2 Answers vary.
Exercise 11.3

1. T	6. T
2. T	7. F (always)
3. F (all)	8. T
4. F (only)	9. T
5. F (invariably)	10. F

Exercise 11.4
1. d
2. a or b for purposes of the exercise, although a is the correct answer

3. d
4. c
5. b or c for purposes of the exercise, although b is the correct answer
6. b or c for purposes of the exercise, although c is the correct answer
7. d
8. b
9. b or c for purposes of the exercise, although b is the correct answer
10. a

Exercise 11.5 Essays vary.

Critical Thinking Application Answers vary.

Chapter 12: Reducing Test Anxiety

Exercise 12.1 Answers vary.

Exercise 12.2

1. She sits alone in her room, breathes deeply, and relaxes to begin the visualization technique.
2. The garden is a peaceful place that does not promote stressful feelings.
3. Other scenes she might imagine are a forest and a seashore.
4. She visualizes the peaceful garden first because the classroom scene is likely to provoke stress unless she is already relaxed. (A person can't be relaxed and anxious at the same time.)
5. Her final image is the instructor's comment on her paper.
6. It is important because it represents a reward for overcoming her anxiety.
7. Because Claudia can control her visualization, she can also control her test anxiety.
8. Answers vary.
9. Answers vary.

Exercise 12.3 Answers vary.

Critical Thinking Application Answers vary.

Chapter 13: Using Critical Thinking Strategies

Exercise 13.1 Answers vary.

Exercise 13.2

1. Answers vary.
2. Answers vary.
3. The passage is about attitudes towards homosexuals.
4. a *Time* magazine poll
5. People with negative attitudes towards homosexuals tend to discriminate against homosexuals.
6. Answers vary.
7. In paragraph 1, sentence 2, *sought* means tried. In paragraph 2, sentence 1, *harbors* means holds or encourages a thought or feeling.

Exercise 13.3
1. No. You do not know whether Susan will apply herself during the rest of the term.
2. No. There is not sufficient information to determine that the instructor is too demanding.
3. Yes. The syllabus may have provided the date.
4. Yes. Some instructors do allow make-up work, so the inference is valid.
5. Yes. Susan's problems resulted from her being absent the first day, so you can make the inference.

Exercise 13.4
1. a
2. c
3. d
4. a

Exercise 13.5
1. D (mostly comparison)
2. G (The steps may follow a sequence, but the emphasis is on how to.)
3. E
4. A
5. D (comparison and contrast)
6. B
7. E
8. F
9. C
10. G (more process than sequence because the emphasis is on how to)

Exercise 13.6 Answers vary.

Exercise 13.7 Answers vary.

Critical Thinking Application Answers can be verified by information given in the ad.

Chapter 14: Becoming an Active Reader

Exercise 14.1 Answers vary.

Exercise 14.2
1. The point is stated in the first sentence.
2. The point is stated in the second sentence.
3. The point is stated in the second sentence.

Exercise 14.3
1. reasons
2. examples
3. facts

Exercise 14.4 Proof:

a. Make note cards.
b. Keep a word list as you read.

Implications:

a. Yes. The methods have worked for many students, so they may work for you.
b. No. The paragraph explains two methods for developing vocabulary, but it does not state that these are the only methods.

Exercise 14.5
1. The point is stated in the first paragraph, sentence 2.
2. The six guidelines are stated as subheadings.
3. You can save $5 to $10 per week.
4. To avoid impulse buying, use restraint.
5. Prices at convenience stores are higher than at supermarkets.
6. When you pay cash, you avoid finance charges and impulse buying.
7. Disposable income is money left over after paying for necessities and bills.
8. Answers vary.
9. Answers vary.
10. Answers vary.

Critical Thinking Application Students should agree that the highlighting and annotation in example A are more useful.

Chapter 15: Becoming a Confident Writer

Exercise 15.1 Answers vary.

Exercise 15.2 Answers vary.

Exercise 15.3 Sentences vary but should resemble the ones in the chapter examples on page 338.

Exercise 15.4 Students' essays will vary but should resemble "Give Mine to the Birds" in structure.

Exercise 15.5
1. The writer's purpose is to entertain. You can tell by the humorous tone of the essay.
2. The last sentence of the first paragraph is the thesis statement.
3. The writer introduces the thesis by discussing a few advantages of worms as a food source.
4. The first sentence of the second paragraph is the topic sentence.
5. The first sentence of the third paragraph is the topic sentence.
6. The first sentence of the fourth paragraph is the topic sentence.
7. Signal words that make the transition are *the most important reason.*
8. The writer uses cause and effect as her thought pattern. She lists the reasons for which she would not eat worms and explains what would result if she did.
9. The word *because* tells you the pattern is cause and effect.
10. b
11. Answers vary.
12. Answers vary.

Critical Thinking Application Students' essays will vary.

Chapter 16: Gaining Math Confidence

Exercise 16.1 Answers vary.

Exercise 16.2
1. Multiply 5,000 (number of brochures needed) by $.20 (cost of one brochure). The answer is $1,000.
2. Four hundred and seventy-seven total miles divided by 50 miles per day is 9.5. It will take Sally and Emi 9.5 days to reach their Montreal destination. All other information is irrelevant to solving the problem.
3. Ten miles multiplied by $1 per volunteer is $10 per volunteer pledge. Three hundred volunteers multiplied by $10 each in pledges is $3,000 altogether. All other information is irrelevant to solving the problem.

Exercise 16.3
1. The careless error is adding the denominators instead of changing both fractions to sixths and then adding them. Correct answer: $4/6 = 2/3$.
2. The careless error is leaving off the sign. Correct answer: $-3x$.
3. The careless error is failing to reduce the fraction. Correct answer: $2x - 2$.
4. The careless error is subtracting denominators. Correct answer: $2/4 = 1/2$.

Exercise 16.4 Answers vary.

Critical Thinking Application Answers vary.

Chapter 17: Developing Science Strategies

Exercise 17.1 Answers vary.

Exercise 17.2 Answers vary.

Exercise 17.3 Answers vary but should reflect the meanings of the textbook definitions.

Critical Thinking Application Answers vary.

Reproducible Masters

This section contains fifteen masters for duplication. You can use these masters in a variety of ways to supplement textbook assignments and exercises in *The Confident Student* Third Edition.

Skill Finder (pages 65–68)

The Skill Finder is a guide to the study skills covered in *The Confident Student* Third Edition. Students can take it on their own to help them assess their skills, or you may assign them to do it as a class activity. If you are teaching a lab course and plan to individualize instruction, the Skill Finder is an excellent way to determine which skills each student needs to work on so that you can plan activities accordingly. Use the master to make copies of the Skill Finder, and present it to students as a post-test at the end of the term or anytime you want to assess progress.

Student Information Sheet (pages 69–70)

One way to get to know your students at the beginning of a term is to have them fill out an information sheet. This one gives you a record of each student's address, phone number, major or career goal, schedule, study problems, and reason for taking the course. If a student misses several class meetings and you do not hear from him or her, you will have a phone number to call. If you want to relate class activities to the courses most of your students are taking, you can look at their information sheets to find out what those courses are. If you schedule periodic personal conferences with students, a review of their information sheets before they come in for a visit will give you something to talk about. For example, you might ask, "How are you doing in your psychology class?" or "I remember that you said at the beginning of the term that you had trouble deciding what to mark in a textbook; do you feel you are making some progress toward solving that problem?"

You can also use the information sheets to help your students evaluate their progress at the end of a semester or quarter. Return the sheets to the students and ask them to read what they wrote down as their study problems and their reasons for taking the course. Then ask them whether they have solved their problems and to what extent the course has been helpful.

Midterm Awareness Check (page 71)

To succeed in college, students must develop an internal locus of control; they must see the connection between the amount of effort they put into their work and the grades they receive. The statements on this Awareness Check call attention to the *students'* behavior and what *they* are doing that is causing them to be either successful or unsuccessful. The purpose of the Awareness Check is to get students to examine their behavior and determine what positive steps they can take to improve their grades, rather than blaming others or making excuses for poor performance.

Students can use the Midterm Awareness Check to assess their progress either in your class or in another one. Their responses to the statements can become the basis for discussion and review of locus of control. For many students, midterm is a turning point. Those who have procrastinated and have done less than their best to this point may still make dramatic improvements by the end of the term.

Speaker Evaluation Form (page 72)

If you plan to have guest speakers talk to your class on topics related to motivation, studying, and learning, or if you plan to have students give oral reports, you may want to use this form. Having students evaluate speakers accomplishes three objectives. First, knowing you expect them to rate the speaker helps them focus attention on the presentation. Second, they become aware of the differences among the speakers' styles and of the qualities that make an effective presentation. This awareness can lead to discussions of what to listen for in a lecture. Finally, as you read your students' evaluations, you will find out whether your students responded positively to the speaker and the topic. This outcome may help you decide whether to invite a speaker again or to schedule more presentations on the same topics.

The following masters are related to specific chapters. For suggestions on how to use them, see "Suggestions for Each Chapter," beginning on page 21.

How Much Control Do You Have? (page 73)	Chapter 1
Goals (pages 74–75)	Chapter 2
Questions for Problem Solvers (page 76)	Chapter 2

How to Calculate GPA (System 2) (page 77)	Chapter 5
Nutrition Record (page 78)	Chapter 6
Course Requirements (page 79)	Chapter 4
Semester or Quarter Calendar Grid (page 80)	Chapter 4
Weekly Schedule (page 81)	Chapter 4
Extreme Modifiers and Qualifying Words (page 82)	Chapter 11
Final Exam Schedule (page 83)	Chapter 11

Skill Finder

This questionnaire will help you determine which learning and study skills you need to develop or improve. Read each statement. If the statement applies to you, check *yes.* If the statement does not apply to you, check *no.* See the end of the questionnaire for suggestions about how to interpret your results.

Motivating Yourself

	Yes	No
1. I know what my basic skills, strengths, and weaknesses are.	☐	☐
2. I know what my learning style is, and I use it.	☐	☐
3. I am able to adapt to others' learning and teaching styles.	☐	☐
4. I do not need anyone to motivate me.	☐	☐

Setting Goals and Using Resources

	Yes	No
5. I usually have a goal I am trying to reach.	☐	☐
6. I have no trouble making decisions about which courses I should take.	☐	☐
7. I know what courses are required at my college.	☐	☐
8. I have a college catalog, and I check it often to keep up with important dates and deadlines.	☐	☐

	Yes	No

Listening and Note Taking

	Yes	No
9. When I am listening to a lecture, I do not become distracted.	☐	☐
10. I know the words to listen for in a lecture that will tell me what is important.	☐	☐
11. I usually take notes during class.	☐	☐
12. When I take notes, I am able to keep up with the lecturer.	☐	☐

Time Management

	Yes	No
13. I know how to manage my time.	☐	☐
14. I almost always arrive on time for classes.	☐	☐
15. Only sickness or emergency prevents me from coming to class.	☐	☐
16. When I have a lot of studying to do, I have no trouble getting started.	☐	☐

Memory and Concentration

	Yes	No
17. I can usually remember what I've studied well enough to get good grades on tests.	☐	☐
18. I associate new material to be learned with what I already know.	☐	☐
19. I have a certain place where I do most of my studying.	☐	☐
20. I am not easily distracted when there is something I need to study.	☐	☐
21. I do not hesitate to ask questions in class.	☐	☐

Using Textbooks Effectively

	Yes	No
22. Before I read a chapter, I look it over briefly to see what it is going to be about.	☐	☐
23. I am able to follow the writer's ideas in a textbook chapter.	☐	☐
24. I am able to maintain my interest in what I read.	☐	☐
25. I read chapter headings and turn them into questions I can answer as I read.	☐	☐
26. I always take a few minutes to examine the tables and other visual aids in chapters I read.	☐	☐

	Yes	No
27. I use mapping techniques to organize information.	☐	☐
28. I almost always underline or highlight my textbooks.	☐	☐
29. I make notes from my textbooks to help me study.	☐	☐
30. I review my notes before and after class.	☐	☐
31. I keep a list of special terms and definitions of words I need to learn for my courses.	☐	☐

Preparing for and Taking Tests

32. I usually know what to study for tests.	☐	☐
33. I am almost always prepared for tests.	☐	☐
34. Taking a test does not make me nervous, if I am prepared.	☐	☐
35. If I don't know the answer to a multiple choice question, I try to guess.	☐	☐
36. I do not usually run out of time when I am taking a test.	☐	☐
37. It doesn't bother me if someone finishes a test before I do.	☐	☐

Critical Thinking

38. Before I attempt to learn anything new, I examine my assumptions about it.	☐	☐
39. When I am listening to a lecture, I can usually predict what the lecturer will say next.	☐	☐
40. I am good at interpreting, or making sense of, what I learn.	☐	☐
41. I am able to evaluate information for its usefulness.	☐	☐

Reading and Writing

42. I know what it means to be an "active" reader.	☐	☐
43. I am able to understand and remember most of what I read.	☐	☐
44. I know how to plan and write an essay.	☐	☐
45. I can usually find and correct my errors.	☐	☐

	Yes	No

Studying Math and Science

	Yes	No
46. I do all math problems at the end of the chapter, whether they are assigned or not.	☐	☐
47. In a math course, I usually know why I make the errors I make on tests.	☐	☐
48. I believe I am capable of doing well in math.	☐	☐
49. I know how to prepare for my science class.	☐	☐
50. Remembering information from science textbooks is easy for me.	☐	☐

Count the number of "no " answers for each section of the questionnaire. If you have more than one per section, you may want to improve or develop the study skill or skills identified by the section heading. Use the list below to locate the part in *The Confident Student* Third Edition that covers these skills; see the Table of Contents or Index if you want to locate a specific topic or discussion. Your instructor may ask you to answer these questions again when you have finished reading this book so that you can see what skills you have mastered.

Questions	*Corresponding Textbook Part*
Questions 1–16	Part One
Questions 17–37	Part Two
Questions 38–50	Part Three
Questions 40–50	Supplementary Chapters A and B in this manual

Student Information Sheet

Name ______________________________ Student I.D.# ______________

Address ____

____

Phone ____

Is this your first semester or quarter in college? ______________________

What is your major/career goal? ______________________________

____

____

Copy your schedule here:

Course	Section	Day(s)	Time	Instructor

What study problems do you have? ____

____

____

____

Please explain your reasons for taking this course.

____

____

____

____

Midterm Awareness Check

As of now you are making a grade of _________ in this course, and you are therefore making (satisfactory, unsatisfactory) progress. If your progress is satisfactory, determine what you are doing that is bringing you success so that you can continue the good work. If your work is unsatisfactory, you need to figure out what you are doing to cause this problem so that you can solve it and start being more successful. Complete the Awareness Check by answering *yes* or *no* to the following statements.

	Yes	No
1. I am rarely, or never, absent or late.	☐	☐
2. I give the class my full attention most of the time.	☐	☐
3. I have completed all assigned work.	☐	☐
4. I almost always hand in work on time.	☐	☐
5. My behavior does not prevent me from listening to lectures or from participating fully in class activities.	☐	☐
6. I have no problem understanding the textbook.	☐	☐
7. I do not procrastinate when it comes to studying.	☐	☐
8. I am generally well prepared for tests.	☐	☐
9. I have applied the study strategies I am learning in this class.	☐	☐
10. I have asked for help when I needed it.	☐	☐

If you are not satisfied with your progress, what action will you take to improve it? Write your plan below.

____

____

____

____

Speaker Evaluation Form

Speaker's name: ______________________________

Topic: ______________________________

Date: ______________________________

Rate the speaker by responding *yes* or *no* to the following statements.

	Yes	No
1. The speaker seemed organized and well prepared.	☐	☐
2. The speaker's topic related to material presented in the course.	☐	☐
3. The topic and the speaker's presentation were interesting and informative.	☐	☐
4. The speaker effectively used visual aids, the chalkboard, or other means to illustrate points.	☐	☐
5. The speaker left enough time for questions and answers.	☐	☐
6. I would like to hear another presentation on the same topic.	☐	☐

Additional comments: ______________________________

____

____

How Much Control Do You Have?

Put a check mark in the column that describes the amount of control you believe you have over these circumstances.

	Very Much	Some	Very Little	None
Grades	☐	☐	☐	☐
Health	☐	☐	☐	☐
Relationships	☐	☐	☐	☐
Money matters	☐	☐	☐	☐
Job requirements	☐	☐	☐	☐
Motivation	☐	☐	☐	☐

Goals

Planning ahead helps you get things done. In setting goals, you are programming yourself for success. You are taking a positive step toward controlling the outcome of your life. Think about what you would like to accomplish, and then answer these questions.

1. By the end of this week I plan to:

   (Academic goal) ______________________________

   ____

   (Personal goal) ______________________________

   ____

   (Work-related goal) ______________________________

   ____

2. By the end of this term I plan to:

   (Academic goal) ______________________________

   ____

   (Personal goal) ______________________________

   ____

   (Work-related goal) ______________________________

   ____

3. Two years from now I plan to:

   (Academic goal) ____

   ____

   (Personal goal) ____

   ____

   (Work-related goal) ____

   ____

4. Five years from now I plan to:

   (Academic goal) ____

   ____

   (Personal goal) ____

   ____

   (Work-related goal) ____

   ____

Questions for Problem Solvers

1. Challenge
   - What *is* my problem?
   - What *causes* my problem?
   - What *result* do I want?
2. Option
   - What are my options?
   - What can I do to eliminate my problem's causes?
3. Plan
   - What plan can I make to act on my options?
   - How long will it take?
4. Evaluation
   - Is my plan working?
   - Have I given my plan enough time to work?
   - Do I still have the problem?
   - Is the situation improving?
   - Should I revise my plan or make a new one?
   - What else can I do?

How to Calculate GPA (System 2)

Formula for calculating grade point average: $GPA = \frac{\text{Grade points}}{\text{Credits}}$

Example:

Course Grades	**GPA Values**		**Credits**	**Grade Points**
A–	3.70	×	4	14.80
C+	2.30	×	3	6.90
D	1.00	×	3	3.00
			10	24.70

$$GPA = \frac{24.70}{10} = 2.47$$

Nutrition Record

Day	Breakfast	Lunch	Dinner	Snacks
Sunday				
Monday				
Tuesday				
Wednesday				
Thursday				
Friday				
Saturday				

Course Requirements

Course	Instructor	Tests %	Projects / Other %	Attendance	Late Work	Makeup Policy

Semester or Quarter Calendar Grid

Sunday	Monday	Tuesday	Wednesday	Thursday	Friday	Saturday

Weekly Schedule

	Sunday	Monday	Tuesday	Wednesday	Thursday	Friday	Saturday
6:00–7:00							
7:00–8:00							
8:00–9:00							
9:00–10:00							
10:00–11:00							
11:00–12:00							
12:00–1:00							
1:00–2:00							
2:00–3:00							
3:00–4:00							
4:00–5:00							
5:00–6:00							
6:00–7:00							
7:00–8:00							
8:00–9:00							
9:00–10:00							
10:00–11:00							
11:00–12:00							
12:00–1:00							

Extreme Modifiers and Qualifying Words

Extreme Modifiers	*Qualifying Words*	
all	some	frequently
every	many	more, less
always	often	good, bad
invariably	usually	better, worse
only	most	best, worst
none	few	sometimes
never	seldom	
absolutely	almost	

Extreme modifiers allow for no exceptions. If you see one of these words in a statement on a true-false test, the statement is probably false unless it is a definition or a mathematic or scientific principle. Why? Because there are very few things in this world that are absolutely true all of the time.

Qualifying words do allow for exceptions. If you see one of these words in a statement on a true-false test, the statement may be true.

When taking a true-false test, read the question very carefully. If you do not know the answer and have to guess, look for extreme modifiers or qualifying words that may help you select the right answer.

The next time you take a true-false test in one of your classes, examine the questions you missed. Try to identify extreme modifiers or qualifying words that could have helped you choose the right answer if you had been looking for them.

Final Exam Schedule

Course	Date	Time	Room	Materials

Bibliography

Anderson, Barry F., *The Complete Thinker* (Englewood Cliffs, N.J.: Prentice-Hall, 1980).

Anselmo, Tom, Leonard Bernstein, and Carol Schoen, *Thinking and Writing in College* (Boston: Little, Brown, 1986).

Bailey, Covert, *Fit or Fat* (Boston: 1978).

Behrens, Laurence, and Leonard J. Rosen, *Writing and Reading Across the Curriculum* (Boston: Little, Brown, 1985).

Benson, Herbert, *The Relaxation Response* (New York: William and Co., Inc., 1975).

Betz, N. L., "Prevalence, Distribution, and Correlates of Math Anxiety in College Students," *Journal of Counseling Psychology*, 25 (1978), pp. 441–448.

Canter, R., J. Forward, J. Mohling, and J. Parent, "Interactive Effects of Teaching Strategy and Personal Locus of Control on Student Performance and Satisfaction," *Journal of Educational Psychology*, 69 (1975), pp. 764–769.

Cremat, Laird S., *Improving Your Memory* (New York: McGraw-Hill, 1976).

Edwards, J. E., and L. K. Walters, "Relationships of Locus of Control to Academic Ability, Academic Performance, and Performance-related Attributions," *Educational and Psychological Measurement*, 14 (1981), pp. 529–531.

Farnan, N., and P. Kelly, "Keeping Track: Creating Assessment Portfolios in Reading and Writing," *Journal of Reading, Writing, and Learning Disabilities*, 7 (1991).

Frase, L. T., and B. J. Schwartz, "Effect of Question Production and Answering on Prose Recall," *Journal of Educational Psychology*, 67 (1975), pp. 628–635.

Fry, Edward B., *Graphical Comprehension* (Providence, R.I.: Jamestown, 1981).

Gardner, Howard, *Frames of Mind* (New York: Basic Books, 1983) and *The Unschooled Mind* (New York: Basic Books, 1991).

Hayes, John R., *The Complete Problem-solver* (Philadelphia, Pa.: Franklin Institute Press, 1981).

Head, L. O., and J. D. Lindsey, "Anxiety and the University Student: A Brief Review of the Professional Literature," *College Student Journal*, 2 (1983), pp. 176–181.

Highbee, Kenneth L., *Your Memory: How It Works and How to Improve It* (Englewood Cliffs, N.J.: Prentice-Hall, 1977).

Kraft, R. G., "Group Inquiry Turns Passive Students into Active," *College Teaching*, 33 (1985), pp. 149–154.

Lakein, Alan, *How to Get Control of Your Time and Your Life* (New York: Signet Books, 1973).

Lorayne, Harry, and Jerry Lucas, *The Memory Book* (New York: Ballantine, 1979).

Lusk, L. S., "Interaction of Test Anxiety and Locus of Control on Academic Performance," *Psychological Reports*, 53 (1983), pp. 639–644.

Mainon, Elaine, et al., *Writing in the Arts and Sciences* (Cambridge, Mass.: Winthrop, 1981).

Murphy, S. T., *On Being LD* (New York: Teachers College Press, 1992).

Nadeau, K. G., *Survival Guide for College Students with ADD or LD* (New York: Magination Press, 1994).

Nowicki, S., and M. Duke, "A Locus of Control Scale for Non-college as Well as College Adults," *Journal of Personality Assessment,* 38 (1974), pp. 136–137.

Nowicki, S., and R. Strickland, "A Locus of Control Scale for Children," *Journal of Counseling and Clinical Psychology,* 40 (1973), pp. 148–154.

Osterhouse, P. A., "Desensitization and Study Skills Training as Treatment for Two Types of Test-anxious Students," *Journal of Counseling Psychology,* 19 (1972), pp. 301–307.

Palladino, C., *Developing Self-Esteem for Students* (Menlo Park, Calif.: Crisp Publications, Inc., 1994).

Pauk, Walter, *How to Study in College,* 4th ed. (Boston: Houghton Mifflin, 1989).

Pauk, Walter, and J. Millman, *How to Take Tests* (New York: McGraw-Hill, 1967).

Rotter, J. B., J. E. Chance, and E. J. Phares, *Social Learning Theory of Personality* (Hillsdale, N.J.: Holt, Rinehart and Winston, Inc., 1972).

Rubenstein, Moshe, and Kenneth Pfeiffer, *Concepts of Problem Solving* (Englewood Cliffs, N.J.: Prentice-Hall, 1980).

Ruggiero, Vincent R., *The Art of Thinking: A Guide to Critical and Creative Thought* (New York: Harper and Row, 1984).

Spielberger, C. D., H. P. Gonzalez, and T. Fletcher, "Test Anxiety Reduction, Learning Strategies, and Academic Performance," *Cognitive and Affective Learning Strategies,* edited by H. F. O'Neil, Jr., and C. D. Spielberger (New York: Academic Press, 1977).

Spires, Hiller A., and P. Diane Stone, "The Directed Note-taking Activity: A Self-questioning Approach," *Journal of Reading,* 43 (1989), pp. 36–39.

Student Learning Styles, National Association of Secondary School Principals, Reston, Va., 1979.

Teaching the SCANS Competencies, The Secretary's Commission on Achieving Necessary Skills (U.S. Department of Labor, 1993).

Tobias, Sheila, *Overcoming Test Anxiety* (New York: Norton, 1978).

Valeri-Gold, M., Olson, J., and Deming, M. P., "Portfolios: Collaborative Authentic Assessment Opportunities for College Developmental Learners," *Journal of Reading,* 35 (1992), pp. 298–305.

Wandersee, James H., "Ways Students Read Texts," *Journal of Research in Science Teaching,* 25 (1988), pp. 69–84.

Weaver, III, Richard L., *Understanding Interpersonal Communication* (Boston: Scott, Foresman and Co., 1987).

What Work Requires of Schools, a SCANS Report for America 2000, The Secretary's Commission on Achieving Necessary Skills (U.S. Department of Labor, 1991).

Zimbardo, Philip G., *Psychology of Life,* 12th ed. (Boston: Scott, Foresman and Co., 1988).

Transparency Masters

Four Keys to Success in College

1. **Assess your strengths and weaknesses.**

2. **Discover and use your learning style.**

3. **Develop critical thinking and study skills.**

4. **Adapt to your instructors' teaching styles.**

WHAT AFFECTS YOUR GRADE IN A COURSE?

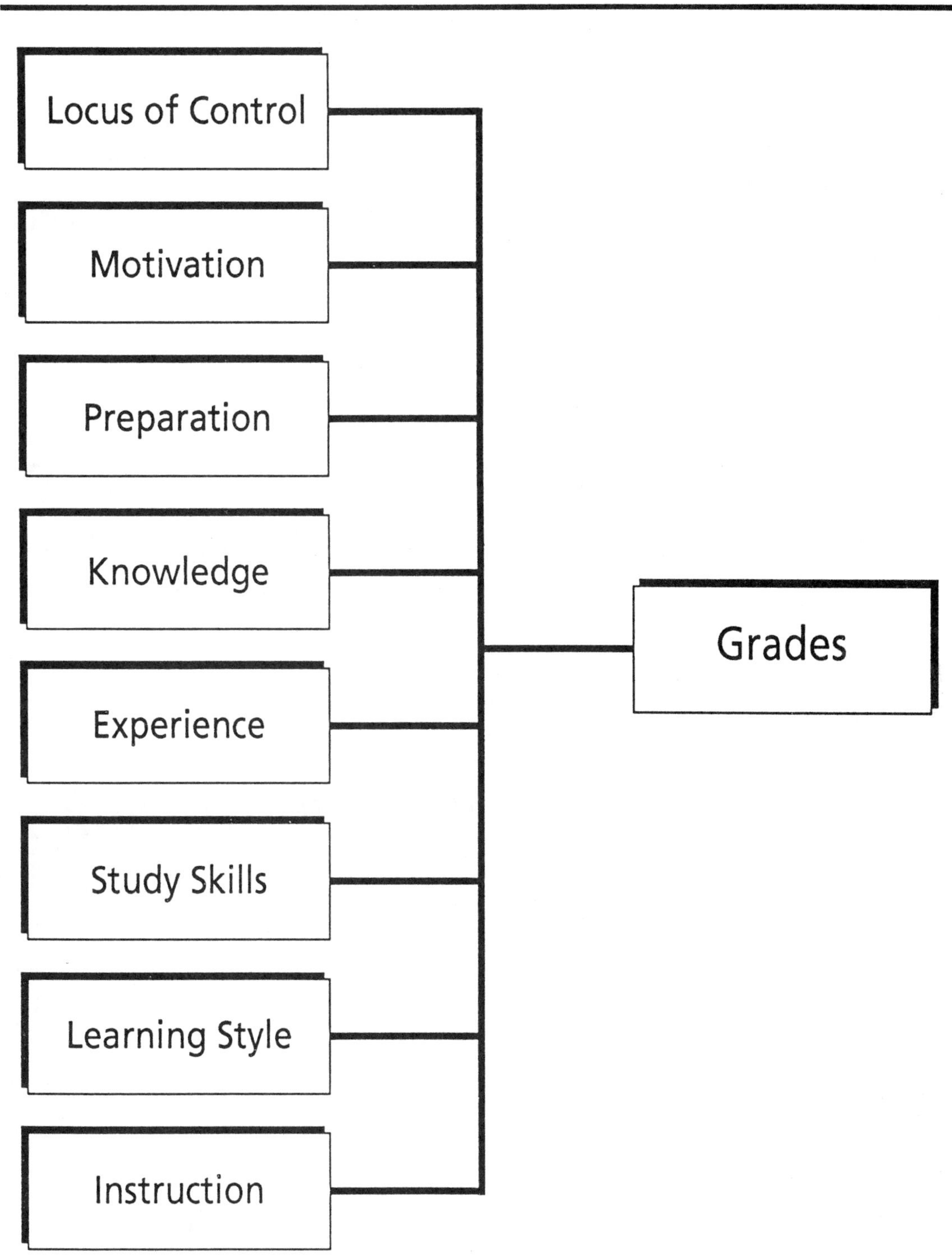

TO SOLVE YOUR PROBLEMS

Challenge: Your problem, its causes, and the results you want

Option: Possible solution among alternatives that are available

Plan: Plan of action for solving your problem

Evaluation: Assessment of plan's success or need for revision

INFORMAL OUTLINE/KEY WORDS SYSTEM OF NOTE TAKING

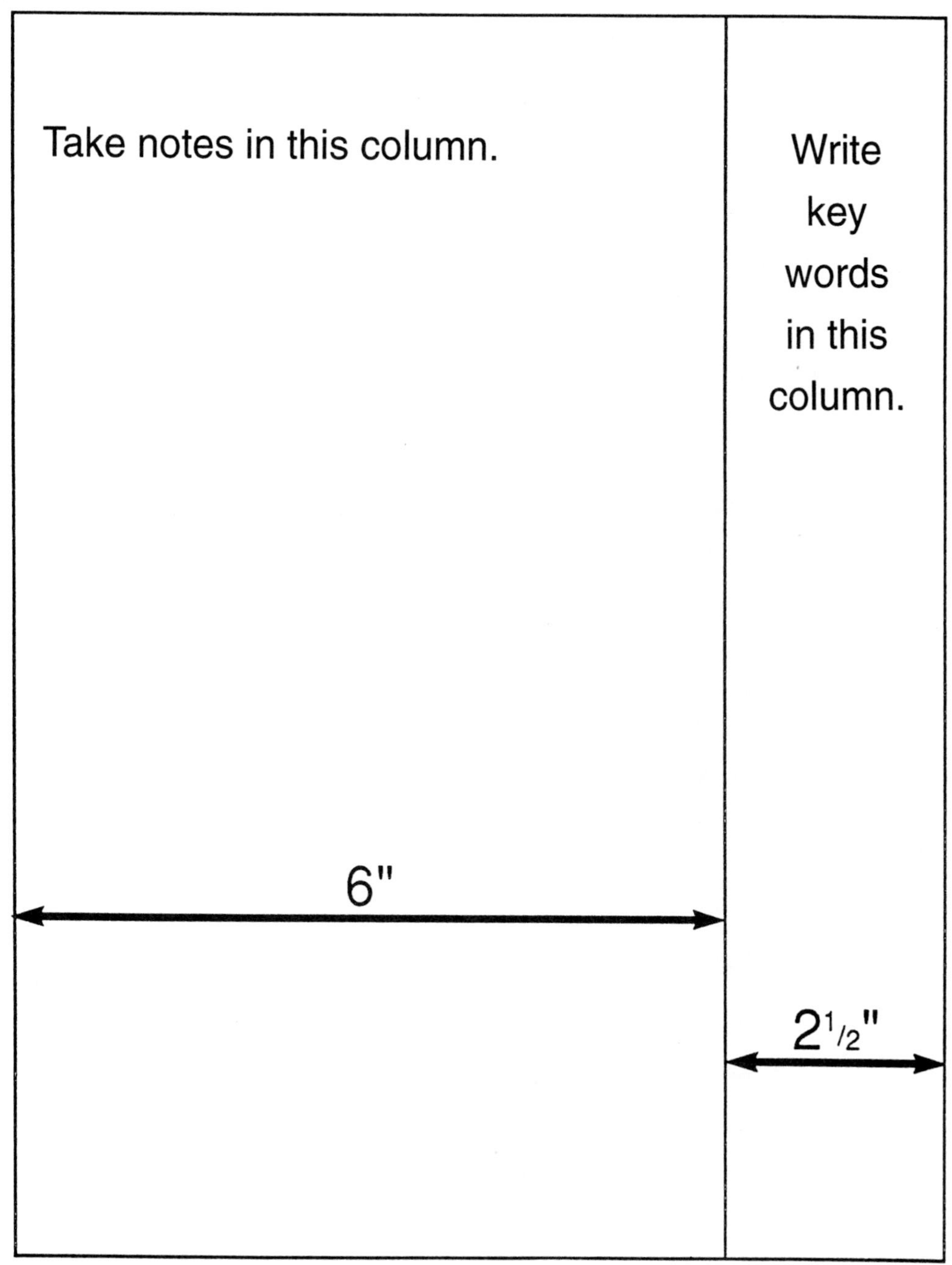

HOW TO *GRAB* TIME TO GET THINGS DONE

GOALS

RESPONSIBILITIES

ANALYSIS

BALANCE

WHY DO YOU PROCRASTINATE?

- **Your tasks seem difficult or time consuming.**
- **You have trouble getting started.**
- **You lack motivation to do the work.**
- **You are afraid of failing.**

SAMPLE SUMMARY OF COURSE REQUIREMENTS

Course	Instructor	Tests (Percentages)	Projects/ Other (Percentages)	Attendance	Late Work	Makeup Policy
English	Ames	Midterm 25% Final 25%	Weekly essays 50%	Withdrawal after three absences	Grade on work lowered one letter for each day late	Midterm: before next class meeting; no others

HOW TO CALCULATE YOUR GPA

GPA Values at System 1 Colleges

A = 4.00
B = 3.00
C = 2.00
D = 1.00
F = 0.00
W = 0.00

GPA Values at System 2 Colleges

A = 4.00	A- = 3.70	
B+ = 3.30	B = 3.00	B- = 2.70
C+ = 2.30	C = 2.00	C- = 1.70
D+ = 1.30	D = 1.00	D- = .70
F = 0.00		
W = 0.00		

HOW TO CALCULATE YOUR GPA

Formula for calculating grade-point average:

$$GPA = \frac{\text{Grade Points}}{\text{Credits}}$$

Example:

Course Grades	GPA Values		Credits	Grade Points
A-	3.70	x	4	14.80
C+	2.30	x	3	6.90
D	1.00	x	3	3.00
			10	24.70

$$GPA = \frac{24.70}{10} = 2.47$$

LEADING A BALANCED LIFE

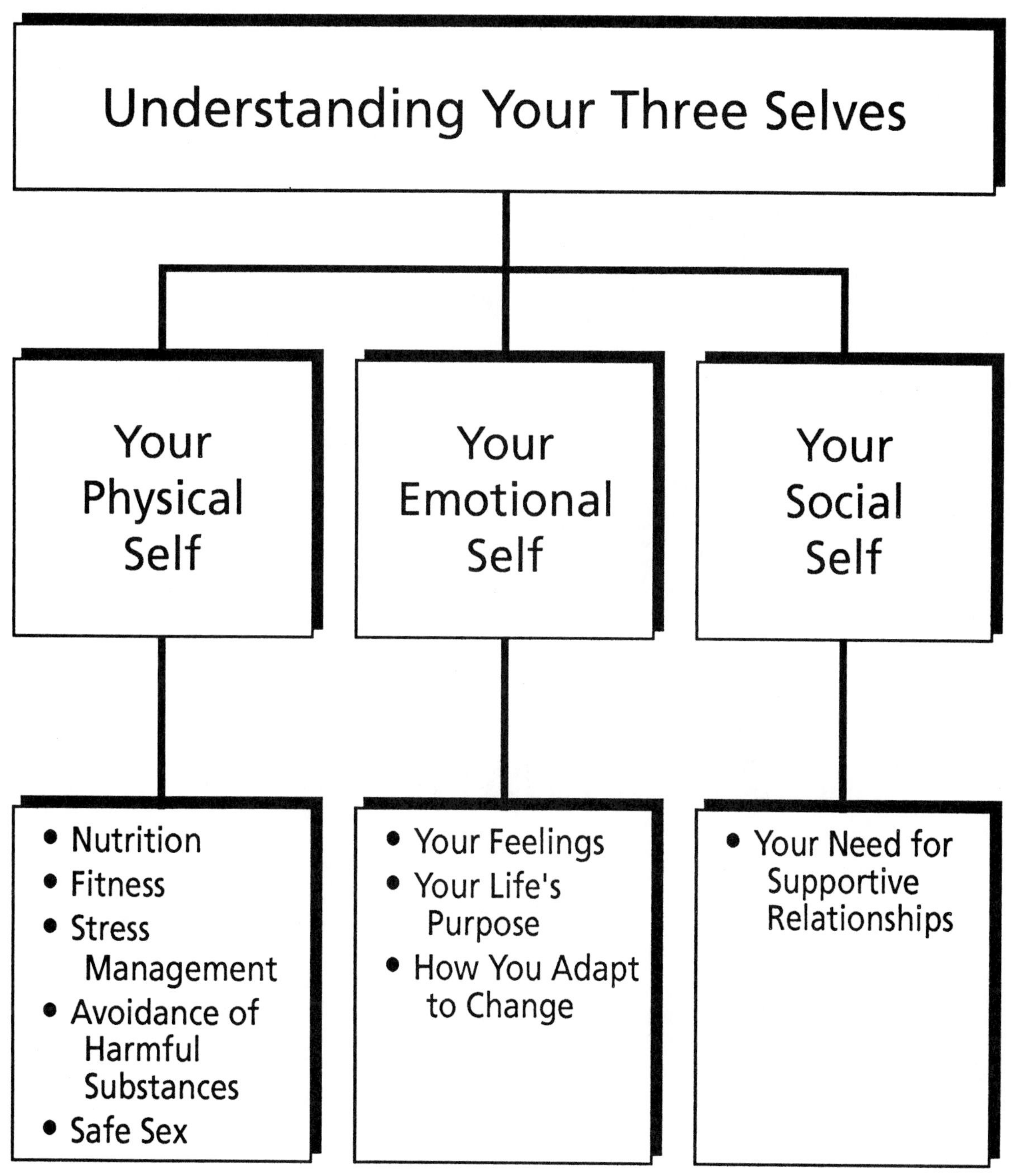

THE *PREP* STUDY SYSTEM

P REVIEW

R EAD

E VALUATE

P RACTICE

THE *SQ3R* STUDY SYSTEM

SURVEY

QUESTION

READING

3 ***R***ECITE

REVIEW

SIX WAYS TO ORGANIZE TEXTBOOK INFORMATION

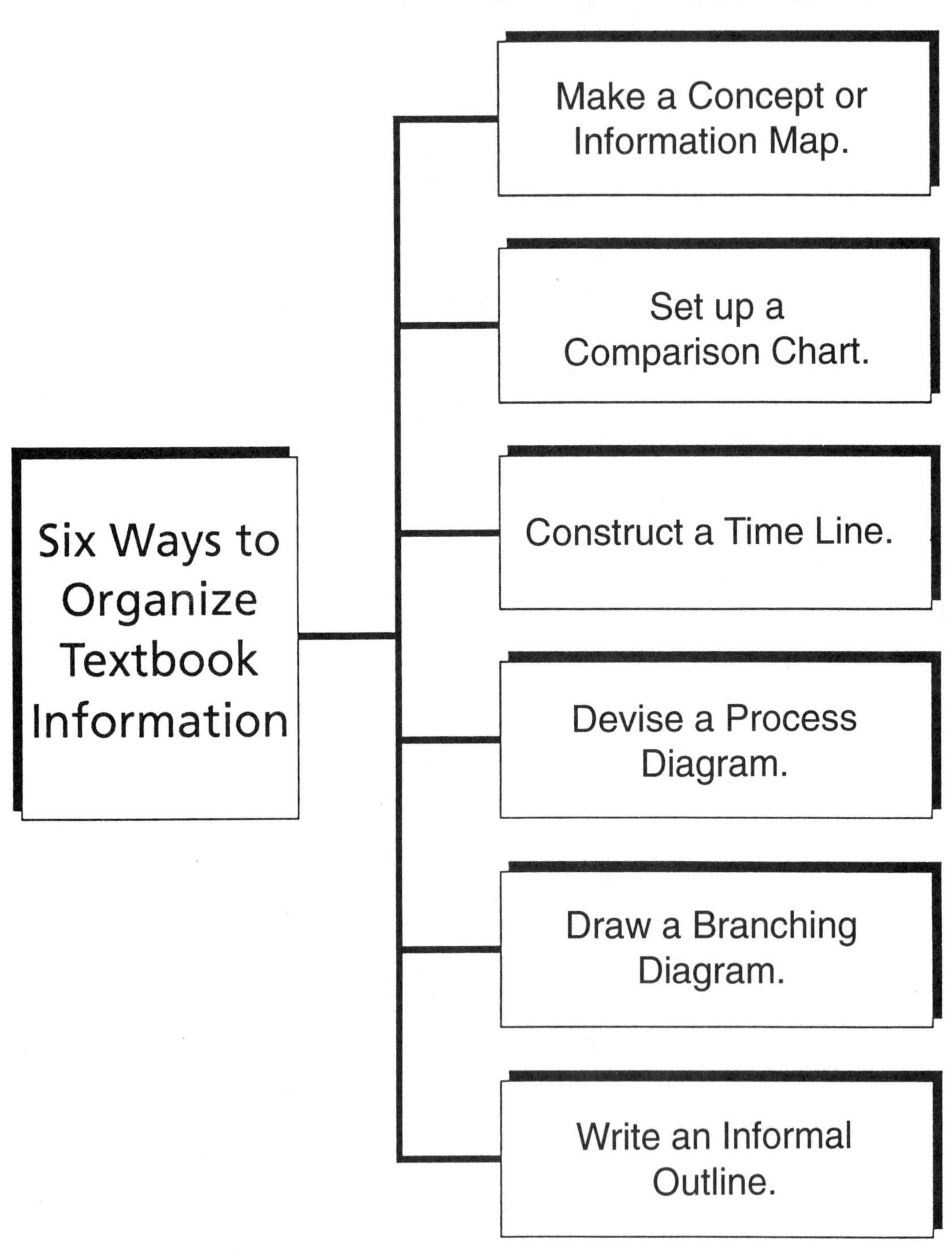

CHARACTERISTICS OF A GOOD STUDY ENVIRONMENT

- **Distraction-free location**
- **Optimal lighting**
- **Comfortable temperature**
- **Suitable furniture**
- **Available supplies**
- **Motivational aids**

THE THREE STAGES OF MEMORY

Reception

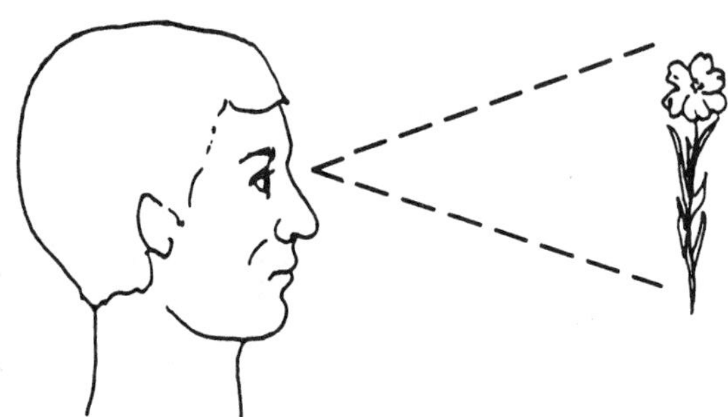

Retention

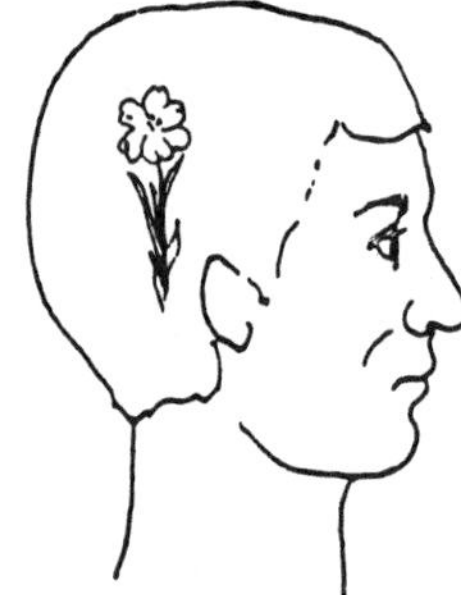

Recollection

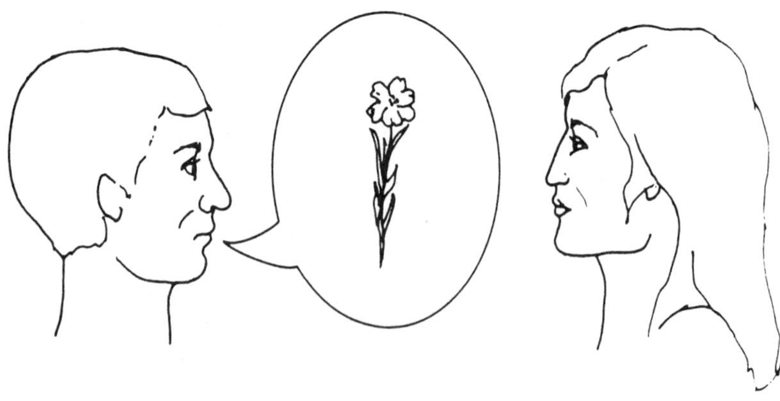

CHECKLIST FOR FINAL EXAMS

- [x] Decide what you have to study.
- [ ] Make a study schedule.
- [ ] Assemble materials for each course.
- [ ] Begin intensive reviews.
- [ ] Concentrate on one course at a time.

WHAT MAKES YOU ANXIOUS ABOUT TESTS?

1. The instructor says, "Now we are going to have a pop quiz."
2. The instructor says, "We are going to have a test next week."
3. You listen to other students talk about what they have studied.
4. You are sitting at a desk waiting for an exam to begin.
5. You can't think of the answer to a question.
6. Students who finish ahead of time begin to leave.
7. You sit down to study for an exam.
8. You even think about taking a test.

The degree of your anxiety is relative to the number and kind of situations that make you feel anxious.

WORDS THAT SIGNAL THE WRITER'S THOUGHT PATTERN

PATTERN	SIGNAL WORDS
PROCESS	Method, how to, follow these steps, process, procedure
COMPARISON/ CONTRAST	Similarities/differences advantages/disadvantages, like, as, different, unlike
CAUSE AND EFFECT	Cause, effect, reason, result, why, because, therefore, due to
CLASSIFICATION	Categories, types, kinds, parts, divisions, characteristics
EXAMPLE	For example, for instance, to illustrate, show, depict
SEQUENCE	Numbers such as first, second, etc.; stages, time periods

Reading Graphics with PRN

P	**Purpose**	**What is the graphic's purpose?**
R	**Relationship**	**What is the graphic's type?**
N	**Narrative Connection**	**How is the graphic explained in the text?**

DO YOU KNOW WHAT TO UNDERLINE OR MARK IN YOUR TEXTBOOKS?

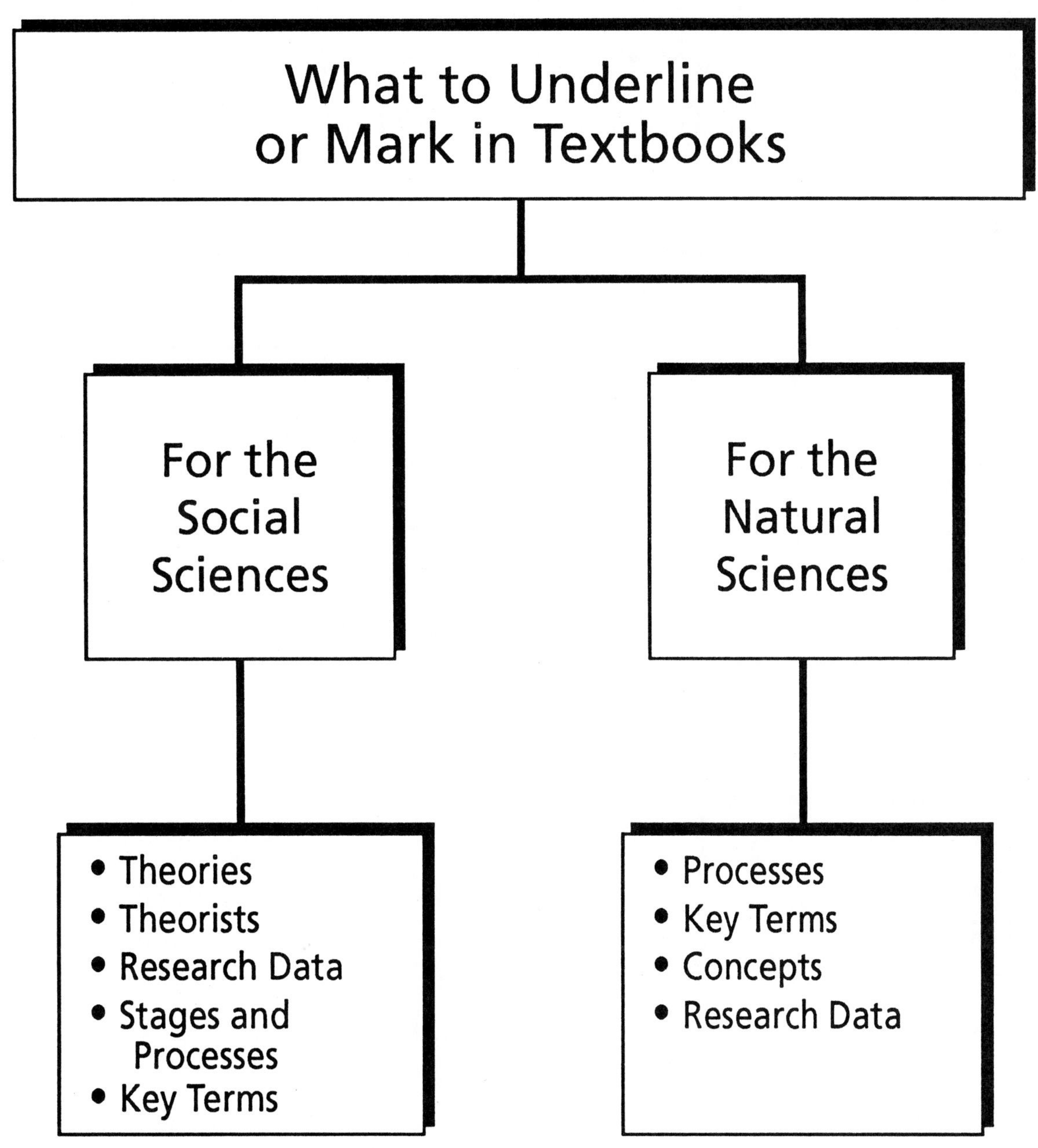

DO YOU KNOW WHAT TO UNDERLINE OR MARK IN YOUR TEXTBOOKS?

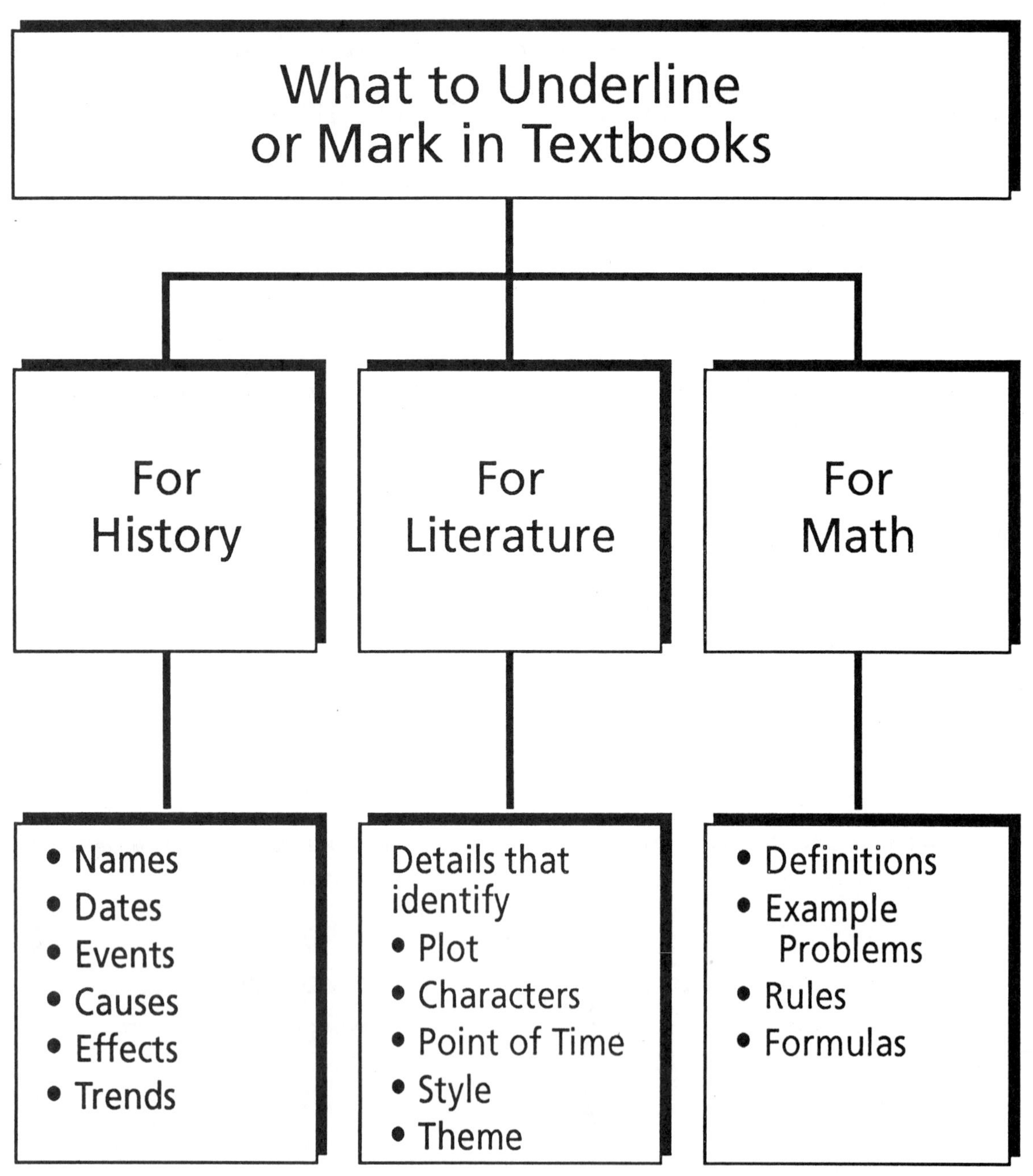

HOW TO BEGIN AN ESSAY

1. Start with an anecdote or brief story.

2. Explain to your readers why the topic is important to them.

3. Use a quotation that sums up, relates to, or leads up to your thesis.

4. Introduce your thesis with a broad, general statement that provides a background or context.

5. Arouse your readers' interest with a surprising statement, statistic, or description.

6. Ask one or more questions so that readers will want to read your essay to learn the answers.

THE *WHISK* METHOD FOR SOLVING MATH WORD PROBLEMS

Ask "What?"

Ask "How?"

Illustrate

Solve

Use two Keys to check:
(1) common sense
(2) computation

THE SCIENTIFIC METHOD

- **Question**
- **Observe**
- **Hypothesize**
- **Research**
- **Analyze**

Chapter Tests and Final Exam

Chapter 1 Test

1. List and explain the four keys to success in college as described in Chapter 1. (8 points)

2. List and explain the four components of learning style discussed in Chapter 1. (8 points)

3. Explain the difference between an internal and an external locus of control. (4 points)

Chapter 2 Test

1. Explain the difference between short-term and long-term goals, and give an example of each. (4 points)

2. List and explain the six characteristics of reachable goals as explained in Chapter 2. (10 points)

3. What is the COPE method, and what do the letters *C, O, P, E* stand for? (5 points)

4. The Confidence Builder in Chapter 2 explains four techniques for developing a positive attitude. Discuss one of these techniques. (1 point)

Chapter 3 Test

1. Discuss how students can improve their skills in each of the four essential areas of classroom performance. (8 points)

   A. Prepare for class:

   B. Become an active listener:

   C. Develop a personal note-taking system:

   D. Participate in class:

2. Discuss your own note-taking system and how this system works for you. (2 points)

Chapter 4 Test

1. Chapter 4 suggests scheduling as a way to manage time. Discuss three types of schedules and the purpose of each. (6 points)

2. Suppose a friend of yours has difficulty getting started when an assignment seems too long or too hard. Using the suggestions offered in Chapter 4 for beating procrastination, what advice would you give your friend? (4 points)

Chapter 5 Test

1. Explain how you are using your college's three major resources—people, places, and publications—to be more successful. (6 points)

2. Where would you go on campus to do the following? (4 points)
   a. Get a transcript of your grades.

   b. Apply for a grant or scholarship.

   c. Take an interest inventory to find out which jobs or careers would be best for you.

   d. Learn how to use a word processor/computer.

Chapter 6 Test

1. What are "your three selves" as explained in Chapter 4? How can you bring them into balance so that you can maintain health and well-being? (5 points)

2. How does your textbook define stress? (1 point)

3. Discuss any two of the "ten stress beaters" explained in Chapter 6. (2 points)

4. Chapter 6 mentions four things you can do to improve the quality of your relationships. Explain two of them. (2 points)

Chapter 7 Test

1. Choose either the SQ3R or PREP study system. List and explain the steps, and explain why a student might want to use the system. (5 points)

2. When is it useful to survey a textbook? A chapter? (2 points)

3. What, in your opinion, is the most useful part of a textbook chapter, and why? (3 points)

Chapter 8 Test

1. Chapter 8 explains six types of graphic organizers (maps, outlines, etc.) that can be used as study guides. Either list and explain the six types, or draw a diagram that illustrates and explains them. (12 points—1 point for correctly naming each type, 1 point for each accurate explanation)

2. Explain how you prefer to organize textbook information for study. (3 points)

Chapter 9 Test

1. Explain the difference between internal and external distractions, give two examples of each, and suggest ways to eliminate them. (6 points)

2. Explain at least four factors to consider when planning a home-study environment or when choosing some other place to study. (4 points)

Chapter 10 Test

1. Explain the three stages of memory. (3 points)

2. Explain the difference among *sensory memory, short-term memory,* and *long-term memory.* (3 points)

3. Chapter 10 explains eleven ways to increase your memory power. Discuss any four of them. (4 points)

Chapter 11 Test

1. What three kinds of reviews can help you prepare for tests? (6 points)

2. Describe your test-taking routine. (2 points)

3. What three strategies can you use for guessing the answer on a true-false test when you are sure you don't know the answer? (3 points)

4. Match the essay instruction words in Column A with their definitions in Column B. (9 points)

Column A	*Column B*
1. _____ contrast	A. Explain by using examples.
2. _____ relate	B. Give a precise and accurate meaning.
3. _____ enumerate or list	C. Describe a series of steps, stages, or events.
4. _____ criticize or evaluate	D. Explain differences only.
5. _____ illustrate	E. Construct argument; support with evidence.
6. _____ summarize	F. State and explain points one by one.
7. _____ compare	G. Show connection among ideas.
8. _____ define	H. Explain similarities and differences.
9. _____ trace	I. Condense main ideas; state briefly.

Chapter 12 Test

1. Define test anxiety as explained in Chapter 12. (2 points)

2. Explain what causes test anxiety. (2 points)

3. Explain how to reduce test anxiety. (2 points)

4. Explain what is meant by "positive self-talk," and give an example. (2 points)

5. Of the techniques for reducing test anxiety that are explained in Chapter 12, which do you think is the most likely to work for you, and why? (2 points)

Chapter 13 Test

1. Define critical thinking as explained in Chapter 13. (2 points)

2. Explain how to use the four critical thinking strategies to improve the way you process information gained from reading and other sources. (8 points)

   a. Examine your assumptions:

   b. Make predictions:

   c. Sharpen your interpretations:

   d. Evaluate what you learn:

Chapter 14 Test

Directions: Read the paragraph. Identify the POINT and outline the PROOF. Then decide whether you can make the IMPLICATIONS, based on the information in the paragraph.

What if you could improve your memory just by listening to music? The authors of *Supermemory,* Sheila Ostrander and Lynn Schroeder, believe that learning to music and other Supermemory feats are possible and that anyone can develop a powerful memory. Two principles underlie the development of Supermemory: You remember what you *want* to remember, and if you are in a relaxed frame of mind when you try to remember something, you will retain more for longer periods of time. To develop a Supermemory, the authors recommend the following steps. First, reduce stress by using a simple technique that involves stretching, then tensing, then relaxing the muscles. Next, visualize a pleasant scene. For example, picture yourself sailing; the day is warm, sunny, and clear. Imagine that whatever it is you want to remember will flow as easily as sailing on a gentle sea. Third, recite or read to music. The authors recommend classical music of the Baroque period. In experimental classrooms students using Superlearning and Supermemory techniques report grade increases of one letter or more. The system seems to work for learning and remembering all kinds of information: spelling words, foreign languages, statistics, and formulas. Could it be that the popular notion that students should not listen to music and study at the same time needs rethinking? Perhaps it all depends on the kind of music students choose to study by.

POINT:

1. ______________________________

   ____

PROOF:

2.

IMPLICATIONS:

3. *You* can develop a Supermemory. YES _____ NO _____

   Use proof from the passage to explain your answer.

   ____

   ____

   ____

4. Listening to rock music while studying will improve your memory. YES _____ NO _____

   Use proof from the passage to explain your answer.

   ____

   ____

   ____

Chapter 15 Test

Demonstrate your understanding of how to apply critical thinking strategies to planning an essay by answering the questions below. First, imagine that you have been asked to plan and write an essay on how students can improve their study skills. Then write your answers in complete sentences. (10 points)

What are your assumptions?

1. Do you believe study skills are necessary for student success?

   ____

2. Which study skills do you think most students need to improve?

   ____

3. Do you think students would welcome advice on how to improve their study skills?

   ____

4. What are your own study problems?

   ____

5. Who will be your audience for this essay?

   ____

What predictions can you make?

6. What is your purpose in writing this essay—to entertain, to inform, or to persuade? Explain your answer.

   ____

7. What kind of evidence will you use to reach your audience?

   ____

8. What points will the essay cover?

   ____

What interpretations will you offer?

9. Formulate a thesis, or controlling idea, for your essay.

   ____

   ____

10. List three details to support your thesis.

    ____

    ____

    ____

Chapter 16 Test

1. What is math anxiety, and what can a student do to overcome it? (2 points)

2. What is the purpose of WHISK? What do the letters mean? (6 points)

3. Discuss the three kinds of math errors and how to eliminate them. (6 points)

4. What is a good way to choose a math instructor? (2 points)

5. When is the best time to take a math course? (2 points)

6. When is the best time to seek help if you are having difficulty in a math course? (2 points)

Chapter 17 Test

1. List and explain the five steps scientists follow to investigate problems, test theories, and define principles. (5 points)

2. What strategies can you use for studying a social science—for example, psychology? (2 points)

3. What strategies can you use for studying a natural science—for example, biology? (2 points)

4. What is the relationship between student motivation and performance in a science class? (1 point)

Final Exam

Directions: Answer each question below. Write your answers in paragraph form and in complete sentences. Use extra paper if you need it. Using specific examples from the textbook to support your answers will increase your chances of making a high score. Each question is worth 20 points.

1. Describe your personal study system and explain what effect this course has had on the way you study. Include any specific methods or suggestions from the textbook that you have tried to apply.

2. Discuss the *one* most helpful thing you have learned from all the chapters you have covered.

3. How has the concept of learning style helped you understand your own strengths and weaknesses?

4. The following is a list of study problems many students have said they would like to overcome. Choose *one* problem from the list, and explain what advice you would give a friend to help him or her overcome the problem.

   - concentration
   - time management
   - note taking
   - studying from textbooks
   - preparing for tests
   - test anxiety

5. Did this review cover what you thought it would? Did you study for a question that your instructor did not ask? Now is your chance to use that information. Write your own question, and answer it.

Answer Key for Chapter Tests and Final Exam

Chapter 1

1. The four keys to success in college are assess your academic strengths and weaknesses; discover and use your learning style; develop critical thinking skills; adapt to your instructors' teaching styles. Explanations of the four keys may vary but should be supported by either an example or a reason for the key's importance.
2. The four components of learning style are your five senses, your body's reactions, your preferred learning environment, your level of motivation. Explanations may vary but should be supported by one or more examples.
3. Students who have an internal locus of control are self-motivated and believe that success results from effort and persistence. They believe they can control what happens to them. Students who have an external locus of control look outside themselves for motivation and believe that success is the result of chance, luck, or fate. They believe they have little or no control over their lives. Explanations may vary but should maintain the gist of this sample answer.

Chapter 2

1. Answers should both define and give an example of short-term and long-term goals.
2. Reachable goals are realistic, believable and possible, measurable, flexible, and controllable. Explanations may vary but should list the characteristics and provide an example of each.
3. COPE is a problem-solving method. The letters mean challenge, option, plan, evaluation, and they stand for the method's four steps. Explanations should name and explain the steps.

4. Four techniques for developing a positive attitude are visualize yourself being successful; control your inner voice; reward yourself for doing well; be a positive listener and speaker. Students should explain *one* of the techniques.

Chapter 3

1. Answers may vary but should include an example of how to improve in each of the areas of classroom performance.
2. Answers may vary but should explain clearly and with examples each student's note-taking system and how it works.

Chapter 4

1. Three types of schedules are the semester or quarter calendar, the weekly schedule, and the daily list. Answers may vary but should name and discuss the three schedules.
2. Students' advice should reflect these suggestions for beating procrastination: break large assignments into smaller units; reward yourself for work completed; schedule long assignments and set goals for their completion; organize your work area; find out what you need to know; be confident.

Chapter 5

1. Answers will vary.
2. a. registrar's office
   b. financial affairs office
   c. career development center
   d. computer center

   Answers may vary but should reflect either chapter explanations or your college catalog's listing of these services.

Chapter 6

1. Your three selves are your physical, emotional, and social selves. Answers may vary but should contain one or more examples of how to maintain physical, emotional, and social health and well-being.
2. Chapter 6 defines stress as "unrelieved anxiety that persists over a long period of time."
3. The ten stress beaters are be realistic; exercise tensions away; learn to say no; ask for help; learn to deal with negative people; lose yourself; treat yourself; get your life in order; make a wish list; help someone else. Answers may vary but should contain an explanation of any *two* of the stress beaters.
4. Four things you can do to improve the quality of your relationships are listen, converse, have fun, and be supportive. Answers may vary but should contain an explanation of any *two* ways to improve relationships.

Chapter 7

1. The steps in the SQ3R study process are survey, question, read, recite, review. The steps in the PREP study system are: predict, read, evaluate, practice. Students' explanations of the steps may vary but should reflect chapter content.
2. Survey a textbook as soon as you get it. You can also survey textbooks in the campus bookstore to help you decide whether to take a course. Survey chapters before reading and again as review after reading.
3. Answers may vary but should discuss at least *one* of the parts of a textbook chapter: title, introduction, headings, visual aids, summary, questions, and exercises.

Chapter 8

1. Six types of maps and outlines that can be used as study guides are concept or information maps, comparison charts, time lines, process diagrams, informal outlines, branching diagrams. Students' explanations may vary but should reflect chapter explanations.
2. Students' answers will vary but should explain clearly and with examples how they organize textbook information for study.

Chapter 9

1. Answers may vary but, like the sample below, should define internal and external distractions, give two examples of each, and suggest ways to eliminate them:

   Internal distractions originate within you, and you can control them. Hunger and tiredness are internal distractions. Eliminate them by studying after you have eaten and when you are rested.

2. When planning a study environment, consider these factors: location, lighting, temperature, furniture, supplies, motivational aids. Answers may vary but should explain any four of the above factors.

Chapter 10

1. Answers may vary but should maintain the gist of the following sample:

   The three stages of memory are reception, retention, and recollection. In the reception stage, information is received or taken in through the five senses. In the retention stage, information is stored in short-term or long-term memory. In the recollection stage, information is retrieved or remembered.

2. Answers may vary but, like the sample below, should briefly describe the three types of memory:

   Everything registers on your sensory memory for only a few seconds. Through selective attention you can transfer information from sensory memory to short-term memory, where you can keep it for less than a minute. To transfer information from short-term memory to long-term memory, you must decide to remember. Verbal, visual, and physical or motor information is stored in long-term memory. Some memories, such as your birth date, can last forever.

3. Students may discuss any *four* of these eleven ways to increase memory power: decide to remember; try relaxed review; combine review with physical activity; use mnemonics; use acronyms; associate to remember; visualize; use an organizational technique; sleep on it; remember key words; memorize.

Chapter 11

1. Three types of reviews that can help you prepare for tests are daily reviews, weekly reviews, and exam reviews. Discussions of the three reviews will vary but should reflect chapter explanations.

2. Students should describe their test-taking routines clearly and with examples.
3. Three guessing strategies to use on a true-false test are (1) Mark a statement true unless you know it is false; (2) assume a statement is false if it contains absolute words such as *always* and *never*; (3) assume a statement is false if any part of it is false.
4. 1. D
   2. G
   3. F
   4. E
   5. A
   6. I
   7. H
   8. B
   9. C

Chapter 12

1. Chapter 12 defines test anxiety as "stress that is related to a testing situation."
2. Answers may vary but should explain at least *two* of these common causes of test anxiety: being afraid that you won't live up to expectations of important others; believing grades are an estimation of personal worth; placing too much emphasis on a single test; giving in to guilt feelings due to poor preparation; feeling helpless and believing that you have no control over your performance.
3. Answers may vary but should explain at least *two* of these ways to reduce test anxiety: set your own goals and live up to your own expectations; realize that grades measure performance, not worth; understand that people like you for yourself, not your test grades; develop an internal locus of control and improve study habits; learn to relax; face your fears; fight distractions; talk positively to yourself.
4. Answers will vary but should maintain the gist of the following sample:

   Students who have test anxiety are frequently plagued with negative thoughts that program them for failure. They may say such things to themselves as "I know I will fail this test." To counter negative thoughts with positive ones and, therefore, to reduce test anxiety, repeat silently such thoughts as "I am prepared and I will try to do my best."

Chapter 13

1. Chapter 13 defines critical thinking as "the process of constructing and evaluating meaning."
2. Answers may vary but should explain clearly and with examples how to use the four critical thinking strategies.

Chapter 14

1. POINT:

   The authors of *Superlearning,* Sheila Ostrander and Lynn Schroeder, believe that learning to music and other Supermemory feats are possible and that anyone can develop a powerful memory.

2. PROOF:

   I. Two principles underlie the development of Supermemory.
      A. You remember what you want to remember.
      B. If you are in a relaxed frame of mind when you try to remember something, you will retain more for longer periods of time.
   II. To develop a Supermemory, the authors recommend the following steps.
      A. Reduce stress by using a simple technique.
      B. Visualize a pleasant scene.
      C. Recite or read to music.
   III. Students report grade increases of one letter or more.
   IV. The system seems to work for learning and remembering all kinds of information.
   V. Could it be that the popular notion. . . .

   IMPLICATIONS:

3. YES. The authors imply that *you* can develop a Supermemory in the last part of the second sentence, which says "anyone can develop a powerful memory."
4. NO. The authors do not say whether listening to rock music while studying will improve your memory, but they do recommend studying to classical Baroque music.

Chapter 15

1.–4. Answers will vary.

5. The appropriate audience for the essay is peers or classmates and instructor.
6. The purpose will probably be to inform, although students' explanations might support one of the other purposes.
7. Evidence for the essay might include facts, examples, or steps in a process.

8.–10. Answers will vary.

Chapter 16

1. Chapter 16 defines math anxiety as: "mental disorganization, fear, or panic associated with math courses and other math-related situations." To overcome it, be well-prepared for tests; jot down on your test formulas or rules you may forget; use a relaxation technique to calm yourself.
2. WHISK is a method for solving math word problems. The letters stand for the steps: What, How, Illustrate, Solve, Key.
3. Three kinds of math errors are concept errors, application errors, and careless errors. Students' explanations will vary but should reflect chapter explanations.
4. Seek out instructors who have a reputation for making math understandable. Ask other students, counselors, and department chairpersons to recommend an instructor. Find out whose classes fill first.
5. The best time to take a math course is in a full semester or quarter, not a short summer term. If you have to take more than one math course, take them one right after another so you don't forget concepts and lose skills.
6. Get help at the first sign of trouble, the first time you make a low test score, or as soon as you start to fall behind.

Chapter 17

1. The five steps of the scientific method are ask questions, make careful observations, formulate a hypothesis based on observations, do research and conduct experiments to test the hypothesis, analyze data and then accept or reject the hypothesis. Students' explanations may vary but should reflect chapter explanations.
2. Three strategies for studying a social science are expand your background by learning established rules and principles of the discipline, look for descriptions of research in your textbook assignments, pay attention to theories and their originators. Students' explanations may vary but should reflect chapter explanations.
3. Strategies for studying a natural science are use PREP to read for explanations of principles and processes, diagram complex information, follow a lab routine. Students' explanations may vary but should reflect chapter explanations.
4. Answers may vary concerning the relationship between motivation and performance but should stress that motivation is the student's responsibility.

Final Exam

Answers to the questions on this review will vary. The questions ask students to apply what they have learned in the course to their own study situations. The best answers—and the ones that should receive the highest scores—are those that demonstrate a thorough understanding of the concepts covered in *The Confident Student* Third Edition and that use specific examples from the text as support.

Exercises for Collaborative Learning

Each chapter of *The Confident Student* Third Edition contains one exercise structured especially for collaborative activity. Of course, any exercise in any chapter, including the Critical Thinking Application, can be done either collaboratively or individually, as the teacher desires, with only a slight change in the directions. Following is a list of the designated collaborative exercises by chapter.

Chapter	*Exercise*	*Chapter*	*Exercise*
1	1.4	10	10.3
2	2.3	11	11.4
3	3.1	12	12.3
4	4.4	13	13.3
5	5.5	14	14.4
6	6.6	15	15.4
7	7.2	16	16.3
8	8.3	17	17.3
9	9.1		

Whenever you do collaborative activities that require students to break into small groups, it is important that everyone has a role to ensure maximum participation.

Different tasks may require different roles. For example, if you design an activity that requires students to time themselves on the completion of a series of tasks, you may modify the roles to include a timekeeper. In the collaborative exercises that follow on pages 147–189, roles are adjusted to the requirements of the activities. Whenever you begin a collaborative activity, make sure your students know what their roles are. Candy R. Ready, an instructor, updated the following exercises to address the SCANS foundation skills and workplace competencies in addition to chapter objectives.

Dear Instructor:

The SCANS competencies on team building and interpersonal skills can be taught by using a pedagogy known as collaborative learning. This section of the instructor's guide includes carefully structured collaborative exercises for each chapter. Collaborative learning provides a structure for group work based on these elements:

Positive Interdependence	Students must share resources and responsibilities in order to complete the task.
Individual Accountability	Each student is responsible and held accountable for his or her own learning.
Social Skills	Interpersonal and communication skills that are necessary for effective group interaction.
Group Processing	Each group is given time to discuss how well they are achieving their goals and maintaining effective working relationships among group members.

By practicing these cooperative skills in the classroom, students become connected with peers and faculty which leads to relationships that continue outside the classroom. You will find that students need to be taught how to work effectively in a group. So, the first lesson is a handout that gives some strategies for effective group communication. However, the most important person in making collaboration in the classroom work is you. By walking around and intervening when necessary you can monitor the progress your class is making.

When deciding how to assign students to groups, you should consider several points:

- Every student has different strengths and weaknesses.
- Heterogeneous groups are the most powerful.
- Groups can be heterogeneous on different variables: ability, sex, ethnic background, perspective, and language.

The most important point to remember is that you are responsible for making group assignments and so must consider all these points. Left to form their own groups, students choose to work with friends and that limits the learning experience.

I hope your students experience as much success with these activities as mine have.

Sincerely,

Candy Ready

Interpersonal Skills Needed for Successful Collaborative Groups

It is important to remember that people do not know instinctively how to interact effectively with others. Nor do interpersonal and group skills magically appear when students are put in a work group. These skills must be taught and practiced. Collaborative groups are people working together cooperatively to achieve a mutual goal.

Rules for Successful Collaborative Groups

1. Students must get to know and trust one another.
2. Students must communicate accurately and clearly with one another.
3. Students must accept and support one another.
4. Students must resolve conflicts constructively.

How to Be an Effective Group Member

When you first join a work group, try to learn the names of the other members of the group. When you speak to your groupmates, use their names. In addition you should do the following:

1. Listen carefully and watch to discover as much as you can about each person's abilities and attitudes.
2. When someone in the group speaks, look at him or her. Scan the other people in the group for nonverbal clues that are signs of enthusiasm or lack of interest.
3. Try to determine who the influential members of the group are. Others tend to agree with them; therefore, they are an important part of the communication flow.
4. Try to identify the group standards for what you can or can't do in the group. For example, how do members encourage or discourage each other? How does the group handle conflict?
5. Listen and try to understand the group's goals and how to best achieve this goal. Ask yourself, "What can I contribute?"
6. Use positive verbal and nonverbal communication. Avoid negative comments and don't talk too much.
7. Ask questions, and give all members time to respond.
8. Use quiet voices so you won't disturb other groups in the room.

Roles in Successful Groups

All members of every group are equally important. However, it is necessary to assign roles to each member. This teaches interdependence and cooperation when the members must rely on one another to accomplish the assignment. Here are some common roles:

Leader Takes charge of explaining the assignment to the group. The leader often repeats ideas to clarify their meaning. The leader sometimes helps resolve conflicts between members by redefining the task.

Reader Reads any information or directions needed to understand the assignment.

Recorder Writes anything down that is needed to complete the assignment.

Researcher Uses reference materials.

Encourager Helps each group member feel successful. The encourager makes sure every member participates in a positive way. An example of how to encourage participation is shown below.

Encouraging Participation	
Looks Like	**Sounds Like**
Smiles	What is your idea?
Eye contact	Awesome!
Thumbs up	Good idea!
Pat on the back	That's interesting.

Collaborative Learning Activity: Chapter 1

General Directions: The work group should have three members. Meet each other and assign each person a role. The Leader is responsible for keeping the group on task and uses the textbook as a reference. The Recorder will write all the group's agreed upon answers. There is only to be one worksheet turned in per group. When the worksheet is completed, everyone should sign the bottom of the worksheet signaling their agreement with the answers. The Timekeeper keeps up with the time. Total time: 20 minutes.

Group Members: ____

Part 1 Directions: Everyone completes Awareness Check #2 and the Recorder records the learning styles of each member below.

Member: ____

Member: ____

Member: ____

Part 2: Study the different learning styles above. Discuss how each one is different. Then think of a learning strategy that would work well for each of the three learning styles and write it below.

Visual: ____

____

Auditory: ____

____

Tactile: ____

____

What are some other factors to consider when you're discovering how you best learn?

Is it important to discover your learning style? Why?

Part 3 Directions: The Leader will use the textbook to lead the discussion on the four keys that lead to college success (from Chapter 1). The recorder will write a brief description of each key and give an example of how the key helps students succeed in college and in the workplace.

1. **Assess your strengths and weaknesses**
   Description of this key:

   Example of how it ensures college success.

   Example of how it ensures quality in the workplace.

2. **Discover and use your learning style**
   Description of this key:

   Example of how it ensures college success.

   Could knowing your learning style be helpful in the workplace? In what way?

3. **Adapt to your instructor's teaching style**
   Description of this key:

   Example of how it ensures college success.

   How do you adapt to an employer's work style? Do employers and employees need to get along? Is this difficult to do? Why?

4. **Sharpen your thinking and study skills**
   Description of this key:

   Example of how this skill ensures college success.

   Critical thinking skills are a requirement in today's workplace. What kinds of study skills will you be using on the job?

Part 4 Evaluate how well you and your group worked together.

We worked well on ____

We could improve on ____

Overall success:

Excellent

Good

Okay

Poor

Collaborative Learning Activity: Chapter 2

The know-how identified by SCANS is made up of five competencies and a three-part foundation of skills and personal qualities that are needed for solid job performance. One of the foundation skills is the ability to recognize a problem then to devise and implement a plan of action for solving the problem. Chapter 2 begins with strategies for setting reachable goals and ends with COPE, a four-step problem-solving technique.

Step 1 Directions: This activity should be completed after the chapter has been read by the group members. There should be three or four members to each group. Assign a role to each group member and distribute the worksheets one per member. Then as a group, complete each question together so that everyone has the same answers. As an evaluation of your group's collaboration, the teacher will randomly select a worksheet to take up and grade as a group grade. Therefore, all answers should be discussed and agreed upon before writing down answers. Only one worksheet will be randomly selected for a group grade so *be sure every group member has the agreed upon answers on their worksheets.*

Step 2: The six characteristics of a reachable goal are listed below. With your group members, describe each characteristic and write which key to college success (from Chapter 1) would help you choose a goal that best fits you.

Six Characteristics of Goals

1. Realistic

   Which key from Chapter 1 fits?

2. Believable and Possible

   Which key from Chapter 1 fits?

3. Measurable

   Which key from Chapter 1 fits?

4. Flexible

   Which key from Chapter 1 fits?

5. Controllable

   Which key from Chapter 1 fits?

6. Ethical

   Which key from Chapter 1 fits?

Step 3: Read the work situation below. Using the COPE method of problem solving, solve the team's problem.

Mark works in the maintenance department of Buzz Industries. The company is using a new cost efficiency policy that requires cost cutbacks. His work team has been assigned the task of refinishing old desks to make them look new. Mark and his teammates look at each other and frown because they don't know how to refinish furniture. So, Mark gets a can of finish and reads the directions: "To begin sand wood with medium grit sandpaper; then immediately with fine grit sandpaper." Mark exclaims, "Piece of cake." Then he continues "Wipe clean before applying a liberal amount of oil on the surface. Wet-sand with wet or dry sandpaper while the surface is still wet." Mark scratches his head. "Anyone know what 'wet-sand' means?" asks Mark. No one knew.

Identify the problem.

Options for solving the problem.

Step 4: Evaluate how well you and your group worked together.

We worked well on ______________________________

We could improve on ______________________________

Overall success:

Excellent

Good

Okay

Poor

Collaborative Learning Activity: Chapter 3

Success in college and qualities of high performance in the workplace require planning, organizing, and commitment on a student's or employee's part. Chapter 3 gives you five strategies that when practiced will ensure success and high performance in the classroom and beyond.

Directions: Meet your group members and assign the following roles. Then turn to Chapter 3 in your textbook. Read the introduction to Chapter 3, then complete Awareness Check #6.

Leader: ______________________________

Recorder: ______________________________

Encourager: ______________________________

1. Compare group members' answers to Awareness Checks #6 and #7. Identify one item from each section that the majority of your group responded "no" to and *explain how these might negatively influence class performance.* If there is no majority response, *unanimously select one from each group to discuss.* Write your response below.

I. Preparing for Class

II. Listening to Lectures

III. Taking Notes

2. Read the section on active listening. Have each member of your group identify whether he or she is an active listener or a passive listener and then identify strategies that he or she practices when listening to a lecture.

   A.

   B.

C.

D.

3. What are the differences between an active listener and a passive listener?

4. How would signal words and phrases help you in taking notes?

5. Turn to Exercise 3.1. In Exercise 3.1, what is the writer's conclusion about listening? Does your group agree? Why or why not?

6. As a group, what have you learned about listening that you didn't know before?

7. Note taking. Read pages 51–59. Summarize the strategies in your own words.

Evaluation

Evaluate how well you and your group worked together.

We worked well on: ______________________________

We could improve on: ______________________________

Overall success:

Excellent

Good

Okay

Poor

Collaborative Learning Activity: Chapter 4

For many people managing time wisely is a difficult task. American lifestyles in the 1990s have become very fast paced. As students, you are faced with the difficulty of balancing classes, outside assignments, and leisure activities. Many students also work and have families to take care of as well. When you graduate and join the workforce, time becomes even more crucial with work deadlines, community commitments, and often family responsibilities. Chapter 4's time management system, GRAB, teaches you how to efficiently manage your time now while you're in school and later when you join the workforce. By using this four-step system, you can easily fix time management problems as they occur.

Directions: Choose roles and fill in names of group members. Complete only one worksheet per group. To check on group participation the teacher will randomly call on different group members to share answers with the class. As the teacher walks around, he or she will be checking for group skills such as encouraging words and everyone contributing.

Group Members: ____

____

Reader: ____

Encourager: ____

Researcher: ____

Checker: ____

1. Using your completed Awareness Check #8, compare your answers with your group members. Who has the most free time? Who has the least? Brainstorm some options for fixing each group member's time management problems.
2. Have each group member complete Exercise 4.3. Use this information to make a to-do list for tomorrow on a 3×5 index card. To make sure each group member's time is spent wisely, prioritize each member's list. In the next class period, bonus points will be given to the group that has the highest percentage of completion of their lists.
3. Answer the questions as a group. Everyone must contribute to the discussion. The Researcher is the only one that can use the textbook.

   A. The author suggests that when making a plan to manage time more efficiently, students must become aggressive and take responsibility for controlling their time. Explain the author's plan for controlling time effectively.

B. Discuss the pros and cons of keeping daily and weekly time logs. List the ones the group decides are valid pros and give reasons that support them.

C. Explain the negative effects procrastination can have on (1) goal setting and (2) time use.

D. As a group, what have you learned about time management that you didn't know before?

E. How does attitude affect studying and using time wisely?

F. Do you believe that students can become successful learners in class without preparing for class beforehand? Discuss this question in your group. Give your group's honest opinion and support it with an explanation.

Evaluation

Evaluate how well you and your group worked together.

We worked well on: ______________________________

We could improve on: ______________________________

Overall success:

Excellent

Good

Okay

Poor

Collaborative Learning Activity: Chapter 5

In today's workplace employees and employers have to be connected and work together in order to produce a quality product.

Today's activity will require that all groups complete their tasks, so that the entire class will become knowledgeable about our campus and its procedures, programs, personnel, and facilities. After each group shares the information they have gathered, there will be a test on our college's procedures, programs, personnel, and facilities. So, do a good job at gathering the information your group is responsible for; then take good notes while the other groups report! Good Luck!

Step 1: Read over the "scavenger sheet" assigned to your group. Decide the most effective way to gather the information needed. These cover People, Places, or Publications.

Step 2: Use the rest of this class period to gather the information needed.

Step 3: Regroup to organize the information found.

Step 4: Present your information to the class.

People

Group Number: ______________________________

Members: ______________________________

List four races or nationalities that are represented on this campus.

____

____

____

____

Give an estimate or percentage of freshmen who are:

Older Returning Adults (Adult Learners) ______________________________

Learning Disabled ______________________________

Physically Disabled ______________________________

Minorities ______________________________

List each of your group members' advisor's name, phone number, and office locations:

Member 1 ______________________________

Member 2 ______________________________

Member 3 ______________________________

Member 4 ______________________________

Member 5 ______________________________

Member 6 ______________________________

Prepare a list of helpful people (other than your advisor) who would be willing to talk with you if you needed advice, had a question, or wanted some help in solving a problem. Include the names, titles, offices, and phone numbers of these people in the spaces provided.

Name and Title: ______________________________

Office: ______________________________

Phone: ______________________________

Name and Title: ______________________________

Office: ______________________________

Phone: ______________________________

Name and Title: ______________________________

Office: ______________________________

Phone: ______________________________

Name and Title: ______________________________

Office: ______________________________

Phone: ______________________________

Evaluation

Evaluate how well you and your group worked together.

We worked well on: ______________________________

We could improve on: ______________________________

Overall success:

Excellent

Good

Okay

Poor

Places

Group Number: ______________________________

Members: ______________________________

List the location of the following places that are found on most college campuses. Then obtain the signature of a person from that facility. Also, give a brief description of what type of information can be found there.

Admissions Office

Location: ______________________________

Signature: ______________________________

Description: ______________________________

____

Registrar's Office

Location: ______________________________

Signature: ______________________________

Description: ______________________________

____

Counseling Center or Career Center

Location: ____________________

Signature: ____________________

Description: ____________________

____

Student Center or Dean of Students

Location: ____________________

Signature: ____________________

Description: ____________________

____

Computer Lab or Center

Location: ____________________

Signature: ____________________

Description: ____________________

____

Financial Aid Office

Location: ____________________

Signature: ____________________

Description: ____________________

____

Public Safety Office

Location: ____________________

Signature: ____________________

Description: ____________________

____

Student Health Services

Location: ____

Signature: ____

Description: ____

____

Learning Lab or Tutoring Center

Location: ____

Signature: ____

Description: ____

____

Evaluation

Evaluate how well you and your group worked together.

We worked well on: ____

We could improve on: ____

Overall success:

Excellent

Good

Okay

Poor

Publications

Group Number: ____

Members: ____

Use your college catalog to find answers to the following questions. (Hint: Some of these questions are found in Exercise 5.6.)

1. How old is your college?

2. Summarize your college's mission statement.

3. List the majors that your college offers.

4. Determine the degrees held and colleges attended of three of your instructors.

5. What is academic probation?

6. What GPA must you maintain in order to avoid being placed on academic probation?

7. What happens if you're placed on academic probation?

8. What is your school's attendance policy?

9. When does the next registration begin?

10. When does this semester end?

11. Give the following information about your college newspaper.

    Name: ______________________________

    Editor: ______________________________

    When it's published: ______________________________

    How to submit an article: ______________________________

    ____

    How to advertise: ______________________________

    ____

12. Describe the information given in your student handbook.

13. Give the locations of bulletin boards around campus where helpful information is posted.

    ____

    ____

14. List any other publication/flyer your college uses.

Evaluation

Evaluate how well you and your group worked together.

We worked well on: ______________________________

We could improve on: ______________________________

Overall success:

Excellent

Good

Okay

Poor

Collaborative Learning Activity: Chapter 6

The SCANS report states that students who graduate from any American educational institution must be competent in interpersonal skills. When you complete this activity with your group members, you are utilizing the skills required in today's workplace to produce a quality product by working on a team.

Directions: With your assigned group members, you will present your assigned topic to the class. Begin with the information in Chapter 6. Then with your group members, continue your research on the topic by using outside resources such as current magazines from the library. The topics are as follows:

- Staying healthy by eating sensibly and improving physical fitness
- Staying healthy by managing stress, practicing safe sex, and avoiding harmful substances
- Staying healthy by controlling your emotions
- Staying healthy by improving relationships and interpersonal skills

After gathering the information needed, your group will then put together a ten-minute oral presentation about the topic. Responsibilities for the presentation must be shared by all group members. Your group's success will be graded by the class. Your grade will be based on content, participation by all group members, and organization and quality of the oral presentation. Be creative! Use visuals, skits, etc. You must contribute to the project in order to receive a grade.

Evaluation

Evaluate how well you and your group worked together.

We worked well on: ______________________________

We could improve on: ______________________________

Overall success:

Excellent

Good

Okay

Poor

Collaborative Learning Activity: Chapter 7

Learning to study using a system such as SQ3R helps you monitor your success while studying. When the test results aren't what you wanted, you can go back through the steps and find out what went wrong.

Directions: Choose a partner and read the following scenario about a student who is having problems adjusting his study habits to the college workload. After reading, design a study system that will enable the student to succeed. Turn in one paper per pair.

Tom is a freshman at IOU College. Tom had done well in high school, graduating with a B average. He never really had to study hard. All he had to do was listen in class and he could understand enough to pass the tests.

Now, after four weeks in college, he finds that just listening in class isn't working. The college instructors expect the students to read on their own, and then they lecture based on that information. Tom is lost. Tom has never really read a textbook. He has skimmed chapters looking for answers to questions, but he hasn't carefully read, so he doesn't even know how to begin.

As a group, using the study guides found in Chapter 7, create a study system that would solve Tom's problem and make him successful in college.

Give an explanation of why your group believes this method will help Tom.

Evaluation

Evaluate how well you and your group worked together.

We worked well on: ____

We could improve on: ____

Overall success:

Excellent

Good

Okay

Poor

Collaborative Learning Activity: Chapter 8

Directions: This collaborative activity will require four roles: A Leader who leads discussion about the group members' most effective learning style and study method. The Recorder will write the answers. The Checker uses an observation sheet (see next page) and checks for group participation. The Timekeeper will keep up with the time. Time limit: 10 minutes.

1. What is your most effective study method?

   Member 1: ____________________

   Member 2: ____________________

   Member 3: ____________________

   Member 4: ____________________

2. What is your preferred learning style?

   Member 1: ____________________

   Member 2: ____________________

   Member 3: ____________________

   Member 4: ____________________

Part 2: As a group, briefly define how each study guide discussed in Chapter 8 would be most effective for which kind of learner and for which kind of course. Support your answer with an explanation.

1. Concept or informal map
   A. Best for ____________________ learning style
   B. Explanation:

2. Comparison charts
   A. Best for ____________________ learning style
   B. Explanation:

3. Time line
   A. Best for ______________________________ learning style
   B. Explanation:

4. Process diagram
   A. Best for ______________________________ learning style
   B. Explanation:

5. Informal outline
   A. Best for ______________________________ learning style
   B. Explanation:

6. Branching diagram
   A. Best for ______________________________ learning style
   B. Explanation:

Checker Observation Sheet				
Members	**Encourages**	**Participates**	**Listens**	**Positive Nonverbal Language**
1				
2				
3				
4				

Evaluation

Evaluate how well you and your group worked together.

We worked well on: ______________________________

We could improve on: ______________________________

Overall success:

Excellent

Good

Okay

Poor

Collaborative Learning Activity: Chapter 9

College success often requires long hours of studying. Learning how to stay focused now will enable you to be successful now in college and also in the workplace later. Because of world-class standards and global competition, many American companies now require employees to work twelve hour shifts.

Directions: With your partner, read the following nine problems and decide which strategy from Chapter 9 will solve the concentration problem. Both of you should be able to support your solutions if the teacher calls on you.

After you finish solving all the problems, turn to the pair on your right and compare answers. If the solutions are different, decide which one is the better solution. The teacher will randomly call on group members to share and support your answers so be sure everyone understands and agrees with all the solutions.

1. John is easily distracted when he studies. He works third shift at a photo-processing plant. He tries to study right after he gets off work, before his ten o'clock class.

   Solution:

2. Mary has problems studying in her apartment with her three roommates. No matter where she goes, someone is always there talking, listening to music, or watching TV.

   Solution:

3. All Sue has to do is sit down to read a chapter in her biology book and her mind begins to wander.

   Solution:

4. Linda is very frustrated at work. She manages an office for a law firm. Every day, each attorney gives her a list of tasks to complete but she just can't find the time to do them.

   Solution:

5. Bob is a team leader in his office. His supervisor meets with all team leaders on Monday and gives them their teams' jobs for the week. Bob often procrastinates and doesn't start on the list, so the team often ends up working longer hours on Thursday in order to get the jobs done by

Friday. The team members are very frustrated with Bob's procrastination problem and would like to help him solve it.

Solution:

6. Will has studied well for his accounting final. Yet, when he sits down to take the test his mind goes blank.

   Solution:

7. General Education courses like English and math are difficult for Tony. He wants to be an automotive technician and can't understand why these courses are needed.

   Solution:

8. Betty graduated from high school in May. She is taking some classes at a local technical college. The problem is that she is failing all her classes and can't figure out why.

   Solution:

9. Barbara is bored with the monotonous tone Dr. Smith uses when he lectures in History 101.

   Solution:

Evaluation

Evaluate how well you and your partner worked together.

We worked well on: ______________________________

We could improve on: ______________________________

Overall success:

Excellent

Good

Okay

Poor

Collaborative Learning Activity: Chapter 10

When you graduate from college you are expected to have mastered certain technical competencies in your area of study as well as some general competencies that enable you to succeed in the twenty-first century workplace. One of the general competencies identified in the SCANS report is lifelong learning. Lifelong learning means that you continue to learn on the job and expand your knowledge base whenever your career field requires it. Therefore, learning how to process information by using the 3R system to improve your memory as described in Chapter 10 will help you not only be successful now in your college studies, but later as you continue to learn in your career.

Group Number: ______________________________

Leader: ______________________________

Timekeeper: ______________________________

Encourager: ______________________________

Directions: Chapter 10 offers some strategies to help you improve your memory. Today, as a group, you are going to put these strategies to use.

Step 1: The leader will go over the Gibbish language rules (see below) with the group.

Step 2: As a group, you will complete the practice exercise. (5 minutes)

Step 3: Group members will help one another memorize the rules for the spelling test. (10 minutes)

Step 4: The spelling test will be taken individually by group members. The grades on the test will be averaged for the group grade.

It is the year 2010. Everybody in America communicates with a network system known as Gibnet. The language used is phonetic, and like most languages, it has some exceptions to its spelling rules.

Your group's objective is to master the Gibbish language. You must memorize the spelling rules and teach these rules to one another. Then everyone will take a spelling test individually. Your test grades will be averaged to give you an overall group grade.

The Gibbish Spelling Rules

1. Gibbish does not have a *v*, *i*, or a *d*. Instead, each letter has the single sound that is written *vid*.
2. A hyphen separates an *r* from the letter that follows it—for example, r-estaur-ant.
3. Whenever *b* and *c* appear together, *c* always follows *b*, except in the middle of the word, when *b* follows *c*—for example, bcaducbous, bcalicber.
4. None of these rules apply to words that begin with *j*. Any word that begins with *j* is correct except that no word that begins with *j* can have a *gh* in it.

Practice Exercise

Using the rules above, indicate whether the following words are spelled correctly by writing C if correct and I if incorrect.

1. _____ jurat
2. _____ gaucbe
3. _____ gvidcbcbr-e
4. _____ r-oguer-y
5. _____ r-uvidose
6. _____ jaught
7. _____ bcearbcat
8. _____ vidcbue
9. _____ cbabcoose
10. _____ bcer-serk

Spelling test

Complete this test individually. If a word is spelled correctly, write C. Write I if the word is misspelled.

1. _____ bcawcbocbk
2. _____ vidar-piscbk
3. _____ junbcture
4. _____ lanviduage
5. _____ jughp
6. _____ r-ectify
7. _____ debclar-ation
8. _____ decbumbcent
9. _____ ghum
10. _____ jurasic

Evaluation

Evaluate how well you and your partner worked together.

We worked well on: ______________________________

We could improve on: ______________________________

Overall success:

Excellent

Good

Okay

Poor

Collaborative Learning Activity: Chapter 11

Being able to follow precise directions is an important step in learning to take tests in college. Successful test taking often requires an understanding of the instruction words being used in the question. Test-taking strategies have also become a necessary tool in the workplace because many companies now require prospective employees to take competency tests in English, math, and critical thinking. Using the strategies in Chapter 11 will help you become more comfortable in answering test questions.

Guidelines for Answering Essay Questions

1. Read the question carefully to make sure you understand what is being asked.
2. Watch for "instruction words."
3. Concentrate on answering the question briefly and precisely.
4. Stay on the topic, and avoid stating your opinion or making judgments unless the question specifically asks for your opinion.
5. Be sure to restate the question in your answer. Doing so will make it easier for your instructor. Also, this approach gives you a starting point and helps keep your answer focused on your topic.

Step 1 directions: Choose roles for each group member.

Leader: ______________________________

Recorder: ______________________________

Encourager: ______________________________

Observer: ______________________________

Step 2: Each member should turn to Figure 11.3 and look at the instruction words and their definitions. The Leader will give each group member two questions to answer. The Recorder will list each group member's answers on the worksheet.

Evaluation

Evaluate how well you and your group worked together.

We worked well on: ______________________________

We could improve on: ______________________________

Overall success:

Excellent

Good

Okay

Poor

Worksheet

Cut apart and give two questions to each group member.

1. Compare/contrast a movie and a television show that you've seen recently.

2. Evaluate Chapter 11's test-taking strategies.

---

1. Explain "A PIE."

2. Describe your college campus.

---

1. Explain the acronym "GRAB."

2. List the 3 P's of college resources.

---

1. Interpret the following saying: "Genius is 99 percent perspiration and 1 percent inspiration."

2. Summarize the four keys to college success.

Worksheet

1. Compare/contrast a movie and a television show that you've seen recently.

2. Evaluate Chapter 11's test-taking strategies.

3. Explain "A PIE."

4. Describe your college campus.

5. Explain the acronym "GRAB."

6. List the 3 P's of college resources.

7. Interpret the following saying: "Genius is 99 percent perspiration and 1 percent inspiration."

8. Summarize the four keys to college success.

Collaborative Learning Activity: Chapter 12

Many people become overanxious and stressed out over the deadlines and pressures that life often sends our way. Students often find themselves unable to take an exam because the importance of getting a certain grade on that exam overrides the purpose of the exam, which is to demonstrate to an instructor your knowledge of the competencies presented in the course. In the same manner, employees often find themselves stressed out because a team leader has asked them to demonstrate their competencies on the job by explaining a process or by applying the technical skills learned in college to troubleshoot and solve problems for their work team.

Directions: In groups of three, complete the following exercise. Choose a Leader. The Leader will choose a role for each member. After completing the worksheet together, sign your names verifying that all members contributed to the worksheet. Turn in one sheet only.

Leader: ______________________________

Reader: ______________________________

Recorder: ______________________________

Encourager: ______________________________

1. Susan hasn't been in a classroom in twenty years. This is her first semester in college. She has her first test tomorrow in BIO 101. Susan is feeling helpless, afraid that she can't perform as well as the other students on the test. What can Susan do to calm down?

2. Barry has studied for three days for his history test. In class, he gets his test and reads the first question. Barry doesn't know the answer. He begins to panic, afraid that he studied the wrong material. Can Barry still be successful on this test? How?

3. Mary Lou is a weak math student, so she got a tutor to help her study for the midterm exam. Mary Lou's tutor assured her that she knew all the formulas and that she was ready. On test day, she got her test and noticed that her palms were sweaty. When Mary Lou read the first problem, her mind went blank. What can Mary Lou do?

4. Walter is the first person in his family to go to college. For years, Walter's parents scrimped and saved their money so he could have this opportunity. Walter is struggling with his freshman courses. Tomorrow is his first scheduled test, and Walter is afraid. What if he fails and lets his parents down? Walter can't even begin to study because he's too busy worrying about failing. Can you help Walter? How?

Evaluation

Evaluate how well you and your group worked together.

We worked well on: ______________________________

We could improve on: ______________________________

Overall success:

Excellent

Good

Okay

Poor

Collaborative Learning Activity: Chapter 13

SCANS research has identified a three-part foundation of intellectual and personal qualities that potential employees need in order to help their businesses compete in today's global market. Intellectual qualities include thinking skills such as: creatively solving problems, making sound decisions, and interpreting printed material correctly. Chapter 13 has a four-part strategy that enables students to critically think through and interpret the author's meaning from college textbooks. Mastering this strategy in college will help you perform better on your job.

Leader: ______________________________

Encourager: ______________________________

Timekeeper: ______________________________

Recorder: ______________________________

Directions: As a group, review the chapter to answer the questions in Part 1. Then the leader will assign each group member a part (2–5) to complete as we begin our study of Chapter 13. After 15 minutes, each group member will share information with others and the group will compose one paper to turn in for a grade.

Part 1

1. Read the introduction. What is critical thinking?

2. Four critical thinking strategies will be covered:

   ____

   ____

   ____

   ____

3. What is the acronym used?

Part 2

Read "Examining Your Assumptions."

1. Briefly explain how we can use assumptions when we study.

2. How do we use assumptions in our daily lives?

3. Define *assumptions.*

Part 3

1. How are predictions helpful when listening to a lecture?

2. Define *predictions.*

3. How do we use predictions in our daily routines?

Evaluation

Evaluate how well you and your group worked together.

We worked well on: ____

We could improve on: ____

Overall success:

Excellent

Good

Okay

Poor

Collaborative Learning Activity: Chapter 14

Reading is a necessary part of any study system. As a college student, you must read, understand, and remember information not only from textbooks but also from journals, periodicals, and other sources when doing research. After you graduate, you will continually be asked to read and understand memos, step-by-step directions, E-mail messages on the computer, manuals to new equipment, and new policies. Practice your reading ability with your group members as you work through this exercise.

Directions: Each group member will complete this lesson. You may do it together and collaborate on the answers. The teacher will select at random one paper from the group to grade, so be sure you agree on the answers. You have 20 minutes.

Leader: ______________________________

Reader: ______________________________

Timekeeper: ______________________________

Encourager: ______________________________

Read this paragraph and pick out the author's point.

> You may frequently hear the terms *drug abuse* and *drug addiction* in certain college classes. Although all forms of drug addiction are classified as drug abuse, not all drug abuse is considered addictive. Drug abuse may be only an occasional indiscretion with a chemical substance, whereas addiction suggests a regular, dependent pattern of substance abuse. The individual who likes to get intoxicated for the weekend game may simply be abusing alcohol, but the person who makes drinking a dominant part of each day's activities is addicted to alcohol.

1. Author's point: ______________________________

   ____

   ____

2. In the paragraph above, underline the sentence or sentences that support the author's central point.

Evaluation

Evaluate how well you and your group worked together.

We worked well on: ____

We could improve on: ____

Overall success:

Excellent

Good

Okay

Poor

Collaborative Learning Activity: Chapter 15

The SCANS report is based on one-on-one interviews that were done with people in America's workforce today. The number one concern overall was quality products that ensure customer satisfaction. Quality products often require many different teams' input as the product is being produced. This means that often the product your team starts, someone else will finish. In order for the product to be done correctly, careful attention must be given to the way instructions are written so that each team can successfully complete its part in the way the job should be done.

Group Number: ______________________________

Leader: ______________________________

Recorder: ______________________________

Encourager: ______________________________

Timekeeper: ______________________________

Directions: Use one of the following story openings to create a collaborative story. The Recorder will write while the others create the story, using the reading and writing connection strategy found on pages 326–333. The group will develop the story for ten minutes. After ten minutes, the Leader will pass your story to the next group. Then, the next group will pick up where you left off and continue to develop the story for ten minutes. You will exchange with another group (chronologically) and repeat the process. Remember to write clearly and legibly so your coauthors can read what you write; also, don't kill off your main characters before the final exchange.

When the Timekeeper indicates the end of the last ten minutes, exchange again, but this time the paper is proofread before being given back to its original group.

Your topic: ______________________________

Suggested Beginnings for Collaborative Stories

- A car was speeding down the highway.
- It was a typical boring lecture until the teacher began acting strangely.
- Tony looked nervously at his watch as he waited for his wife to arrive.
- My husband (or wife) woke up and said, "I hear noises downstairs."
- I'm going to tell you the most exciting experience of my life.
- The trouble started when I left my science class.
- As I walked across campus, I had this strange feeling.

These titles should be given out one to a group.

Evaluation

Evaluate how well you and your group worked together.

We worked well on: ______________________________

We could improve on: ______________________________

Overall success:

Excellent

Good

Okay

Poor

Collaborative Learning Activity: Chapter 16

The personal skills that enable success in college, such as coming to class prepared and on time, doing your homework, applying math strategies to solve problems, and working together in a group, also will help you be successful in your career.

Directions: Turn to the student next to you and work on the following chart together. One person reads the behavior and one fills in the chart.

Evaluation

Evaluate how well you and your partner worked together.

We worked well on: ____

We could improve on: ____

Overall success:

Excellent

Good

Okay

Poor

Course Activity	Successful Student	Unsuccessful Student
1. Attending Class	never misses except for illness or unusual reasons	cuts classes often, especially on Fridays
2. Studying Math Textbooks		
3. Doing Homework		
4. Asking Questions		
5. Getting Help Outside of Class		
6. After Working a Problem		
7. Math Notebook		
8. After Being Unsuccessful on a Test		
9. Attitude and Approach		
10. Making Use of Old Tests and Homework		

Collaborative Learning Activity: Chapter 17

Leader: ____________________

Timekeeper: ____________________

Researcher: ____________________

Encourager: ____________________

Learning to study using a system such as SQ3R helps you monitor your success while studying. When the test results aren't what you wanted, you can go back through the steps and find out what went wrong.

Choose a chapter to survey from a science text used on your campus. Everyone must complete an activity. The teacher will randomly select a paper from your group to grade. You have 45 minutes.

1. What kind of science book did your group choose?

   ____

2. Which of these parts are included? Circle the letter of the answer or answers that apply.
   a. questions
   b. objectives
   c. introductory paragraph
3. Based on the chapter opening, what is the chapter about? Summarize your answer in one or two sentences.

4. What would be the major purpose for reading this chapter? Write your answer in one or two sentences.

5. Are there introductory questions? If so, can you tell which topics will be covered?

6. Show how the body of the chapter is organized by writing the headings in outline form.

7. Turn each heading into a question that will guide the reading of this chapter.

Evaluation

Evaluate how well you and your group worked together.

We worked well on: ______________________________

We could improve on: ______________________________

Overall success:

Excellent

Good

Okay

Poor

Developing Your Vocabulary

Try this exercise. Close your eyes and think "chair." As you think about what the word means, try to picture a chair in your mind's eye. When the image is very clear to you, open your eyes and draw the chair that you pictured. Don't worry about the quality of your art work; just draw a chair in the box below.

Compare your drawing with other students' drawings. How many different kinds of chairs are represented? How would you classify the chair you drew? Is it an early American ladder-back, a Victorian wing chair, a wrought-iron garden chair?

Whenever students do this exercise, their drawings are all a little different, but they are similar in one respect. The object drawn by each student is a piece of furniture that can comfortably seat one person; it has four legs and a back, and it may have arm rests. This object is clearly distinguishable from benches, sofas, stools, porch swings, and other pieces of furniture designed for sitting.

The point of the exercise is that "chair" means the same thing to everyone, but the chair you picture in your mind is a personal image based on your experience with certain kinds of chairs. *A word is a symbol that represents an idea, object, or meaning that exists, or has existed, in reality.* As you develop your vocabulary, you will become sensitive to words and the meanings they represent. The more words you know, the more choices you have for conveying accurately and precisely what you mean both in speaking and in writing. Developing your vocabulary will also improve your reading comprehension as you become aware of terminologies essential to your understanding of the course material.

This chapter has three objectives:

- To teach you new ways to think about words
- To explain strategies that have helped many successful students develop their vocabularies
- To encourage you to come up with your own system for learning and remembering new words.

LINKS IN THE CHAIN OF MEANING: PREFIXES, ROOTS, SUFFIXES

Words are made up of parts called *prefixes, roots,* and *suffixes.* The word *root* suggests origin or foundation. A root is the basic part of a word. A *prefix* is a word part often added to the beginning of a root; it usually changes the root's meaning. A *suffix* is a word part added to the end of a root; it may change the root's part of speech, or grammatical form, and it may expand the root's meaning. When you find the meaning of a prefix, root, or suffix of a word, you have found a link in the chain of meaning. Find out how many meanings of common word parts you already know by completing Awareness Check A.

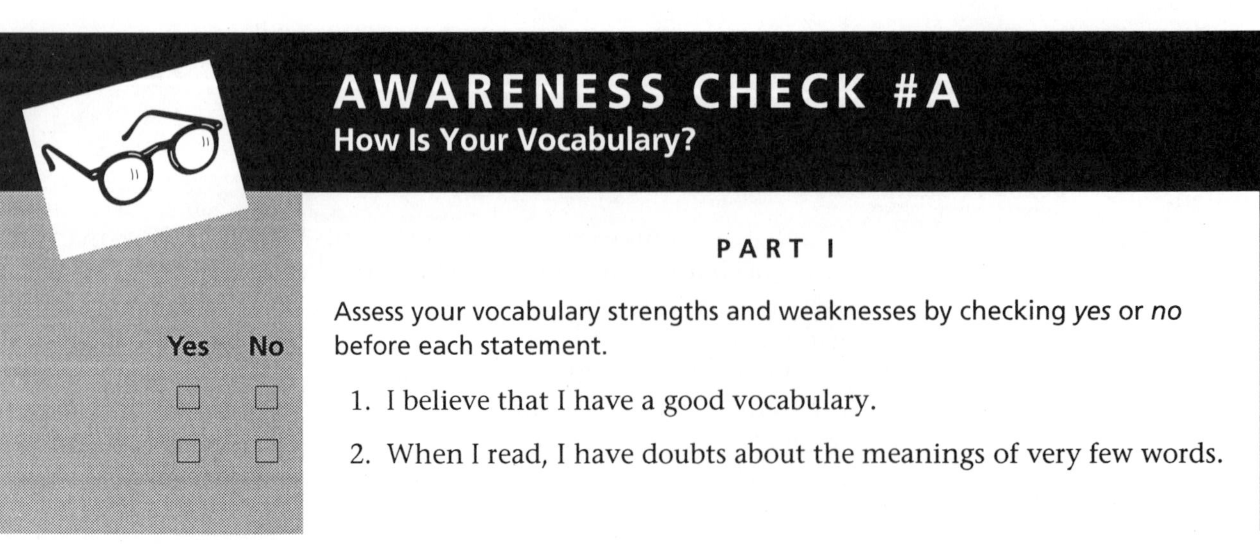

AWARENESS CHECK #A

How Is Your Vocabulary?

PART I

Assess your vocabulary strengths and weaknesses by checking *yes* or *no* before each statement.

Yes	No	
☐	☐	1. I believe that I have a good vocabulary.
☐	☐	2. When I read, I have doubts about the meanings of very few words.

Yes	No	
☐	☐	3. I use a dictionary when I *am* in doubt about a word's meaning.
☐	☐	4. I always keep a dictionary within reach when I read, write, or study.
☐	☐	5. I usually have no trouble reading a dictionary entry and finding the information I need.
☐	☐	6. I am often able to determine a word's meaning based on its context (sentence or paragraph in which a word appears).
☐	☐	7. I am aware that many of the courses I take have special vocabularies or terminologies that I should learn.
☐	☐	8. I know the meanings of many of the parts that make up a word: prefixes, roots, and suffixes.
☐	☐	9. I am not at a disadvantage when I write because I do not have a limited vocabulary.
☐	☐	10. I have a reliable strategy for learning words and terms, and I use it.

PART II

To find out how many common word parts you already know, match the underlined word parts in column A with their meanings in column B. The meaning of the whole word in which each underlined word part appears may provide you with a clue to the meaning of the underlined part.

Column A

1. _______ <u>in</u>sensitive
2. _______ <u>bi</u>focal
3. _______ auto<u>graph</u>
4. _______ <u>astro</u>naut
5. _______ re<u>tain</u>
6. _______ <u>sub</u>merge
7. _______ <u>pre</u>vent
8. _______ sym<u>phony</u>
9. _______ <u>re</u>call
10. _______ <u>post</u>pone

Column B

A. two
B. under
C. after
D. not
E. before
F. write
G. star
H. back, again
I. hold
J. sound

If you checked *yes* to most of the items in Part I, you may already have a strong vocabulary. If you checked *no* to most of the items, you may need to develop your vocabulary. To assess your knowledge of the ten common word parts covered in Part II, check your answers with this key: 1(D), 2(A), 3(F), 4(G), 5(I), 6(B), 7(E), 8(J), 9(H), 10(C).

If you know the meaning of one word part, you can figure out the meaning of many words that contain that part. Look at this word.

microbiology

Micro is a root that means "small," and *bio* is a root that means "life." The combining form *-logy* is a root, *log,* combined with a suffix, *-y,* that means "study of." Thus, *microbiology* means "the study of the smallest living things." The smallest living things are called *microorganisms,* and they must be viewed through a *microscope.* The root *scope* means "look."

Do you see how the parts of a word form links in a chain of meaning that connects other words having the same parts?

Here are some more words that contain the roots found in the word *microbiology.*

micro-	**bio-**	**-logy**
microscope	biotic	anthropology
microfilm	bionic	archaeology
microfiche	biosphere	paleontology
micrometer	biomass	zoology
microwave	biography	ecology

Some words are made by adding a prefix to one or more roots. For example, *re-* is a prefix that means "back" or "again." The root *tract* means "to pull." The word *retract* is made by attaching the prefix to the root. *Retract* means "to pull back." In the sentence "The *New York Times* agreed to retract a statement that proved to be inaccurate," *retract* means to "pull back" the statement, or to say that it was a mistake.

How many other words can you think of that begin with the prefix *re-* or that contain the root *tract*? Here are a few examples.

re-	**tract**
refrain	attract
rebate	detract
reduce	protracted
reload	extract
relocate	contract

You can change the part of speech of a word by adding a *suffix.* For example, *attract* is a verb. If you add the suffix *-ion* to this word, it becomes *attraction,* a noun. The suffix *-ed* is used to form the past tense of verbs. For instance, the past tense of *attract* is *attracted.* Someone who is pleasant to look at is *attractive.* This word is formed by adding the adjective suffix *-ive* to the base word. To describe someone who is wearing a nice-looking outfit, you might say, "That person is *attractively* dressed." You make the adjective into an adverb by adding the suffix *-ly.* Adding suffixes does not change the meaning of the base word, *attract.* All that changes is the part of speech.

Look what happens to the following words when you attach the prefix *un-*, which means "not." This prefix, when added to some words, changes those words into *antonyms*, words having the opposite meaning.

attractive	unattractive
attractiveness	unattractiveness
attractively	unattractively

Other prefixes that can change words into antonyms are *in-*, *im-*, and *il-*.

attentive	inattentive
active	inactive
mobile	immobile
efficient	inefficient
substantial	insubstantial
legal	illegal

The chart that follows contains commonly occurring prefixes, roots, and suffixes, along with their meanings, and some example words. If you learn to recognize these word parts on sight so that you can recall their meanings instantly, two interesting things may happen. First, your awareness of words containing these parts may increase. They'll jump out at you from the pages of your books as well as from lectures, movies, and television programs. Second, you'll notice and be able to define common prefixes, roots, and suffixes in new words that you encounter. This ability may help you determine the meanings of new or unfamiliar words.

Common Prefixes, Roots, and Suffixes

PREFIX	MEANING	EXAMPLE WORDS
anti-, ant-	against	antisocial, antacid
bene-	good, well	benevolent, beneficial
co-, col-, com-, con-, cor-	together, with	cooperate, collection, commiserate, convene, correlate
dis-	apart, not	distract, disable
e-, ec-, ex-	out	elicit, ecstasy, exit
equa-, equi-	equal	equation, equivalent
il-, im-, in-, ir-	not	illegal, impossible, inept, irrational
mal-	bad, harmful	malevolent, maladjusted
re-	back, again	revitalize, recreation
se-	away, from	seduce, secession
sub-	under	subterranean, substandard
ROOT	**MEANING**	**EXAMPLE WORDS**
ann	year	annual, annuity
chron	time	chronometer, chronicle
clud, clus	shut	include, recluse

Common Prefixes, Roots, and Suffixes (continued)

ROOT	MEANING	EXAMPLE WORDS
cred	believe	credible, credit
dict	speak	dictation, prediction
duc, duct	lead	deduction, reduce
graph, gram	write	biography, telegram
gress, grad	go, step	regress, graduate
path	feeling, disease	sympathy, pathology
ped, pod	foot	pedestrian, podiatrist
scrib	write	scribble, transcribe
spec	look	spectacle, inspection
tain, ten	hold	abstain, retention
vers, vert	turn	conversation, divert
vit, viv	life	vitality, vivid

ADJECTIVE SUFFIX	MEANING	EXAMPLE WORDS
-able, -ible	capable, able	portable, reversible
-al	related to	musical, comical
-ant, -ent	related to	resistant, dependent
-ful	full of	flavorful, shameful
-ive	tending to act	attentive, communicative
-less	without	merciless, humorless
-ous	full of	delicious, ambitious

ADVERB SUFFIX	MEANING	EXAMPLE WORDS
-ly	in the manner of	quietly, forcefully
-ward	to, toward	forward, homeward

NOUN SUFFIX	MEANING	EXAMPLE WORDS
-ance, -ence	state, condition, quality	governance, dependence
-er, -or, -ar	one who	trainer, conductor, registrar
-ion	state, condition, act, process	sensation, reaction
-ity	state, condition, quality	validity, mediocrity
-ment	state, condition, quality	commitment, inducement
-ness	state, condition, quality	receptiveness, kindness

VERB SUFFIX	MEANING	EXAMPLE WORDS
-ate	act, cause	originate, eliminate
-ed	past-tense ending	walked, mended
-ify	make, perform	amplify, verify
-ize	make, perform	rationalize, characterize

There are many more prefixes, roots, and suffixes than are listed here, but these should stimulate your interest in thinking critically about words.

EXERCISE A.1

Working on your own or with a partner, use the list of common prefixes, roots, and suffixes to help you match the words in column A with their definitions in column B.

Column A		Column B
1. ______	secreted	A. device that records time
2. ______	discredit	B. writing or carving on a surface
3. ______	convivial	C. one who opposes
4. ______	chronograph	D. having all sides equal
5. ______	residue	E. a part of a whole
6. ______	inscription	F. hidden away
7. ______	antagonist	G. kept or shut out
8. ______	component	H. sociable, enjoying being with others
9. ______	equilateral	I. remainder; what is left behind
10. ______	excluded	J. to cast doubt upon

ANOTHER LINK: ETYMOLOGY

Etymology is the study of a language's origin—where words come from. Many English words are composed of word parts, or elements, that come from Latin or Greek. For example, *uni-* is a Latin word part that means "one," and *mono-* is a Greek word part that means "one." Look at these two lists.

unicycle	**mono**poly
uniform	**mono**gamy
unique	**mono**graph
unilateral	**mono**rail
universe	**mono**logue

You probably know the meanings of most of these words. Now you know also that the first part, or prefix, of each word means "one." When you encounter an unfamiliar word that begins with the prefix *mono-* or *uni-*, you will at least know that the concept of oneness is part of that word's definition.

Word parts form links in a chain of meaning. Knowing one word can help you understand another. In the following diagram, arrows indicate the links in the chain, showing how a word part in one word is linked to a word part in another.

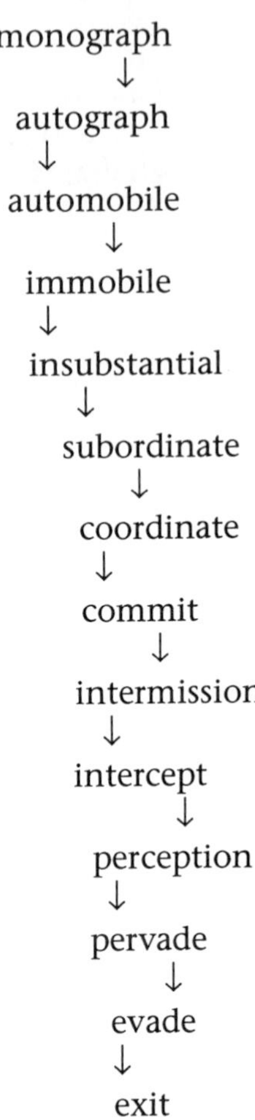

If you don't know what a *monograph* is but you do know that an *autograph* is a signature and that *graph* means "write," then you also know that part of the meaning of *monograph* has to do with writing. Knowing part of a word's meaning can help you make assumptions about the whole word's meaning. You can test your assumptions by looking up the word in a dictionary.

The words in the next two lists all begin with a prefix that means "with" or "together." As you think about the meanings of these common words, try to get a feeling for the way in which each one conveys a sense of "withness" or togetherness. For example, the first word, *connect,* means "to join together."

connect	**con**struction
convention	**com**mittee
contest	**col**lect
concert	**cor**rect

Notice that three of the words begin with *com-, col-,* and *cor-*. These are spelling variations of one prefix that means "with" or "together." Ease of pronunciation determines the spelling of the prefix. Once you know the meanings of several example words such as those in the lists above, it is easy to spot other words that begin with the same prefix, whether it is spelled *co-, con-, com-, col-,* or *cor-*. Knowing the meanings of word parts and some example words that contain them may help you analyze the meanings of unfamiliar words as you encounter them in your reading.

EXERCISE A.2

Find the links in this chain of meaning. Draw arrows to connect the parts that these words have in common. Then, using the list of common prefixes, roots, and suffixes on pages 195–196, list the word parts you linked, and define them on the lines provided. The first one is done for you.

pertain
↓
retain

reduce

conduct

conclude

inclusion

incredible

credulous

vivacious

vitality

Word Part	Meaning
tain	hold

CONNECTIONS IN CONTEXTS

Combining your knowledge of the meanings of common word parts with information that you have picked up from the context in which a word appears may make it possible for you to determine the meaning of a word even if a dictionary is not available. To use context to help you determine the meaning of a word, look for one of four common connections that relate an unfamiliar word to its context: The definition connection; The example connection; The contrast connection; The experience connection.

The Definition Connection

Sometimes a writer states the definition of a word he or she feels you may not know. Find the definitions of the boldface words in these two sentences.

1. **Redundancy,** or repetition, is something you may want to avoid when giving a speech, unless you use it sparingly and for emphasis.
2. Because of falling plaster, students were asked to **convene** (assemble) in another classroom.

In the first sentence, the definition is set off by commas and introduced by the signal word "or." In the second sentence, the definition is in parentheses immediately following the boldface word. To find the definition connection, look for the following:

1. **A stated meaning following or preceding the unfamiliar word**
2. **A stated meaning set off by marks of punctuation, usually commas**
3. **A stated meaning given in parentheses**
4. **Other signals such as "the definition is," "the meaning is," or "called"**

EXERCISE A.3

Sometimes an author states a definition in a sentence to help you connect an unfamiliar word to its context. Read the following sentences, then circle the correct definition of each boldface word.

1. There is enough financial aid available to students today so that no one should be **precluded,** or prevented, from getting a college education for financial reasons.

   a. inspired

   b. barred or stopped

   c. pushed

2. The Tolland Arts Institute is a **consortium** (partnership) of ten universities that researches funding for the arts.

   a. association of institutions

   b. scholarship fund

   c. set of connected buildings

3. The experimental music sounded **dissonant,** or harsh, to her ears.

   a. not professional

   b. not harmonious

   c. loud

The Example Connection

When a simple definition isn't enough to explain the meaning of a word or expression, a writer may provide an example. Writers use the signal phrases *for example, for instance, to illustrate,* and *such as* to indicate that an example follows. If an unfamiliar word causes you to pause in your reading, read a little farther or go back a sentence or two to see if the writer provides an example to explain what he or she means. The two sentences that follow contain examples that define the boldface words.

1. To ward off a vampire, lock all doors and windows and **festoon** them with strings of garlic; for example, drape the garlic strings between two nails driven into either side of each door or window.
2. People such as chronic complainers who find fault with everything and everyone around them are regarded as **malcontents** by those who have to work with them.

In the first sentence, "for example" signals that a description of *festoon* will follow. From this example, you can determine that *festoon* means "to drape from one point to another." In the second sentence, the words "such as" signal an example of the kind of people that most others would call *malcontents:* people who see the bad side of everything.

When a writer uses examples to define a word, you may not get an exact definition. Instead, you may have to infer, or figure out, the meaning from information provided in the example. By the way, in the preceding sentence, what does *infer* mean? How do you know? Is an example or definition connection provided in the sentence?

EXERCISE A.4

Writers often provide an example to help explain the meaning of a word in context. Read the following sentences, then circle the correct definition of each boldface word.

1. People from all over the United States showed their **beneficence** by offering help to the victims of Hurricane Andrew.

   a. sorrow

   b. anger

   c. kindness

2. The couple felt they could not endure the **cacophony** of loud music and all-night partying coming from the apartment next door.

   a. humor

   b. melody

   c. harsh sound

3. The antique sofa was so large that the movers had to **dismantle** it and carry it into the house in four pieces.

   a. take apart

   b. destroy

   c. uncover

The Contrast Connection

Another common technique that writers use to reveal what a word means is to say what it does *not* mean. Look at the next two sentences. See if you can guess the meaning of the boldface word by finding its *antonym,* opposite, in the sentence.

1. No two people could be more unalike than my brother Carlos, who is stubborn, and my brother Victor, who is **tractable.**
2. My friend thought my excuse—my dog chewed up my essay—was unbelievable, but I hoped my instructor was inexperienced enough to find it **credible.**

In the first sentence, Victor is not like Carlos. If Carlos is stubborn, then Victor must be easy to control or manage, because *stubborn* means "not easy to persuade." In the second sentence, the friend finds the excuse unbelievable. The student hopes that the instructor won't feel the same way and that the instructor will find the excuse *credible,* or believable.

If you think a sentence might contain a contrast connection, look for an antonym of the word you are trying to define. Look for a comparison or a contrast of ideas or meanings. Also look for signal words such as *but, however, unlike,* and *different.*

EXERCISE A.5

An author can define a word in context by stating the antonym, or opposite, in the sentence. Read the following sentences, then circle the correct definition of each boldface word.

1. Because Julia was an **introspective** person by nature, she preferred to solve her own problems instead of talking about them.
   a. artistically talented
   b. talkative
   c. looking inward
2. The Rembrandt forgery was not discovered until an **authentic** painting by the artist was examined next to it.
   a. genuine
   b. colorful
   c. antique
3. For Keenan and Andrew to be able to enjoy working together cooperatively, they would have to overcome their **antipathy.**
   a. commitment
   b. fear of failure
   c. strong dislike

The Experience Connection

Sometimes it is difficult to see any connections in the contexts in which new or unfamiliar words appear. When this happens, you may be able to find an implied meaning, or you may have to rely on your experience with the situation described in the context. It also may help to read a little farther to see if the writer defines the word later on, or you might try looking back a few sentences to see if you missed something that might clarify the meaning of the unfamiliar word. If all else fails, use the dictionary.

See if you can use your experience to determine the meanings of the boldface words in the next two sentences.

1. Maria felt **elated** when she found that after studying especially hard for a test she had made an A.
2. Jay really wanted the job, but after the interview he was **disconsolate** because he knew the employer's attitude was definitely "Don't call us; we'll call you."

Your experience probably tells you that most students feel happy about receiving A's on tests. Therefore you can assume that Maria, in the first sentence, felt happy. To get the exact definition of *elated,* you would have to look the word up in the dictionary. *Elated* means "joyful." Your experience tells you that most people who believe they are going to be turned down for a job would feel unhappy or depressed. You could therefore conclude that *disconsolate,* in the second sentence, means "hopelessly sad, cheerless, and gloomy."

To make the experience connection, ask yourself what you know about the situation described in the context. Ask yourself what you would be likely to do in that situation or how you would probably feel. Also consider how most people would act or feel in the situation described.

EXERCISE A.6

Your experience can help you determine the meanings of words when you cannot find any other connections. Read the following sentences, then circle the correct definition of each boldface word.

1. Although Nancy and Alan had been looking forward to seeing the latest action movie, they decided to wait a week for the crowds to **subside.**

   a. increase

   b. decrease

   c. exit

2. Clarence was **incredulous** that he hadn't won the lottery because he was sure his new mathematical system had picked the winning numbers.

   a. excited

   b. filled with disbelief

   c. depressed

3. Instructors become frustrated when their questions **elicit** nothing from students but blank stares.

   a. close up

   b. demand

   c. bring out

YOUR DICTIONARY: THE LAST WORD

If you learn how to use word parts and context connections effectively, you may need to use your dictionary only as a last resort or to verify your construction of a word's meaning. To improve your use of the dictionary, make sure you know how to read each entry. A *dictionary entry* consists of a word and its definitions. An entry contains five common parts.

The Word Divided into Syllables. Words are broken down into syllables for ease of pronunciation—for example,

pe·des·tri·an

Pronunciation. There is a pronunciation guide at the bottom of each page of the dictionary. Within each entry, the pronunciation of each syllable is indicated by a mark above the vowel or by a special symbol. Accent marks show which syllables to emphasize. The full pronunciation for a word appears in parentheses beside it:

pe·des·tri·an (pə-dĕs′-trē-ən)

The upside-down *e* indicates a special vowel sound similar to the sound of the *a* in *about* and the *e* in *item.* Every dictionary contains a pronunciation key in its introductory pages. Following are common pronunciation symbols for the vowels (*a, e, i, o,* and *u*) and example words to show how they sound.

Symbol	**Example**
ă	**a**crobat
ā	displ**ay**
â	b**a**re
ä	f**a**rther
ĕ	m**e**t
ē	fl**ee**
ĭ	s**i**t
ī	r**i**pe
î	we**i**rd
ŏ	r**o**t
ō	h**oe**
oi	p**oi**se
ou	p**ou**t
o͝o	c**oo**k
o͞o	b**oo**t
ŭ	b**u**t
ûr	p**ur**ge

Part of Speech. The part of speech follows each word and is indicated by an abbreviation—for example, *n.* for *noun, v.* for *verb, adj.* for *adjective.* When more than one definition is given, a part of speech indicator appears before each definition. This can be very useful if you are writing a paper and you need to check whether you have used the correct form of a word.

Definitions. Most words have more than one definition; each one is numbered. Don't make the mistake of looking up a word, reading the first definition, and believing you have found the appropriate meaning. The first definition may not fit the context in which your word appears. For example, do you remember this sentence from a previous section in the chapter?

It is strange how an experience can seem unique or unusual to some people and merely ***pedestrian*** *to others.*

Now read the *American Heritage Dictionary*'s entry for *pedestrian.*

pe•des•tri•an (pə-dĕs′tre-ən) *n.* One who travels on foot; a walker. —*adj.* **1.** Of, relating to, or made for pedestrians. **2.** Going or performed on foot. **3.** Undistinguished; ordinary: *pedestrian prose.* [< Lat. *pedester, pedestr-,* going on foot < *pedes,* a pedestrian < *pēs, ped-,* foot. See **ped-***.] —**pe•des′-tri•an•ism** *n.*

You can see that the definition numbered 3 best fits the meaning intended in the sentence.

Some words or terms have specialized meanings, which are indicated by the abbreviation of a subject-area word preceding the definition. For example, if a word is used as a biological term, the abbreviation *Biol.* appears in front of the term's definition. In what subject area is the following term used?

pedal point *n. Mus.* A note, usu. in the bass and on the tonic or dominant, sustained through harmonic changes in the other parts. [POINT, musical note.]

As you can see, *pedal point* is a musical term.

Etymology. A dictionary entry also contains the word's origin in square brackets. Look again at the entry for *pedestrian.* The explanation that follows the abbreviation *Lat.* in brackets tells you that *pedestrian* comes from a Latin root meaning "foot."

In some dictionaries, a list of synonyms (words similar in meaning) may be included in an entry. Some dictionaries even include a sample sentence to show how a word is used.

You need a desk dictionary in your study area—in addition to any paperback version that you take to class. A desk dictionary contains more complete entries for each word.

CONFIDENCE BUILDER

How to Learn Specialized or Technical Terms

Many of your courses employ a specialized vocabulary or set of terms to describe problems, principles, concepts, and situations unique to the subject area. A major task for you as a college student is to learn and use this new language. Instructors use special terminology in their lectures, and they expect you to use it when you write reports, essays, and answers to test questions. Textbook writers often call attention to terms that you should learn by introducing them at the beginning of the chapter or including them in a "words to learn" list at the end. Specialized terms are often printed in italics, boldface, or a special color; at the back of your textbook you may find a glossary that lists the terms and their meanings.

Use these three strategies to learn the specialized language essential to your understanding of a subject.

1. Apply your new knowledge of prefixes, suffixes, and roots to help you identify the word parts that commonly occur in the terms of one of your courses. List these word parts and learn them. They are clues to the meanings of any terms in which they appear. For example, here is a short list of word parts and example terms from a biology course.

Word Parts	Meanings	Example words
anthropo-	human	**anthropo**id
anti-	against	**anti**body, **anti**toxin
-oid	like	anthrop**oid**
photo-	light	**photo**synthesis, **photo**tropic

2. Learn the symbols and abbreviations that stand for special terms and formulas. In science courses, learn symbols such as F = force, W = work, D = distance, and T = time. In math courses, learn symbols such as r = radius, x^2 = square, π = pi; learn formulas that combine the terms, such as the formula for the area of a circle: $A = \pi r^2$.

3. Make a *personal glossary* for each of your courses that employs a specialized vocabulary. Add to your list each time you encounter a new term. You can organize these terms by chapter and record them on flash cards, in a notebook, or in your computer.

YOUR SYSTEM FOR LEARNING NEW WORDS

If you really want to learn a new word, you must make it your own. Words that you look up once and forget and words that you memorize for a test and never review again are quickly forgotten. To keep words in your long-term memory, you have to use them, review them often, and make them part of your *working vocabulary,* the words you use regularly.

You need a system for learning and remembering words. The best system is one that you devise yourself, that fits your learning style. Many students make flash cards for learning words, terms, formulas, and other information. Vocabulary flash cards are easy to make and fun to use. If you would like to try this strategy, here's how to do it.

Buy a pack of 3″ by 5″ note cards. You might want to get cards in different colors for different courses. Print the word on one side of the card and the definition on the other side (see the example in Figure A.1). Include other information that will help you remember the word, such as a memory cue for quick recall, the word in a sentence to show its meaning, and the part of speech. If you often misspell words, use a color to highlight spelling problem areas.

To learn your words, recite from your note cards. Keep the cards with you so that you can review them between classes, while traveling to and from campus, or while waiting in offices or lines. Follow these steps.

1. **Turn all cards so that just the words you are learning are showing.**
2. **Look at each word, and recite its definition.**
3. **Turn the card over and check yourself.**
4. **If you are right, lay the card down.**
5. **If you are wrong, or if you can't remember, put the card at the bottom of the deck in your hand to review again.**
6. **Keep on until there are no cards left in the deck you are holding.**
7. **Turn all the cards so that just the definitions are showing. Repeat steps 2–6, but this time look at the definitions and then recite the words.**

Another way to study vocabulary is to keep a vocabulary notebook. A notebook does not offer the flexibility of cards because it is not as easy to carry around, but many students find this method useful.

1. **Draw a line down the left side of a notebook page so that there is a 3″ margin.**
2. **Write the word in the left column.**
3. **Write the definition directly across from the word in the right column.**

FIGURE A.1 Vocabulary Flash Card

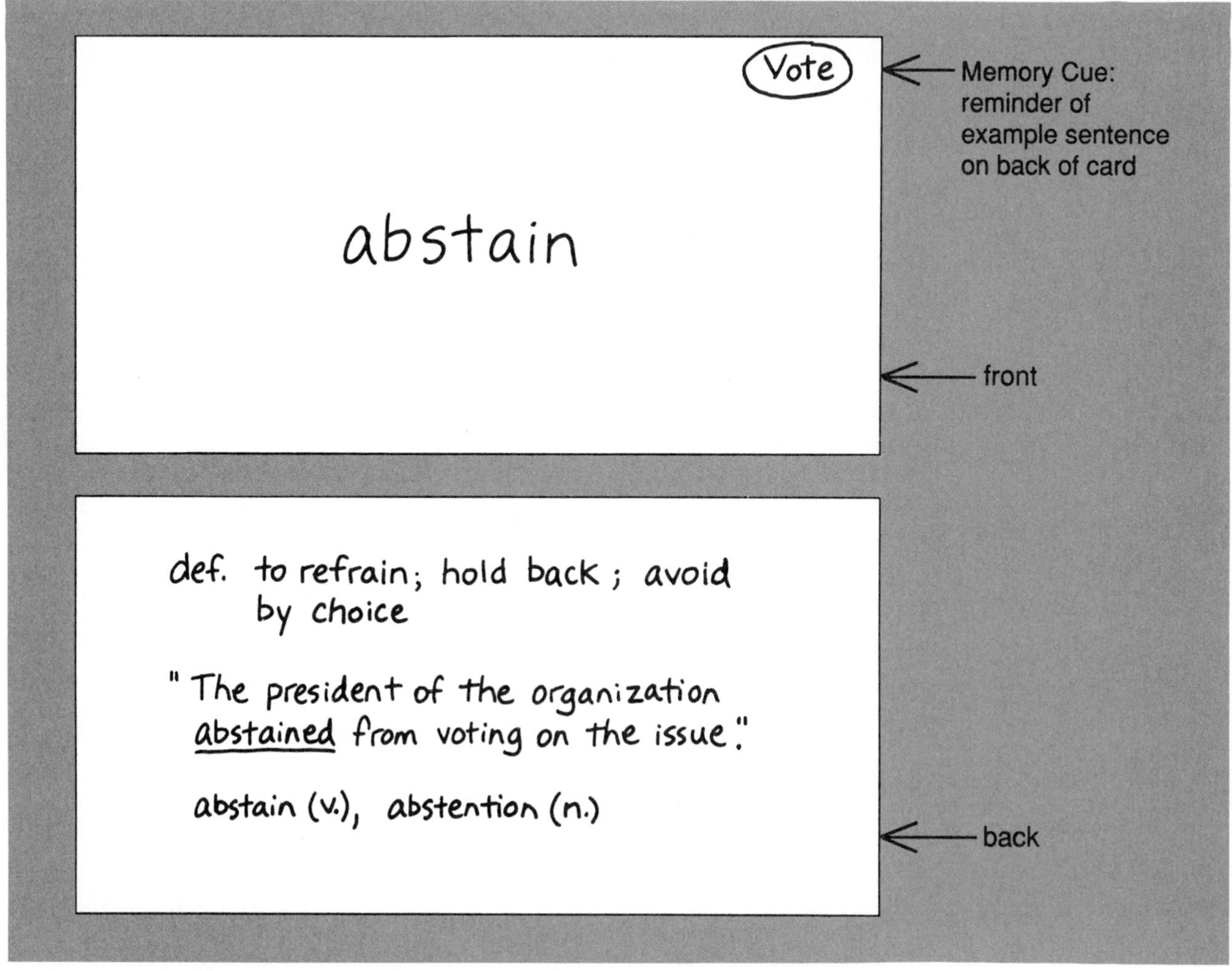

4. **Cover up one of the columns and recite. Slide a sheet of paper down to check each answer as you go.**
5. **To make a quick practice test, cover one column with a clean sheet of paper. Write the words or definitions on this paper; then check your answers.**

Review your flash cards or the words in your notebook frequently. Each time you add new words to your list, review all of your words. Use them in writing and speaking. Frequent use and review is the key to making new words part of your working vocabulary.

EXERCISE A.7

Try the flash card system for learning new words. Imagine that you are taking an art history course. Two of the specialized terms used by your instructor are *triptych* and *pointillism.* Fill in the blanks below to show how you would make a complete flash card for each word. Use a dictionary or a glossary from an art book to obtain the information.

Side 1: **triptych**

(Highlight spelling problem areas in color.)

Memory cue: ______________________________

Side 2: definition: ______________________________

Use the word in a sentence: ______________________________

____

Word(s) plus part of speech: ______________________________

Side 1: **pointillism**

(Highlight spelling problem areas in color.)

Memory cue: ______________________________

Side 2: definition: ______________________________

Use the word in a sentence: ______________________________

____

Word(s) plus part of speech: ______________________________

Using this format, you may want to make a full set of flash cards for any course that uses specialized terms. Consult with your instructor for a list of words to learn.

COMPUTER CONFIDENCE

Use a Computer to Make a Glossary

Many college courses require knowledge of a specialized vocabulary. As the semester or quarter proceeds, your instructor will begin to assume that you have learned the jargon and terminology of your course's subject matter. Your computer can help you with this learning if you take the time to input new words and copy them into a glossary file.

Create your own glossary by following these simple steps:

1. As you take notes during a lecture or while you are reading a textbook, underline specialized terms or difficult words that you need to learn or review. When you enter your notes into the computer,

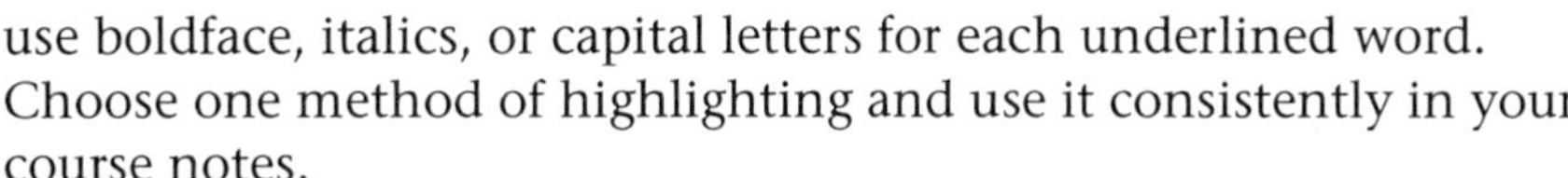

use boldface, italics, or capital letters for each underlined word. Choose one method of highlighting and use it consistently in your course notes.

2. Create a new file for each of your courses. After inputting the day's notes for each class, scroll through the notes and copy each highlighted word into the glossary file for that course.
3. Using a dictionary and your textbook as references, write a definition for each word in the course glossary. If you need further clarification, write a sentence using the word in context. Try to note any memory cues that relate to the instructor's specific use of the word in class.
4. Alphabetize the words in your glossary so that you can find words with ease. Many software programs have an alphabetizing feature. Constantly update your glossary as the course proceeds. For a science or engineering class that has dozens of technical words, classify the words into categories for easy access.
5. Print out each glossary as often as you update it. Make a separate glossary for each of your classes, and keep it with each course notebook. These glossaries will become handy personal dictionaries that you can study from and refer to in class.
6. When you are studying for an exam, review the course vocabulary by scrolling through your glossary. Look at a word alone and try to define it before scrolling forward to check your accuracy.
7. At the end of a semester, keep your printouts as references for more advanced or interrelated courses that you might take in the future.

CRITICAL THINKING APPLICATION

Form a group according to the guidelines explained in Chapter 1. Select five words from your reading or from one of your courses. On one sheet of paper, list the words and their definitions. On another sheet of paper, write a sentence using each of your words. Underline your word in each sentence. To make your sentences clearly show the meanings of the underlined words, build into them the context connections explained in this chapter: *definition, example, contrast, experience.* Review the connections, if necessary, before you begin. Use the sentences in Exercises A.3–A.6 as models for constructing your own sentences.

When you finish, exchange papers with another group and try to determine the meanings of each other's underlined words. If you have made good use of context connections in writing your sentences, you should have no trouble figuring out the words' meanings. Verify your answers by reading each other's definitions.

SUMMARY

Following is a summary of the chapter and an outline of its important points.

Words are made up of prefixes, roots, and suffixes. These word parts work together to construct the meanings of words. Knowledge of common prefixes, roots, and suffixes will help you determine the meanings of unfamiliar words. When you combine your knowledge of word parts with the four context connections of *definition, example, contrast,* and *experience,* you will have a reliable system for constructing word meanings.

Most dictionary entries have five parts: the word divided into syllables; the word with symbols for pronunciation; an abbreviation for part of speech; definitions; and an etymology. Some dictionary entries list synonyms. Understanding and using these parts will help you get more out of your dictionary.

To retain new words in your long-term memory, review them often. Devise a system for learning and remembering words, such as the flash card and notebook systems discussed in this chapter.

How To Develop Your Vocabulary

I. Be able to recognize common word parts and their meanings:

- **A.** Prefixes
- **B.** Roots
- **C.** Suffixes

II. Look for connections between unfamiliar words and the contexts in which they appear:

- **A.** The definition connection
- **B.** The example connection
- **C.** The contrast connection
- **D.** The experience connection

III. Know what the common parts of a dictionary entry are and how to use them:

- **A.** The word divided into syllables
- **B.** The pronunciation symbols
- **C.** The word's part of speech
- **D.** The definitions of the word
- **E.** The etymology of the parts that make up the word

IV. Apply strategies to learn and retain new vocabulary words in your long-term memory:

- **A.** Frequent review
- **B.** A system for learning new words, such as the flash card and notebook systems explained in the chapter
- **C.** A system you develop

YOUR SUCCESS JOURNAL

For your next journal entry, explain how vocabulary is important in the courses you are taking now. For example, which courses require you to learn and remember technical words or terms and definitions? What strategy do you use for learning words and terms? How do you plan to modify your strategy as a result of reading this chapter?

Date: ______________________________

SUPPLEMENTARY CHAPTER B

Using Your Library, Doing Research

In every subject you take in college, there are issues to consider. In a psychology class, the issues include the ways different personality theories explain human behavior. How do we learn? How does the memory work? What behaviors are normal or abnormal? In a literature class, the issues may include different ways of reading or interpreting great works of fiction. A related issue you may debate is what *are* considered great works and why? Issues in a business course revolve around management styles, marketing theories, or accounting procedures, for example. Any one of these courses, as well as many others, may require you to write a research paper or report on an issue the class has explored. Or you may have the option of choosing your own topic on a related issue or one that interests you.

An *issue* is a matter of controversy that is difficult to resolve because people may have strong opinions about it. An issue may be a problem that needs a solution or a question that needs answering. Few issues are simple, and most are affected by related issues. To have an informed opinion about any issue, you must carefully weigh the evidence on all sides.

WHY DO RESEARCH?

There are many purposes for research: to define an issue, to add to the accumulated evidence on one side of an issue, and to propose a resolution to an issue are a few of them. Your instructors also have a purpose in asking you to do research. There are few other course-related activities in which critical thinking plays as significant a role. You grow intellectually as you wrestle with different opinions you encounter in your research; in addition, you may arrive at a more informed opinion and perhaps even add to the body of information available.

To do effective research, you must become *information literate;* that is, you must know what kind of information you are looking for and how to use the resources that will enable you to find it. Knowing how and where to find information in the library is only the first step. Knowing what to do with that information once you've found it is a much more critical skill. This chapter explains how to use your library and how to conduct the research needed for writing a research paper.

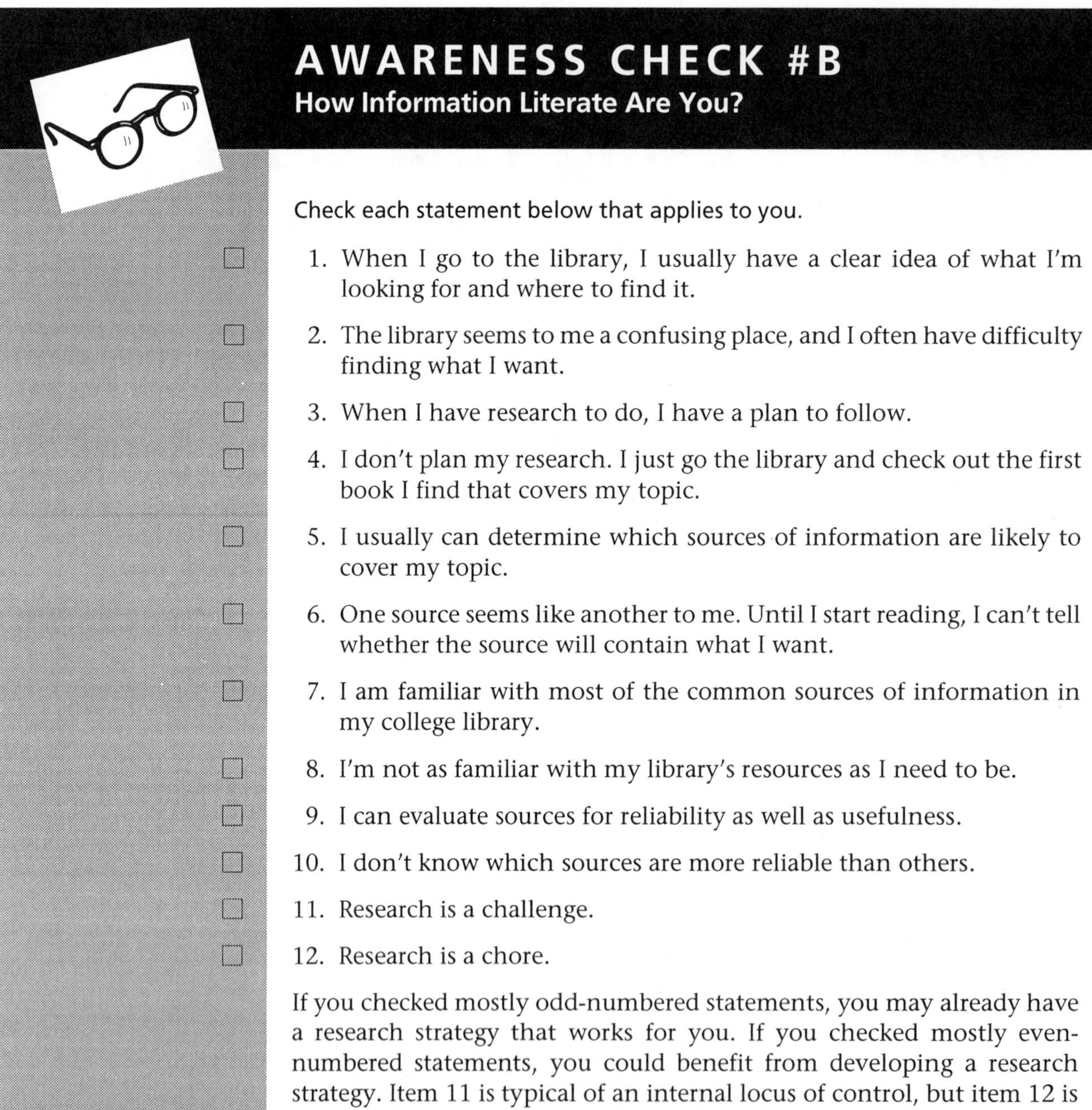

AWARENESS CHECK #B

How Information Literate Are You?

Check each statement below that applies to you.

- ☐ 1. When I go to the library, I usually have a clear idea of what I'm looking for and where to find it.
- ☐ 2. The library seems to me a confusing place, and I often have difficulty finding what I want.
- ☐ 3. When I have research to do, I have a plan to follow.
- ☐ 4. I don't plan my research. I just go the library and check out the first book I find that covers my topic.
- ☐ 5. I usually can determine which sources of information are likely to cover my topic.
- ☐ 6. One source seems like another to me. Until I start reading, I can't tell whether the source will contain what I want.
- ☐ 7. I am familiar with most of the common sources of information in my college library.
- ☐ 8. I'm not as familiar with my library's resources as I need to be.
- ☐ 9. I can evaluate sources for reliability as well as usefulness.
- ☐ 10. I don't know which sources are more reliable than others.
- ☐ 11. Research is a challenge.
- ☐ 12. Research is a chore.

If you checked mostly odd-numbered statements, you may already have a research strategy that works for you. If you checked mostly even-numbered statements, you could benefit from developing a research strategy. Item 11 is typical of an internal locus of control, but item 12 is typical of an external locus of control. Whether research is a chore or a challenge is largely a matter of attitude. To develop an internal orientation toward research, think positively about the activity. Ask yourself, "What's in it for me?" Then expect to be rewarded, and you will. The reward may be an enlarged frame of reference, new facts or insights to add to your increasing store, or a feeling of accomplishment, which is always a confidence builder.

FINDING YOUR WAY AROUND THE LIBRARY

You are living in what many have called *the information age*. Knowing what information you need, where to find it, and how to use it are skills essential to success in college and in any kind of work that requires you to find information and either report on it or use it to complete a task. Many business transactions involve an exchange of information, and entire careers are built around information processing. Your introduction to the information age begins in the library. Keys to getting around in your college library are the following:

- Library Personnel
- Information Retrieval Systems
- Your Library's Resources

These three keys unlock the mystery of research and make it possible for you to find the information you need.

Library Personnel

Whether you are researching several sources in the library or trying to find one magazine article, the process of locating that information can be an overwhelming experience. If you are like many students, you may not know where to begin. Some students enter the library with good intentions, but become frustrated and either leave without finding what they came for or settle for the first piece of information they *can* find even though it may not be exactly what they want. An important part of a librarian's job is to help you overcome that frustration.

Librarians and their assistants know the library well. Furthermore, they are usually people who love books and who are fascinated by the search for information. If you have a research project to do or a piece of information to find, ask a librarian or library assistant to point you in the right direction. If you need a general orientation to the library and its resources, ask if there is a guided tour or a videocassette recording that explains what your library provides. Some libraries have a printed guide or handbook available that explains their resources and where they are located.

There is no way to avoid the time it takes to find information in the library, but you can make that time productive and rewarding if you know *how* to find information.

Information Retrieval Systems

Suppose you are interested in the possible effects of nutrition on memory, and you wonder whether eating certain foods or lacking vitamins or other nutrients affects your brain's ability to process and retain information. A book on how memory works or an article about the effects of nutrition on memory might contain the information you want. To find a book, you could use the library's *card catalog*. This file is a set of drawers that contain a card for each book in the library. Books are organized by *subject, author,* and *title.*

More likely than not, however, your library may be using a computerized card catalog. Here books and audiovisual materials are also classified by subject, author, and title and are usually organized according to the Library of Congress system of numbering. Furthermore, the catalog may be networked with other libraries' holdings so that you can access them to find what you need.

To access a listing for a book or videocassette recording from a computerized card catalog, type responses on a keyboard in answer to questions that come up on the computer screen. First decide which file you want: subject, title, or author. Once you're in the file, use key words to find what you need. For example, if you type in "memory," a list of your library's holdings on this topic will come up on the screen. If you see a title of a book that interests you, print out the listing, which also has the book's call number. Taking the printout with you, go to the stacks and look for the book.

Your library may have other computerized information retrieval systems. For example, there are computerized indexes to periodicals, newspapers, journals, and other resources. These too may be networked with other listings, and each may require access using a different set of commands. Systems vary from one library to another, so your best bet is to first find out what computerized systems your library has and what kind of information they contain. Then have a librarian demonstrate each system's use. Computerized systems are efficient, but they are only one of your library's many resources.

Your Library's Resources

In addition to books, your library contains many other sources of information including *reference works* and *periodicals* (magazines, journals, and newspapers). There probably is a map or drawing posted that shows where you can find these resources. Some of them wiil be shelved, others may be collected on microfilm or microfiche. *Reference works* include encyclopedias, dictionaries, almanacs, atlases, books of quotations, biographical indexes, indexes to newspapers and periodicals, and government documents. If you want to find Lapland on a map, look in an *atlas,* which is a collection of maps. If you want to know the batting average of a favorite baseball player or the average rainfall in your state, you can find that and other statistics on such subjects as sports, commerce, and politics in an *almanac,* which is published yearly. If you want to know the site of a geographical area such as a river, volcano, mountain range, or a sea, look in a *gazetteer.* A reference book such as *Bartlett's Familiar Quotations* contains well-known sayings by noteworthy people. You can use this source to find an appropriate quotation to use as the opening of a speech, for example. If you want to find a magazine or journal article on memory, try the *Reader's Guide to Periodical Literature* or the index of a journal that is likely to contain articles of the type you are looking for. For statistics or other information on AIDS in the United States, you might turn to a *government document* on the subject, or

EXERCISE B.1

Either working with a partner or on your own, go to the library and find the answers to the following questions. Indicate the resource that contains the information. This exercise will introduce you to some resources you may not have realized are in your library and will serve as a guide to the kind of information they contain.

1. What was the most frequent cause of death among women in 1962? In 1992?
2. Who wrote *The Big Sea,* and when was it published?
3. Who flew the first manned space vehicle?
4. What is the population of Washington D.C.?
5. What is the definition of *burnout?*
6. What college or university did Dr. Martin Luther King, Jr. attend?
7. Who said "I shall return"?
8. An article written by Mike Pride about Christa McAuliffe appeared in the February 10, 1986 edition of *Newsweek*. What is the title of the article? Who was Christa McAuliffe?
9. People of what age and sex had the highest number of traffic fatalities in 1992?
10. What teams played in the World Series in 1980? Who won?

your college may have a file on AIDS in its vertical file. The *vertical file* contains large manila envelopes or folders filled with clippings, pictures, pamphlets, and other pieces of information on certain topics. It's a good place to get an overall feel for a subject you might want to explore in depth, using other resources.

Finding your way around your library and getting the information you need, is a matter of knowing what the resources are, where to find them, and how to use them. Library personnel are there to assist you, but you must ask for their help.

STARTING YOUR RESEARCH PAPER

It is important to allow the necessary time to complete a research project. Getting started is much easier if you know what is involved and plan accordingly. Figure B.1 is an overview of the research and writing process that lists typical steps you might follow to complete your project.

FIGURE B.1 Overview of the Research and Writing Process

1. Choose a topic.
2. Narrow topic to an issue (problem or question to be researched).
3. Determine audience and purpose (who will read your paper and why).
4. Write preliminary thesis statement (the central idea, or point of your research paper).
5. Gather and evaluate information.
6. Compile a working bibliography (list of possible sources).
7. Write final thesis statement.
8. Synthesize (put together) information from all your sources using an outline, chart, or other organizer.
9. Draft your paper.
10. Revise your paper and write final copy.
11. Compile a final bibliography (list of sources actually used).

You may not follow all the steps listed in Figure B.1; for example, you may decide not to try to write a thesis statement until after you have gathered your information and done some thinking about it. Furthermore, the steps don't necessarily have to be followed in the order listed. During the drafting process you may decide that you need more information and that another trip to the library is necessary. However you adapt the steps to fit your project, schedule your time so that you are not trying to complete the work at the last minute.

EXERCISE B.2

Either working with a partner or on your own, discuss the eleven steps listed in Figure B.1. Talk about research assignments you have done and problems you had completing them. Even if you have not, as yet, done a research project, determine how much time you think it would take you to complete each step on the list effectively. Which steps do you think will require the most time? Finally, imagine that it is midterm, and you have a research paper due at the end of the term. Using a calendar and the chart below, work out a possible schedule for completing the project.

Steps in the Process	Complete by (date)
Choose topic.	______________
Narrow topic to an issue.	______________
Determine audience and purpose.	______________
Write preliminary thesis statement.	______________

Gather and evaluate information.	______
Compile working bibliography.	______
Write final thesis statement.	______
Synthesize information on outline or chart.	______
Draft paper.	______
Revise paper and write final copy.	______
Compile final bibliography.	______

Choosing and Narrowing Topics

Though some instructors assign specific research topics, you will often have the opportunity to select your own. When choosing a topic, keep these guidelines in mind:

- **Be realistic.** Select a topic for which resources are readily available, either from your college library or through interlibrary loan.
- **Choose a significant topic.** Choose a topic of general interest and concern that allows you to think critically about the information and opinions you encounter in your research. Avoid trivial, overly technical, and overworked topics such as abortion, capital punishment, and gun control. Though these are significant, they are emotional hot spots, and it may be difficult to find information on them that is free of bias and logically supported.
- **Choose a topic of personal interest.** Since your research project will take some time, avoid boredom and burnout by selecting a topic that arouses your curiosity or that you think is important.
- **Ask your instructor for ideas.** Your instructor may have some suggestions or helpful hints for narrowing topics. He or she will also be able to tell you the names of major works or authors in your field of interest and steer you in the right direction as you begin your research.

Suppose the human memory has always interested you. "Why do we forget?" and "How can we improve memory?" are questions for which you would like answers. Let's say you do some research into ways to improve memory and stumble upon the idea that listening to music may enhance learning and improve retention. "That's strange," you think. For haven't you always heard that listening to music interferes with learning and remembering? You begin to wonder what kind of music could enhance learning, and under what conditions it could act as a memory cue. Does listening to music work as a memory aid for only certain kinds of information, or can it improve retention of any material? Now you have an issue to research, a question to answer, and a way to narrow your topic: Does listening to music help or hinder your memory? The topic of memory itself is too broad for a research paper. Your narrowed topic deals with only one of the many possible aids to memory.

The prewriting strategies discussed in Chapter 15 are useful for narrowing a topic for a research paper. To help you generate ideas, try *brainstorming.* Another useful strategy is *clustering,* or making an *idea cluster.* To make a cluster, draw a circle in the middle of a sheet of paper and write your topic in the circle. As you get an idea, draw a line out from the center of the circle, make a new circle, and write your idea in it. As you think of related ideas, connect them to this circle. If you get a different idea, go back to the center circle and start a new cluster. See Figure B.2 for an example.

Sandy, who made this cluster, wanted to write about animal rights, but she didn't know how to narrow her topic. She started with animal rights in the center circle. As ideas came to her, she added more circles to her diagram. She stopped when it occurred to her that what she most wanted to write about was one animal under attack: the spotted owl. Making the cluster helped Sandy zero in on a specific topic related to the larger issue of animal rights. Her narrowed topic became *what we can do to save the spotted owl.*

EXERCISE B.3

Following is a list of ten possible research topics. Choose any three and narrow them down to topics you could write about if they were assigned to you.

1. gang violence
2. sports in your city
3. AIDS awareness or education
4. animal communication
5. mandatory drug testing
6. children's TV programs
7. an environmental issue
8. diets
9. cults
10. the works of an artist

Limited topic #1 ______________________________

Limited topic #2 ______________________________

Limited topic #3 ______________________________

FIGURE B.2 Clustering to Generate Ideas for Writing

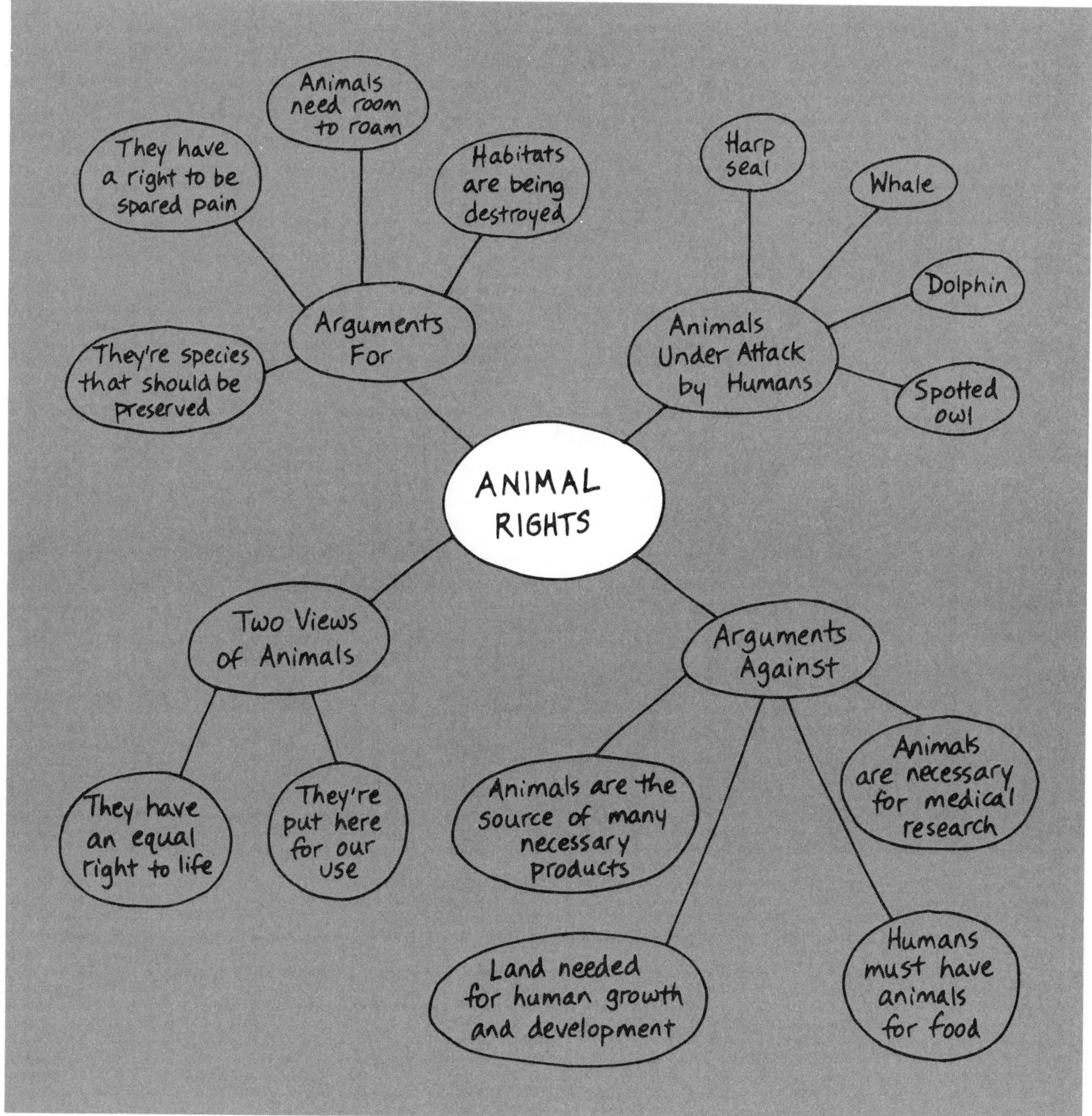

Determining Audience and Purpose

The *audience* for your paper may be just the instructor, or it may include students. Students and instructors are members of the general public. You can assume that they have some knowledge about your topic, and may have some personal interest or concern as well. To improve your **awareness of your audience,** answer these questions:

Why is my topic important?

What can I assume readers already know about my topic?

What more can I assume readers want or need to know about my topic?

How will their lives or thinking be affected by my research?

The *purpose* for your paper will be either to inform or persuade readers. To determine a purpose, turn your topic, or issue, into a question. If the question can be answered by facts and an explanation, your purpose is to inform. If the question can be answered by your opinion based upon a consideration of the evidence you've gathered, then your purpose is to persuade. Consider the following questions:

What kinds of music enhance learning and retention of information?

Should students listen to music while studying?

The first question can be answered by facts gathered from research; the purpose, therefore, is to inform. The second question can be answered by stating your opinion based upon your understanding of the evidence; the purpose, therefore, is to persuade.

Another way to arrive at a purpose for writing is to consider what effect you want your research to have on your audience. If you expect your readers to be enlightened (to know more about your topic than they did before reading your paper), then your purpose is to inform. If you expect your readers to change their minds or decide to act after reading your paper, then your purpose is to persuade.

EXERCISE B.4

For the topics you narrowed in Exercise B.3, would your purpose be to inform or to persuade? Why?

1. Topic ____________________

   Purpose ____________________

   Explanation ____________________

2. Topic ____________________

   Purpose ____________________

   Explanation ____________________

3. Topic ____________________

   Purpose ____________________

   Explanation ____________________

Writing Your Thesis Statement

The thesis statement of any essay, including a research paper, is its central idea. To arrive at a thesis statement, ask yourself these questions and answer them:

What is my narrowed topic (issue)?	*sex education in middle school*
What question do I have about my topic/issue?	*Why should sex education begin in middle school?*
What is my answer (thesis statement)?	*For sex education to have an impact on teenagers, it must begin in middle school as children near puberty.*

It is common to write a *preliminary,* or working, thesis statement before you begin your research so that you have a clear direction to follow. Knowing the central idea of your paper may guide your research because your primary purpose in writing a research paper is to support the thesis statement. As you learn about your topic, you may revise your thesis statement many times until you arrive at a final thesis statement. On the other hand, you may prefer to wait until you have done some research before you write your first thesis statement.

Suppose that after writing the above thesis statement about sex education and researching several sources, you decide that focusing on the age sex education should occur is too narrow. What you really want to write about is what makes an effective sex education program. Therefore, you come up with the following revised thesis statement:

> *An effective sex education program should begin before children reach puberty, and it should include an ethics and values component as well as instruction in birth control methods and safe sex.*

A good thesis will control your research paper's development and help you separate relevant from irrelevant information.

EXERCISE B.5 Using the topics and purposes from Exercise B.4, now write a thesis statement for each one. Follow the steps outlined below.

Topic #1

1. What is my narrowed topic (issue)?

____

2. What question do I have about my topic/issue?

____

3. What is my answer to the question (thesis statement)?

____

____

____

Topic #2

1. What is my narrowed topic (issue)?

   ____

2. What question do I have about my topic/issue?

   ____

3. What is my answer to the question (thesis statement)?

   ____

   ____

   ____

Topic #3

1. What is my narrowed topic (issue)?

   ____

2. What question do I have about my topic/issue?

   ____

3. What is my answer to the question (thesis statement)?

   ____

   ____

   ____

Developing Your Research Strategy

There is no single best way to conduct research. However, without a plan to follow you may spend hours searching through sources without finding anything pertinent. To avoid wasting time, you need a research strategy that will help you zero in on the sources most likely to address your topic. If you go to the library with a narrowed topic and perhaps even a preliminary thesis in mind, you have a good chance of finding the information you need. Furthermore, you will have something specific to tell your librarian if you decide to ask for assistance in getting started. A *research strategy* is a plan for finding information that leads you first to general references and then to more specific sources on your topic. The following typical research strategy steps will help you identify key words, know how to document your paper, and evaluate your sources.

1. **Identify key words** that will help you search for information on your topic. Key words and related terms that clearly identify your topic will

help you skim through tables of contents in books and headings in periodical indexes to find relevant information. Key words also are necessary to access information from a computerized card catalog or other data base. If your topic is AIDS, for example, the key words and terms *AIDS, STD (sexually transmitted disease), venereal disease,* and *immune disorders and deficiencies* may be useful. Because your librarian may have helped other students find information on your topic, he or she can probably help you compile a list of helpful key words and terms.

2. **Know how to document your paper.** Besides listing all your sources in a bibliography, you must document ideas you take from sources, or you run the risk of plagiarism. *Plagiarism* is writing someone else's ideas as if they were your own; it is a type of stealing. Different academic disciplines have their own *documentation styles,* or preferred ways of indicating the sources from which information is taken. The *MLA style,* developed by the Modern Language Association, is characteristic of research done in the humanities. Those who write in the biological sciences use the *CBE style,* developed by the Council of Biology Editors. If you write a paper for your psychology class, your instructor may want you to use the *APA style,* developed by the American Psychological Association for use in the social sciences.

   Before beginning your research, find out which documentation style your instructor requires. Then, as you are taking notes, be sure to record the information needed for documentation in the style you plan to use. Style manuals are available in your college bookstore and in commercial bookstores. You will probably want to purchase one or more for easy reference. Handbooks used in composition courses usually contain a section on style for research papers. If you have a handbook, check to see if there is a section on the style required for your research project. This may save you buying an additional manual.

3. **Evaluate sources** for reliability, objectivity, and usefulness. Primary sources are generally more reliable than secondary sources. *Primary sources* are an author's original work: poems, novels, short stories, essays, autobiographies, diaries, letters, speeches, first-hand reports of research experiments, surveys, and observations. If you use data from any of these sources, you have used primary sources. If you interview an expert or write and conduct your own survey, the data from either are primary sources. *Secondary sources* interpret data from primary sources, analyze experiments and surveys, draw conclusions, and explain events. A news reporter's analysis of a politician's speech is a secondary source. A sports writer's description of a game and conclusion regarding why a team won or lost is a secondary source. A recording of the game or a telecast of the players' and coaches' play analyses are primary sources. Book, film, and play reviews are all secondary sources. How many times have you read a film review (secondary source), then gone to the movie (primary source) and drawn a different conclusion from the reviewer's? A secondary source is only as reliable as its author's quality of research and degree of expertise in the subject.

An objective author reports facts and avoids using unsubstantiated opinions to support claims or draw conclusions. An author who gives even-handed treatment to both sides of an argument and acknowledges opposing views is considered more objective than one who does not. How objective, for example, is the Vatican's or NOW's (National Organization for Women) position on abortion? Objectivity may be difficult to determine unless you are familiar with an author's qualifications or have extensive background in your subject.

A source is only useful if it is relevant to your topic. Does the research address your subject? Does it provide new data to support your thesis? Furthermore, is it current? Check the publication date of the source before

CONFIDENCE BUILDER

Evaluating Sources of Information

You may have asked yourself, "How am I supposed to know whether an author is being objective or whether a secondary source is reliable?" You may also have had second thoughts about a source's usefulness. The following checklist for evaluating sources of information may be helpful to you in conducting your research.

- **Is the author an authority?** Check the author's background (degrees held, colleges attended, major field of expertise, works written, accomplishments) in a biographical reference such as one of the *Who's Who* references or the *Dictionary of American Biography.* Ask your librarian which biographical references are in your library's holdings.
- **Is the author a "name" in his or her field?** A recognized expert will be cited in textbooks, reference works, bibliographies, journal articles, and will be well known among other experts in the field. In addition, your librarian will either know or will help you find out how well known an author is.
- **Is the source reliable?** Newspapers and magazines having a wide readership and reputation for accuracy such as the *New York Times* and *Washington Post, Time,* and *Newsweek* are generally reliable. Academic journals are also reliable sources as are books published by large well-known publishers and university presses.
- **Is the source current?** The more recent the copyright date the more likely a source is to contain new research and discoveries. This is especially important in medicine, the sciences, engineering, and computer technology, where research is ongoing and information quickly outdated.
- **Is the source free of bias?** Read carefully to determine whether ideas are supported with hard evidence and logical reasoning. Unsupported opinions and emotional language are not characteristic of authoritative or scholarly research.

EXERCISE B.6

Prepare a report for the class on a current topic that interests you or choose one from the list in Exercise B.3. Then go to the library and gather information from three different sources: a newspaper, a magazine, and an additional periodical or government document. Then note any similarities and differences in the way the information is reported. Finally, evaluate your three sources for reliability, objectivity, and usefulness.

using it. In addition to these suggestions for determining reliability, objectivity, and usefulness, see also Chapter 13, pages 290–294.

TAKING EFFECTIVE NOTES

Three skills essential to taking notes and avoiding plagiarism are *quoting, paraphrasing,* and *summarizing.* These are all ways of indicating that some information is not your own, and all require documentation. Index cards are useful when you are taking notes. See Figure A.1 on page 209 for examples of index cards.

Quoting

At times you may want to *quote,* or state directly, what an author has said. Use quotations sparingly and use them only to support your ideas. Do not use a quotation as your thesis or topic statement. Quotations should be integrated within the text of your paper and *framed* by introductory and concluding remarks that explain the quotation's significance, as in the following example from a paper on Edith Wharton's *The Age of Innocence.*

> *As the novel opens, the Archers and Wellands are attending the opera. They are only peripherally interested in the music and story; their primary interest is to see who is there and to be seen. The opera is more a social obligation than an entertainment as the narrator suggests in Chapter 1 when commenting on the hasty departure of the spectators after the opera: "It was one of the great livery-stableman's most masterly intuitions to have discovered that Americans want to get away from amusement even more quickly than they want to get to it." This observation hints at one of the novel's minor themes that European art and culture were merely affectations of old New York's upper class, things they knew they should appreciate but did not enjoy, or if they enjoyed them then they did so for the wrong reasons.*

Remember to set off direct quotations in quotation marks and to document them according to the style you are using. When your quotation is five lines or longer, single space, indent, and omit quotation marks.

Paraphrasing

Like quotations, paraphrases should be used to support your thinking and should not form the bulk of your evidence. A *paraphrase* is a restatement in your own words of someone else's words or ideas. A paraphrase restates the entire passage, whether it be a sentence, paragraph, or longer piece of writing, so your paraphrase should be about as long as the original. Paraphrasing from authorities adds weight to your conclusions. To paraphrase accurately, use your own words and sentence structure to restate what the author says. Maintain the intent and emphasis of the original passage, and make sure you copy into your notes all the information you need to correctly document the source, such as page numbers, title of work, and author. The following example shows an original passage, and a paraphrase of it. The passage is about Maria Mitchell (1818–1889) who was the first professional woman astronomer in the United States.

Original

> *Mitchell was a self-taught astronomer, reading mathematics and science while a librarian at the Nantucket (Mass.) Atheneum (1836–56). In 1847, while helping her father, William Mitchell, survey the sky for the U.S. Coast Survey, she discovered a comet, for which she received worldwide attention. In 1848 she became the first woman elected to the American Academy of Arts and Sciences.*
>
> *In 1865 Mitchell was appointed professor of astronomy at Vassar College. There she gained distinction as a teacher of some of America's leading women scientists, including Christine Ladd-Franklin and Ellen Swallow-Richards. In 1873 her concern with the status of professional women led her to help found the Association for the Advancement of Women.*
>
> *Mitchell pioneered in the daily photography of sunspots; she was the first to find that they were whirling vertical cavities, rather than clouds, as had been earlier believed. She also studied comets, nebulae, double stars, solar eclipses, and the satellites of Saturn and Jupiter.*
>
>

Paraphrase

> *Maria Mitchell was a librarian in Nantucket from 1836 to 1856. During that time she studied mathematics and science and taught herself astronomy. In 1847, she discovered a comet while working with her father, William Mitchell, on the U.S. Coast Survey. The discovery brought her recognition, and led to several honors and appointments.*
>
> *In 1848, the American Academy of Arts and Sciences elected her as its first female member. In 1865, Vassar College appointed her as professor of astronomy. She was a noteworthy professor who taught other women of science; among them were Ellen Swallow-Richards and Christine Ladd-Franklin. In 1873 she was also one of the founders of the Association for the Advancement of Women.*
>
> *Mitchell was the first to discover through photography that sunspots were cavities, not clouds, and her studies led her to observe a wide range of astronomical phenomena: among them were the satellites of Saturn and Jupiter, solar eclipses, nebulae, double stars, and comets.*

Summarizing

A *summary* condenses into a few sentences the central idea of a passage. Therefore, your summary of a passage will be much shorter than the original. The following example is a summary of the passage about Maria Mitchell.

> *Maria Mitchell, daughter of the astronomer William Mitchell, was a Nantucket librarian who taught herself astronomy. Her discovery of a comet led to worldwide recognition and honors. She became professor of astronomy at Vassar where she taught other women of science. She was the first female member of the Academy of Arts and Sciences and the first to discover the true nature of sunspots. She was a founder of the Association for the Advancement of Women. Her studies led her to observe a wide range of astronomical phenomena.*

Whether you quote, paraphrase, or summarize, use a note-taking system that will help you keep track of your sources and compile a bibliography later. Take notes on index cards, because they are much easier to organize than pages. You can lay the cards out on a table and experiment with different ways of putting your information together. If you have more than one card for a source, number the cards. Use a different card for each topic you take notes on from the same source. Identify the source by title, author, and page number at the top of your index card, and indicate what type of note it is, quotation, paraphrase, summary, or your own idea. Use a symbol or a different color ink to distinguish notes that are your own independent ideas from those you get from sources. Once you have decided that you will definitely use a source, make a bibliography card for it. Later, when you compile your bibliography, arrange your cards in alphabetical order and type directly from them. Figure B.3 on pages 232–233 shows examples of four different kinds of note cards.

GATHERING INFORMATION

Now that you have a research strategy, you are ready to begin the search for information. There are many ways to find information; which ones you choose are up to you. You will do most of your research in the library, but there are other useful ways to gather information.

Interviewing Experts

An expert can offer an opinion on your topic or provide information either to support or deny what you have already found out. An expert may even suggest ways to approach your topic that you have not considered. Experts include college faculty, business and professional people who know something about your topic, and public officials and employees who act as spokespersons for their various agencies or corporations. To conduct effective interviews, try these tips.

FIGURE B.3 Index Cards for Quotation, Paraphrase, Summary, and Bibliography

Quotation

"Those two forces—a powerful surge among American blacks toward freedom, mostly inspired by the *Brown* decision, and a quantum leap in the power of the media—fed each other; each made the other more vital, and the combination created what became known as the Movement. Together, the Movement and the media educated America about civil rights."

Halberstam, David, *The Fifties.* New York: Villard Books, 1993, p. 429.

Paraphrase

The Civil Rights Movement, that began with the outcome of the *Brown* case, was the effect of two events: a growing desire among blacks for freedom and a powerful media that brought their struggle into America's living rooms.

Halberstam, David, *The Fifties.* New York: Villard Books, 1993, p. 429.

- **Schedule far ahead.** Most people have busy schedules, and you will probably have to make an appointment for your interview. Therefore, if you plan to use interviews as a source of information, get started right away.
- **Prepare a list of questions.** Go to the interview with a clear idea of what you want to find out. If you have thought through the questions you want to ask, you will make better use of the interview time. Be sure to phrase your questions so they call for an explanation rather than a yes or no answer.
- **Seek permission to quote the expert.** Also, ask permission if you plan to tape the interview to review later. If your expert does not want to be taped, be prepared to take notes.

FIGURE B.3 Index Cards for Quotation, Paraphrase, Summary, and Bibliography (continued)

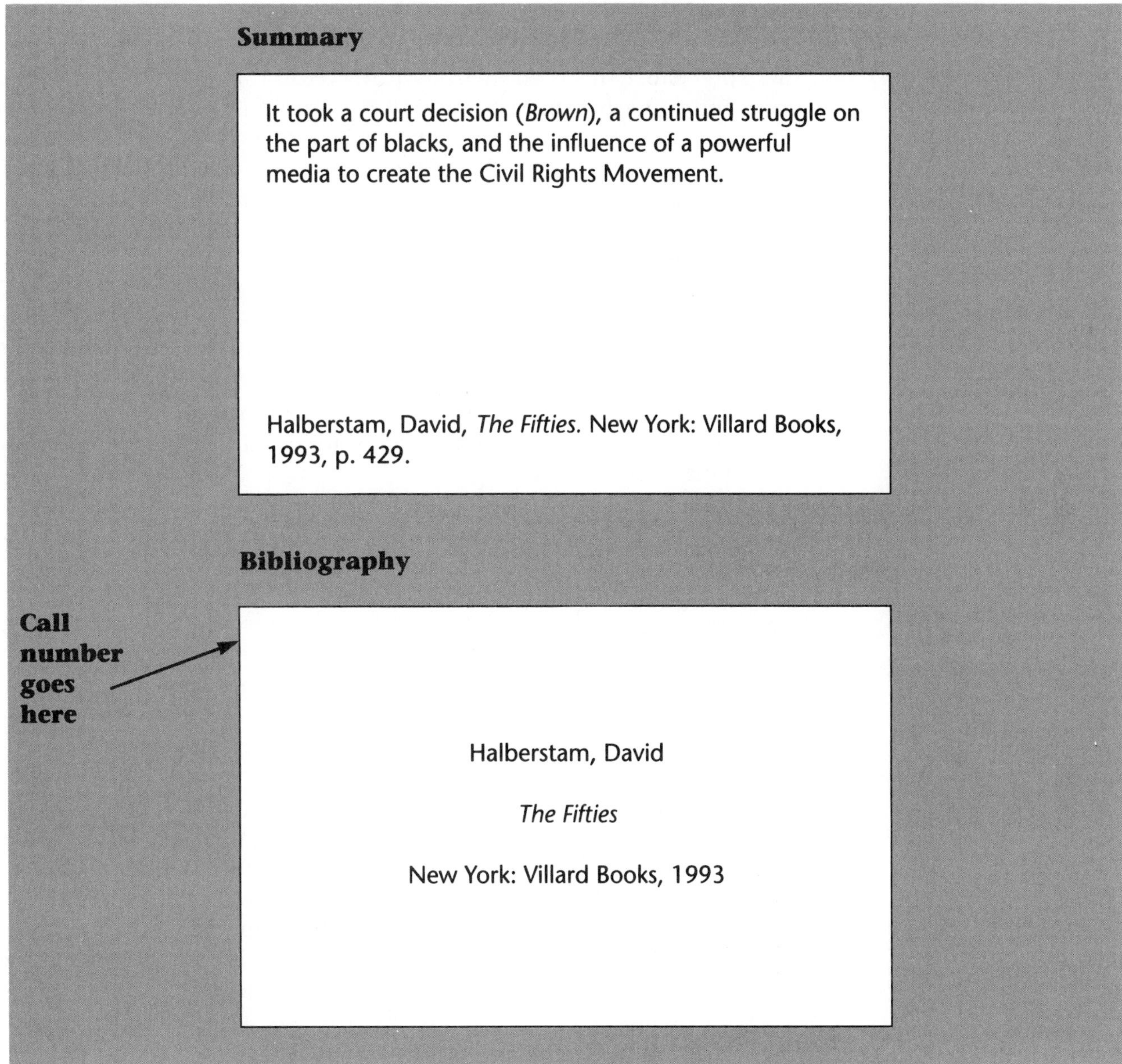

- **Evaluate information.** An expert may have a personal bias or special interest that colors his or her views on your topic. It may be useful to interview several people or to weigh the interview information against that gathered from other sources.
- **Express your thanks.** Show your appreciation by thanking the expert and sending a thank-you note.

Making Observations

Suppose you decide to write a paper on criminal justice in your state. The early-release program, whereby criminals who have not served their full sentences are released to make way for new offenders, is a controversial issue. You believe this is an ineffective answer to the problem of crowded prisons and decide to explore the topic further. In addition to any interviews and library research you may do, you decide to spend a few days observing court proceedings to get an idea of the number of prosecutions in a given day and the type of crimes being committed in your city or county.

To *observe* is to watch with a purpose and take notes on what you see. Your observations should be objective or based only on what you see or hear, not on what you think. Thinking about your observations and drawing conclusions come later. During the observation process, your purpose is only to gather facts. This is often difficult, because your mind will try to interpret the facts in spite of your efforts to be objective. For this reason, you should decide in advance what kind of information you are looking for. Make a checklist of facts you want to find out, or write a series of questions to be answered.

Locating the Best Sources

Plan to spend a minimum of fifteen to twenty hours doing research for a short (5,000–10,000 words) paper. A longer project will take more time. Also, some people work faster than others and some information takes a while to find. Take all of these factors into consideration as you plan your time. You will have to look through many sources, reading some carefully and taking notes and skimming others. Some of the material you want may not be available, and you will have to find alternative sources. All this takes time. Your librarians' assistance is invaluable, and though they will not do the research for you, they will point you in the right direction and teach you how to use any computerized search services your library provides.

A good place to start is with general reference works as explained on pages 218–219, which summarize a tremendous amount of information. From these you will want to move to more specialized references in an academic discipline that relates to your topic. Next you will want to check articles in periodicals that you can find by looking up your topic in a periodical index, such as the *Reader's Guide to Periodical Literature* or the *New York Times Index*—both are general indexes. Even more helpful in locating articles pertaining to your topic are the specialized periodical indexes, such as the *Education Index, Humanities Index,* or *Psychological Abstracts.* Finally, you will want to consult books for a more in-depth treatment of your topic. As explained on pages 217–218, most libraries now have a computerized card catalog and other data bases that make conducting an information search easier and more efficient.

EXERCISE B.7

Find out what specialized references are available in your library. Form small groups or pairs to complete this class project. Each group or pair should select an academic discipline from the list below. Go to the library and make a list of up to five specialized references available in your discipline. Ask a librarian to help you if necessary. List the title, author, publisher, and date of the reference and briefly summarize what kind of information it contains. Share your list with the rest of the class.

business and economics
education
fine arts
history
literature
mathematics
philosophy and religion
political science
science and technology
social sciences
performing arts (film, television, theatre)

PUTTING IT ALL TOGETHER

Your research paper should demonstrate that you understand your information. Rather than being a summary of what you have found, the research should support your thesis by providing the facts to support your opinion or to answer a question. Writing a research paper is the same as writing any other paper, except that, first, you are using other people's research to support your thesis instead of your own experience; and, second, because your research comes from other sources, you must document your paper.

To write an effective paper, start with an *outline.* Also, you will have to write several drafts to organize and present your ideas effectively. The *first draft* is your first attempt to put your notes together in a coherent way. As you write *additional drafts,* you will refine your organization. You may discover new ways of looking at your topic, leading to additional revisions until you have a *final draft* that is ready to hand in. A research paper develops from the introduction, to the body of the paper, to the summary or conclusion. In the introduction, get your readers' attention by telling them what your topic is, what you're going to say about it, and why it should interest them. In the body of your paper, explain your topic in detail by supporting your thesis statement with evidence you've gathered from your research. In the conclusion, summarize what you have said and leave your readers with a fresh insight in the form of a final thought you have on the topic or a challenge for them.

Figure B.4 is a checklist for revising your research paper.

FIGURE B.4 Revising Your Research Paper: A Checklist

Yes	No		
		1.	Do I have an effective introduction?
☐	☐		a. Audience identified
☐	☐		b. Topic and purpose stated
☐	☐		c. Thesis statement made
		2.	Have I supported my thesis well?
☐	☐		a. Important questions answered
☐	☐		b. Only relevant information included
☐	☐		c. Quotation and paraphrase used effectively
☐	☐		d. Flow of ideas smooth
☐	☐		e. Organization logical
☐	☐		f. Topic maintained
		3.	Have I concluded my paper effectively?
☐	☐		a. Research findings summarized
☐	☐		b. Final insight or challenge for readers given
☐	☐	4.	Have I documented correctly and where necessary?
☐	☐	5.	Have I used references from a variety of sources?
☐	☐	6.	Have I used correct grammar, punctuation, and spelling?
☐	☐	7.	Have I used the proper format for my paper?

CRITICAL THINKING APPLICATION

Practice paraphrasing, summarizing, and making note cards using the explanation and Figure B.3 on pages 232–233 as a guide. If you have a research assignment for one of your classes, select a passage from one of your sources and do a paraphrase and summary of it. Not only will you be practicing the skills, but you will be taking notes on information you can use in your research. If you do not have a research assignment, select a passage from one of your textbooks or from a magazine article to paraphrase and summarize.

SUMMARY

A summary, as explained on page 231, condenses the central idea of a passage into a few sentences. Following is a summary of this chapter and then a list of key ideas.

Research, a purposeful search for information, is key to writing a research paper. Because researching a topic takes time and planning, you need a strategy for getting started and completing the task. A good way to begin is to choose and narrow a topic, determine an audience and purpose for the research, and write a thesis statement. With topic, audience, purpose, and thesis in mind, you can find your way through the maze of resources in your library to get to the information you seek. Your strategy might include identifying key words to help you in your search; choosing a documentation style and using it as you make your notes; and evaluating sources for reliability, objectivity, and usefulness. Having a note-taking system is also an important part of your strategy, especially being able to quote, paraphrase, and summarize information from sources. Bolstered by an effective strategy, you can begin to gather information from interviews, personal observations, and your library's resources that include general and specialized references, periodicals, books, and other materials.

To organize your information into a unified paper, plan on writing several drafts. Your finished paper should have an introduction, body, and conclusion that support the thesis. Use an appropriate format, correct grammar, and accurate documentation. A checklist, such as the one in Figure B.4, p. 236 will guide your revision process.

- **The purposes of research include**

  to define an issue
  to add to accumulated evidence
  to propose a resolution to an issue
  to examine your thinking about an issue

- **To do effective research you must**

  become information literate
  know the steps to follow to plan and write a research paper
  be able to find your way around the library

- **To develop your own research strategy**

  identify key words for doing an information search
  know how to document papers
  evaluate sources of information

- **To take effective notes and avoid plagiarism**

  use quotations effectively, and cite sources
  paraphrase information and cite sources
  summarize information and cite sources
  make note cards to keep track of information

- **To gather information from various sources**

  interview experts
  make your own observations and take notes
  use all your library's resources

- **To write an effective paper**

  choose and narrow your topic
  make an outline
  write several drafts
  check for introduction, support, and conclusion
  document your paper

YOUR SUCCESS JOURNAL

To make research as enjoyable and challenging as possible, choose topics that are of vital interest to you whenever you have a choice. Take a moment to think about some possible research topics. What idea, discovery, issue, matter of controversy, or social problem is of great importance to you? Is there something you have always wanted to know more about but never had the time to research? Make a list of possible research topics. Let this journal entry be the start of an idea journal that you can use as a resource whenever you need a writing topic.

Date: ______________________________

Using the "Roundtable Discussions" Videotapes

The "Roundtable Discussions" videotapes are structured according to major tasks and their logically related skills. For example, Segment One focuses on taking notes in class along with active listening and on taking notes while studying along with the Cornell Method. Understanding this approach may be helpful as you integrate the video segments and activities with your textbook material and exercises.

In general, each videotape segment presents "the task" as a challenge for one of the students and "the skills, tools, and techniques" as helpful solutions that work for his or her friends. This approach is designed to introduce each challenge area in a context that will

- show students the actions that can be taken to deal with the challenge.
- show students that they probably already have many of the skills needed to succeed.
- stimulate students to identify their own challenges and begin to formulate ways of improving.
- motivate students to develop a personal approach to effective learning.

The sequence in which you use the video segments will depend upon the structure of your course and the ability level of your students. In most instances, you will probably want to play a specific video segment through as an introduction to the topic at hand, then replay appropriate portions of that segment as you address particular tools or techniques. Before showing each segment of the videotape, you may decide to conduct a brief discussion or self-assessment of your students' current attitudes, habits, and difficulties relating to the particular topic.

Part One presents a segment-by-segment description of the videotape contents and suggests classroom activities to help you link the videotape with your existing curriculum. In Part Two, you will find a summary exercise for each segment. These exercises are designed to demonstrate to students the practical value of the skills presented, not just in the classroom but also in many aspects of personal, academic, and professional life.

Part One: Segment Activities

Tape One—Study Strategies, Segment One: Note Taking

This segment of the videotape introduces the skills required for effective note taking and specifically addresses active listening, deciding what is important, mind mapping, and the Cornell Method of note taking. Students' note-taking skills can be measured by how well they are able to answer the questions provided below.

Active Listening

1. In the videotape, Pham has trouble taking notes in class. What do his friends mention as the possible sources of his problems?
2. List the five elements of active listening.
3. Which of these elements might you be able to control?
4. Identify all the factors that might hinder your ability to listen actively.
5. For each of these hindrances, identify how you might eliminate it or otherwise neutralize it so as to enhance your ability to listen actively.

Deciding What Is Important

In the videotape, one of the first suggestions Maria makes to Pham is that he has to decide to listen. Pham accepts her suggestion, but he still feels frustrated by his difficulty in evaluating the importance of what he is hearing.

1. What ideas do Pham's friends offer for deciding what is important?
2. List the cues identified in the video, and provide examples of each.
3. What other indicators is Pham told to look for?
4. Identify any ways (not mentioned in the video) *you* have of deciding what's important in a lecture.

Mind Mapping

Beverly shows Pham how to use mind mapping as a way to capture a lot of information quickly and succinctly.

1. Select a hobby, sport, or other activity you are especially good at or know a lot about.

2. Write a summary (of no more than one page) of the information you know about the activity, providing enough information for someone new to the activity to get started.

3. Draw an information or concept map of the activity.

4. Compare your narrative summary and mind map. How are they different? How are they alike?

Extended Activity: Ask several students to give short oral presentations on the hobby or sport they selected in the previous activity. Have the rest of the class draw concept maps while they are listening to the presentation. Then compare the maps drawn by the class with the one drawn by the presenter.

The Cornell Method

In the videotape, the last suggestion Pham's friends make is that he should have a note-taking system. Maria demonstrates the Cornell Method.

1. On a blank sheet of paper, show the Cornell Method for taking notes and indicate the purpose of each component.

2. Describe the steps for studying notes taken by using the Cornell Method.

3. List the aspects of the Cornell Method that are part of the note-taking system you currently use.

4. Identify aspects of the Cornell Method you are not currently using but that you think will enhance your note-taking skills.

Reminders to Students

- Be honest with yourself about why you might have difficulty concentrating in certain subject areas.
- Find new motivations and methods for staying focused even when your level of interest may be relatively low.
- Decide for yourself which note-taking methods work best for you. Create your own approach.

Segment Two: Reading

This segment of the videotape addresses students' reading-related difficulties and introduces skills and techniques needed to improve study efficiency and comprehension. Specifically, this segment focuses on improving concentration, active reading, and the SQ3R system.

Concentration

1. In the videotape, Beverly seems to have difficulty with the amount of reading required in her courses. Based on what you saw in the flashback to her study session, identify the aspects of Beverly's study habits that hindered her ability to concentrate.

2. For each item you listed in #1, describe what Beverly could do differently that would improve her concentration.

3. Review the list you made in #1 and identify any items that also describe *your* study habits.

4. Identify any additional distractions to which you know you are susceptible.

5. For each item you identified, describe how you might change your approach for the better or otherwise deal with the distraction. (Be realistic about any limitations imposed by your particular situation.)

Active Reading

1. What suggestion does Pham offer Beverly for improving her reading skills?

2. List the six elements of active reading.

3. Review your notes to find the guidelines for "Deciding What Is Important" p. 242 that were introduced in the segment on note taking. Then create a new set of guidelines for active reading.

Extended Activity: To reinforce the idea that reading with a purpose makes a difference, have students survey the media for one week, making a note of each item (e.g., stories, editorials, and advertisements) connected to a topic you are currently studying.

SQ3R Reading System

1. In the videotape, Tina describes the SQ3R reading system she uses. Describe what "SQ3R" means and give a brief definition of each step in the process.

2. Select a chapter in a textbook (or some other multi-page passage) and read it according to whatever system you currently use.

3. Summarize for a partner what you read, providing as much detail as you can.

4. Select another chapter (or multi-page passage) and read it, using the SQ3R system.

5. Again, summarize for a partner what you read, giving as much detail as possible.

6. Compare the two reading methods in the following ways:

   a. Assess your own confidence that you understand the material you read.

   b. Ask your partner to evaluate your ability to articulate what you read.

   c. Identify the aspects of each system that were most helpful and effective for you.

   d. Integrate the best of both methods to create your own reading system.

Extended Activity: To heighten students' awareness that some reading tasks are more difficult than others, ask them to find and bring to class examples of material that they find especially difficult. In class, conduct a discussion of the impact an author's writing skills (or lack thereof) have on the reader's ability to concentrate and learn. Then ask students for examples illustrating the points you've covered (e.g., convoluted writing style, lack of organization, or poor topic sentences).

Reminders to Students

- Always keep a dictionary at hand, and use it to clarify the meanings of words of which you are not absolutely sure.
- Practice silently paraphrasing each paragraph as you complete it to help stay focused and to confirm your understanding of the material.
- Keep a list of new concepts you want to remember from every reading session.
- When faced with a passage or concept you don't understand, "talk it out" with yourself or with a study partner.

Segment Three: Memory

This segment of the videotape introduces the memory process and presents techniques for strengthening memory.

Extended Activity: To show that *remembering is a choice,* select a series of numbers or a phrase and write it on the chalkboard (either before students arrive or at the beginning of class), but do not make any comment about what you have written. Begin class as you normally would and then introduce the videotape segment. When the videotape segment ends (again without comment or explanation), erase what was written on the chalkboard and move on to the first activity.

Memory Process

1. What are the stages of memory?

2. What are the different kinds of memory?

3. In the videotape, what tips do Maria's friends offer her for strengthening her ability to remember?

4. Can you remember what was written on the chalkboard at the beginning of class?
5. Why do you think you remember what was written there? Or why do you think you don't?
6. Do those numbers (or words) have some particular meaning for you?
7. Do you think you remember what was written because it was on the board?

Memory Techniques

1. Identify the memory techniques Maria's friends suggest in the videotape.
2. Identify any additional memory techniques you use or know about.
3. For each of the memory techniques you've identified, describe why and how you think it works. Give any examples of times you have used these techniques.

Extended Activity: To help students understand how memory operates, ask students to work (either individually or in small groups) to complete the following assignment. Adapt this activity to fit the level of computer literacy of your students.

1. Create a concept map on whatever topic you choose.
2. Think about the three types of human memory—sensory, short-term, and long-term—and show how human memory parallels a computer's operation.

With class participation, discuss similarities in how human memory and computer memory operate. Summarize the activity by pointing out that decisions are made moment by moment (not always consciously) about which information will be stored for future retrieval and that everyone can exert conscious control over remembering and recalling information. (The drawing shown below may be helpful as a discussion guide. The information in boldface on the computer screen shows human processes.)

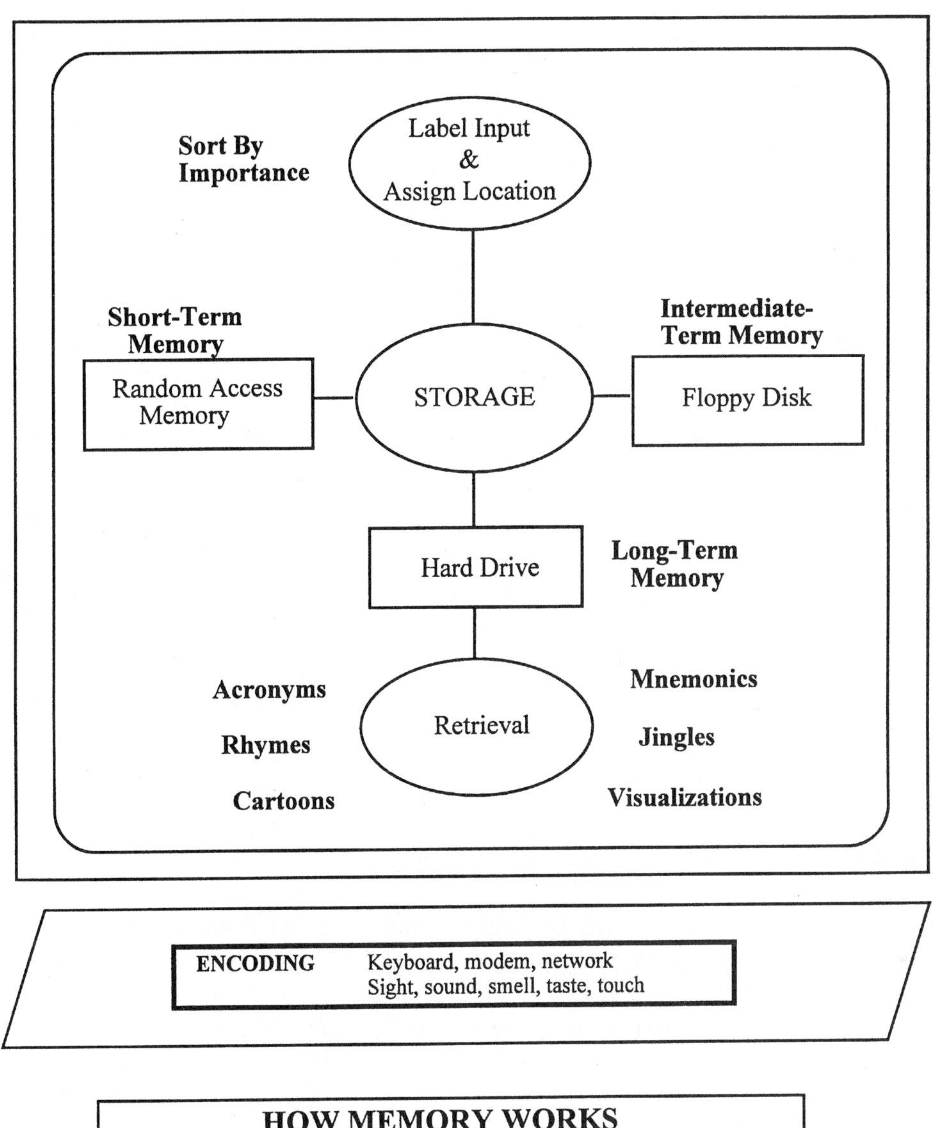

HOW MEMORY WORKS

Reminders to Students

- There are no "right" or "wrong" memory techniques—if something works for you, use it.
- Don't forget to choose to remember.

Segment Four: Test Taking

This segment of the videotape addresses test anxiety, test preparation, taking tests, and understanding different types of tests.

Test Anxiety

1. In the videotape, what kinds of problems is Rob having in taking tests?
2. What solutions do his friends offer to help with each of these problem areas?
3. What are the most important factors in trying to cope with test anxiety?
4. Choose a situation in which you recall being anxious, and describe what happened to you (e.g., how you felt and what you were thinking at that time).
5. Looking back on that situation, can you identify some of the reasons behind your anxiety?
6. List some ways you might address each of those reasons in the future.

Test Preparation

1. Pham and the others offer some concrete suggestions to Rob about preparing for tests. List as many of those suggestions as you can remember.
2. Describe the system you use to prepare for tests.
3. Compare your current system with the suggestions given in the videotape, and then integrate the two to create a new system for yourself.
4. Evaluate your new test preparation system to see if it is realistic for you. If there are aspects you are not comfortable with, alter them to meet your individual needs.

Test Taking

1. List the test-taking strategies Rob's friends suggest.
2. List any additional strategies you have for taking tests.
3. Identify the aspect of test taking that is most difficult for you.
4. What are the reasons behind this difficulty?
5. How might you overcome this difficulty in the future?

Understanding Different Types of Tests

1. What guidelines for answering essay questions were given in the videotape?

2. Devise a system for remembering these guidelines, describe it in writing, and commit it to memory.

3. Using the guidelines, write an essay describing your personal history with taking tests. Include how you feel about taking tests, how well you generally perform on tests, the types of tests on which you perform well/poorly, the reasons behind your success or lack of success on that type of test, and any other issues related to the testing situation that you think are interesting or important.

4. When taking true-false tests, you should answer only those questions of which you are absolutely sure. True ______ False ______

5. On true-false tests, you should choose true if only a small part of the statement is false. True ______ False ______

6. You should always choose true unless you know the statement is false. True ______ False ______

7. Devise a method of remembering the guidelines for taking true-false tests, describe it in writing, and commit it to memory.

8. What system does Pham suggest to Rob for taking multiple-choice tests?

9. Devise a method of remembering how to approach multiple-choice tests, describe it in writing, and commit it to memory.

10. List the guidelines mentioned in the videotape for taking fill-in-the-blank tests.

11. List any additional guidelines or techniques you use on this type of test.

12. Devise a system for remembering these guidelines, describe it in writing, and commit it to memory.

Reminders to Students

- Mastery of a topic is the best reducer of test anxiety.
- You need a system for preparing yourself academically, physically, and emotionally to take tests.
- You need a system for taking each type of test.
- The best system is one that makes sense to you and that you create for yourself.

Tape Two—Life Skills, Segment One: Goal Setting

The purpose of this segment is to provide insight into how to set achievable goals, monitor progress toward them, and remain appropriately flexible in revising them over time. The presentation is structured around the idea that students can easily get sidetracked when they do not have clearly defined goals.

Long- and Short-Term Goals

1. In the videotape, Beverly seems to have lost her sense of direction. What advice do her friends offer her with regard to setting goals for the future?
2. What is Beverly's long-term goal?
3. What are Beverly's short-term goals?
4. Describe one of your personal long-term goals and the shorter-term goals toward attaining that goal.
5. Describe a long-term academic goal and the short-term goals required to reach it.

How to Write Effective Goals and Reach Them

1. List the criteria for writing effective goals that Beverly's friends mention in the videotape.
2. Look at each of the goals you wrote for yourself in #4 and #5 of the previous activity, and evaluate each against the criteria for effective goals. Rewrite your goals, if necessary.
3. What suggestions do Beverly's friends offer for ensuring that she reaches her goals?
4. Revisit your list of long- and short-term goals, and note the steps you can take to ensure that you reach them.

Extended Activity: Use the following process to push personal and academic goal setting to an even greater level of detail.

1. Identify goals that will take the longest amount of time to reach.
2. Work backwards in small steps to identify what must happen in order to achieve each goal.
3. For each short-term, intermediate, and long-term goal, identify any anticipated obstacles and ways to handle them.
4. Identify areas in which help is needed for realizing each goal.
5. Establish milestones for tracking progress and for revising plans, if necessary.